76.50
2732

Historical Dictionaries of Ancient Civilizations and Historical Eras

Series editor: Jon Woronoff

Historical Dictionary of the Enlightenment

Harvey Chisick

Historical Dictionaries of Ancient Civilizations and Historical Eras, No. 16

The Scarecrow Press, Inc.
Lanham, Maryland • Toronto • Oxford
2005

SCARECROW PRESS, INC.

Published in the United States of America
by Scarecrow Press, Inc.
A wholly owned subsidary of
The Rowman & Littlefield Publishing Group, Inc.
4501 Forbes Boulevard, Suite 200, Lanham, Maryland 20706
www.scarecrowpress.com

PO Box 317
Oxford
OX2 9RU, UK

British Library Cataloguing in Publication Information Available

Library of Congress Cataloging-in-Publication Data

Chisick, Harvey, 1946–
   Historical dictionary of the Enlightenment / Harvey Chisick.
      p. cm. — (Historical dictionaries of ancient civilizations and
historical eras ; no. 16)
   Includes bibliographical references and index.
   ISBN 0-8108-5097-4 (hardcover : alk. paper)
   1. Enlightenment—Encyclopedias. I. Title. II. Series.
B1925.E5C45 2004
940.2'5'03—dc22

                                        2004012054

For my parents
in memoriam

The picture on the cover of this book, "Reading of the *Tragedy of the Orphan of China* by Voltaire in the salon of Madame Geoffrin," is the most famous of Gabriel Lemonnier's paintings. Lemonnier, who was born in Rouen in 1743 and died in Paris in 1824, painted this work in 1814. It was not intended as a realistic portrait but rather an idealized version of the celebrated reading, in the salon of Madame Geoffrin, which was one of the main centers of intellectual life of the times and did receive many Enlightenment figures, the most famous of whom appear here. However, it was never host to the assembly in this painting, many of whom were not in Paris at the time, and some of whom had never attended her salon, nor did the salon look like this. But there is no doubt that Voltaire—whose bust appears in the painting—was one of the most admired of the leading lights, and the reading, by Lekain, of his *Tragedy of the Orphan of China* (1755) would be a defining moment. The assembly includes, starting with Buffon in the red coat on the not quite far left, and in the front row, from left to right: Mlle Lespinasse, Mlle Clairon, Lekain, Dalambert, Carle Vanloo, Helvetius, Duclos, Piron, Crebillon, Abbe de Bernis, Duc de Nivernois, Duchesse d'Anville, Prince de Conti, Madame Geoffrin, Fontenelle, Joseph Vernet, Comtesse d'Houdetot, and President de Montesquieu. In the back row, from right to left: Claireau, Dageufseau, Mayran, Maupertuis, Marcehal de Richelieu, Mallesherbes, Turgot, Diderot, Quesne, Abbe Barthelemy, Comte de Caylus, Danville, Soufflot, Bouchardon, St-Lambert, Dargental, the bust of Voltaire, Duc de Choiseul, President Henault, Rameau, Jean-Jacques Rousseau, Raynal, La Condamine, Thomas, Vien, Marmontel, Marivaux, Gresset and Vaucanson, and clustered to the left of Buffon, Pigalle, Bernard de Jussieu, Daubenton, Abbe de Condillac, Madame de Grassigny, Reaumur and Madame du Bocage. The image for the cover was graciously provided by the Museum of Fine Arts in Rouen, where the painting hangs.

Contents

Editor's Foreword

While every historical era is important, there are some that seem particularly relevant because they direct us more specifically toward where we are today. In this respect, the Age of the Enlightenment clearly stands out in helping humanity turn its back on the old regime of absolutism and obscurantism and move toward a new civilization of democracy, equality, reason and tolerance. Admittedly, these goals were not really achieved during the Enlightenment, nor even during the following centuries to the present day, but they remained cherished goals and progress has certainly been made. For that alone, it is worthwhile reviewing the period, to see what things were like before, how the calls for change emerged and what was accomplished in that day and age. But such a review is even more vital at a time, and not the first, when many of these goals—still loudly proclaimed and, indeed, fought for in many places—are being questioned, and suppressed, in others.

Books and writings of all sorts were one of the keys to the Enlightenment, especially the *Encyclopédie* and other works which not only summed up the accumulated knowledge of the past, but pointed toward other possible futures. These historical dictionaries, in a more modest manner, do much the same. The *Historical Dictionary of the Enlightenment* includes a chronology charting the progression of the time period, an introduction summing the era up more broadly, and a dictionary presenting significant persons, places, events, institutions and literary works. The bibliography lists more detailed studies with alternative views. Together they provide a good feel for that age. They also force us to reflect on why humanity took that turn and why so frequently it has been so hard to continue along the path.

The author, Harvey Chisick, has an encyclopedic knowledge of the period. He has been teaching history for more than three decades. His specialization has been the French Enlightenment, on which he wrote his doctoral thesis, and he has also carried out research on the French Revolution. He has produced numerous articles on these and related topics as well as two edited books and three books of his own. One of these is *The Limits of Reform in the Enlightenment*. Thus it is not surprising that Dr. Chisick deals with the period realistically, since it was not generally so "enlightened" as has often been claimed. In addition, and certainly more unusual, his writing is certainly not cut and dried—a collection of facts and figures—but rather a reasoned presentation highlighting strengths and weaknesses and introducing a bit of philosophy or whimsy on occasion. This historical dictionary is not only informative, it is also a good read, which is definitely welcome.

Jon Woronoff
Series Editor

Preface

It is not easy to justify another reference work on the Enlightenment after the recent appearance of the two major collections, both entitled *Encyclopedia of the Enlightenment*, the one edited by Jean Delon and translated from the French in two large, handsome quarto volumes, and the second edited in four quarto volumes by Alan Kors. A dictionary in a single volume done mostly by one author cannot compare in scope or erudition with the impressive collaborative projects directed by Delon and Kors. However, for readers who do not have the leisure to enjoy entries that in these two encyclopedias are often substantial essays, the shorter format of this dictionary may be more convenient. And while no single author can equal the erudition of teams of specialists, a work produced largely by one person might have a greater measure of coherence.

There are, further, a number of advantages to this dictionary that follow from the requirements of the series of reference works to which it belongs. Scarecrow's historical dictionaries include chronologies, which provide a factual overview of the period, and concentrated bibliographies, which provide a broader context than the brief and sharply focused bibliographies included in individual entries in other encyclopedias and dictionaries. The introduction here is more comprehensive than is usual for a reference work, and offers, in effect, a broad definition of the Enlightenment which takes into account main trends in contemporary scholarship, but does not restrict itself to summarizing received wisdom. Scarecrow favors a length for dictionary entries that allows more than a summary statement of fact, but avoids long essays that, whatever their interest and value, are not economical.

Finally, though the main author has tried to provide the basic information relative to the subject and time, he has placed most emphasis on what is alive, meaningful and relevant in the Enlightenment. He would also admit to being a believer in the validity and feasibility of many of the key ideas, assumptions and objectives of the Enlightenment. For better or for worse, this is an engaged treatment of the Enlightenment.

Cross-references are indicated by bold type. In phrases, the word under which the entry appears, and not the whole phrase, is bolded. Thus, for example, "cultural **relativism**" directs the reader to the entry "**Relativism, Cultural**," and the phrase "natural **law**" refers to the entry "**Law, Natural**." Variant forms of key words for entries have sometimes also been bolded, with, for example, **absolutist** referring the reader to the entry **Absolutism**, and **empiricist** to **Empiricism**.

Articles are signed by collaborators. Unsigned articles are by the main author.

Harvey Chisick

Acknowledgments

The opportunity to write this dictionary presented itself a number of years ago when Emmet Kennedy, who had been approached by Scarecrow Press but could not then undertake the project, asked me whether I might be interested. After some initial hesitation I decided that I was. What more suitable project for a student of the Enlightenment than to undertake a treatment of the movement using one of the tools that writers and publishers and the public of the time so favored and used so often and with such relish? Scarecrow allowed itself to be convinced that the dictionary might be entrusted to me, and since doing so has been unfailingly generous and understanding in accommodating an author whose book did not always proceed as quickly or as well as might have been hoped.

I would particularly like to thank Jon Woronoff for having patiently and helpfully read the first drafts of this dictionary. His encouragement, support and flexibility helped greatly in moving the writing along, and his sense of what was feasible and realistic has saved me from a number of errors that a less careful and critical editor might have let slip by. Kim Tabor and Nicole Carty were unfailingly efficient and helpful, and allowed a degree of flexibility to the author on technical details for which he remains grateful, and for which he thinks the better of the press.

This dictionary differs from many other reference works on the Enlightenment in that it relies more on the contributions of the editor than a team of collaborators. Nevertheless, I was not able to do many of the entries myself and wish to thank the friends and colleagues who agreed, often at the expense of their own pressing work or obligations, to contribute items that were beyond my competence. It is not in the nature of a work such as this to include entries on all relevant and desirable subjects, but certainly without the collaboration of those who wrote articles on their special areas of expertise this would have been a more limited and less complete effort than it is with their participation.

I wish to thank a number of colleagues who were particularly forthcoming and supportive. Emmet Kennedy, after having decided not to take on the responsibility of the dictionary, nevertheless contributed willingly to it. Roger Emerson, despite an extremely heavy research and writing schedule of his own, not only contributed a number of entries when asked, but also volunteered to look at the items I had done on the Scottish Enlightenment, and saved me from many errors in this area which he knows so very well. I am indebted to Bertram Schwarzbach not only for a series of rich articles on the theological and humanistic erudition of the period, but also for his interest in this project and constant encouragement. The participation in the writing of this dictionary of Robert Forster, my thesis advisor, was a source of special satisfaction. The combination of expert knowledge, a practical and businesslike approach and the warm good will and concern with which he related to the project would have been refreshingly welcome in any collaborator. In the case of a person who initiated one into the *métier*, one's appreciation is all the greater.

This dictionary has also benefited from critical readings of different sections by various friends and colleagues. The introduction, particularly, was read and helpfully commented on by Brad Chisick, Bob Kaplan, Jon Petrie, Norbert Ruebsaat, Stan Wallach, and by a number of students, Dennis Yoffe, Kalman Maler and Betty Shamash, who went well beyond the bounds of their duties in doing so. The task of proofreading was shared by my long-suffering wife, Tammy Chisick, who, with her usual good grace and slightly pongy sense of humor, carried out this least rewarding, but most necessary, task. By giving her a limited number of items to read as they were ready I obviated her usual (and usually fair) comment that the book is too long.

Etti Marom and Livnat Nissim printed up files many times over without losing their good humor or helpfulness. The formatting of the camera-ready copy was done with her usual efficiency and resourcefulness by Danielle Friedlander.

Chronological Table

DATE	MAIN FIGURES	POLITICS AND SOCIETY	SCIENCE, ARTS, LETTERS
	Bacon (1561-1626)		
	Jansenius (1585-1638)		
	Richelieu (1585-1642)		
	Descartes (1596-1650)		
1605			Bacon, *Advancement of Learning*
1610		Henri IV assassinated; reign of Louis XIII (to 1643)	
1611			Oratory founded
1614		meeting of French Estates General	
1618		Thirty Years' War (1618-1648)	
1620			Bacon, *Novum Organum*
	Molière (1622-1673)		
	Pascal (1623-1662)		
1624		administration of Richelieu (to 1642); salon of Marquise de Rambouillet	
1625			Grotius, *De jure belli et pacis*

	Bossuet (1627-1704)		Gazette de France founded
1631			
1632	Spinoza (1632-1677) Locke (1632-1704)		Galileo, Dialog on the Two Principal Systems of the World
1635		Académie française founded	
1637			Descartes, Discourse on Method
	Louis XIV (1638-1715) Racine (1639-1699)		
1640		Puritan Revolution	Jansenius, Augustinus
	Newton (1642-1727) Leibniz (1646-1716) Bayle (1647-1706) Mme Lambert (1647-1733)		
1648		Peace of Westphalia; Fronde (1648-1653); Academy of Castres founded	
1650		Academy of Caen founded	
1651	Fénelon (1651-1715)		Hobbes, Leviathan
1653		Protectorate of Cromwell	
	Thomasius (1655-1728) Fontenelle (1657-1757)		
1658	Saint-Pierre (1658-1743)	Academy of Avignon founded	
1659		Treaty of the Pyrenees	

1660	Defoe (1660-1731)	Restoration in England; Royal Society founded	
1661		personal Rule of Louis XIV (to 1715)	
1663		Academy of Inscriptions founded	
1664	Meslier (1664-1729)		
1665			*Journal des Savants* founded; La Fontaine, *Contes*
1666		Paris Academy of Sciences founded	
1667	Swift (1667-1745)	War of Devolution (to 1668); Academy of Arles founded	
1668			La Fontaine, *Fables*
1670	Mandeville (1670-1733)		Spinoza, *Tractatus Theologico-politicus*; Pascal, *Pensées*
1671	Shaftesbury (1671-1713)		
1672	Peter I (1672-1725) Muratori (1672-1750) Addison (1672-1719) Steele (1672-1729)		Pufendorf, *De Jure naturae et gentium*; *Mercure gallant* founded
1674		Academy of Soissons founded	
1675			discovery of calculus by Leibniz and Newton

	Robert Walpole (1676-1745)		
1677	Mme Doublet (1677-1771)		Spinoza, *Ethics*
1678	Bolingbroke (1678-1751)		Simon, *Critical History of the Old Testament*; Mme de La Fayette, *La Princesse de Clèves*
1679	Wolff (1679-1754)	Habeas Corpus	
1680		Comédie française founded	
1681	Mme Tencin (1681-1749)		Bossuet, *Discourse on Universal History*
1682	Campbell (1682-1761) Charles XII (1682-1718)	Academy of Nîmes founded	*Acta Eruditorum* founded; Bayle, *Thoughts on the Comet*
1683	Réaumur (1683-1757) Fourmont (1683-1745)		Fontenelle, *Dialogs of the Dead*
	Rameau (1683-1764)		
1684	Watteau (1684-1721) Astruc (1684-1766)		Bayle, *Nouvelles de la République des Lettres* (1684-1687)
1685		Reign of James II (to 1688); Revocation of the Edict of Nantes	
1686			Fontenelle, *Discussions on the Plurality of Worlds*
1687			Newton, *Principia*; Fontenelle, *History of Oracles*

1688	Marivaux (1688-1763) Pluche (1688-1761) Pope (1688-1744) Vico (1688-1744)	Glorious Revolution; War of the League of Augsburg (to 1697)	La Bruyère, *Characters*
1689	Montesquieu (1689-1755) Richardson (1689-1761)	William III of England (to 1702); Declaration of Rights; Act of Toleration; Peter I Czar (to 1725)	
1690	Bachaumont (1690-1771)		Locke, *Essay Concerning Human Understanding*; Locke, *Two Treatises of Government*
1692			Simon, *Critical History and Commentary on the New Testament*
1694	Voltaire (1694-1778) Hutcheson (1694-1746)	Bank of England founded	*Dictionary* of the Académie française
1695	Mme Graffigny (1695-1758) Mme du Deffand (1696-1780)	Academy of Toulouse founded	
1697	Prévost (1697-1763)	Reign of Charles XII (to 1718)	Bayle, *Historical and Critical Dictionary*
1698	Maupertuis (1698-1759)		
1699	Mme Geoffrin (1699-1779) Mme de Warens (1699-1762)		Fénelon, *Telemachus*

1700	Academy of Sciences of Berlin and Academy of Lyon founded	
1701	Act of Settlement; War of Spanish Succession (to 1714)	*Journal de Trévoux* founded
1702	reign of Anne (to 1714)	
1703	Camissard rebellion	
	Boucher (1703-1770)	
	Wesley (1703-1791)	
1704	Jaucourt (1704-1779)	Leibniz, *New Essays on Human Understanding*; Newton, *Opticks*
1705		Mandeville, *Fable of the Bees*
1706	Academy of Montpellier founded	
	Mme de Châtelet (1706-1749)	
	Franklin (1706-1790)	
1707	Union of England and Scotland	
	Buffon (1707-1788)	
	Coyer (1707-1782)	
	Fielding (1707-1754)	
	William Pitt I (1708-1778)	
1709	crisis in French economy	Bossuet, *Politics derived from Holy Scriptures*
	Johnson (1709-1784)	
	La Mettrie (1709-1751)	
	Mably (1709-1785)	
1710	salon of Mme Lambert (to 1733); Port Royal des Champs destroyed	Leibniz, *Theodicy*
	Louis XV (1710-1774)	
	Reid (1710-1796)	

1711	Hume (1711-1776)		Addison and Steele, *The Spectator* (1711-1714); Shaftesbury, *Characteristics*
	Rousseau (1712-1778) Frederick II (1712-1786)		
1713	Diderot (1713-1784) Mme Riccoboni (1713-1792) Sterne (1713-1768)	Unigenitus; Academy of Bordeaux founded	
1714	Condillac (1714-1780) Maupeou (1714-1792)	George I accedes to throne of England (to 1727)	Leibniz, *Monodology*
1715	Helvétius (1715-1771)	Death of Louis XIV; Regency; polysynody; Jacobite rising in Scotland	Lesage, *Gil Blas*
	Mlle Volland (1716-1784)		
	Maria Theresa (1717-1780) Alembert (1717-1783)		
1718			Watteau, *Embarkation for Cythera*
1719	Fréron (1719-1776)		Defoe, *Robinson Crusoe*
1720	Mme de Pompadour (1719-1764)	Pragmatic Sanction adopted; South Seas Bubble	Dom Calmet, *Dictionary of the Bible*
1721	Robertson (1721-1793) Malesherbes (1721-1794)	Pope Innocent XIII (to 1724); administration of Robert Walpole (to 1742)	Montesquieu, *Persian Letters*
1722		Universities of Dijon and Pau founded	Rameau, *Treatise on Harmony*

1723	Holbach (1723-1789) Smith (1723-1790) Ferguson (1723-1816) Marmontel (1723-1799)	Louis XV of age; Academy of Béziers founded	Voltaire, *Henriade*
1724	Kant (1724-1804)	Pope Benedict XIII (to 1730); Academy of St. Petersburg and Club de l'Entresol founded	*Mercure de France* founded
1725	Greuze (1725-1805) Casanova (1725-1798)	first masonic lodge in Paris established; Academy of Orléans founded	Vico, *New Science*, first edition
1726	Mme d'Épinay (1726-1783)		Swift, *Gulliver's Travels*; Rollin, *Traité des Etudes*
1727	Turgot (1727-1781) Morellet (1727-1819) Pidansat de Mairobert (1727-1779)	George II reigns (to 1760); beginning of phenomenon of convulsionaries in Paris	
1728	Catherine II (1729-1796) Lessing (1729-1781) Mendelssohn (1729-1786) Burke (1729-1797)		*Nouvelles ecclésiastiques* (to 1803)
1730	Palissot (1730-1814)	Pope Clement XII (to 1740); salon of Mme du Deffand (to 1780)	Marivaux, *Le Jeu de l'amour et du hazard*

1731	Academy of Surgery in Paris founded	Prévost, *Manon Lescaut*; Marivaux, *La Vie de Mariane* (to 1741)
1732	Beaumarchais (1732–1799) Thomas (1732–1785) Mlle de Lespinasse (1732–1776) Necker (1732–1804) Fragonard (1732–1806) Haydn (1732–1809)	Academy of La Rochelle founded	Pluche, *Le Spectacle de la nature* (to 1742); Pope, *Essay on Man*
1733	Priestly (1733–1804)	Prussia enacts conscription	
1734	Restif de la Bretonne (1734–1806) Mesmer (1734–1815)		Voltaire, *Letters on England*; Montesquieu, *Considerations on the Romans*; Réaumur, *History of Insects*
1735	Millar (1735–1801)		Dom Calmet, *Universal History*; Marivaux, *Le Paysan Parvenu*
1736	Linguet (1736–1794)	beginning of Methodist revival in England	
1737	Gibbon (1737–1794) Geddes (1737–1802) Paine (1737–1809) Mme Necker (1737–1804)	Academy of Arras founded	

Year		Events	Works
1738	Beccaria (1738-1794)		Voltaire, *Elements of the Philosophy of Newton*; Chardin, *La Gouvernante*; Boucher, *Le Déjeuner*
1739			Hume, *A Treatise of Human Nature*
1740	Mercier (1740-1814)	Pope Benedict XIV (to 1758); War of Austrian Succession (1740-1748); Frederick II accedes to throne of Prussia (to 1788); reign of Maria Theresa (to 1780); Academy of Dijon founded; Mme du Deffand opens her salon (to 1780)	Richardson, *Pamela*; Boucher, *Birth of Venus*
1741	Joseph II (1741-1790) Houdon (1741-1828)	grain shortages in Paris	Hume, *Essays, Moral and Political*; Fielding, *Joseph Andrews*; Chardin, *L'Enfant au tonton*
1742		Academy of Rouen founded	Boucher, *Dianna*; *Leda*; Voltaire, *Mohammed*
1743	Lavoisier (1743-1794) Condorcet (1743-1794) Jefferson (1743-1826)	Academy of Denmark founded	Alembert, *Traité de dynamique*
1744		Academy of Montauban founded	Vico, *New Science*, third edition

1745	Jacobite rising in Scotland; beginning of influence of Mme de Pompadour; Academy of Amiens founded	La Mettrie, *Natural History of the Soul*
1746	Mme Genlis (1746-1830)	Condillac, *Essay on the Origin of Human Knowledge*; Diderot, *Philosophical Thoughts*
1747	Leopold II (1747-1792) Monge (1747-1818)	Voltaire, *Zadig*
1748	Bentham (1748-1832) David (1748-1825)	Montesquieu, *Spirit of the Laws*; Hume, *Enquiry Concerning Human Understanding*; La Mettrie, *Man a Machine*; Diderot, *Les Bijoux indiscrets*
1749	Laplace (1749-1827) Goethe (1749-1832)	salon of Mme Geoffrin; Academy of Auxerre founded; *vingtième* tax instituted	Diderot, *Letter on the Blind*; Buffon begins *Natural History*; Fielding, *Tom Jones*
1750	Grégoire (1750-1831)	Pombal minister in Portugal; Academy of Nancy founded	Rousseau, *First Discourse*; Rameau, *Demonstration of the Principle of Harmony*

1751	Benedict XIV condemns freemasonry	*Encyclopédie*, first volumes; Voltaire, *The Century of Louis XIV*; Hume, *Enquiry Concerning the Principles of Morals*; Fielding, *Amelia*
1752	Kaunitz Chancellor of Austria; Affair of receipts for confession in Paris; Academy of Besançon founded	Rousseau, *Le Devin du village*; quarrel over Italian music; Alembert, *Resistance of Fluids*
1753	Great Remonstrances of Parlement of Paris; famine around Paris and in south	Buffon, *Discourse on Style*; Grimm begins *Correspondance littéraire*
1754	Louis XVI (1754-1793) Destutt de Tracy (1754-1836)	Diderot, *Thoughts on the Interpretation of Nature*; Condillac, *Treatise on Sensation*; Fréron begins *Année Littéraire* (to 1790); Hume, *History of England* (1754-1762); Boucher, *Mme de Pompadour*
1755	University of Moscow founded; Lisbon earthquake	Rousseau, *Second Discourse*; Morelly, *Code of Nature*; Johnson, *English Dictionary*; Greuze, *A Father Explaining the Bible*; Montesquieu dies

1756	Mozart (1756-1791)	Seven Years' War (to 1763); France allies with Austria	Voltaire, *Essay on Manners*; Mirabeau, *L'Ami des hommes*; Messance, *Recherches sur la population*; Chardin, *Kitchen Table*; *Journal Encyclopédique* (to 1793)
1757		Attempt on life of Louis XV; Academies of Metz and Châlons-sur-Marne founded	Burke, *Sublime and Beautiful*
1758		Pope Clement XIII (to 1769)	Rousseau, *Letter to d'Alembert*; Quesnay, *Economic Table*; Helvétius, *On Mind (De l'Esprit)*
1759	Schiller (1759-1805) Wollstonecraft (1759-1797)	British Museum and Academy of Cherbourg founded	Smith, *Theory of Moral Sentiments*; Voltaire, *Candide*; Johnson, *Rasselas*; Sterne, *Tristram Shandy*
1760	Saint-Simon (1760-1825)	George III accedes to throne (to 1820); Voltaire moves to Ferney	Rousseau, *La Nouvelle Héloïse*; D'Alembert, *Differential Equations*; Macpherson, *Poems of Ossian*; Mirabeau, *Theory of Taxes*; Quesnay, *Maximes générales*; Palissot, *Les Philosophes*
1761		Turgot Intendant of Limoges	Marmontel, *Contes moraux*; Holbach, *Christianity Unmasked*; Greuze, *L'Accordée du village*

Year		Events	Works
1762		reign of Catherine II (to 1796); suppression of Jesuits in France; trial and execution of Jean Calas	Rousseau, *Social Contract*; *Émile, or On Education*; Diderot, composition of *Rameau's Nephew*
1763		Treaty of Paris; salon of Julie de Lespinasse	Voltaire, *Treatise on Tolerance*; La Chalotais, *Essay on National Education*
1764		*Nakaz* of Catherine II; Stanislas Poniatowski elected king of Poland; Brittany Affair; Mme de Pompadour dies	Voltaire, *Philosophical Dictionary*; Rousseau, *Letters Written from the Mountain*; Beccaria, *On Crimes and Punishments*
1765		Leopold II begins rule in Tuscany; Bank of Berlin founded	Goldsmith, *Vicar of Wakefield*
1766	Malthus (1766-1834)	France annexes Lorraine; Chevalier de la Barre executed	Lessing, *Laokoon*; Turgot, *Essay on the Formation and Distribution of Riches*
1767			Holbach, *Christianity Unmasked*; Marmontel, *Bélisaire*; Voltaire, *L'Ingénu*; Mercier de la Rivière, *Natural and Essential Order of Political Societies*; Ferguson, *Essay on the History of Civil Society*
1768		France acquires Corsica	Quesnay, *Physiocracy*

1769	Napoleon (1769-1821)	Pope Clement XIV (to 1774)		Diderot, *D'Alembert's Dream*; Robertson, *History of the Reign of Charles V*; *Letters of Junius* (to 1772)
1770	Hegel (1770-1831)		marriage of future Louis XVI and Marie Antoinette; administration of Lord North (to 1782)	Holbach, *System of Nature*; Raynal, *History of the Two Indies*
1771			Maupeou reforms	Mercier, *L'An 2440*; Millar, *Observations concerning the Distinction of Ranks*; Diderot begins *Jacques le fataliste*
1772			first partition of Poland; suppression of Cossack rising in Russia	Diderot, *Supplement to Bougainville's Voyage*; Helvétius, *Of Man (De l'Homme)*; publication of *Encyclopédie* completed
1773			Clement XIV dissolves Jesuit Order; formation of the Grand Orient Lodge in France; Boston Tea Party	Holbach, *Système social*; *La Politique naturelle*; Diderot visits Catherine II
1774			Accession of Louis XVI (to 1793); reversal of Maupeou reform	Goethe, *The Sorrows of Young Werther*; Mettra, *Correspondance littéraire* (to 1793)

1775	Flour War; Pope Pius VI (to 1799)	Beaumarchais, *The Barber of Seville*; Herder, *Philosophy of History and Culture*
1776	American Declaration of Independence	Smith, *Wealth of Nations*; Gibbon, *Decline and Fall of the Roman Empire* (to 1788); Paine, *Common Sense*; Bentham, *Fragment on Government*
1777	Necker Controller General (to 1781); Franco-American treaty	*Journal de Paris* founded; Bachaumont begins *Mémoires secrets*; Greuze, *The Paternal Curse*
1778	France supports America; first provincial assembly in France	exeunt Voltaire and Rousseau; Marmontel, *The Incas*
1779	abolition of serfdom on royal domain in France	
1780	Joseph II sole ruler of Habsburg possessions (to 1790); first *musée* founded in Paris; France abolishes torture; Gordon riots in London	Lessing, *On the Education of the Human Race*; Condillac, *Logic*

1781	abolition of serfdom in Austria; Yorktown	Rousseau, *Confessions*; *Reveries*; Kant, *Critique of Pure Reason*; Mercier, *Tableau de Paris* (to 1788)
1782	Joseph II closes monasteries; Wilkes seated in Parliament	Laclos, *Les Liaisons Dangereuses*
1783	American independence recognized; Joseph II abolishes *corvée*; administration of William Pitt the Younger (to 1801)	Bernadin de Saint-Pierre, *Studies on Nature*; Herder, *Ideas on the Philosophy of the History of Humanity*
1784	Academies founded at Valence and Orléans	death of Diderot; Beaumarchais, *Marriage of Figaro*; Lavoisier, *Treatise of Chemistry*; David, *Oath of the Horatii*
1785	Diamond Necklace Affair	Kant, *Foundation of a Metaphysics of Morals*; Mozart, *Marriage of Figaro*
1787	First Notables in France; Protestants accorded civil status	Bernadin de Saint-Pierre, *Paul and Virginia*
1788	Six Edicts; Estates General summoned; Second Notables; insanity (temporary) of George III	Kant, *Critique of Practical Reason*; Grégoire, *Essay on the Moral and Political Regeneration of the Jews*

Year	Events	Publications
1789	Estates General convenes; becomes National Assembly; destruction of privilege; Declaration of the Rights of Man and the Citizen; Nationalization of Church property	Blake, *Songs of Innocence and of Experience*; Lavoisier, *Elementary Treatise on Chemistry*; Sieyès, *What is the Third Estate?* David, *Brutus*; Bentham, *Introduction to the Principles of Morals*
1790	Civil Constitution of Clergy	Burke, *Reflections on the Revolution in France*; Kant, *Critique of Judgment*; Wollstonecraft, *Vindication of the Rights of Men*
1791	flight to Varennes; Constitution of 1791; Legislative Assembly	Paine, *Rights of Man, Part I*; Mackintosh, *Vindiciae Gallicae*; Volney, *The Ruins*
1792	War of the First Coalition (to 1797); second revolution of 10 August; September Massacres	Paine, *Right of Man, Part II*; Wollstonecraft, *Vindication of the Rights of Woman*
1793	Vendée rising; federalist rebellions; Terror; academies suppressed; second partition of Poland	Godwin, *Enquiry concerning Political Justice*; Condorcet, *Essay on the Progress of the Human Mind*; Restif de La Bretonne, *Nights of Paris*; David, *Marat*

1794	Rousseau's remains moved to Pantheon; Thermidorean reaction; Jacobin clubs closed; treason trials in England	Restif de la Bretonne, *Monsieur Nicolas* (to 1797); Volney, *Natural Law*
1795	freedom of religion asserted; separation of church and state; *écoles centrales* established; Directory; Institut established; third partition of Poland	Hutton, *Theory of the Earth*
1796	Italian campaign begins; Conspiracy of Equals	Paine, *Age of Reason* completed; Maistre, *Considerations on France*
1797	Babeuf tried and executed	
1798	War of the Second Coalition (to 1799)	Mercier, *Le Nouveau Paris*; Barruel, *History of Jacobinism*; Wordsworth and Colderidge, *Lyrical Ballads*
1799	Consulat	David, *The Sabine Women*
1800		David, *Bonaparte Crossing the Alps*
1801	Concordat between France and the Papacy; union of Great Britain and Ireland	Destutt de Tracy, *Eléments de l'Idéologie*

Introduction

In 1784 Immanuel Kant wrote an essay entitled "What is Enlightenment?" in response to a question posed by a Berlin newspaper. The answer he gave was that it could best be understood as man's emergence from self-imposed nonage or immaturity.[1] While it is not easy to argue with one of the greatest and most respected representatives of a movement about the nature of that movement, both the question posed and Kant's answer have drawbacks from the point of view of the historian. For historians set out to study not "enlightenment" as a state of mind, but an intellectual movement known as the Enlightenment, and they are less concerned with the universal category "man" than with specific people and groups of people whose life experiences have been shaped by their gender, upbringing, education, occupations, the economic opportunity available to them, the cultures in which they moved and the technological and administrative capacities of the societies in which they lived.

This dictionary takes the Enlightenment as an intellectual movement that played a key role in the culture of Europe in the years between roughly 1687 and 1789. Of course the Enlightenment was not restricted to the continent of Europe, but it remains accurate to say that the Enlightenment was a European movement. It existed in its most concentrated form in the area lying between the great urban centers of Paris, London and Amsterdam. With certain striking exceptions, such as Scotland, the farther one moved away from the wealthy and urbanized French-British-Dutch heartland, the weaker and more isolated the concentrations of Enlightenment culture became.

If it is convenient to date the inception of the Enlightenment from the publication of Isaac Newton's *Principia* in 1687, this does not imply that basic scientific attitudes constituent of the Enlightenment view of the world were absent before then. Nevertheless, the publication of the *Principia* remains a cultural watershed of major importance, and insofar as any single event can be said to do so, signals the beginning of a great movement. The outbreak of the French Revolution in 1789 is a much weaker candidate for the terminal date of the Enlightenment. Despite the rise of Romanticism and growing political conservatism, many of the basic assumptions of Enlightenment thought and the projects associated with the Enlightenment retained their vitality well into the 19th century, and some to the present day. Nevertheless, there was a change in the climate of opinion in Europe between 1789 and 1815, and during that time the complex of ideas and values associated with the Enlightenment lost the prominence they had enjoyed among wealthier and more prominent elements of European society during most of the 18th century.

Since the Enlightenment is basically an intellectual movement, most of this introduction will deal with the structure and nature of the ideas that characterize it. There are three sets of assumptions that inform the thought of the Enlightenment, that orient and distinguish it from the intellectual movements that preceded and followed it. These can be called paradigms, as they are models that underlie all Enlightenment thought. The first of these is associated with the name of Newton, and concerns the way we understand the material world and the methods by which things material should be investigated. The second paradigm follows directly from the work of John Locke on the way human beings develop their ideas. As Newton had provided a new model for thinking about the material universe, so Locke, who was a physician as well as a political theorist, provided a new way of thinking about man.

The third paradigm that informed Enlightenment thought can claim neither the originality nor the authority of those grounded in the work of Newton and Locke. This is the humanist paradigm, the recovery of which was the great achievement of the Renaissance, but which remained vital through the 18th century. The heritage of Greco-Roman classicism continued to provide the core of advanced education during the Enlightenment, and if the habit of writing in Latin lost ground over the 18th century, the practice of reading it was retained widely. However, rather than being used as a tool for the recovery of the civic spirit or for a better critical appreciation of the texts of Scripture, in the hands of Pierre Bayle the works of classical antiquity and the early history of Christianity became the basis for questioning the historicity of much that was reported in those sources. Far less constructive than the humanism of the scholars of the Renaissance and Reformation, the critical humanism of the Enlightenment was nevertheless a key constitutive element of the movement, and so deserves a place beside the Newtonian and Lockean paradigms.

After an account of the three main paradigms which shaped and directed Enlightenment thought, attention will be directed to a number of principles and characteristics that follow from these paradigms, and which give the thought of the Enlightenment its distinctiveness. These principles and values include reason, nature, secularization, individualism, liberalism, *humanité*, beneficence and moralism. It is worth pointing out before approaching each of these ideas individually that they existed in a common climate of opinion of which a broad optimism was an important feature. This optimism was grounded in the assumptions that the world was both lawful and intelligible. But the men and women of the Enlightenment did not assume that their minds and the intellectual tools available to them were capable of comprehending the whole world. Of great importance to the thinkers of the Enlightenment was the conviction that they were able to distinguish between areas in which clear and certain knowledge was possible, and others in which it was not. From this basic distinction two potentially contradictory attitudes followed. One, which emphasized the limits of possible knowledge, tended toward intellectual modesty. The other, which focused on areas in which certain knowledge could be attained, encouraged a sense of empowerment that sometimes bordered on arrogance. For the most part the arrogance that tended to accompany the bracing new sense of intellectual competence was kept in check by recognition of the limitations of the competence of the mind and an awareness of the precariousness of man's place in the world.

While the Enlightenment must be defined primarily in terms of its intellectual achievements and values, a characterization of the movement cast exclusively in these terms would be incomplete. Such a characterization would not tell us anything about either the way these ideas circulated, or what levels of society were affected by them. These are issues which, if not of great importance to philosophers, cannot be overlooked by historians. Accordingly, after an account of the main ideas and values of the Enlightenment, a description will be given of the more important institutions and forms of communication through which the men and women who made up the enlightened community engaged in debate, and shared and articulated their ideas.

The last section of the introduction will return to the ideas that characterized the Enlightenment to show how they developed and changed between the late 17th and the late 18th century. There was a dynamic to Enlightenment thought that caused certain assumptions or principles that initially were regarded as solutions, to become themselves problematic as they developed. The order and lawfulness of the Newtonian universe would come to be seen as materialistic determinism. The attempts to loosen the bonds of corporatism and absolutism for the benefit of the individual, as they succeeded, in turn raised the problem of state legitimacy and social cohesiveness. The rejection of a system of morality based on the authority of church and state resulted in an ethics based on utility and the inherent dignity of the human being. But the values of beneficence and *humanité* came to be questioned by thinkers who pushed the logic of radical individualism to its conclusion.

To appreciate the Enlightenment it is necessary to gain a clear notion of the basic assumptions and values that structured the movement, and also to know how these ideas were articulated and the paths of communication they followed. But to avoid a static and simplified view of the Enlightenment, it is also necessary to see how its key ideas grew, developed and were refracted, and how new problems grew out of what were advanced as solutions to older problems.

The Paradigms of Enlightenment Thought

The Newtonian Paradigm

Probably the most characteristic feature of what was to become the Enlightenment worldview found its classic expression in Newton's *Principia Mathematica*, which was published in 1687. The book can rightly be seen as the culmination of the scientific revolution of the 16th and 17th centuries, building as it does on the work of Nicolas Copernicus, Johann Kepler, Galilei Galileo and others, and providing compelling answers to problems of astronomy that Newton's distinguished predecessors had posed, but had not been able to solve. But the *Principia* was written as a technical scientific treatise and used sophisticated mathematics—Newton had invented the calculus for the purpose of solving the problems involved in writing the book—and was inaccessible even to the reasonably well instructed layman. While Newton's findings were immediately accepted as conclusive by the scientific community, at least in England, it took a generation or more for the implications of the work to become diffused among the general public.

What Newton demonstrated in the *Principia* was that movements of the planets and terrestrial physics could be reduced to two basic laws, the laws of gravitation and of inertia. The law of inertia states that an object in motion will continue to move at the same speed and in the same direction until it is acted upon by another force. The law of gravitation states that bodies attract each other in direct proportion to their mass and in inverse proportion to their distance from each other. Newton put forward these laws not as philosophical principles, but as empirically and mathematically demonstrable generalizations. He could show that planets, comets and stars appeared when and where his principles predicted they should, and he could calculate the tides in the same way. Whatever one's feelings about the implications of Newton's concept of the universe, one could not well deny that his explanations effectively accounted for the workings of many previously unexplained phenomena.

Scientifically, the significance of Newton's achievement was that it validated the assumptions and methods of scientists working in the tradition of Kepler and Galileo. And representing the culmination of the scientific revolution, it drove the last nail into the coffin of Aristotelian astronomy and physics. This is a point of more than strictly scientific significance, in that today we have for the most part lost any sense of a comprehensive and integrated view of the world, and instead depend on a series of fragmented sciences to describe the nature of reality.

Up to and well into the 18th century it was generally assumed that the universe formed an integrated and largely harmonious construct. There was no sharp division between theology and physics, and in the case of the Catholic Church, Aristotelian physics was accepted as the theologically correct interpretation of the universe. In an age that thought in terms of integrated constructs, it was almost inevitable that certain propositions about the physical universe be given a religious or philosophical significance. It was equally inevitable that Newton's science be construed as problematic for Catholic orthodoxy. Perhaps this is one reason that Newton's theory took longer to find acceptance in France than in Holland and England, though Newton's discrediting of the cosmology of René Descartes, which represented a more theory-oriented facet of the scientific revolution, may have played a role here too. In any case, the separation of science from dogma is one implication of Newtonian science that was to gain importance in the Enlightenment and the 19th century.

Arguably, Newton's methodology was of as much significance for the Enlightenment as was his cosmology. Newton combined empirical and deductive methods in a way that remained a model for scientific research well into the 20th century. But in the balance between observation and theory, he gave priority to observation and fact. It is well known that Newton had hit upon his theory of gravity as a young man, but that when he tried to demonstrate it, he found that his calculations did not bear him out. So he set his theory aside, assuming that it was incorrect. Only when a more accurate value for a degree of the earth's meridian became available thanks to the work of a French astronomer did Newton again make his calculations and, finding them satisfactory, present his theory to the scientific community. For the development of Enlightenment thought Newton's subordination of theory to empirical evidence was probably as important as his demonstration of the lawfulness of the physical universe.

It was characteristic of the comprehensive and integrative systems of the world that had predominated until the 17th century that the need to find meaning in the universe contributed to giving theory, whether metaphysical or dogmatic, precedence over fact. Newton reversed this order, and pointedly stated "I pose no hypotheses." Today it is clear that theory does not emerge of itself from a set of facts, no matter how voluminous and comprehensive, and that fact and theory are inseparable in scientific investigation. If this sort of thoroughgoing empiricism seems to us naïve, it is worth bearing in mind that until the time of Francis Bacon, the great theorist of empiricism who himself made no significant scientific discoveries, and of Newton, one of the greatest practitioners of science, an urgently felt need for meaning almost always caused fact mercilessly to be subordinated to theory. It was subordinating his own mental constructs to the evidence of the external world that, as much as his actual discoveries, made Newton probably the greatest culture hero of the Enlightenment. And it was turning away from theory toward empirically verifiable external realities that as much as anything else characterized and defined Enlightenment thought.

The discovery that the movements of all heavenly bodies and many terrestrial phenomena conformed to a few basic laws and were amenable to calculation contributed mightily to a disenchantment of the world that was initially grasped as liberating and empowering. Peter Gay has aptly described this development as a "recovery of nerve."[2] The sense of liberation from inscrutable mystery in the generation following the publication of the *Principia* is reflected in Alexander Pope's *Epitaph: Intended for Sir Isaac Newton in Westminster Abbey* (1730) in the lines:

Nature and nature's laws were hid in night
God said let Newton be, and all was light.

To a generation that experienced eclipses and comets as portents, and perceived irregularities of nature as intimations of conflicts between forces of good and evil, the prospect of a regular and intelligible nature offered both relief and a sense of power. The educated began to feel more at home in a world the mechanics of which they understood better than they had ever done before.

And yet for Newton and his contemporaries the new understanding of nature did not reduce the sense of wonder that they felt in contemplating the world, and this for two reasons. First, they did not perceive wonder and order to be incompatible. Indeed, for most of the 18th century the very fact of cosmic order was cause for wonder, and deists argued that the order of nature reflected the ordering hand of a Divine Artificer. Secondly, the data available to Newton were not so accurate as they might have been, so that his calculations yielded a system that was not altogether self-sustaining and contained a blessed imperfection.

Newton's revised calculations were a great improvement on his earlier ones, but they were not altogether accurate. According to his figures, the orbits of the planets would not remain completely stable, so that over time the equilibrium of the solar system would not be maintained. While not willing to disregard facts, Newton himself was profoundly concerned with finding meaning in nature. As a deeply, if idiosyncratically, religious man, he hypothesized that the fact of stability of the solar system could be explained by periodic divine intervention to put the planets back onto their appropriate courses. This was to save science while recognizing the existence of an active, interventionist and well-intentioned Deity. Initially, then, Newton's cosmology provided both a comprehensive explanation of the workings of the physical world and a theology that had a place for divine intervention. If Newton reduced the world to order, he did not deprive it of meaning. Of course more accurate observations were made, and toward the end of the 18th century it became apparent that Newton's assumption of a divine hand gently returning wayward planets to their proper orbits was superfluous.

Though not himself a positivist, Newton contributed significantly to setting modern science on the road to positivism, the school of thought that maintains that beyond hard facts and the relations between such facts there can be no certain knowledge. But he himself did not live to see, nor for the most part did the Enlightenment have to confront, a world radically deprived of meaning and of mystery. That did not come into focus until well into the 19th century. The Enlightenment celebrated an ordered vision of the world only rarely troubled by the deterministic implications of the cosmic order it believed immanent in all aspects of the physical, social and moral spheres.

The Lockean Paradigm

John Locke's *Essay Concerning Human Understanding* of 1690 holds the place in the Enlightenment's conceptualization of man that Newton's *Principia* has in its understanding of nature. In this seminal work Locke approaches man as a physical being whose intellectual capacities develop from his senses. Man is born, according to the naturalistic approach adopted by Locke in the *Essay*, as pure potential, or a *tabula rasa*. At birth a human being is no more than matter organized in such a way that it has sensation. The experiences that the infant undergoes determine the way its mind develops. The richer and more coherent the sensory experiences of the child as it grows, the better and clearer its ideas will be. But ideas do not exist in their own right. According to Locke they are no more than the comparison of sensations. On this view of things the moral and intellectual faculties of mankind are grounded in sense experience. And sense experience for the most part is amenable to empirical verification.

Locke's project was similar to Newton's in two important ways. First, both adopted an empirical approach to their subjects, attempting to establish the facts, and only afterwards to offer broader explanations or theories to account for them. Secondly, while both men were sincerely believing Christians, both avoided adducing theological premises as parameters for their investigations. Both proceeded as scientists. Indeed, one of the features of empiricism was that it helped to separate science from religion.

The basic question that Locke asked was: what is the source of our knowledge? His answer was that all certain knowledge originates in the senses, and can be traced along a chain of sensation to its inception. There was nothing in the mind that was not first in the senses. This simple but nevertheless revolutionary doctrine was rich with implications that contributed to allowing men to empower themselves, to regain their nerve and to continue the process of disenchantment.

The notion of human beings beginning their lives at a point zero of pure potential is liberating from two points of view. First, it negates the doctrine of original sin, which, whatever its theological status, and however well it accounts for the general nastiness of human beings, is psychologically oppressive. Secondly, it offers the possibility of building new and better social institutions. For if human nature is malleable, it is possible by appropriately supervising and ordering life experiences to make people better, more able and more moral than they might otherwise have been. On the assumptions of Locke's psychology it is possible by means of education to improve each individual and society as a whole.

There is also a negative implication of Locke's theory of knowledge that had great positive value. If the only knowledge of which certainty is possible is knowledge based on the senses or on calculation, then it follows that in areas in which data amenable to the senses and to empirical or mathematical verification are not available, it is not possible to claim certainty, or true knowledge. If we consider that most areas of intellectual endeavor at the time were ones in which logic and metaphysics prevailed, then the significance of Locke's position becomes clear. All of revelation-based theology and the entire scholastic project could no longer lay claim to certainty. Locke thus reduced the area of appropriate intellectual activity enormously. But he did so willingly and knowingly,[3] and in this he was followed by virtually all thinkers of the Enlightenment. Indeed, Locke was here laying the groundwork for much of modern liberalism. By denying the epistemological certainty of most theological and metaphysical propositions, Locke and those who followed him were undercutting sanctions that had been and might be applied to enforce compliance with such propositions. Where there was no certainty, there were no grounds for coercion. Locke's epistemology encouraged both a massive reorientation of intellectual effort away from the abstract and toward the concrete, and a concomitant extension of personal freedom.

Locke's theory of knowledge and psychology were not essays in particular disciplines. They amounted to a theory of man. And they contained a system of ethics. In the *Essay* Locke pointed out that human beings are so constructed that they enjoy and seek to maximize pleasurable sense stimuli, while they suffer from, and seek to avoid, stimuli that cause pain. It follows that "Things then are good or evil, only in reference to pleasure and pain."[4] Responses are not based on value judgments, but on physiological impulses, and so are rooted in human nature, which is by definition universal. Of course different cultures define and value pleasures and pains differently, so that cultural determinations are of great weight. This was apparent both to Locke and to most Enlightenment thinkers. But the fact of cultural diversity could not obscure two implications of Locke's theory of man that are of critical importance.

First, Locke's notion of an unspoiled and uniform human nature based on physiology defined human beings in terms of what they had in common. Biology is a great equalizer. If one accepted Locke's account of human development, one could not well be a racist. On the most fundamental level, that of their physiological composition, all men are indeed broadly equal. Differences of physical appearance, class, status and culture, however important, could not be construed as primary.

Secondly, Locke's emphasis on the natural proclivity of human beings to maximize pleasure and to minimize pain entails a break with the great classical systems of ethics based on virtue. For Plato, Aristotle and many Christian moralists, right action was directed to some higher good, which was intended to serve the community, or involved a higher form of knowledge. Locke, by contrast, laid the foundation for the validation of happiness as a moral category. He further asserted the legitimacy of self-interest against all forms of other-oriented ethical systems. He did not, however, advocate bald egoism. Indeed, Locke maintained that no one person by nature had titles to better treatment than another. The aspiration to happiness was universal. It was logical for Enlightenment thinkers such as Claude Adrien Helvétius and Jeremy Bentham to draw the conclusion that while the goal of the individual was to maximize his or her own happiness, the goal of society was to achieve "the greatest happiness of the greatest number." This doctrine, called utilitarianism, was characteristic of Enlightenment ethical thought in that it recognized the legitimacy of the individual's aspiration to his or her own happiness, while asserting a universal right to happiness for all and making society responsible for generalizing this good as far as possible.

Locke was one of the leading spokesmen for what was to become modern individualism. But in Locke's account of the legitimate pursuit of self-interest, the collectivity always benefited. It is in the notion of the pursuit of self-interest as the optimal means of achieving the general good that Locke can be seen as one of the most important founders of modern liberalism. Locke thus stands at the beginning of a number of the most dynamic, but also most problematic and contested, of the ideological currents of the Enlightenment.

Critical Humanism

Obviously, the critical study of the texts and history of classical antiquity was not new to the 17th and 18th centuries. The Greek and especially Roman classics had been central to the intellectual life of the elites of Europe since the Renaissance. Nor can we point to any innovations in the study of the classics to compare in scope or power with Newton's cosmology or Locke's psychology. Nevertheless, the place that the study of classical texts played in the Enlightenment entitles it to be considered one of the paradigms that structured its thought.

If one views the Enlightenment primarily as a struggle to overcome the Christian tradition, then the classics take on a central importance as a body of knowledge which was both pagan and philosophical. It is in this sense that Peter Gay has written of the Enlightenment as the "Rise of Modern Paganism."[5] Gay's treatment of classical culture as a store-house of secular values and critical attitudes that could be used by the *philosophes* to free themselves from the extensive and dogmatic claims of the Catholic Church on all aspects of life is, on the whole, convincing. From the Renaissance, and especially the Counter-Reformation on, the Greek and Latin classics formed the backbone of the curriculum of secondary education in most of Europe. In France the *collèges* run by the Jesuits taught a carefully expurgated version of the classics that might eliminate particular offensive passages, but could not destroy the basic character of these texts redolent with the atmosphere of a fundamentally different culture. In the hands of scholars no longer committed to the orthodoxies of the various churches, the classics could provide the inspiration, and often the means, of calling the basic assumptions of Christianity into question.

In the 15th and 16th centuries humanism played a largely positive role. The Italian humanists studied and purified Latin in order to recover the civic values of the classical polity and to attempt to capture for themselves something of an ethos that now had renewed relevance for the city-states of their times. Erasmus, on the other hand, studied Greek not primarily for its philological interest, but in order to restore the texts of the Greek Scriptures to as close to their original form and meaning as possible. By the 17th and 18th centuries, however, the cutting edge of intellectual advance had moved toward the natural sciences, as the examples of both Newton and Locke indicate. Humanism did not so much lose its interest for the educated classes of Europe as experience a change in the uses to which it was put.

In 1697 Pierre Bayle, a refugee from the religious persecution that Louis XIV inflicted on the Protestants of France and one of the greatest intellectuals of the 17th century, published his *Historical and Critical Dictionary*. This was a work of immense erudition. It appeared first in two folio volumes, then in three (1702), four (1720 and 1730), and finally in five (from 1734). It was also translated into English and German. The work was studded with citations in the original Greek and Latin, and usually contained a much higher proportion of notes than text. Despite its intimidating bulk and format, this work was reprinted frequently, and was found more often than any other by Daniel Mornet in his study of 500 libraries toward the end of the 18th century.[6]

The erudition of Bayle's *Dictionary* is remarkable. So too were the uses to which it was put. By close critical evaluation of the sources of history, both sacred and secular, Bayle showed how tenuous is our knowledge of the past. Corruptions of texts, contradictions among authors and variations in editions of the same work all pointed to the problem of establishing historical certainty. In Bayle's hands the very possibility of certain historical knowledge became problematic, and he is often regarded as one of the main advocates of skepticism between Michel Montaigne and David Hume. The uncertainty of source materials that Bayle emphasized was a major obstacle to historians trying to establish conclusive accounts of the pasts of their countries, and it was no less so for historians of religion, for whom, after initial acts of revelation, everything depended on the integrity of the written record.

Far though Bayle's subject matter was from that of Newton and Locke, the implications of his work were similar. All three men contended with the problem of the limits of human knowledge, and all three opted for restricted criteria of certainty. Unlike representatives of the established intellectual traditions of their own day, they were all prepared not only to admit their ignorance of large areas of intellectual endeavor, but also to insist on the impossibility of achieving certain knowledge in many areas. All three sought to encourage further work in areas in which certain knowledge was attainable, and all three wished to work more with empirically verifiable facts and were mistrustful of sweeping generalizations and theory.

In practice all three, despite their widely recognized achievements, counseled intellectual modesty. And from intellectual modesty to toleration and respect for the opinions of others is a small step. Indeed, it was arguably the intention of Bayle's monumental *Dictionary* to demonstrate the uncertainty of religious history, and so to lay the groundwork for toleration. Despite the fundamental differences in the subject matter of Newton, Locke and Bayle, all three scholars sought to limit the areas within which certain knowledge was attainable, and all viewed with equanimity, if not positive approval, the extension of those areas in which proof was impossible, and one opinion as good, more or less, as another. It is in this sense also, and not only in their positive achievements, that Newton, Locke and Bayle laid the groundwork for so much of what was liberal and tolerant in the Enlightenment.

The Key Values and Assumptions of the Enlightenment

Reason

The Enlightenment has often been referred to as the "Age of Reason" and this designation is not without justification. In contrast to the traditional Christian view of man as radically corrupted by sin and unable to achieve his salvation by his own efforts, the Enlightenment assumed that reason was a powerful and effective force for good. And in contrast to secular thinkers such as Machiavelli and Thomas Hobbes, who regarded man as a creature driven by irrational and violent passions that left reason only an instrumental and subordinate role, the thinkers of the Enlightenment on the whole regarded reason as capable of ordering and directing human life effectively. There was, further, a widespread belief in the goodness of reason in the 18th century in the sense that it was assumed that reason would be able to discover in the immanent order of the world solutions that would be to the general good.

Mainstream Enlightenment thought operated on the assumption, generally abandoned in the 19th century and merely quaint today, that there were no (or almost no) conflicts that could not be settled with a modicum of common sense and goodwill. It was assumed that at bottom reasonable solutions would be acceptable solutions. Harmony, conciliation and peaceful resolution of social and diplomatic problems on the basis of reason and fairness remained key Enlightenment aspirations as long as the movement retained its vitality. Similarly, it was assumed that men and women would prefer the general good to their own immediate self-interest not on the basis of altruism, but after rational calculation that demonstrated that the well-being of the individual was bound up with the well-being of the society and subgroups of which the individual was a part. The self-interest legitimated by the Enlightenment was enlightened other-regarding, and reasonable self-interest.

But to characterize the Enlightenment as an age of reason should not obscure the fact that "reason" in the 18th century was a more limited and more humble concept than it had been for the scholastics and for the great system builders of the 17th century. Peter Gay has reminded us that, as in the methodology of Newton and Locke, reason was limited by, and subordinated to, reference to the material world. Hypothesis was subordinated to fact. In this sense the 18th century saw, as Gay rightly argued, "a revolt against rationalism" in the name of empiricism.[7] The reason that the Enlightenment advocated was strictly fact-limited.

The implications of this fact-oriented and limited notion of reason are far-reaching. Abstract reason, metaphysics and logic were mistrusted by Enlightenment thinkers. Words not directly related to things were not to be relied on. Hence Voltaire's disdain for Cartesian physics.[8] Propositions that cannot be demonstrated by precise calculations or by recourse to the facts were suspect. They might be entertained, but they were not to be acted upon. Propositions of this sort include almost the entire realm of theology and much of ethics. And so prescriptive theology and prescriptive ethics find themselves largely delegitimized, for the Enlightenment concept of reason cannot assure their certainty. It follows that one of the main sources of Enlightenment liberalism is negative. It rests on the proposition that directives that cannot be shown to be true should not be enforced by society or the state. Beliefs or actions that did not cause direct harm were to be tolerated. Together, the insistence on the rationality of social norms and a notion of reason limited by empirically verifiable fact did much to lighten the weight of scholastic science, on the one hand, and of religious dogma, on the other.

Nature

Interest in nature grew during the 18th century. This was partly a consequence of achievements in the sciences during the 16th and 17th centuries, especially in astronomy, which made the world appear a more intelligible and less mysterious place than it had previously seemed. These advances in science allowed men and women who had the economic and cultural means to make themselves familiar with them to feel more at home in the world, and more the masters of it, than they had before. The scientific method developed by Newton and others held the promise that achievements comparable to those made in astronomy could be expected in other disciplines, so that eventually all of nature would be understood clearly and comprehensively. The appeal of the study of nature came to be expressed in the heightened prestige and activity of scientific academies, as well as in a vogue for the natural sciences among laymen, who frequented classes on experimental physics and chemistry, took up botany and established cabinets for the display of geological samples. Among the best sellers of the 18th century we find multi-volume works such the *Spectacle de la nature* of the abbé Pluche and the Count de Buffon's *Histoire naturelle*.

The Enlightenment concept of nature differed both from that of the Middle Ages, in which nature was often portrayed as standing in opposition to the Divine, and from the Darwinian view, which highlighted competition and irreconcilable conflict. Based largely on the Newtonian model of celestial physics, the Enlightenment concept of nature emphasized order and harmony. The deists of the 18th century were not original in seeing in the orderliness of nature a manifestation of the Divine. This is a position found both in the Hebrew Scriptures and in medieval philosophy. Moreover, the argument from design was often used at the time to prove the existence of a Divine Creator. But unlike medieval thinkers, the deists of the 18th century disregarded revelation, and based their ethics on the assumed benevolence of the Creator who had taken the trouble to make an orderly and hospitable world for mankind to inhabit. Nature came to be perceived as inherently orderly, and beyond this, as broadly beneficent. This ethical twist is one of the distinctive features of the Enlightenment view of nature.

Educated men and women in the 18th century generally assumed that nature was morally good and could serve as a model for social behavior. Jean-Jacques Rousseau is the best known and greatest exponent of the goodness of nature, but this view was one that Rousseau articulated rather than originated. Few writers of the time would have stated as boldly as Rousseau did, that "All is well as it comes from the hands of the Author of things: all degenerates in the hands of man,"[9] but few adherents of Enlightenment thought would have allowed that nature was itself in any way corrupt, or denied that the orderliness of nature also implied goodness. By assuming the original and natural goodness of man, the thinkers of the Enlightenment shifted the emphasis in the search for the origin of evil from theology and metaphysics to history and society. It is, then, a thoroughly Newtonian view of nature that much Enlightenment social thought rests upon.

The hypothetical "state of nature" dear to social theorists of the 17th and 18th centuries was used to spell out the social and moral implications of a rehabilitated concept of nature. If equality was the original condition of mankind, then classes and estates must be products of historical processes, or perhaps simply accidents, and if they were to be defended, they would have to be defended in terms of utility or historical contingency rather than natural right. Similarly, the original liberty of mankind in the state of nature called into question the limitations on liberty found in different degrees in different societies. And again, the original, essential and normative status accorded to liberty, as was the case with equality, put defenders of established regimes at a disadvantage. It is perhaps usual for broad notions of nature to correspond to principles of social organization in most periods of history and in most societies, but this correspondence is particularly close in the case of the Enlightenment.

Secularization

One of the basic assumptions of the Enlightenment, which followed from its view of nature and scientific method, was that virtually all phenomena were amenable to empirical investigation and that they could be explained in rational and often mechanistic terms. For European elites in the 18th century the realm of mystery shrank while that of rational explanation expanded. This resulted in the diminution of the roles of both theology and superstition, and an increasing belief in the ability of mankind to understand and to moderate the world in which it found itself. This shift has been referred to both as secularization and as disenchantment.

For the illusion of an enchanted universe, the Enlightenment substituted the illusion of a transparently intelligible universe. Something was lost and something gained. While the enchanted universe was rich with a sense of the wonder and mystery of being, it was also thick with unpredictable occult forces that men and women feared and sought to propitiate as best they might.

It is probably true that by the 18th century the domesticated enchantment of Catholicism and Protestantism had gained ascendancy over the older pagan forms of enchantment that permeated all levels of society. But it was also true that in the battle for control of enchantment one might fall victim to repression by the authorities of the dogmatically constrained enchantment of established religion as easily as to the spells of a witch. In rejecting both the enchantment of witchcraft and that of theology, as well as the conflicts between them, the Enlightenment lost something of the sense of mystery and beauty permeating the older worldview. But it is not clear how people could have retained a belief in the enchanted universe without also finding themselves burdened with beliefs in sorcery and *autos-da-fé*. Probably to be rid of the one, it was necessary to eliminate the other. But this did not inevitably remove all sense of wonder from the world. Deists such as Voltaire and Rousseau could also express their awe at the orderliness of the scientifically verifiable workings of nature, and see behind natural mechanisms the designs of the world's Creator. Materialists such as Denis Diderot, the Baron d'Holbach or Claude Adrien Helvétius, who denied the existence of an ordering force beyond nature, were scarcely less impressed with the beauty and order of nature itself.

If the achievements of science resulted in a demystified account of nature, abuses within the Church contributed powerfully to undermining the status of that institution, and often its ministers. While it is generally true that parish priests in the 18th century performed essential religious and social functions and retained the respect and appreciation of their parishioners as well as of men of letters, wealthy prelates, cloistered monks and nuns, worldly *abbés* and friars who had irregular contacts with the population came in for strident and sometimes justified criticism. The anticlericalism, which abuses within the Church called forth, was usually based on pragmatic and utilitarian considerations. Enlightenment critics of the Church were generally not inclined to enter into debates over dogma, but for the most part restricted their demands to reforms in areas of social and sexual behavior, and for greater toleration. In other words, religion came to be judged more in terms of material and secular considerations, and the fierce conflicts over dogma, which had characterized the Reformation, gave way to arguments on a more concrete and mundane level. This too was a part of the movement toward secularization and disenchantment.

Individualism

In virtually all societies the questions of the degree of individual autonomy and of responsibility toward the collectivity, or collectivities, to which one belongs are central issues. In traditional societies the balance is usually in favor of the group or collectivity. During most of the Old Regime, one's identity was constructed from the groups or corporations—state, family, parish, church, guild, confraternity, professional association and clubs—to which one belonged. Membership in multiple corporations defined one's status, and these corporations gave society its structure. Hence the respect accorded them. During the 18th century, however, more extensive claims were put forward on behalf of the individual. Emphasis shifted gradually and unevenly away from one's obligations to various corporations and toward the rights, aspirations and satisfaction of the individual.

A sense of self and recognition of the force of self-interest did not, of course, originate with the Enlightenment. Both Machiavelli and Hobbes were acutely aware of the potential of the passion-driven and anarchic individual, and both sought means of channeling or limiting such individuals. In the case of Hobbes, contemporary science, which was atomistic, suggested that the individual was to be given a higher ontological status than the collectivity. Individuals existed necessarily and physiologically, and so were logically prior to any groups that they made up. The assumption of a state of nature from which individuals emerge by means of an agreement or contract objectified this point of view, making the state secondary and derivative, while the individual was primary and constitutive.

It was in this context that the Enlightenment conferred on the individual and on individual self-interest a degree of legitimacy that they had not previously enjoyed. But unlike the power-oriented and radically egoistic individualism of Machiavelli's *Prince*, mainstream Enlightenment individualism was democratized and socialized. Legitimate self-interest for most thinkers of the 18th century could not disregard the rights of others, and in that each person was expected to calculate the implications of his or her actions, and to avoid actions harmful to himself, nor would he or she fail to do so. Moreover, the pursuit of self-interest, as conceived by Bernard Mandeville, Adam Smith and the physiocrats, would automatically maximize the general good, as in the case of a baker who would from pure self-interest strive to provide the best quality bread at the cheapest possible price, for in this way his product, and he with it, would prosper most. It is not simple egoism that Enlightenment thinkers sought to legitimize, but rather the rational pursuit of self-interest modified by an objective and self-regulating mechanism that would reward individual industry while maximizing social well-being.

Though the tendency to find harmonious solutions to all issues, including the tension between self-interest and the common good, was always prominent in Enlightenment thought, there was also an awareness that conflicts were sometimes irreconcilable. The economic success of a family, for example, was often dependent on an intentionally unequal division of the family's resources. In the nobility, especially, elder sons normally succeeded to the estate, while younger sons were forced to accept subordinate positions in the Church or the army, or to seek their own fortune as best they might. Daughters often suffered even more from accepted strategies of family advancement. Many nobles allowed only the eldest daughter to marry. Others suffered enforced celibacy, or were deprived of the emotional and social satisfactions of stable and regular relationships, and of families of their own. It is a situation such as this that Diderot dramatized in his novel *The Nun,* in which a young woman was forced into a convent against her will. Her plight reflects the complete negation of her right to happiness and self-determination at the hands of corporate authorities. In allowing the victim of this system to escape so as to live her life as she chose, Diderot sided with the individual against life-denying authority.

Liberalism

Liberalism is a doctrine that maintains that it is appropriate and desirable to allow individuals as much freedom as possible and compatible with a minimalist view of social order. It is a position that can be maintained only if one makes a number of assumptions about man and the world.

Maximal freedom for the individual makes sense only so long as human beings are conceived in such a way that this freedom does not become self-destructive, and so long as circumstances do not require strict discipline and a high degree of social integration. Authority is a means by which societies that are, or feel themselves to be, threatened, attempt to assure their security. Whether the perceived danger comes from within or without, from a human or a natural agency, is irrelevant from the point of view of the degree of liberty allowed the individual.

It follows that on a Hobbesian view of human nature, a high degree of individual liberty is an intolerable danger to society. A strong central authority is a condition for the very existence of society for Hobbes because the inherently aggressive and irrational nature of men would destroy any form of social organization were it allowed free rein. Similarly, a society threatened by invasion and conquest would have to maintain a high level of social discipline to assure its continued existence, and this at a high cost to the liberty of individuals.

For those who accepted Locke's analysis of human nature, the need for authority and social discipline was minimized, and it was safe to accord greater liberty to individuals. Locke denied that humans were ineluctably driven by irrational and aggressive passions, asserting instead that they were creatures who were morally neutral from birth and developed in interaction with the world around them. The human body contained its own control mechanisms directed by the senses, so that an insatiable drive for domination was not an integral part of human nature. And while Locke certainly acknowledged that humans were primarily motivated by self-interest, he argued that in pursuing their self-interest they would consult reason and calculate the advantages and disadvantages of any course of action, and make decisions accordingly. It is the reasonable, calculated and enlightened concept of self-interest formulated by Locke and his followers that allows them to reduce the role of authority in society and significantly to extend the scope of liberty and self-determination the individual might enjoy.

While a domesticated and rationalized notion of self-interest is necessary for a liberal revision of the relation between individual and collectivity, it does not by itself assure the feasibility of such a revision.

In societies experiencing serious tensions that result in civil wars or wars with neighbors, order remains the primary objective of social and political organization. During the 16th and 17th centuries wars in which religion played an important role, at least as an ideology of domination, civil wars and wars between dynastic states all made the central political problem in Europe achieving and maintaining order. Probably Hobbes gave this problem its most striking formulation, and Richelieu and Louis XIV did most, through the construction of the absolutist state, to provide a practical solution. Indeed, until the problem of order had been solved, it did not make much sense to raise the issue of individual liberty.

By the early 18th century a degree of political order had been achieved in Europe that made it possible to regard the most basic of all problems in political theory as solved, and allowed attention to shift to the question of freedom. Europe did not enter into a period of universal peace during the 18th century, though this was an aspiration of thinkers as diverse as the abbé de Saint Pierre and Immanuel Kant. But it is fair to say that levels of violence within societies and between states fell from the excesses of the preceding centuries. This was not, of course, an achievement for which the Enlightenment could claim responsibility, but it was one on which it built.

If the stabilization of the European states system and of European societies contributed to laying the groundwork for the development of liberalism in the 18th century, it does not by itself explain the extent to which this new attitude rooted itself in the consciousness of the progressive elements of European elites. Returning briefly to the achievements of the founding thinkers of the Enlightenment will help to put this issue into perspective.

The disenchantment of the universe effected by Newton in his demonstration of the regularity and pervasiveness of the laws of nature reduced the need for appeals to inscrutable forces and to authority. And the orderliness discovered by Newton in all branches of physics served as the basis for a presumption of comparable orderliness in other sciences, natural and social, provided the appropriate data could be subjected to suitable analysis. Thus, as numerous historians have pointed out, thinkers of the Enlightenment sought the laws of society, which they assumed would be few and comprehensive, and which they also assumed would reflect immanent order and harmony. It was on this set of assumptions that Adam Smith claimed to have discovered economic laws that existed objectively, and which men needed only to be free to follow to maximize social well-being.

Smith recognized that the infinitely complex bureaucratic regulations of mercantilism were intended to achieve benefits for the state and its population, but argued that they were fundamentally misconceived in that they intruded state control into areas best left to individual initiative. The market automatically adjusted supply to demand so as to assure both plenty and prosperity, and the self-interest of the individual would automatically engage him or her in economic activity in a way that would maximize the well-being of both the individual and society. It was the assumed underlying harmony of individual and social objectives that made state intervention so retrograde and regrettable. Smith's doctrine did not come to command wide acceptance until the 19th century, for in his own time most statesman and theorists of economics hesitated to leave the vital question of the supply of subsistence goods to the vagaries of a supposedly harmonious market. It was only after the stakes involved in deregulating the market were reduced that economic liberalism gained the wide support that it enjoyed among the middle and upper classes.

Like Newton's physics, Locke's epistemology also contributed to accrediting liberalism. One of the main points of the *Essay Concerning Human Understanding* was to show that certainty of knowledge could only be achieved under restricted conditions and in only some areas. It follows that society should not have recourse to coercion where certainty is lacking. Following this logic, Montesquieu and Cesare Beccaria argued for the decriminalization of offenses based on opinion and for the separation of civil judicial procedures from religion.[10] Here we see a different side of the liberalism, and with it toleration, of the Enlightenment. By emphasizing what we cannot know, Locke restricted the areas in which society might be entitled to interfere. While Newton encouraged people to think in terms of an underlying order and harmony that men were naturally drawn to, Locke, at least by implication, contributed to extending the scope of individual self-determination by undercutting the grounds for the exercise of authority.

Pierre Bayle also furthered liberalism by largely negative means. Like Locke, he emphasized the limits of our knowledge, especially in the areas of history and religion. Where sources are unreliable and contradictions abound, there is little justification for constraint. The skepticism that shows through Bayle's massive erudition was not so much a denial of the possibility of sound knowledge as denial of the appropriateness of persecution on the basis of belief or dogma.[11] The demand for individual liberty and social toleration that grew during the 18th century depended on both a positive evaluation of the competence and rights of individuals as opposed to collectivities, and on a sense of intellectual modesty that took into account the limits of what it was possible to know.

Humanity and Beneficence

As central as was individualism to the Enlightenment, and as important as was liberalism as a framework for the elaboration of individualist values, the atomizing tendencies of these values were offset by a value no less characteristic of the Enlightenment: *humanité*. It is a notion the sense of which we have for the most part lost, and so requires explanation.

Humanité was a notion that made little sense to ages and civilizations that defined themselves in terms of their religious allegiances. For them mankind was divided primarily between believers in the true faith and heretics. Still less does an all-inclusive notion of humanity appeal to racists, for whom differences between racial groupings, however defined or imagined, are of primary significance and, moreover, insuperable. Similarly, extreme nationalists subordinate all other considerations to their loyalty to particular states and their ideologies. During the Enlightenment the notion of a community of humanity was more convincing and more powerful than the notions of communities of faith, race or nation.

The value *humanité* was rooted in a Lockean approach that emphasized the common biological bases of all human beings. As creatures that have broadly the same physiologies, whose responses to pain and pleasure, however culturally varied, can be recognized, and who exist within certain minimal social frameworks, the similarities among humans were perceived as greater than the differences. The borders of humanity are not altogether clear. For instance, the primal humanoid creature of Rousseau's *Second Discourse* cannot be distinguished from other animals except by a capacity for improvement that initially is not apparent. Its humanity is realized only through a long process of evolution.[12] But it is less the vagueness of the border between men and animals that is relevant for thinkers of the Enlightenment than the assumption of community among all human beings. It is this assumption, based on physiological similarity that overrides cultural diversity, that is at the core of the Enlightenment notion of *humanité*. And it is this assumption of community that raises the notion of *humanité* from a scientific observation to a moral imperative.

For the Enlightenment, *humanité* meant more than recognition that human beings could not survive unaided in extreme conditions, or could not develop normally, or maintain their existence at all, beneath a given nutritional level, or could not develop linguistic skills in isolation. It meant that as creatures of a similar sort among whom a broad community was believed to exist, one human being, or group of human beings, was morally obligated toward others, that there are certain minimal standards that need to be honored and that human beings are obliged to behave with a degree of respect and consideration for others.

Humanité, then, was not only a recognition of common humanity, but also a set of moral imperatives that followed from this recognition. This is not to say that there were no racists in the 18th century, or that all *philosophes* placed equal weight on the concept. While Diderot emphasized the centrality of an all-inclusive world community of mankind in his article "Natural Law" in the *Encyclopédie*, Rousseau, in a chapter of the *Social Contract* which he did not publish,[13] questioned, not the validity of the notion of *humanité*, but its effectiveness, and insisted on the importance of collectivities intermediate between the individual and mankind in structuring human life. But on the whole it was the notion of membership in a broadly conceived humanity that inclined the men and women of the Enlightenment to reject and oppose racist doctrines and to assert a set of rights applicable to all mankind. The notion of *humanité* helped to offset the individualistic strain of Enlightenment thought, and it was to a considerable degree the ideological basis for the criticism of European racism and colonialism produced by the abbé Raynal and his collaborators in the multi-volume best seller, *The History of the Two Indies.*

The term "beneficence," or *bienfaisance*, entered into usage during the 18th century. The notion of doing good to one's fellow was not a new one, but the terminology did reflect a new understanding of what that meant. Beneficence has often been taken as a secularized counterpart of the Christian virtue of charity, and to a degree it is. But beneficence is both more and less than charity. It is less in that it does not entail an inner emotional state, an outpouring of love, an awareness of cosmic unity and belonging. Rather it was the impulse to relieve evident want and discomfort, conditions that can be determined by empirical observation and alleviated by appropriate actions.[14] Nor was beneficence indiscriminate. It was not intended to encourage the lazy or improvident in their ways, but to reflect a concern on the part of society for those who, by no fault of their own, found themselves in need. Charity was rather less judgmental.

Beneficence was also more than charity in that charity was a virtue that was normally exercised toward members of one's own religious community, or at least prospective members of that community. Catholics were not always encouraged to be charitable toward Protestants or

Anabaptists, or heretics, or adherents of other religions, and other Christian denominations, while disagreeing with Catholics on much else, seemed to agree with them on this. The referent of beneficence, on the other hand, was humanity. One was obliged to do good, and entitled to expect comparable aid oneself, solely on the basis of one's status as a human being. The cohesive forces of beneficence and *humanité* held the centrifugal forces of individualism and self-interest in check, at least for a time. Charity might be regarded as having universal application by certain currents (often marginal and persecuted) within Christianity, but for the most part the established denominations tended to limit the exercise of this virtue to members of the same denomination. Beneficence had a comparable metaphysical grounding, but the Divine Artificer of deist theology being conceived as universal and nondenominational, so too was application of the virtue of beneficence. Indeed, beneficence was both the sum total of the social gospel of deism, and, for atheists such as Diderot and d'Holbach, nature's directive to all its sentient creatures, which amounts to pretty much the same thing.

Moralism

Historians have recognized in the Enlightenment the beginnings of the social sciences and of the assumption that human actions are subject to laws that follow from climate, economic conditions and principles of social and political organization. There is no doubt that the demography of Thomas Robert Malthus, the economic theory of Adam Smith, David Ricardo, Karl Marx and others, and theories of social reorganization on the basis of supposedly scientific principles put forward by Henri Saint Simon, Charles Fourier and Auguste Comte are rooted in basic assumptions of Enlightenment thought and that some of these authors claimed to be building on Newton's method in order to subject society to the same kind of rigorous analysis that had been achieved in the natural sciences. Further, the interest that historians normally show in the origins of movements and ideas that subsequently exercise great influence has reinforced this tendency to see the Enlightenment as the point from which originated the desire to comprehend the social and political worlds scientifically, and then to modify and improve them.

Arguably the origins of the social sciences and the positivist mentality are one of the most original and important features of the Enlightenment. What this development tends to obscure, however, is that the Enlightenment probably placed more reliance on moral agency, and expected more of morality, than ages before or since. This reliance on moral agency and emphasis on ethics to achieve social goals will be referred to as moralism.

Enlightenment moralism developed in a period after Augustinian rigorism had lost its grip on most thinking people, but before the social sciences gained the ascendancy that they enjoyed from the 19th century on. In Augustine's view of the world the greatness of the Divine precluded effective moral action on the part of human beings. All were the sons and daughters of Adam and Eve, all bore the burden of original sin. Since all men were radically corrupt, they were unable to achieve their own salvation. However, by divine grace some might be saved. According to Catholic doctrine the Church could and did assure the salvation of its members, so salvation remained within reach of mankind even in its fallen condition. But salvation, while still attainable, could not be effected by unaided right will and action alone. Divine grace and the offices of the Church were necessary. Moral agency by itself was inadequate.

The rise of the social sciences also tended to diminish the role and importance of moral agency. Economics demography, and sociology all emphasize the lawfulness of larger systems, and individuals, being part of these larger systems, are restricted in their freedom of choice. If the determinism inherent in the social sciences failed to reach the comprehensiveness of the doctrine of original sin, it nevertheless caused people in the 19th century and later to recognize that their freedom of choice and action were severely limited. In the work of Montesquieu, Anne-Robert-Jacques Turgot, the Marquis de Condorcet, Adam Smith, Adam Ferguson, John Millar and others, the groundwork of the social sciences was being laid. But there were other forces at work in the Enlightenment that nevertheless allowed the notion of moral agency to achieve a more central role than it had had in previous centuries or in those that followed.

One of the legacies of the classical world valued by the Enlightenment was republicanism. This was a school of thought that validated active citizenship, which included the right directly to take part in the framing of laws and the administration of the state, as well as the obligation of military service. In the formulations of Aristotle, Plutarch and Cicero, citizenship required responsibility and imposed obligations on the citizen, but in return provided him—and citizenship in the classical world was the prerogative of males—with a context in which he could fully realize his human potential. The key value that bound the citizen to the state was virtue, which was often interpreted as the identity of the citizen with the state, or the readiness of the citizen to subordinate his personal interests to those of the state, or the common good.

There can be little doubt but that the classical republican notion of virtue ran against the rehabilitation of self-interest that occurred in the 18th century. Nevertheless, the older idea of civic virtue had wide currency, and was not without gifted spokesmen. The classical curriculum of *collèges* made the values of the ancient city-state part of the consciousness of all who attended them, and the fullness of the life that active citizenship in the classical world conferred was attractive to young men constrained within the politically passive status of subjects of a monarch. To the degree that the ideology of absolutism was breaking down, classical republicanism offered the most fully articulated and most attractive alternate model of political participation. Probably the most eloquent writer of the Enlightenment, Jean-Jacques Rousseau, was the foremost advocate of the classical notion of citizenship, and with it, the idea of virtue.

A second source for the validation of moral agency in the 18th century was the period's notion of nature. As noted above, the ordered and harmonious conception of nature common in Enlightenment thought itself had an ethical aspect. The ordered universe of Newton was amenable to rational understanding and appeared to be the handiwork of a beneficent Creator. Rousseau's assertion of, and faith in, the goodness of nature would seem to be based on the partial disenchantment effected by Newton. But it also rested on the psychology of the senses put forward by Locke.

By making pain and pleasure the things that ultimately directed all human behavior, Locke made his psychology into a system of ethics. One of the distinctive features of this ethics is that it is not based on concepts of right and wrong, but on immediate sensation. Of course it is still a moral judgment to assert that pain is bad and pleasure good, but it is not a judgment that is abstracted from ordinary experience. And while recognizing that there are many situations that vary from culture to culture in which it is deemed appropriate for individuals to accept considerable pain, we generally assume that such situations aside, individuals from whatever culture will prefer pleasure or non-suffering to pain. Insofar as this position is physiologically based, it is valid cross-culturally, and so can be claimed to be natural.

Locke's ethically inclined psychology was taken up by a number of 18th-century moralists known as the moral sense school, of whom Francis Hutcheson and Adam Smith were leading figures. In his significantly entitled *Theory of Moral Sentiments* (1759), Adam Smith argued that all human beings, including even "ruffians," naturally felt sympathy with the suffering of others.[15] To make this claim good required nothing more than the assumptions that pain was unwelcome, and that by associating our own experiences of pain with the outer signs of distress in others we to some degree come to share in their distress. The mechanism of association in Locke's psychology made this second assumption readily acceptable. Thus for Smith, men were naturally moral beings.

Interestingly, though Rousseau differed from Smith in many basic ways, in the first part of the *Second Discourse* (1755) he proceeds from the same assumptions to the same conclusion. According to Rousseau, self-interest and pity are the only primal inclinations that man receives from nature. By pity he means the sympathy (literally "feeling-with") that one sentient creature feels at witnessing the distress of another creature, providing that the observer has had a similar experience. The pity of which Rousseau speaks here is not a matter of judgment, but a physiological response to a known sense experience.[16] In this sense the notions of sympathy and pity described by Smith and Rousseau, based firmly in the categories of Lockean psychology, serve as the basis for the natural existence in human beings of a moral sense or proclivity.

We might assume that in the 18th century, as today, the theories of moral philosophers did not get much public exposure, and so had relatively little influence. Such was not the case. First, both Smith's *Theory of Moral Sentiments* and Rousseau's *Discourse on the Origins of Inequality* were best sellers. Further, both works, at least with respect to their psychological assumptions, drew on and popularized the work of Locke, which was well received and formed one of the basic elements in the Enlightenment worldview.

Secondly, primacy of moral agency was popularized in the literature of the time. Jean-François Marmontel's *Contes moraux* went through numerous editions and found many imitators. Newspapers and literary periodicals often carried filler items entitled "Traits de Bienfaisance" or something similar, which gave accounts of acts of kindness or beneficence performed, often across barriers of class, and demonstrated to a public that feared that social bonds were dissolving and had need of reassurance, that virtue would find its reward. Indeed, the last decades of the Old Regime saw the organization of numerous clubs and groups whose explicit purpose was to reward acts of kindness or patriotism on the part of those in need. These groups included freemasons, who indulged in often sentimental acts of beneficence, a *maison philanthropique* founded in Paris in 1780, and voluntary associations dedicated to providing basic education for those who could not afford it, dowries for virtuous but poor young women or pensions for the aged. Reports on all these activities were frequently found in the periodic press, and were even collected in anthologies published separately.

The importance of moral agency, then, was founded in one of the constitutive paradigms of Enlightenment thought, drew sustenance from classical republicanism, and was spun out into the literature and social activism of the last decades of the Old Regime. Probably these tendencies were in part responses to a concern that socially cohesive values were being attacked by the newly rehabilitated notion of self-interest, and to socio-economic tensions that were misperceived in moral terms.[17] What is significant here is the tendency of the men and women of the Enlightenment to assume that the problems they faced could best be met by means of moral agency. Certainly earlier generations, which saw human activity as less autonomous because vitiated by original sin, or following generations, which believed human choice to be limited by broader social and economic forces, would not have shared this assumption. Arguably the French Revolution was the last great event in Western history in which the assumptions of moralism carried great weight. But that, while one of the more important and less recognized legacies of the Enlightenment to the Revolution, is another story.

The Social Dimensions of Enlightenment

The Complex Elitism of Enlightenment Culture

The question of who shared in the Enlightenment is a very different one from the question of what the thought of the Enlightenment was like. Culture is not dissociated from social standing, and while there are cases of people from the lower levels of society achieving functional membership in elite culture, such cases are rare. And for the authorities, they are problematic. The prospect of young men from economically deprived backgrounds gaining a degree of competence in the skills of literacy and seeking to become writers or intellectuals troubled administrators and social conservatives who tended to believe that those who did not benefit from existing social and economic relations would become critics of those relations, and that such voices were best not heard. It is the well-known fear of an "intellectual proletariat."

Robert Darnton has done more than any other scholar to elucidate the nature and implications of the lives of impecunious writers and intellectuals during the second half of the 18th century in France. He has shown that while a few such men might succeed in rising into the establishment, where they enjoyed the fruits of patronage, the great majority of the inhabitants of Grub Street were subject to grinding poverty that forced them to do hackwork, turning out translations, compilations and pamphlets, were constantly in danger of lapsing into various forms of petty crime, or could be forced to become police spies. Darnton has argued that the degradation of Grub Street often resulted in an emotive and visceral radicalism that later found expression in the French Revolution.[18] The milieu of Grub Street is also significant from another point of view. It represents one of the lower limits to which Enlightenment thought extended.

In cultural terms 18th-century France was a deeply divided society. The culture of the Enlightenment was emphatically that of an elite. Membership in that elite was conferred in the first place by the possession of wealth, and secondly by a willingness to invest some of that wealth in education and in cultural artifacts, such as books, periodicals, paintings and musical instruments, and then to participate at some level, be it as audiences for plays or concerts, or actively, as members of academies or any of a range of discussion groups. Those with access to the culture of the Enlightenment and choosing to actualize that potential to some degree can be seen as constituting an enlightened community.

How big was this enlightened community? This is a question to which no precise answer is possible and to which historians have offered varying estimates. Daniel Roche, for example, has recently emphasized that the culture of the Enlightenment was intimately bound up with the urban environment.[19] On the one hand, this indicates that the royal court, which played a dominant role in the articulation of high culture from the Renaissance through the 17th century, had a diminished part in the culture of the Enlightenment, and on the other hand, that the overwhelming majority of the 80 percent of the population living in the countryside could not have been expected to have access to the movement. In towns the working population would for the most part have been excluded from the world of the Enlightenment, though access would appear to have been a real if remote option from the level of master artisan up. Diderot, for example, was the son of a master cutler, and Rousseau of a master watchmaker, but both men are highly exceptional.

More specific indicators, such as subscription lists to periodicals and pressruns of books suggest that only a very small proportion of the population was directly involved in Enlightenment culture, even in the relatively passive function of readers. Successful periodicals toward the end of the Old Regime published between one and two thousand copies of a number, and though there are examples of journals publishing larger pressruns, they were few. Assuming that each copy of a periodical reached on average 20 readers by being passed around among friends, left around for casual use in private homes, or kept in cafés for the use of customers, that periodical would still only have had a readership of 40,000 or 50,000 people out of a total population of 27 or 28 million. Robert Darnton has found that close to 25,000 copies of the *Encyclopédie* were published before the outbreak of the French Revolution.[20] However one may multiply the total number of readers of this work, the result is still that only a tiny proportion of the population might have had access to it.

Most modern authorities would not allow that the enlightened community consisted of more than 1 or 2 percent of the population of France. In his *Philosophical Letters* Voltaire asserted that 95 percent of the population would not be able to read his book, and of those who could, the great majority would not be interested in doing so. Nor did this bother him.[21] An estimate of the size of the enlightened community as about 5 percent of the population of France is probably as liberal a one as can be sustained for western Europe, and would probably have to be considerably reduced for the eastern parts of the continent. It would also be extremely inclusive, granting membership in the community to those whose participation was marginal.

In cultural terms, the great majority of the population of 18th century Europe lived generations, if not centuries, before Montesquieu and Voltaire. The weight of material necessity circumscribed their world within the narrowest of boundaries. Their most immediate concern was assuring enough to eat, a task in which they were too often unsuccessful, and their ability to learn was limited as much by malnutrition and exhaustion as by lack of access to secondary education. Most rural children in France did attend primary schools or *petites écoles,* but these schools, which often functioned irregularly, were run by the Church and village community, and were conceived in terms of acculturation, which included minimal religious instruction, but not necessarily the skills of literacy. Protestant societies generally had higher rates of school attendance and literacy than Catholic ones, but this is not to say that they sought to encourage habits of critical thought among lower-class children. Most men and women in the 18th century still lived in an enchanted universe in which witches or priests were seen as the agents of authority and sources of wisdom, and in which the local seigneur and notary were the arbiters of material well-being. The mentality of the enlightened was both a badge of elite status and a tool of domination, while the mentality and culture of the poor were geared to surviving in conditions of subjugation and deprivation. How the men and women of the Enlightenment related to their social inferiors is one of the more complex and interesting features of that movement.

In order to understand the Enlightenment it is well to keep in mind that in social terms it excluded, though never hermetically, some 95 percent of the French population, and so was thoroughly elitist. The social composition of this elite, however, was far from uniform. It used to be maintained that the Enlightenment was essentially a bourgeois movement. While it is certainly fair to claim that it was thoroughly urban, this is not to say that it was necessarily bourgeois. In light of recent research it makes better sense to claim that it had a significant bourgeois component. Information derived from subscription lists to periodicals or publishing projects like the *Encyclopédie* and from membership lists of academies indicates that the enlightened community included important, and often dominant, representation from the nobility and the clergy.

It was common, for example, to find 30 or 40 percent of subscribers to literary periodicals to be nobles and clerics, though they together represented only 3 or 4 percent of the population. Of regular members of French provincial academies in the 18th century nearly half were nobles, though of the less prestigious corresponding members just under a third were.[22] Of known subscribers to the *Encyclopédie* in the area in and around Besançon, just over 40 percent were nobles, slightly more than 10 percent clerics, and roughly half belonged to the upper ranks of the third estate.[23] Clearly, in social terms it will not do to ignore the very substantial rates of participation of the privileged elites of old-regime society in the collective undertakings of the enlightened community. The high proportions of nobles and clerics in Enlightenment cultural activities has led historians to speak of the social basis of the movement being made up of a composite elite in which talent and wealth count for more than birth or social standing.

This is not to say, however, that the bourgeoisie did not play a significant role in the Enlightenment. But the sources cited above indicate that bourgeois who took an active part in Enlightenment culture were educators, doctors and above all a rich variety of legal professionals, and not businessmen and manufacturers. In other words, the bourgeoisie participating most visibly in the Enlightenment was a bourgeoisie of "old-regime type." This is not surprising. Members of the liberal professions are trained in disciplines that draw from and feed into high culture. It was not just a matter of lawyers and doctors having libraries with more works representative of the Enlightenment in them than merchants and manufacturers, it was a question of those engaged in commerce rarely having the time or interest or willingness to buy books at all. They were engaged in building their fortunes. Often their children or grandchildren would make the transition to the world of the learned professions, and their cultural outlook would change accordingly. It is also worth pointing out that at least better-off merchants and manufacturers would have had family ties with the liberal professions, and that merchants would often have had occasion to consult lawyers for business purposes. In this way businessmen would have had direct contact with more active participants in Enlightenment culture, and would have been exposed to their attitudes and ideas. Rather than excluding themselves from the culture of the Enlightenment, members of the commercial bourgeoisie can be seen as associating with it more passively and in more restricted fashion. While there is a real distinction between the participation of a commercial and a liberal bourgeoisie in the culture of the Enlightenment, it is not sharp.

There is another sense in which it is possible to speak of the Enlightenment as a bourgeois movement. This is with respect to the overall tendency of its ideology. Insofar as the Enlightenment favored universal values, individual endeavor and utilitarian criteria and was critical of corporatism and of hierarchy, it makes sense to argue that the movement favored the interests of those sectors of the population engaged in the rational maximization of their self-interest. In the long run, liberty and equality were compatible with the civic vision and interests of the bourgeoisie. This is not to say that progressive elements of the privileged orders did not often share the universalist and egalitarian ideals that appealed directly to many members of the elites of the third estate, or that they did not work actively to reform society along these lines. Clearly they did, and this is one of the things that gives Enlightenment culture its richness and complexity. But the long project of reform on which thinkers and administrators of the time were engaged and which might, given world and time enough, have resulted in a society transformed and modernized along the lines of the British model, was interrupted by a complex set of events beginning in 1787/89, which, for the sake of simplicity, is referred to as the French Revolution.

By destroying the main corporate structures and status systems of the Old Regime within a very short time, the Revolution created a world largely in harmony with the universalist ideals of the Enlightenment and the immediate interests of the bourgeoisie. But this does not mean that the bourgeoisies of the Old Regime advocated violence in politics or planned the overthrow of the regime in which they lived and flourished. In the sense that key Enlightenment values such as universalism and individual rights were compatible with long-term bourgeois interests, it makes sense to describe the Enlightenment as "bourgeois." But it is surely incorrect to deny that the nobility and clergy played central roles in the movement, or to assert that the objectives striven for by the complex of intellectual elites that formed the backbone of the enlightened community involved more than gradual and pacific reform.

The Structure of the Enlightened Community

If the enlightened community included from several hundred thousand to a million or so members, including family of those more active, and excluded roughly 95 percent of the population, it still had a complex institutional structure and a sophisticated system of communication. The institutions that structured the enlightened community ranged from the august academies, of both capitals and provinces, to informal reading circles and cafés. An understanding of them is essential to any appreciation of Enlightenment thought.

Perhaps the most basic distinction among institutions of the enlightened community is between those that were patronized or chartered by the state and those that were voluntary associations. In the first category there is the court, whose cultural role has been better studied for the 17th century than for the 18th century, and the academies.

During the Renaissance and through the 17th century the court played a central role in supporting and directing the development of high culture. Royal patronage was eagerly sought by artists and writers, and the crown, in return for the pensions, official posts and sinecures it conferred, usually expected that the artists and intellectuals it supported do something for the regime. By the 18th century artists and intellectuals had found additional resources. The most important of these was the market for books and periodicals, but probably its role has been exaggerated. Only a handful of writers could support themselves by their writings in the age of Enlightenment. In France, at least, the bookseller or publisher seldom proved more generous than aristocratic patrons had been. Patronage by the court, however, could still prove vital to an artist's or writer's career. The commissioning of the *Devin du village* for presentation before Louis XV not only increased Rousseau's standing as a composer, it also prepared the way for his being offered a pension. The court also provided a substantial number of pensions to writers and intellectuals, on the assumptions for which authorities normally provide such benefits. Direct control of intellectual life by the court and government was far from negligible during the Enlightenment. Such influence was probably greater in Germany, with its many small but active princely courts, but even more restricted in England where the monarchy was weaker than in France and the commercialization of culture had gone further.

Academies were also official institutions in that they received and functioned under government charters. The Académie française was established by Richelieu with explicitly statist intentions in 1635 and its letters patent were registered two years later. It was intended to provide accomplished authors prepared to support or glorify the regime with a prestigious platform, as well as an income, and beyond this was expected to help achieve the standardization of French culture. It is in this context that the production of the Dictionary of the Académie française should be seen. The great Parisian academies, and to a lesser extent the provincial academies, adopted the aesthetics of classicism with its emphasis on rules and order, and contributed significantly to the long task of cultural integration according to the lights of the state-building administrations of the time.

The French provincial academies, of which there were roughly 40 by the end of the 18th century, have been the subject of a basic study by Daniel Roche. Roche has demonstrated clearly the official and elitist nature of these academies, but he has also shown that in the subjects to which they gave their attention and in their approaches to them they were very much a part of the Enlightenment. Indeed, it is one upshot of Roche's work to show in the provincial academies an important moderate, responsible, sometimes even conservative, current of thought and action within the Enlightenment.[24]

At the beginning of the 18th century, most academies were engaged in polite literary and rhetorical exercises, often involving adulatory accounts of the great figures of French and classical politics and culture. Toward the middle and end of the century subjects treated in sessions of the academies and in the essay contests proposed to the general public shifted toward the scientific and practical, and included agriculture and social problems such as crime, poverty and education. The very fact that these issues were being taken up by the social and intellectual elites is itself significant. But the spirit in which they were developed was even more so. Serious social problems were being addressed not from the point of view of those for whom repression was an acceptable response provided it were effective, but on the assumption that such issues could be solved constructively for all concerned. We find in the provincial academies faith in the pragmatic application of knowledge, belief in the rightness of humanitarian reform and conviction that these things not only did not threaten, but supported, the continued functioning of old-regime society. Though the radicalism of the Enlightenment has often received considerable attention, it is probably fair to see the optimistic, moderately reformist but still broadly conservative attitude of the academies as more representative of the enlightened community.

Had the academies discussed the subjects mentioned above in closed sessions, their impact would have been minimal. In fact, however, they consciously sought to reach a wider public. They did this in a number of ways. First, the provincial academies accredited corresponding members in addition to regular ones. This opened them geographically as well as socially. Over the 18th century French provincial academies had slightly more corresponding than regular members. While just over half of the regular members were commoners, more than 70 percent of the correspondents were. This suggests that for non-residents interest and willingness to participate in the exchanges that occupied the academies was given greater weight than status. Secondly, the academies made a point of holding public sessions. At these events, which played an important social role, members of the public could hear academicians present their work, and beyond this could meet them. Thirdly, most academies published volumes of their proceedings, making their work available to anyone with the interest and the means to purchase them. Edward Gibbon may have been exceptional in buying and then devouring with pleasure 20 volumes of Memoirs of the Academy of Inscriptions,[25] but he was merely availing himself of an opportunity that others of his social and cultural class also shared. Finally, the academies proposed essay contests that anyone could enter, and provided both prizes and prestige for the winners. These were probably the means by which the academies influenced the public most directly and effectively.

In setting subjects for essay contests the academies were in a sense setting the agenda for the enlightened community. And in deciding which essay to award the prize to, they gave direction to opinion. A winning essay would normally be published by the academy under its prestigious imprint, or with the distinction of having won the contest would readily find a publisher. Usually prizes were awarded to essays that best responded to the question while respecting the proprieties to which the academies, as representatives of the established order, were obligated. Occasionally, however, an academy might reward sheer originality or brilliance, as did the Academy of Dijon when in 1750 it awarded first prize to Rousseau's essay arguing that the arts and sciences had contributed to moral corruption, though the contest question was clearly designed to elicit answers in praise of Enlightenment.

Rousseau tells us in his *Confessions* that he came upon the advertisement for the Dijon essay contest in the *Mercure de France* while on his way to Vincennes to visit Diderot, who was imprisoned there. The question raised by the academy caused Rousseau something of an illumination, and set the pattern for his subsequent career. What is significant here, though, is the function performed by the journal he had with him. The *Mercure*, as well as many other periodicals, routinely carried news from the academies, including announcements of subjects of essay contests and of winners. In this way subjects of importance to the academies would be brought to the attention of anyone who subscribed to a periodical, or who could borrow one from a friend or consult one in a café or reading room. Thanks to the lively periodical press of the time the work and interests of the academies were brought to the attention of virtually the whole enlightened community, and the influence of these formal institutions with roughly six thousand members over the entire 18th century reached almost all of those with access to Enlightenment culture.

Collectively, then, the academies played a central role in shaping enlightened opinion. And while they were officially established, they were not simply instruments of government propaganda. Their self-image as centers of learning and research conferred a degree of independence on them. Moreover, both Crown and academies saw themselves engaged in an extended project to better understand the world and better organize society that would contribute to the improvement of the country without compromising its stability. Both administration and academies shared a progressive, reformist and moderate mentality. In the academies is found a version of the Enlightenment that, while progressive and reformist, was also fully integrated into the structures of the Old Regime and loyal to its principles.

In addition to the official and formal frameworks discussed so far, Enlightenment culture also flourished in an array of contexts based on voluntary association. The most glamorous and best known of these were the salons, which met in private homes, usually once or twice a week, and which brought invited members of the social and intellectual elites together for discussion and recreation. With rare exceptions they were presided over by capable and intelligent women, and salons were indeed the place where women played the most important role in a culture generally dominated by men. It has been argued convincingly that the influence of women as interlocutors in salons contributed significantly to the domestication of intellectuals and to encouraging them to speak and write in a way that was accessible to intelligent lay folk. By the same token, however, salon hostesses could not tolerate the expression of views that might offend the sensibilities of their guests. For all their glamour, free food and value as social and professional clearing-houses, salons were not the place for putting forward daring ideas. Propriety has its price and its limitations.[26] If Diderot and Rousseau had attended the same salons, they would not have been able to say the same things there as they said to each other in a café of the Palais Royal, or wandering along the quais.

The network of lodges of freemasons formed another key structure of the enlightened community. This organization spread at a remarkable rate throughout 18th-century Europe. By the 1780s France had hundreds of lodges with some 50,000 members, males who ranged from the very highest levels of society to respectable but modest merchants. Membership was conferred through selection and approval by the members and entailed the payment of fees. Masonry involved adherence to a set of metaphysical but not quite religious principles, which in practice amounted to little more than an assertion of the existence of a divinely based order and a commitment to fraternity. Harmless and indeed socially beneficial as these beliefs were, since they were maintained in strict secrecy masons almost immediately became suspect. In practice freemasonry allowed its adherents to meet outside the usual formal structures of old-regime society and gave them a framework for the performance of acts of beneficence that addressed their concerns about the strains their society was experiencing. It is probably unfair to see the freemasons simply as middle and upper-class gentlemen whose religious faith was not so robust as that of their grandfathers, but who nevertheless retained a taste for ceremony. Rather, the masonic movement seems to reflect a constructive response to anxieties generated by the disenchantment of the world, the threat of individualism and the increasing economic pressures of the last decades of the Old Regime.

Another context for the meeting of individuals interested in the culture of the Enlightenment was a variety of courses intended for the instruction of the general public. These courses were often *ad hoc* sets of lectures on subjects of general interest, especially in the sciences and in areas for which no regular means of instruction existed. For instructors, offering sets of lectures on electricity, mineralogy or chemistry was a way of trying to keep out of Grub Street. For the public such courses offered both instruction and polite recreation, and brought them into contact with new developments in the sciences. More ambitious people also established ongoing centers of education for adults. These included lectures, demonstrations and often reading rooms and discussion groups, which were sometimes termed *musées* or *lycées*.

It is worth noting that the vogue of such courses owed much to the absence of new subjects in established educational institutions. During the 18th century European universities, with the notable exceptions of some in Scotland and in Germany, were intellectual backwaters. Faculties of Arts were in effect high schools teaching a heavily, and sometimes exclusively, classical curriculum, while the professional faculties of Theology, Law and Medicine were geared to occupational training and not to research or critical enquiry. Generally dominated by Faculties of Theology, most universities in the 18th century were expected to contribute to maintaining the ideological integrity of the regime and to training those who undertook careers in the liberal professions. It is in the light of the conservatism, orthodoxy and professionally weighted curricula of the universities that it is possible to appreciate both why so few professors played significant roles in the French Enlightenment, and why intellectuals and cultured elites turned to other institutions such as academies, masonic lodges and informal courses in order to pursue their intellectual interests.

An institution about which regrettably little is known, but which no doubt played an important role in Enlightenment sociability, was the reading room, or *cabinet de lecture*. Usually organized by booksellers on a commercial basis, these reading rooms made available to whoever could afford a modest monthly fee a variety of books and periodicals for use on site. Potentially this was an extremely effective way of multiplying the readership of printed materials. Unfortunately we do not possess lists of clients of these reading rooms, and can only speculate about how they were used and who attended them. Often we are aware of their existence only from announcements in the periodical press. It is clear, however, that these facilities increased in number after mid-century and especially after 1770, and that they would have appealed to the less wealthy members of the enlightened community. Probably the importance of *cabinets de lecture* and of similarly humble institutions has been underestimated for the simple reason that few records on them have survived. Conversely, because academies and masonic lodges kept formal registers of members and minutes of their proceedings there is a good deal of information available on them. Likewise, much is known about salons because they were frequently discussed in the writings and letters of important Enlightenment figures. It is because the archives have so little to offer on more humble forms of sociability and their role in the dissemination of ideas, and not because they were not important, that so little can be written about them.

There is not much more information available about the cafés in which all levels of society congregated to eat and drink and to socialize. From the point of view of the historian, cafés have the advantage of being older, better established and more numerous than *cabinets de lecture*. As centers of sociability where people gathered to talk, they also received the attention of police spies, whose reports sometimes provide valuable insights into the exchange of ideas that took place there. Upscale literary cafés, such as the Procope or certain of the cafés in the Palais Royal, provided an informal and inexpensive setting for men of letters to meet and discuss their ideas unconstrained by the proprieties of salons or the protocol of learned societies. They were particularly convenient for writers and artists who did not have homes of their own in which they could entertain, as was the case with bachelors such as Diderot and Rousseau in their earlier years in Paris.

Owners of cafés often subscribed to gazettes and literary periodicals for their customers' use, and so provided an important means of communication of news and ideas of interest to members of the enlightened community. In England cafés became meeting places for informal clubs, such as those presided over by Joseph Addison and Dr. Johnson in London. Cafés frequented by the working population would not normally play any significant intellectual role, but it was not easy to draw the line between highbrow and other cafés, and it was not impossible for a certain amount of cultural cross-fertilization to occur there. It was, for example, to a café that the glazier Jacques-Louis Ménétra retired to talk with Rousseau.[27]

The importance of these various institutions through which the enlightened community structured itself and articulated its thought is basic. For ideas do not exist independently in isolation, but are worked out in the give-and-take of social contact, conversation and written communication. In academies, salons and masonic lodges people met in a non-commercial atmosphere to engage in polite discussion, both serious and amusing. In reading rooms, public lessons of various sorts, cafés and the harsh realities of Grub Street, fees or payment of some sort was the rule, but it cannot seriously be maintained that Enlightenment culture can be separated from the social and commercial conditions in which it developed. The essential point is that together these various institutions provided the structures that brought people together, exposing them to the literature and art of the Enlightenment and allowing them to explore and develop the ideas and values they embodied.

Access to these various organs of the enlightened community varied considerably. Only members of the elite could be members of academies or would have been invited to salons, but almost anyone could attend a literary café. A courtier might well have had access to the world of academies and salons, and any of the more humble forms of enlightened sociability that he chose. A law clerk with literary aspirations would probably not have been able to attend anything more than a reading room or café, though he, like anyone else, might have submitted a response to an essay contest proposed by an academy. So while access to the various institutions through which enlightened thought was articulated and disseminated was uneven, it was through the existence of the distinct structures just described that this thought was able to spread as far and as effectively as it did.

The Circulation of Ideas

Establishing the social composition and institutional structure of the enlightened community allows us to appreciate which kinds of people were likely to have participated in Enlightenment culture, and how that culture was organized. How ideas in fact circulated among individuals and organizations belonging to the enlightened community is another matter, and a particularly delicate one, for sources here are even more incomplete than those for social composition and structure.

The main channels of communication during the 18th century were conversation, letters and print. Of course, they tended to spill over into each other. Nor were any of them new then, and none have been superseded since. If there is any distinctiveness in the patterns of communication characteristic of the Enlightenment, it probably lies in the weighting of each of these elements, and in the growing importance of unlicensed discourse as opposed to officially approved or licensed discourse.

It is probably fair to say that in the 18th century conversation in polite society verged on being an art form. In the absence of electronic media, entertainment was much harder to come by than it is today, and people had either to betake themselves physically to plays or concerts, or to provide their own amusement. Arguably, entertainment was the primary function of salons where, typically, cultured and gifted women entertained and regulated meetings of carefully selected members of the social and cultural elites. Thinkers and artists gave dramatic readings or performances of their works, sometimes modifying them in response to comments and criticisms, and chatted politely, and hopefully wittily, with their hostesses and other guests. If there were significant innovations in salon society it consisted in bringing writers and artists together with those who had formerly been their patrons and employers on a footing of cultural equality and in the influence of women, who encouraged intellectuals to express themselves in terms accessible to intelligent lay folk and insisted on strict observation of the proprieties without which no socially and culturally mixed gatherings could long have continued. Less witty or more serious conversations would normally have been relegated to other contexts.

Letter writing flourished during the Enlightenment as it had before and continued to do well into the 20th century. Voltaire's correspondence, to take only the most outstanding example, is a virtual encyclopedia of the concerns of progressive thinkers of the time and a *who's who* of the enlightened community. It has been called Voltaire's greatest work and readily invites comparison with the correspondence of Erasmus, another intellectual leader of his generation whose letters vividly reflect the main issues of the high culture of his time. The collected letters of Diderot and Rousseau are scarcely less important for illuminating both the intellectual life of the time and the lives of the *philosophes* in question. Diderot's letters to Sophie Volland are more personal and informal than the more learned and business-oriented correspondences of Voltaire, Montesquieu, Helvétius, the abbé Morellet and a host of others.

In addition to the correspondence of Diderot and Sophie Volland, there were a number of other correspondences between men and women who belonged to the enlightened community and who sought to continue their relations beyond direct meetings, which often took place in salons. Madame d'Epinay and the abbé Galiani, Madame de Graffigny and Devaux, and Julie de l'Espinasse and the Comte de Guibert all engaged in protracted exchanges of letters in which the traditional learned correspondence is balanced by a concern for personal relations. In this sense some of the correspondences of the Enlightenment differ from the largely learned correspondences of European savants in the 16th and 17th centuries.

The practical business of letter writing also spilled over into literature. Many of the novels of the 18th century were cast in the form of an exchange of letters. This device presented a story in a familiar form, and provided a measure of verisimilitude for the fiction. From Montesquieu's *Persian Letters* to Samuel Richardson's *Pamela* and *Clarissa* to Rousseau's *Nouvelle Héloïse* to Choderlos de Laclos's *Les Liaisons dangereuses*, authors presented their stories in the form of letters, and their readers found themselves readily drawn into the fictions presented therein. The epistolary novel owed its success, at least in part, to the central role that writing and receiving letters played in the elite culture of the time.

Print was, however, the most effective means by which ideas circulated. Conversation would carry only as far as the voice, and letters, even if passed from hand to hand, could reach only a restricted number of readers. But once set in print, a text could be reproduced an indefinite number of times, depending on demand. More than anything else, it was the printing press that kept the enlightened community informed and assured its coherence.

Michel Vovelle has suggested that the cultural revolution quietly underlying the development of the Enlightenment was the dramatic growth of literacy over the 18th century. From the late 17th century to the late 18th century rates of literacy rose from 14 to 27 percent for women and from 29 to 47 percent for men. Moreover, the sharp demographic expansion that occurred over the 18th century meant that the number of consumers of the printed word increased in absolute terms.[28] Works of literature and scholarship had been printed and circulated from the time of Gutenberg on, and pamphlets had also been published virtually from the inception of printing, though in different circumstances. Such works of course played a central role in the Enlightenment. Indeed, with the effort made by writers to present their works clearly and intelligibly for a general audience, it is likely that serious works of history, such as David Hume's *History of England,* Voltaire's *Essai sur les moeurs* and Edward Gibbon's *Decline and Fall of the Roman Empire*, reached far wider audiences than had been the case for comparable works in the previous century.

The taste of the reading public in the 18th century was less earnest than it had been a century earlier. Studies of censors' permissions to publish carried out by François Furet and a team of researchers show that the number of works in theology fell significantly over the 18th century, while literature and the arts and sciences took up the slack. There was also a sharp decline in the proportion of books published in Latin and a proportionate increase in those in the vernacular, indicating the growth of a public more interested in entertainment than traditional learning.[29] The rise of the novel was accompanied by a growth of a female readership. It has also been shown that over the 18th century books were published in smaller formats, weighty folios giving way to smaller and cheaper formats more suited to casual reading.

If there was a trend toward secularization and a movement away from professional and toward works of general interest in the book trade at the time of the Enlightenment, this was a modification of established patterns. The most important innovation of the time was the proliferation of periodical literature. Periodicals seem to have been founded first in the 17th century. The *Gazette de France* was a government-controlled publication founded in 1631 by Théophraste Renaudot under the auspices of Richelieu. Initially it simply provided an officially sanctioned version of the news. Pierre Bayle's *Nouvelles de la République des Lettres* (1684–1687), by contrast, was a literary journal that gave extensive reviews of recent works. It provided a model for the literary periodicals of the 18th century. While both France and England had only a few periodicals at the beginning of the 18th century, by its end France had some 70, and England well over a hundred.[30]

As the market for periodicals broadened, different types emerged. The literary periodical, such as the *Mercure* and the *Année Littéraire* in France and the *Gentleman's Magazine* and *Annual Register* in England, played a central role in Enlightenment culture by providing news and critical evaluations of new books in substantial reviews. They also, as noted above, carried news of the activities of academies and other literary information, and so contributed significantly to keeping members of the enlightened community aware of new developments. Journals which specialized in providing news on national and international politics, generally under strict government supervision, also proliferated, as did newspapers that gave space to advertisements and commercial news. In England such papers appeared in a daily format in the first half of the century, but France's first daily, the *Journal de Paris*, did not appear until the 1770s.

The role of the periodical press in the Enlightenment can hardly be overestimated. Periodicals often carried announcements of new books, their prices and where they could be obtained, thus bringing booksellers and potential purchasers together, and of course their book reviews provided an initial evaluation of new works. Announcements concerning courses available, sessions of academies, essay contests, subscriptions for engravings, activities of masonic lodges and other events of interest helped to inform and so minimally to integrate virtually the entire enlightened community, while letters to the editor allowed the readers of periodicals a means of making their voices heard.

Important and far-reaching as was the scope of the periodical press, however, it was not altogether comprehensive. Because of the ease with which the government in France could control the circulation of periodicals through the postal service, censorship of the periodical press was, with a single exception, particularly effective. Journals could not comment on any publication or subject they chose. Works that received government approval or even tacit toleration were fair game. Others were off bounds. One of the most widely sold works of the late Old Regime, Louis Sébastien Mercier's *L'An 2440*, which was banned by the government, was not discussed in the accredited periodical press, and was barely mentioned in the manuscript newsletters of the time. Thus, mainstream periodicals are good reflections of the officially acceptable literature of the Enlightenment, but not of its radical and clandestine currents. They capture the realities of the salons and academies, but not of Grub Street.

In fairness to the administration of the Old Regime it should be said that its censorship was neither obscurantist nor bloody-minded. Indeed, over the 18th century, the categories of censorship were loosened to allow a greater range of opinion to be expressed than had been the case previously. Works that might not have been officially endorsed were allowed to publish with what was called "tacit permission" or simple toleration. And for a considerable time around mid-century, supervision of censorship was entrusted to Christian-Guillaume de Lamoignon de Malesherbes, one of the gentlest, fairest and most enlightened of 18th-century administrators, and a friend of the *philosophes*. Still, the concept of government current under the monarchy regarded the state as responsible for the moral well-being of its subjects, and so refused legitimacy, and permission to publish, to works that were believed to threaten the security of the state, religion or public morals. This left a rather wide field of endeavor for more adventurous authors and publishers.

The unlicensed literature of the Enlightenment represents a fascinating but problematic field of study. As the focus of radicalism, it has always drawn the attention of historians. As an illegal undertaking subject to severe penalties, it was intentionally hidden from the authorities and so has left few traces in the archives. It is to the credit of Robert Darnton that he has undertaken massive research projects to unearth the existence and workings of the clandestine book trade of the Old Regime.

Darnton has worked both on the milieu of Grub Street, described above, and on foreign publishers of French-language works in England, Holland and especially the Société Typographique de Neuchâtel, Switzerland. He has uncovered the business practices, production techniques, distribution networks, including smuggling, and methods of dealing with the authorities of those engaged in the illegal book trade. He has also discovered lists of clandestine works bought by booksellers or seized by the police, and so has been able to offer a detailed analysis of this literature, in which he has also read extensively. What Darnton found was a combination of pornography, books and pamphlets offering damning accounts of the aristocracy and court society and radical works by the *philosophes* offending state, religion and morality. The radicalism of this clandestine literature was more theoretical and personal than it was social or political, and it is far from clear that it was intended as anything more than an argument for reform. Interestingly, Darnton has found that the most widely sold clandestine text of the last decades of the Old Regime was Mercier's *L'An 2440*, a rather dull utopia that offended royalist susceptibilities and the church establishment, but which was thoroughly moralistic and pragmatic throughout.[31] Just how to balance the staid productions of the academies with the sometimes radical unlicensed books and pamphlets so as to arrive at a fair evaluation of the character of Enlightenment thought is not easy.

The Movement of Ideas

While there was a basic coherence to Enlightenment thought, it did not remain static from the late 17th to the late 18th century. Since the Enlightenment developed to a significant degree in opposition to intellectual currents and institutions that had long been predominant in Europe, it will appear that the dialectic of engagement with traditional modes of thought and institutional structures imposed a dynamic upon Enlightenment thought that was not directly of its choosing. As key ideas and values of the Enlightenment changed their status from marginal to mainstream, these ideas took on a different significance and generated new sets of problems.

It was one thing, for example, to advocate a thoroughgoing empiricism in order to limit a metaphysically based dogmatism; it was another to conceptualize all aspects of life in purely empirical terms. If the early Enlightenment was concerned with freeing the individual from the weight of social and institutional authority, by the end of the 18th century thinkers had begun to worry about the implications of an individualism that recognized no fundamental social or institutional bounds. And if in the earlier part of the 18th century writers were much concerned with excessive authority of the state, by its end they began to ask whether individual liberty might be carried too far and whether it was ultimately compatible with social responsibility. These and similar issues, together with the expansion of the social scope of the Enlightenment, are what gave the movement its characteristic dynamic.

From Empiricism to Materialism

If the Enlightenment is seen largely as the triumph and extension of the assumptions of the scientific revolution of the 16th and 17th centuries to areas beyond the natural sciences, then the methodological shift from idea and deduction characteristic of scholasticism toward empiricism, was, perhaps, the most basic shift in the development of Enlightenment thought. The devaluation of abstraction and shift of emphasis to the specific and concrete was fundamental for the attitudes identified with the Enlightenment. During the 18th century this distinction was often formulated as one between "words" and "things." One of the few areas where there was something approaching unanimity among Enlightenment thinkers was in their assertion of the primacy of the study of things and their scorn for what they called sciences of words, sciences that they generally associated with scholasticism and metaphysics.

Scholasticism was, among other things, a blend of Aristotelian science and Catholic dogma. It worked in terms of broad assumptions and logical principles, which interlocked effectively. Its criterion of truth was compatibility with the system. In this way scholasticism excluded from consideration any phenomenon or principle incompatible with its basic assumptions and methodology, and so secured itself against fundamental criticism. Intellectuals and scientists of the 16th and 17th centuries who were critical of the dogmatically sanctioned Aristotelian science that was the accepted wisdom of the universities could not well challenge the system from within.

The appeal to fact against principle was in the centuries preceding the Enlightenment often an appeal against scholasticism. It was also an acceptance of a science without meaning, largely because it was not possible convincingly to challenge the established sciences, so rich in broader meanings, on their own grounds. Initially, then, the founders of the Enlightenment turned to empiricism as a means not only of reconceptualizing science, but also as a way of avoiding the crushing weight of an older intellectual tradition.

This is not to say that scientists such as Copernicus or Kepler were indifferent to broader questions of significance, only that having opted for observation and calculation, the meanings they projected onto their work were not integral to it the way that the meanings of scholastic science were built upon and into Aristotle's philosophy and Catholic dogma. In a sense the sciences that developed empirically from the 16th through the 18th centuries disoriented Europeans in that they tended to substitute a world of perceived phenomena exhibiting lawful regularities for one steeped in meaning. Newton restored meaning to the physical universe by making cosmic order a metaphysical principle from which an Ordering Force was derived. However, as the century wore on and astronomical data improved, it became clear that the anomalies that Newton had used to argue for continued direct intervention by the Creator were a result of imperfect observations. A system in perfectly balanced equilibrium did not require the ordering hand of a cosmic architect to explain its continuing orderliness.

Materialists and atheists were a small minority among the thinkers of the Enlightenment. But including authors such as Diderot, La Mettrie, d'Holbach and Helvétius, they were a significant minority. In part their materialism was a scientific endeavor to explain the world exclusively in terms of facts that could be observed and measured; in part, it was a polemical one, being consciously directed against the prevailing metaphysics and theology. Disproving the divine origins of Catholic dogma meant revoking the license for coercion claimed by the Church. It was an argument for tolerance as well as for sounder science.

It appears to many scholars, as it did to some contemporaries, that in looking to develop the sciences in purely physical terms and denying the validity of metaphysics, the materialists of the 18th century risked reducing the world to a single dimension, the dimension of sense experience. But thinkers of the Enlightenment assumed that if the main uses of metaphysics were repressive and obscurantist, then the elimination of metaphysics was liberating. Of course in establishing positive values, such as *humanité*, and in conceptualizing nature in ethical terms, the materialist thinkers of the 18th century were far from abandoning all metaphysics, even though they might have believed they were.

The logic of radical empiricism, however, did limit the role of theory in science, and so contributed to the negation of metaphysics. Only on the margins of the Enlightenment, in the brutal and stultifying works of the Marquis de Sade, or in Diderot's *Rameau's Nephew*, was the problem of a world deprived of all metaphysical meaning addressed. This became one of the central problems of Western thought in the 19th and 20th centuries. But it was scarcely apparent in the 18th century.

Having posited the irrelevance of metaphysics, many thinkers of the Enlightenment also assumed the self-sufficiency of the sciences. This notion, which originated in the 18th century, found a far greater appeal in the 19th century. Known as positivism, and finding its most comprehensive expression in the work of Auguste Comte, this tendency to see the sciences as autonomous contributed to progress in the natural sciences and to attempts to develop social sciences on the model of the natural sciences. While positivist science resulted in a better understanding of many aspects of the material world, to which it intentionally limited itself, it failed to produce an adequate model for the appreciation of human needs and motives, which are not always reducible to a calculus of material interests or a sound knowledge of mechanics.

The spiritual desolation to which the assumptions of positivist science gave rise in the 19th century and beyond was not obvious in the 18th century. But as the power of the paradigm of positivist science grew, it delegitimated not just scholastic metaphysics and theology that were perceived as threats by Enlightenment liberals, but all metaphysics. That life devoid of some faith or assumptions beyond positive fact is problematic has since been made abundantly clear.

Liberty and Authority

In a famous essay, Isaiah Berlin distinguished between two main varieties of liberalism. He defined "positive liberty" as the set of rights that allowed the citizen direct and active participation in the formulation and administration of laws. By "negative liberty" he designated the civil rights that protected the individual from infringement by the state, or social groups or their agents, on activities that did not violate the law.[32] Negative liberty, which required a minimalist state and conceived the individual in atomistic terms, came to characterize 19th-century liberalism. Montesquieu and Voltaire were early spokesmen for this kind of liberty. Positive liberty, which was an integral part of the classical republican tradition, and which demanded a high degree of involvement of the citizen in civic matters, had relatively few spokesmen in the 18th century. Rousseau was the most prominent of them.

Though the ideals of classical republicanism retained their moral and intellectual appeal, they did not have much practical effect, for they were inappropriate to the political and social conditions of the 18th century. In a political system in which all dominant players were hereditary monarchies with greater and lesser degrees of central control over their extensive territories, the republican ideal was simply inapplicable. And since classical republicanism was based on a citizen body that both was relatively well educated and had at its disposal considerable leisure, it necessarily excluded the great majority of the population of 18th-century Europe. Where the republican ideal was invoked in the decades before 1789 in Europe, it usually involved the issue of political competence, and required minimal standards of culture and well-being. As a result, "democracy" in 18th-century usage for the most part referred to a regime that would enfranchise only a small proportion of the total population. From our point of view today this is regressive, but it was not so at the time. However, since the republican ideal was in practical terms incompatible with monarchy, it tended to disqualify itself as a serious contender for political power. The notion of positive liberty to a degree retained its resonance as a cultural model, and was to have a great impact during the French Revolution, but during the Enlightenment it was of little practical importance. The same cannot be said of negative liberty.

In their arguments for constitutional limits on government, for tolerance in religion and for humanitarian reform in the legal system, thinkers of the Enlightenment contributed significantly to extending civil liberties. It was this strain of "negative liberty" that became the basis of most liberalism in the 19th century. In addition to the clearly enunciated respect for the rights of the individual, liberals from Locke and Montesquieu to Mill and Acton and beyond were suspicious of authority, and assumed that its very existence was a temptation to abuse too strong for mortals to resist. For them, liberty of the individual depended on the ability to check and limit the exercise of power by those in authority. Beyond this, the broad assumption that economic and social structures were inherently lawful also contributed to undermining the legitimacy of extensive state authority.

Just as the notion of a self-adjusting market caused state interference in economics to appear unnecessary, and even harmful, so the notion of the responsible individual rationally pursuing his or her interests rendered a strong concept of the state superfluous. For most liberals of the 18th and 19th centuries, the role of the state was to be reduced to minimal rule setting, policing and administration. The state in their eyes was a necessary evil whose scope was to be reduced as far as possible. While Voltaire, for one, did look to existing governments to implement necessary reforms, he expected those reforms to come from above, and not from the body of citizens. This is far from the classical valuation of the state as the necessary framework in which male citizens could realize their human potential. Rather, it seems a matter of a society of Cyclopes clever enough to understand that infringing on the rights of others would result in curtailment of their own. By the end of the 18th century demands for greater individual autonomy and reduced state and corporate control had not had much practical effect. It is true that in France censorship had become more flexible, guilds had been abolished and the legal system had begun to be reformed. Even taken together, these changes do not amount to a dramatic shift away from corporate controls and toward individual liberty. They do, however, reflect movement in that direction. On the level of theory, there was a strong tendency in Enlightenment thought toward the moral and social enfranchisement of the individual. Most *philosophes* denied the need for high levels of state or corporate authority, preferring instead to rely on enlightened self-interest to direct the individual. Those who suspected that self-interest would not always result in enlightened or responsible action were faced with the problem of how the individual newly and imperfectly liberated from the overwhelming weight of church and state authority could be restrained. While this issue became central to Western thought in the 19th and 20th centuries, its importance was only beginning to be perceived during the Enlightenment.

Individual and Community

The Old Regime was a corporate society in which the identity of individuals was derived from the associations to which they belonged and their places within them. During the early modern period it was generally held that political authority had a theocratic component, and established churches regarded it as their responsibility, as well as their right, to define and limit acceptable opinion in the areas of religion, morality and politics. At the same time, the very weakness of the nation-state in terms of the resources it commanded, the degree of control it could exercise over its elites and the general population and the inadequacy of its administrative agencies, led to overstated assertions of competence and authority. The ideology of absolutism reflected its aspirations more than its actual power, as Pierre Goubert has demonstrated.[33] Harsh social and economic conditions also contributed to strengthening corporate structures and authority, for the harsher these conditions, the greater the need for cooperation and integration to assure effective functioning, and ultimately, survival.

The Enlightenment tended to conceive the individual as less integrated into social structures and more independent than had earlier periods. In the realm of politics the tendency was to reduce what was regarded as the excessive authority of the state to the benefit of the individual, usually by insisting on constitutional and legal safeguards. Montesquieu, for example, argued passionately against the use of arbitrary power by the state, and insisted on the need for law courts to be fully independent of government.[34] The constitutionalism he advocated was intended to prevent legitimate government from degenerating into despotism, which he believed would inevitably follow on violation of the principle of the separation of powers. Critics of old-regime legal practice, such as Montesquieu, Voltaire and Beccaria, sought to decriminalize opinion and to reduce unnecessary use of coercion in judicial procedure. In France judicial torture was eliminated in 1787, and is an example of enlightened reformism achieving its objective before the Revolution.

With respect to religion, it was the view of the great majority in the enlightened community that the coercive powers of the Church should be reduced or even eliminated. Montesquieu showed that the world's major religions contradicted each other on any number of points, and concluded that their value must be relative. If it was impossible to prove the rightness of the claims of competing revelations, it followed logically that each should be tolerated and none should be imposed by force. Both Voltaire and Rousseau posited a divine Creator who had little if any interest in ritual and required only adherence to a minimal and clear ethical code. For thinkers of the Enlightenment, actions were properly subject to legal sanctions, while opinions, even religious opinions, were not. Religion ceased to be regarded as an object of obligatory conformity and became a matter of individual choice.

The absolutist state of the 17th century felt that it had the right and obligation to direct economic activity. The system of mercantilism, elaborated most notably by Colbert, set out to regulate production, prices, exports and imports according to the interests of the state. During the first half of the 18th century writers such as Jean François Melon and David Hume argued that the market functioned as a self-regulating mechanism that achieved maximal benefits by allowing free action to the self-interest of agents competing in the market. This view was adopted by the physiocrats in France and was most forcefully expressed by Adam Smith in *The Wealth of Nations,* which appeared in 1776.

The Wealth of Nations is in many ways an adaptation of Newton's harmonious physical universe to the realms of society and economics. Self-interest in Smith's economics plays the role of gravity in Newton's system, while the market mechanism automatically balances and harmonizes opposing forces. Whether or not this is an accurate description of economic forces, it is certainly an optimistic one. And it empowers the individual while delegitimizing state intervention in economic life. But its long-term significance extends beyond economics.

Smith's argument in *The Wealth of Nations* is a classic statement of economic liberalism. His broader assumptions are, however, no less important than his economic argument. The notion that pursuit of enlightened self-interest maximizes social well-being is perhaps the most powerful myth generated by the Enlightenment. It both legitimizes self-interest in an unprecedentedly effective way, and undercuts one of the key values of classical social and political thought. For if self-interest can achieve the common good so effectively, what need is there of virtue? Smith's validation of enlightened self-interest calls into question not just virtue, but all corporate and socially cohesive values. Though it does not negate them, it reduces their importance. Self-interest, which is rooted in human nature, is a value of the first order; beneficence, humanity and dedication to the common good, are still recognized as positive values, but they are values of the second order.[35]

The devaluation of virtue in favor of self-interest is one of the lasting consequences of the Enlightenment. In *The Persian Letters* Montesquieu relates the parable of the Troglodytes, a people whose short-sighted greed resulted in the destruction of their society.[36] The point of the fable is that society could not exist without the other-regarding values. In 1748, in *The Spirit of the Laws,* he discussed political virtue, defining it as patriotism or devotion to the fatherland, but located it safely in antiquity.[37] His contemporaries, who did not live in republican governments, were not expected to attain it. During the early 1760s, a full decade before the publication of *The Wealth of Nations,* Diderot wrote, but did not publish, what is arguably his masterpiece, *Rameau's Nephew.* This work, brilliant and enigmatic throughout, is among other things a meditation on the implications for society of calculating but unenlightened, materialistic and passion-driven self-interest. The "I" figure in the dialogue represents, among other things, traditional virtues of responsibility to friends, family and society, while the Nephew, or "He," is the spokesman for an amoral, uninhibited but coherent form of radical egoism. The spokesman for traditional values is unable to show any logical weaknesses in the world view of the eccentric nephew of the great musician, and the two part with the issues raised unresolved.

In the thought of the mature Enlightenment self-interest was balanced by the socially cohesive virtues of humanity, beneficence and by a keen sense of social responsibility. Diderot was precocious in focusing on the probability that these virtues would not withstand the acid critique of radical egoism. During the 1770s and 1780s, and increasingly as social and economic conditions deteriorated, the successful rehabilitation of self-interest resulted in a sense of insecurity and a growing fear of social disaggregation. The anxiety generated by these perceptions is reflected in the attempt to reinforce the socially cohesive virtues in the "moral stories" and "traits de bienfaisance" published in the periodical press and in special collections. It is part of the background to the attitude that has been described above as "moralism."

There was, however, one figure who, more than any other, argued eloquently against the spread of radical individualism. This was Rousseau, the great advocate of both virtue and community in the 18th century. Like Diderot, Rousseau saw beyond the liberating aspects of enlightened individualism to its dangers. At a time when most of his contemporaries focused on liberation of the individual from the weight of corporate authority, Rousseau maintained that the social context in which the individual had his or her being was constitutive of, and not merely contingent to, the kind of human being that he or she might be. Inspired by classical republicanism, but also elaborating it in his distinctive manner, Rousseau was probably the last great spokesman of republican virtue. Despite his immense popularity, he was no doubt in a minority in the enlightened community in seeing virtue as the necessary prerequisite to individual freedom. Classical virtue made its last major resurgence during the French Revolution. But 19th-century liberalism effectively reasserted the dominance of Enlightenment individualism over republican virtue.

At the beginning of the 18th century people who had a degree of material security and well-being were narrowly constrained by a variety of corporate authorities, so that restraint of the individual did not pose a major problem. Traditional Catholicism, absolutist political theory and classical republicanism all tended to make the individual aware of his social obligations. By the end of the century, the questioning of traditional moralities, religious and secular, and the rehabilitation of self-interest caused concern about social cohesiveness. Having successfully laid the foundation for the loosening of corporate restraints for those elements of 18th-century society that had risen above the continuous struggle to assure bare subsistence, the Enlightenment then created a new problem: how to restrain the liberated individual who, as a radical egoist, no longer found compelling either the traditional religious and social ideologies of restraint or the newer socially cohesive values of humanity and beneficence. This problem the Enlightenment bequeathed to later periods, and we contend with it still.

Notes

1. Immanuel Kant, "What is Enlightenment?" in *What is Enlightenment? Eighteenth-Century Answers and Twentieth-Century Questions,* ed. James Schmidt (Berkeley, University of California Press 1996), pp. 62-63.

2. Peter Gay, *The Enlightenment: An Interpretation* (New York, Knopf, 2 vols., 1966 and 1969). This is the title Gay gives to the first chapter of the second volume of his study.

3. John Locke, *Essay Concerning Human Understanding,* introduction, and bk. IV, chaps. 3 and 12.

4. It follows that "Things then are good or evil, only in reference to pleasure and pain." *Essay Concerning Human Understanding,* bk. II, chap. 20.

5. The first volume of Peter Gay's synthesis, *The Enlightenment,* is subtitled *The Rise of Modern Paganism.*

6. Daniel Mornet, "Les Enseignements des bibliothèques privées: 1750–1780," *Revue d'histoire littéraire de la France,* 17 (1910), pp. 449-96.

7. "In its treatment of the passions, in its treatment of metaphysics, the Enlightenment was not an age of reason but a revolt against rationalism." Peter Gay, *The Enlightenment,* II, 189.

8. Voltaire said of Descartes that he was "born to uncover the errors of antiquity but to substitute his own" for them. *Letters on England,* trans. Leon-

ard Tancock (Harmondsworth, Penguin, 1986), Letter 13, p. 63. See also Letter 14.

9. This is the first sentence of the first book of Rousseau's great treatise on education, *Emile*.

10. Montesquieu, *Spirit of the Laws,* bk. XII, chaps. 11-12 and bk. XXVI, chaps. 7-12. Cesare Beccaria, *On Crimes and Punishments*, trans. David Young (Indianapolis, Hackett, 1986; 1764), pp. 16-17, 64-66 and 72-73.

11. Bayle's, *Commentaires philosophiques sur ces paroles de Jésus-Christ: "Contrains-les d'entrer"* of 1686 is perhaps his most concentrated and forceful argument for toleration.

12. It is worth noting that Rousseau was consistent in claiming rights for animals as fellow sentient creatures. *Discourse on the Origins of Inequality,* in *The First and Second Discourses,* ed. Roger D. Masters, trans. Judith R. Masters (New York, St. Martin's, 1964), p. 96.

13. Diderot, "Natural Law," in *Denis Diderot: Political Writings*, ed. John Hope Mason and Robert Wokler (Cambridge, Cambridge University Press, 1992), pp. 17-21, and J.-J. Rousseau, "Geneva manuscript of the *Social Contract*," in *The Social Contract and Discourses*, ed. G. D. H. Cole (Toronto, Fitzhenry and Whiteside, 1986), pp. 69-77.

14. Adam Smith, *The Theory of Moral Sentiments,* ed. D. D. Raphael and A. L. Macfie (Oxford, Oxford University Press, 1976).

15. Smith, *Theory of Moral Sentiments*, p. 9.

16. Rousseau, *Discourse on the Origins of Inequality.*

17. See Harvey Chisick, *The Limits of Reform in the Enlightenment: Attitudes toward the Education of the Lower Classes in Eighteenth-Century France* (Princeton, Princeton University Press, 1981), chap. 4.

18. Robert Darnton, "The High Enlightenment and the Low-Life of Literature in Pre-Revolutionary France," *Past & Present,* no. 51 (1971), pp. 81-115.

19. Daniel Roche, *France in the Enlightenment*, trans. Arthur Goldhammer (Cambridge, Mass., Harvard University Press, 1998; 1993), chaps. 6 and 20.

20. Robert Darnton, *The Business of Enlightenment: A Publishing History of the* Encyclopédie (Cambridge, Mass., Harvard University Press, 1979), p. 37.

21. Voltaire, *Letters on England*, Letter 13, p. 67.

22. Daniel Roche, *Le Siècle des lumières en province: Académies et académiciens provinciaux, 1680-1789* (Paris, Mouton, 2 vols., 1970).

23. Robert Darnton, *The Business of Enlightenment,* pp. 287-99, and John Lough, *The Encyclopédie* (London, Longman, 1971), pp. 59-60.

24. Daniel Roche, *Le Siècle des lumières en province.*

25. Edward Gibbon, *Memoirs*, ed. Dero A. Sanders (New York, Meridian, 1961), p. 121.

26. The most extensive recent treatment of the salons, but one which perhaps claims too much for them, is Dena Goodman, *The Republic of Letters: A*

Cultural History of the French Enlightenment (Ithaca, N.Y., Cornell University Press, 1994).

27. Jacques-Louis Ménétra, *Journal of My Life*, introduction and commentary by Daniel Roche, trans. Arthur Goldhammer (New York, Columbia University Press, 1986; 1982), pp. 182-83.

28. Michel Vovelle, "The Prerevolutionary Sensibility," in *Ideologies and Mentalities*, trans. E. O. Flaherty (Chicago, University of Chicago Press, 1990), pp. 183-84.

29. François Furet, ed., *Livre et société dans la France du XVIIIe siècle* (Paris, Mouton, 2 vols., 1965-1970).

30. Steven Botein, Jack R. Censer, and Harriet Ritvo, "The Periodical Press in 18th-Century English and French Society," *Comparative Studies in Society and History*, 23 (1981), pp. 464-90, and Jack R. Censer, *The French Press in the Age of Enlightenment* (London, Routledge, 1994).

31. Robert Darnton, *The Literary Underground of the Old Regime* (Cambridge, Mass., Harvard University Press, 1982), *The Great Cat Massacre and Other Episodes in French Cultural History* (New York, Basic, 1984), *The Kiss of Lamourette: Reflections in Cultural History* (New York, Norton, 1990), and *The Forbidden Best sellers of Pre-Revolutionary France* (New York, Norton, 1995).

32. Isaiah Berlin, "Two Concepts of Liberty," in *Four Essays on Liberty* (Oxford, Oxford University Press, 1969).

33. Pierre Goubert, *Louis XIV and Twenty Million Frenchmen*, trans. Anne Carter (New York, Pantheon, 1970; 1966).

34. Montesquieu, *Spirit of the Laws*, bk. II, chap. 4 and bk. XI, chap. 6.

35. Smith might well have argued that he had established sympathy and other other-regarding values as rooted in human nature and physiology, and so primary, in the book that established his reputation, *The Theory of Moral Sentiments*, which had appeared in 1759.

36. Montesquieu, *Persian Letters*, Letters 11-14.

37. Montesquieu, *Spirit of the Laws*, "Author's Explanatory Note," and bk. III, chap. 3, bk. IV, chap. 5, bk. V, chaps. 2-3, and bk. VIII, chaps. 2-3.

The Dictionary

A

ABBÉ. Formally the title of a head of an abbey or the superior of a monastery. The English equivalent is abbot, and for the equivalent position in a woman's order, abbess. In France the meaning of the term was modified in two important ways.

First, the king was able to appoint an *abbé commendataire* to the headship of certain religious houses. An *abbé commendataire* enjoyed the revenues of his position without being obliged to fulfill any of its duties, or to reside in the abbey of which he was nominally the superior. Such a position was in effect a sinecure awarded by virtue of **patronage**, and was a means of channeling the revenues of Church property to families, generally noble, favored by the crown.

Secondly, during the 18th century the term abbé took on another meaning and became a courtesy title for a wide range of ecclesiastics. Sometimes it was applied to the *curés* of a parish, as was the case with the abbé **Grégoire**. More commonly, however, it was used to designate those who had taken a degree in theology, but who did not have a benefice. During the **Old Regime** the Church was the biggest single employer of the highly educated and it happened then, as it does today, that one could complete one's university degree without finding appropriate employment. According to John Andrews, an English traveler who published his impressions of French society: "These abbés are very numerous, and no less useful. They are in colleges instructors of youth; in private families, the tutors of young gentlemen: and many procure a decent livelihood by their literary and witty compositions of all kinds, from the profoundest philosophy to the most airy romances. They are, in short, a body of men who possess a fund of universal talents and learning; and are incessantly employed in cultivation of every various branch of literature and ingenuity" (*Comparative View*, p. 96). This is to say that abbés were to be found wherever there were intellectuals, whether in prestigious **academies** and **salons**, or in **Grub Street.**

There were no doubt thousands of graduates of seminaries and holders of degrees in theology who were without benefices, who wore a clerical collar and simple black coat, and performed the kind of functions that Andrews describes. Some of them played central roles in the **Enlightenment**, and their status on the edge of the Church and engagement with advanced thought indicates something of the complexity of the social and intellectual reality of the time. The abbé **Condillac** was one of the main popularizers of Lockean psychology; his brother the abbé **Mably** wrote important historical works; the abbé **Raynal** was both a key figure in the world of the *philosophes*, and the main author of a best-selling radical critique of European imperialism, the *History of the Two Indies*; the abbé **Pluche** was a leading popularizer of science; and the abbé **Prévost** both contributed to the *Gallia Christiana* and wrote one of the great romantic novels of his generation, *Manon Lescaut.*

ABSOLUTISM. During the Enlightenment the term absolutism was used interchangeably with **despotism** to designate a form of government in which the crown, representing the central authority, concentrated power in its own hands at the expense of the other constitutionally established agencies, privileged social groups and autonomous or semi-autonomous regions.

Modern historians agree that absolutism, best exemplified in the regime of Louis XIV, embodied a tendency to centralize power in the hands of the monarchy, and that this process entailed a reduction in the status and power of the aristocracy and the subordination of local and regional authorities to the central administration. In the view of Alexis de Tocqueville, for example, Louis XIV, Robespierre and Napoleon were all engaged in the same project, namely, the building of a strong, uniform and centralized state. It was under the absolute monarchs, and in large part dependent on the degree to which these rulers were able to impose their programs and their wills, that European states made the transition from diffused feudal organization to the centralized nation-state.

It follows from this that the absolute monarchs and their servants were generally innovators and reformers, and that their usually aristocratic opponents had precedent and the constitution on their side. This is not to say, however, that monarchs claimed to be above the law. French kings, including Louis XIV, recognized both the fundamental laws and the complex existing legal codes of the land. The notion of an arbitrary power above the law, which served an important ideological and polemical function during the second half of the 18th century, was usually designated as despotism. Historians speak indifferently of enlightened absolutism and **enlightened despotism**.

ACADÉMIE FRANÇAISE. Founded by the Cardinal de Richelieu in 1635, this academy initially reflected the cultural aspirations of **absolutism**. By the end of the 18th century, it had become an arena for the cooperation of a generally progressive Bourbon monarchy and the established sectors of the enlightened community.

Membership in the Académie française was restricted to 40 persons at one time and was for life. In principle membership was conferred by election, but in fact the crown, as sponsor and patron, exercised a veto in the selection of candidates. Elections were complicated exercises in cultural politics, involving the court, ministers, the academicians themselves and leading Parisian **salons**. Often a candidate's **patronage** network proved more decisive than anything that he had written, as is sometimes still the case in academic life.

As a result of its royal patronage and standing as the most prestigious cultural institution in the country, membership in the Academy was highly desirable. Because of the corporate nature of the **Old Regime**, it included great nobles, prelates and magistrates who chose to have their preeminence demonstrated in this way, as well as many of the outstanding literary figures of the century, such as **Montesquieu, Voltaire,** Jean le Ronde d'**Alembert**, who was secretary from 1772, and the Marquis de **Condorcet,** who succeeded him in that capacity. Accordingly, the Académie française was rather more of a gentleman's club than is the case with its contemporary counterpart, the **Institut**. The prestige of membership in the Academy was increased by pensions for members and the added benefit of an apartment in a state building, often a royal palace.

The main task of the Académie française at its foundation was the production of a **dictionary** of the French language, a task that reflected the aspirations to order, authority and centralization characteristic of absolute monarchy. Regular weekly meetings of the members of the Academy engaged in the project pushed the monumental task forward slowly. The first edition of the Academy's dictionary did not appear until 1694, with further editions in 1718, 1740 and 1762. The contribution of this project to setting standards for the French language should not be minimized, especially because during the 17th and 18th centuries the majority of French men and women spoke and wrote local dialects rather than French.

In addition to its more formal task, the Académie française sought increasingly to engage with and influence **public opinion**. Probably its most effective means of doing this was in setting essay contests. Choosing the subject assured that it would be discussed, and a cash prize and the publication of the winning entry with the Academy's endorsement were strong incentives to potential participants. Initially subjects ideologically suitable to the monarchy and old-regime values were set, but over the 18th century subjects of a more utilitarian nature or general interest to enlightened opinion were chosen.

Over the 18th century the Académie française ceased to be the preserve of learned clerics and protégés of the powerful, and was increasingly made up of thinkers and writers associated with the *philosophes*. More than a takeover of a key institution of high culture by progressive forces, the membership and character of the Académie française seems to reflect the adoption of a more progressive outlook by the Court, on the one hand, and a basic acceptance of the values of the Old Regime by the thinkers of the Enlightenment who had the good fortune to achieve membership in the Academy, on the other. To the radicals of the **French Revolution** the Académie française and the other main Parisian **academies** were elitist institutions that deserved to be, and were, closed.

ACADEMIES. The term derives from Plato's school at Athens, and has become a generic expression for organized learning that proceeds on philosophical or scientific principles. The history of the West, of course, has examples of other sorts of organization by which knowledge was acquired and transmitted. The monastic model of learning, dominant during the Middle Ages and still vital, though modified, during the early modern period, sought to preserve and to perpetuate theological and related forms of knowledge. What distinguished the academic model from others was that academies were generally devoted to open-ended methods and inquiry, usually in the fields of the arts and sciences.

From the Renaissance on, there were two basic kinds of academy. One was private, and informally brought together scholars and amateurs to discuss matters of common interest. Meetings of such groups, which typically flourished in a context of sociability, might also include reports or papers by members. Widespread in Italy since the

Renaissance, by the 18th century such academies had developed into, or beside, **clubs** and **salons** that varied widely in their objectives, degrees of openness and membership, but which had in common the characteristics of voluntary association and selectiveness. Examples include the **Club de l'Entresol** in Paris, the Academy of Fists in Milan, to which Cesare **Beccaria** belonged as a young man, Dr. **Johnson**'s Literary Club held in the Turk's Head Tavern in London, the Select Society of Edinburgh and many other clubs and associations described by Alexander Carlyle in his *Autobiography*.

The proliferation of informal academies, clubs and salons in the 18th century was in large part a consequence of the inability of professionally oriented **universities** of the time to provide intellectual stimulation or guidance to a small but growing public. At roughly the same time, representatives of the nation-state took an active interest in ways the world of learning could contribute to improving its functioning and enhance its status.

Large, formal, court or state-sponsored academies (*see* **Academies, State-Sponsored**) became an important part of the cultural scene of early modern Europe. Cosimo de Medici supported Marsilio Ficino's Platonic Academy in Florence in the mid-15th century, and many courts sought to attract artists and scholars. Statesmen pursuing the centralizing policies of absolute monarchs, and adherents of classical values, among which order, clarity and authority figured prominently, sought to concentrate cultural authority in the hands of institutions that would have broad influence, and over which they would have a significant degree of control.

ACADEMIES, PROVINCIAL. A specifically French phenomenon, provincial academies were a form of cultural association intermediate between **clubs** and state-sponsored academies (*see* **Academies, State-Sponsored**). Unlike clubs and other informal associations, provincial academies received letters patent from the government. Unlike the academies of capital cities on the continent, they did not benefit from direct government support. Provincial academies in France became regional centers of high culture, contributing significantly to an important strain of moderate and responsible, but still progressive and reformist, Enlightenment thought and practice. There were 31 such academies in 1789.

Membership in these academies was divided into three broad categories: honorary, ordinary and associate. Each was heavily weighted in favor of the elites. According to the research of Daniel **Roche,** among 664 honorary members, 17.6 percent were clerics, and generally prelates, 71.2 percent were nobles and 11.1 percent belonged to the Third Estate. For the 2,807 ordinary members the figures are 22.2 percent clergy, 39.9 percent nobles and 37.7 percent commoners. In the case of 2,931 associate members the proportion of commoners rises to 55 percent, while that of clerics is 19 percent and that of nobles 25.7 percent. If we bear in mind that the nobility accounted for only one or two percent of the population and that the commoners belonging to academies were generally members of the upper reaches of the liberal professions and represented probably less than 10 percent of the Third Estate, then the elitist nature of the provincial academies becomes clear. In mixing clerics, nobles and cultured commoners, however, these academies contributed to the development of a more variegated and integrated elite than had formerly been the case.

The provincial academies both grew in number and changed in function over the 18th century. Initially they were basically gentlemen's clubs with an interest in literature, and sometimes the arts and sciences, as in the case of the Academy of Bordeaux, of which **Montesquieu** was an active member. Around mid-century they began to show a greater interest in social and economic issues and to give evidence of a more utilitarian orientation, thus shifting the emphasis of provincial high culture from literature and refined enjoyment to an engaged and pragmatic reformism.

Like the great academies of the capital, the provincial academies held a few open gala sessions a year and many closed sessions in which their regular work was carried out. Like the great Parisian academies, too, the provincial academies held essay contests. At the beginning of the century they were generally on literary or patriotic themes, but after 1750 they shifted increasingly toward confronting social and economic problems. In 1753, for example, the Academy of Dijon posed its question on the origin of social inequality, famously answered by Jean-Jacques **Rousseau** in his *Second Discourse;* in 1764 the Academy of Lyon posed a question on the quality of air in poorhouses and prisons and how it might be improved; in 1779 the Academy of Châlons-sur-Marne proposed as the subject of its essay contest, "What would be the best plan for the education of the lower classes?"; and in 1787 the Academy of Metz posed the question, "Are there ways of rendering the **Jews** more useful and happier in France?" and received the best answers from the abbé **Grégoire** and Zalkind Hourwitz, a Jew of Polish origin.

Broadly advertised in the periodical press and open to the public at large, these essay contests were a means by which the provincial academies effectively stimulated debate and set the agenda for large sections of the enlightened community. In this way the academies were able both to maintain positions of leadership, and to reach out to audiences far broader than their immediate memberships. Winning an essay contest conferred considerable prestige, and was the means by which figures such as Rousseau, Grégoire and Antoine Léonard **Thomas** first came to public notice.

ACADEMIES, STATE-SPONSORED. One of the main models for the relation between state power and high culture. In France four great academies located in Paris set the standards and tone in their respective fields. These were the **Académie française** (1635), which was expected to watch over linguistic usage and the field of literature; the Académie des Inscriptions et Belles-Lettres (1663), which was initially required to design medals and study the antiquities in the royal collections, but which broadened its mandate to include historical studies, especially of Celtic Gaul and the Middle Ages; the **Royal Academy of Painting and Sculpture** (1665), which provided a framework for the training of artists and set standards in the representational arts; and the Royal Academy of Sciences (1666), which encouraged and carried out scientific research and evaluated claims of new discoveries and theories, such as those of the doctors Anton Mesmer and Jean-Paul Marat.

These academies and others like them, such as the Academy of Berlin (1702) and the Academy of Saint Petersburg (1724), were formed on state initiative, usually with the intentions of increasing control and enhancing prestige. The Académie française, for example, had as its founding task the production of a **dictionary** to encourage uniform usage in French, and the Royal Academy of Painting and Sculpture was seen by Louis XIV as a way of mobilizing art for the greater glory of himself and his court (*see also* **Salon, Art**). The academies were conceived as instruments of cultural **absolutism**. They also fit well with the aspirations to control, order and hierarchy, which are characteristic of the esthetics of classicism.

The State defined the objectives and rules of academies in letters patent. It also maintained a considerable degree of control over academicians, in the first instance by monitoring candidates for election, and in the second by providing various perquisites for which the academician remained dependent on the authorities. For the main Parisian academies the Crown and government exercised an informal veto. Beyond this they could, and did, back candidates close to them, and in this way many a great noble or tutor in the royal household gained membership in academies for which their learning or talents would not have made them obvious candidates. If they were neither objectionable to the court nor strongly backed by it, candidates would have to win the support of members who had the right to vote, and in practice this often meant gaining the backing of a powerful noble or politician, or of a prominent **salonnière**.

Once elected, academicians enjoyed both material and honorific benefits. Academicians in full standing received annual stipends, and often accommodation in royal palaces, such as the Louvre. The status of academician was also an advantage in the unending competition for pensions, sinecures and soft jobs that was an integral part of the life of intellectuals at the time.

Membership in academies also conferred prestige, being both recognition of achievement, for those engaged in the arts and sciences, and a mark of official approbation. Indeed, membership in an academy was an indication of acceptance into the socio-cultural elite, and of the individual in question having "arrived." The world of officially sanctioned learning and culture stood in sharp contrast to the social and cultural realities of poor, aspiring artists, thinkers and writers who were dependent on the market for books, and those who controlled it (*see* **Grub Street**).

The academies and their members also occupied positions of cultural leadership. The rare public sessions of the academies were social as well cultural events, and were well attended by members of higher social circles. The annual salons of the Academy of Painting, held in the Louvre and open to the public, set the tone for the world of art. The Académie Royale des Sciences was responsible for verifying the claims of inventors and scientists, and the Académie française was recognized as the arbiter of linguistic usage and literary taste, and in repeated editions of its dictionary sought to provide the public with a guideline to standard French.

To appeal to and interact with a broader public, the Académie française also set essay contests that were advertised in the periodical press and open to the general public. There is good reason to think that essay contests of this sort, which were also sponsored by provincial academies (*see* **Academies, Provincial**), effectively stimulated discussion and mobilized opinion. For a narrower and more learned public, the academies also published proceedings, which gave a comprehensive view of their deliberations and their closed meetings.

Though the state-sponsored academies of the 17th and 18th centuries were initially conceived as tools of cultural absolutism, their achievements extended beyond offering ideological legitimation and support to the States that founded and nurtured them. These academies provided the stable institutional frameworks in which scholars could pursue research in areas such as the natural sciences and history, which were not treated beyond the secondary level in the existing educational system, and so helped develop areas of learning excluded from the professionally oriented contemporary **universities**. By opening themselves to cooperation with scholars from other countries, in many cases by allowing for corresponding memberships for foreign nationals, the academies furthered the internationalization of the learned community, as did the publication of their proceedings.

Though founded by centralizing monarchies as tools of state building, and retaining a degree of conservatism inseparable from elite status, the academies not only adapted to, but led, cultural changes over the 18th century. This can be seen in the fact that by roughly 1770 the *philosophes* had come to control the Académie française, and had considerable, if not predominant, influence in the Académie Royale des Sciences as well. The themes of essay contests sponsored by the Académie française shifted from eloquence to subjects of social and political significance, and the very opening of the academies to **public opinion** indicates a shift away from the assumptions of absolutism. It is probably better to see the growing influences of the *philosophes* in the academies more as an indication that the court felt that it could live with, and indeed benefit from, Enlightenment culture than as forces hostile to the monarchy somehow managing to take over key cultural institutions over which it maintained control.

Like **salons**, the academies proved arenas in which old-regime society and Enlightenment culture could coexist comfortably and with mutual benefit. During the radical phase of the **French Revolution** the academies were not maintained as forces that had furthered Enlightenment and helped undermine the **Old Regime**, but were closed because of their perceived elitism.

ADDISON, Joseph (1672-1719). One of the leading literary figures of early 18th-century England, Addison wrote in a variety of genres, mixed his literature with politics and prospered as few men of letters did in his time.

The son of the Dean of Lichfield, Addison attended the Charter-house school of that town, where he became friends with Richard **Steele**, with whom he collaborated over many years on some of his most successful literary projects. He continued his education at Oxford, first at Queen's, and then at Magdalen College, where he became a fellow. Addison was a talented classical scholar, writing Latin poetry that was particularly well regarded, and doing, upon request by a London publisher, a translation of Herodotus. He considered a career in the Church, but, apparently because some of his poems appealed to the future Earl of Halifax, was given a government pension.

From 1699 to 1703 Addison travelled widely in Europe in order to prepare himself for a diplomatic career. In the event, he did play an active role in politics as an adherent of the dominant **Whig** party. Continuing to write for the government, and being well rewarded for it, Addison received a number of lucrative political offices through **patronage**, among them the office of under-secretary of state in 1706. Two years later he was elected to **Parliament** and remained there, though without making much impact, for life. In 1709 he became the chief secretary to the Lord Lieutenant of Ireland. When his political patrons fell from power he lost his various offices, though not his seat in Parliament. By this time, however, Addison was well off, for in 1711 he was able to buy an estate valued at 10,000 pounds.

When the Whigs returned to power in 1714 Addison again enjoyed the fruits of political patronage. He got his old office of secretary back and a further post as commissioner of trade. Addison's association with the Whigs went beyond formal politics. He was a member of the **Kit-Cat Club**, which was a sort of cultural committee to which the leading Whigs belonged, and in 1716, in one of the most remarkable matches of the century, he married the Countess of Warwick, of a powerful and wealthy Whig family. Few marriages brought together spouses from such different social backgrounds. In this case the result was not happy. Addison retired from his political offices in 1718, comfortably pensioned, and died the following year.

As a politician Addison was no more than mediocre. He is remembered today as a writer. Although his corpus is varied, including poetry in Latin and English, a highly successful tragedy, *Cato*, a failed comedy, *The Drummer*, and a range of political journalism, his greatest achievement was as an essayist. When Richard Steele, a friend from youth and frequent collaborator, began a periodical called the *Tatler* (1709-1711), he invited Addison to contribute. He did so, and soon showed himself to be as, if not more, proficient in the genre than the founder. Addison reduced the importance of the news component in the journal while increasing that of the familiar essay.

It was again Steele who took the initiative in founding a new periodical, the *Spectator*, a few months after he had ended the *Tatler*. The new journal appeared daily in the form of a single familiar, often humorous, essay on social, moral or critical subjects. It was an immediate and huge success, both commercially and in the opinion of literary critics. The journal consisted of 555 numbers, roughly half by Steele and half by Addison, with some others by collaborators, and appeared between March 1711 and December 1712. It was immediately followed by another periodical that Steele established, the *Guardian*, to which Addison also contributed. The popularity of the *Spectator* was such that it became the model for many more such periodicals, both in England and on the continent.

In some ways Addison's career is typical of the transition of the status of the **author** over the 18th century. He began his literary career as an Oxford classicist noted especially for his Latin poetry, and came to the notice of the government by the traditional means of dedicating poems to people of influence whose patronage he hoped for, and indeed was successful in gaining. He also engaged in political journalism for the Whigs from his entry into public life into his retirement, editing and writing the *Freeholder* during 1715-1716. However, Addison also played a conspicuous role in laying out the groundwork for a **public sphere** independent of political authority. His contributions to the *Tatler* and the *Spectator* helped to establish the autonomy of already existing frameworks, such as **cafés, clubs** and social and cultural gatherings in private homes or public spaces in which sociability was enjoyed for its own sake. The popularity of his writings also made of Addison one of the happy few who could make a respectable living in the literary marketplace, though he never depended solely on his writings for his income.

By temperament Addison was somewhat bashful and withdrawn, but once at his ease was a pleasing and considerate companion and a brilliant conversationalist. His friends included Richard Steele, Jonathan Swift and many of the men of letters and Whig grandees whom he met regularly in the Kit-Cat Club. He was also the center of a small circle that met at Button's coffeehouse.

Addison's last years were not happy, his financial and political successes notwithstanding. His marriage to the Countess of Warwick was more a social triumph than a matter of affection, and brought him little satisfaction. During 1715 he became engaged in a political disagreement with his lifelong friend, Richard Steele, Steele writing in the *Plebeian*, and Addison responding in the pages of the *Old Whig*, and as a result of this, as well as some unpleasantness over a loan, the two men fell out. Addison was buried in Westminster Abbey and satirized by Alexander **Pope**.

ALEMBERT, Jean-Baptiste le Ronde d' (1717-1783). One of the most important of the *philosophes*. His career brought him into contact with many of the key figures and most of the main institutions, both formal and informal, of the Enlightenment.

Exceptionally, Alembert was a foundling. The name Jean le Ronde is derived from the church on whose steps he was abandoned. Exceptionally, too, we know who his parents were. The mother was the society hostess and *salonnière*, Mme de **Tencin**, and the father an obscure gentleman, the Chevalier Destouches. Abandoned babies taken to the Paris Foundling Hospital had a one in 10 chance of surviving their first year, and little chance of making anything of themselves if they survived to adulthood. Apparently Destouches saw to it that his natural son was put in the care of a reliable wet nurse, one Mme Rousseau, whom Alembert came to regard as a mother. Destouches also made sure that his son got a good education, first in private *pensions*, then at the Collège des Quatre Nations in Paris. Alembert did the practical thing and took a degree in law, but having done so then turned to his real interest, mathematics.

In 1743 Alembert published the *Traité de dynamique*, which immediately won him a European reputation. The previous year he had been admitted as a junior member to the Academy of Sciences, and eventually became a full member. In 1747 he began work with Denis **Diderot** as co-editor of the *Encyclopédie*, and in 1751 published the *Preliminary Discourse* to it, a work that can be regarded as a manifesto of the Enlightenment. In 1755 Alembert was elected to the **Académie française**, and in 1772 became its permanent secretary. He was also offered the headship of the Berlin Academy by **Frederick II**, but declined it, though he did accept Frederick's offer to visit him in Berlin during 1762. He also corresponded with **Catherine II**. In late 1757 or 1758 he abandoned co-editorship of the *Encyclopédie*, though he remained on good terms with Diderot.

Having gotten his start in a **salon**, it was only fitting that he continued to attend these meetings once he had established himself. He was a regular participant in those of Mme **Geoffrin**, Mme du **Deffand**, and then Mlle de **Lespinasse**. Alembert used his connections in the academies and salons to further the careers of talented young mathematicians, scientists and thinkers such as Pierre Simon Laplace and the Marquis de **Condorcet**.

Alembert's writings include, in addition to his scientific works, and the *Preliminary Discourse*, a book on music (1752), another on the condition of writers, entitled *Essai sur la société des gens de lettres et des grands* (1753), the article "Geneva" in the *Encyclopédie* in 1757, to which Jean-Jacques **Rousseau** responded in his *Letter to d'Alembert* of the following year, the *Eléments de philosophie* (1759), in which he expresses his secular and anti-religious views, a book celebrating the expulsion of the **Jesuits** from France (1763), and a history of the Académie française in the form of biographies of the members who died between 1700 and 1762.

Alembert led a quiet, but not uninteresting, personal life. He lived until his late forties with the woman who nursed and brought him up, and only left her house to move in with Julie de Lespinasse, the love of his life. Unfortunately for Alembert this clever and sociable woman was deeply attracted to two other men. He nevertheless remained with her until her death, and grieved her loss intensely. Alembert also figures in a number of works of fiction, among them Diderot's *d'Alembert's Dream*, finished in 1769, but not published during the *philosophe's* life, in which Mlle de Lespinasse also appears, and Andrew Crumey's imaginative and insightful *D'Alembert's Principle* (1996).

ANNÉE LITTÉRAIRE. One of the most important literary **periodicals** of the Enlightenment, it appeared between 1754 and 1790. The founder of the journal was Elie Catherine **Fréron**, one of the outstanding literary critics of the 18th century, who edited and directed it from its inception to his death in 1776. Thereafter, thanks to the strong reputation of the journal, to the competent team of writers that Fréron had put together and to the effective management of his widow, née Anne Françoise Royou, the *Année Littéraire* continued to appear until 1790. In that year Mme Fréron made over the *Année Littéraire* by contract to an unknown young cleric, and in collaboration with her brother, the abbé Royou, launched a conservative political daily, the *Ami du Roi*, which proved a great publishing success.

In format the *Année Littéraire* was fairly typical of serious French literary periodicals. It was published in duodecimo and intended to be bound, so that it would appear on the shelf like a set of books. A year of the journal comprised eight volumes of roughly 360 pages each, divided into 15 numbers or "Letters."

Initially, about 95 percent of its content was book reviews containing extracts of works reviewed, usually with introductory and closing comments by the reviewers. In this Fréron remained close to the model of the learned periodical established by Pierre **Bayle** in his *Nouvelles de la République des Lettres* and the *Journal des Savants*. The *Année Littéraire*, however, was geared to more literary themes and directed to a broader readership, which included a significant female component.

Fréron himself reduced the amount of space devoted to book reviews to just under 90 percent of copy, and his successors went farther in this direction. The rest of the space in the journal was made up of articles, letters to the editor, occasional poems, announcements of new books and classes (a commercial element) and activities of **academies**, news and anecdotes.

The main categories of works reviewed were: theology, history, literature, arts and sciences and law. Like other French periodicals of the time that have been studied, Fréron's journal reviewed fewer works in theology as the century progressed, maintained a high level of interest in history and increased coverage of literature and the arts and sciences.

It has been argued, and is sometimes still said, that the *Année Littéraire* was an organ of conservatism, and was fundamentally opposed to the Enlightenment. This view is based more on the animosity of such important spokesmen of the Enlightenment as **Voltaire** and Denis **Diderot** to Fréron. Their animosity, however, is based more on their belonging to opposing parties within the **Republic of Letters** and differences of opinion about literary competence than on matters of substance.

Fréron's difference with Voltaire revolved about the fact that the author of the *Henriade* regarded himself as a great poet, while Fréron expressed his doubts on this score. Voltaire, for his part, satirized Fréron in his play, *L'Ecossaise*, and devoted a pamphlet, "Anecdotes sur Fréron," to defaming him. Still, Fréron was one of the few contemporaries whose erudition and taste were on a level with, if not above, those of Voltaire.

A visitor to Ferney recounts that the patriarch subscribed to the *Année Littéraire*, which he thought the best of the literary periodicals of the capital, and that when he read it his hand shook, "like a criminal about to hear his sentence" (*Mémoires secrets*, vol. 9, p.29).

There exists a portrait of Voltaire holding an open copy of the *Année Littéraire* and pointing at the text.

In *Rameau's Nephew* Diderot presents Fréron as an habitué of a **salon** of anti-philosophes, and a member of a literary faction opposed to his own. There is no argument here, simply denigration, which is an unfortunate but common aspect of factional disagreement. Anyone who takes the trouble of looking at the reviews of the works of **Montesquieu** or Jean-Jacques **Rousseau** in the *Année Littéraire* will find them fair, and, indeed, sympathetic.

ARGUMENT FROM DESIGN. An argument seeking to prove the existence of the Divine from inferences about the way the world is organized and functions. It is a central feature of what in the 18th century was known as "natural theology," or theology based on nature, rather than revelation.

The basic assumption of the argument from design is that an ordered, rational system is evidence of the existence of a systems designer. An example commonly used in the 18th century was that of the Divine as Artificer, and more specifically, as Clockmaker. If one were to find a watch, the argument goes, would it be more likely that this watch would be the product of chance, or the work of a watchmaker whom one does not know and may never meet? The more probable—and the question is framed as one of probability verging on certainty, but still of probability—alternative is that the watch is presumptive proof of the existence of a watchmaker.

In the framework of Newtonian physics, in which the universe is conceived as a finely calibrated mechanism, this analogy appears convincing. Indeed, the existence of a deity seems, on Newtonian assumptions, to be proven scientifically. During the Enlightenment the fortunes of **deism** were closely related to those of Isaac **Newton**'s science. Whether or not the argument from design still carries conviction in a world of quantum physics, the big bang and superstrings, is a matter for individual judgment. This judgment will generally come down, however, to the same issue that it involved in the 18th century, namely, whether order and lawfulness exist inherently in nature, or whether they indicate the existence of an ordering principle.

The argument from design was not restricted to thinkers who identified exclusively with the Enlightenment. Traditional and pious Christians, such as the abbé **Pluche**, also used it as proof of the existence of the Divine, and they regarded this proof from nature as complementary to orthodox theology. The argument from design was thus common to traditional Christian theologians of the 18th century and to enlightened adherents of deism. It was one of the areas in which Enlightenment and traditional Christianity proved compatible.

ASTRUC, Jean (1684-1766). Son of a Huguenot minister in Sauve (Gard) who would abjure his faith during the persecution that accompanied the revocation of the Edict of Nantes, Jean Astruc studied, first with his father, from whom he learned Latin, Greek and even Hebrew, then medicine at the University of Montpellier. He served briefly as professor of medicine at the University of Toulouse before being called to Paris where he was a remarkably successful practitioner and was eventually (1731) named Royal Professor of "general therapeutics," that is to say, professor in what is now known as the Collège de France, the only institution of instruction which was independent of the Church.

It is hard to know what degree of collegiality there was among the royal professors, but Astruc had at least one relatively radical colleague, Étienne **Fourmont**, Royal Professor of Arabic, who held, and expounded in public, very advanced views regarding the composition and transmission of the biblical texts. During his career in Paris Astruc frequented the literary and political **salon** of the dissolute novelist and former nun, Mme de **Tencin**, together with Bernard Le Bouvier de **Fontenelle**, the playwright, Pierre Carlet **Marivaux**, the novelist, Charles Pinot Duclos, the physicist, Mairan, Jean-Baptiste Mirabaud, author of **clandestine** tracts on the soul, on the **Jews** and on the Gospels, the political philosopher Charles de Secondat de **Montesquieu** and, until they left Paris for Cirey, Mme du **Châtelet** and her lover, the poet, **Voltaire,** which is to say free-thinkers but, except for the very cautious Mirabaud, not radical iconoclasts like Nicolas Fréret of the Académie des Inscriptions. Despite such dubious company, Astruc was not rumored to have been himself heterodox, and was in fact reproached with the contrary, with being a bigoted Molinist and with supporting the **Jesuits** against the **Jansenists**.

Astruc wrote a "natural history" of his native Languedoc (1737), embarked upon, but never completed, a history of the medical faculty of Montpellier and published treatises on venereal diseases (1736, translated into French, 1740). He also wrote on midwifery (1765), though he had never seen a childbirth, based on a course he gave in 1745 to prepare midwives—this was one of the very rare learned/practical professions open to **women**, and when the surgeons refused to continue teaching them anatomy and whatever else they knew that was pertinent to midwifery, Astruc accepted the responsibility of providing suitable instruction. He also published an astonishing number of more banal medical papers. His medical research was conservative and even reactionary, insofar as he opposed smallpox inoculations. But the same can hardly be said for his biblical criticism.

Astruc published, anonymously, the *Conjectures sur les mémoires originaux dont il paroît que Moyse s'est servi pour composer le livre de la Genèse, avec des remarques, qui appuient ou qui éclaircissent ces conjectures* (Bruxelles [Paris], Fricx [Cuvellier], 1753). This remarkable analysis decomposes—Astruc's expression!—Genesis and the first two chapters of Exodus into four principal, recoverable documents and nine other fragmentary ones because Moses could only have described the creation and early history of mankind and of his ancestors on the basis of earlier documents. (Pascal had argued in the *Pensées* that the lives of the descendents of Adam had overlapped, so there could well have been a transmission of authentic memories of the earliest history of mankind!) The criterion Astruc proposed for distinguishing the four main documents is the epithet each used to designate God. This (literary) analysis led directly to the German school of Bible criticism of Johann Eichhorn, Karl David Ilgen and eventually Julius Wellhausen.

Astruc's good faith in this work is highly questionable, first, because of the need to avoid **censorship** and the stake, had he been suspected of iconoclastic intentions, and secondly, because his list of orthodox Catholic thinkers who preceded him in admitting that Moses exploited earlier documents is, at the very least, disingenuous. His analysis exposed contradictions and anachronisms in Genesis that are incompatible with the generally (but not universally) held theory of verbal inspiration and inerrancy of the Scriptures. The dubious company he kept at Mme de Tencin's salon suggests a certain duplicity, which is consistent with Voltaire's reading of the *Conjectures* as an iconoclastic analysis. He complained in his *Bible enfin expliquée* (1776) that Astruc did not go far enough and he extended Astruc's argument, in a less formal version, to the historical books of the Bible.

Bertram Eugene Schwarzbach

AUTHOR. In normal usage, a writer who intends that his or her work be published, usually for payment, and usually under the writer's signature. In the romantic tradition, the author is regarded as a fount of cultural wisdom, and at higher levels of achievement, as a genius.

By contrast, during the Middle Ages, when the source of truth was thought to be found in Scripture and the writings of the Church Fathers, authorship was a category of minor significance. Thomas Aquinas was responsible for the *Summa Theologica*, but how much of the Angelic Doctor is there in that compilation? In the 18th century it is possible to trace the names of many of those who worked on the *Gallia Christiana*, but this great survey of ecclesiastical history in France is presented as the collective work of the Benedictine Order. The period of the Enlightenment would seem to be the time during which authorship was significantly personalized, and concomitantly, commercialized.

In his brief essay, "What is an Author?" Michel Foucault analyzes the impact of commercialization on authorship, and considers the disappearance not only of the author, but also of a more abstract "author function." He also considers the possibility of all discourse being reduced to a "murmur" in the absence of the author function. At the beginning and again at the end of the essay Foucault poses the question formulated by Samuel Beckett, "What does it matter who is speaking?"

One answer to Beckett's question is that it does not matter, and that the essential point is the text (or discourse) and what it says (or signifies), not its source. Another answer is that it matters a great deal to know who is speaking because texts or discourses do not and cannot exist apart from their speakers or writers, and that the life experiences and situations of the writers or speakers necessarily influence what they say. Foucault does not indicate which possible response to Beckett's question he prefers, and it is not unlikely that he ends his essay on a note of irony.

Robert **Darnton** approaches authorship during the Enlightenment from a more concrete and pragmatic point of view. In his 1987 essay "The Facts of Literary Life in 18th-Century France," he attempts to determine how many authors there were in France at this time and what their condition was. Accepting the rough contemporary rule of thumb that an author was anyone who had published a book ("book" is sufficiently loosely defined to include pamphlets and virtually any composition published separately, and some that were not), and using as his main source *La France littéraire*, a sort of who's who of French writers published in progressively larger editions between 1752 and 1784, Darnton provides as complete a picture as we are likely to have of the historical condition of French writers during the 18th century.

After careful analysis of this source, Darnton found evidence of 1,187 writers in 1757, 2,367 in 1769 and 2,819 in 1784. Given that the source was necessarily incomplete and that other countries had higher proportions of writers, Darnton regards the figures he derived from *La France littéraire* as underrepresenting the number of active writers. This was certainly the case. If we include the large number of anonymous books and the practice of anonymous journalism at the time, then the total number of authors would be significantly higher.

The 18th century still had a relatively high proportion of gentle-manly and scholarly authors who wrote from gentlemanly and schol-arly motives, men such as the President **Montesquieu,** Lord **Shaftes-bury,** Baron d'**Holbach** and Johann Wolfgang von **Goethe.** The au-thors who most interest Darnton, however, are those caught in the transition from literary life dominated by **patronage** to that ruled by the market. With the exception of a few dozen writers, many of them compilers, most men of letters without independent fortunes could not make a living by writing. The literary marketplace, and the pub-lishers and booksellers who controlled it, were no kinder to aspiring writers than the older system of personal patronage had been. Indeed, Darnton argues convincingly for the continued importance of patron-age. But there was sufficient patronage for only a few writers, and the market consigned most of the others to the rigors of **Grub Street.**

The wretched moral and economic conditions that almost inevita-bly became the fate of aspiring authors without independent means did not prevent their numbers from increasing. Since it was all but impossible for writers to make a living by their pens alone, it was the norm during the 18th century for aspiring authors to engage in a number of professions at once. Rare was the author during the Enlightenment who had not acted as tutor or secretary or clerk at some time in his or her career. It is only a small proportion of authors today who can make a living from writing. During the 18th century the multi-occupational author was even more common.

On the other hand, the status of the writer improved as the more successful adopted the pose of, and came to be accepted as, intellec-tual and community leaders. In a small book on authors and literature published in 1778, L. S. **Mercier** portrayed the public man of letters as something between an engaged spokesman for Enlightenment val-ues and a secular prophet. In his view, "Every Writer is particularly bound to justice in a solemn manner & before any other obligation.

The infraction of justice is an insult to the human species; that is why every Author worthy of this name feels sharply the wrong done to his fellow; he is unable to tolerate it. He is the avenger of the public interest, & the oppression that has fallen on his neighbor, must be personal to him; he cannot permit himself not to raise his voice in response, & the most respected Writer will always be he who demands with more force the imprescriptible rights of justice and Humanity." (*De La Littérature et des littérateurs*, p. 3).

There is no doubt but that Darnton's account of the increasingly crowded and harsh world of professional writers reflects the constrained condition of those who wrote to make a living. Just as obviously, the view presented by Mercier represents a very real, if highly idealized, conception of the man of letters. Though largely contradictory, these two views of the profession of letters are valid on different levels. The condition of the professional writer during the 18th century was no doubt as harsh as Darnton asserts. Nevertheless, the writer as independent intellectual, as opposed to cleric, propagandist or entertainer, would seem to be have emerged at this time.

AUTHORITY. A key concept of the Enlightenment that also indicates how scholars understood the movement. Historians who emphasize the importance of **individualism** and **liberty** in the thought of the Enlightenment tend to see the movement as opposed in principle to the established authorities of the time, and particularly to certain agencies of the Church and State, such as **censorship**, administrative detention and the Inquisition. On this view of things the Enlightenment is taken to stand against an authoritarian and hierarchical state and to embody the values of liberty and **equality**.

There is some validity to this portrayal of the Enlightenment and its relation to the **Old Regime**. But only some. It was not authority itself, but placing authority where it did not belong that was objectionable to the thinkers of the Enlightenment. Authority based on natural **law**, **reason** or the common good they accepted willingly. But authority grounded in the arbitrary will of a ruler, in **superstition**, or in mere force, they criticized and condemned as despotic. Further, an antagonistic portrayal of the attitude of the Enlightenment toward the institutions and authorities of the Old Regime could lead to seriously underestimating the degree of cooperation between enlightened thinkers and established authorities.

A conflict-oriented model will have difficulty making sense of the phenomenon of **enlightened despotism**, which was based on the cooperation between *philosophes* and progressive rulers. Nor does it offer a fair appreciation of the projects of enlightened reform carried out by administrators such as Anne-Robert-Jacques **Turgot** or Chrétien-Guillaume de Lamoignon de **Malesherbes** from within the royal bureaucracy. In other words, positing an antagonistic relationship between the Enlightenment and the state of the Old Regime makes it difficult to appreciate the interpenetration of interests and attitudes between Enlightenment thinkers, monarchs and administrators. Emphasizing this antagonism also makes it difficult properly to appreciate the opposition of the **parlements** to the crown in France, an opposition that was sometimes principled and constitutionalist, and sometimes simply self-interested.

Geared as it is to opposition and conflict, the model that posits a progressive and liberal Enlightenment set against a repressive old-regime state also misses the cultural accommodation between the Church and the Enlightenment that occurred over the 18th century. Not only did the **Jesuits** adopt and teach the classics and modern science, and Christian moralists articulate the notion of a Christian patriot, but the *philosophes,* even while they criticized worldly prelates and wealthy *abbés* who collected their stipends without fulfilling any ecclesiastical function, often praised and idealized parish priests for filling the roles of social worker, link to the outside world and source of spiritual comfort. Though the thinkers of the Enlightenment had reservations about certain forms and uses of authority, they were far from rejecting authority itself.

B

BACHAUMONT, Louis Petit de (1690-1771). A gentleman and amateur of independent means with an interest in art and literature, best known for his role in producing one of the more important literary newssheets of the time, the *Mémoires secrets.*

Bachaumont came from a family active in the liberal professions, his father being a lawyer and his grandfather a doctor. Though he himself inherited an important office in the *Parlement* of Paris, he was not tempted by a career in the law, and sold it. He lived in Paris, taking an active interest in the arts of the capital, on which he published a number of works around mid-century. Bachaumont's importance for the Enlightenment, however, derives not from his interest in the fine arts, but from his association with the **salon** of Mme de **Doublet.**

About 1730 Bachaumont began to attend the salon of Mme de Doublet, and continued to do so assiduously for the rest of his long life. The relationship between the two is not clear, though it may well have been simply a sincere friendship between an already middle-aged man and a woman 16 or 17 years his senior. Bachaumont took an apartment beside hers, at the present site of the Bourse, which is about a five-minute walk from where Mme **Lambert** held her salon. Bachaumont and Mme de Doublet spent some 40 years in close proximity. They also died within a few days of each other.

Most Parisian salons produced a good deal of gossip. Mme de Doublet's was the only one to produce a journal. From 1738 she provided two registers for news items for those who frequented her salon. One was for items deemed certain, the others for those less so. One would like to know just how it was decided what went where. In any case, as of 1762 a printed and edited version of this newsletter began to appear as the *Mémoires secrets pour servir à l'histoire de la république des lettres en France, depuis 1762 jusqu'à nos jours [1789]* (London, 36 vols., 1762-1789). This collection of reviews of books and plays and comments on the literary and artistic life of the capital is a valuable source for the intellectual history of the period. It is also the only known instance of a journal being produced by the members of a salon, though these institutions commonly functioned as sounding boards for all manner of literary production.

The *Mémoires secrets* are normally associated with Bachaumont, who edited them from 1762 to his death in 1771. It was then edited by **Pidansat de Mairobert** from 1771 until 1779, and by Mouffle d'Angerville from 1779 to 1789. Use of this collection is greatly facilitated by the publishers having produced an index volume for it.

BACON, Francis (1561-1626). An English legist, politician and philosopher whose work on the nature, methods and organization of science was highly influential during the Enlightenment. His advocacy of induction and criticism of older approaches to knowledge, such as **scholasticism,** humanism and occultism, made him one of the main inspirations for the *Encyclopédie*.

Bacon's father came from a relatively humble background, but nevertheless rose to high office as Lord Keeper. Bacon studied at Cambridge as an adolescent, but was averse to the traditional curriculum he found there. The death of his father in 1579 made it necessary for him to choose a career, and like many an ambitious young man at the time, he opted for law. In 1582 he became a barrister and two years later was elected to the House of Commons.

In his political choices, Bacon showed himself far more a courtier and willing servant of the crown than a parliamentarian. Like most politicians at the time and since, he sought preferment through **patronage**. The distrust of Queen Elizabeth, his rivalry with Edward Coke and his inability to cultivate an effective patron kept him out of office during Elizabeth's reign. With the accession of James I, however, Bacon's fortunes improved dramatically.

In 1607 Bacon was named Solicitor General, in 1612 Attorney General, in 1617 Lord Keeper, and the following year, Lord Chancellor. In addition to offices, he also acquired titles, in 1618 becoming Lord Verulam and in 1621 Viscount St. Alban's. Shortly thereafter, however, he was convicted of bribery, and lost both his offices and good name. If Bacon's political career was successful to a point, it was by no means distinguished. His reputation was assured by his philosophical works, and by advocacy of a new approach to science. Bacon married in 1606, but had no children. He died in 1626 at the age of 65.

Bacon made an important contribution to English literature with his *Essays*, the first of which he published in 1597, and to which he kept adding until the last edition, a year before his death. He also wrote a history of Henry VII. His most important work from the point of view of the Enlightenment, however, is to be found in his writings on science. His project for the renewal of the sciences he called the "Great Instauration" and it is described in fragmentary form in a series of books beginning with *The Advancement of Learning* (1605), and continuing in *New Atlantis* (1610, but not published until 1626), *The New Organon* (1620), and a number of elaborations on these works.

The main features of Bacon's project were shifting the thrust of science from speculation to utility, giving scientists effective institutional frameworks in which to work, such as **academies** or research institutes, and basing science on induction and experiment. Bacon offered scathing criticisms of the abstraction of scholasticism, the practical inutility of humanism and the illusions of occult studies. Bacon's emphasis on the practical uses of science and his concept of the unity of knowledge, taken over by Jean Le Ronde d'**Alembert** in his *Preliminary Discourse* to the *Encyclopédie*, appealed greatly to the thinkers of the Enlightenment, who saw him as one of the main founders of their movement.

BAYLE, Pierre (1647-1706). One of the great founding figures of the Enlightenment, but exceptional in making his contribution through traditional humanist learning, not uninfluenced by the work of René **Descartes**, rather than the new sciences and their implications. Bayle was also far more engaged in religious controversy than were the *philosophes* of the High Enlightenment, and himself was probably a sincere believer in Protestant Christianity. This was not unusual for the great thinkers of the late 17th century who helped lay the groundwork for much Enlightenment thought, such as Isaac **Newton** and John **Locke.**

Bayle was born in the south of France to a Calvinist, or Huguenot, family. His father was a pastor, and highly committed to his Church. This was not an easy period for Protestants in France. From the time of Richelieu and Louis XIII the crown worked to reduce the generous settlement for the Huguenots made by Henri IV in the Edict of Nantes, and in 1685 Louis XIV revoked this edict completely, depriving the Protestants of civil status, and driving many, Bayle among them, abroad. Bayle's life was deeply marked by religious persecution, for not only did he lose his teaching position at the Protestant Academy of Sedan when Louis XIV had all Protestant schools in France closed, but also one of his brothers died in jail as part of an effort to force him to convert to Catholicism. Subsequently he also suffered from the fanaticism of his fellow Protestants.

Bayle's education was begun at the Protestant Academy of Puylaurens, then continued at the **Jesuit** college of Toulouse. Under the influence of his new teachers Bayle abjured his native religion for Catholicism. However, he was quickly persuaded by his family to return to Protestantism, and was sent to Geneva in August 1670 to strengthen his Calvinist faith. He subsequently returned to France, and worked as a tutor in various places until in 1675 he was named professor of philosophy at the Protestant Academy of Sedan. When this school was closed by the Crown in 1681, he moved to the more liberal Dutch Republic, where he took up a teaching position in Rotterdam.

In Holland Bayle devoted himself to teaching and increasingly to writing. His concept of scholarship was traditional, and he apparently regarded it as incompatible with the duties of family life. In many ways he was a transitional figure, combining features of the Christian humanism and scholarly ideals of Erasmus with more modern enterprises. Bayle did not care for the easy sociability of most of the *philosophes*, and there was something almost monkish in his devotion to his work. While many *philosophes* had nothing but disdain for **scholasticism,** Bayle was content to use its categories, though he rejected its basic premise that faith and reason were compatible.

Bayle pioneered two literary forms that proved central to the Enlightenment: journalism and encyclopedism. He did not, however, write fiction. His *Nouvelles de la république des lettres*, which he edited and wrote between 1684 and 1687, showed keen critical skills and proved a model for later enlightened journalism, while his *Historical and Critical Dictionary*, the first edition of which appeared in 1697, and of which there were eight editions by 1740 as well as translations to English and German, was one of the most influential works of the 18th century.

Among Bayle's other works were *Diverse thoughts on the Comet* (1681), a devastating criticism of **superstition** based more on traditional humanistic learning than on the new science, of which, at that time, **Cartesianism** was the dominant variant; the *General Criticism of the History of Calvinism of Father Maimbourg* (1682), which offered a moderate criticism of a work designed to provide ideological justification for persecution of the Huguenots; and *A Philosophical Commentary on these Words of Jesus Christ: "Compel Them to Come in"* (1686), a response to the Revocation of the Edict of Nantes, and one of the strongest and most sweeping assertions of religious **toleration** published at that time.

Bayle is one of the most enigmatic figures of the early Enlightenment. While his criticism of superstition and dogmatism, his relentless pursuit of intellectual error, his forceful assertion of toleration and his questioning the competence of **rationalism** make him a founder of central strains of Enlightenment thought, his acceptance of the Calvinist version of Christian revelation seems to distance him from it.

Scholars are divided as to whether Bayle was a skeptic, and possibly an atheist, or whether, as he claimed, he accepted his religion fully on the basis of faith. In the fourth item of the third "Clarification" to his *Dictionary*, Bayle writes as follows: "A true believer, a Christian. . . is well aware that natural things are not proportional to supernatural ones, and that if a philosopher were asked to put on a level basis and in perfect harmony the Gospel mysteries and the Aristotelian axioms, one would be requesting of him what the nature of things will not permit. One must necessarily choose between philosophy and the Gospel" (Popkin, 1965, pp. 428-429).

This statement has the ring of sincerity to it. Beyond that, it reflects a historical moment when the most educated men of the age were still able to believe in the mysteries of religion. Today, and indeed probably from the generation following Bayle, a growing proportion of the educated elites could no longer sustain the kind of faith Bayle appears to have had. For **Voltaire** and his contemporaries, belief in revelation was not an option, but nor was finding one's way in the world without the help of **reason** modified by experience and a morality that included values such as **beneficence** and **humanity.** During the 19th and 20th centuries, when belief in these values has become progressively more difficult, more people find themselves in a world deprived not only of divine mercy, but also of rationality. This is one of the things that separates us from the world of the Enlightenment, and even more so, from that of Bayle.

BEAUMARCHAIS, Pierre Augustin Caron (1732-1799). Perhaps the most remarkable example of upward social and cultural mobility in the period. Born in Paris to a watchmaker, young Caron studied in a *collège* for a few years before being apprenticed to his father. Thanks to his own truly exceptional abilities, he rose to occupy a position at the royal court, to achieve great wealth, to acquire noble status, to be entrusted with more than one sensitive mission for the French government and to produce a number of works that are still regarded as classics. A series of fortunate marriages also contributed to his advancement. His first two marriages to wealthy widows were both terminated by the death of the wife within roughly a year. It was from an estate belonging to his first wife that he took the name Beaumarchais. His third wife, much his junior, was a wealthy orphan and survived him.

Beaumarchais's career was highly unusual. At age 21 he discovered a new escapement, and when it was claimed by a competitor appealed to the Academy of Sciences, which found in his favor. Through an acquaintance with the husband of Mme de **Pompadour**, Beaumarchais was introduced at court, and his musical ability resulted in his being appointed in 1759 teacher of the harp to the daughters of **Louis XV**. While at court he came to know the financier Pâris-Duverney, and began working with him. By 1761 he was able to buy an ennobling office. That the ascent from common to noble status usually took five or six generations under the **Old Regime** is an indication of how exceptional Beaumarchais's rise was.

Beaumarchais was a more prolific author than his two famous plays suggest. His first play, *Eugénie*, was consciously modelled on the dramatic theory of Denis **Diderot**, who argued for abandoning the classical and aristocratic figures of the tragedies of Corneille and Racine and their followers in favor of the "drame bourgeois" (*see* **Bourgeois Drama**) with its domestic scenes and humble characters. A second play, *Les Deux Amis, ou Le Négociant de Lyon*, was performed in 1770, but was not a success. *The Barber of Seville*, which was produced in the summer of 1775, initially met with a cool reception, but following a series of revisions was acclaimed. **Louis XVI** initially opposed the production of *The Marriage of Figaro* because of its criticism of the aristocracy and basic values of the Old Regime, but eventually relented, and when it was produced in 1784 it proved a great success, as much among the aristocracy as the wider public. In 1787 Beaumarchais put on *Tarase,* a philosophical opera with music by Antonio Salieri, but it was not well received. Nor was a sentimental sequel to the *Marriage, L'Autre Tartuffe, ou La Mère coupable.*

Beaumarchais's other literary enterprises include a number of very popular legal briefs he published against the judge Goëzman in 1773, and a polemic with Nicolas Bergasse in 1787. In 1777 he organized a Society for Authors of Dramas to represent them in their dealings with the main theater companies. The following year he became involved in a printing venture to produce a complete edition of the works of **Voltaire**. The result was the Kehl edition that for years was standard.

Despite the sharpness of his criticism of the Old Regime, Beaumarchais sought reform, not revolution. He adapted reasonably well to the **French Revolution** when it came, and though he was imprisoned for part of 1792, and spent time abroad as an *émigré*, he was able to return to France in 1796.

BECCARIA, Cesare Bonesana, Marchese di (1738-1794). A noble from Milan and author of *On Crimes and Punishments.* Beccaria studied with the **Jesuits** of Parma, and then took a degree in law at the Univeristy of Pavia in 1758. In 1761, against parental wishes, he married a woman of lower social standing than his own, but eventually father and son were reconciled, and the young man was able to keep both his bride and his inheritance.

Beccaria's career was unexceptional. In 1768 he was appointed to the chair of political economy in the Palatine School of Milan, and from 1771 held various positions in the civil service of his native city, distinguishing himself in none of them. Indeed, Beccaria was outstanding in neither personality nor ability. Yet as the author of *On Crimes and Punishments* he played an important and indeed distinguished role in the Enlightenment. Yet it is not a role to which he had an exclusive claim.

The writing of *On Crimes and Punishments* is as instructive as it is curious, for though the book bears his name it was the product of a strange and fruitful collaboration. In 1761 the shy and introverted Beccaria met Pietro Verri and his brother Alessandro. Pietro especially was a bright, accomplished, energetic, outgoing and curious man who in his travels had been exposed to, and positively impressed by, Enlightenment ideas. In Milan he became the leader of a circle of young men who met for pleasure and serious discussion, and which is a good example of the sociability of enlightened male elites. The group termed itself the Academy of Fists, and produced a short-lived journal, *Il Caffè* (The Coffeehouse). It was in this circle that Beccaria was encouraged to write on legal reform. He did so, but needed both constant stimulation from his friends in the writing of the work, and Pietro Verri's editorial skills in putting it into final form. The book was, in a real sense, a collaborative effort.

The immediate success of *On Crimes and Punishments* won Beccaria an invitation to visit Paris, which he did in the company of Alessandro Verri in 1766. His shyness and social incompetence made his reception in overwhelmingly sympathetic and admiring Parisian society a burden. He returned to Milan long before he had intended to, disappointing the polite society of Paris and his friends at home, whom he soon stopped seeing. He wrote a number of other works, but none of them were better than mediocre. Outside the congenial, challenging and supportive Verri circle he proved unable to produce anything comparable to the great book which made his reputation. If there is a case in which the life of the mind was dependent upon sociability, it is Beccaria's.

BENEFICENCE/*BIENFAISANCE*. A term originated in the 18th century to designate the social virtue of doing good, usually to the unfortunate and deserving. In the enlightened view of the world *bienfaisance* took the place that charity had held in Christianity. However, whereas charity, as traditionally conceived, had its origins in divine goodness and love for radically corrupt fellow beings, beneficence, which was sometimes conceived as a virtue, and sometimes as a duty, was rooted either in an implied directive of a beneficent Supreme Being, or in the value of **humanity.** Unlike Christianity, which saw mankind as fundamentally corrupt, Enlightenment thinkers tended to see the human species as not only uncorrupted by original sin, but also as inclined to good (*see Second Discourse*) and as rational.

Beneficence, then, was the appropriate ethic for a creation myth that posited human beings to be whole and good. David **Hume** noted that compared to **self-interest**, in society as it was then constituted, beneficence was necessarily a weak motive (*A Treatise of Human Nature*, Bk. III, part iii, chap. 3). While Hume was no doubt right that most people prefer their own interests to those of others, the attention paid by the enlightened public to the virtue and social value of beneficence grew over the 18th century.

From roughly 1750 some newspapers and journals printed sections under the rubric "Acts of Beneficence." Normally inserted as filler, these items usually took the form of short reports or anecdotes of acts of exceptional devotion or goodness, whether of a responsible, wealthy person for a less fortunate one, of one family member for the rest of the family or of a member of the lower classes coming to the aid of a fallen member of the elite, as, for example, of a servant who used his savings to support a master who had ruined himself through gambling. The common feature of these accounts is the socially cohesive power of acts of beneficence in the face of forces of socioeconomic and moral dissolution.

The value of beneficence, then, played a key role both in the Enlightenment myth of a regenerate humanity and in offsetting by moral prescription the signs of socio-economic crisis that caused so much anxiety to contemporaries.

BENTHAM, Jeremy (1748-1832). An English legist, philosopher and reformer best known for his advocacy of **utilitarianism.**

Bentham's father and grandfather had both practiced law, and Bentham himself studied the subject and was called to the bar in 1772. However, his interest in the law was more theoretical than practical. An independent income made it possible for him to devote himself to his broader interests. Bentham accepted the view of a number of Enlightenment thinkers, and especially of Claude Adrien **Helvétius**, that the proper goal of society was to achieve the greatest **happiness** of the greatest number, happiness being defined in terms of pleasure and pain. Though this idea was not original with Bentham, he developed and applied it more thoroughly than others.

Bentham held a strongly liberal view of society and politics, believing that the greatest happiness of the greatest number could best be assured by leaving each individual to pursue his or her interests with due regard for others. The only proper role of government, in his view, was to offer disincentives to interference with the free activities of others. He thus reduced the functions of government to establishing and administering criminal law. Like Cesare **Beccaria**, by whom he was also influenced, he insisted that punishments be those minimally necessary to deter wrongdoing. The infliction of excessive or unnecessary pain was both barbaric and counter-productive.

Bentham carried certain strains of Enlightenment thought, such as **individualism**, **liberalism**, laissez-faire and reformism well into the 19th century. He was typical in preferring reform from above, and only when it became obvious to him that the elites who controlled the political system in England opposed any sort of significant change or modernization did he lend his support to reform of **Parliament**. His solidly empirical outlook, however, made him hostile to certain other key Enlightenment concepts, such as the **social contract**, and natural **law**, which he genially dismissed as nonsense.

Bentham wrote a great deal, not much of it readable. He was sensitive to the ambiguities and imprecisions of language, and like the Marquis de **Condorcet** in the 18th century, and Auguste Comte in the 19th, aspired to a reformed scientific language of mathematical exactness. His first published work, *A Fragment on Government* (1776), was a criticism of William Blackstone's *Commentaries* on English law, and particularly his use of the notion of natural law. In 1787 Bentham published *A Defense of Usury*, which extended the principles of laissez-faire to credit, and which Adam **Smith** approved. Perhaps his best-known work is the *Introduction to the Principles of Morals and Legislation* (1789), which sets forth the greatest happiness of the greatest number principle and is another instance of the aspiration, characteristic of the Enlightenment, to reduce politics to a science.

The reform project for which Bentham is best known is the Panopticon, a prison designed to allow the warder complete and unobstructed surveillance of the inmates. It was much discussed, but never built, and has seemed to some scholars, such as Michel Foucault, to embody a tendency toward excessive control in Enlightenment thought.

Bentham's embalmed body, the head in a pan between the feet, and an artificial head wearing a somewhat enigmatic expression on the neck, can be seen today in the boardroom of University College, London. The utility of this is not immediately apparent.

BOLINGBROKE, Viscount, Henry St. John (1678-1751). An English politician and writer of the early 18th century, Bolingbroke combined the roles of practical politician and **Tory** ideologist and publicist. His preferred lifestyle included an element of libertinism.

Born to a wealthy and influential family, which controlled a borough seat in **Parliament**, Bolingbroke attended Eton and possibly Oxford. He went on the grand tour in 1697, and in the course of it acquired a number of European languages and developed his taste for the good things in life. Not long after returning to England he entered the House of Commons, taking the family seat, which his grandfather had occupied.

Bolingbroke's political career was marked by sharp successes and reverses. He held high office between 1704 and 1708 as secretary of war, and between 1710 and 1714 as a secretary of state. In this latter capacity he played a significant role in negotiating the Treaty of Utrecht. He was raised to the peerage in 1712 with the title Viscount Bolingbroke, and took his seat in the House of Lords. Bolingbroke achieved these positions and honors under Queen Anne and in the framework of Tory ministries. With the death of Anne and the accession of George I in 1714, Bolingbroke's political fortunes were quickly reversed.

There was no place for Bolingbroke in the **Whig** ministry of the new king. He left England for France in 1715. There he served the Stuart Pretender for a short time, and enjoyed the free and open atmosphere of the **Regency**. Bolingbroke was a welcome participant in the **salons** and learned gatherings of the capital, including the **Club de l'Entresol**. He became something of a *philosophe* in his own right, and made the acquaintance of figures such as the President **Montesquieu** and **Voltaire.** At home, however, his association with the Pretender was, not unreasonably, construed as treasonable. He was pardoned in 1723, and his attainder reversed, but under conditions that excluded him from direct participation in parliamentary politics. He returned to England in 1725 and became the unofficial leader of the opposition to Sir Robert Walpole's Whig government, which effectively dominated political life in England for the next 20 years. Excluded from Parliament, this former minister now appealed to **public opinion** by means of the printed word.

Between 1727 and 1733 Bolingbroke directed and wrote for, together with a number of friends, among whom were Jonathan Swift and Alexander **Pope**, a weekly periodical entitled *The Craftsman*, which directed criticism and satire against Walpole's administration. This journal is an illustration of significant differences between the cultural and political life in England and on the continent at this time. Most obviously, explicit political criticism was not permitted in France, and writers such as Voltaire were shown the inside of the Bastille for less than Bolingbroke and his collaborators printed as a matter of course. No less significant is the fact that in France outstanding writers might contribute from time to time to periodicals, but they did not edit or contribute regularly to them. By contrast, in England the great writers of the time such as Joseph **Addison**, Daniel **Defoe**, Jonathan Swift and Dr. **Johnson** all directed or wrote for periodicals and engaged in political journalism. Some British periodicals, such as *The Craftsman* and the *Spectator*, were produced by a few friends or a circle of acquaintances, and as long as they were commercially successful, enjoyed virtually complete independence.

The Craftsman, in fact, was one facet of the activity of a circle that Bolingbroke presided over at his estate near Oxford. It consisted of men of letters and aristocrats critical of Walpole and the Whigs, many of whom had previously been members of the Scriblerus Club of Tory wits and the Brothers Club, which Bolingbroke had organized in 1711 as a focus of sociability and patronage for Tories, in many ways similar to the Whig **Kit-Cat Club**, though on a more modest scale. Two of Bolingbroke's more important works, *Remarks on the History of England* and *A Dissertation Upon Parties,* grew out of *Craftsman* essays.

Following a sharp response by Walpole in Parliament to his criticisms in 1735, Bolingbroke found it prudent to travel to France. He returned to England in 1738, again taking up his criticism of the government. It was in this context that he wrote what is probably his most important work, *The Idea of a Patriot King*. Though this work was written during the late 1730s, it was not intended for publication, and Bolingbroke published it in 1749 because Pope, with whom he had left the manuscript, had had copies printed without his permission. The book was an indictment of the manipulativeness and corruption of the management of parliamentary politics that Walpole used so effectively in the interests of the Whig magnates. It is an odd work for a Tory, in that its key values include the republican notions of **virtue** and the common good. This is not, however, an illogical position for a critic of the Whig oligarchy to take, and the appeal to a monarch who embodied political virtue was perhaps the only line of criticism left open to someone who regarded Parliament as radically corrupted, and who could not conceive of a democratic alternative.

Bolingbroke was an example, perhaps more common in the first half of the 18th century than later, of a thinker who was also actively engaged in politics. Pope was much influenced by him, especially in his *Essay on Man* and *Moral Essays*. Certainly there is no parallel on the continent to a minister fallen from office who then wrote and published extensively on politics, in effect leading an opposition, and this activity being tolerated.

BOUCHER, François (1703-1770). One of the most prolific and important French painters of the mid-18th century, and one of the outstanding representatives of the **rococo** style in France.

Boucher was the son of an undistinguished artisanal painter. The son's talents were precocious and soon recognized by the father, who apprenticed him to a respectable atelier. Boucher was taught decoration, and his first assignments were apparently in decorating the door frames in the royal chateau of Fontainebleau and in the residence of the Soubise family in Paris, which today houses the National Archives. This beginning to what was to prove a highly successful career was appropriate in that Boucher was to spend much of his active life at the royal court and executing commissions for the aristocracy of the capital.

Boucher's career took off when he won the Roman prize of the **Royal Academy of Painting**, which allowed him to study in Italy. On returning to France in 1731 he was elected to the Academy, of which he eventually became the director. He also met and won the **patronage** of Mme de **Pompadour**, whose portrait he painted on a number of occasions, always in the pose of a patron of the arts and learning. Among other lucrative positions that his patrons were able to arrange for him were the posts of Painter to the King and Director of the Gobelins tapestry works, for which he produced designs, as he did for the porcelain workshops of Sevres.

Although Boucher painted portraits, landscapes and a number of charming scenes portraying the everyday life of ordinary people, such as a breakfast scene and a saleswoman, he is best known for his scenes of classical mythology featuring female nudes. Canvases such as *Rinaldo and Armida* (1734), *Aurora and Cepahalus* (1739), the *Birth of Venus* and *Leda and the Swan* (1740) and the *Bath of Diana*

(1742) take an obvious, sensual and often erotic delight in the human body, and particularly in the youthful, shapely bodies of women. Usually commissioned by aristocratic patrons, and often intended to serve a decorative function in their luxurious residences, these paintings embody a validation of this world and its pleasures that are central to the Enlightenment project of rehabilitating **happiness** in general and physical pleasure in particular.

One the greatest art critics of the 18th century, Denis **Diderot**, said of Boucher that his work contained everything but truth. This is a harsh judgment. Boucher's painting did not convey, and did not try to convey, the moral messages of the work of Jean-Baptiste **Greuze** or of Jacques-Louis **David**. His truth was not their truth. The explicit validation of the beauty of the human form and the implicit appeal to pleasure in his painting, presented for the most part in the idiom of the classical tradition of the West, expressed an important current of Enlightenment thought and sensibility. That this view of the world, once generalized, offered little in the way of social or ethical direction, shows only that in itself it was not an adequate guide to life. Its achievement, nevertheless, was a lasting one.

BOURGEOIS DRAMA/DRAME BOURGEOIS. If the Greek term drama (action) evolved in numerous European languages to designate a theatrical work in general, the theatrical meaning of the term was more specific in French. It came to designate a definite genre, and later the "romantic and lyric" drama of the 19th century. Concern in France to renew the classical traditions with more realism, foreign influences (mostly English) and the growing power of the bourgeoisie together gave birth to the "bourgeois" drama, also called the "serious genre." With respect to form, it defined itself as opposed to both tragedy and comedy.

The "drame bourgeois," which is characteristically a "mixed" genre, was invented to represent on stage the bourgeoisie and its values. The content of the drama was generally of a contemporary and social nature. However, it preserved the seriousness of the tragic ethos and its dramatic qualities, though without its quasi-spiritual ambiance.

The poetics of the bourgeois drama is governed by two principles: the first is to create a realistic effect on stage while reinforcing the illusion it fosters; the second is to further the moral education of the spectator, and to render the viewer morally sensitive through examples.

Denis **Diderot** is considered the main theoretician of the bourgeois drama, but many others also tried to define it, among them Pierre Augustin Caron de **Beaumarchais**, who wrote an *Essai sur le genre dramatique sérieux* (1767). In his *Entretiens entre Dorval et moi* (1757), Diderot explains that the theater must become an art based on the imitation of **nature** and truth. It should strive to become an art form capable of correcting morality by moving the spectators and involving them personally. Drama should paint the humble problems and adventures of ordinary people from the bourgeoisie and the lower classes. It should describe social conditions, problems of daily life or domestic disasters. It should aim to show, for example, the worthiness of trade and those engaged in it, or the virtue of thrift, or of domestic life, or of simple, productive work. Prose is preferred to verse because it imitates better the spoken language of ordinary life.

Pantomime is privileged, too, because, according to Diderot, it intimately connects the dramatic action with the sighs, screams and tears that are part of it. Changes of physiognomy portray emotion more directly and better than long tirades. It is important to endeavor to reproduce on stage "animated tableaux" whose models are found, for example, in the painting of Jean-Baptiste **Greuze**. Diderot was among the first to insist on the importance of directing, for in his view this permitted a closer imitation of reality. He favored the insertion of explicit stage directions into the text of the play itself. Finally, Diderot advocated renunciation of the unity of place to reinforce the visual illusion of the theater.

It is noteworthy that the bourgeois drama developed throughout Europe during the Enlightenment, with France following the lead of others. Diderot or Bernard-Joseph Saurin imitated English dramatists such as George Lillo and Edward Moore. In Italy, Charles Goldoni oriented the comedy in this direction. In Germany, Gotthold Ephraim **Lessing**, Jean-Michel Reinhold Lenz or Frederick Schiller gave the genre a degree of fame that was never attained in France. In spite of the relative success of Sedaine, and in spite of the influence of the drama on authors such as Pierre Carlet **Marivaux** and **Voltaire**, the bourgeois drama led quickly to the melodrama through an exaggeration of pathos.

Isabelle Martin

BUFFON, Georges Jean Louis Leclerc, comte de (1707-1788). An important *philosophe* and leading scientist of the Enlightenment. His father was a magistrate of the *Parlement* of Dijon. Buffon received his secondary education at the **Jesuit** *collège* of Dijon, and then, apparently in accordance with family tradition, studied law. However, his interest in the sciences soon asserted itself, and he was able to devote himself to them.

Buffon's career proceeded smoothly. In 1733 he was appointed in a junior capacity to the Academy of Sciences. Six years later he was made curator of the King's Gardens, an important position that he kept for life, and filled with distinction. In 1753 he was elected to the **Académie française**, thus sealing his reputation. Though he spent considerable periods on his Burgundian estate, which provided him excellent conditions for his work as a naturalist, when in Paris he was welcome in the **salon** society of the capital.

The work for which Buffon is best remembered is the *Histoire naturelle*, published in 15 volumes between 1749 and 1767 with a further nine volumes on birds, five on minerals, and a seven-volume supplement appearing down to and beyond his death. While this huge work is properly Buffon's, he did benefit from the collaboration of other distinguished scientists, among them Louis-Jean-Marie Daubenton and Bernard-Germain-Etienne de la Ville de Lacépède. An outstanding work of science of the time, the *Histoire naturelle* is a typical product of the Enlightenment in that it was written in an admirable style and appealed to a wide readership. The emphasis in the work is more theoretical than empirical, which may also have enhanced its appeal. In it Buffon treats not only animals, but also human beings, and has a claim to be considered a founder of anthropology. The *Histoire naturelle* having been denounced as heterodox by the theologians of the Sorbonne in 1749, Buffon inserted a formal acceptance of the authority of Church doctrine at the beginning of the fourth volume of his work, and then continued with it. Unlike Denis **Diderot**, however, he did not see science as irreconcilably and necessarily opposed to religion.

Buffon also contributed the article "Nature" to the *Encyclopédie*, and toward the beginning of his career translated a number of works from English, among them Isaac **Newton**'s *Method of Fluxions* (1740). Though a leading savant, Buffon also took a strong interest in social questions. He showed considerable concern for the condition of the peasantry, which as a seigneur he knew at first hand, and denounced **slavery**.

BURKE, Edmund (1729-1797). Best known as the founding thinker of the modern conservative political tradition, Burke nevertheless for most of his career would have been placed by most observers toward the liberal end of the political spectrum.

Burke was born in Ireland to a Catholic mother and Protestant father who made his living from the law. He was sent to Trinity College, Dublin, where he received a sound secondary education, but went to London to make his career. There he studied, but did not practice, law, wrote, and became involved in politics.

While still in his twenties Burke published two significant works. The first, *A Vindication of Natural Society*, published in 1756, was a critical comment on contemporary social theory. The second, the *Philosophical Inquiry into our Ideas on the Sublime and the Beautiful*, which appeared the following year, proved to be a key work of Enlightenment esthetic theory that shifted emphasis from the values of **Neoclassicism** toward those of Romanticism. He also worked as a journalist and editor of the *Annual Register* from 1758. However, after an initial attempt to establish himself as a writer, he opted for a career in politics.

In 1761 Burke began working for the Duke of Hamilton, who headed the British administration in Ireland. In 1765 he became the secretary of the Marquis of Rockingham, one of the great **Whig** magnates of the time. This determined Burke's political future, as he became and remained Rockingham's man. Burke's three seats in **Parliament** between 1766 and 1794 were all within the gift of his patron, and whether he was making a speech in Parliament, writing a pamphlet or attending to political business, his position was that of the Rockinghamite faction of the Whig party. Of course, a mind as active and comprehensive as Burke's could not be reduced to reiteration of a party line, and within the confines of Whig interests and policies he creatively balanced pragmatism and principle.

Burke supported the British Empire, but his vision of the Empire was restrained and humanitarian. He favored recognizing many basic claims of the American colonists, and counseled avoiding direct confrontation with them. Without giving up British control of Ireland, he advocated greater freedom and consideration for the Irish, both on humanitarian and practical grounds. In his prosecution of Warren Hastings for misdeeds and corruption as head of the East India Company, Burke argued for moral limits on commercial profit-making. If a supporter of the British Empire, Burke at least worked to make the Empire more humane and enlightened.

Today Burke is best known for his criticism of the **French Revolution**, first expressed in his *Reflections on the Revolution in France*, published in November 1790. Alfred Cobban wrote of this work that "As literature, as political theory, as anything but history, his *Reflections* are magnificent" (Cobban, *Aspects*, p. 32). And so they are. As in many of his speeches and political writings, Burke identified and related to broad issues of principle behind the specifics of the case. It is this quality in the *Reflections* that made it the founding text of modern conservatism. Burke questioned the wisdom of attempting to remake on rational grounds the social and political structures that had been worked out over millennia in a protracted process of trial and error, and his argument applied to his own country, and indeed to every country and society, as well as to France. In arguing for the organic nature of societies and the dangers of unadvisedly intervening in their functioning, Burke also defended existing practices and institutions, regardless of their unfairness or irrationality. He insisted, for example, that property should have the preponderant voice in determining policy, and he justified the system of rotten boroughs on the grounds of their historicity.

What remains valuable in the *Reflections* is the understanding of the interrelatedness of social phenomena and their evolutionary growth over long periods of time. In these respects Burke offered a searching critique of Enlightenment **rationalism**, and contributed to both the emergence of romantic sensibility and to a better appreciation of history.

Burke's *Reflections on the Revolution in France* opened what turned out to be a debate of great extent and, in the contributions of Thomas **Paine**, Mary **Wollstonecraft**, William Godwin, James Mackintosh and others, of high quality. In his last years Burke became somewhat obsessed with the revolutionary movement in Europe and spoke and wrote on it repeatedly. In addition to his speeches in Parliament, Burke wrote *An Appeal from the New to the Old Whigs* (1791), a number of *Letters on a Regicide Peace* and *Thoughts on French Affairs*, which was written in 1791, but not published until 1797.

C

CABINETS DE LECTURE/READING ROOMS. *Cabinets de lecture* were commercial enterprises established by booksellers to rent books and periodicals, and to profit from the increasing literacy of the French public, as well as an increasing discrepancy between wages and the cost of reading material that effectively limited purchase to monied gentlemen of leisure. The first *cabinet de lecture* was opened by a Parisian book dealer, Jacques-François Quillau, in 1761, and became the prototype for such institutions. Subscribers to Quillau's *Magasin littéraire* had access not only to books and newspapers, but also to a warm, well-lit and comfortable space in which to read them. Membership (which included a free catalog) was paid on a weekly, six-month, or annual basis, at fees of 3 *livres*, 15 *livres* and 24 *livres* respectively. While not inexpensive, the cost was modest when contrasted with the price of a short novel (up to 4 *livres*) or a journal subscription (up to 30 *livres* a year). Quillau inspired other Parisian booksellers, including Grangé, Lejay, Mérigot and Couturier, who opened similar *cabinets* in the 1770s and 1780s.

The phenomenon spread to provincial cities, first to Lyon (which had three *cabinets* before the Revolution) then to Poitiers, Besançon, Metz, Montpellier and beyond. To judge from surviving catalogs, censorship in the provinces was more readily evaded than in the capital: provincial book lists included *livres philosophiques* and *nouveautés*, code words in the underground book trade for pornographic, irreligious and seditious publications, among them *Thérèse philosophe, Dictionnaire philosophique* and *L'An 2440*. Many such works, as well as counterfeited editions of works by established authors, were published by the Société Typographique de Neuchatel, Switzerland, which built up trade by establishing sales territories, calling on clients and arranging (sometimes clandestine) deliveries of goods.

The popularity of *cabinets de lecture* continued into the early part of the 19th century, when 463 of them existed in Paris alone.

Paul Benhamou

CAFÉS/COFFEEHOUSES. Commercial establishments that sold coffee and other drinks, as well as prepared food, and which came to play a central role in the culture of the Enlightenment.

Coffee was introduced into Europe during the last decades of the 17th century. Due largely to the lack of comparable beverages, coffee, and tea as well, enjoyed great popularity. By the 1730s London had more than 500 coffeehouses, which exceeded the number of taverns, and, according to Louis Sébastien **Mercier**, by the end of the century Paris had between 600 and 700, as well as vendors who sold coffee to workers in the streets. It has been argued that coffee was in part responsible for the more pacific tone of 18th century sociability, in that up to its introduction into Europe the drinks used in places of public gatherings were alcoholic.

From their appearance toward the end of the 17th century cafés played a number of roles. One was commercial, as members of the same professions, such as lawyers, publishers and insurers frequented the same establishments and transacted business there. And coffee-houses were famous as meeting places for men of letters. In Paris the *philosophes* and their associates met at the café Procope, while Denis **Diderot** and Jean-Jacques **Rousseau** first met at the Café de la Régence in the **Palais Royal**, and it was there that Diderot set his masterpiece, *Rameau's Nephew*. In London John Dryden and Alexander **Pope** were regulars at Will's in Covent Garden, Dr. **Johnson**'s circle met at the Turk's Head, and Scottish men of letters, such as David **Hume** and William **Robertson**, when in the capital met at the British Coffeehouse at Charing Cross. But the importance of coffee-houses extended beyond these more or less formal functions.

Cafés were perhaps the most popular and basic institutions of the emerging **public sphere** in the 18th century, and probably the main foci of the new sociability. They provided an open, egalitarian environment in which opinions could be, and were, exchanged freely, either in conversation, or by reading periodicals, which were routinely kept by owners of coffeehouses both in England and on the continent.

This freedom of association and opinion was a matter of concern to governments who regarded it as their responsibility and prerogative to monitor and control opinion. In 1675 Charles II tried to force the closure of London coffeehouses, but was unable to do so, and had to back down. Just over a hundred years later **Frederick II** of Prussia issued an edict to control cafés, and the Bourbon monarchy in France maintained a network of spies to monitor opinion in the cafés of Paris. While considerable freedom of opinion was achieved in Britain following the Glorious Revolution, on the continent governments that retained absolutist ideologies continued to attempt to control the expression of opinion. As contemporaries recognized, cafés were everywhere foci for the formulation and expression of opinion, political and other.

For Joseph **Addison,** however, cafés were to play primarily a cultural role. He wrote, "It was said of *Socrates* that he brought Philosophy down from Heaven, to inhabit among Men; and I shall be ambitious to have it said of me that I have brought Philosophy out of Closets and Libraries, Schools and Colleges, to dwell in Clubs and Assemblies, at Tea-Tables and in Coffee-Houses" (*The Spectator*, no. 10; 12 March 1711).

CAHIERS DE DOLEANCES. These notebooks were lists of grievances drawn up by some 40,000 towns and villages of France in 1789. They included grievances from the Clergy and **Nobility** as well the common people (the Third Estate). They constitute a remarkable survey of **public opinion**, not the public opinion of intellectuals or social elites, but what we can call popular opinion. True, since most peasants and artisans were illiterate and not used to public speaking, country lawyers, tenant farmers and local officials usually presided over the village assemblies which drew up the *cahiers*. Nevertheless, given the specificity of the grievances expressed and their correlation with earlier court cases, the *cahiers* have authenticity. They are a valuable source of grass-roots opinion at an important moment in European history.

A distinction should be made between the *cahiers* of the villages and those of the towns. The villages were most concerned with economic grievances. They demanded the reduction or abolition of church tithes and seigneurial dues, abolition of seigneurial justice, voiced support for village claims to common meadow and woodland and for a reduction of royal taxes, especially taxes on consumption of such commodities as salt, wine and tobacco. The overall message of the village *cahiers* was a rejection of the seigneurial system (*see* **Seigneurie**) and a plea for tax equality. The town *cahiers* also asked for reform of the tax system, but they were more concerned with political reforms. They asked for regular meetings of the Estates-General (*see* **Constituted Bodies** and **Notables**), transfer of the tax power from the King to this national representative body and a complete overhaul of the law and judicial system, eliminating privileges of institutions and persons and guaranteeing civil rights.

Now this tissue of demands was radical indeed. It amounted to the rejection of a society based on legalized **privilege** and royal **absolutism**. It anticipated the Declaration of Rights of Man and the Citizen promulgated by the National Assembly. At the same time, the *cahiers*, especially the village *cahiers*, were very respectful of the Monarchy and the Church. They wanted a reforming monarchy, not a republic, much less a democratic one. The *cahiers* are also significant for certain ambiguities and omissions. There is almost no voice for the poor, except in the *cahiers* of the Clergy. Property, large and small, was sacred, especially landed property (*see* **Physiocracy**). Should landlords therefore be compensated for the abolition of seigneurial dues and church tithes? Should common land be divided, and if so how? Although the *cahiers* of the Clergy and Nobility represented only a tiny minority of the total number, they expressed views concerning civil rights and legal privileges contrary to those of the vast majority. Hence the *cahiers* reflect certain fissures in French society as well as a common program of reform.

Robert Forster

CALMET, Augustin (1672-1757). Augustin Calmet was born in Mesnil-la-Horgne in Lorraine and, except for 10 years in Paris and a short voyage in Switzerland, spent his entire career in the Benedictine monasteries of his native province, culminating his itinerary as the abbot of Senones. His enormous literary output concerns ecclesiastical subjects exclusively, and was written with the (acknowledged) collaboration of the brothers in the monasteries where he worked. The more iconoclastic *philosophes* regarded Calmet as an archconservative but still read his works, especially the 23-volume Bible commentary (*Commentaire littérale et historique de tous les livres de l'ancien et du nouveau Testament*, Paris, 1707-1716), because it was encyclopedic and accessible, having been written in French. Indeed he was, if not quite an archconservative, at the very least impeccably orthodox for the period, with a strain of nearly pathological antisemitism and misogyny. His orthodoxy did not prevent him from entertaining friendly relations with **Voltaire**, nor did his misogyny prevent him from corresponding in friendly terms with Voltaire's mistress, Mme du **Châtelet**, who was a radical deist if not quite an atheist and a vigorous proto-feminist. A confirmation of his status as the oracle of the Church on matters biblical can be seen in the articles on biblical subjects in Denis **Diderot**'s *Encyclopédie*, which were necessarily confided to respectable theologians who were heavily in Calmet's debt.

The reasons for Calmet's specialization in Bible and related questions are multiple. Without ever committing himself to the **Jansenist** cause, he seems to have been strongly influenced by Pasquier Quesnel's teaching that Bible reading should be an important part of Catholic piety. Since Richard Simon's *Histoire critique du vieux testament* (Paris, 1678) it had become possible and even increasingly important to write about the Bible in French rather than in Latin because the Bible had entered French popular culture. There was therefore a need for a detailed commentary on and apology for the Bible in French.

The notes that were an integral part of the Port-Royal translation of the Bible were so completely oriented toward edification and piety that they were inadequate to anticipate and answer the questions of the freethinkers and philosophers hostile to the Bible and religion, like Benedict **Spinoza**, and did not seek to harmonize the Bible with itself, nor to demonstrate, point by point, the biblical authority for post-Tridentine Catholic theology. For the pious "solitaires" of Port-Royal, that was evident and not too important because they hardly distinguished between Patristic opinion and Biblical teaching, but to judge from Calmet's commentary, he thought that it had become necessary.

Calmet's command of Hebrew was weak, his knowledge of rabbinic literature weaker, and of the natural sciences weaker still, and based on authority, including that of Aristotle, Pliny and the ancient Greek doctors, rather than on modern experimentation. For Calmet, what the authorities asserted needed no verification; his idea of what constituted historical proof was quite erratic, while he often suspended his critical judgment in the cause of apologetics. He thus believed in all the biblical **miracles**, and in particular in New Testament demons. He was sufficiently consistent not to question the contemporary "apparitions, ghosts and vampires of Hungary and Moravia" (1746). Nevertheless he had an enlightened side.

When Catholic doctrine and apologetics were not in question, he could produce some remarkable specimens of Bible criticism, distinguishing, for example, several different literary styles and thus different authors in the book of Proverbs, and setting out the problem of the complicated relationship of the books of Chronicles with the historical books of the Bible and their mutual dependence upon (lost) sources. He might have advanced biblical studies rather than retarded them had these astute observations not been buried in the mass of his credulous and uncritical commentary. Subsequent editions of his commentary became increasingly orthodox, which suggests that Catholic orthodoxy in 18th-century France against which Voltaire and the other anti-religious *philosophes* railed, was neither monolithic nor always reactionary.

Bertram Eugene Schwarzbach

CAMERALISM. An approach to government and administration originated in central Europe toward the end of the 17th century and developed over the 18th century. The term "cameralism" derives from "kammer," the chamber, or exchequer, of the territorial lord. In its assumptions concerning the necessity of state control of economics, cameralism is close to mercantilism. However, unlike the mercantilists, cameralists tended to define their objective as the general well-being of the people rather than the power and prestige of the state.

During the 18th century cameralism became a central feature of the **enlightened despotism** of the German-speaking areas of Europe and Russia. It can be seen as an early attempt to establish a discipline or science of government and administration. Cameralism was traditional in regarding the state as responsible for the well-being of the population, but innovative in seeking in a systematic way to achieve this end through administrative and economic modernization.

Unlike the enlightened despotism of western Europe, cameralism had an established institutional base. In 1727 chairs of Administrative Science (*Cameralwissenschaft*) were established in the Univerities of Halle and Frankfurt an der Oder. Another such chair in the University of Vienna was held by Johann H. G. von Justi, whose *Foundations of the Power and Happiness of States* (1760-1761) was one the earliest authoritative texts of cameralism. Another occupant of this chair at the University of Vienna was Joseph von Sonnenfels, one of the leading figures of the Enlightenment in Austria, a counselor of **Joseph II** and author of the influential *Basic Principles of the Science of Administration, Business and Finance*, which appeared in three volumes between 1765 and 1776.

In its statism, elitist paternalism and aspiration to rationalizing reform, cameralism deserves to be regarded as an integral element of one of the dominant currents of the Enlightenment.

CAMPBELL, Archibald, 1st Earl of Ilay (or Islay) and 3rd Duke of Argyll (1682-1761). Lord Ilay, as he was known from 1707 until 1743, attended Eton, Glasgow University and the University of Utrecht, where he studied law and probably a variety of other subjects including mathematics, medicine, chemistry and history. His intellectual commitments were those of a late 17th-century virtuoso and scientist. Ilay was a competent mathematician, astronomer, chemist and botanist who held an honorary M.D. and prescribed for his friends. For a generation (c.1735-1760) he maintained one of the best botanical gardens in England, one in which 22 new species of plants were naturalized. This was located near London on reclaimed wasteland, one of several estates he much improved.

His personal religious views were deistical and rooted in his Newtonianism. He collected a large library of over 12,000 volumes, which contained many science books and a good selection of economic tracts. As an economic manager, he supported the views of his old friend John Law of Lauriston. They saw a managed economy with an expanding money supply as a good thing. Ilay in Scotland helped to secure these through the creation of the Scottish Board of Trustees for Arts, Fish and Manufactories (1727), the Royal Bank of Scotland (1727) and the British Linen Bank (1743). While not much of a patron of the arts, he did build one of the largest Gothic structures erected in 18th-century Britain, and had fashionable interests in chinoiserie and Palladian architecture. He also furthered the careers of the artists William Aikman and Allan Ramsay the younger.

Ilay's career was primarily a political one. Although he spent some time in the army, rising to the rank of colonel commanding his own regiment, his political work was more important. He served as Lord Treasurer of Scotland in 1705, helped to arrange the Treaty of Union with England (1705-1707) and was rewarded with largely honorary, but lucrative, positions in the Scottish courts and administrative offices. Generally out of power between 1707 and c.1724, he thereafter managed Scotland for Sir Robert Walpole's ministries until 1742 when again he lost power until c.1747. From then until 1761 he handled most government patronage in Scotland.

In office, Ilay used his power to further his own interests, which were often those of the enlightened. Despite his dislike and distrust of clerics, he sometimes sat in the General Assembly of the Kirk, which he also tried to manage as a patronage politician. His enduring monument is the Scottish culture, which he did so much to change through his patronage appointments of enlightened men. Most of the Scots who are today of interest to Enlightenment scholars were patronized by him and his political machine. The list is long but includes mathematicians like Colin Maclaurin, the teachers at the Edinburgh medical school (1726-1761), clerics like John Home, William **Robertson**, Hugh Blair, distinguished social thinkers such as Henry Home, Lord Kames and Adam **Smith**, as well as many more who made Scotland more utilitarian in outlook, science oriented, secular, tolerant and humane.

Roger Emerson

CANDIDE (1759). **Voltaire**'s best known and most popular work, and a classic example of the *conte*. It is the account of a good-natured and naïve young man who in the course of his adventures in pursuit of his beloved Cunégonde is gradually disabused of his idealism. Like Fénelon's *Telemachus*, but in a very different key, *Candide* is a sort of novel of the road in which the protagonist is educated by being confronted with different cultures and experiences.

The framework that Voltaire chose for his philosophical fantasy allows him to direct withering criticism against corporations and values of the **Old Regime** that he despised. Cunégonde's father and brother are the butt of most of his barbs against the **nobility**; the **Jesuits** and the Inquisition are made to represent all that is worst in organized religion; and the inhumanity of warfare is used to highlight the harm perpetrated by the State. Nor do merchants and commerce get off lightly, as Voltaire subjects the slave economy of the sugar islands in the Caribbean to scathing criticism. Pangloss, whose doctrinal denial of the very real evils of which the story offers instance after horrifying instance, exemplifies the fatuous intellectual whose main function is to justify the status quo.

If criticism of the Old Regime and of a philosophy of optimism (defined by one of the characters in the book as the mania for maintaining that all is well when it is not) were all there was to *Candide,* it is unlikely that the work would still sustain the interest it does. Beyond the criticism of the institutions and prejudices of the Old Regime there is a critique of **human nature** that still holds our attention.

In the stories of Candide and Cunégonde, Pangloss, Martin, the Old Woman and the rest, Voltaire portrays the world as a scene of endless crimes and men as creatures driven by greed, lust and aggressiveness, who balk at no manner of violence or cruelty to achieve their ends. Even the cultured and wealthy Venetian, Pococurante, with all his luxury and leisure is bored and incapable of **happiness**. Similarly, the **utopia** of Eldorado is well enough for those who have known nothing else, but cannot restrain Candide in his erotic quest for Cunégonde. Nor is the world in which the adventures of Candide unfold a hospitable place. There are storms and earthquakes that kill innocent and guilty alike, and time and experience reduce the once lovely Cunégonde to an ugly, shrewish old hag.

Despite the comic-book character of the violence in *Candide,* the world in which the book's protagonist moves is harsh and somber. Voltaire implies that we do better to recognize unpleasant facts than to tax our intellects to find ways of denying them. At the end of *Candide,* Pangloss observes that the necessary interrelations of things, implicitly good, have brought the hero and his friends and associates to the relative peace of the farm near the Bosphorus. His argument shows that he has learned nothing from his experiences, and modified nothing in his philosophy. Candide observes that his former instructor's views were very well formulated but also that "it is necessary to cultivate our garden."

Unhappy though Candide's experiences were, he has learned from them the futility of unfounded speculation and the importance of practical work. This implies that while the world is in most cases harsh and inhospitable, our stay in it can be made worse by ignoring our objective situation in favor of unprovable fantasies. By the same token it can be improved by a realistic understanding of our situation and by hard work. This attitude, which we might term a mitigated and pragmatic pessimism, is characteristic of Voltaire in his other works, and of those thinkers of the Enlightenment who reject both metaphysics and utopia.

CARTESIANISM. The complex of ideas associated with the French philosopher of the 17th century, René **Descartes**, and elaborated by scientists and philosophers who found inspiration in his work. The place of Cartesianism in the Enlightenment is ambiguous. On the one hand, it formed the core of the world view of the early Enlightenment, or perhaps more correctly the pre-Enlightenment, and it has been argued that it remained at the center of the radical thrust of Enlightenment thought up to and into the **French Revolution**. On the other hand, in its comprehensiveness, **rationalism** and deductive methodology, Cartesianism ran counter to the empirical and inductive approaches dominant during the High Enlightenment.

One aspect of Descartes's thought that appealed to virtually all Enlightenment figures was his criticism of **scholasticism**. Like Francis **Bacon** before him, and Jean le Ronde d'**Alembert** and **Voltaire** after, Descartes had nothing but scorn for a system of thought that sought to circumscribe the workings of the material world within categories of logic, which took words for things, and which preferred authority to evidence. On these points Descartes enjoyed the approval of most Enlightenment thinkers.

Descartes's description of the world in purely mechanistic and mathematical terms also pleased many of the scientists of the time. However, his aspiration to comprehensiveness and his attempt to base his science on assured metaphysical principles were suspect in the eyes of most later *philosophes*. Indeed, the inability of scientists sympathetic to Descartes's ideas to elaborate them successfully, and then the development of a more convincing system of physics by Isaac **Newton**, effectively discredited Descartes's theories of subtle matter and vortices, and called into question the entire enterprise of deductive and metaphysically based science.

Descartes aspired to produce a perfectly intelligible and thoroughly comprehensive explanation of the world. Newton, by contrast, sought only to provide an adequate explanation for observed phenomena. Whereas Descartes tried to provide a rational and intelligible account of physics—and whatever its drawbacks, movement caused by impulsion is intelligible—Newton readily admitted that he could not explain the causes of gravity or what it was, but he could accurately describe the workings of celestial mechanics by positing the law of universal gravitation. Some contemporaries complained that gravity was a return to occult forces in science. Newton replied that so long as he could describe how it worked, he was not troubled by what ultimately it might be. This willingness to accept a limited but precise form of knowledge is one of the things that separates Newton and his followers from Descartes.

The aspiration to universal knowledge was, for many thinkers of the time, a gateway to error, for it invited those who sought such knowledge to fill in gaps in substantiated knowledge with speculation that would likely prove false. Voltaire said of Descartes that he was "born to discover the errors of antiquity, but also to substitute his own for them" and that he had been "carried away by that systematic spirit that blinds [even] the greatest men" (***Letters on England***, Letter 13). This is not a bad appreciation of Descartes's role in the history of science.

Descartes was, among other things, a magnificent builder of **systems**. This aspect of his work allowed him to posit comprehensive theories that explained much but often lacked a sound empirical base. It was the comprehensiveness of this thought that made Cartesianism a real rival of the scholastic synthesis that dominated European high culture to the end of the 17th century. The rationalism and mechanistic character of Descartes's basic assumptions contributed to the disenchantment of the world, but it retained space for imagination and projections that **empiricism** rejected as unfounded. It was because of its contradiction of scholasticism and its broad incompatibility with traditional theology that Cartesianism was condemned by the Catholic Church in 1663 and by the French state in 1691. It was because of its comprehensive and systematic nature that it was rejected and mocked by the more empirically minded *philosophes* of the High Enlightenment.

Descartes's influence was immense. Among those who sought to elaborate his ideas and make use of his method were the **Jansenists** Antoine Arnauld and Pierre Nicole, the Oratorian Father Malebranche, the scientists Jacques Rohault and Pierre Sylvain, the philosophers Gottfried Wilhelm **Leibniz** and Benedict **Spinoza**, and, some maintain, the scholar and polymath, Pierre **Bayle.**

CASANOVA, Giacomo Girolamo (1725-1798). Casanova was a Venetian, a fact the importance of which exceeds the bounds of a simple statement of biographical fact. It is significant for his later career, for his profound sense of attachment and for his general outlook.

The son of Venetian actors (though according to rumor probably the bastard son of a Venetian patrician, Michel Grimani) and abandoned by his mother after the early death of his father, Casanova was brought up by his grandmother. He studied law and theology at Padua, was tonsured in 1740, then took minor orders the following year before abandoning the possibility of a career in the Church in order to move more freely in the world. He tried his hand at, or practiced, dozens of ways of making a living, among them law clerk, secretary, alchemist, violinist, soldier, then military officer, a diplomatic post, director of the lottery in France, author, dramatist, poet, translator and textile manufacturer. Giving up establishing himself in any fixed profession, he seems to have opted to become an intellectual adventurer.

Having already traveled much in his youth, Casanova found an adoptive father in 1746 in the Venetian senator Bragadino, who considered him as his son. In order to amuse his adoptive father and his friends, he developed a cabbalistic design in the form of a pyramid, which allowed him to fabricate predictions of the future and initiated him in the somewhat questionable disciplines of magic and alchemy. He was arrested on the orders of the Inquisitors of the Republic of Venice in 1755 and incarcerated in the fear-inspiring Prison de Plombs.

The reasons for his arrest have never been adequately explained in that there was no documented charge against him. Among the more plausible reasons are his knowledge of magic and alchemy, his ties with foreign diplomats, among them the Cardinal de Bernis, French ambassador at Venice, and his familiarity with the Venetian senator already mentioned. Casanova succeeded in doing the impossible and escaping from the Plombs on 31 October 1756 after more than a year of captivity. He fled to France, where he was able to profit from his earlier friendship with the Cardinal de Bernis, and to make some important new acquaintances, among them the Count de Lamberg and some other well-known figures. He never stopped travelling around Europe, principally Germany, Italy and England, and in 1765 he went as far as Russia. In 1759 he made up the name of the chevalier de Seignalt in order to pass as a noble.

The number of Casanova's amorous adventures, made famous by his memoirs, *The History of My Life*, is not so imposing in quantitative terms (a total of 122 verifiable affairs) as by the way he succeeded in transposing his lived experiences into his writings. There is every reason to believe that he intentionally made use of libertine and picaresque literary models to portray his life as a story in a novel. In the field of autobiography, his great innovation was to elevate his private life to the rank of facts worthy of narration. Beyond this, the text as a whole revives daily life of the 18th century as vividly as that of **salons** and courts, and so serves as a living encyclopedia of the whole period.

Casanova is not the author of a single book, since his essays, poems, a utopian novel, *Icosaméron*, and a good many political texts bear witness to his talent as a writer beside his memoirs.

In his last years, after a failed attempt to return to Venice and to earn his living there as an informer for the Inquisition, Casanova was obliged to retire to Bohemia, where he accepted a position as librarian of the Count of Waldstein in the castle of Dux, today Duhcov in the Czech Republic. It was there that he dedicated the last ten years of his life to writing his memoirs in which he immortalizes himself as the lover and hero of innumerable adventures. In order to judge the literary merit of his work it is sufficient to remark that he is one of the few persons who actually lived to succeed in giving his name to a character type, which soon became a noun, and a synonym for "seducer."

Ilona Kovacs

CASSIRER, Ernst (1874-1945). A philosopher and historian who wrote one of the classic accounts of the Enlightenment. Cassirer was born to a Jewish family in the sometime German, sometime Polish, city of Breslau. He studied at the University of Marburg under Hermann Cohen, one of the leading philosophers of Judaism of his time. He taught in a junior capacity at the University of Berlin between 1909 and 1919, and then moved to Hamburg where he held a professorship and for a short time acted as chancellor. Cassirer was among the more fortunate German-Jewish academics who were able to leave their homeland when the Nazis came to power in 1933. He went first to England and taught at Oxford, then to Sweden, and finally to the United States, where he taught at Yale and Columbia.

Cassirer's philosophical position was Kantian and idealist. His work extended from editing the writings of Gottfried Wilhelm **Leibniz** and Immanuel **Kant** to extensive studies in the history of ideas, and to original contributions to philosophy, most importantly his *Philosophy of Symbolic Forms* (1923-1929; English trans. 1955-1957). Cassirer's most important contribution to Enlightenment studies is his appropriately named *The Philosophy of the Enlightenment*, which was first published in 1932 (English trans. 1951), and can fairly be seen as a defense of the liberal, rational and humane values of the Enlightenment against the rising tide of Nazism and its ideology of extreme nationalism, corporatism and **racism**. In a restrained and scholarly way it makes a strong case for the relevance of the Enlightenment, and for the practical importance of its key values.

The Philosophy of the Enlightenment is not an easy book, but the effort of studying it is amply rewarded, for it provides what is probably still the best treatment of the ideas that inform, and to a considerable degree define, the movement. The opening chapter, entitled "The Mind of the Enlightenment," remains one of the best introductions to the subject available. The other six chapters systematically treat nature, psychology, religion, history, society and esthetics. Written by a trained and highly competent philosopher, *The Philosophy of the Enlightenment* is sometimes formal and dry, but it is always lucid and faithful to its subject. It has the added advantage of giving more weight to the thinkers of the German Enlightenment, who are often overlooked in general studies in favor of the French and English.

Cassirer also produced two short monographs on the Enlightenment that emphasize the role of Jean-Jacques **Rousseau**. These are *The Question of Jean-Jacques Rousseau* (1932; trans. 1954) and *Rousseau, Kant and Goethe* (trans. 1945).

CATHERINE II (1729-1796). Czarina of Russia from 1762 until her death. Born to the ruling house of the minor German principality of Holstein-Gottorp, Catherine married a Russian prince, who ruled briefly and badly until deposed by a plot to which his wife was party, and killed not long after, almost certainly with Catherine's knowledge and complicity.

One of the leading practitioners of **enlightened despotism**, Catherine combined great energy and intellectual curiosity with a desire to reform her realm internally and to extend its borders. She succeeded better in her second objective than her first. Under Catherine's direction Russia increased its territory by annexing the greater part of **Poland** between 1772 and 1795, and the Crimea and part of the Black Sea littoral in 1783.

Catherine's attempts at internal reform include an Instruction or Nakaz (1767) intended as the basis for a new law code for Russia, on which Denis **Diderot** wrote an extensive commentary, a provincial statute (1775), a police ordinance (1782), charters for the **nobility** and towns (1785) and a program of national **education**, restricted to the larger towns (1786). In general these plans were intended to centralize, rationalize and modernize the country. That these projects had little practical impact is a consequence of the social and cultural conditions of Russia at the time. Overwhelmingly agricultural, dependent on serf labor and dominated by the nobility, Russian society of the 18th century was backward in the extreme, and even the most enlightened of rulers could not overcome this set of circumstances. In practical terms Catherine's only potential local partners were the nobles, and in the attempt to win their support, she abandoned the wretched peasantry to their discretion.

Catherine's ties with the advanced thinkers of the time were strong. She corresponded with Diderot, **Voltaire** and Jean le Ronde d'**Alembert** among others, encouraged leading writers to visit her court, which Diderot did during 1773-1774, and was often generous in the extreme in supporting them. For example, she bought Diderot's library while he was still alive, then left it in his possession and paid him to act as her librarian. After his death his books and manuscripts were shipped to Russia. She was also an active patron of the arts.

In her politics Catherine consulted the national interest of Russia and the imperatives of power. What she took from the Enlightenment in her political endeavors was instrumental rather than substantial, though the harsh international environment in which she functioned may well have left her little alternative. Her ascent to power was almost certainly criminal, though her exercise of it was, in the circumstances, moderate. Her personal life was not marked by the regularity or discretion she sought to impose on the State, and with the **French Revolution** she tended toward reaction. But then there is no necessary correlation between participation in the culture of the Enlightenment and support for the French Revolution.

CENSORSHIP. The practice of examining writings in order to determine whether there is anything in them that is considered detrimental to the State, the Church or morality. The mentality supporting censorship was one that distinguished clearly between truth and error, and assumed that it was in possession of the truth. Virtually from its inception the Catholic Church had sought to control the expression and dissemination of views it deemed unorthodox or heretical. In the same manner, the early-modern State denied legitimacy to, and strove to control, ideas or opinions that called its legitimacy into question or might otherwise destabilize it.

During the 18th century in Europe censorship took many forms. In Spain, for example, the Inquisition exercised the function of censorship, and did so with great rigor. In England, by contrast, the censorship of printed materials before publication was abandoned in 1695, and the State relied on libel laws to keep the expression of opinion within acceptable limits. Austria retained the practice of censorship, but shifted responsibility for it from a commission of **Jesuits** to a board including laymen and clerics. Enlightened despots moderated, but still retained, mechanisms of censorship, and adjusted their use to changing conditions.

Old-regime France remained a corporate society in which the authorities, ecclesiastical and secular, regarded it as their responsibility to control the expression of opinion, especially in the print media. It had a number of institutions that were empowered to act as censors. These include the Faculty of Theology of the Sorbonne, the *Parlement* of Paris and the office of the Chancellor of France.

Normal procedure for an author or publisher was to submit a manuscript intended for publication to the office of the Chancellor, which would then pass it on to an officially appointed censor to read. If the censor found that the book had nothing in it contrary to religion, morality or the government, he would usually issue it a privilege allowing it to be printed. If the book were deemed offensive, it would be denied permission to be published, and would then either be shelved, revised or become part of the clandestine book trade. Works that were neither clearly orthodox nor plainly unacceptable might be granted a simple tolerance or tacit permission to publish. These intermediary categories reflected the readiness of the government to adapt to new conditions and to become more flexible in its treatment of the growing volume and variety of literature being produced. The use of tacit permissions increased roughly tenfold between the 1730s and the 1760s, when Lamoignon de **Malesherbes** was given responsibility for control of the book trade.

To representatives of the **Old Regime** censorship was not only a right, but also an obligation. It was seen as part of the responsible exercise of authority, in which those with knowledge and understanding sought to protect the less educated from false or dangerous opinions. In general the Enlightenment objected to censorship on the grounds that the individual had the capacity and the right to decide for himself or herself what to think or believe.

CHÂTELET, Gabrielle Emilie Le Tonnelier de Breteuil, Marquise du (1706-1749). One of the most remarkable women of the Enlightenment. Her father, the baron de Breteuil, was responsible for introducing ambassadors at the court of Versailles. As a girl Mme du Châtelet received a fairly typical convent education, but her father, recognizing her outstanding intellectual abilities, arranged for her to be tutored in Latin and mathematics. Among her private math teachers were the distinguished mathematicians Alexis Claude Clairaut and Pierre Louis Moreau de **Maupertuis.**

Mme du Châtelet is best known today as the companion in love and intellectual pursuits of **Voltaire.** She met him in 1733 and the following year he came to stay with her at her country residence of Cirey in Champagne. The estate served the couple as both resort and research institute. Their studies covered physics, history and the Bible. Voltaire began his *Essay on Manners* for Mme du Châtelet and published his popularization of Newton in 1737 while at Cirey. Mme du Châtelet published a basic text on physics in 1740 and did the first French translation of **Newton**'s *Principia*, which did not appear, however, until after her death. She also did a translation of Bernard **Mandeville**'s *Fable of the Bees*, though it too remained in manuscript. Among her other writings is a long manuscript on biblical criticism that is now being edited and published by B. E. Schwarzbach. In 1738 both Mme du Châtelet and Voltaire submitted entries to an essay competition on the nature of fire to the Academy of Sciences, though neither won a prize. In her own time Mme du Châtelet was best known for her work in physics, particularly in the field of kinetic energy, and had the unusual honor for a woman of being elected to the Academy of Sciences of Bologna.

Mme du Châtelet's private life was no less remarkable than were her intellectual achievements. Her extended affair with Voltaire was accompanied by mutual respect and affection. However, this did not prevent her from falling in love with the army officer, poet and minor *philosophe*, Jean François de Saint-Lambert, in 1747. Voltaire initially took this development badly, but then reconciled himself to it, so that Mme du Châtelet and her two lovers formed a *ménage à trois* (four if M. du Châtelet is counted, but whether husbands count in such situations is unclear). This arrangement did not last long. Mme du Châtelet gave birth to a child of Saint-Lambert in September of 1749 and died a week later.

CITIZENSHIP. A status assuring varying rights of political participation to certain classes of the population, usually on the basis of birth, **gender**, race, age and **property**. The model of citizenship current in the 18th century was derived from the literature of classical antiquity, which was widely diffused because it served as the core curriculum of secondary **education** throughout Europe at this time.

In that monarchies regarded the making and implementation of policy as the prerogative of the king and his council, and as the king had the right of appointing and dismissing his ministers and most members of his administration, citizenship and with it **democracy**, which implied a sovereign citizen body, were of only theoretical significance for most of Europe during the **Old Regime**. With the exception of a few politically powerless **republics** in Italy and Switzerland, Europeans were subjects, not citizens. Nevertheless, the ideal of citizenship persisted in the educational system and in the discourse of the time, and, as Louis Sébastien **Mercier** pointed out, it was potentially subversive (*Tableau de Paris*, chap. lxxxi).

Unexpectedly, the notion of citizenship was transferred from theory to practice over the course of the 18th century. Following the American War of Independence against the British in 1776 and the **French Revolution** of 1789, one of the founding documents of which was the *Declaration of Rights of Man and the Citizen* of August of the same year, citizenship was extended to extensive portions of the population. Unlike the republics of classical antiquity, which were direct democracies, the American Republic and the regimes of revolutionary France, like modern democracies, practiced indirect, or representative, democracy. However, the American and French democracies of the 18th century defined citizenship more narrowly than do modern democracies.

In America **slaves** were without either rights of political participation or protection of the civil laws. In both America (with the exception of the State of New Jersey) and France, **women** were as a matter of course excluded from citizenship. The French Constitution of 1791 distinguished between active and passive citizens. The latter enjoyed the full protection of the law, but only the former had the right to vote and to stand for office. Access to the franchise was relatively easy, being set at the payment of taxes equivalent to three days' salary. Under these conditions about 60 percent of adult males could vote.

The French Constitution of 1793, which was never implemented, accorded universal male suffrage. This was a highly unusual measure for the time. Subsequent regimes instituted progressively higher property qualifications for voting, until under the Bourbon Restoration only the richest one percent of adult males had the right to vote.

Today citizenship is usually a matter of one's birth and passport. In the 18th century, by contrast, it was generally assumed that decisions that citizens were required to make demanded a certain level of competence. This was usually measured in some combination of education, leisure and wealth, with property often the decisive factor. The debate and conflicts over the franchise were intense in Europe from the later 18th century to the mid-19th century, when universal male suffrage began to be instituted. Women in Western democracies only received the right to vote around the time of, and following, World War I.

CLANDESTINE MANUSCRIPTS. The **censorship** of the print media in France is almost as old as printing in the realm, dating to François I, who censored Bibles in the vernacular along with tracts by the early reformers (1526). In the 18th century, the level of public literacy had increased and the control of printing had improved considerably. As a result, what could not be published because of its iconoclasm could be, and often was, diffused among "the happy few" in manuscript. These copies were in turn copied, sometimes with embellishments to render them more literary, or more moderate or, sometimes, more radical, which is to say that many of these texts have both an author, though he or she has rarely been rigorously identified, and a metahistory, which is sometimes no less interesting than the original author's intentions.

The first students of the phenomenon of a corpus of clandestine manuscripts assumed that the radicalism of early 18th-century France found expression in that corpus, and that it inspired the Encyclopedists, **Voltaire**, Denis **Diderot** and the other radical writers of the second half of the century. Localization lists of 1996 identify 269 different tracts, including many that were written for publication, some that were copies of contemporary printed books, others that date from the Renaissance, like Machiavelli's *Il Principe*, or Bonaventure Des Périers's *Cymbalum mundi*, or Giordano Bruno's *Spaccio della bestia trionfante*; still others emerged from the circle of the so-called "libertins érudits" of the 17th century, the French expression of Padovan "naturalism."

This was an attractive scheme, bridging the formative years of the Enlightenment, 1685 to 1715, that Paul Hazard would call the "crisis of European consciousness," and the mid-century when Enlightenment writers like Voltaire and Jean-Jacques **Rousseau** would be openly critical of the old order and its institutions, and would propose a variety of political, cultural and religious reforms. It is now obvious that this scheme is not satisfactory.

In the first place, the clandestine tracts are quite diverse, and include propositions of moderate religious reform, deistic tracts, materialist tracts and tracts that profess outright atheism, even though the latter two tendencies would not find many disciples among the major writers of the Enlightenment except the Baron d'**Holbach** and Julien Offray **La Mettrie**. We would add that this literature was in direct relation with 18th century apologetics echoing the doubts of the apologists while they, in turn, tried to refute the attacks against religion and the Church that they imagined the freethinkers were making. In particular, perhaps because apologetics stress the biblical basis for religion and for church authority, many of the clandestine tracts sought to weaken that support by exposing the Bible to criticism, especially normative criticism, whose sophistication varied from tract to tract.

It has been demonstrated that there was considerable iconoclastic publishing in French in France and in adjacent countries that was tolerated or had escaped the censors, so one can no longer argue that manuscript diffusion was the only medium or the alternative medium for the expression of radical ideas, especially in the second half of the century. Furthermore, not every tract that has survived in manuscript was necessarily radical for its time. Despite these reservations, the clandestine tracts still offer a privileged look at amateur philosophizing in 18th-century France that may be more representative of the thought and values of educated men and women of the time than mainstream publications that were necessarily autocensored and sought to appeal to the widest possible public.

Bertram Eugene Schwarzbach

CLUB DE L'ENTRESOL. A gathering in Paris of a group of clerics, intellectuals, administrators and nobles that met once or twice a month on Saturdays from 1724 to 1731. It was located in the residence of the Président d'**Hénault** on the Place Vendôme, but named for the mezzanine, or entresol, where the abbé Alary had an apartment, and where the meetings were held. Alary, who was the founder of the club and had been one of the tutors of **Louis XV**, was something of a linguist, and was a member of the **Académie française**. Other members included the abbé de **Saint-Pierre**, in many ways the animating spirit of the group, the marquis d'Argenson, the chevalier de Ramsay, President **Montesquieu,** an English visitor, the Viscount **Bolingbroke** and a number of **abbés** and nobles. Though **salons** were being established in Paris at this time, the Club de l'Entresol remained exclusively male, and was frequented predominantly by members of the privileged orders.

The Club de l'Entresol has been described as a sort of academy dedicated to moral and political questions. This was the forum before which the abbé de Saint-Pierre presented many of his reform projects, and where projects of a similar sort were discussed. The business of offering governments unsolicited advice is not without its risks, and the meetings of this club ended when Cardinal Fleury, in effect the head of Louis XV's government at the time, expressed his wish that they cease. One of the earliest groups to act as a sort of unofficial think tank advocating a broadly enlightened program, the Club de l'Entresol was in many ways similar to the **Mittwochsgesellschaft** that was active in Berlin at the end of the century.

CLUBS. Voluntary groupings of men with common interests, whether occupational, artistic, intellectual or simply social. It was common, especially in Great Britain, for clubs to meet in coffeehouses, but they might also gather in private homes. Clubs were run on the basis of recognized membership, so in terms of sociability they fell between the complete openness of the **café**, where for the price of one's drink the client could speak to, or forebear from speaking to, whomever he wished, and the highly formalized sociability of state-sponsored **academies**.

In their criteria for membership and degrees of formality, clubs differed widely. To attend organized meetings of men of recognized status as writers, artists, administrators or thinkers, it was usually necessary to have been chosen a member, and minimally to have received an invitation. This was the case, for example, with the **Club** de l'Entresol of Paris, which flourished during the early years of the reign of Louis XV and discussed political issues; the aristocratic Kit-Cat Club of London; Dr. Johnson's Literary Club (1764-1794); the Mittwochsgesellschaft, or Wednesday Club (1783-1798), in Berlin, where intellectuals and bureaucrats met to discuss the issues of the day; the Select Society of Edinburgh (1754-1764), which brought together leading academics, clerics and local notables; or the Lunar Society of Birmingham, which included a high proportion of scientists (many of whom where also members of the Royal Society), and exceptionally, practical businessmen and manufacturers, and whose members modestly referred to themselves as "Lunatics." The main figures in this club were Erasmus Darwin, the grandfather of Charles, Matthew Boulton, James Watt and Josiah Wedgwood. On the other hand, reading rooms (see Cabinets de lecture), which were largely commercial enterprises providing access to books and periodicals in comfortable conditions, often formed the basis for literary societies with fairly open membership. In France some of these associations called themselves "clubs" or "societies" before the French Revolution, and became local branches of the Jacobin Club once the Revolution began.

The importance of clubs to the development and spread of Enlightenment culture was great, but it consisted less in the content of whatever was said than in the fact that they provided a framework in which the members of civil society—overwhelmingly male and middle class—could meet freely and express their views without regard for authority, whether civil or ecclesiastical. These clubs, whether as serious as Johnson's Literary Club, as practical and useful as the Lunar Society or as frivolous as the Sublime Society of the Beefsteaks, which met in a London coffeehouse, all contributed to furthering the openness and freedom of the public sphere, which according to some scholars provided the necessary space in which the Enlightenment could develop. The clubs were, of course, only one part of the broader public sphere, and often overlapped in membership with other institutions, from humble cafés and reading rooms to masonic lodges, and clearly elitist salons and academies.

CODE OF NATURE/CODE DE LA NATURE. One of the more radical statements of Enlightenment social thought. It was published in 1755 and is generally attributed to the abbé Morelly. In some ways the work is altogether typical of the Enlightenment, in others exceptional.

The full and enthusiastic acceptance of the contributions of John **Locke** and Isaac **Newton** to modern thought is shared by the author of the *Code*, as well as by virtually all major proponents of Enlightenment ideas. Morelly accepts the notion of the infant at birth as a *tabula rasa* and sees human beings as physiologically disposed to their own interests. However, like Jean-Jacques **Rousseau**, he sees human beings as naturally good and inclined toward **beneficence**. Morelly also admires the scientific synthesis achieved by Newton, and like other Enlightenment thinkers, sought to find social and political analogies to Newton's simple and harmonious laws of **nature**. He refers to **self-interest** as a social force equivalent to gravity in physics (Morelly, *Code de la Nature,* Paris, Éditions sociales, 1970, pp.43 and 55-56), and assumes that just as the forces of gravity and inertia result in stable equilibria, so when rightly understood, self-interest and the general good are harmonized by complementary needs.

Nevertheless, the *Code de la Nature* belongs less to Adam **Smith**'s than to Rousseau's intellectual world. While both were moral Newtonians, Smith saw the **laws** governing society as already existing and needing only a change in legislation to be activated. Both Rousseau and Morelly, by contrast, regarded contemporary society as radically corrupt because of departures from natural norms of human relationships that occurred at the inception of civil society, and so regarded contemporary society as being in need of fundamental restructuring. Like Rousseau, Morelly sought to discover mankind's primal and natural condition, and to apply the principles that informed that original condition to restructuring society in such a way that it would achieve general well-being. And again like Rousseau, Morelly held man's primal nature to be good. Morelly was not, however, a follower of Rousseau. At the time of the publication of the *Code de la Nature* only Rousseau's *First Discourse* had appeared, and Morelly referred to its author as a "bold sophist" (p. 116). While the *Second Discourse* would have been far more to Morelly's liking, it could not have influenced his writing of the *Code*, and the two men seem to have worked out their ideas independently.

There are also aspects of the *Code de la Nature* that are atypical of mainstream Enlightenment thought. These include the emphasis on consanguinity as the basis of sociability, a position that is used to qualify contract theory (*see* **Social Contract**) and that serves as the theoretical basis for the heavily patriarchal structure of the polity described in Part IV of the *Code*. The identification of **property** as the root of all social and political evil and the concomitant presentation of a weak form of communism as the kind of society most conducive to general well-being is also unusual for the period. While the value of beneficence is indeed a central feature of the thought of the Enlightenment, few writers attach as much importance to it as does Morelly.

The final section of the *Code de la Nature* is an outline of a society in harmony with nature that assures biological well-being, which was a much more immediate problem in the West during the 18th century than it is today, and social harmony. The key features of this code are the absence of private property and a form of communism that includes institutions to assure social order and welfare, such as schools, old-folks homes and prisons, and a loose but obligatory system of labor. Politics, which are formally republican and paternalistic, are conceived in administrative terms. In many ways Morelly's *Code* recalls More's *Utopia*, but without the stylistic grace, depth or humor of the great humanist's work, though also without some of its harshness.

In an age which required that philosophical works be attractively written and its proposals for social change not wildly impractical, it is not surprising that the *Code de la Nature* never achieved a particularly wide circulation. Indeed, it had only one edition in the 18th century. Nevertheless, it remains a minor Enlightenment classic.

Perhaps this is because it posits a theory of man and of society that is significantly different from contemporary assumptions and practice, and in doing this creates a tension between existing social and political conditions and social and political ideals by which these realities might be measured and modified. The attempt to imagine and describe a world better and more decent than the one they lived in was one of the ways the thinkers of the Enlightenment created the conceptual space for change, and it is as part of this effort that the main significance of the *Code de la Nature* is to be found. *See also* **Utopia**.

COLLEGES. In France *collèges* were in effect secondary schools concerned with preparation of students for **university**. Their curricula have been described as Latin, more Latin and yet more Latin. While this can be seen as a continuation of the Renaissance secondary curriculum, such a course of studies was not unreasonable at the time, since the language of instruction of all the senior faculties of the universities was Latin. A command of the rudiments of Latin was a prerequisite for acceptance into *collèges*, where class exercises entailed not only the reading of Latin texts, often bowdlerized by conscientious pedagogues, but also translation from Latin into French and composition in Latin. In Paris most *collèges* were attached to the University. However, the colleges of Oxford, Cambridge and Paris, which today receive students in their late teens and early twenties, in the 18th century were frequented by young gentlemen and scholarship students who began their studies at 13 or 14, though sometimes earlier, and finished them a little before students today graduate from high school.

Attendance at municipal *collèges* was generally free, though parents were responsible for the student's room and board, and the student's family also had to bear the cost of his primary **education**, including Latin rudiments. The Parisian *collèges* had a considerable number of scholarships available to gifted students with some patronage, but as many of these scholarships were originally pious foundations, they were restricted to the training of clerics.

Most *collèges* were run by the clergy, especially the Oratorians and the **Jesuits**, both of whom had reputations for excellence. This reflected a cultural environment in which an adequate knowledge of the Latin language and classics was restricted and the function of teacher badly paid. The near monopoly of the teaching orders on secondary education resulted in most of the *philosophes* (and leading revolutionaries) having received their educations from clerics. **Voltaire** and Denis **Diderot**, for example, studied under the Jesuits, **Montesquieu** with the Oratorians. Following the disbanding of the Jesuits in France in 1762 their *collèges* were taken over by secular authorities and reorganized.

COLONIES. By the 18th century the expansion of Europe to other continents had three centuries behind it, if one excepts the Crusades. A widening technological advantage, epitomized in the phrase "guns and ships," gave Western Europeans an opportunity to use the Atlantic to extend their dominance—economic, military, political—to all four of the other continents and even to Oceania. Their technological advantage included an advanced form of capitalism, characterized by concentrations of investment capital, rationalized markets and new sources of labor.

The Europeans employed at least three methods of domination. First, trading posts, forts and warehouses were built along the coasts of Africa and Asia in order to tap trade from deep in the interior. One can debate whether trading posts constituted "colonies." Cultural exchange here between Europeans and non-Europeans was minimal. Second, Europeans developed slave colonies, especially in the Caribbean, Brazil and British North America (the future U.S. South) with a minimum of European settlers (except in North America) but a large number of imported Africans. African slave labor resisted tropical diseases and worked sugar, coffee, rice and tobacco **plantations** more effectively than European labor, albeit at staggering death rates (*see* **Slavery**). Third, the Europeans developed settlement colonies on the two American continents. Here large numbers of Europeans founded permanent communities, implanted their own religion and customs and relegated the indigenous Amerindian population to heavy labor. Disease (smallpox) or the destruction of their communities further decimated these populations. In its ultimate effects on the Amerindian, the encounter with the Europeans can be called genocidal.

The settlement colonies in the Americas developed different cultures, depending partly on their country of origin, partly on the local milieu, and partly on the result of intra-European colonial wars. Spain had the largest empire, stretching from Cape Horn to the Great Plains of North America. It imparted a highly centralized state, Catholic religion modified by important Amerindian accretions, and a hierarchical society with racial elements but modified by a high rate of miscegenation, which eventually created multi-cultural societies. French Canada had such long and harsh winters that there were few immigrants, especially females. Canada's main economic activity was the fur trade, which depended on Amerindian cooperation to function. This, added to the need for Amerindian auxiliaries in the wars against the British to their south, led to better interracial relations than between the British settlers and the Indian tribes. The British immigrated in large numbers and in complete families, especially to the Massachusetts and Virginia colonies. They implanted British institutions, including legislatures, civil law and Protestantism. They developed a strong sense of "American" identity (excluding slaves), which led to increasing colonial resistance to even minimum control from London.

Robert Forster

COMÉDIE FRANÇAISE. The "Comédie française," also known as the "Maison de Molière," was established in 1680, that is to say, after the death of Molière. By a "lettre de cachet" Louis XIV ordered the troupes of the Hôtel de Bourgogne and the Hôtel Guénégaud to merge and become one company. At the same time, they obtained the monopoly of being the only theatrical company authorized to play in French in Paris.

The French Royal Company operated, and still operates, under the name of Comédie Française as a cooperative. Although protected by the king and receiving an allowance, the members were, in common with their heirs, responsible for the debts they contracted. They had to invest in the Theater if it was necessary. The society, or company, which was independent, was composed of 23 shares; only the senior members could own a whole share.

Generally an actor began with half a share and then acquired quarters or half-quarters. The actors gathered every week to decide on the upcoming program, listen to the reading of new plays, and accept or reject them by vote, establish and control the expenses, and the like. Living authors had the habit of giving the best roles to their favorite actors, but for plays by dead authors, the actors chose roles by deliberation. When they retired, the actors got a pension of 1,000 *livres* a year, a sum that allowed them to live modestly.

From 1689 to 1770, the Company was located at rue des Fossés Saint-Germain, in a building especially designed for them by the architect François d'Orbay. The auditorium could accommodate about 1,500 spectators. From 1770 the Company stayed for a few years at the Tuileries, in the Machines room conceived in 1660 by Le Vau, which was used by the Opera. In 1782 it moved to a modern theater specifically designed for the Company, and which has not changed a lot since then: the Odeon.

In 1791 ideological conflicts and the official proclamation of freedom of the theater provoked a split within the Company. The more moderate members stayed at the Odeon and the more revolutionary ones, among them François-Joseph Talma, settled at rue de Richelieu, in a theater built by Victor Louis, using an innovative technique: structure, roofing, ceiling and box frames were made entirely of metal.

The Comédie Française continued to be in the 18th century the Royal Company with exclusive rights to the whole classic and modern repertoires. It was this company that mounted the plays of Crébillon the elder, Alain René Lesage, **Voltaire**, Pierre-Augustin Caron de **Beaumarchais** and Alexis Piron. The actors struggled, sometimes aggressively, against all attempts by the **Italian Comedy** and the

fairground theaters to interfere with their control over the repertoire.

The Comédie Française was at the center of Parisian life as a result of the importance of the theater in the 18th century. Therefore, the French *philosophes* tried to annex it in order to spread new ideas. It was at the Comédie Française that the first tearful comedies, or **comédies larmoyantes**, were played, but the French tragedy was still very predominant. It was at the Comédie Française, too, that Voltaire's bust was crowned shortly before his death.

Three of the most famous actors of the 18th century who appeared at the Comédie Française were Claire Josèphe (called Mlle Clairon), Henri Louis Cain, known as Lekain, and Pierre Louis du Bus Préville. This last succeeded in developing the art of direction, in making costumes more authentic and in improving body movement.

Despite many misadventures due to changes of the political system, the Comédie Française has kept, in an architecture of the time, esthetic and theatrical functions that were defined during the 18th century.

Isabelle Martin

COMÉDIE LARMOYANTE/**TEARFUL COMEDY.** The "comédie larmoyante" is similar in many ways to the **bourgeois drama**. It appeared during the years 1730-1750, but only became really popular around 1760. Moral rectitude, stereotypic feelings and affirmation of a social and moral ideal constitute its main themes. The outstanding success in England of the *London Merchant* (1731) of George Lillo illustrates well the drift toward moral tales based on the private life of the bourgeoisie that would also inspire Denis **Diderot** and Gotthold Ephraim **Lessing**. In this genre with invariably happy endings, the spectator becomes emotionally involved and cries in sympathy with the extreme distress of the characters, who include the virtuous in exile, abducted children and divided families.

Pierre Claude Nivelle de la Chaussée (1691-1754), author of *l'Ecole de la jeunesse, l'Ecole des mères*, and *l'Ecole des amis* is identified in France with this genre, which constitutes an essential transition between the "molièresque" comedy and the thesis theater of the 19th century.

The melodrama opens the way to the new theater of the Enlightenment: it strives toward a naturalistic, non-grotesque description of the moral hopes and the ideals of contemporary society. Its morality is militant, and aims at reuniting broken couples, reconciling generations and defending the virtuous. This genre avoids the comic and the vulgar as much as it does the tragic, for all of these modes are irrelevant to the upper middle class. The conventional and classical language that connects it to "high" comedy is undoubtedly the main reason for its disappearance, because it contrasts too much with the modernity of its topics.

Isabelle Martin

COMEDY. Several types of comedy were prominent in the 18th century. Two of the more important were based on character and on manners. By the 18th century, the comedy of character, which had been most fully developed by Molière, had reduced the importance of intrigue and unpredictable circumstances to comic situations. These in turn were used as the framework for presentation of character in the manner of La Bruyère, namely, as the psychological and moral description of a universal type. Numerous plays that depict conventional types were staged in the 18th century, and illustrate the resilience of the genre. Among them are *Le Petit-maître corrigé* of Pierre Carlet **Marivaux** and *Le Méchant* of Jean-Baptiste-Louis Gresset.

The comedy of manners is characterized by the treatment of a failing peculiar to a social group or period, and is less interested in character development. It also owes a good deal to Molière, especially in a play such as *Les Femmes savantes*.

This type of comedy developed in two periods over the 18th century. The first is characterized by the cynical comedy that depicts unscrupulous financiers, depraved noblemen or representatives of other social groups that Alain-René Lesage and Jean-François Regnard had already portrayed with success in the last years of the reign of Louis XIV. The second period covers almost the whole reign of **Louis XV**, and culminates towards 1760. The major theme developed in this genre is the description of true feelings and simple moral behavior opposed to the snobbery and affectation of high society. A good example of this genre is *Les Mœurs du temps* of Joseph Saurin. *See also* **Italian Comedy** and *Comédie larmoyante*.

Isabelle Martin

CONDILLAC, Etienne Bonnot de, abbé (1714-1780). The younger brother of the abbé **Mably,** and probably the French thinker who did more than any other to work out the implications of John **Locke**'s psychology. Condillac was the son of a tax official whose fortune allowed him to buy the office of Secretary to the King, which brought with it immediate noble status. Condillac thus belonged by birth to the elite ranks of his society. His career reflects this clearly. But it also reflects a rich ambiguity of interests and activities typical of the Enlightenment.

Condillac received his early **education** at home. In 1733 he entered the leading Parisian seminary of Saint Sulpice together with his brother, the abbé Mably. Seven years later he was ordained, but subsequently performed no regular clerical duties, though he did retain clerical dress and behaved in his personal life with the reserve appropriate to a man of the cloth. His formal clerical status did not, however, prevent him from keeping company with the likes of Denis **Diderot** and Jean-Jacques **Rousseau,** and as both a gentleman and a recognized scholar he was welcome to the **salons** and other social foci of polite society.

In 1758 Condillac was appointed preceptor to the Prince of Parma. By this time he had already published his main studies on epistemology and so was recognized as a leading intellectual, but appointments to courts, even minor courts, were not won without the recommendations of well-placed friends and patrons. Condillac spent the period between 1758 and 1767 attending to the education of his less than gifted student. Many Enlightenment figures exercised the function of tutor. Condillac was fortunate to be able to do so at the very highest social level. After leaving Parma he published a 16-volume set of texts that derived from his teaching experience, the *Cours d'études pour le Prince de Parme* (1769-1773). Condillac thus not only wrote theoretical works for the intellectual elite, but also, like many of his fellow *philosophes*, engaged in popularization.

On his return to France in 1767 he was appointed abbot of Mureau, and was, according to the custom of the time and his position as *abbé commendataire*, able to enjoy the revenues of the abbey without performing the duties of abbot. The following year he was elected to the **Académie française**, thus consolidating his social and intellectual status. But Condillac was not content to rest on his laurels. In 1773 he bought a country estate and moved there. He was elected to the local Royal Agricultural Society in whose activities he took a serious interest, and in 1776 published a treatise on political economy in which he argued in favor of free trade and the importance of industry. In the wide range of his interests and writing for a broad as well as more learned audience, Condillac is typical of enlightened intellectuals. Even his clerical dress, if unusual for a thinker of the Enlightenment, was not without precedent. Indeed, together with the abbés **Raynal,**

Coyer, his brother Mably and many others, Condillac was able to balance his active participation in the Enlightenment with continued membership in the Church.

Condillac's most important contributions to Enlightenment thought are his treatises on epistemology, the *Traité sur l'origine des connaissances humaines* (1746), the *Traité des Systèmes* (1749) and the *Traité des sensations* (1754). In addition to his course of studies for the Prince of Parma, he also published *Le Commerce et le gouvernement considérés relativement l'un à l'autre* (1776), and toward the end of his life a treatise on logic and another entitled *Langue de calculs* (1779).

CONDORCET, Marie Jean Antoine Nicolas de Caritat, Marquis de (1743-1794). A leading *philosophe* who combined scientific and social interests in a way that foreshadowed the social sciences. Condorcet was born to an old and wealthy family of the **nobility** of the sword. He studied at the **Jesuit** *collège* of Reims and the Parisian *Collège* de Navarre, where he received a solid grounding in the sciences.

Initially Condorcet devoted himself to science and to mathematics. A first book on calculus published in 1765 was well received. In 1769 he was elected to the Academy of Sciences (*see* **Academies, State-Sponsored**) and four years later became its secretary. In this capacity he wrote the biographies of its members, much as his friend and patron, Jean le Ronde d'**Alembert**, did for the members of the **Académie française**. In 1770 Alembert had taken Condorcet on a pilgrimage to visit **Voltaire**, and also introduced him into Parisian **salons**. From 1774 he began to devote his attention to broader social and political issues. In that year he wrote a polemic against a traditionalist history of thought by the abbé Sabatier de Castres. In 1775 and 1776 he wrote works on economics arguing for free trade and against state intervention. His comprehensively humanitarian outlook expressed itself in support for and defense of various minorities. In 1781 Condorcet wrote in favor of civil equality for Protestants and against the **slavery** of blacks, and in 1790 was among the first to argue for the conferral of political rights on **women**. In 1785 he produced an important work applying the theory of probability to voting. In his attempts to apply mathematics and scientific methods to social issues Condorcet deserves to be regarded as one of the founders of the social sciences.

Unlike many of his fellow *philosophes,* Condorcet welcomed the **French Revolution** and became actively involved in it. During 1790 he wrote some 20 pamphlets on a variety of social and political questions. He was elected to the Legislative Assembly in 1791 and then to the Convention in 1792. He associated with the Girondins, and was active both as a writer and a legislator on such central issues as **educational** reform and the constitution. Having been outlawed by the Mountain, he went into hiding, and in his retreat wrote the *Sketch of the Progress of the Human Mind.* In this work, which some see as the testament of the Enlightenment, Condorcet expressed his belief in the inevitable progress of mankind thanks to advances in the arts and sciences.

On leaving his hiding place in Paris, Condorcet was soon captured. He committed suicide in jail during the night of 28 to 29 March 1793, and was survived by his wife since 1786, Sophie de Grouchy, and their young daughter, to whom he wrote at length while in hiding. One of the most liberal and courageous figures of the Enlightenment, Condorcet came to grief over the politics of the French Revolution, not its philosophy.

CONSTITUTED BODIES. Social groups in 18th Europe west of Russia were grouped into "orders" or "**estates**," each with its own **privileges** and obligations. Rather than being part of a uniform citizenry loyal to a sovereign state, individuals were defined above all by their station in a multi-tiered hierarchy ranging from the clergy and **nobility** at the top of the social pyramid to the craft guilds and professional associations at the bottom. These "estates" existed at all levels, local, municipal, provincial and national.

In France these estates periodically came together at the provincial level as Clergy, Nobility and the Third Estate in two institutions that claimed to represent them. These were the five provincial estates and the 31 sovereign courts of law. (The Estates General, a national representative body, existed in theory, but it was not convoked by the Crown between 1615 and 1789.) These bodies were not elected like modern Western legislatures. The members were either chosen by the royal administration or they inherited their positions by tradition or literally as family property, since in France many offices were sold by the Crown as a means of raising revenue. Among the provincial estates only those of Languedoc and Brittany had important local powers, which largely affected the distribution of taxes. The sovereign courts of law, however, were more important, especially the 15 *par-*

lements. These had the power to review royal decrees and refuse registration, a stamp of judicial approval that gave the royal decree the full force of law. Although there were constitutional procedures permitting the king to override a refusal, the publicity surrounding such a "remonstrance" made the king hesitate to confront the parlements.

After 1760, the parlements became more systematic in their opposition to royal tax and religious policies and defended their positions to the public in the press, pamphlets and books. The opposition to the French monarchy did not come only from theoretical tracts of the *philosophes*, but also from controversies over public policy generated by the parlements. The magistrates claimed to be bulwarks against "ministerial despotism" and disciples of **Montesquieu**'s theory of "intermediary powers" between the monarch and the people. However, their principles coincided too closely with their own tax privileges and landed interests. When the **French Revolution** of 1789 came, the magistrates were identified with a retrograde nobility and a corporate "**Old Regime**" that would be replaced by a whole set of new political and judicial institutions. The regime of "estates" would be succeeded by a uniform citizenry with universal rights and a sovereign National Assembly.

Robert Forster

CONSTITUTIONALISM. An orientation in political thought that emphasizes obedience to law and due process, and recognizes norms, written or unwritten, governing political behavior. Constitutions, as they were understood in the 18th-century, were bodies of law laying the groundwork for political life, and in practice were seen as ways of limiting the power of the monarch and his administration, and hence of assuring the **liberty** of subjects. Constitutionalism was generally taken to stand in opposition to **absolutism**.

Emphasis on respect for existing legal structures tends to be conservative. Spokesmen for constitutional rights in 18th-century France, such as the sovereign courts or *parlements*, usually opposed significant deviations from established legal norms, something which reforming monarchs sought to undertake in order to modernize their realms. The sovereign courts acted in the name of historically sanctioned laws, and the security and liberties assured the subjects of the monarch. In their suspicion of governments and potential abuses of power, and in their concern for the rights of subjects, spokesmen of constitutionalism, such as **Montesquieu**, who was himself a magistrate in the sovereign court of Bordeaux, tended to **liberalism**. In their opposition to reforms proposed by the monarchy, however, they appear conservative. Some historians believe that the effective opposition of the parlements to reform programs of the central government blocked gradual reform and contributed to bringing about more fundamental and radical changes in French government and society known as the **French Revolution**.

CONTE. A short, often fanciful, prose narrative. As a genre it was developed in the Enlightenment, following the vogue for fairy tales (*contes de fées*) at the end of the 17th century, such as Charles Perrault's *Tales of Mother Goose* (1697).

A *conte* is generally shorter than a novel, and usually does not attempt the realistic drawing of character or credibility of plot that is found in most novels. It is particularly suited to the informal discussion of ideas, and often takes the form of a thought experiment written with an eye for entertainment. In this way it is typical of the Enlightenment aspiration to arouse thought and instruct in an accessible and amusing way. It frequently uses exotic and marvelous themes for serious and critical purposes.

Voltaire did most to develop this genre, and the most famous example of it is his *Candide*, which is, among other things, a send-up of Gottfried Wilhelm **Leibniz**'s philosophy, and especially his optimism, which appears to deny the reality and horror of human suffering. Voltaire presents the horrendous injustices and brutality as comic-book violence, which is to say violence without consequences. Having created an atmosphere of unreality, he deploys murders, rapes, theft and swindling as so many little jokes, and builds his argument against optimism and its fatuous spokesmen.

Other examples of Voltaire's short, fanciful, pointed fictions of this sort are *L'Ingénu, Micromégas, Zadig, Le Taureau Blanc* and *Le Monde comme il va*. Other examples of the genre in France include *Le Sopha* of Crébillon *fils*, Charles Pinot Duclos's *Acajou et Zirophile*, some of Denis **Diderot**'s fiction, which are *contes* in spirit and novels in length (something which could also be said of Lawrence **Sterne**'s *Tristram Shandy*), and going against the licentious tone of many of the above works, Jean François **Marmontel**'s *Contes moraux*. Probably the most famous *conte* in English is Samuel **Johnson**'s *Rasselas*, which in the guise of a novel of the road explores the theme of human **happiness**. *Rasselas* was published at the same time as Voltaire's *Candide*, and shares many features with it, though for incisiveness and wit it can hardly compare with Voltaire's tale.

CORVÉE. An obligation on peasants to perform labor without pay. The duration of this service was not fixed and varied from region to region. There were two distinct kinds of *corvée* under the **Old Regime**. The *corvée royale* was the obligation of peasants to maintain at their own cost and without receiving payment any royal roads or highways that passed through their parishes. This was the *corvée* commuted by Anne-Robert-Jacques **Turgot**. The other *corvée* was one of the **seigneurial** obligations owed by the peasant to the holder of the eminent domain of his land. This obligation to work on the land of the seigneur, or for him, was often poorly defined and open to abuse.

COSMOPOLITANISM. Literally, citizenship of the world. The term is derived from the Greek *kosmos,* meaning world or universe, and *polites*, citizen. It reflects the Enlightenment belief that one was first and primarily a member of a common **humanity**, and only secondarily the member of a specific state or nation. The tension between one's duty to humanity and to the state of which one was a member was heightened during the Revolutionary and Napoleonic wars, and from the 19th century onwards, the force of **nationalism** increased. During the Enlightenment national characteristics and stereotypes were recognized, but the differences they implied were regarded as secondary to the things that all humans have in common.

Partly because it was socially and culturally an elitist movement, the Enlightenment crossed national boundaries with ease. Aristocratic and elite English, Scots, Italians, Poles, Germans and Americans all met on a friendly footing in the **salons** and **cafés** and theaters of Paris, and Frenchmen, whose language had become the common property of the elites of all European nations, were received equally well abroad. Similarly, the international community of the **Republic of Letters** was open to all men and women of ability. Both the social composition of the enlightened community and the basic universalistic values of the Enlightenment inclined the enlightened elites to set world citizenship and belonging to a common humanity above national loyalties.

COUNTER-ENLIGHTENMENT. A movement or trend in 18th- and 19th-century thought fundamentally opposed to the basic assumptions and beliefs of the **Enlightenment**. This notion was first put forward by Isaiah Berlin in an article in the second volume of the *Dictionary of the History of Ideas*, which was published in 1973, and which has since appeared in his collection of essays, *Against the Current*.

How one understands the Counter-Enlightenment depends very much on how one defines the Enlightenment, for the former is basically an inversion of the latter. According to Berlin, the distinguishing features of the Enlightenment are a belief in an all-pervasive and natural lawfulness, which includes adherence to a doctrine of natural **law**, an assertion of the autonomy of **reason** together with a concomitant mistrust of tradition and authority, the assumption that **human nature** is the same at all times and in all places, and faith in **empiricism** as the method appropriate for investigating all questions, moral as well as physical, accompanied by a sweeping denial of the validity of transcendental ideas or entities.

The Counter-Enlightenment, by contrast, is characterized by a thoroughgoing relativism, which rejects objective natural standards. It also denies that it is possible rationally to reorganize society according to universally valid norms, for the nature of man is neither uniform nor rational. The thinkers of the Counter-Enlightenment regarded mankind as motivated by instinct rather than reason, and so needing to be governed by force, persuasion being generally ineffectual. A concomitant of these points of view was a radical **individualism** that had little regard for the interests of others or of society as a whole.

In many ways the Counter-Enlightenment as presented by Berlin differs little from the Romantic movement of the late 18th and early 19th centuries. With few exceptions, the key figures of the Counter-Enlightenment all belonged to that movement, and few of them were French, as were most of the leading thinkers of the Enlightenment whom Berlin adduces. Germans predominate with Johann Georg Hamann, Justus Moser, Friedrich von Schiller, Johann Gottfried von Herder, Friedrich Heinrich Jacobi and Friedrich Wilhelm Joseph von Schelling, while the British are represented by Edmund **Burke,** William Blake and occasional reference to William Wordsworth. Among the French Jean-Jacques **Rousseau,** who belonged fully if uneasily to both worlds, is touched on, as is the Marquis de **Sade**, but the main figures are two aristocrats, Joseph de Maistre and Louis de Bonald, whom the **French Revolution** had frightened into theocracy and autocracy. The one important thinker from the early 18th century whom Berlin associates with the Counter-Enlightenment is Giambatttista **Vico**, an enigmatic figure whose originality makes him hard to place. Whether he properly belongs to the Enlightenment or not, and if so to what degree, is a moot question (*see New Science*).

The notion of Counter-Enlightenment suggests a polarized view of intellectual development. There is a movement, and then there is its opposite. This model calls for sharp distinctions and mutual incompatibilities. In discussing what he regarded as oversimplified views of the Enlightenment, Peter **Gay** once referred to a strategy he called "definition by larceny." Take away all that is various and diffuse in a movement, and it will necessarily be reduced to uniformity, and probably dullness. But, Gay asked, can we properly define the Enlightenment in such a way as to exclude the emphasis on sentiment and morality in Rousseau, or the appreciation of historical development found in Burke, or the awareness of the force and omnipresence of the darker instincts in the works of Denis **Diderot**? Does this not both distort and diminish the Enlightenment? The question remains relevant.

COYER, François Gabriel, abbé (1707-1782). A marginal cleric who advocated advanced ideas and was part of the established Enlightenment. One of 13 children of a cloth merchant, Coyer was educated by the **Jesuits**, and for a time taught in their *collèges*. He left the order in 1736 to take up the post of tutor to the future Duc de Bouillon. After four years in this position he served for a time as a military chaplain. Coyer's student became his patron, and he was henceforth, unlike many aspiring writers of the time, assured a reasonably comfortable situation. He also had pensions from the houses of Soubise and Condé, as well as several Church benefices. At the time of his death the abbé enjoyed the substantial annual income of roughly 13,000 *livres*.

Coyer made his literary reputation with a number of satirical sketches entitled *Bagatelles morales* in 1754. Two years later he published an argument in favor of permitting nobles to engage in trade. This book, *La Noblesse commerçante*, initiated a lively debate on the status and function of the **nobility**, and is probably Coyer's best known work. He also wrote a *Plan d'éducation publique*, and two other works which indirectly had a wide influence. Both his *Dissertation sur la nature du peuple* and *Histoire de Jean Sobieski* were used by the Chevalier de **Jaucourt** as the basis of articles in the **Encyclopédie**, the former for "Peuple" and the latter for "Polonais." In 1763 Coyer was named a member of the Academy of Nancy (*see* **Academies, Provincial**). However, despite the support of **Voltaire** he was unable to win election to the **Académie française**. Nevertheless, Coyer's career is an example of a talented young man from a modest family making a successful literary career by the traditional means of service in the Church and in a great noble family, but at the same time advocating ideas and values characteristic of the Enlightenment.

CURCHOD, Suzanne/Mme NECKER (1739-1794). Suzanne Curchod was the daughter of a Swiss Protestant pastor who lived not far from Lausanne. He was not well-off, but provided his daughter with an admirably sound and well-rounded education. Beautiful, intelligent and cultured, Mlle Curchod won the heart of the young Edward **Gibbon** during his stay in Lausanne, but being forced to choose between his inheritance and his prospective bride, he opted for the former. Gibbon's loss was the gain of Jacques **Necker**, a wealthy banker and future minister of finance of **Louis XVI**.

After the death of her parents, Mlle Curchod moved to Geneva, where she met and favorably impressed a Parisian society figure, Mme de Vermenoux, who offered her a position as her companion. Once in Paris, she met Necker at her mistress's **salon**, and the two married in 1764. They became devoted to each other, and their married life was exceptionally harmonious. They had one daughter, famous as Anne Louise Germaine de Staël.

Shortly after marrying, Mme Necker set about setting up her own salon. Her motive for doing so was to further her husband's career and interests. Mme Necker was thus one of the few *salonnières* not to be independent or to use her salon primarily as an arena for cultural sociability. She received men of letters of all inclinations on Fridays, while Tuesdays were reserved for the nobility.

In 1770 after a dinner at Mme Necker's a decision was taken to erect a statue to **Voltaire**, and the hostess was entrusted with responsibility for the contributions. From that time, her salon had arrived. It was open to men of letters and politicians of all points of view, for in this way it would be most useful to M Necker. Interestingly, though established at roughly the same time as Mlle de **Lespinasse**'s salon, Mme Necker's preserved the forms of the older models of Mme **Lambert** and Mme **Geoffrin**.

Mme Necker was traditional in her religious beliefs and conventional in her morality. She was also charitable and contributed to founding a new hospice in Paris. Her *Reflexions sur le divorce* (1794) argued against the propriety of dissolving marriages, an interesting position for a Protestant. She also translated Gray's *Elegy*. She did not, however, write much for publication, which her husband thought inappropriate for a woman of her standing. The most extensive work we have from her is an eight-volume collection, *Pensées et mélanges extraits des manuscripts de Madame Necker*, published by her husband in 1798.

CURÉ. In France the parish priest of the Catholic Church who was charged both with administering the sacraments to his parishioners and with serving as the agent of the government by keeping the parish register and reading out royal directives after mass on Sunday. In practice the *curé* was responsible for the modern equivalent of social services in his parish, and generally acted as a community leader.

A *curé* under the **Old Regime** received his jurisdiction from the bishop of the diocese, under whose spiritual authority he remained, but his benefice from the person or corporation in whose gift it was. In cases where the original curate was an abbey, the full revenues from the tithe went to the abbey, which then paid the cleric actually performing the duties of *curé* a modest stipend known as the *portion congrue*. This uneven division of the clerical revenues of the parish contributed to a widely felt hostility to the regular clergy that was cloistered and performed few, if any, services for the **population** at large, while it often enjoyed the incomes from extensive estates. By contrast, the secular clergy that saw to the spiritual and often the social needs of the faithful were appreciated and respected because of their positive contribution to the community. It was true, however, that in some cases curates who were overly exacting in claiming their fees for the performance of such necessary services as baptisms, marriages and burials, aroused considerable animosity.

From the 17th century on the parish clergy in most of Europe tended to be well educated and to behave with appropriate decorum and responsibility. There were, to be sure, complaints about overly worldly prelates and monks, but such criticism did not generally extend to the parish clergy, whose role, not only in administering the sacraments, but also in overseeing **education** and in providing advice and charity, was widely appreciated. No doubt there were few parish clergy as saintly as the protagonist of Oliver Goldsmith's *Vicar of Wakefield* or as the Savoyard vicar in Jean-Jacques **Rousseau**'s *Émile*. On the other hand, there must have been few as obsequious and foolish as Jane Austen portrayed Mr. Collins to be in *Pride and Prejudice*. For the most part the thinkers of the Enlightenment tended to respect and even to idealize the parish clergy, largely for the practical and very real services they rendered the communities they served.

D

DARNTON, Robert (1939-). Probably the best and most imaginative North American historian of the Enlightenment. His work is characterized by extensive archival research, searching reflection on the materials uncovered and an exceptionally clear and pleasing sytle.

Darnton is not much interested in the history of ideas as practiced by Ernst **Cassirer**, Paul Hazard or Peter **Gay**. His Enlightenment, rather, is one of the marginals of **Grub Street**, the authorities they confronted and the writing they produced, not of the **salons**; of the print workers and businessmen who made the *Encyclopédie* such a financial success, not of the writers who provided the copy; of the profession of **authorship** under the **Old Regime**, quantitatively determined and minutely analyzed, not of the careers of leading *philosophes*; of the books and pamphlets, many of them all but forgotten, that the public actually bought and read in the 18th century, not of the classics of **Montesquieu** and **Voltaire**; and of the mechanisms by which books were produced and the means by which they were distributed rather than an analysis of their content, though Darnton has shown himself to be a close reader of the clandestine literature that has generally been disregarded by historians of ideas.

Darnton has extended our knowledge of the business of publication and the distribution of printed matter, especially illegal and clandestine literature, in his collection of essays, *The Literary Underground of the Old Regime*, in his recent *The Forbidden Best sellers of Pre-Revolutionary France*, together with its companion volume of sources, *The Corpus of Clandestine Literature*, and in his overly long monograph, *The Business of Enlightenment*, which treats the publishing history of the *Encyclopédie*. He has further innovatively explored aspects of 18th-century French history from the point of view of cultural anthropology and tried to understand the mentality of administrators in *The Great Cat Massacres and Other Episodes in French Cultural History* and *The Kiss of Lamourette: Reflections on Cultural History*.

Though Darnton's corpus is impressive in its range and extent, possibly his most influential work was an article entitled "The High Enlightenment and the Low-Life of Literature in Pre-Revolutionary France" published in *Past & Present* in 1971. In this article Darnton drew a distinction between the established intellectuals of the salons, who enjoyed the status, pensions and sinecures that the regime provided for those whom it favored, and the excluded, frustrated and bitter world of Grub Street. Proposing a new solution to one of the perennial problems of early-modern historiography, he further suggested that a link between the Enlightenment and the **French Revolution** could be made through Grub Street rather than, as had usually been argued, through the major *philosophes* and their influence. This, in any case, is the theme presented as the "Darnton thesis" in the volume of *Studies on Voltaire and Eighteenth Century* (vol. 359) dealing with this subject. This collection of essays is a rare tribute offered to a living historian. It contains 12 for the most part excellent essays, the best of which, as might be expected, is by Darnton himself.

DAVID, Jacques Louis (1748-1825). One of the most important painters of the 18th century, and in France, the leading exponent of **Neoclassicism**. David was born to a comfortable commercial family, which apparently had social pretensions, as the father was killed in a duel. He was related to the celebrated **rococo** painter François **Boucher**, who directed him to another artist's workshop for what was in effect an apprenticeship, during which he spent four years in Italy.

David gained fame through his paintings on subjects from classical antiquity. In 1781 his *Belisarius*, which some have construed as a criticism of monarchy, gained him acceptance to the **Royal Academy of Painting**, and three years later he was made a regular member. His stark, sharply focused painting, *The Oath of the Horatii*, which was taken as an embodiment of classical **patriotism** and exhibited in 1785, contributed to making Neoclassicism the dominant style of the time. His canvases the *Death of Socrates* (1787) and *Brutus* (1789) continued his exploration of the same themes in the same classical context.

The **French Revolution** brought David the possibility of continuing his artistic career while combining it with one in politics. He was exceptional among the figures of the Enlightenment in adopting a position on the far left of the revolutionary spectrum. He joined the Jacobin Club fairly early, and was commissioned by it to do a painting of the *Tennis Court Oath* in 1790, though this was one monumental canvas that he never completed. He was elected to the Convention in 1792, sat with the Mountain, was a member of the important Committee of General Security and supported Maximilien Robespierre. His cultural activity during this time included intensive work on the staging of revolutionary festivals, a role in the dismantling of **academies** of the **Old Regime**, and painting. Probably his most famous canvas of this time was that of Marat dead in his bathtub (1793). He also did portraits of two other republican martyrs, Lepeletier de Saint-Fargeau and the drummer boy Bara, this latter a strangely feminine portrayal of a youth, as well as a portrait of the abbé Sieyès and a self-portrait. In 1789 he had done an impressive portrait of the farmer general and chemist Antoine-Laurent Lavoisier and his wife.

David was imprisoned for a time following the fall of Robespierre, and while in jail began painting *The Intervention of the Sabine Women*, which has been seen as a plea for conciliation. He rallied to Napoleon, painting an impressive portrait of him on horseback (1805), a portrait that is more romantic than neoclassical. He also did an elaborate painting of his coronation (1805). With the fall of Napoleon, David seems to have been prepared to rally to the Restoration, but even to the moderate Louis XVIII and a regime that favored forgetfulness and conciliation, a man who had voted the death of **Louis XVI** and glorified Napoleon was beyond the pale. David had therefore to live out the last 10 years of his life in Belgium producing more conventional paintings for which there was a market.

A basic difficulty in interpreting David's career is determining the significance of the French Revolution in it. That Neoclassicism found inspiration in ancient **republicanism** and patriotism and was thus potentially anti-monarchical seems clear enough. That this movement in art and literature was revolutionary in the sense that it contributed to the events of 1789 to 1794 and beyond is less clear, though much of the rhetoric and imagery of the revolutionary period had a significant classical component. Advocacy of **virtue** and moral reform are not necessarily a call to violent revolution. It is unlikely, however, that without a set of events of considerable magnitude David's art would have extended to the stark realism of his portrait of Marat, or the romantic tension of his painting of Napoleon mounted on a rearing horse and pointing the way to Italy.

DECLINE AND FALL OF THE ROMAN EMPIRE, THE. Probably the greatest history in English. Written by Edward **Gibbon,** it is a massive work of roughly one-and-a-half-million words that was published in six quarto volumes between 1776 and 1788. It was also an immediate best seller.

The scope of the work is remarkable. It begins with the Roman Empire at the time of Trajan (ruled 98-117) and concludes 1,350 years later with the fall of Constantinople to the Turks in 1453. It thus encompasses not only imperial Rome, but also the fortunes of the Mediterranean world and considerable parts of Asia, the barbarian invasions, the rise of Islam and the history of the Middle Ages. The popularity of the *Decline and Fall* is sometimes attributed to the way it is written, and there is little doubt but that Gibbon is one of the great stylists of the English language. But the appeal of the book extends beyond this.

In 1764 Gibbon visited Rome, where, as he writes in his *Memoirs*, seeing barefoot friars saying vespers in the Temple of Jupiter, he decided to attempt the history of the fall of Rome and the rise of the civilization that replaced it. One of the central themes of Gibbon's book is the conflict between the culture of pagan classical antiquity and Christianity, and the surprising victory of the latter. In a sense the *Decline and Fall* was a lament for the loss of the ordered, rational, tolerant, humanistic world of civic responsibility and classical **republicanism**, and its replacement with the mystical, other-worldly and inscrutable culture of Christianity. Although Gibbon was much criticized for his treatment of Christianity in the *Decline and Fall*, especially chapters 15 and 16, his analysis of the rise and triumph of the new religion is informed and closely analytical. Neither the Protestant tradition nor enlightened historiography treated the miraculous narratives and atmosphere of early Christianity in a way that orthodox Catholics would have approved.

The popularity and durability of the *Decline and Fall* derive in part from the great cultural conflicts that Gibbon presents, and in part from the immense erudition that the author combines with the critical and analytical approach of the Enlightenment. And like many works of historical scholarship, the *Decline and Fall* has as much to tell us about the period in which it was written as it does about the times it treats. The *Decline and Fall* and its author are the focus of J. G. A. Pocock's *Barbarism and Religion*, a searching examination of Gibbon's world and Enlightenment historiography, three volumes of which have appeared so far.

DEFFAND, Marie de Vichy-Chamrond, Marquise du (1696-1780). Among the *salonnières* of Paris, she was one of the most aristocratic and least sympathetic to the *philosophes*. Born to a noble family in Burgundy, she was educated in a convent school in Paris, where she failed to develop either affection or respect for religion. She was married in 1722 to the Marquis du Deffand without her wishes being consulted, and the match was without affection. She entered immediately into aristocratic libertinism of the **Regency**, taking as her first lover the regent himself.

In 1728 Mme du Deffand decided to regularize her life, and while she could never adopt orthodoxy, she did become a lapsed libertine. Her reform began by her distancing herself from her husband and establishing a stable relationship with the President **Hénault**. She began to modify her sociability by frequenting **salons**, among them that of Mme **Lambert**. When her husband died she was left both her freedom and a good deal of money (behind many a *salonnière* there was a wealthy but deceased husband). She then moved to a larger apartment in the Convent of Saint-Joseph on the rue Saint-Dominique, and there began the salon for which she is famous.

At about this time her sight began to fail. A number of years later, while visiting her brother on his estate of Chamrond in Burgundy, she met the young Julie de **Lespinasse** and engaged her to come to Paris as her companion and reader. Between 1754 and 1764 Julie fulfilled these functions, learned the manners of Parisian society, and helped run Mme du Deffand's salon. This salon attracted a more aristocratic set of guests with fewer men of letters than did most others, and this trend was accentuated when Julie de Lespinasse was dismissed, and most of the men of letters, led by Jean le Ronde d'**Alembert**, followed her. Indeed, while Mme du Deffand remained on good terms only with **Voltaire**, her salon became somewhat hostile to the *philosophes*.

Mme du Deffand seems to have been more than usually unhappy toward the end of her life. Her blindness weighed upon her, as did her extreme *ennui* (an exaggerated but fashionable form of boredom) and tendency to despair. She did not write for publication, but carried on an extensive correspondence. According to Charles Augustin Saint-Beuve, one of the great literary critics of the 19th century, her prose style was on a level with Voltaire's. She died with benefit of clergy and was buried in the Church of Saint-Sulpice, not far from where she had lived.

DEFOE, Daniel (1660-1731). Defoe came of Flemish ancestry. For reasons unknown to us, he changed his original surname, Foe, in 1703. He attended Charles Morton's Academy (a dissenting academy) and was intended for a life in the Church by his nonconformist father.

By 1683 Defoe was earning his living as a merchant, a hosiery maker and commission merchant. He married about this time, and subsequently had six children. In 1685 he participated in the Duke of Monmouth's rebellion against James II. He then became a staunch supporter and leading pamphleteer for William of Orange. In 1701 he published a poem, "The True Born Englishman," in defense of the "foreign" king and then in 1702 he penned a pamphlet, "The Shortest Way with the Dissenters," which was intended to discredit the High Churchmen using their own arguments but carrying them to absurd extremes.

The pamphlet resulted in libel charges. In 1703 he was pilloried, jailed and fined for it. The crowd expressed its sympathy for him by placing flowers on the pillory and protecting him from insult. While in jail Defoe began to publish the journal *A Review of the Affairs of France and of all Europe, as influenced by that Nation*, which came to be known simply as *The Review*. Having shown Defoe's abilities as a publicist to Robert Harley, the future first Earl of Oxford, the journal was largely responsible for getting him released from Newgate Prison in August 1704. The Earl's intervention on Defoe's behalf seems to have been acquired in return for Defoe's services as a pamphleteer and intelligence agent.

Defoe continued to publish the *Review*, which was soon appearing three times a week, with almost all copy supplied by Defoe himself, until 1713. At the same time he produced a wide variety of pamphlets and contributed to other periodicals, as well as acting as an agent for the government in Scotland. A degree of direct participation in politics of this sort for a man of letters was beginning to appear in England at this time, but would have been highly unusual on the continent. Defoe was broadly aligned with the **Whigs**, but he was also prepared to work for **Tory** administrations, though he never abandoned his loyalty to the House of Hanover.

Toward the end of his life, Defoe was comfortably off. This makes him one of the first writers to owe his economic independence to his pen, though he was also well paid for other political services. He was amazingly prolific, producing, in addition to reams of political pamphlets and periodicals, a number of important works of literature. In 1719 he published *Robinson Crusoe*, which achieved great and immediate popularity. Jean-Jacques **Rousseau** made this the only book that he would allow **Émile** to read as a child. Defoe's rogue novel with a female hero, *Moll Flanders*, appeared in 1722, and in the same year he brought out his *Journal of the Plague Year*. Between 1724 and 1726 he published his *Tour through Great Britain*, and between 1725 and 1727 the *Complete English Tradesman*.

In many ways Defoe is a transitional figure. He is an early example of a man of letters working as a superior government hack to help influence **public opinion**. He was one of the first authors to actually succeed in making a living by his pen, something that remained highly exceptional to the end of the century and beyond. While much of his political journalism and pamphleteering, as well as his novels and reportage, and his interest in commercial subjects fed directly into the Enlightenment, his traditional, if dissenting, position on religion and his acceptance of many popular superstitions showed him to inhabit a still enchanted world that was hardly acceptable to the thinkers of the High Enlightenment.

Peter Sorek

DEISM. A theological and philosophical position that asserts the existence of a Deity, but which denies the legitimacy of specific revelations such as the Jewish, the Christian or the Muslim.

Deism reflects the desire, widespread in the 18th century, to provide a rational and scientific approach to religion. The deists abandoned the Judeo-Christian notion of an ultimately inscrutable Deity shrouded in mystery and speaking to certain ethnic groups through specially chosen intermediaries for a concept of a divine Creator who was accessible to all human beings capable of **reason**. Conceived as beneficent, the only ethical imperative of this impersonal Deity was to do good to one's fellow, or at least to refrain from causing harm unnecessarily. The existence of the Supreme Being was deduced from the orderliness of nature by the **argument from design**. Deism can be seen as providing a broad underpinning for the key Enlightenment values of **universalism** and **humanity**.

There was also a negative side to the deism of the 17th and 18th centuries. The very limited theological and ethical precepts of this approach to religion implicitly (and in the hands of critical deists such as John Toland, Anthony Collins and Matthew Tindal, explicitly) called into question the highly complex and mutually contradictory dispensations of revealed religions (*see* **Relativism, Cultural**).

For deists, the ritual and material demands made by priests of most religions were without spiritual value, and served, rather, to control and exploit the masses. Among the deists of the French Enlightenment, **Voltaire** was particularly polemical, directing his unending animosity to organized religion primarily against Roman Catholicism and biblical Judaism. Jean-Jacques **Rousseau,** for his part, gave a more lyrical formulation of the doctrine, most fully elaborated in book IV of *Émile*, and came close to a form of nature worship.

The deists opposed not only the orthodoxies of revealed religions, but also the atheism of contemporary radicals such as the baron d'**Holbach**, Denis **Diderot**, and Julien Offray **La Mettrie**.

Deism has sometimes been dismissed as a philosophy without religious content. The genuine sense of awe before the orderliness of nature expressed by deists as diverse as Voltaire and Rousseau, however, would suggest that the doctrine did have a properly religious dimension.

DEMOCRACY. Literally, rule by the citizenry, or **people**. The term varies significantly according to historical context. In the ancient world democracies enfranchised only adult males belonging to families of citizens born within their jurisdictions, so that women, slaves and aliens, who together formed the overwhelming majorities of the populations of democratic states, were excluded from the rights of **citizenship**. These rights, however, were far more comprehensive than those attached to citizenship in the modern world. The small city-state of antiquity practiced direct democracy, which allowed citizens to participate in person in making and adjudicating the laws and offered a very good chance for all to hold public office.

The notion of representation, on which more inclusive modern democracies are based, was foreign to the ancient world. Though modern democracies extend the rights of citizenship more generously than did ancient democracies, these rights are more circumscribed, and the duties attendant on them less burdensome than in antiquity. In politics, as in economics, one generally gets what one pays for. The main thing ancient and modern democracies have in common is the doctrine of popular sovereignty.

During the 18th century, at least until its last decade, democracy was of marginal or academic interest. While a few **republics**, such as the Swiss republics and Venice, which because of their oligarchic structures cannot well be regarded as democracies, did exist, political power was concentrated in the hands of nation-states ruled by monarchs. Democracy retained a theoretical interest because it played an important role in classical history and political theory. Its legacy, however, was ambivalent. On the one hand, democracies and republics were associated with **liberty**, one of the key values of the Enlightenment; on the other, the people were mistrusted by classical authors and most aristocrats as unstable, uninformed and unreliable, and so unsuited to political responsibility.

Montesquieu regarded the people as capable of judging fairly matters of which they had immediate experience, such as choosing leaders from among their neighbors, but incompetent for more comprehensive tasks. He also laid it down as a principle that democracies were suitable for small states, but inappropriate for large ones, thus denying this form of government any contemporary relevance (*Spirit of the Laws,* Bk. II, chap. 2). In this, as in much else, Montesquieu's views were taken as authoritative by his contemporaries.

Jean-Jacques **Rousseau**, who of all Enlightenment political theorists was most sympathetic to democracy, maintained that it was a form of government that had never been fully realized, and never would be, in that its demands were so great as to be more suited to gods than to men (*Social Contract,* Bk. III, chap. 4). Democracy was not a practical option for the men and women of the Enlightenment, and its sudden emergence during the **French Revolution** came as a shock.

DESCARTES, René (1596-1650). Probably the most important and influential philosopher of the 17th century. His influence on the Enlightenment was considerable, but ambivalent.

The son of a magistrate in the southwest of France, Descartes received a sound secondary **education** from the **Jesuits** at their *Collège* of La Flèche. From the age of 10 to 18 he followed the complete course of studies offered by what were likely the best teachers in Europe at the time, though it was not until his last two years at the school that he was exposed to mathematics and physics, as was then the practice. In 1618 Descartes took a law degree at the University of Poitiers, but he never practiced. Instead, he decided to enlist as a volunteer in the army of Maurice of Nassau in Holland, apparently as the first stage of a military career.

On his arrival in Holland in 1618, Descartes met and became friends with the physician Isaac Beekman, with whom he discussed mathematics. In the course of a journey, on 10 November 1619, Descartes experienced a mystic vision in which he saw that the universe was pervaded by a comprehensible cosmic order.

Following his vision, Descartes continued for a time in his military calling, then spent the years 1623-1625 in Italy, and then two more years in Paris. Conditions in the France of Louis XIII and Richelieu being turbulent, and the social and political disorder being aggravated by religious tensions, Descartes opted to move to Holland, then the most tolerant and open state in Europe. During his stay there he became involved in a number of acrimonious philosophical and theological disputes, and after nearly 20 years, returned to his native country. Failing to find a position or **patronage** in the agitated conditions of France in 1648, after some justified hesitation he accepted an invitation to the court of Queen Christina of Sweden. Between the harsh Swedish winter and the indignity of being reduced to writing a comedy to amuse the court, Descartes did not survive long. He died on 11 February 1650.

Descartes is distinguished as a mathematician, a scientist and a philosopher. His view of the world is thoroughly naturalistic and mechanistic, and so broadly conceived as to be taken as a viable alternative to the complex and deeply entrenched scholastic synthesis. He conceived of the material world as consisting of extension and motion, and as such it was amenable to purely mathematical analysis. Indeed, for Descartes science was a matter of reducing problems to mathematical, and hence manageable, terms.

His physics posited the existence of an ether, or subtle matter, and thus a plenum in which objects moved by impulsion. Together with his theory of vortices, by which he explained the movement of the planets, his physics was discredited both by the research of sympathetic scientists, who found that they could not get his system to work, and by the incompatible findings of Isaac **Newton**. However, during the second half of the 17th century Descartes's notions of science were regarded as a serious threat to established scholastic learning. His works were put on the Index of the Catholic Church in 1663, and in 1691 Louis XIV forbade the teaching of any of his views in France.

Though the implications of Descartes's work might be seen to challenge the dogmas of established religions, the man himself was conventionally pious, making a pilgrimage to Our Lady of Loretto in thanks for his vision, and allied himself with progressive clerics, such as Father Marin Mersenne and Cardinal Pierre Berulle, in seeking to give religion a sound philosophical basis. Descartes sought to prove the existence of the Divine in his *Discourse on Method*, and he explicitly argued for the existence of an immortal soul. Nevertheless, religious traditionalists found the implications of his science more worrying than his explicit and orthodox statements on matters of faith were reassuring.

As might have been expected from a mathematician, Descartes favored the deductive method. He sought first to establish absolutely true basic propositions, and then logically to deduce the consequences that followed from them. This was a system that worked well enough in mathematics, but less well in physics. It was an approach that was independent of authority, whether philosophical or theological, but for the thinkers of the Enlightenment it also gave too much weight to abstract ideas, too little to facts.

Descartes argued that two basic modes of existence were to be found in the world, the one consisting of matter, the other of spirit. This position is known as dualism. From a philosophical point of view, though not from a religious one, the relation between these two modes was problematic. Those who defined reality as consisting in spirit are termed idealists. The outstanding representative of this position in the 18th century was the English cleric George Berkeley. Those who assert that reality consisted in matter are termed materialists, and during the Enlightenment the better-known exponents of this position were Denis **Diderot**, the Baron d'**Holbach**, and Julien Offray de **La Mettrie**.

Descartes's main works include *Rules for the Direction of the Intelligence*, which was written about 1627 but not published during his lifetime; *Discourse on Method of Rightly Conducting the Reason*, his most famous work, published in 1637 as the introduction to three essays on optics, meteorology and geometry, which were meant as illustrations of his scientific and philosophical methods; *Meditations on First Philosophy* (1641); *The Principles of Philosophy* (1644); and *Treatise of the Passions of the Soul* (1649). *See also* **Cartesianism**.

DESPOTISM. A form of government characterized by the arbitrary exercise of authority, and hence the negation of the rule of law and of **constitutionalism**.

During the Enlightenment "despot," "despotic" and their derivatives became key terms in the delegitimization of monarchical authority deemed to have exceeded its proper limits as determined by constitutional norms. The broad currency of the term dates from the *Spirit of the Laws* of **Montesquieu**, which appeared in 1748. In this hugely influential work Montesquieu designated despotism as one of only four basic forms of government. While Aristotle defined despotism or tyranny simply as the corrupt counterpart of monarchy, for

Montesquieu it was a distinct regime characterized by a principle proper to it—fear—and by a distinct structure, the key feature of which was the destruction of all intermediary political agents, such as independent law courts or a constitutionally recognized **nobility**. Montesquieu maintained that infringement of the **separation of powers** resulted in despotism.

Despotism was a form of government that Montesquieu associated with the East, and particularly with Turkey. In his hands the term was given a powerful emotional charge by being associated with radical debasement, verging on dehumanization, exemplified in the relation of a harem to its proprietor or a slave to his or her master. Montesquieu builds on the distinction, at least as old as Herodotus, between an oriental political culture characterized by unlimited authority of the ruler and total subordination and debasement of the subject, and a free European political culture in which the government is constitutionally limited and the **citizen** enjoys a set of clearly defined rights. The tension between monarchy and despotism is the central issue in Montesquieu's political theory. Nor was this a bad assessment of European politics of the time.

Voltaire used the terms despotism, **absolutism** and tyranny interchangeably, and all with a strong negative connotation. It became common during the second half of the 18th century for critics of the government to denounce "ministerial despotism," thus avoiding calling the status of the monarch himself into question. The term **"enlightened despotism"** is used by historians to designate regimes that preferred far-reaching reforms to respect for constitutional norms.

DESTUTT DE TRACY, Antoine Louis Claude (1754-1836). Tracy descended from a Scottish family named Stutt. Four sons had served as archers in the Hundred Years' War under Charles VII, who ennobled them. Tracy's father, an officer in the Seven Years' War, was killed in Tracy's childhood. His mother (née Verzure) saw her son gain the honors of the court, a brief university education at Strasbourg, a regiment (Penthièvre) and a marriage with the daughter of a high and powerful noble family (Dufort de Civrac, 1779).

Seigneur of Paray-le-Frésil, Destutt de Tracy was elected to the noble delegation of the Estates General from Moulins. In the Constituent Assembly he habitually took the patriot side. After serving as a commander of the Army of the Center in 1792, he retired to Auteuil. He was imprisoned in Carmes, where he devoted himself to philosophy. Released on 6 October 1794, he was elected in 1796 as associate member of the Class of Moral and Political Sciences of the National Institute (*see* **Institut**). In June 1796 he gave the "science of ideas" established by John **Locke** and Étienne Bonnot de **Condillac** the name **Ideology.**

As a member of the Council of Public Instruction from 1799-1801, Destutt de Tracy led the effort to disseminate "Ideology" in the secondary "central schools." The Council, the schools and the Class of Moral and Political Sciences were successively dismantled between 1801 and 1803 by Napoleon Bonaparte, who coined the pejorative name "**Ideologue**" to designate his liberal opponents. Nonetheless Tracy doggedly continued to publish his four-volume *Éléments d'idéologie* (1801-1815), which reduced all thought to sensation, systematically excluding centers and processes of thinking that smacked of "spiritualism."

Emmet Kennedy

DICTIONARY. A book consisting primarily of lists of words, usually in alphabetical order, with definitions. It was common during the Middle Ages for students to compile lists of Latin words with their equivalents in the vernacular. Vernacular same-language dictionaries began to appear in the 17th and 18th centuries, and became a favored genre, with the alphabetical arrangement of subjects in different sorts of reference works and pseudo reference works being extended far beyond the function of definition.

The context in which dictionaries appeared was one of regional, cultural and linguistic diversity. In Europe same-language vernacular dictionaries were initially sponsored by monarchies and produced by **academies** supported by them. They were conceived as part of the projects of standardization and centralization carried out by the absolutist state. The first edition of the *Dictionnaire de l'Académie française* appeared in 1694, a Spanish dictionary by the Royal Spanish Academy between 1726 and 1739 and a Russian dictionary by the Academy of Arts of Saint Petersburg between 1789 and 1794. The first vernacular dictionary in Europe seems to have been prepared precociously outside of the cultural aspirations of centralizing monarchies by the Academia della Crusca of Florence and published in 1602.

In England the production of dictionaries was left to the initiative of booksellers and scholars. The most famous of these, though not the first, was that published by Samuel **Johnson** in 1755. In France, in addition to the Dictionary of the **Académie française,** multi-volume, folio-sized, same-language vernacular dictionaries were published by César-Pierre Richelet (1679-1680), Antoine Furetière (1690) and the **Jesuits,** who took Richelet's dictionary as their point of departure, but greatly modified and expanded it in their own *Dictionnaire de Trévoux* (1704). All of the above dictionaries were published repeatedly over the 18th century in ever larger editions.

The impetus to defining the elements of language and, subsequently, other branches of knowledge, and presenting the results in an orderly and easily accessible way can be seen as part of classical esthetics and of the assertion of cultural authority on the part of centralizing monarchies. However, simply by ordering subject matter according to rational criteria and in a critical spirit, the making of dictionaries and encyclopedias could also play a subversive role. It did so not so much in the case of dictionaries proper, but in the extension of the dictionary that played an important role in the intellectual and publishing history of the Enlightenment, namely, the encyclopedia.

Encyclopedias were a publishing phenomenon during the 18th century. They reflect a demand by the public for the popularization of knowledge, and publishers found that meeting this demand could be highly profitable. The many dictionaries, philosophical dictionaries and encyclopedias produced during the Enlightenment were as good as the teams, or **authors,** that produced them. Some were works of polemical genius and critical acumen, others were mere compilations provided on order from booksellers by hacks, and some were a combination. Pierre **Bayle**'s *Historical and Critical Dictionary* and **Voltaire**'s *Philosophical Dictionary* are examples of the former, the *Encyclopédie* of Denis **Diderot** and his collaborators of the latter. Dictionaries and encyclopedias were produced on all manner of specialized subjects, from commerce and manufacturing to police to ecclesiastical organization and social commentary, such as the *Dictionnaire philosophique, ou Introduction à la conoissance de l'homme* (1762) of D. P. Chicaneau de Neuville, or the *Dictionnaire social et patriotique, ou Précis raisonné des connoissances relatives à l'économie morale, civile & politique* (1770) of Pierre Lefebvre de Beauvray.

The public's taste for alphabetically organized compilations of various sorts has persisted, and is still exploited by publishers. In today's book trade there is a small American company based in Lanham, Maryland, that has found that if it can convince someone to do a dictionary on virtually any subject, it will be able to sell enough copies to turn a profit. This is not a small advantage today, and it was not in the 18th century. The literature that advanced Enlightenment values had to have something worthwhile to say; it had to say it in an accessible and attractive way; and to be effective, it had to sell.

DIDEROT, Denis (1713-1784). Of the major *philosophes*, Diderot was the least appreciated by the broad public of his time, but is among the most admired and most closely studied by students of the Enlightenment today. Warm, open, with a great capacity and perhaps need for friendship, Diderot is among the most personally attractive of the main figures of the Enlightenment.

Diderot was born in Langres. His father was a well-off master cutler who was able to assure his son's education, first at the **Jesuit** *collège* of Langres, then in Paris. Diderot alienated his father's affection and lost his material support by refusing to take up a profession in the Church or the law and by **marrying** without parental permission. Though eventually reconciled to his family, he had to make his way by his wits in the harsh economic conditions of the capital. He did so by tutoring and hackwork, which included translations from English, for publishers. Diderot was among the fortunate few who, having begun his career in **Grub Street**, was able to rise above it. As a youth and young man he frequented the taverns, **cafés** and public places open to all with friends such as Jean-Jacques **Rousseau** and Friedrich Melchior Grimm; by middle age and in later years he was welcomed in **salons** and the courts of monarchs such as **Frederick II** and **Catherine II**, whose court he visited from the autumn of 1773 to the spring of 1774.

Diderot's literary output was unusual. He was the only major *philosophe* not to publish a best seller in his lifetime. He wrote prolifically enough, producing a variety of serious philosophical and scientific works that rightly gained him a reputation for radicalism, among them *Philosophical Thoughts* (1746), *Letter on the Blind*, as a result of which he found himself imprisoned in the fortress of Vincennes for three-and-a-half months in the summer and fall of 1749, *Letter on the Deaf and Dumb* (1751) and *On the Interpretation of Nature* (1753). He also wrote a witty and mildly pornographic novel, *Les Bijoux indiscrets* (1748), sentimental plays of a genre known as the *drame*, or **bourgeois drama**, of which he was also a theoretician, and art criticism. But none of these went through more than a few editions.

He was unusually active in collaborative works, pre-eminently the *Encyclopédie*, which he undertook for reasons of economic necessity as a piece of hackwork, and, with Jean le Ronde d'**Alembert**, turned into one the major collective enterprises of the Enlightenment. Other collaborations, however, were extensions of his friendships, as was the case with Grimm's *Correspondance Littéraire*, beginning from 1756, or parts of works in which a group of *philosophes* took an interest, such as the abbé **Raynal**'s *History of the Two Indies* from 1772.

Diderot's generous use of his time and energies for the benefit of his friends has often been noted, as has the openness of his personality, which is reflected in his reputation as a great conversationalist and in his correspondence. His letters to the great love of his life, Sophie **Volland**, reflect both his social and intellectual activities and his intense affection for his friend and mistress.

Were Diderot remembered only by the works cited above, it is unlikely that he would hold the commanding position he does in Enlightenment studies. For reasons that are not altogether clear, he did not publish his greatest works during his lifetime. These include *The Nun*, written in 1760 but not published until 1796, *Jacques le fataliste*, written around 1773 and also published in 1796, *Alembert's Dream,* written in 1769 but which did not appear in print until 1830 and pre-eminently *Rameau's Nephew,* written probably between 1762 and 1764 and first published in a German translation by Johann Wolfgang von **Goethe** in 1805.

Arguably Diderot, who had spent time in the prison of Vincennes because of views expressed in print, may have regarded these works as offensive to the authorities, and so refrained from publishing them from prudence. He may, however, have been differently motivated. Some of these works, especially *Rameau's Nephew*, can be read as criticisms of basic Enlightenment values or assumptions. While Diderot's intellectual acuity and honesty may have led him to formulate fundamental criticisms of the movement of which he was a leading spokesman, he may not have wanted to make these criticisms available to those hostile to it. That would also explain why he did not publish a refutation of **Helvétius** that he wrote (1773).

DOUBLET, Marie-Anne, née Legendre, Mme (1677-1771). Married in 1698 to an intendant de commerce and widowed in 1723, Mme de Doublet is a typical case of a woman who achieved freedom through widowhood. Her income was modest, but sufficient for her to rent an apartment in the Convent of the Filles-Saint-Thomas, just a few minutes' walk from Mme de **Lambert**'s residence, and there held for 40 years one of the most remarkable **salons** of the time.

Mme Doublet's salon was exceptional in many ways. First, she presided over the salon together with her friend and companion, the wealthy amateur of the arts and gentleman, Louis Petit de **Bachaumont**, who was 16 years her junior. The direction of this salon was thus gender inclusive. Secondly, those attending the salon seemed to have formed a more close-knit group than was usual in salon society, and referred to themselves as "the parishioners." These included, in addition to Bachaumont, Mme Doublet's brother, the abbé Legendre, the abbés Chauvelin and Xampi, the medievalist Lacurne de Sainte-Palaye and his brother, the sculptor Étienne Maurice Falconnet, the doctor and thinker Jean-Jacques Dortous de Mairan, the diplomat, jurist and writer, the Comte d'Argental, Jean-Baptiste de Mirabaud, cleric, educator, and from 1742 Perpetual Secretary of the **Académie française**, and the political commentator, **Pidansat de Mairobert**.

Thirdly, this salon kept its distance from the *philosophes*, most of its members being sympathetic to the **Jansenist** cause. Intensification of the persecution of Jansenists around mid-century led Mme de Doublet's "parishioners" to take a strong and consistently anti-absolutist political position and to support the *Parlement* of Paris in its opposition to the crown's religious policies and the **Maupeou** reforms of 1771-1774.

Finally, Mme de Doublet's salon produced a journal that was first distributed in manuscript, and then published as the *Mémoires secrets pour servir à l'histoire de la république des lettres* (London, 36 vols., 1762-1789). The *Mémoires* are usually associated with Bachaumont, though after his death Pidansat de Mairobert and Mouffle d'Angerville were responsible for it. It is a particularly valuable source for the history of the later Enlightenment.

Mme de Doublet died in 1771, and was followed a short time later by Bachaumont. Pidansat de Mairobert claimed that he was the product of the union of Mme de Doublet and Bachaumont. Whether this was in fact so is unknown.

E

EDUCATION. Like any society, 18th-century Europe provided training and instruction for the young. For the popular classes this usually included attendance at primary schools, the chief purpose of which was religious instruction and acculturation. The skills of **literacy** were generally regarded as of secondary concern. However, in Protestant countries literacy was seen as necessary to sound religious instruction, and hence taught more effectively at the popular level than in Catholic countries. Primary schools were influenced by the Church, but usually only functioned during the slack periods of the agricultural year. They tended to be irregular in duration, in the abilities of the teachers and in the kinds of tasks required of students.

On secondary and higher education *see* **Colleges** and **Universities.** *See also* **Educational Theory.**

EDUCATIONAL THEORY. Few if any intellectual movements had greater expectations of **education** than did the Enlightenment. The groundwork for this optimism is to be found in John **Locke**'s *Essay Concerning Human Understanding*, which assumes all human beings to be equal at birth, in the sense that they are pure potential, and to develop according to the sense stimuli to which they are subjected and the experiences they undergo. This is, to be sure, education broadly conceived, but it is in precisely this way that Enlightenment thinkers as diverse as Jean-Jacques **Rousseau** in *Émile* and Claude Adrien **Helvétius** in *De l'homme* conceived it. The notion of the human being at birth as a *tabula rasa*, or to use another metaphor common at the time, as a ball of wax, implied that people were highly malleable, and that educators could shape them in virtually any way they pleased. The assumption of unlimited malleability leads logically to a belief in the unlimited power of education. Helvétius made precisely this claim, asserting that "Education can do everything" (*De l'homme*, Bk. x, chap. 9).

Another reason that education had so prominent a role in Enlightenment thought is that it offered a peaceful means of social change to a movement that sought both extensive reform and the maintenance of social order. The thinkers of the Enlightenment expected that appropriate education could gradually and peacefully effect the most extensive changes without threatening governments in power or existing social structures. For the same reasons educational reform usually played a significant role in programs of **enlightened despotism.** This is one of the ways the social thought of the Enlightenment differed from that of the 19th century, in which conflict was usually taken as a given.

EGOISM. The evil twin of **self-interest.** Both terms refer to the same basic idea, but with different connotations.

Self-interest is usually qualified by modifiers such as "enlightened" and is generally understood to be both reasonable and socially responsible. A person motivated by enlightened self-interest is aware that his or her well-being is inseparable from that of the society to which he or she belongs. Moreover, in the social world self-interest was seen as the equivalent of the force of gravity in physics, so it was thought to belong to the realm of **nature**.

Egoism, by contrast, connoted an excessive and unenlightened concern with the self. The egoist was caught up in a search for his or her own pleasure and self-enhancement without regard for society or for others. Typically, an egoist refused the social and natural responsibilities of **marriage** and raising children, while enjoying the pleasures of the company of the other sex. Self-indulgence, **luxury** and disregard for society, the State and the poor were characteristics usually attributed to egoists in the literature of the time.

The rehabilitation of the **individual** and of self-interest was one of the main innovations of Enlightenment ethical thought. Given the difficulties in balancing the rights and obligations of individuals and the groups to which they belong, it is not surprising that the Enlightenment developed two distinct models of this value. The implications of the form of self-interest that is unrestrained by **reason** or social responsibility is analyzed most incisively by Denis **Diderot** in *Rameau's Nephew*.

ÉMILE, OR ON EDUCATION (1762). Jean-Jacques **Rousseau**'s great treatise on **education**, and one of the great conspectual treatments of what it means to be human in Western literature. Despite its bulk and high seriousness, *Émile* was one of the leading best sellers of the Enlightenment. Though full of good sense, compassion and concern for humanity, it was one of Rousseau's most controversial works. The theistic but profoundly felt confession of faith of the Savoyard vicar in book IV angered the orthodox magistrates of the *Parlement* of Paris, who had the book burned and a warrant issued for the arrest of the author. The treatment of gender in book V has been found objectionable by many feminists.

In *Émile*, as in his other writings, Rousseau viewed human beings as creatures defined by their senses, and education as the ordering and training of the senses. He derives his basic assumptions from John **Locke**, but goes beyond him in seeing infants, and even embryos, as amenable to education. Rousseau was the first notable theoretician of education to take seriously the physical upbringing of small children. His denunciation of swaddling contributed significantly to the reduction of this practice, and his advocacy of mothers breast-feeding their own children led to many upper-class women doing so. His emphasis on physical training during the early years of a child's development and on the desirability of leaving the skills of **literacy** and exercises depending on **reason** to an age at which reason had begun to develop must have made life better for children whose parents and teachers came under Rousseau's considerable influence. Similarly, Rousseau's insistence on teaching by arousing the child's curiosity and having him learn from things rather than theory would also have rendered the lot of children easier. One cannot say the same for his recommendation that infants be given cold baths in all seasons to toughen them, which we know that in at least some cases was done.

The student Émile of Rousseau's treatise is an ideal construct, akin to the statue that the abbé **Condillac** brings to life in his explanation of Lockean psychology. Since man in the state of nature is good, and since Rousseau conceives of evil originating in society, or more accurately, abuses arising from society, so he views the infant at birth as good. Much of education for Rousseau is thus negative, consisting in protecting the unspoiled child from the corrupting influences of socially generated dishonesty, hypocrisy and error. Rousseau is also consistent in subordinating proficiency in the sciences and arts to morality.

While beginning from a physiological, even materialist, view of man, Rousseau places as much emphasis as any thinker of the Enlightenment on moral and spiritual matters. The profession of faith of the Savoyard vicar in book IV of *Émile* is a closely reasoned, passionately informed argument for the existence of a Divinity beyond particular revelations, a Divinity that imposes a universally valid set of ethics on all humanity.

In book V Rousseau puts forward his views on gender relations. He argues, among other things, that the natural domination of women over men requires an artificial or social constraint of women by men. Rousseau's notion of eros is complex, assuming a fundamental and complementary difference between men and women. He conceives the formation of the couple, and then the family, as a bonding in which each of the individuals is modified and the result is more than the sum of two equal contracting parties. Whatever the advantages and disadvantages of this view of gender relations and of love, it seems to be at the base of the romantic notion of the couple and of the emerging affectively oriented family. While Rousseau had a large and devoted female readership in his own time, his views on gender relations have been vigorously attacked by feminists from Mary **Wollstonecraft** on.

EMPIRICISM. A methodology that bases its investigations on fact and observation. It accumulates facts in order to provide grounds for the formulation of a theory, and it uses conformity to fact as the main criterion of the adequacy of theory.

This methodology has been used most successfully in the natural sciences and in disciplines modeling themselves on the natural sciences. In these instances satisfactory conceptualization and results are narrowly dependent on an adequate factual basis. It has been least effective in areas such as metaphysics and theology, where facts either cannot be determined or are largely irrelevant. As a methodology, empiricism stands against **rationalism**, though the two approaches are not mutually exclusive.

The main advantage of empiricism is that it keeps investigations close to material reality. It lends itself to standardized, quantifiable analysis of natural phenomena that can be readily verified. Taking fact as a starting point and checking any theory for conformity to fact has the great virtue of constraining speculation and restricting the influence of already formulated ideas in science. With fact as the criterion of validation or falsification, hypothesis is narrowly limited. Nevertheless, empiricism does have significant drawbacks.

The first of these is that facts are in themselves inert. They do not normally present themselves to observers in ready-formed patterns. The relations among facts need to be imagined or postulated by critical intelligence. Theories thus formed can be subjected to empirical verification, but unfortunately theories do not emerge ready-made if we simply collect enough facts. Hence empiricism is more a basis for a scientific method than a method in its own right.

Secondly, empiricism narrows our view of reality. By defining as unreal those things that cannot be weighed or counted or observed or repeated in laboratory experiments, it implies that such things cannot be the subject of a science, which is to say that they cannot be taken seriously. Whether we approve of it or not, empiricism was a powerful agent of disenchantment. And it was clearly the preferred methodology of the Enlightenment.

The founding philosopher of modern empiricism was Francis **Bacon**. Not a practicing scientist in his own right, Bacon nevertheless forcefully argued that unless narrowly constrained by fact, observation and experiment, natural science would remain trapped in the series of vicious circles elaborated by **scholasticism**. Bacon argued for a science of things, not of words. As taken up and interpreted by the thinkers of the Enlightenment, Bacon's methodology contributed significantly to a shift away from unverifiable abstractions, whether philosophical or theological. It is in large part to the empirical method that we owe the scientific and concrete view of the world that has become predominant since the 18th century.

ENCYCLOPÉDIE. The short name by which the *Encyclopédie, ou Dictionnaire raisonné des sciences, des arts et des métiers* is generally known. It was published under the direction of Denis **Diderot** and Jean le Ronde d'**Alembert** unevenly between 1751 and 1765 in 17 folio volumes of text, with a further 11 volumes of plates which appeared between 1762 and 1772. A supplement of four volumes of text, which unlike the original volumes includes biographical entries, and one of plates, was published between 1776 and 1777, and a two-volume index followed in 1780. Alembert withdrew from the project in 1759, and Diderot, who is most closely associated with it, was not responsible for the supplement.

The project originated with the publisher Le Breton, who initially intended nothing more than a translation of Ephraim Chamber's *Cyclopedia*, successfully published in England in 1728. Le Breton arranged in 1746 to have a member of the Academy of Sciences, the abbé Gua de Malves, edit the work, and only the following year, on the abbé's withdrawal, put the work into the hands of Diderot and Alembert. He got more than he bargained for.

The *Encyclopédie* is often regarded as the most representative work of the Enlightenment. While it unquestionably played an important role in the movement, this is probably to overstate its importance. It is true that among its roughly 140 known collaborators we find most of the great figures and outstanding writers of the Enlightenment. It is also true that the *Encyclopédie* was extremely widely distributed. Thanks to the work of Robert **Darnton** we now know that a total of some 25,000 sets in different formats and at different prices were sold by the end of the century. The first edition cost 960 *livres*, which represents perhaps twice the income of a working family at the time, with the editions in smaller formats costing proportionately less. The *Encyclopédie* was probably the most profitable publishing venture of the 18th century. Nevertheless, the content of the work hardly justifies the high regard in which it is usually held.

Most of the articles by Diderot, **Montesquieu,** Jean-Jacques **Rousseau, Voltaire,** Anne-Robert-Jacques **Turgot,** the Baron d'**Holbach** and other *philosophes* were striking and sometimes brilliant. But they formed a tiny proportion of the whole. The most prolific *encyclopédiste* was the Chevalier de **Jaucourt,** who was responsible for roughly a quarter of the text. He effectively popularized ideas and values central to the Enlightenment, but he did so by citing extensively from existing works. He worked diligently and selected intelligently. Most of the political articles for which he was responsible, for example, he simply cut and pasted from the *Spirit of the Laws.* What he selected was good, but it was not original. Nor was Jaucourt, the great workhorse of the *Encyclopédie,* exceptional in this regard. Many of the collaborators of the project, Diderot among them, had recourse to the same method. But then notions of literary property were much looser in the 18th century than they are today.

In addition to being derivative, much of the content of the *Encyclopédie* was uneven. Diderot's political articles ("Political **Authority,**" "Natural **Law,**" "Representatives," "Sovereign") made utility the criterion of politics and inclined toward popular sovereignty; those of Jaucourt ("**Democracy,**" "**Despotism,**" "**Law,**" "Monarchy," "**Nobility,**" "**Republic**") recycled Montesquieu; and those of Boucher d'Argis ("Public Law," "Paternal Power") took the side of Sir Robert Filmer against John **Locke,** deriving political legitimacy from patriarchal authority. It appears that the intellectual integrity of the work was compromised by restrictions of state **censorship,** on the one hand, and by the commercial interests of the publishers, on the other.

The *Encyclopédie* in part owes its eminent position in the Enlightenment to attempts by forces hostile to the movement to quash it. Due to criticism of the **Jesuits** and politicking at court, its production was suspended for a time in 1752. With the help of Christian-Guillaume Lamoignon de **Malesherbes,** this decision was reversed before it could do much damage. However, in 1759 the *Parlement* of Paris had the privilege of the *Encyclopédie* revoked, and this resulted in serious difficulties. The work was also placed on the Index the same year. Volumes VIII to XVII were printed in Switzerland, and could only be distributed to the subscribers in 1766. Whatever the content of the *Encyclopédie,* the opposition of Jesuits, **Jansenists,** the Papacy and political conservatives assured that the work would have a high profile.

ENLIGHTENED DESPOTISM. A term used by historians to indicate certain 18th-century monarchies more concerned with modernization and rationalization of state and social structures than with constitutional forms. For the most part these regimes were located on the peripheries of Europe, in countries such as Austria, Prussia and Russia, and occurred where progressive and modernizing monarchs ruled over traditional or backward societies. Typically, societies likely to experience enlightened despotism were those with strong aristocracies, weak middle classes and suppressed peasantries that were often, as in the cases of Russia and Prussia, in a condition of serfdom.

Political modernization consisted in concentrating powers to levy taxes, to raise armies and to strengthen the state administration in the hands of the central government. In this sense its project was identical with that of the **absolutism** of the 17th and 18th centuries. As western European states had more developed social and economic bases and more effective state structures, the countries to the east, which operated in the same diplomatic sphere, found themselves in a position of inferiority. Enlightened absolutism was an attempt to bridge this gap. It sought to speed up the process of modernization by appealing to leading intellectuals, often French *philo-sophes*, for advice, and in strengthening central bureaucracies to enable them to carry out those recommendations of the thinkers that the monarchs wished to implement.

An example of this approach is the **cameralism** of many small German states. **Catherine II** corresponded with a number of *philosophes*, among them Denis **Diderot,** who also made the trip to Russia to instruct and confer with her, and **Frederick II** of Prussia acted as host to **Voltaire** for a number of years and courted a number of other *philosophes*. The relations between kings and the thinkers of the Enlightenment seldom resulted in mutual satisfaction, for the rulers were primarily interested in practical applications of power and the *philosophes*, be it said to their credit, would not compromise their principles to curry favor with the rulers. The phenomenon does reflect, however, a rise in the status of intellectuals, and a new awareness of the potential uses of knowledge by those in power.

Politically, the key practical problem of the enlightened monarchs was coming to an accommodation with their national aristocracies. **Joseph II** of Austria tried to impose his policies on his nobles, ultimately without success. Catherine II of Russia and Frederick II of Prussia abandoned their peasants to the discretion of their lords in return for state service by the nobles in the army and bureaucracy. In both cases this model of reform from above resulted in a strong but autocratic state and a society largely impervious to **liberalism**. **Louis XVI** of France is sometimes seen as an enlightened despot because he too sought to modernize and rationalize his administration, and he too faced in an aggressive aristocracy his main political challenge.

ENLIGHTENMENT. The process of spreading certain kinds of information, knowledge, understanding and attitudes.

The name of the movement is its own key metaphor: light spreading and driving out the darknesses of **ignorance, superstition** and **fanaticism**. This metaphor is preserved in most European languages designating the movement: Enlightenment in English, *siècle des lumières* (century of light) or simply *les lumières* in French, *Aufklärung*, or coming of light in German, and *l'Illuminismo* in Italian, which like the French *lumières,* is derived from the Latin word for light.

Light is often associated with understanding. To say that something is clear indicates that we see or understand it. Sufficient light (in French *clarté*) is a necessary condition for seeing things, as it is for understanding them. Identifying true knowledge and proper understanding with light, the Enlightenment portrayed itself as a movement that would extend knowledge and understanding within specific societies and among mankind as progressively and non-violently as light dispels darkness. But darkness did need to be overcome, and this caused the Enlightenment to develop a militant and polemical side.

ENLIGHTENMENT, DARK NARRATIVE OF. Max Horkheimer and Theodor Adorno, two of the leading thinkers of the Frankfurt School, wrote *Dialectic of Enlightenment* during World War II. The "Introduction" is dated 1944 and signed Los Angeles, California. As Marxists and Jews, Horkheimer and Adorno were unwelcome in Nazi Germany, and the two men were fortunate in having left while they could. Their book was copyrighted in New York in 1944, though in their "Preface to the New Edition" written in Frankfurt in 1969, it is stated that it was first published in Amsterdam in 1947.

The date of the writing of *Dialectic of Enlightenment* is important because it puts the work in the category of what might be called crisis literature. Faced with the collapse of Western civilization in the technologically sophisticated barbarism of Nazism and other fascist and totalitarian regimes, Horkheimer and Adorno asked what had gone so badly wrong. Perhaps regarding the virulent nationalist, racist and expansionist ideologies of the Nazis as too obvious or inadequate an answer, perhaps habituated by long exposure to Hegelian and Marxist thought to expect things dialectically to change into their opposites, Horkheimer and Adorno asserted that the source of the ills of modernity were to be found in the Enlightenment. This notion of the Enlightenment as the origin of the alienation, dehumanization, oppression and totalitarianism characteristic of the modern world is what is known as the "dark narrative of Enlightenment."

Horkheimer and Adorno's thesis has been influential, especially in the field of cultural studies, and to a lesser degree among historians of the Enlightenment. Whatever the value of their analysis to the understanding of modern cultural trends, and it is generally considered to be great, their book has a number of shortcomings as a work of history.

First, Horkheimer and Adorno did not undertake specifically to write the history of the Enlightenment of the 18th century. Their book is entitled *Dialectic of Enlightenment*, not of "the Enlightenment," and treats a set of attitudes and assumptions that stretch from Homeric Greece to the mid-20th century.

Secondly, when Horkheimer and Adorno come to the Enlightenment of the 18th century they treat it from a narrow and restrictive point of view. It is not wrong to say that "The program of the Enlightenment was the disenchantment of the world" (*Dialectic*, p. 3), but it is misleading to imply that the Enlightenment was not engaged in a number of other projects which were political and ethical in nature. Again, it is not wrong to see in the Enlightenment a will to master **nature** for human benefit, or to see in "instrumental reason" the key tool for the analysis of nature, but without also taking into account the subversive mockery and whimsy of **Montesquieu**, **Voltaire** and Denis **Diderot**, and the moral earnestness of Jean-Jacques **Rousseau**, the Enlightenment is impossibly distorted.

Thirdly, while it is perfectly legitimate to follow up the repressive and dehumanizing features of a worldview based on instrumental reason from Francis **Bacon** to the scientists and technicians of the 18th century and beyond, this is not a fair summary of the content and implications of Enlightenment thought. Without taking into account the key values of **humanity, beneficence**, **toleration**, **liberty**, **equality** and the public good, and strenuous efforts actually to implement these values in a practical way, we cannot be said to be speaking of the Enlightenment at all.

Finally, even if it is conceded that, taken on a sufficiently abstract level, the Enlightenment was carried forward by, and tended toward, a potentially totalitarian organization of society and the dehumanization of mankind, it is not even vaguely apparent how the writings and activities of Voltaire, Montesquieu, Diderot, Rousseau and the rest can be fit into this story line.

Developing a narrative that explains how the modern world has come to the social, political, environmental and ideological impasses and catastrophes that it has experienced, and continues to experience, is a valid and important project. It is not surprising that the outstanding Nazi ideologist, Karl Schmidt, and certain of his students have maintained that Nazism drew on the Enlightenment, but that position does not deserve more credence than the rest of Nazi ideology. That the Enlightenment of the 18th century merits so central and causative a place in Horkheimer and Adorno's narrative of the ills of modernity is questionable.

ENLIGHTENMENT, RELEVANCE OF. Perhaps as little as 20 years ago there would have been little point in discussing the relevance of the Enlightenment to contemporary culture. The scientific and technological achievements of the movement were widely recognized and appreciated, though some thinkers questioned the implications of instrumental reason. There was general agreement in the West, at least, that the validation of individual **happiness** and **liberty**, mutual **toleration** and separation of church and state were the means for achieving a desirable form of society. Today, both the rightness and effectiveness of these assumptions are called into question.

Insofar as the Enlightenment has provided the intellectual framework in which capitalism has developed, it has released forces that are greater and more destructive than first believed. The belief that pursuit of **self-interest** would automatically result in the general good is no longer tenable. Nor is the presumed **beneficence** of technology. Though modern technology has the potential for furthering human welfare, as Francis **Bacon** rightly saw, if it is not subjected to appropriate social controls, it turns its power against both mankind and the environment. When what Jean-Jacques **Rousseau** would have termed partial interests gain control over technologies so powerful that they can fundamentally modify the environment and use these technologies to further their own restricted interests in the absence of significant countervailing interests representing the general good, then the promise of technology becomes an all-encompassing threat. The Enlightenment maintained a balance between the traditional notion of the common good and a newer **individualism**. The 19th and 20th centuries have lost this balance, and having eclipsed notions of the common good and the value of community, have seen corporate interests replace those, as well as individual values.

As for the broadly secularist outlook that underlay separation of church and state and validated toleration and individual liberties, though taken for granted less than a generation ago, it is now under attack. The most striking source of this challenge to toleration and secularism is the resurgence of fundamentalist religion, whatever the denomination with which it is associated. Returning to literal readings of texts ascribed the status of sanctity and absolute validity, fundamentalists insist on the enforcement of commandments and directives that take no account of the liberal and humanitarian elements of Enlightenment thought. Indeed, fundamentalists reject the man-centered ethics of the Enlightenment for a theocentric ethic, and the modest epistemology of John **Locke** and his followers for an assertion of absolute truths.

Some of the tensions in Enlightenment thought were not, and could not have been, worked out during the 18th century because many of the projects of the Enlightenment were ongoing and unresolved at that time. But issues which not that long ago we believed had been resolved, are again open to question. The battles that **Montesquieu**, **Voltaire**, **Diderot**, the abbé **Raynal** and others had fought over issues such as **racism**, toleration and individual rights will have to be fought over again. Apparently the key values of the Enlightenment are not acquired once and for all. Rather, they must be appropriated by each generation and each culture in turn, or they will be submerged and lost.

ENTHUSIASM. A state of mind fundamentally opposed to Enlightenment values. Etymologically the term derives from the Greek "en," meaning in, and "theos," meaning the divine. Hence, to have the divine within oneself, or to be possessed by the divine. During and since the 18th century "enthusiasm" is also used in secular contexts to indicate a state of being carried away by ideas or forces that are not subject to rational or objective control.

One of the basic assumptions of Enlightenment thought was that human behavior should be directed by norms that assure the well-being of the individual and of society. These norms were defined in rational, scientific, pragmatic and utilitarian terms. Enthusiasm was a frame of mind determined by forces that were not generally identified with these things, and might well be opposed to them. Moreover, because enthusiasm internalized such forces, it severed the link between the individual enthusiast and the regular structures and functions in **nature** on which Enlightenment thinkers sought to base their worldview.

ÉPINAY, Louise Françoise Pétronville Tardieu d'Eschevelles dame de la Live, Marquise d' (1726-1783). Mme d'Épinay was born to a family of the nobility of the sword. On the death of her father she and her mother went to live with Mme Bellegrande and she was educated with the daughter of the house, the future Mme d'Houdetot, who was to provide the model for the heroine of *Julie, ou La Nouvelle Héloïse*, and was the great passion of the mature Jean-Jacques **Rousseau.** Exceptionally, Mme d'Épinay was married on her own initiative and without family approval, and so without a dowry (*see* **Marriage)**, at the age of 19, to her cousin, the farmer general La Live d'Épinay. D'Épinay proved exceptionally dissipated and worthless. He separated from his wife, and in 1762 came close to ruining her financially.

Mme d'Épinay was not without the means of leading an independent life of her own. At her chateau of La Chevrette she hosted *philosophes* such at Denis **Diderot**, the Baron d'**Holbach**, Jean-Jacques Rousseau and Friedrich Melchior Grimm, who became and remained her lover for 30 years, on and off. She is best known for her **patronage** of, and quarrel with, Rousseau.

In 1755 Mme d'Épinay generously outfitted a comfortable cottage on her property, the Ermitage, for Rousseau who had decided to leave Paris for a simpler way of life. Rousseau's *Confessions* paint a picture of Mme d'Épinay much influenced by the animosity that subsequently developed between them, and between Rousseau and Grimm. Mme d'Épinay responded with her own account of their relations in an autobiographical novel of great length, the *Histoire de Mme de Montbrillant*.

Not only the friend and hostess of *philosophes*, Mme d'Épinay was also an author in her own right. In 1774 she published an educational treatise, *Les Conversations d'Emilie*. She contributed significantly to Grimm's manuscript newsletter the *Correspondance Littéraire*, and her correspondence with the abbé Galiani, for a time the representative of Naples in France but then required by his government to return home, has recently been published and provides valuable insights into the life and activities of the *philosophes* and their friends.

EPISTEMOLOGY. The branch of philosophy that deals with the origins and nature of knowledge. For most broad movements of ideas this often technical branch of philosophy is neither central nor vital. For the Enlightenment it is both.

One approach to the Enlightenment is to see it as a new and coherent way of seeing the world, more specifically, a scientific and objective way of seeing it. For most scientists from the 17th century on, their disciplines required clear proofs, cast in mathematical and/or empirical terms, and the application of a clearly defined method. These issues played a far more central role in the Enlightenment than they had in the Renaissance or Reformation, where the main questions were textual, philological and theological.

It follows, then, that the question of what things can be known and how one can gain knowledge came to be central and even defining features of Enlightenment perceptions of the world. The methodology favored by the Enlightenment is **empiricism**.

EQUALITY. One of the key values of the Enlightenment, but certainly not new. Classical Greece assured broadly equal rights to citizens, while withholding political and civic rights from **women**, **slaves** and resident foreigners. Christianity asserted the equality and preciousness of all souls. The indifference of the founders and early adherents of this faith to things material and to authority fostered egalitarianism, but as the Church developed and legitimized things material, so it tended to favor hierarchy above equality.

The society of the **Old Regime** was in principle radically unegalitarian. It defined the individual in terms of the corporation, **estate**, occupation and religion to which he or she belonged, ascribing different dignities and statuses to each. The **law** was particularistic, recognizing **privilege** and varying rights and customs throughout the country and across the social scale. It is worth bearing this in mind in considering the place of equality in Enlightenment thought.

The thinkers of the Enlightenment abstracted individuals from their social contexts to see them simply as human beings. Coming from the hands of **nature**, or a Creator, they were equal in rights and dignity. This assumption formed the basis of contract theory without necessarily negating notions of authority or hierarchy (*see* **Social Contract**). Figures as conservative as Thomas Hobbes, David **Hume** or

Edmund **Burke** accepted the primal equality of all human beings; but they denied this hypothesis relevance to constituted societies. Radicals, on the other hand, treated the equality of the state of nature as a moral imperative and guideline for the shaping of modern societies. This was the position of Jean-Jacques **Rousseau**, Thomas **Paine** and most reformers. Conservatives and radicals differed not on the hypothesis of a primal state of equality, but on its relevance to established societies, particularly their own.

The tendency of Enlightenment thought was to extend the circle of equality beyond the narrow bounds of **citizenship** of classical antiquity or the corporate hierarchies of the Old Regime, and to conceive equality in broadly theoretical and civic terms. However, the thinkers of the Enlightenment denied the propriety of enforcing equality, and generally regarded "absolute" equality as a "chimera" (Voltaire, *Philosophical Dictionary,* art. "Equality"). Rousseau's guideline for practical politics was that no man should be so poor that he would be obliged to sell himself, and none so rich that he could buy another (*Social Contract,* Bk. II, chap. 11). This is to say that in practice the Enlightenment recognized legitimate forms of inequality.

Talent, ability, intelligence and industry all resulted in differences of fortune that the thinkers of the Enlightenment found eminently acceptable. With rare exceptions, Enlightenment thinkers measured the capacity of individuals by their ability to acquire **property**, and made active participation in politics dependent on a property qualification. Though the Enlightenment extended a broad notion of equality to **humanity** as a whole and widened the scope of civil **rights**, it was, again with rare exceptions, far from seriously considering the possibilities of socio-economic equality or **gender** equality. Still, equality of opportunity and equality before the law were highly progressive values in a hierarchical society, which determined the place of the individual by birth and corporate affiliation.

ESTATES. Traditional European societies were usually divided into three broad status groups or estates, the first of which was the clergy, the second the nobility and the third, which in France included more than 95 percent of the population, the commons. Each estate had certain legally defined rights and prerogatives, or **privileges**, particular to itself. Privileges often took the form of exemptions from general obligations, and these could be regional or institutional as well as a matter of formal status. In general the first and second estates were more privileged than the third, towns were more privileged than the countryside, and peripheral regions were more privileged than the center.

Under the **Old Regime** representation was by estate, and took two main forms. Provincial Estates, or assemblies, existed in the more peripheral regions of France, such as Brittany, Provence, Languedoc, Dauphiny and Artois, known as *pays d'états*, and were an indication of at least a tradition of regional autonomy. The main functions of the provincial estates were to raise taxes and carry out certain administrative duties. Restricted though these functions were, they were often real advantages to the regions that had provincial estates, as they were able to moderate the level of taxation to which they were subject.

The Estates General were a properly political body. They consisted of representatives of each estate of the realm who met when convened by the crown to offer advice on affairs of state and to approve extraordinary taxes. These assemblies are usually identified with **constitutionalism**, and, representing the interests of the aristocracy, usually opposed the extension of royal authority. For this reason the crown convened it only when necessary, and having been given the right to collect the main direct tax on commoners, the *taille*, without regular approval by the Estates General in 1614, did not call another session until forced by its aristocratic opposition to do so in 1789.

ESSAY ON MANNERS/ESSAI SUR LES MOEURS (1756; 1769).
Voltaire's great universal history, covering all of European and world history from Charlemagne to Louis XIV. A huge work of 1,650 pages in a modern edition, the *Essay* took shape over more than 20 years and was constantly reworked by Voltaire. Of all his books, it was the one in which he invested most time, energy and care.

Together with David **Hume**, Edward **Gibbon** and William **Robertson,** Voltaire is considered one of the four great historians of the Enlightenment. His contribution in the *Essay on Manners* was to pioneer a secular cultural history, and to expand its scope beyond the Christian world to include China, India and the Islamic world. Voltaire had great appreciation for these other cultures, and often used them as points of comparison to bring out the shortcomings of European Christianity.

It is probably no coincidence that Voltaire begins the *Essay on Manners* where Bishop Bossuet had left off his Eurocentric and profoundly Christian *Universal History*. One of the reasons that Voltaire invested the enormous amount of time and work he did in the study of the civilizations of Asia was to de-center Europe and Christianity in his narrative. Once he had described the parallel and often demonstrably older civilizations of China, India, Egypt and the ancient Near East, it became untenable to maintain the uniqueness and greater antiquity of the Judeo-Christian tradition. Indeed, undermining the claim of Christianity to exclusive legitimacy was one of Voltaire's main objectives in the *Essay*, as it was in many of his other writings.

Another of Voltaire's goals in the *Essay* was to redefine the nature of history. Up to the 18th century most history was written around politics and war, usually from the point of view of a certain country or ruling house. For Voltaire, wars, regardless of who, or what, was involved, were occasions for barbarity and brutality, and conquerors and generals were in his eyes little more than glorified bandits. Similarly, he regarded the kings and barons who, with the complicity of priests, ruled the wretched and downtrodden populations of the medieval West as oppressors and extortionists.

Having devalued war and politics as subjects for history, Voltaire substituted culture and commerce. His heroes were the thinkers who provided a more accurate portrayal of the world and its workings, and so helped limit the hold of **ignorance**, **superstition** and priests on society. They were also those rare politicians, like Henri IV, who were able to assure their peoples peace and well-being. And the states of which he wrote with greatest sympathy were those, like England and Holland, which assured their citizens personal security, freedom and **toleration**.

As Voltaire saw it, the historical record was bleak. It showed innumerable cases of confusion, conquest, oppression, fraud, extortion, murder and suffering, but few of decency and **humanity**. The historical world of the *Essay* is of a piece with the world of *Candide*. Yet the few periods in which reasonable and well-intentioned rulers effectively established their authority and overcame the centrifugal forces of local interests, **prejudice** and superstition are grounds for hope and represent goals for which humanity must strive.

F

FABLE OF THE BEES, THE. A complex and highly controversial work by Bernard **Mandeville**. The core of the book was a rhymed fable entitled *The Grumbling Hive: or Knaves Turn'd Honest*, which Mandeville published anonymously in 1705, and which was soon pirated and sold at a half-penny for the four-page poem. In 1714 Mandeville published, again anonymously, *The Fable of the Bees: or, Private Vices, Publick Benefits*, a substantial volume that consisted of the original poem, a brief "Enquiry into the Origin of Moral Virtue," and 20 alphabetically designated "Remarks." By 1723 the "Remarks" were increased to 25 and expanded, and two more essays had been added to the volume, "An Essay on Charity and Charity Schools," and "A Search into the Nature of Society." Together with a "Vindication" defending the book against allegations of immorality, irreligion and subversiveness in a law case brought against it, these items make up the first volume of the complete *Fable of the Bees*. In 1728 Mandeville brought out another volume of comparable size, which he designated Part II. The two volumes were not published together until 1733. The work went through many editions and was translated into French and German.

What made Mandeville's book so controversial was the combination of its views on **human nature** and on society. Against the view of the Earl of **Shaftesbury**, who maintained that human beings were naturally sociable and beneficent, Mandeville argued that human nature was radically egoistic. He gave this position a novel twist, however, by maintaining that it was thanks to the passions and vices of its basically flawed nature that mankind was induced to live in society, to develop the arts and sciences and to enjoy all the advantages of civilization. In Mandeville's own terms, private vices were the source of public benefits.

In its qualified rehabilitation of **self-interest**, its criticism of an ethic consciously directed toward the common good and its emphasis on unintended consequences, *The Fable of the Bees* contributed to the development of liberal economic thought and helped to prepare the way for David **Hume** and Adam **Smith**. For the same reasons, Mandeville's outlook was in fundamental opposition to that of Jean-Jacques **Rousseau**. There are, however, some points of convergence between the two thinkers.

Mandeville and Rousseau were at one in regarding the arts and sciences as resulting from vice and corruption. Both saw large societies and large cities as necessarily corrupt. And both felt that **happiness** could best be achieved in small, undeveloped and largely static societies. Where they differed was in Mandeville's regarding the benefits of development and civilization as worth the cost. For the naturalized Englishman, self-interest provided a functional and acceptable basis for social and political organization, while for the

Genevan, without **virtue** there could be no legitimate and viable social order.

FAIRGROUND THEATER/THÉÂTRE DE LA FOIRE. The origin of this theater can be traced to the last years of the 16th century when some wandering players settled in Paris and began to entertain the public at fairs with performing monkeys, trained dogs, acrobats, tightrope walkers and puppet shows.

The fairs of Saint-Germain and Saint-Laurent, which featured small stages, were especially famous in the 18th century. They were much commented upon in the guides of Paris for strangers, such as the well known one of Nemeitz (1727). The fair of Saint-Germain on the left bank ran for three months in winter, that of Saint-Laurent on the right bank, for three months in summer.

In 1697, when the **Italian Comedians** fled Paris, the fairground troupes took over part of the newly available repertoire and hired some members of the former company. At the same time, they benefited from a public avid for stage entertainment. They also benefited from the collaboration of talented authors like Alain-René Lesage, Louis Fuselier, Dorneval and Alexis Piron—who introduced a progressively more elaborate repertoire, whose comedy was less coarse and less raw. The first three of the authors mentioned above left posterity a two-volume collection entitled *Le Théâtre de la Foire ou l'Opéra-Comique, contenant les meilleures Pièces qui ont été représentées aux Foires Saint-Germain et Saint-Laurent* (1737), which was made up of what they thought were the best of the repertoire of the fairground theater.

However, the success of these small stages triggered a war of the theaters. The **Comédie Française** fought to keep the **privilege** of its monopoly as the only French-speaking theater in Paris. From 1701 the courts upheld the claims of the Comédie Française and forbade the fairground entrepreneurs, first to stage plays with consistent plots, then to use dialogue, or even monologues, and finally, to speak at all. These successive interdictions became themes of **comedies** in polemical and satirical plays, and comforted the entertainers through the support of a sympathetic public. Their pugnacity enhanced their popularity and greatly increased their vogue among the stages of Paris.

A kind of agreement was reached when the Opera sold part of its own privilege, the permission to sing, to a fairground troupe. This was the official birth of the *opéra-comique* as a distinct genre. As part of the text was sung on airs of **vaudevilles**, it permitted, little by little, the reintroduction of spoken dialogue. But hostilities were renewed when actors from the new Italian troupe decided, for economic reasons, to take over the fairgrounds. Finally, in 1762, the Italian theater and the Opéra-Comique merged to become officially the new Opéra-Comique with a set repertoire.

The importance of the fairground theater is that it popularized a number of interesting formal inventions and innovations of theatrical and para-theatrical techniques, some of popular origin. The authors used, successively or simultaneously, monologues, "pièces à écriteaux" (the fairground actor carried rolled-up sheets of paper—as many sheets as the scenario had lines—and unfurled words from his pocket; when his pocket was emptied, words written on a blackboard flanked by cherubim descended from the rafter), "pièces à la muette," or dumb shows, or actors reciting gibberish to convey the sense, or pantomime. All of these genres were born of enforced silence. These techniques in turn influenced the official theaters. The fairground theaters also represent the first attempt to establish in Paris theaters based on private investments, and intended to make a profit. In this respect they parallel the commercialization of leisure in the popular Vauxhall Gardens of London.

Isabelle Martin

FANATICISM. What idolatry was to the prophets of the Hebrew Scriptures, fanaticism was to the *philosophes* of the Enlightenment. It combined intellectual and moral error and resulted in harm to individuals and to society.

Typically, fanaticism involved blind adherence to beliefs or doctrines that were not open to rational investigation or empirical verification. For thinkers of the Enlightenment this generally meant the revelations of positive religions and the authority of established churches.

Blind belief in Church dogma was an aspect of fanaticism that involved the believer in intellectual error. While from the point of view of enlightened thinkers adherence to Aristotelian physics and cosmology had become untenable, and so foolish, and insistence that there was no salvation outside the Catholic Church was inconsistent with the even-handed **beneficence** of the **deist** Supreme Being, such beliefs were not regarded as dangerous. When, however, such dogmas were enforced by coercion, as in the case of the Inquisition, or when clerics sure of their dogmas enlisted blindly enthusiastic masses to enforce such beliefs, as happened during the Crusades and the wars of religion, then the full weight of fanaticism made itself felt in human suffering, death and destruction.

As an intellectual movement, the Enlightenment opposed purely intellectual error, which included taking as certain things that could not be clearly proven. Emphasizing humanitarianism, the thinkers of the Enlightenment passionately condemned the unwarranted infliction of suffering and loss of life. It was intellectual error manifesting itself as threats to individual well-being and social order that the thinkers of the Enlightenment saw as one of the primary objectives of their polemic. Their response was to demonstrate the uncertainty of dogma, and in the light of this uncertainty to put forward the counter-value of **toleration**.

Fanaticism refers more to the way beliefs are held than to their content. And of course they are not limited to the field of religion. Indeed the Enlightenment saw the development not only of a moderate and ethically-oriented deism, but also of an enlightened Catholicism. Other forms of belief that can be held fanatically—that is, without regard to fact, evidence or **reason**—include the political, ethnic, nationalist, racial and scientific, of all of which there are notable illustrations after the 18th century.

FERGUSON, Adam (1723-1816). Scottish minister, professor and social analyst, best known today for his *Essay on Civil Society*, which is now seen as an important contribution to the establishment of a systematic approach to social thought.

Ferguson was born in Perthshire, and like many of the leading figures of the Scottish Enlightenment, he was the son of a parish minister of the established Presbyterian Church. He received his first instruction at home, and was then sent to his parish school and a grammar school in Perth before going on to St. Andrew's University, where he excelled in Latin. Ferguson prepared for a position in the Church of Scotland, but on graduating in 1742 moved to Edinburgh, where he became friendly with John Home, Robert Adam and William **Robertson**, and worked as the private secretary to Lord Milton while waiting for a more regular position.

In 1745 Ferguson began his clerical career by becoming an army chaplain. His knowledge of Gaelic, unusual for the educated at the time, endeared him to the soldiers of the highland regiment with which he served, as did his propensity to take a more active role in battle than his clerical status properly allowed. Not receiving the preferment within the Church that he felt he deserved, he left it in 1754.

Like many intellectuals at the time, Ferguson was dependent on his friends and connections for finding work, or better, sinecures. He became private secretary and tutor to the sons of Lord Milton, a Scottish judge, and then in 1757 he succeeded his friend, David **Hume**, as librarian to the Faculty of Advocates of Edinburgh. He also tutored the sons of Lord Bute. His career as a professor became firmly established in 1759 when he was appointed to teach natural history in the University of Edinburgh, and then in 1764 when he took over the chair of moral philosophy, which was more to his taste. It is worth noting that the university instructors who contributed so much to the Scottish Enlightenment did not belong, with the exception of physicians, ministers and the lawyer John **Millar**, to professional faculties, and that many of them, including Francis **Hutcheson**, Adam **Smith** and Thomas **Reid**, taught moral philosophy, which included a broad range of social and historical subjects.

Ferguson was a popular teacher, and in addition to his duties at the university tutored the sons of the Earl of Warwick and a son of the Chesterfield family, whom he took on the tour of the continent. In 1778 Ferguson was secretary to a British commission sent to negotiate with the Americans. When he retired from his chair of moral philosophy in 1785, the university conferred another position on him to provide a retirement income. With the income from this sinecure and pensions from the Chesterfield family and the British government, Ferguson spent a comfortable and long retirement.

The work which made Ferguson's reputation was *An Essay on the History of Civil Society* of 1767, which went through a number of editions, and was translated into French and German. Though this book is regarded as an important contribution to the development of a science of society, his fellow Scots literati were cool to it. Hume did not care for it, though he did not specify his objections, and the usually supportive Alexander Carlyle said that "it ought only to be considered as a college exercise" (*Autobiography*, p. 299). In 1772 Ferguson published the *Institutes of Moral Philosophy*, which reflected his teaching, and in 1792 another textbook, the *Principles of Moral and Political Science*. Like many members of the enlightened community, Ferguson retained a strong interest in the classical history that he had been exposed to as a student, and which continued to serve as a point of reference. His *History of the Progress and Termination of the Roman Republic* of 1782 forms part of the ongoing debate on Roman history and its significance to which **Montesquieu** and Edward **Gibbon** notably contributed.

Like many of the leading figures of the Scottish Enlightenment, Ferguson was eminently clubable. He was a member of the Select Society of Edinburgh, and one of the founders of a **club** to further the cause of a Scottish militia, for which he suggested the name Poker Club. Ferguson supported Robertson's project for the founding of a Royal Society of Scotland, and following a journey to Italy and Germany in 1793 was named an honorary member of the Berlin Academy. Recognized at home and abroad, Ferguson lived a long, healthy and comfortable rural retirement. He died aged 93 and was buried at St. Andrew's, where his monument bears an inscription composed by Sir Walter Scott.

FIELDING, Henry (1707-1754). Fielding was born on 22 April 1707 to a family not of the upper class itself, but having familial connections to the aristocracy. His father was an officer in the army, who gradually reached the rank of major general in 1735 and was finally promoted to lieutenant general in 1739. He died soon afterwards in 1741.

Henry was educated by a Mr. Oliver, curate of Motcombe, at Eton. He is said to have acquired a considerable knowledge of the classics. Of great constitutional vigor, and towering over six feet tall, Fielding was a powerful and active figure in London. He threw himself recklessly into the pleasures of life in the great city. When forced to work, he turned to the stage, having been influenced by Molière's *Le Médecin Malgré Lui* and *L'Avare,* which both left a lasting impression on him. For a decade Fielding was the most successful dramatist in London, focusing his skills on domestic comedies and political satires, and producing a total of 25 plays in this period.

He took up the study of law and engaged in political journalism. His exposure to this underside of life led to his developing some of his favored fictional themes of crime, punishment, justice and trials.

Sir Robert Walpole was a frequent target of Fielding; in 1737 he published *Historical Register, For the Year 1736* aimed against the Prime Minister. In 1743 he produced the play *Jonathan Wild,* a mock retelling of the life of a notorious criminal, which was in effect a satire on the penchant for mistaking power for greatness. So piqued was Walpole that the government was moved to pass the Licensing Act, which effectively put an end to Fielding's theatrical career.

It was Samuel **Richardson**'s *Pamela* (1740) that galvanized Fielding into becoming a novelist, publishing *Shamela*, a satire on prudish morality and sentimentality, in 1741. This success led directly to Fielding's next novel, *Joseph Andrews*, an entertaining work in its own right, in 1742. Fielding's debt to Cervantes and other earlier fiction has been widely noted. He swiftly established a model for the novel, which differed significantly from that of Richardson, that is, as a comic epic poem in prose.

In 1745 Fielding published an anti-Jacobite pamphlet and in 1748 he was rewarded for his loyalty with an appointment as a magistrate. In 1749 he published his masterpiece, and one of the greatest novels in English, *Tom Jones*, portraying high and low life in an enormous variety of situations and presenting a vast gallery of characters and scenes. In 1751 he brought out *Amelia*, a domestic novel treating the relationship between a man and his wife, and lauding womanly virtues.

Fielding died in 1754 in Lisbon, Portugal.

Peter Sorek

FIRST DISCOURSE, or *DISCOURSE ON THE SCIENCES AND ARTS* (1750). This work was written by Jean-Jacques **Rousseau** in response to the question proposed by the Academy of Dijon for its essay contest of 1750, "Has the restoration of the sciences and arts tended to purify morals?" Rousseau's composition, which was elegantly written, though less well formulated and argued than most of his work, won first prize, and its publication, with ensuing polemics, established his reputation.

The question posed by the Academy of Dijon was clearly intended to offer an occasion for praise of culture and enlightenment, and particularly for the assumption that intellectual advances were morally beneficial. Rousseau, with Denis **Diderot**'s encouragement, argued the opposite. His point was not that intellectual and cultural progress were bad in themselves, but that they were the products of sophisticated societies characterized by the polarization of wealth and were inevitably accompanied by social inequality, injustice and oppression. There was gain, but in Rousseau's view the cost was prohibitive.

Rousseau thus denied the central optimistic assumption of the unity of intellectual and moral aspects of enlightenment and proposed instead a tragic view of enlightenment in which the inevitable result of intellectual advance and sophistication was social injustice. Moreover, he gave morality precedence over learning. This position, from which he never deviated, separated him from mainstream Enlightenment thinkers who made the easier and less complicated assumption that intellectual and moral advances proceed in tandem. *See also* **Equality**.

FLOUR WAR. The name given to a series of grain riots that occurred in the Paris region and northeastern France in the spring of 1775. These riots, which were an instance of a structured and well-defined form of popular protest, were a response to two distinct developments. First, the harvest of 1774 was poor and resulted in relative scarcity of grain and higher prices for bread. The higher prices were felt most severely in the spring and early summer months before the new harvest. Secondly, in September 1774 Anne-Robert-Jacques **Turgot** had deregulated the grain trade. His expectation was that by opening the production and distribution of this basic staple to market forces he would give farmers the incentive to produce more, and in the long term match supply to demand at reasonable prices.

For small consumers the short-term result of Turgot's liberalizing measures, which were exacerbated by the bad harvest of 1774, was an increase in the price of bread that made it impossible for families that were able to feed themselves in normal times to continue to do so. Those so affected responded in traditional fashion by blocking the shipment of grains away from their vicinity, and by enforcing the sale of grain at a "fair" price, namely, a price that working families could afford in normal times, rather than the increased market price (*see* **Taxation populaire**). The government repressed these risings with force, and executed many of those involved.

The Flour War is an instance of the incommensurability of enlightened and popular values. The government believed that it was acting in a progressive and responsible fashion to stimulate agricultural production by deregulating the market in grain. Possibly this policy would have had its desired effect in the long term. Significant sections of the working population did not have a long term available to them. For them high grain prices meant destitution, and possibly starvation. They put little faith in enlightened economic theories if these entailed hunger and suffering. Rather, they had recourse to an ideal of a fair price and to regulation as the responsibility of the authorities to assure that this price was not exceeded. The Flour War is an instance of this ideology being imposed by collective and traditional popular action, and being met by effective repression.

This conflict points to a contradiction between enlightened and popular outlooks that is not easily reconciled. From the point of view of macro-economic analysis, Turgot's reform had much to recommend it. For net consumers of grains, however, the micro-economic implications of this policy were unacceptable. Enlightenment programs of economic reform, while well intentioned and progressive, were often unable to overcome conditions of underdevelopment, on the one hand, and popular mentalities that were rooted in centuries of adapting to and coping with these conditions, on the other.

FONTENELLE, Bernard le Bovier de (1657-1757). One of the key figures in the transformation of high culture from the 17th to the 18th century. Fontenelle's father was a practicing lawyer in Rouen, and his mother a sister of the great dramatist, Pierre Corneille. Fontenelle attended the **Jesuit** *collège* of Rouen, and then took a degree in law. In a pattern that was to be repeated many times over the course of the 18th century, the young man abandoned a career in law for a more attractive one in letters.

Like many Enlightenment figures Fontenelle's literary output is marked by diversity. During the 1670s he wrote mostly poetry and plays and provided copy for the fashionable journal, *Mercure galant*. The particularly hostile reception given one of his tragedies in 1680 caused him to return from Paris to Rouen, and there in the following years he produced many of the works for which he is best remembered. These include *Dialogues of the Dead* (1683); *Discussions on the Plurality of Worlds* (1686), a highly accessible and successful popularization of **Cartesian** science; *History of Oracles* (1687), a criticism of **superstition**, ancient and modern, in some ways similar to Pierre **Bayle**'s *Diverse Thoughts on the Comet* published a few years before; and *Digression on the Ancients and the Moderns* (1688), an argument for the comparability, and in some cases superiority, of modern culture to that of the classical world.

Unlike Bayle, Fontenelle was by no means a reclusive scholar. He played an active part in both the learned societies and **salons** of the time. In 1691 he was elected to the **Académie française** and returned to the capital. While continuing to write drama and poetry, his main area of activity shifted to the sciences when he was elected, in 1697, a member of the Academy of Sciences (*see* **Academies, State-Sponsored**), and then became its secretary. In this capacity he edited the proceedings of the Academy, and wrote some 70 eulogies of academicians who died between 1699 and 1740. Once established in

Paris, Fontenelle not only attended virtually all of the important salons, but also played a central role in them.

In his personal life Fontenelle was rather self-centered, a tendency that was no doubt strengthened by poor health, which he managed to survive for a century. He was an early apologist of hedonism, and in this way validated the this-worldly attitude that became prevalent in the Enlightenment.

Fontenelle's views on science remained Cartesian to the end. He still had not accepted Newtonian physics by 1754, when he published a *Theory of Cartesian Vortices*. Yet if his rejection of Newtonianism was retrograde, his adherence to the broadly rational, lawful and naturalistic view of the world characteristic of Cartesianism was not.

No other important figure of the Enlightenment lived as long, and possibly as happily, in his own terms, as did Fontenelle. His career, however, reflects a number of characteristic features of Enlightenment culture: the ability to bridge comfortably the domains of literature and science; a willingness to spread learning beyond the confines of **universities** and academies (though not so far as to reach the common people); and a sophisticated sociability that made verbal communication and a degree of informality an integral part of the lives of men and women of letters.

FOURMONT, Étienne (1683-1745). Etienne Fourmont was born in Herblay, northwest of Paris, to a pious family on the lower edge of the magistrature. As a child he studied with the family's parish priest, who recognized his talent and then, at the age of 11, or a year or so later, entered the *Collège* des Quatre Nations that had recently been founded with a legacy of the Cardinal Mazarin. He studied there until the age of 17, and then continued his studies at the Séminaire des trente-trois, an institution for poor students, but was expelled for reading more Greek, Latin and possibly Hebrew than was compatible with preparation for the priesthood. He then studied at the Collège de Montaigu and finally the Collège de Navarre, which he left to teach Hebrew at the Collège d'Harcourt. (These were all constituents of the Sorbonne.) He was a gifted student of Greek, Latin and Hebrew but it is not known who initiated him in Hebrew since there were no distinguished Hebraists at any of the colleges of the Sorbonne in the period, and there is no tradition that he had contacts with Jews who might have taught him outside the university. He must have been largely an autodidact.

Fourmont seems to have been a sufficiently successful teacher to have provoked the envy of his colleagues, and, to add insult to injury, he accepted the pronunciation of Hebrew and the grammatical analysis traditional among Jews rather than the heuristic methods of the Abbeville canon, François Masclef, who thought that he could read and understand Hebrew independently of the Jewish tradition.

Fourmont was forced to leave the Sorbonne, married in 1711 and after the death of his first wife remarried in 1737. He made a lay career as the Royal Professor of Arabic, Royal Interpreter of Oriental languages, Royal Librarian, was elected in 1715 to the Royal Academy of Inscriptions and Belles-Lettres–the only institution where freethinkers and pious scholars might meet, discuss and differ–and taught privately because the salaries of Royal professors were very modest and irregularly paid.

Fourmont's earliest works are a series of three very vigorous, ironic and iconoclastic polemics against leading Catholic writers. In two of them he writes disguised as a Jew! In the first, written while he was still teaching in the Collège d'Harcourt, he argues against the Benedictine exegete Augustin **Calmet** (*Lettres à M*** sur le Commentaire du père Calmet . . .*, Paris, 1709), that the necessary tools for biblical interpretation include a thorough knowledge of Hebrew and rabbinic exegesis and, by implication, that Patristic exegesis does not have a privileged exegetical status. Against the apologist François-Claude-Alexandre Houtteville (*Lettre de R. Ismael ben Abraham, juif converti . . .*, Paris, 1722), he argued that the Old Testament prophecies that he (and the Catholic apologetic tradition) applied to Jesus were in fact misapplied. Against the "figurist"/milleniarist Jacques-Joseph Duguet (*Mouaâcah. Ceinture de douleurs, . . . composé par rabbi Ismael Ben-Abraham, juif converti. . .*, Paris, 1723) he maintained that the only suitable method for interpreting the Bible is to seek the direct, literal sense of the texts which alone has a privileged epistemological status. No more polemics followed these three, as though he had gone as far as he dared in illustrating the value of his Hebrew learning without compromising his career.

Manuscript drafts of many of his public lectures and private courses have survived and they show Fourmont to have been an unavowed disciple of Richard Simon, demonstrating the breadth and depth of Jewish culture to a public that, in its profound ignorance, despised it, and holding that the Old Testament text is a composite of various sources that had suffered in its millennial transmission. Apparently this could be said in public lectures, but not published. (His lectures on the Psalms, however, contain apologetic elements, whence our hesitation in classifying him as a closet iconoclast).

Fourmont also left a manuscript Hebrew grammar which has its quirks but which is fundamentally an algebra isomorphic to David Kimhi's classical *Torath ha-nikkud*, theory of vocalization.

Bertram Eugene Schwarzbach

FRANKLIN, Benjamin (1706-1790). Born in Boston in the American colonies and the son of a candle-maker, Franklin was to become an important figure of the Enlightenment, active not only in North America, but also in England and France. His talents included business, literature, science, diplomacy and politics.

Apprenticed to his brother to learn the trade of printing, but feeling himself too harshly treated, Franklin left Boston for Philadelphia in 1723. He apparently learned the trade well and combined his skill with a shrewd business sense, for by 1730 he was proprietor of his own establishment, and by 1748 he had made enough to be able to retire. Franklin not only managed his printing business, but also wrote, with outstanding success, some of the materials he published, among them the *Pennsylvania Gazette* and *Poor Richard's Almanach*. In 1725 he had already published *A Dissertation on Liberty and Necessity, Pain and Pleasure*, but this was a young man's attempt at philosophy, and did little to gain him either wealth or reputation.

Some 20 years later Franklin began working on electricity, and in 1751 published his *Experiments and Observations on Electricity*. This work brought him international recognition, and in 1756 he was made a fellow of the **Royal Society** of London. In his scientific work Franklin combined theoretical originality with practical applications, as in the cases of the lightning rod, bifocals and the stove that bears his name.

Having retired from business, Franklin began a long and fruitful political career. He was elected to the Pennsylvania Assembly in 1751, and served as that Assembly's agent, as well as that of a number of colonies, in London between 1757 and 1762, and again between 1764 and 1775. During this second term he did his homeland the considerable service of providing Thomas **Paine** with letters of recommendation to friends in Philadelphia. Though initially a supporter of the British Empire, Franklin was alienated by the arrogance and flawed policies of the mother country toward its colonies. He helped to discredit the Stamp Act, and became a leading advocate of independence.

Franklin returned to Philadelphia in 1775 and so was able to take an active part in the events of the following year. He was elected by Pennsylvania as a delegate to the Second Continental Congress, served on a number of committees of that body, and was a signatory of the Declaration of Independence. He was then elected President of the Pennsylvania State Constitutional Convention, and appointed commissioner to France. Between 1778 and 1785 he served in effect as American ambassador in France, and in that capacity took part in the negotiations for the Treaty of Paris of 1783, which regularized relations between the United States and Britain.

In 1785 Franklin again returned home and took an active part in the politics on both the state and national levels. As of 1787 he served as President of the Society for Promoting the Abolition of **Slavery**. There is no parallel in Europe of the time for a young man of humble background rising to such high office and playing so central a role in the politics of his country for so long a time.

FREDERICK II (1712-1786). King of Prussia from 1740 until his death, and an outstanding exemplar of **enlightened despotism**. Frederick was brutalized as a child, but developed into probably the most successful and effective state-builder of the 18th century. He was, moreover, hugely and diversely cultured.

Frederick was an unscrupulous politician, a hard-working administrator and a brilliant military commander. He understood power and the mechanisms of power as well as any statesman of his time, and through a combination of force and judicious diplomacy turned Prussia from a minor state into one of the leading powers of Europe. Inheriting a well-disciplined army of about 80,000 men from his father, Frederick William I, he expanded it two-and-a-half times. This he achieved by keeping down personal and state expenses and expending 80 percent of a balanced budget on the military.

In 1740, shortly after his accession, Frederick attacked and annexed Silesia. During the Seven Years' War (1756-1763) Prussia, with British support, faced a powerful coalition that included France, Austria and Russia. Frederick proved himself a superior military strategist and commander, and made good use of his well-trained troops. However, it was largely through good fortune, when the bitterly hostile Czarina Elizabeth II died in 1762 and was replaced by Peter III who admired him and negotiated Russia's withdrawal from the war, that he escaped with Prussian territory intact. Frederick was also largely responsible for instigating the first partition of **Poland** in

1772, by which he achieved territorial continuity between East and West Prussia.

In addition to expanding the Prussian state, Frederick worked assiduously to rationalize and modernize it. He favored mercantilist economic policies, but also moderate taxation. He worked throughout his reign on a uniform code of law, which was implemented after his death in 1794. He also instituted obligatory primary instruction under state rather than church supervision. Though Frederick significantly rationalized and centralized the administration, he did not, and perhaps could not, liberalize Prussian society.

Frederick's rule was absolute, but it was also enlightened. Shortly after ascending the throne he decreed religious **toleration**, eliminated torture from judicial proceedings (something the French did not do until 1787) and limited **censorship**. He was genuinely interested in the arts and letters, playing and composing music, writing on politics and other subjects, corresponding with a number of *philosophes* and inviting them to his court. He also reinvigorated and took an active interest in the Berlin Academy (*see* **Academies, State-Sponsored**). But where the imperatives of power politics and state building came into conflict with values of the Enlightenment, it was the former that prevailed.

It would be unfair to ignore the predatory international climate and the economics of underdevelopment with which Frederick had to contend. And if one bears in mind the extreme penalty imposed on the Chevalier de la Barre for sacrilege, it is hard not to appreciate Frederick's response to a similar case. With respect to a man condemned for speaking disrespectfully of religion and the secular authorities, Frederick ruled: "That he blasphemed against God proves that he does not know Him; for his slander of me I forgive him; but to insult a noble Counsellor calls for exemplary punishment: imprison him for half-an-hour" (Bruun, 1967, p. 52).

FREEMASONRY. A movement founded in Scotland in the early 17th century, and spreading from there to England and thence to continental Europe. It grew rapidly over the 18th century, and still exists today.

Originally the freemasons were indeed building workers organized in a guild. However, from the middle of the 17th century membership was conferred without regard to occupation, and the varieties prevalent in the 18th century were almost entirely middle and upper class in social composition. At one point the masonic lodges formally excluded women, and despite occasional acceptance of women to membership, the movement remained overwhelmingly male. Freemasonry was introduced into France during the 1720s, and by the late 1780s had approximately 50,000 members in perhaps 1,000 lodges.

The beliefs and values of the freemasons were a combination of Renaissance Neoplatonism and mainstream Enlightenment science and ideas. The values of **equality,** fraternity and **beneficence** played a key role in masonic sensibility, and were combined with a taste for ritual and soft-core occultism, which perhaps had the function of bringing members together in a common status and attitude before the inscrutable. The activities of the masons included a good deal of banqueting, socially conscious outreach and formal meetings. Overall, these societies tended to be socially conservative. They were nevertheless suspect to authorities, and this for a number of reasons.

First, all proceedings of the freemasons were strictly secret. While this would not necessarily disturb agents of modern states, it was highly suspect in the context of **absolutism**. The absolutist state did not recognize a right of free association and felt it necessary to authorize and scrutinize all meetings.

Secondly, the broad values of freemasonry, such as equality and fraternity, stood in contrast to the key values of the **Old Regime**, such as hierarchy, status and **privilege**. Beyond the matter of values there was also the question of procedures. By adhering to a fixed and recognized set of rules and choosing officers by election, the freemasons appeared to favor **constitutionalism** and to approach **republicanism**, and even **democracy**. Historians generally agree that in its development in Britain, masonry was influenced by constitutionalist, and during the 17th century, even republican, ideas, and that these ideas were retained, though not given radical application, thereafter. Freemasons consistently asserted their loyalty to the crown and the constituted authorities, and they were no doubt sincere in this.

It is one of the more interesting features of masonry that its explicitly stated conservatism was implicitly contradicted by the egalitarian and open sociability it practiced. Masonic projects of beneficence were directed both to assisting the needy and virtuous and to reducing strains in a society perceived to be undergoing a crisis of disaggregation. The efforts of the freemasons were directed to smoothing the functioning of the Old Regime, not to disrupting it. The attempt of reactionary Catholics such as the abbé Barruel and Joseph de Maistre to portray the **French Revolution** as a result of the nefarious activities of an unholy trinity of freemasons, Protestants and **Jews** is utterly misguided.

Though far from atheism, the forms of **deism** common among the masons was unacceptable to established churches, and it was to be expected that the Catholic Church would condemn the movement and forbid the faithful to belong to it, as it did in 1738, and again in 1751. In addition to the loose and universalistic theology of freemasonry, the Church also looked askance at its rituals. However, this did not prevent some clerics from participating in the movement.

The disapproval of the authorities notwithstanding, freemasonry had great appeal for the middling and upper levels of 18th-century society. In part this can be explained by the attraction of the new civic and egalitarian sociability it cultivated, and to which contemporaries clearly responded. Masonry also had the virtue of offering a secular and rationalist metaphysic to those who could no longer believe in traditional theology, and a set of constructive and cohesive social values for those who no longer found the **master fictions** of the Old Regime convincing. A rational basis to the overall system of masonic ideas satisfied the mind, while a learned, quasi-scientific, soft-core occultism appealed to the imagination.

FRENCH REVOLUTION. A set of events occurring in France and exerting great influence throughout Europe between roughly 1787 and 1815, though there is no general agreement on its duration. Politically, the Revolution made France a constitutional monarchy, then a republic, then an empire. Socially, it changed France from a society of orders based on **privilege** to a society in which all citizens were broadly equal before the law, though for most of the Revolution some political rights were made to depend on wealth. The Revolution eliminated such major institutions of the **Old Regime** as the **seigneurial** system, **noble** status (partially restored under Napoleon) and guilds, and fundamentally reorganized the Catholic Church in France.

The relationship of the Enlightenment to the French Revolution has been much debated by historians. Conservatives portray the Enlightenment as a complex of abstract ideas without practical application to the social and political realities of the 18th century. In their view the Enlightenment resulted in the destabilization of the basically viable and decent Old Regime, and in the excesses of the Revolution, which they perceive to be ideologically motivated. In the view of most conservatives, the Enlightenment has much to answer for. Liberal and left-wing historians tend to see the Old Regime as fundamentally flawed, and the Enlightenment, among other things, as a program for humanitarian reform and modernization, that failing the obstructionism of the privileged orders, might well have brought France to modernity without the kinds of violence that occurred during the Revolution, and more or less in line with the British model.

The issues here are complex. However, a number of points are fairly clear. First, since the origins of the French Revolution contain an inextricable mixture of social, economic, administrative, fiscal and cultural elements, any analysis that focuses primarily on intellectual causes will be badly distorted. Secondly, struggles for political power in France had traditionally been accompanied by high levels of violence, as, for example, in the wars of religion, the League and the Fronde. It seems superfluous to invoke the Enlightenment, as some historians have done, to explain the violence of the Revolution. Indeed, if we look at the writings of even such radical *philosophes* as Jean-Jacques **Rousseau** and the Baron d'**Holbach**, we find that they warn that the use of force to achieve desirable reforms may prove counterproductive. Finally, the legislation of the revolutionary assemblies contains a high theoretical component and a remarkably clear view of the kinds of social organization and political arrangements that they wanted to replace those of the Old Regime. Without comprehensive alternate social and political visions, which do here seem to have come from the Enlightenment, movements for reform tend to result in little more than changes in personnel, or simply to peter out.

FRÉRON, Elie Catherine (1719-1776). One of the leading journalists of the **Old Regime**, famous both for his **periodical**, the *Année Littéraire,* and for his long-standing animosity to **Voltaire**. Fréron came from a Protestant family that had returned to Catholicism with the Revocation of the Edict of Nantes in 1685. His father was a goldsmith, but was never well-off. In 1730 Fréron was attending the **Jesuit** *collège* in Quimper, his birthplace, and in 1734 he was at Louis-le-Grand in Paris. He prepared to become a Jesuit, teaching at the Order's *collège* in Caen and then at Louis-le-Grand. However, in 1739 he was deprived of his status of novice for having attended the theater in lay dress.

Fréron was attracted not only to teaching, but also to writing. He produced some poetry and plays, but only found his vocation when he began to work with the abbé Desfontaines on his journal, the *Observations sur les écrits modernes*. In 1745 Fréron began a journal of his own, the *Lettres de la Comtesse de* ***. Four years later he published a new journal entitled *Lettres sur quelques écrits de ce temps*. When in 1754 he began publication of the *Année Littéraire*, the journal with which he is most closely associated, he had considerable experience in writing and running a periodical. The *Année Littéraire* became something of an institution and survived its founder by 15 years.

Fréron has been described as "Voltaire's greatest enemy" and his journal as fundamentally opposed to the Enlightenment. The first characterization is fair enough, but it does not justify the second. Fréron consistently questioned the quality of Voltaire's work, and generally denied it, especially the poetry and dramatic productions, the high status it was accorded by contemporaries. There was also a good deal of personal animosity between the two men, with Voltaire far outdoing Fréron in personal denigration. Fréron's critical evaluation of Voltaire as a writer, which is now seen to be for the most part justified, does not put him beyond the limits of Enlightenment thought. It does put him outside of, and in opposition to, one of the most powerful and influential literary circles and systems of **patronage** of the time.

Fréron's reviews of the President **Montesquieu** and Jean-Jacques **Rousseau** show him to be open minded and appreciative of much mainstream Enlightenment thought. Nor does the structure of his journal, and the views it expressed, differ much from those of the *Journal Encyclopédique*, which is identified with the Enlightenment, and enjoyed close relations with Voltaire. It makes better sense, therefore, to see Fréron and those associated with his journal as representing a current of thought within, or at the least compatible with, the Enlightenment, and not fundamentally opposed to it.

For a writer who was supposed to act as a spokesman for the established church and state, Fréron experienced considerable adversity. His journals were suspended a number of times, and the journalist himself spent time in state prisons, including the Bastille, on at least three occasions. Fréron, like Voltaire, was a **freemason**. He also enjoyed the patronage of the enlightened ruler Stanislas Leszczynski (1677-1766), who saw to it that he was appointed to the Academy of Nancy in 1753 (*see* **Academies, Provincial**). Fréron's career suggests that one could both be at odds with Voltaire and an active participant in Enlightenment culture.

G

GAY, Peter (1923-). One of the leading living historians of the Enlightenment. Peter Gay was born in Berlin, and given that his family was Jewish, he was fortunate to have emigrated to the United States. He received his B.A. from the University of Denver, and his M.A. and doctorate from Columbia University, where he began his teaching career in the Department of Political Science before switching to History. He subsequently held a distinguished professorship at Yale University.

Gay is one of the most prolific scholars of his generation, and has worked in more fields than is common in an age of narrow specialization. His interest in and major publications on the Enlightenment are centered on the decade of the 1960s. His monograph, *Voltaire's Politics: The Poet as Realist*, was published by Yale in 1959, and a collection of essays entitled *The Party of Humanity: Essays on the French Enlightenment* appeared with Knopf in 1964. His well-known and influential synthesis, *The Enlightenment: An Interpretation*, was also published by Knopf in two volumes in 1966 and 1969. The first volume had the subtitle *The Rise of Modern Paganism*, and the second, *The Science of Freedom*. Gay summarized his views on the Enlightenment and its significance in a speculative essay, which he structured as a discussion between Lucian, Erasmus and **Voltaire**, and called *The Bridge of Criticism: Dialogues on the Enlightenment*. In addition to these critical and synthetic studies, Gay also translated Ernst **Cassirer**'s *The Question of Jean-Jacques Rousseau* (1954), Voltaire's *Philosophical Dictionary* (1962) and *Candide* (1963), and edited an appropriately entitled *Comprehensive Anthology of the Enlightenment* (1973).

Gay's approach to the Enlightenment is characterized by an interest in the practical and reformist implications of the movement and its struggles against conservative forces. Unlike Cassirer, he wants to do more than provide a full philosophical description and analysis of the main areas of Enlightenment thought, and unlike Robert **Darnton**, he is more interested in the ideas than in clandestine literature, the history of books and the way they were distributed. Gay's history of the Enlightenment is an engaged one, and to a considerable degree partisan. Against Carl Becker (*see Heavenly City*) he argues for the modernity of the Enlightenment, and against Theodor Adorno and Max Horkheimer (*see* **Enlightenment, Dark Narrative**), he sees the Enlightenment as fundamentally **liberal** and **democratic**. He focuses on the *philosophes*, whom he describes as a family, a characterization which both insists on the overall unity and coherence of the group and recognizes significant differences within it.

Gay's treatment of the Enlightenment attempts to capture both its unity and its rich diversity. This is not to say that he argues two contradictory theses. Rather, he insists on the overall liberal, liberating, humanitarian and modernizing core of Enlightenment thought while recognizing that differences of opinion and strategy were common among the exponents of enlightened ideas.

How to weight unity and diversity is a problem that all historians of ideas face. Gay's solution, while clear enough overall, sometimes leads him to enunciate a position and then to qualify it in such a way that the reader is uncertain what he is really arguing. This situation is not the consequence of confusion on Gay's part, but rather of a felt need to do justice of the complexity of the ideas and movement he is dealing with.

Unlike most contemporary historians, Gay has a distinct style. He has an eye for the catching phrase ("definition by larceny") and takes pleasure in paradox (in "The Party of Humanity" he suggested that the Enlightenment could be characterized by "aristocratic liberalism," "Epicurean Stoicism," "passionate rationalism" and "tragic humanism," and elsewhere asserted that "the Enlightenment was not an age of reason, but a revolt against rationalism"). This makes him eminently readable, but sometimes adds to the confusion caused by his fuller than usual qualifications of his main theses. Interestingly, Roy Porter's important recent study of the Enlightenment in Britain, *The Creation of the Modern World* (2000), while in places critical of Gay, shares some of the stylistic features of his writing.

Most outstanding Enlightenment scholars, such as Daniel **Mornet**, Daniel **Roche** and Robert Darnton have spent their whole working lives, or nearly so, in the 18th century. For Gay the Enlightenment was one subject of research among others. Other areas he has published in include the history of 20th century Germany, Puritan historiography, pychoanalysis and Sigmund Freud. In fact, Gay's record of publication would do credit to many a small history department. There are, however, other scholars who work at a different pace and in a different way, and who establish a lasting reputation on the basis of a single comprehensive work. A case in point is Arthur Wilson, whose *Diderot*, it is safe to assume, will remain a basic point of reference in Enlightenment studies.

Peter Gay's conceptualization of the Enlightenment is, likely, one that would have pleased the main thinkers of the movement. He gives us a set of protagonists who are good and noble, though not without foibles and shortcomings, and it is well to be reminded that there is much that is good and noble in the Enlightenment. In Gay's rendition emphasis is placed on the progressive, liberal and democratic aspects of the movement. In the opinion of the present writer, for all his careful qualifications, Peter Gay underestimates the forces limiting and constraining the generous and liberal aspects of the Enlightenment. It is also the opinion of the present writer that Gay's history of the Enlightenment would be the one that most *philosophes* (or at least Voltaire), given a choice, would have preferred. One need not subscribe to Peter Gay's view of the Enlightenment, but no serious student of the period can ignore his work.

GEDDES, Alexander (1737–1802). Geddes was born in Rathven, Aberdeenshire. Despite its Catholicism, his family read the Bible in the (Anglican) King James translation, and Geddes's elementary education was acquired together with Presbyterian neighbors, but soon, because Catholicism was illegal in both Scotland and England, though in practice it was tolerated in Aberdeenshire, where Presbyterian peasants respected even Catholic neighbors' rights of conscience, he had to pursue his further education in the "minor seminary" of Scanlan, and then in the **Jansenist**-leaning Scots' College in Paris, from 1758 to 1764, where he studied Hebrew in addition to the usual preparation for the priesthood.

Upon ordination Geddes returned to Scotland to assume priestly functions at Traquair House, where he served as chaplain to a prominent family and began his serious biblical studies in its well-stocked library. However, after four years he was removed from his chaplainry, apparently because his criticism of the Catholic hierarchy scandalized his straight-laced employers, and possibly because of a romantic attraction to one of the ladies of the house, though this may be mere conjecture that has been endlessly repeated.

Geddes returned to France for a brief period, from 1767 or 1768 to 1769, and then accepted a curacy in Auchinhalrig, 50 miles from Aberdeen, where he served until 1781, when he was forced by his bishop to resign because he had attended an Episcopalian service. He had already begun his literary career with a much admired *Select satires of Horace translated into English verse* (1779) and, after leaving Auchinhalrig, settled in cosmopolitan London to live by his pen. This precarious existence was made somewhat easier by a generous pension from a prominent Catholic nobleman for whom he wrote several pamphlets.

Geddes's two sojourns in Paris correspond to the period when the radicalism that had been implicit in French thought since the "crise de conscience" of 1685-1715 was finding explicit expression. As a seminarian, his contacts with Enlightenment thought would have been indirect at best and hidden from the directors of his seminary, but during his second visit, about which nothing is known, he would have been freer to read **Voltaire**, the *Encyclopédie* and even more radical texts. He may have made contacts among the French scholars of the time, or among the dissident intellectuals and would-be writers scrounging for a livelihood in what Robert **Darnton** describes as the Parisian **Grub Street**. There are few explicit references in his writings on the Bible to what he might have read in Paris; the inventory of the books he possessed at his death includes many titles in French, but few radical books, either in French or in English.

Geddes pursued the career of a biblical scholar and translator while writing poetry in English and Scots, notably his *Three Scottish poems with a previous dissertation on the Scoto-Saxon dialect* (1792). The poems are a long and satiric demonstration of the power and suppleness of the Scots language, while the dissertation is a survey of the Celtic, Norse and Anglo-Saxon influences upon the English language. His idea of the Scottish tradition embraced both Calvinist, Episcopalian-rationalism and pre-Reformation, and thus necessarily Catholic, writers and philosophers, so he has been hard to classify.

There was also a radical element in his work visible in pamphlets in favor of Catholic emancipation in England and Scotland and criticism of the curtailments of **liberty** in England during its conflicts with Napoleonic France; he wrote a satirical defense of **slavery** and supported the **French Revolution**, even during its more radical phases. Several of his poems were good enough to have passed until 1999 as the work of Robert Burns, while other texts of considerable literary and historical interest remained unpublished. His literary reputation suffered in the 19th century because, as a representative of the cosmopolitan Scotto-Latin tradition rather than the more familiar Scottish Presbyterian tradition, he did not quite fit in any of the standard literary categories, which imagined authentic Scottish voices to be necessarily more comic and demotic than the one Geddes adopted. He even had a pre-romantic side, influencing William Blake and Samuel Taylor Coleridge.

Geddes is best known for his Bible translation—the Pentateuch (*The holy Bible, or the books accounted sacred by Jews and Christians; otherwise called the books of the old and new covenants*, v. I, London, 1792), Earlier Prophets and Chronicles (*The holy Bible, or the books accounted sacred by Jews and Christians; otherwise called the books of the old and new covenants*, v. II, London, 1797), a volume of *Critical remarks on the Hebrew scriptures corresponding with a new translation of the Bible* (London, 1800), which justify his translation of the Pentateuch, and a posthumously published *A new translation of the Psalms (1-118) from corrected texts of the originals, with occasional annotations* (London, 1804). He translated from the Hebrew into very vigorous English, though taking many liberties with the masoretic text, which he held to be unreliable. He assents to the more radical Bible criticism of the Enlightenment, in particular to its denial that the Old Testament contained figures and prophecies of Jesus, its criticism of the authenticity and integrity of the biblical texts and their inerrancy and its normative Bible criticism, which sapped a fundamental argument of apologetics that claimed that biblical ethical teaching was transparently excellent.

Accepting these arguments that had been advanced by the likes of Benedict **Spinoza**, David **Hume** and Voltaire rendered Geddes unique among religious writers of the period. He prefers what he thinks he knows about ancient history and natural science to what he finds in the Bible, explaining miracles as natural phenomena when he can, and de-emphasizing or even denying them when he cannot, and especially one sees that his ethical values are largely independent of those implicit and explicit in the Bible. Now, reconciling contradictions between what the Bible took for fact and what later generations accepted as fact, and between biblical ethics and the ethics of its readers was, since the most ancient times, the business of interpreters and apologists. Geddes poses those problems, but avoids apologetics almost entirely.

Bertram Eugene Schwarzbach

GENDER. The difficulty with which we define gender today finds its origins, paradoxically, in an 18th-century medical and literary culture in which the anatomical differences between men and women were unequivocal. At once the object of normalizing forces and the site of an ambiguity with regard to sexual difference dating from the Renaissance, Enlightenment medical science in particular made irreconcilable what had previously been considered symmetrical in female and male anatomy.

Due in part to the advent of the microscope in the previous century, which made visible the *animalcules* necessary for reproduction in humans and the taxonomic disposition of the age, male and female body parts were invested with a range of differentiating qualities. However, for every effort to oppose the two genders and to draw fixed and stable lines between them, the 18th-century critical spirit countered with an emblematic refusal of normalizing and constrictive systems of thought. This refusal was born out in both the philosophy of the period and in the social practices that in the end called into question any stable or essentializing understanding of gender in the Age of Enlightenment.

A clear illustration of this point is to be found in one of the Enlightenment thinkers *par excellence*, Denis **Diderot**, who in his *Elements of Physiology* assigns the female body not just anatomical difference with respect to the male body, but monstrosity in relation to her own. As a medical layman of significant erudition, Diderot's views were influenced by the case histories of the medical and surgical establishments of the day, which were themselves littered with accounts of aberrant forms of the female body, especially in its reproductive capacity or incapacity. Yet it is the same Diderot who coins one of the most ingenious Enlightenment commentaries on gender in his *D'Alembert's Dream*: "Man is perhaps but the monster of woman, and woman but the monster of man."

Indeed, the key terms for understanding medical, philosophical and social ideas concerning gender during the 18th century are those of the monstrous and the liminal, given the assumption that **nature** took up residence in an ever-shifting terrain. In the *Encyclopédie* article "Eunuch," the Valencian physician d'Aumont conflates the natural and the artificial in a meditation on the ostensibly contrary anatomical attributes that men and women possess. Absolute attributes dissipate as the body of the castrated man takes on a plethora of meanings, ranging from the gentle and soft signifiers for "woman" to the abhorrent and violent for "man." At either end of this traditionally gendered spectrum, the eunuch occupies a place of excess. Here a third gender of sorts finds itself uniquely at home in a realm informed by human intervention and artifice. In the articles "Man" and "Woman" Diderot navigates a similarly ambiguous set of characteristics that do not so much define male and female genders as set them adrift in a taxonomical system that worked against the normalizing force of its own efforts of categorization.

If the *Encyclopédie* represents a vexed repository for gender, the social practices of the 18th century illustrate a relatively egalitarian stage upon which the **Republic of Letters** played itself out. While the **cafés**, scientific **clubs** (or *musées*) excluded women, the literary **salons** of Paris and its outskirts were run by women. *Femmes de lettres* such as Mmes **Lambert**, du **Deffand**, de **Tencin**, **Geoffrin**, **Doublet**, de Brienne, **Necker** and d'**Épinay** (also sometime editor of the *Corréspondance littéraire*) were instrumental in the promotion of the careers of their male counterparts, the circulation of letters and manuscripts among philosophical and literary circles and the arbitration of an increasingly democratized form of cultural exchange that revolutionized the strict elitism of the previous century that would have excluded the likes of a Mlle de **Lespinasse**, Jean le Rond d'**Alembert** and Jean-Jacques **Rousseau** from its inner circles.

Dianah Leigh Jackson

GENLIS, Marie-Félicité du Crest, Countess (1746-1830). The daughter of an impecunious noble of Autun, Mme Genlis was both beautiful and talented. Though poorly educated, she nevertheless came to play a significant role in the high culture of her time.

Mme de Genlis was married at he age of 16 to a well-connected colonel of the Grenadiers. They became retainers in the Orléans household. When, in 1770, the Count de Genlis was made captain of the guard of the Duke d'Orléans, and his wife was appointed lady in waiting to the Duchess de Chartres and governess of the two daughters of the Duke d'Orléans, the couple moved into the **Palais Royal**. In 1782 Mme de Genlis was named governess of the Orléans princes, an exceptional honor for a woman.

The key formal role of Mme de Genlis in the Orléans household was that of tutor. In this capacity she produced two texts for the edification of her charges, *Adèle et Théodore, ou Lettres sur l'éducation* (1782), and *Veillées du château* (1784), neither of which have achieved the status of classics. She also sought to further the interests of the house of Orléans in the **salons** she attended, especially that of Mme **Necker**.

During the **French Revolution** Mme de Genlis's husband was executed as a Girondin, and she went abroad between 1793 and 1800. Her literary output is immense, but the quality is not equal to the quantity. Her *La Religion considérée comme l'unique source du* *bonheur et de la vérité* (1787) is thoroughly orthodox and reflects her consistently anti-*philosophe* outlook.

GEOFFRIN, Marie Thérèse Rodet (1699-1777). One of the most important, most generous and most traditional of the **salonnières** of the 18th century. The daughter of a valet at the Court at Versailles, Mme Geoffrin was orphaned at an early age and married when only 14 to a wealthy businessman. They had one daughter, the marquise de Ferté-Imbault, whose memoirs are a valuable source for her mother's **salon**.

Mme Geoffrin received little formal education and was without intellectual pretensions. However, her neighbor on the rue St. Honoré, Mme de **Tencin**, invited her to her salon on a regular basis, and in this way she received her apprenticeship in the demanding craft of being hostess to the social and cultural elites of Paris. When her husband died in 1749 he left her a wealthy woman. The death of Mme de Tencin the same year was the opportunity for her to continue her friend and mentor's salon in her own home.

Mme Geoffrin received artists for dinner on Mondays and men of letters on Wednesdays. Among the latter were Bernard le Bovier de **Fontenelle, Montesquieu,** Pierre Carlet de **Marivaux,** Jean-François **Marmontel,** the abbé **Morellet,** Jean le Ronde d'**Alembert,** Friedrich Melchior Grimm, Claude-Adrien **Helvétius** and the Baron d'**Holbach,** as well as distinguished foreigners who visited Paris. Mme Geoffrin was herself observant, and she kept the views expressed at her home within the bounds of good taste, gently steering discussion away from perceived dangers with the comment "Yes, yes, that is all very well." If the *philosophes* who attended her salon were limited in what they might say there, they received in return convivial company, excellent food and the cachet of respectability.

Mme Geoffrin bought canvases at prices advantageous to the artists who were admitted to her Mondays, offered generous financial help to authors who needed it, among them Denis **Diderot**, and even conferred a life pension of 3,000 *livres* on Mlle de **Lespinasse.** Through her salon and other connections Mme Geoffrin played an important part in the informal cultural politics of the time. Like other *salonnières* she played an important if unofficial role in appointments to the **Académie française**.

In addition to her salon, Mme Geoffrin also carried on extensive correspondences with **Catherine II** of Russia and Stanislas Poniatowski, King of Poland. She even visited his court, but was taken

aback at the moral looseness prevalent there. Her main contribution
to the culture of her time, however, was her salon, which brought the
social and intellectual elites together and tended to keep expressions
of advanced thought within the bounds of discretion, so conferring on
it a degree of respectability that it might otherwise have been unable
to claim.

GIBBON, Edward (1737-1774). An English gentleman and historian.
Gibbon was born to well-off gentry, but his family life bordered on
the tragic. He was the only one of seven siblings to survive, and lost
his mother when a child of nine. His father was distant and often
harsh in his relations with him.

Gibbon's early education was interrupted by frequent illnesses that
kept him away from school, but gave him ample opportunity to in-
dulge his taste for reading. He was sent to Oxford, where he decided
to abandon Anglican religious practice for Catholicism. On learning
of this decision his father sent him to Lausanne in Switzerland where
he lodged with a Protestant clergyman, read widely and with time returned to Protestantism. While in Lausanne Gibbon fell in love with
Suzanne **Curchod**, but was forbidden to marry her by his father.
Gibbon records this event with the aphorism that he sighed as a lover
and obeyed as a son. What emotions lie behind that statement one can
only guess. Mlle Curchod became Mme Necker, wife of Jacques
Necker, the Swiss banker and minister of Louis XVI, and hostess of
one of the most important **salons** of the late Enlightenment.

Gibbon returned to England in 1758, and served as captain in the
Hampshire militia from 1759 to 1763. When his father died in 1772
Gibbon was left enough money to live independently. He moved to
London, sat in **Parliament,** where he said nothing but voted with
Lord North, and pursued the life of a gentleman scholar. The first
volume of the *Decline and Fall of the Roman Empire* appeared in
1776, and was an immediate and huge success. Two more volumes
appeared in 1781. In 1783 he moved back to Lausanne where he
completed the last three volumes of this monumental work, which
were published in 1788. He returned to London where he lived with
his friend the Earl of Sheffield. Though radical in his views on religion, Gibbon was socially and politically conservative, and hostile to
the **French Revolution**.

Gibbon's first book was the *Essai sur l'étude de la littérature*,
which appeared in 1758. In addition to his great history of Rome,
Gibbon also wrote an autobiography, or rather a series of autobiogra-

phies, which reveal a remarkable consciousness of his own development.

GOETHE, Johann Wolfgang von (1749-1832). Probably the most important writer in German literature. His work expressed and helped form the outlooks of both the Enlightenment and Romantic movement in Germany and beyond. In an age of writers and thinkers of broad interests and capabilities, Goethe's literary output was remarkable for its scope and variety as well as the aesthetic standards it set.

Goethe was born in Frankfurt to an influential and cultured family. His mother was the daughter of the mayor of the city, while his father was a cultivated and leisured gentleman of independent means who, exceptionally for the time, was sufficiently interested in his children's education actively to take a hand in it himself. Goethe's formative years were thus passed in a cosmopolitan city, in comfortable circumstances and in a family that willingly provided him with the intellectual training and stimulation that helped develop his outstanding abilities.

At age 16 Goethe was sent to the University of Leipzig to study law. Like so many of his contemporaries in the same situation, he found little interest in his legal studies, devoting his time instead to literature and the arts. Because of an illness he returned to Frankfurt, but was then sent by his father to Strasbourg to finish his degree in law. This he did, and even practiced for a number of years, but the law never held his interest as a discipline or a profession.

While in Strasbourg Goethe met Johann Gottfried Herder, came to appreciate gothic architecture, was influenced by English novelists, particularly Richard **Fielding** and Laurence **Sterne**, and began to think in terms of national culture and identity. In 1771 he returned to Frankfurt, where he frequented **salons** and read Jean-Jacques **Rousseau**, Johann Georg Hamann and Herder, who together oriented him toward Romanticism. He also wrote two pamphlets on **toleration**. In 1772 he fell in love with Charlotte Buff, who was already engaged. This episode was the basis of Goethe's internationally acclaimed novel, *The Sorrows of Young Werther*, which appeared in 1774 and made his reputation.

In 1775 Goethe was invited by Carl August, Duke of Weimar, to come to his court. He did so, and until the middle of the following decade took an active part in the administration of the duchy, became good friends with the duke and led an active social and intellectual life. In 1782 he was granted a patent of nobility. Goethe's experience at Weimar was perhaps the happiest instance of cooperation between a leading intellectual and a ruler at the time. Certainly the relations of **Voltaire** with **Frederick II**, or of Denis **Diderot** with **Catherine II**, were neither so harmonious nor so fruitful. During his time in Weimar Goethe's aesthetic preferences shifted from romantic to classical, though, especially in his case, the distinction was never a neat one.

By 1786 Goethe felt that his duties at court had become overly onerous, and he left secretly for a two-year stay in Italy. On his return to Weimar, Goethe was relieved of his administrative duties, and his interests broadened to include philosophy, science and the fine arts. He studied the works of Immanuel **Kant**, Plato and Homer, became friends with such leading intellectuals as Wilhelm von Humboldt and from 1794 Johann Christoff Friedrich von Schiller, who taught at the University of Jena, over which Goethe had considerable influence. During the 1790s and until roughly 1805 Goethe, together with Schiller, Johann Gottlieb Fichte, Wilhelm Joseph Schelling and Georg Wilhelm Friedrich Hegel made of Jena and Weimar a focus not only of a vibrant, emerging German culture, but also a great European intellectual and cultural center.

Goethe's creativity never waned, though it took different forms and reflected changing interests, and for the last 20 years or so of his life he was no longer so closely integrated into the cultural life of his time as he had been. His very stature set him apart. Indeed, there was probably no other figure in the intellectual life of the time who enjoyed the sustained success and recognition that Goethe did with both men of letters and the authorities.

The literary output of Goethe is immense, and not easily classified. He made his name early with lyric poetry, plays and the short novel, *The Sorrows of Young Werther*, which, though tremendously popular in the years after its appearance, appears stilted and awkward today. The process of composition and revision of many of his major works often extended over decades. This was the case with the *Meister Wilhelm* trilogy, the first part of which was published in 1795 and 1796, the second part, *Elective Affinities*, in 1809 and the third part, *Meister Wilhelm's Travels*, in 1821. Similarly, he began writing the work that is usually regarded as his masterpiece in the 1790s, but only completed it in the year before his death. The first part of *Faust* was published in 1808, the second part in 1832. He also published a long, anti-Newtonian scientific treatise on color in 1810, but had been working on the subject for the previous 20 years.

During his early sixties Goethe wrote his autobiography, which he entitled *From My Life: Poetry and Truth* and which was published between 1811 and 1813. It was translated into English and published 10 years later as *Memoirs of Goethe, Written by Himself.* Goethe was also responsible for the discovery of Diderot's *Rameau's Nephew* and its first publication in his own German translation.

GRAFFIGNY, Françoise Paule d'Issembourg du Buisson d'Happoncourt (1695-1758). Born to a family of the nobility of the sword in Lorraine, Mme de Graffigny was married at the age of 17 to a man of suitable social standing. Her husband, who had the post of Chamberlain to the Duke of Lorraine, treated her brutally. His death in 1725 was her liberation.

When in 1738 the Dukedom of Lorraine was given to Stanislas Leszczynski, Mme de Graffigny lost the **patronage** she had until then enjoyed. She was without resources and for a time lived in the households of a number of wealthy society women, the first of whom was Mme du **Châtelet**, who at the time was also hosting **Voltaire**. In 1745 she opened her own **salon** in Paris on the rue Saint-Hyacinthe.

Mme de Graffigny also wrote a number of plays and novels. Her best known work, the *Lettres d'une Péruvienne*, first published in 1747, is a minor classic. It is in some ways an imitation of **Montesquieu**'s *Persian Letters*, but in addition to criticisms of French society by an outsider, it also contains powerful denunciations of European colonialism in the New World. Her comedy *Cénie,* which was produced in 1750, was also a success. Her other published works were not. Today Mme de Graffigny's extensive correspondence is considered her most valuable work.

GRÉGOIRE, Henri, abbé (1750-1831). A Catholic priest of the kind that gives Christianity a good name, the abbé Grégoire began his career as an erudite and humanitarian parish priest in northeastern France, and with the outbreak of the **French Revolution** became an ardent advocate of social and political change. He was elected to the Estates General to represent the clergy of his region, in which capacity he contributed significantly to keeping the movement for reform viable. Between 1790 and 1801 he served as bishop in the Constitutional Church put in place by the Revolution, and continued to sit in the revolutionary assemblies. He opposed Napoleon, and was forced into exile during his rule. His role in the Revolution made him unwelcome to the regimes of the Restoration.

Grégoire's father was a tailor of the parish of Vého in Lorraine. Though his family was not well-off, it provided him, an only child, with a warm upbringing and a sound **education**. After attending the parish school of Vého, Grégoire was taken into the private school of the *curé* of the nearby parish of Emberménil, apparently in recognition of his ability and seriousness. From 1763 to 1768 he studied at the **Jesuit** *collège* of Nancy, and though he himself was to become a firm adherent of **Jansenism**, he never spoke of his teachers other than with respect and affection. The next four years Grégoire spent studying theology at the **University** of Nancy. In 1772 he entered a seminary at Metz, and also taught in the nearby *collège* of Pont-à-Mousson. Grégoire was ordained in 1776 and received his first post immediately. In 1782 he succeeded his old teacher, the abbé Charrier, as parish priest of Emberménil.

Grégoire seems to have had a genuine vocation, and to have derived great satisfaction from his duties as *curé* of his parish. It should be borne in mind in this respect that the parish priest of the **Old Regime** was charged not only with the spiritual care of his flock, but also, in the almost complete absence of secular social assistance, with their material and social well-being. On the local level, the rural parish priest was the Old Regime's system of charity and social services. Grégoire also established a library for his parishioners that included works on practical matters such as agriculture and hygiene, as well as works of religious instruction. He seems from the beginning of his career to have been devoted both to the Enlightenment and his Church.

In many ways Grégoire appears a typical representative of the enlightened clergy. Apart from his revolutionary career, he is today best known for his concern for two oppressed minorities of his time, **Jews** and blacks. It is probably fair to see this concern as the product conjointly of the traditional Christian values of charity and care for the poor and downtrodden, and the newer enlightened values of **beneficence** and **humanity**. It may also be that as a Jansenist, and so a member of an oppressed and persecuted minority, Grégoire identified with other minorities whose treatment was in some ways similar.

Grégoire first gained a reputation among his educated compatriots as a result of his participation in essay contests set by provincial **academies**. In 1773 he won the prize set by the Academy of Nancy for an essay, *In Praise of Poetry*, which was also published, and in 1788 he shared the prize for the subject set by the Academy of Metz, "Are there means for rendering the Jews more useful and happier in

France?" In 1789 Grégoire's essay appeared with the title *Essay on the Physical, Moral and Political Regeneration of the Jews.*

This is not to say, however, that the abbé had shown interest in the condition of the Jews of northeastern France simply because they appeared as the subject for an essay contest by a local academy. Grégoire had already written on the Jews in response to an earlier contest sponsored by a philanthropical society in 1779, and in 1785, at the opening of a synagogue in Lunéville, he preached a sermon strongly advocating **toleration**. Moreover, Grégoire himself knew a number of Jews, among them Isaac Berr Bing, a leader of the local Jewish community, and he traveled in his region specifically to learn about the Jewish communities there.

As a member of the Constituent Assembly Grégoire was among the leading advocates of Jewish emancipation, which was achieved at the very end of that Assembly's tenure, in September 1791. This legislation allowed the Jews as individuals full French **citizenship**, but it refused to recognize the traditional organization of Jewish communities, which went the way of other old-regime corporations, or to make allowances for particularly Jewish customs, such as Sabbath observance. That is to say, the kind of emancipation legislated by the Constituent Assembly fell short of pluralism and recognition of the cultural integrity of religious minorities, while at the same time it made France the only state in the world to offer Jews equal civic standing and full citizenship. Citizenship was a great boon, but its price was high. This price has been demanded by all subsequent regimes in France, and remains unchanged today.

As a member of the Convention Grégoire was a forceful advocate for the abolition of **slavery** in the French colonies, a subject on which he had already begun to speak and write in 1789. Gregoire's career during and after the French Revolution, which is extremely full and important for the history of France, no doubt has its relevance to the fortunes of the Enlightenment after 1789. The abbé's personality and values, however, were formed well before then, and provide a case of a harmonious blending of Enlightenment and traditional Catholic values that were, in exceptional circumstances, able to find expression not only in theory, but also in practice.

GREUZE, Jean-Baptiste (1725-1805). An important genre painter whose popularity was eclipsed long before his death. Greuze's father was a master roofer, and like most members of the working classes hoped that his son would study something practical. He finally agreed to him beginning an apprenticeship to a painter in Lyon. Greuze later returned to Paris, where he followed lessons of the **Royal Academy of Painting**. In 1755 he was admitted to the Academy, and in 1769, by which time he had achieved fame, he became a full member. However, it was from roughly this time that his popularity began to fail. He lost his fortune during the **French Revolution,** and was reduced to giving lessons to make a living.

Greuze is one of the painters of the 18th century for whom it is difficult for modern viewers of his work to feel sympathy. This is largely because the paintings for which he is most famous, and was most appreciated in his own time, are today thought to be maudlin, overstated and melodramatic. Greuze typically sought to portray scenes of domestic concord and the unheroic virtues, usually in rustic settings. His paintings of this sort include *A Father Reading the Bible to His Children* (1755), *Village Betrothal* (1761), *The Paralytic Tended by His Children* (1761) and *The Wicked Son Punished* (1765/1778). Goodness and harmony are much more difficult to portray convincingly than conflict and evil, which seem to be, for whatever reason, more inherently interesting.

What led Greuze to attempt the portrayal of humble virtues among simple folk? As a participant in Enlightenment culture, Greuze read Denis **Diderot** and Jean-Jacques **Rousseau** on the function of art, and sought to put into practice what they preached. He sought to give art a moral function, and to represent **sentiment** in images. And his work did strike a responsive chord with contemporaries. Many of his compositions were engraved, thus reaching a far wider audience than they could have by being exhibited alone. Diderot praised him without restraint. In a way, Greuze is to painting of the Enlightenment what Samuel **Richardson** is to its literature, and one might apply to the viewing of Greuze what Dr. **Johnson** said of the reading of Richardson: "if you were to read Richardson for the story, your impatience would be so much fretted that you would hang yourself. But you must read him for the sentiment" (*Life of Johnson*, p. 480).

A turning point in Greuze's career came when in 1769 he exhibited an historical painting of *Septimus Severus and Caracalla*, in which the father rebuked the son. Contemporaries did not like it, and Greuze was so taken aback at the criticism that he did not exhibit at the Salon again. The picture is in a Roman setting, and the rendering more restrained than in his paintings portraying the common people. In many ways this canvas seems neoclassical. Certainly the 1769 painting has the same moral emphasis that is found in his genre pictures. It would seem that either the public was not yet ready for **Neoclassicism**, or Greuze did not have the ability to excel in that style as well as the one in which he made his name.

In his later years Greuze turned his hand to historical and mythological subjects, though without much success. Throughout his career he produced a series of portraits that are still appreciated, and which included, in addition to members of his family, the Dauphin and Fabre de l'Eglantine. Though the genre paintings for which he is most famous are now generally held in low esteem, if we do not appreciate what contemporaries found compelling and moving in them, we miss an important element of Enlightenment sensibility.

GRUB STREET. A street in London where, during the 18th century, the less elevated and more dependent sectors of the literary profession were concentrated. Usually employed on specific projects by publishers or booksellers, the writers of this milieu produced the translations, almanachs, reference works, pamphlets, chapbooks, histories, compilations of travelers' tales and other varieties of hackwork that fed the appetite of an expanding reading public. Publishers, as entrepreneurs, often became rich from the proceeds of such work, while most of the writers engaged in it barely managed to keep body and soul together.

There were writers and thinkers of exceptional ability, such as Denis **Diderot** and Samuel **Johnson**, who succeeded, by dint of hard work and talent, to write their way out of the harsh milieu of Grub Street. Such writers were few. For the most part, the hacks who produced what the booksellers wanted at the prices the booksellers and publishers were willing to pay were as surely caught in a poverty trap as were unskilled laborers who possessed no property.

The French equivalent of Grub Street has been analyzed with exceptional skill and insight by Robert **Darnton**. In addition to describing the basic conditions of a poor and dependent class of intellectuals, Darnton has added important psychological, social and political dimensions to his treatment of the inhabitants of the Parisian equivalent of Grub Street. He has argued that young provincials coming to the capital to make their careers in literature were well-intentioned, idealistic, and probably naïve in their expectations of the openness of the **Republic of Letters** of which they hoped to become a part.

Most failed to produce the books that would have won them the recognition and status they craved, and access to the world of **salons** and **academies**, sinecures and pensions to which they aspired. To live they had to accept whatever commissions booksellers or publishers were willing to give them, and their poverty was aggravated by the surveillance of the police. If they drifted into crime, which was all too likely, or simply from a need for money, the inhabitants of Grub Street could be recruited as police spies and made to work on behalf of a regime they despised.

Suffering economic deprivation, professional frustration and falling self-esteem, their idealism eroded, and being excluded from the cultural world to which they believed they deserved to belong, the writers of Grub Street were reduced to impotence and rage. According to Darnton, they "hated the **Old Regime** in their guts" and "ached with hatred of it" (*Literary Underground*, p. 40). They expressed this rage and hatred in *libelles*, vicious pamphlets often combining pornography and political criticism, to discredit and delegitimize the regime that had debased them.

Normally the suffering of impecunious intellectuals is part of the human misery routinely generated in hierarchical and inegalitarian societies. But France during the 1770s and 1780s was exceptional. It was a society about to undergo fundamental social and political change. Darnton has plausibly argued that the frustrations and hatreds engendered by Grub Street, together with a certain residual idealism, fed into the radical and egalitarian revolutionary sentiment of such former victims of the culture of Grub Street as Jean-Paul Marat and Jacques-Pierre Brissot.

GUILDS. In the 18th century a guild, called *corporation* in France, was an association of craftsmen with a written charter of by-laws and legal **privileges**. Each craft—carpenters, glassmakers, metalsmiths, weavers, butchers, grocers, tailors, printers, etc.—had its own guild, and its members were fiercely loyal to their own association or brotherhood. There were guilds for master craftsmen who owned their own shops, and guilds for journeymen, artisans who had not yet presented their masterpiece to a board of examiners (not unlike graduate students in our universities).

The guild provided three primary services to its members—ceremonial, welfare and working conditions. The ceremonial aspects were important. The guild was a quasi-religious brotherhood that performed Catholic mass (or communion service in Protestant countries) before each assembly, prescribed elaborate initiation rites and organized festivals, processions and banquets. It had a complex code of secret signs and communication, not unlike a modern fraternal association. Welfare consisted of a dense network of "mother houses" or hostels, where journeymen could lodge during mandatory training tours in different regions of the country. This "lodging" included free meals, mutual aid in case of illness, accident or destitution, and common funds for proper burials.

Working conditions could be a source of dispute between masters and journeymen. Masters' guilds attempted to enforce work rules and quality controls and to prevent work stoppages; journeymen's guilds attempted to improve working conditions, increase the prices paid for their product and expand leisure time, which they often preferred to higher pay. Although strikes were illegal in the 18th century, work stoppages to protest working conditions did occur and the journeymen's guilds had the potential of becoming modern labor unions.

Guilds had existed in the towns of Europe since the 12th century and would last in many regions until the 19th century. However, already in the 18th century administrators, wholesale merchants and economists began to question the usefulness of the guild structure. As economies grew, guild regulations tended to limit labor mobility, raise unit costs and block innovation. An economic policy of "*laissez-faire*," which tended to base all entrepreneurial decisions on market forces, gained acceptance, especially in Britain and France. The guilds were weakened in France in 1776 and died out in Britain even earlier. They persisted in the small towns of central and southern Europe until the late 19th century. Many of the welfare functions of the guilds were adopted by modern labor parties.

Robert Forster

H

HAPPINESS. A condition of moral and physical well-being. In antiquity happiness was given philosophical justification by Epicurus and his followers, but was not regarded as a prime good by either Plato, who emphasized transcendental values, or Aristotle, in whose views science and civil responsibilities were more important.

Early Christianity took over Plato's emphasis on the spiritual and other-worldly. Influenced by a particularly negative reading of the Fall of man, the mainstream Christian tradition not only devalued the material world and its pleasures, but also regarded them as obstacles to achieving the supreme good, which was, of course, salvation of one's immortal soul. It is in this context that the rehabilitation of happiness by the thinkers of the Enlightenment should be seen.

The revaluation of happiness as a legitimate aspiration for human beings is part of a broader shift from the metaphysical to the material and the empirical, and from a spiritual to a generally this-worldly outlook, that occurred over the 18th century. The aspiration to comfort, which for a Carthusian monk in the Middle Ages would have been negatively valued, came to be viewed as reasonable and positive. As intellectuals came to understand, accept and appreciate the material world, so they came to feel more at home in it, and to aspire to a greater degree of material comfort.

Utilitarians defined happiness in terms of pleasure and pain. It should be noted, however, that in the 18th century happiness still had an important moral and other-regarding component, and though it included pleasure or fun, it also implied considerably more. The argument that happiness could be reduced to physical sensation was a kind of *reductio ad absurdam* of this idea that we find among critics of the Enlightenment, such as the Marquis de **Sade** or the Nephew in *Rameau's Nephew*, and rarely if ever among its exponents.

Happiness is the subject of one of the major thematic monographs devoted to Enlightenment thought by Robert Mauzi.

HEAVENLY CITY OF THE EIGHTEENTH-CENTURY PHI-LOSOPHERS, THE. The title of a short book calling into question certain basic assumptions about the progressiveness of the Enlightenment published by Carl Becker (1873-1945), a leading historian who taught at Cornell University.

The early 1930s was a remarkably fruitful time for Enlightenment studies. Ernst **Cassirer**'s *The Philosophy of the Enlightenment* appeared in 1932, as did Becker's *Heavenly City*. Daniel **Mornet**'s *Les Origines intellectuelles de la Révolution française* was published in 1933, and was followed by Paul Hazard's *La Crise de la conscience européenne*, translated as *The European Mind*, in 1934-1935. All have become classics of Enlightenment historiography. Of these four books, Becker's is the one that doesn't fit with the rest. Cassirer, Mornet and Hazard all sought to present comprehensive views of what the Enlightenment was, and all tended to view the movement as progressive. Becker, by contrast, focused on a few key issues and argued that the Enlightenment was not really the gateway to modernity as was generally believed.

Historians who see the Enlightenment as progressive do so largely because for them it represents the transition from a theological or enchanted worldview to a secular one, and because it asserted individual autonomy against the collectivist demands of church, state and corporation. Becker focused on different criteria. He regarded the key move in the shift to modernity the abandonment of systems of thought that posited objective realities in favor of others that instead assumed unlimited subjectivity and relativity. In philosophical terms, this shift can be described as the rejection of a correspondence theory of truth for voluntarism.

The correspondence theory of truth maintains that objective truths exist independently of observers, and that it is the task of philosophers, or other thinkers, such as theologians, to coordinate their views of the world with objective external realities. In this sense, Becker argued, Thomas Aquinas and **Voltaire** (and, we might add, Fox Mulder) held the same basic assumptions about the world. The truth, whatever forms it may take, is out there: we need only search it out, and it is assumed that we are capable of carrying out such investigations appropriately, and of recognizing the truth when we find it. By contrast, voluntarism maintains that there is no truth independent of the perceptions and desires of the person or persons perceiving, thinking or desiring. It is will that determines and defines reality, which now comes to be seen as subjective and relative. For the voluntarist, truth as a notion has no validity, and is demoted to the status of a kind of preference.

With the rise of **nationalism** in the 19th century it became common for one national or ethnic group to assert its superiority, however defined, over others without regard to objective criteria. Romanticism reinforced the appeal to **sentiment** and validated group association. For thinkers such as Arthur Schopenhauer and Friedrich Nietzsche, will, idea and desire were the dominant categories. The applications of such views could result in murder being conceived merely as a game, as in the case dramatized in the film *Compulsion*, or in the brutal and irrational politics of fascism and Nazism. Seen against such phenomena, Becker seemed to suggest, the Enlightenment was moderate and far from threatening, and it was not so very daring intellectually after all.

Better to believe that the truth is out there, and, the skeptics notwithstanding, that with the proper intentions and methodologies we can find and recognize it, than to posit that truth is simply an illusion and our unregulated personal and collective wills the prime reality. On the basis of its belief in objective criteria of individual and social well-being, the Enlightenment could and did plan reforms to assure greater productivity, fairer distribution, improved government efficiency and due process. Whatever the metaphysical status of such changes, they reflect an aspiration to reduce human suffering and increase human dignity. This was something that could not be said of the extreme nationalisms and irrational, violent and relativist ethics already prominent in the 1930s, and to which Becker was in all likelihood reacting.

Becker's *Heavenly City* had been through 11 editions by 1957, and was the subject of a colloquium held at Colgate University in 1956, the papers from which were edited by Raymond O. Rockwood under the title *Carl Becker's Heavenly City Revisited* (1958). The subject that Becker raises, the relation of the Enlightenment to modernity, is still relevant, and has received considerable attention since his book first appeared. The "dark narrative of Enlightenment," which derives from the analysis of Theodor Adorno and Max Horkheimer in their *Dialectic of Enlightenment*, and the postmodernist view, which rejects notions of objectivity and fixed determination, both take a harsher view of intellectual developments in the 18th century than did Becker. *See also* **Enlightenment, Dark Narrative.**

HELVÉTIUS, Claude Adrien (1715-1771). One of the most audacious thinkers of the Enlightenment. His book *De l'Esprit* (1758) ranks among the clearest and most forceful statements of materialist philosophy of the time. Taking up the basic theses of John **Locke's** *Essay Concerning Human Understanding*, he analyzed human behavior in purely utilitarian terms. His analysis of nature was mechanistic. Curiously for so radical a work, *De l'Esprit* was published with the approval of a censor who saw in it only a work of science and philosophy. The authorities soon reversed themselves, with the royal council, the *Parlement* of Paris, the Sorbonne and the Archbishop of Paris all condemning the work, and the author was forced to retract the views expressed in it. That the retraction was the effect of coercion rather than conviction is apparent from the posthumous publication of *De l'Homme* (1772) in which Helvétius expressed much the same views as he had in *De l'Esprit*. These works remain classic statements of Enlightenment materialism, but were not convincing even to all materialist philosophers of the time. Denis **Diderot** wrote, but did not publish, a criticism of *De l'Esprit* in which he brought attention to some of the main philosophical weaknesses of the book.

Helvétius is an example of an author who combined theoretical radicalism with high social status and great wealth. Though from a family of successful doctors, Helvétius pursued a career in public finance as a *fermier général*, or director, of one of the cartels that collected indirect taxes for the government. He retired in his mid-thirties to devote himself to study and writing and congenial society, dividing his time, like a comfortable noble, between his country estate and the capital. Together with his wife, Anne Catherine de **Ligniville**, he hosted an important **salon**.

HÉNAULT, Charles Jean François (1685-1770). An important magistrate of the *Parlement* of Paris and man of letters. His most important literary work was the *Abrégé chronologique de l'histoire de la France* (1744), but he also wrote plays and essays for contests set by academies. Very much a member of the cultural and intellectual elite, Hénault was elected to the **Académie française** (1723), was a regular participant in many of the **salons** of the capital, particularly that of Mme du **Deffand**, with whom he enjoyed a long and stable relationship, and later in life became a member of the royal court. Apparently under the influence of a good woman, Mme de Castelmoron, he returned to religious orthodoxy, which was, for intellectuals of the period, rather unusual. His memoirs, which give a good account of the elite culture of the time, are generally regarded as his most interesting work.

HIDDEN HAND. A metaphor used to explain a paradox in liberal economic theory. The paradox is that single-minded pursuit of **self-interest** is assumed to result in optimal benefit for society as a whole. Individual self-interest is said to be moderated by the mechanism of the market, which is presumably kept on track by a "hidden hand."

This metaphor was used occasionally by Adam **Smith**, but only casually. The phrase seems to allude to the way Isaac **Newton** solved a problem in his celestial mechanics.

Due to the imperfect data available to him, Newton found through his calculations that the orbits of the planets were not quite regular, so that eventually the equilibrium of the solar system would break down and the planets would go shooting off in all directions. Why, Newton asked, had this not yet occurred? Because, the theologically orthodox scientist asserted, the Divine hand intervened when necessary to put the planets back into their proper orbits. Thus at one stroke Newton was able to explain the workings of the stars and planets, and to avoid the embarrassment of a superfluous Deity.

For Newton, whose data indicated that the equilibrium of the solar system would break down if left to itself, the hypothesis of Divine intervention served to explain an observed phenomenon. With more accurate data, the feared coming apart of the solar system ceased to be a threat, and there was no longer a need for the Divine to lend a hand from time to time.

Adam Smith and his followers thought of the marketplace as a self-regulating mechanism analogous to Newton's celestial mechanics. Self-interest was the force that drove the market mechanism, and by rewarding industry and intelligence, arranged all things economic in the best way possible. That the market rewarded those with commodities that were in demand was obvious. That those whose labor or goods were not in demand did well from this system is less obvious.

The hidden hand, with its theological and scientific connotations, was invoked to underwrite the overall efficiency and benignity of the unregulated, yet self-regulating, market. This was less a matter of clarification than of mystification. The hidden hand is probably the most powerful and longest-lived myth that we have taken over from the **Enlightenment**.

How people view the hidden hand depends on how they have been treated by it. Let us say that Jones goes to his bank, and finds that his account has $10,000 more in it than expected. Being an honest fellow, he brings this discrepancy to the attention of the bank manager. The bank manager checks the account, and is pleased to inform Jones that the balance is correct. The hidden hand has intervened in Jones's favor. Most probably Jones would have felt well disposed toward the author of his unexpected prosperity.

Let us now assume that two weeks later Jones again visits his bank, but this time is told by a soulful manager that his account is overdrawn by $10,000, and offered the explanation, "the hidden hand, you know." Likely, Jones's attitude to said appendage would change significantly.

Metaphors and mystifications are usually short-lived in the natural sciences. In more imprecise areas of study, and in ideology, they tend to do better. The metaphor of the hidden hand is a case in point.

HISTORICAL AND CRITICAL DICTIONARY/DICTIONNAIRE HISTORIQUE ET CRITIQUE. Written by Pierre **Bayle** and published in 1697, this erudite work, replete with quotations in Greek and Latin and comprising four or five folio volumes, became one of the most popular and influential works of the Enlightenment. It had been through nine French editions, three English ones and one German edition by 1750, and Daniel **Mornet** found it to be the most commonly owned book in the catalogs of libraries of the second half of the 18th century, occurring 288 times in the 500 catalogues examined. ("Les Enseignements des biliothèques privées"). There is also evidence of heavy use of the work in public libraries.

Bayle, who was among the most learned men of his time, originally got the idea of writing this work in order to correct the errors he found in *Le Grand Dictionnaire historique* of Louis Moreri, first published in 1674. While he went beyond this plan to produce a historical work organized around hundreds of biographies of figures, many of them thoroughly obscure, from classical antiquity to his own time, the critical enterprise of uncovering sources and pointing out errors and inconsistencies was retained.

In format Bayle's great folio volumes reflect the erudition of the humanistic and theological traditions on which he drew. A typical page has a few lines of text in French at the top, usually consisting of straightforward narrative, and beneath them appear, in twin columns and in smaller print, notes or comments, which often include quotations in Greek and Latin, and raise questions about, in the process often subverting, the text to which they refer. In the ample margins are scattered bibliographic references to the thousands upon thousands of volumes of classical scholarship, theology and history which Bayle had read and could conjure up at will. The visual effect of the pages of the *Historical and Critical Dictionary*, while intricate, complex and esthetically intriguing, reflects a tradition that has reached maturity and perhaps exhausted itself. It was a book produced by an exceptionally erudite scholar for a community of the learned. From a modern point of view it is surprising how extensive that was.

The content of Bayle's dictionary is almost infinitely varied, treating the Hebrew Bible, the history and culture of classical antiquity and the history and theology of Christianity down to his own time. Nevertheless, certain themes recur. There are repeated demonstrations, in the form of contradictions within sources, uncertainty of testimony, gaps in chains of tradition and inherent improbability, that absolute certainty is not to be had in history. And where facts cannot be known, unaided speculation is worse than useless. There is a tendency to separate theology from morality, and a preference for the latter over the former. The article "David" suggests that whatever his status in the Jewish and Christian traditions, King David's ethics would not be tolerated in any decent society, while the article **"Spinoza"** conversely shows that however absurd his philosophy, Benedict Spinoza's personal morality was above reproach. Similarly, an article devoted to the utterly obscure Reformation sectarian Thomas Knuzen, whose theology outraged any orthodoxy, but whose ethical teachings were (though Bayle implies this without saying it explicitly) compatible with those of primitive Christianity, underscores the independence of ethics from dogma.

What the *Historical and Critical Dictionary* showed was that faith should be restricted to those areas of life above or beyond **reason**, and that the two spheres were not compatible. In the sphere of reason, however that was defined, reason was sovereign. And within that sphere all things were to be approached critically and factually.

This message was adopted readily by the *philosophes* of the Enlightenment. However, the broader reading public emerging over the 18th century was not always inclined to take the *Historical and Critical Dictionary* neat. **Voltaire**, among others, adhered to Bayle's spirit, but eliminated his heavy scholarly apparatus, wrote in a more graceful style, had his ideas packaged in convenient, pocket-sized editions, and so made more generally available the basic outlook, as well as many of Bayle's values, in works such as the *Philosophical Dictionary*. The *Encyclopédie*, too, popularized Bayle's outlook, though where the *Historical and Critical Dictionary* discreetly tucked away many of its most radical ideas in footnotes, the writers of the *Encyclopédie*, doing without the labyrinthine notes beloved by Bayle, often put them in unlikely places, then directed readers to them by cross-references. The system of cross-references, however, was already well developed in the *Historical and Critical Dictionary*.

HISTORY. There was a tendency among teachers of history during the 18th century, many of whom taught at the secondary level, to treat history as a branch of ethics. Even the great historians of the Enlightenment, such as Edward **Gibbon**, William **Robertson**, David **Hume** and **Voltaire**, sought to draw a lesson or point a moral more frequently than do academic historians today. Though it is probably inaccurate to ascribe an excessive optimism or a naïve faith in **progress** to thinkers as knowledgeable and disabused as those just mentioned, it is fair to say that the Enlightenment expected more in the way of guidance from history than we do today.

A criticism widely made of Enlightenment historiography is that, because of its belief in a uniform **human nature**, it tended to favor the universal, and often missed, or denied, the significance of the particular. In other words, by looking for general laws and tendencies, it failed to come to grips with the lived realities and specific value systems of different societies, which are often viewed as the real stuff of history. This criticism, which was leveled against the Enlightenment by the Romantic and nationalist thinkers of the 19th century, has several weaknesses.

First, in treating history or society, there is an irreducible tension between the general and the particular. The criticism of 19th century nationalists that Enlightenment historiography fails to appreciate the particularity of specific societies and cultures may just as well reflect the tendency of these critics to undervalue things that human beings as human beings have in common. This shortcoming commonly occurs in nationalist or racist historiographies. Belief in a common human nature, and with it a value of **humanity**, is not necessarily incompatible with sound history.

A second reservation concerning the ability of Enlightenment historians to deal adequately with societies fundamentally different from their own is the fact that they did so repeatedly and well. Pierre **Bayle**, Edward Gibbon and Voltaire, to name but a few, saw and appreciated the fundamental differences between the pagan civilizations of classical antiquity and the norms and values of Christianity with great clarity. They all, to greater or lesser degrees, were critical of Christian civilization and of religious sectarian violence, at which **Jews** and Christians excelled, and emphasized the incompatibility of Christianity with civic responsibility.

These were judgments of value on their part, not blind spots in their treatment of history. But then the notion of history and historians who are without (or above) values is itself a myth usually propagated by historians who are reticent about the values they hold and the role of these values in their writing of history.

***HISTORY OF ORACLES/HISTOIRE DES ORACLES* (1687).** The year that Isaac **Newton**'s *Principia* appeared, Bernard de **Fontenelle** published a short, accessible historical study, the *History of Oracles*, which, in its own, more modest way, has a claim to be regarded as a founding work of the Enlightenment.

The *History of Oracles* contributed to the project of demystification and disenchantment by undertaking to show that the oracles of pagan antiquity, far from having a demonic origin, were a form of deception and manipulation practiced by the priestly classes on the ignorant. Pagan oracles did not cease with the advent of Christianity for the simple reason that the new religion did not, unhappily, bring an immediate end to either human manipulativeness or human folly.

Fontenelle's argument here is in keeping with the historical and critical trends of Enlightenment thought, but it is also profoundly unoriginal. The argument, in fact, Fontenelle had found intact in a Latin treatise by the Dutch scholar Antonius Van Dale. Fontenelle's innovation here was not in originating a theory or argument, but in taking these things from another scholar, transposing them from the closed field of humanistic scholarship and making them available to the lay readership of his time, a readership that included both women and men without training in the classical languages. Simply put, Fontenelle took a weighty Latin treatise of more than 500 pages octavo first published in 1683 (and nearly 700 quarto pages in its second edition of 1700) and rendered its progressive key ideas much more briefly in lucid, readily accessible French.

Pierre **Bayle**'s *Historical and Critical Dictionary* was a work that attracted virtually all the serious thinkers of the Enlightenment, but it could not reach a wide public in the form in which it was written. Fontenelle's *History of Oracles*, by contrast, was readily accessible to a broad readership from the day it was published. Indeed, it was probably the first major work of the Enlightenment intentionally geared to popularization.

HOLBACH, Paul Henri Thiry, Baron d' (1723-1789). One of the most radical and militant of Enlightenment thinkers. Holbach produced a large number of materialist and anti-Christian tracts, among them the *Système de la nature* (1770), which Robert **Darnton** has shown to be among the top clandestine best sellers of the late **Old Regime**. Most of these works were published anonymously in Holland, and exceptionally, the secret of their authorship was kept from contemporaries.

Holbach's philosophy was rigorously materialistic in that he denied the existence of anything other than matter and motion. Unlike other materialists of the 18th century, such as the Marquis de **Sade**, or of later periods, Holbach found no difficulty in combining his materialism with a profoundly moral view of man and the world. Like Jean-Jacques **Rousseau** he conceived **nature** as **beneficent**. Indeed, in the *Système de la nature* he comes close to deifying it. Nor did his utilitarian ethics require more than a demonstration of a general tendency in living creatures to avoid pain and to seek pleasure. Yet this view of the world and of man as subjected to unvarying laws of physics and biology is ennobled by what Basil Willey has called "the passion for human improvement" (*The Eighteenth Century Background*, p. 167).

Born in Germany, Holbach was raised in Paris by an uncle who left him both his title of baron and wealth enough to live in the manner of a great lord. A considerable portion of this wealth he used to further collective projects of the Enlightenment. In his Paris residence he hosted the most important all-male **salon** of the time. The absence of women and their requirements of decorum allowed for more radical and potentially disconcerting exchanges of ideas than was the norm in most salons. At his country estate of Grandval Holbach generously received his philosophical friends. The tenor of life there has been memorably described by Denis **Diderot** in his letters. Holbach played a key role in popularizing by print radical criticisms of the Bible and of Christianity that had circulated clandestinely in manuscript during the first part of the century (*see* **Clandestine Manuscripts**). His most important contribution to this literature was *Le Christianisme dévoilé*, or *Christianity Unmasked* (1761), which appeared under the name of a recently deceased friend. Holbach also contributed hundreds of articles to the ***Encyclopédie***, which is often regarded as the flagship of the Enlightenment cultural project.

Holbach is an example of an Enlightenment intellectual who combined high social status and great wealth with radical ideas. He informally provided the material conditions, financial support and direction for collective intellectual projects typical of the modern research institute.

HUMAN NATURE. A fixed core of common characteristics shared by all human beings. From the later 19th century the apparently limitless ability of human beings to adapt to different cultures, the powers of societies to acculturate their young to the most diverse values and the difficulty of agreeing on the features that constituted human nature led many social thinkers to deny the notion altogether. This is a fairly modern position.

In traditional Christian theology human nature is taken as uniform, but also as irremediably corrupted by the Fall, and consequently vicious. However, it is redeemable through the ministrations of the Church. We find a secularized version of this outlook in thinkers such as Machiavelli and Thomas Hobbes, who observed the social and political behavior of men, and found them to be radically selfish, passion-driven, avaricious and violent. During the Renaissance there were also those who, like Pico della Mirandola in his *Oration on the Dignity of Man*, regarded human nature as indeterminate. The notion of human nature as fundamentally good was developed during the Enlightenment.

Notions of human nature are usually closely connected to assumptions about nature itself. In an interpretation of the world influenced by Charles Darwin, conflict and struggle are taken as the norms. The Newtonian view of physics, which found the world to be ordered in a lawful, simple and harmonious fashion, inclined toward the expectation that human behavior could also properly be so ordered, and indeed had a natural tendency in this direction. And in the basically physiological view of man predominant in the Enlightenment, human beings are relieved of the weight of original sin, and the bases laid for a view of human nature that justifies **individualism** moderated by **reason** and respect for others. **Nature**, and the Creator of nature, the Supreme Being or Divine Artificer, who informed nature with its own rationality and **beneficence** (*see* **Argument from Design**) was perceived in the 18th century as harmonious and beneficent, and so too was human nature. But getting at this nature was no simple matter.

In the *Second Discourse*, Jean-Jacques **Rousseau** sought to demonstrate that the behavior of his contemporaries reflected the demands and pressures imposed by an imperfect civil order, and that discovering the true character of human nature required moving back in time to a condition before socialization could have influenced the basic proclivities of human nature. Rousseau proceeded by stripping away layers of socializing and civilizing influence until he arrived at a humanoid creature without society, culture or language, and that for him represented mankind in its primal—and hence true—condition. The characteristics that this creature received from nature were an inclination toward self-preservation, and a physiologically grounded aversion to seeing other creatures suffer. Living in isolation from other members of his own species, this primal humanoid was also characterized by independence. There was nothing evil or hurtful in human nature so understood, and Rousseau did not hesitate to describe it as good. **Voltaire**, who disagreed with Rousseau on many things, agreed with him on this.

HUMANITY/*HUMANITÉ*. An abstract noun that in contemporary usage refers to the collectivity of all human beings, but in the 18th century was also taken as a value and a moral imperative.

As one of the key values of the Enlightenment, *humanité* asserted a fundamental kinship of all people and demanded that all human beings be approached with respect and treated according to basic standards of fairness and decency.

Care for others and compassion obviously did not originate with the Enlightenment, but the assumption that we owe such care and compassion to people to whom we are not related and with whom we share no common ties of nationality or religion probably is. Certainly, recognizing the integrity and dignity of other human beings on the basis of their physiological organization, more or less as the basic assumptions of John **Locke**'s view of man requires, is not a position that we find clearly articulated and widely accepted before the Enlightenment. The value of humanity shows the Enlightenment in a universalist and ethically responsible light. But of course humanity remained at the time an ideal to which to aspire much more than a value that had been realized.

That ethnocentrism and economic **self-interest** often caused the demands of humanity to be ignored during the 18th century is only too clearly a matter of record. That this value was used by the thinkers of the Enlightenment as a criterion by which to judge such institutions as **slavery** or exceptionally harsh legal sanctions is as clearly a matter of fact. **Voltaire**, for example, could both denounce the exploitation and abuse of black slaves on sugar **plantations** (*Candide*, chap. 19; interestingly, the case cited here is that of the Dutch colony of Surinam, and not of the equally reprehensible French colonies of the Caribbean) and express views that were clearly racist (*Essay on Manners*, chaps. 1, 141 and 145). But with Voltaire, as with most of the thinkers of the Enlightenment, the ethical imperative of *humanité* took precedence over flawed anthropology.

HUME, David (1711-1776). Scottish gentleman, essayist, historian and philosopher, and one of the few thinkers of the Enlightenment to make a lasting contribution to Western philosophy.

Hume was the youngest of three children born to a family of the Scottish gentry, which owned an estate at Ninewells near Berwick-upon-Tweed. He was sent to the **University** of Edinburgh for his secondary **education** when 12 years old. Since his older brother would inherit the family estate, Hume had to consider how to make a living. Like so many families looking for profitable employment for their children, Hume's chose the law. And like so many thinkers and writers of the Enlightenment, Hume could not endure the tedium of legal studies, and turned instead to letters. Hume had the advantage over many of his contemporaries who were about to begin a literary career of having a small but still valuable annuity at his disposal. Though it required time, he eventually achieved both fame and considerable fortune.

For a gentleman, Hume had a checkered career. It is a remarkable irony that Hume, who is today studied intensively in university philosophy departments, twice tried, and on both occasions failed, to get university appointments, largely because his religious views were suspect. The Universities of Edinburgh and Glasgow are probably both still kicking themselves. Instead, Hume took positions, usually thanks to the recommendations of well-placed friends and relatives. In this way, altogether typical of the time, he became a clerk in a company dealing in sugar; a tutor; secretary on a military expedition headed by a relative; aide-de-camp to the same relative in a military embassy to Vienna; librarian to the Faculty of Advocates of Edinburgh; and secretary to the British ambassador in Paris.

On his return from Paris in 1766 Hume offered Jean-Jacques **Rousseau** refuge in England, and did his best to provide him with comfortable conditions in which to live and work. Rousseau was initially appreciative of Hume's considerable efforts on his behalf, but, apparently as the result of paranoia, came to view his well-intentioned friend as part of an elaborate conspiracy against him. The result was a highly publicized quarrel between two of the leading thinkers of the Enlightenment, something that conservatives and opponents of the *philosophes* savored. By 1769 Hume was able to return to Edinburgh, where he settled with his sister in the New Town with a more than comfortable income, much of it derived from his writings.

As an author, Hume tended to do things backwards. His great work of philosophy, *A Treatise of Human Nature: Being an Attempt to Introduce the Experimental Method of Reasoning into Moral Subjects* (1739-1740), was the product of his earlier years. A large and difficult, though beautifully written book, which has since achieved the status of a classic, it was an utter failure when it first appeared, though it does seem to have set Thomas **Reid**, then minister in a rural parish near Aberdeen, on the road to philosophy. Feeling that his book failed largely because of poor presentation, Hume reworked the *Treatise*, publishing its main arguments in the shorter and more attractive *An Enquiry Concerning Human Understanding* (1748) and *An Enquiry Concerning the Principles of Morals* (1751). He also published a series of essays on economics, politics, religion and literary criticism. These essays, elegantly written and incisive, first won him widespread recognition. However, it was his *History of England*, published in six volumes between 1754 and 1762, beginning with the Stuarts and working back to the Roman period, that assured both his fame and fortune.

While it is certain that Hume adhered to no officially established religion, scholars are divided on whether he was a skeptical **deist** or an atheist. He refrained from publishing one of his more controversial works, *Dialogues Concerning Natural Religion*, during his lifetime from concern about orthodox reactions.

Hume had the reputation of being particularly sociable, pleasant and good-humored. His devoted lifelong friend, Adam **Smith**, wrote of him: "Upon the whole, I have always considered him, both in his life-time, and since his death, as approaching as nearly to the idea of a perfectly wise and virtuous man, as perhaps the nature of human frailty will admit." (Letter to William Strahan, 9 November 1776).

HUTCHESON, Francis (1694-1746). One of the key figures of the early Scottish Enlightenment, important particularly for his development of the notion of "moral sense."

Hutcheson was born in Ireland, where his father was a Presbyterian minister. His early **education** was seen to by his grandfather, also a Presbyterian minister, and then by the schoolmasters of private schools. In 1710 he was sent to the **University** of Glasgow, where he studied for the ministry until about 1717. He returned to Ireland but instead of following the family tradition and going into the Church, he opened a private school in Dublin, and published a number of essays on esthetics and ethics. Among the works he published between 1725 and 1728 is *An Inquiry into the Original of our Ideas of Beauty and Virtue, in two treatises, in which the Principles of the late Earl of Shaftesbury are examined and defended against the author of the "Fable of the Bees" and the "Ideas of Moral Good and Evil" are established, according to the Sentiments of the Ancient Moralists, with an attempt to introduce a mathematical calculation on subjects of Morality*, the title of which gives a good idea of his philosophical concerns.

In 1729, on the basis of his publications, his success as a teacher and through family contacts, Hutcheson was offered the chair of moral philosophy at the University of Glasgow. He accepted and filled it with distinction until his death in 1746. Though his style of writing lacks grace, Hutcheson was an outstanding lecturer noted not only for his eloquence, but also for his kind and warm manner. Like many others in the Scottish universities, his career offers an outstanding example of the bond between Enlightenment and higher education, something that was lacking in France and England, but not in Holland or Germany. The chair in moral philosophy at Glasgow was filled from its inception in 1727 until the 1780s by a series of exceptional and enlightened men: Gersom Carmichael occupied it before Hutcheson, Adam **Smith** and Thomas **Reid** after him.

Hutcheson's main contribution to the thought of the Enlightenment was his elaboration of a doctrine first put forward by the Earl of **Shaftesbury**, namely, that of a moral sense, which served for him, and for other thinkers of the time, such as David **Hume** and Adam Smith, as a basis from which to contest the view of morality based on **self-interest**. This might be individualistic and self-centered, as with Thomas Hobbes and Bernard **Mandeville**, but also theological, as with Archibald **Campbell**. Though Hutcheson was probably the first to use the phrase "the greatest happiness of the greatest number" as early as 1726 in the second edition of his *Inquiry concerning Moral Good and Evil*, he is more properly associated with the moral sense school of ethical thought than with **utilitarianism**, at least as it came to be developed in the work of Claude Adrien **Helvétius** or Jeremy **Bentham**.

As a professor at Glasgow Hutcheson published a number of texts in Latin for his students, and was recognized as an authority on esthetics and ethics, but wrote little that was original after 1729. In 1755 a *System of Moral Philosophy* appeared under his name, but it was more a reformulation of his essays of the 1720s than a new work. He seems to have been satisfied, once at Glasgow, scrupulously to fulfill the very onerous duties of his chair and to develop the moral theory the basis of which he had worked out while in Ireland. At Glasgow he also aided in the establishment of the Foulis Press, for which he provided part of a translation and life of Marcus Aurelius.

I

IDÉOLOGIE. A term coined by Antoine Louis Claude **Destutt de Tracy** in 1796 to designate the "science of ideas" begun during the Enlightenment. In particular it referred to an epistemology based on that of John **Locke** and the abbé de **Condillac**. The latter had surpassed Locke by claiming that all ideas are "transformed sensation" and Tracy went even further, arguing that "to think is to sense, nothing but to sense." Condillac had maintained the term "soul"; Destutt de Tracy denied any spiritual center of the self in his correspondence with Maine de Biran. Idéologie, with Tracy, Pierre-Jean-Georges Cabanis and Constantin-François Chasseboeuf de Volney, was generally hostile toward religion. Tracy made a formal but anonymous declaration of agnosticism in his *Analyse de tous les cultes par Dupuis* (Paris, an XII [1804]).

In his four-volume *Éléments d'idéologie* (1801-1815), Destutt de Tracy developed the most systematic organization of knowledge since the *Encyclopédie*, beginning with the science of ideas and proceeding through "general grammar," logic and political economy. Cabanis' *Rapports du physique et du morale de l'homme* (1802) became a manual of materialism, seeing most psychological phenomena caused by the body rather than the mind. In his posthumous "Lettre à Fauriel," Cabanis professed the likelihood of an intelligent cause of the universe.

Emmet Kennedy

IDÉOLOGUES. A term coined by Napoleon Bonaparte to disparage those men of the *Institut* (Class of Moral and Political Sciences), who pursued the new **Idéologie**, or "science of ideas" staked out by Antoine Louis Claude **Destutt de Tracy**. Other ideologues included Constantin François Chasseboeuf de Volney, the historian and anthropologist; Pierre Jean Georges Cabanis, the physician and physiologist; and Dominique Garat, the former minister who had given the first courses in Idéologie at the École Normale in 1794 before the discipline acquired its new name.

Ginguené and P. Laromiguière were more "spiritualist," less "materialist" than Tracy, Cabanis and Volney, arguing for a more active, unitary and less psychological "self" as the center of perception. Maine de Biran had the longest lasting influence.

Derogatory synonyms for the Ideologues included "dreamers" and "metaphysical faction," pointing to their alleged impracticality and dissidence. Napoleon disapproved of them due to their opposition to some of his reforms, among them the Concordat with the Church, but he never really considered them dangerous. They did pursue epistemology, **history** and physiology at a high, if not uncontested level, continuing trends by the **Enlightenment** proper.

Emmet Kennedy

IGNORANCE. A condition of not knowing. For the Enlightenment, following John **Locke**'s *Essay on Human Understanding*, the original condition of mankind. Hence it was both natural and superable.

As conceived by Locke, not-knowing is a sort of ground zero of intellectual and moral being, as reflected in his metaphor of the newborn infant as a blank sheet of paper, or *tabula rasa*. Sub-zero conditions were of course worse than ground zero. It is, for example, worse, from many points of view, to begin one's life with the burden of the accumulated interest of original sin on one's back, as Catholic dogma maintains, than to begin it in a state of moral and intellectual neutrality. Similarly, Jean-Jacques **Rousseau** argued, corrupt or vicious societies are worse than those still at ground zero of political development.

For most Enlightenment thinkers, ignorance was not in itself necessarily a bad thing. It was natural, and at the time **nature** was believed to incline its creatures toward goodness or **beneficence**. Further, it was a temporary condition, for as Locke argued, we learn by experience, which depends on no more than the functioning of the senses. So while the Enlightenment did not look with favor upon ignorance, nor did it regard ignorance as its greatest enemy. Though ignorance could not recognize truth, nor did it ascribe to error or falsehood the status of truth. Ideologies that did make this attribution were for the Enlightenment the worst and most implacable enemies. *See also* **Fanaticism; Scholasticism; Superstition.**

INDIVIDUALISM. A set of assumptions about man and society that validates the individual and asserts his or her priority to collectivities, from the family and social **club** to the state. This position was given expression by theoreticians of the **social contract,** who posited the existence of autonomous individuals in a state of nature who came together to overcome the difficulties of their unregulated natural condition by forming a society along lines mutually agreeable to the contracting parties. Though there is a wide variety of contract theories, all assume that the individual is prior to society, that society is instrumental and that its purpose is to serve the needs and interests of its members.

In the conditions of the society of the **Old Regime**, individualism implied opposition to existing social norms and an attempt to liberate the individual from the demands and requirements of family, corporation, church and state. It tended to delegitimize most forms of corporatism and regulation.

To the degree that the individual is liberated from social and corporate constraints, the danger of a return to the inconveniences of an unregulated state of nature increases. For Thomas Hobbes, who saw **human nature** as both radically egoistic and passion-driven, there was no middle ground between a strong state able to impose order by force on its recalcitrant subjects and the anarchy characteristic of the state of nature. Because he assumed that freedom would necessarily be abused, he cannot well be regarded as a liberal. Other thinkers, however, sought ways to conciliate the freedom of the individual with social order.

John **Locke** agreed that men were self-interested, but assumed that they were also sufficiently rational to restrain themselves when their **self-interest** required it. This allowed Locke to assign the state a minimal refereeing role, while leaving individuals extensive **liberty** to pursue their goals as they saw fit. Adam **Smith** likewise assumed human motivation to be driven by self-interest, and he ascribed to self-interest the role in economics that Isaac **Newton** assigned to gravity in physics. The result in Smith's case is a lawful, natural harmony that results from the workings of the laws of supply and demand in an unregulated, or minimally regulated, market. The market mechanism, Smith held, allows each person to pursue his or her self-interest and in doing so to maximize general well-being. The market could only achieve this goal, however, if it was left to find its own level without excessive state intervention. Smith thus provides a rationale for both economic individualism and economic liberalism.

Individualism is a viable position for those who assume that human beings are naturally reasonable enough to restrain their own asocial impulses, or for those who believe that there is an immanent lawfulness and harmony in social phenomena. It is not acceptable to theologians who believe that all humans were radically corrupted by the Fall and hence dependent on the Church for their salvation, or for Hobbesians, who view the individual as primary but also, because of his or her passion-driven nature, incapable of self-control.

One of the main trends of Enlightenment thought was to free the individual from the weight of corporate authority. Some of the more thoughtful advocates of this position, such as Jean-Jacques **Rousseau** and Denis **Diderot**, also pondered the questions of how the newly liberated individual could also be a responsible citizen, and whether the ethic of individualism was not in danger of becoming an anarchic and morally corrosive **egoism**.

INQUIRY INTO THE NATURE AND CAUSES OF THE WEALTH OF NATIONS, AN. The founding text of modern political economy published by Adam **Smith** in 1776, and commonly known by its abbreviated title, *The Wealth of Nations.*

Smith's book was the result of 20 years of reading, discussions and thinking. It reflects an impressively broad erudition, critical acumen and a comprehensive view of human activities that is often lacking in modern economic theory.

Smith divided his masterpiece on economics into five books. The first deals with methods of production and the working of the market. It contains Smith's famous statements on the division of labor, illustrated with material drawn from the *Encyclopédie* article "Pin," (Bk. I, chap. 1), and on **self-interest,** to the effect that, "It is not from the benevolence of the butcher, the brewer, or the baker, that we expect our dinner, but from their regard to their own interest. We address ourselves, not to their humanity but to their self-love, and never talk to them of our own necessities but of their advantages" (Bk. I, chap. 2; Oxford ed., pp. 26-27). The first book also includes an outline of a theory of the market as a self-adjusting mechanism, cast largely in terms of the interplay of wages, capital and rent.

Book Two offers an analysis of capital, while Book Three, most of which is a treatment of the economic history of the late Roman Empire and early Middle Ages, considers how wealth is increased. The fourth book contains Smith's celebrated attack on **mercantilism** and monopolies, and his treatment of **physiocracy.** The last book deals with taxation, and more broadly, the relation of the state and of the public interest to economics, which is driven by private interests.

Given its size and complexity, *The Wealth of Nations* did not sell badly. On the other hand, it did not immediately become a best seller, nor did it win uncontested approval during the author's lifetime. The status of the book as a classic dates from the 19th century, and owes more to facets of the work that became obvious in the course of the Industrial Revolution, and which appealed to the beneficiaries of the Industrial Revolution, than to Smith's immediate concerns (*see also* **Hidden Hand**). There is a danger that the reception and near canonization of *The Wealth of Nations* in the 19th and 20th centuries may distort the book's relation to its own time.

It should be noted, first, that Smith was no prophet of industrialization. The economy of Europe, and even of Britain, in the years during which *The Wealth of Nations* was being meditated and written, remained traditional and basically agricultural, and if there were significant innovations at this time they were more in the field of commerce than that of manufacturing. There were few signs of approaching industrialization for Smith to contemplate. He took for granted, and lived in the midst of, a still largely traditional economy.

Secondly, Smith was also, and obviously, very much a part of the Enlightenment. Arguably his greatest and most lasting contribution to this movement was his application of the Newtonian paradigm of physics to economics. Playing the role of gravity in Isaac **Newton**'s system is self-interest in Smith's. Parallel to the harmony of celestial bodies moving in their naturally determined orbits is Smith's assurance that left to themselves, economic processes will find their own optimal levels. And against Newton's cosmic optimism is the assumption that general well-being could be maximized by the pursuit of self-interest mediated by the market mechanism.

Finally, Smith was concerned not only with the economic advantages of the division of labor, but also with its costs. He observed that "The man whose whole life is spent in performing a few simple operations, of which the effects too are, perhaps, always the same, or very nearly the same, has no occasion to exert his understanding, or to exercise his invention in finding out expedients for removing difficulties which never occur. He naturally loses, therefore, the habit of such exertion, and generally becomes as stupid and ignorant as it is possible for a human creature to become" (Bk. V, chap. 1; p. 782). Smith's broad civic vision, which includes concern for extra-economic factors, such as **education**, has largely disappeared from subsequent economic theory, which focuses more narrowly on profit and loss.

The Wealth of Nations is a work of wide-ranging erudition and considerable wisdom. It also puts forward an economic theory with a vibrant social and political dimension. It is a matter for regret that most economists in the West seem indifferent to something that Smith and his contemporaries knew full well, namely, that economics cannot properly be separated from social and political policy.

INSTITUT/**NATIONAL INSTITUTE OF SCIENCES AND ARTS.** Even before the Jacobin Convention abolished the old-regime **academies** in 1793, Honoré Gabriel Riquetti de Mirabeau, Charles Maurice Talleyrand and the Marquis de **Condorcet** had proposed such an institution under different names and different attributes. The Daunou Law of October 1795 obviated criticism by creating a unified body and omitting appointment of many old-regime academicians.

The first class, Physical and Mathematical Sciences, enjoyed great prestige due to the fact that it contained some of the world's most famous scientists, among them Pierre Simon Laplace, Joseph Louis de Lagrange, Joseph Jerome Lalande, Gaspard Monge, Antoine François de Fourcroy and Jean Baptiste de Lamarck. The second class, the Class of Moral and Political Sciences (*see* **Idéologues** and **Idéologie**), institutionalized the Enlightenment social sciences on a national level for the first time, putting themselves at the service of the nation through efforts at staffing the faculties of the newly created central schools and holding prize competitions or "concours" on subjects like "What are the means of founding morality in a people?" and "What is the influence of habit on the faculty of thinking?" Members of the second class included Constantin François Chasseboeuf de Volney, Pierre Jean Georges Cabanis, **Destutt de Tracy** (correspondent), Dominique Joseph Garat, the abbé Sieyès, Dupont de Nemours, Talleyrand, Louis Antoine de Bougainville, the abbé **Grégoire** and Pierre Claude François Daunou.

Napoleon suppressed the second class of the Institute in 1803 and restored the survivors of the **Académie française** to the Institute.

Emmet Kennedy

ITALIAN COMEDY. The existence of companies of Italian actors was well established in France, mainly in Paris, from the 16th century. In 1680, at the time of the establishment of the **Comédie française**, the Italian troupe received from Louis XIV the old theater of the Hôtel de Bourgogne, where, in principle, they could only perform in Italian. In 1697, they had to leave the kingdom because the monarch thought he had recognized Madame de Maintenon in a satirical comedy entitled *The False Prude*. After the death of Louis XIV, in 1716 the Regent allowed a new Italian company, directed by Luigi Riccoboni, to return to Paris. In 1723, he designated them as the second official theater company, the first being the Comédie française: the "Comédiens ordinaires du Roi de la troupe italienne." They preserved the traditional stock characters of the *commedia dell'arte* (Arlecchino, Colombina, and the rest), the techniques of improvisation on scenarios (*canevas*), the use of sumptuous settings and of an odd and picturesque repertoire that extended from farce to tragedy.

Obliged to adapt to changing tastes, the Italian players blended the art of improvisation with exceptional skills of poetic grace, psychological sharpness and gentleness in expression of feelings. From the 1720s they introduced a new French repertoire to which we owe the works of Delisle de la Drevetière and Pierre Carlet **Marivaux**. After some compromises (for example, "Italian scenes" inserted into plays in French), they had, in order to survive, to compete on its own ground with the Comédie Française. Finally, in 1762 they were obliged to merge with the company of the Opéra-Comique, born of the **fairground theaters**.

The influence of the Italians, revived by the small fairground companies, was significant for the style of acting and for the French repertoire, from Molière to Marivaux. The character types of the Italian comedy became French national types like Pierrot or Arlequin, and inspired poets, as well as artists, such as Antoine **Watteau**.

Isabelle Martin

J

JANSENISM. A rigorist current within the Catholic Church that originated in the mid-17th century, and which played an important part in the religious, intellectual and political life of France in the later 17th and 18th centuries. The movement derived its name from Cornelius Otto Jansen (1585-1638), Bishop of Ypres, whose most important work, *Augustinus*, was published posthumously in 1640. Because Jansen's theology, which emphasized the radical corruption of mankind and the inability to achieve salvation without divine grace, though firmly based on the views of Saint Augustine, was thought by Church authorities to be too close to Calvinism, it was condemned by the Sorbonne in 1649 and by the papacy in 1653. This was only the first of a series of condemnations and persecutions that helped shape and define Jansenism. Jansenists, however, regarded themselves as orthodox Catholics.

Jansenism began as a spiritual movement that encouraged its adherents to withdraw from the world to devote themselves to religious exercises and meditation, but because of the persecutions to which it was subjected, it came to be an engaged and important force of political opposition. At first the movement was focused on the convent of Port Royal just outside Paris. The convent accepted Jansenism under the influence of its spiritual director, the abbé Saint-Cyran, and the community's superior, Mother Angélique, who was the sister of Antoine Arnauld, one of the leading Jansenist spokesmen of the time. Also associated with this convent were Pierre Nicole, a theologian and co-author with Arnauld of the *Logic of Port Royal*, an important text, and Blaise Pascal, the great mathematician, scientist and religious thinker whose *Provincial Letters* (1656-1657) was an outstanding defense of Jansenism, and whose fragmentary *Pensées* (1670) remains one of the great explorations of religious sensibility.

None of the outstanding intellectual figures who adhered to Jansenism during the 17th century could be described as social or political activists, or as opposed in principle to authority. Time and experience changed this. Louis XIV's style of government was comprehensively authoritarian. He did not believe that his subjects were entitled to beliefs or opinions that went against those preferred by the State, and if admonition would not have the effect he desired, he readily had recourse to coercion. In principle there should have been no reason why Louis's subjects should not have practiced a rigorist Augustinian version of Catholicism if they so chose. Difficulty arose because the king favored the laxer and more worldly theology of the **Jesuits**.

Issues such as frequency of communion or the strictness of direction of conscience by confessors, which concerned the Jansenists, did not require state intervention. However, once the king had taken a position, he did not regard alternatives as legitimate. He had little trouble in winning the papacy, which saw itself as exercising a sort of absolute spiritual authority, to his position. A formula of adherence to the officially sanctioned view of the issues in question was drawn up, and when the nuns of Port Royal refused to sign it, their convent was razed, and their order disbanded by the pope in 1709. Pasquier Quesnel's popular text of religious instruction, the *Moral Reflections*, was condemned in 1708, and in 1713 was the object of the papal bull *Unigenitus,* which condemned 101 propositions in it and by implication Jansenism as a whole. In 1730 *Unigenitus* became law in the French state. The prelacy was gradually purged of bishops with Jansenist leanings, but the lower clergy was not.

Rather than being effectively suppressed as the authorities of church and state hoped, Jansenism persisted and organized to defend itself, and where possible, to take the offensive. Convinced Jansenists published the *Nouvelles ecclésiastiques,* the only serial publication to succeed in appearing clandestinely over an extended period during the **Old Regime**. Moreover, Jansenism retained adherents both among the lower classes and among the magistrates of the *Parlement* of Paris.

From 1727 a number of miracles was supposed to have occurred at the tomb of a saintly cleric, the Deacon Pâris, in the graveyard of Saint-Médard in the capital. Pâris was reputed to have been a Jansenist, and the miraculous cures that were said to occur at his grave were accompanied with violent convulsions. To assure public order the authorities ordered the graveyard closed, whereupon a wit posted a mock announcement on the gates of the cemetery "By order of the King, God is hereby forbidden to perform miracles in this place." The king's religious advisors were inclined to see the hand of the devil in these outbreaks, and the *philosophes* an extreme example of popular **superstition** and credulity. What this episode seems to reflect is the inability of power to coerce belief.

A similar instance occurred between 1749 and 1756, when the Church authorities sought to separate the faithful from *curés* thought to be tainted by Jansenism. To prevent people from seeking the ministrations of such priests the Archbishop of Paris declared that without an attestation of confession from an orthodox priest, the faithful would be denied the last rites. Known as the "affaire des billets," this act of spiritual coercion, in which the Church had the support of the crown, provided the magistrates of the *Parlement* with an occasion to confront the crown, and protect simple folk threatened with a terrible sanction. The crown proved unable to impose its policy, or even to silence discussion of the issue. Again, a failed attempt to coerce conscience contributed to undermining secular authority.

In the late 1750s, when the Jesuits became involved in a complicated court case before the *Parlement* of Paris concerning its activities overseas, a minority of Jansenist magistrates of that court saw the possibility of exacting revenge for a century of persecution. They extended their investigation beyond the immediate issue to include the legal establishment of the Jesuits in France, and succeeded in showing that by law there was no such right. The case was heavily influenced by nationalist sentiment and by resentment of Jesuit loyalty to the papacy rather than their country of residence. With the disbanding of the Jesuit Order in France in 1762 and the expulsion of Jesuits who remained faithful to the Order two years later, the Jansenists had effectively and definitively defeated their old foe.

Jansenism was significant for the history of the Old Regime on a number of levels. Beginning as an intensely spiritual reformist tendency within the Catholic Church it was obliged, in dealing with the persecution to which it was subjected, to stand against the combined authority of church and state, and thus developed into a sort of diffuse mentality of opposition. It has been argued that the defense of individual conscience in religious terms prepared the way for the **individualism** of the Enlightenment. During the 18th century the main spokesmen of Jansenism were no longer theologians and outstanding thinkers, as they had been in the 17th century, but tended to be lawyers who treated political questions from the point of view of a republic rather than that of the monarchy. It has been shown by Dale Van Kley that some of the pamphlets produced by parlementaire and Jansenist critics of the crown and of the Jesuits were republished by the patriot opposition during the Pre-Revolution.

JAUCOURT, Louis, Chevalier de (1704-1779). The writer who contributed more copy to the *Encyclopédie* than any other. He is responsible for roughly a quarter of the text of the whole.

Jaucourt came from a family of the sword **nobility** that had only recently converted to Catholicism. He studied theology in Switzerland, mathematics in England and medicine in Holland, receiving his medical degree from the University of Leyden in 1730. However, Jaucourt devoted himself to study and writing rather than to a regular medical practice. He produced a multi-volume dictionary of medicine, the only copy of which was lost at sea on the way to the printer. He was also a member of the **Academies** of Bordeaux, Stockholm and Berlin, as well as of the **Royal Society** in London.

It is his role in the production of the *Encyclopédie* that confers on Jaucourt his importance in the history of the Enlightenment. And this role was that of a popularizer, not an original thinker. The *Encyclopédie* contains entries by Denis **Diderot**, Jean-Jacques **Rousseau** and others of undisputed brilliance. But these are far from being the majority. Most of the huge work consists of excerpts and summaries from recognized authorities. Jaucourt, who hired a number of secretaries to help him in his task, was a tireless compiler. For example, most of the articles on politics in the *Encyclopédie* are borrowed by Jaucourt from **Montesquieu**'s *Spirit of the Laws*. Whole sections of that work are simply broken down appropriately for the articles in question, and sent to the printer. In this way Montesquieu and other authors acceptable to the enlightened editors and compilers of the *Encyclopédie* reached a wider audience in a more manageable form.

This is not to denigrate Jaucourt's contribution. To select appropriately and intelligently from a huge literature and to craft comprehensive articles from much larger and sometimes composite sources requires no little application and skill. Jaucourt's contribution to the *Encyclopédie* was seldom original, but it was vital. Although Diderot had overall responsibility for the *Encyclopédie*, Jaucourt produced far more of the text, perhaps as much as a quarter of the whole.

JEFFERSON, Thomas (1743-1826). Author of the American Declaration of Independence, governor of Virginia, secretary of state, vice-president, third president of the United States, founder of the University of Virginia, planter, architect and philosopher, Jefferson was probably the most notable figure of the Enlightenment in America.

Jefferson came from a comfortable family whose wealth consisted primarily in land. He enjoyed a healthful upbringing and good relations with his father. Between 1760 and 1762 he studied at William and Mary College, taking pleasure in his studies, which included the classics, leading an active social life and preparing for a career in law. He began practicing as a lawyer, but was soon drawn into politics. Jefferson sat in the Virginia House of Burgesses from 1769, and in 1775 was chosen a delegate to the Continental Congress, where he became the principal author of the Declaration of Independence, one of the key statements of values, not only for the emerging United States of America, but for the Enlightenment generally. Indeed, the Declaration of Independence was more suited to Western Europe than to America in that the contradiction between a universalist ethic and racially-based **slavery** did not exist in the Old World, whatever its other shortcomings.

Jefferson's political career was just taking off. Between 1779 and 1781 he served as governor of Virginia, and undertook to modernize and liberalize that state's constitution, effectively passing legislation to assure comprehensive freedom of religion. In 1784 he tried, but failed, to have slavery blocked from the new western states. During the critical five years preceding the outbreak of revolution in France, Jefferson served as his country's ambassador in Paris. When he returned home he acted as George Washington's first secretary of state, and from 1796 to 1800 as vice-president. He then served two terms as president. On leaving office Jefferson retired to his **plantation**, where he continued to think, write, invent and to lay plans for the University of Virginia.

Thomas Jefferson is one of very few American presidents with a claim to outstanding intellectual abilities. In outlook he was a **deist**, and adhered to the moral sense school. Like many of the thinkers of the Enlightenment, he accepted the existence of natural **rights**, and with a minority, he upheld the **social contract** as the basis for political association. He believed in and furthered **democracy**, but, like many of his contemporaries, he recognized that political independence necessary for **citizenship** required a significant degree of economic independence. This is one way that notions of democracy in the 18th century differ from views of democracy today. Certainly Jefferson was one of the very few theorists of politics of his time who had as much opportunity to take a direct part in the formation and implementation of policy.

Among Jefferson's many talents was architecture. Monticello, the home he designed and directed the building of on his plantation, is a gem of neoclassical style. The Daughters of the American Revolution who show visitors the building and grounds point out that the materials, including wooden nails, all came from the plantation. They do not offer the information that the labor used to build this elegant and luminous building was slave labor, but they can show the visitor, if asked, where the slaves lived, though their dwellings were not thought worth preserving.

It is a puzzle how a thinker who believed in natural rights and the **equality** of mankind could have accepted the institution of slavery. Probably Jefferson did not accept it. He tried to limit it in legislation, and he freed some of his slaves in his will. But the institution was one that he had no choice but to live with if he was to continue to be a part of the social milieu into which he was born. The aspiration to eliminate this blight on his time and society reflects a key Enlightenment ideal; Jefferson's inability to convince his contemporaries to act on this value, and his attempt to proceed toward abolition by gradual reform, shows up the weakness of ideals opposed by powerful economic and political interests.

JESUITS. The Society of Jesus was an order of the Catholic Church founded by Ignatius Loyola in Paris in 1534 and approved by Rome in 1540. It was intended to support and reinvigorate Catholicism both internally and in its struggle against Protestantism. The Jesuit Order was directly and immediately subordinate to the papacy.

Members of the Order were required to undergo vigorous training, and on the whole were well educated, highly competent, completely assured of their vocations and altogether obedient to their superior and to the pope. Because the Jesuits set themselves the task of strengthening the Church and fighting its enemies in the context of existing cultural and political conditions, they tended to be actively engaged in politics and seldom exhibited the pious withdrawal from secular concerns and intense spirituality that characterized cloistered monasticism at its best.

In their interpretation of Catholic doctrine the Jesuits tended to take a more optimistic view of the human condition than did

Augustine, the Calvinists or the **Jansenists**. This is to say that grace was not all-determining, but that people could, by good deeds and piety, and through the offices of the Catholic Church, contribute toward their salvation. Their opponents alleged that they were overly accommodating to human weakness, especially in the cases of the wealthy and powerful. Certainly the Jesuits sought to influence the social and political elites, as they saw this as the most effective way of influencing society at large.

Education was one of the social tasks the Jesuits took upon themselves, and specifically secondary education, since it brought them into contact with those who could be expected to become community leaders. The Jesuit *collèges,* of which there were more than 100 in France toward the middle of the 18th century, based their curricula on the classics, appropriately expurgated, and taught them superbly. The members of the Order were also open to the sciences, and were generally progressive in outlook. Insofar as there was a middle ground between enlightened thought and Church doctrine, the Jesuits were delighted to occupy it. Even **Voltaire**, who studied at the leading Parisian *collège* of Louis-le-Grand, remembered his Jesuit schoolmasters with affection.

The Jesuits were also actively engaged in spreading the Catholic religion. Their missions in China, India and South America were remarkably successful. In part this was a consequence of the willingness of the Jesuit missionaries to adapt local beliefs and customs to their teachings rather than simply condemning them. To some Catholic theologians, especially among rival missionary orders, this appeared as a culpable deviation from strict Church doctrine, and Church authorities tended to accept this criticism.

In their political work the Jesuits usually allied with kings and absolutist states so as to gain as much influence as possible. Their ultimate loyalty, however, was not to secular monarchs, but to their Church, and more specifically to the papacy. This was a position that did them little harm during the struggles of the Counter-Reformation with Protestantism, but caused them to be viewed with suspicion as a sense of national identity emerged, and elites and rulers became less sympathetic to the uncompromising ultramontanism they embodied. In 1759 the Jesuits were expelled from Portugal; in 1762 they were condemned by the traditionally Gallican *Parlement* of Paris, which was, moreover, influenced by a small but determined group of Jansenist magistrates, and in 1764 expelled from France; and in 1767 they met the same fate in Spain. The papacy was prevailed upon to dissolve the Order in 1773, and it was not restored until 1814.

JEWS. The Enlightenment opens at a moment when Jews were authorized to return to and reside in Western European countries after expulsions in the 13th century (England), 14th century (France), and the 15th century (Spain and Portugal). There were also smaller-scale, local expulsions from German and Counter-Reformation Italian states in the second half of the 16th century that were, along with the censoring of Jewish books and the burning of copies of the Talmud, expressions of Counter-Reformation piety.

At the same time, the Counter-Reformation came to Poland which, together with Eastern Europe as far east as the Ukraine, had been the refuge of the Jews formally expelled from the Western states, or driven from them by persecution or economic disabilities, and who had found relative tolerance there. There remained some crypto-Jews in Spain and Portugal, but, contrary to the legends about heroic "marranos," most had become sincere "conversos" or "new Christians" according to modern research, but were nonetheless suspected by the Inquisition of Judaizing, and a significant number were tried and not infrequently burned at the stake.

Crypto-Jews who succeeded in leaving the Iberian peninsula settled in the Bordeaux and Bayonne regions of France, where they remained "in the closet" until the mid-18th century but were not persecuted, or in London, Amsterdam and Italy where they lived openly as Jews, and became relatively acculturated, even if they still used their Spanish or Portuguese or Judeo-Spanish for many religious and communal purposes. The fact that their ancestors had lived several generations as Christians, cut off from the practice of Jewish law (*halakhah*) and its study tended to orient them more towards the Bible, which their dissimulation did not prevent them from reading in Latin or in a vernacular translation, than Ashkenazic Jews who were never obliged to abandon the study of rabbinic texts, and induced a resentment of the rabbis and religious authorities who tried to bring them into conformity with strict *halakhic* practice.

That orientation, plus their entry into states where there were no Jews or Jewish institutions (England, southwest France) led them to prefer a certain rationalism to traditional authority, and to acculturate more completely than most Ashkenazic Jews in Eastern France, in Amsterdam and in Germany. But their acculturation, which is the model for that of all of today's Jews, except for a fundamentalist fringe which still yearns for the closed world of the East-European Ghetto, was without ideology until the Haskalah movement in late 18th-century Germany, inspired by Moses **Mendelssohn** (1729-1786) and, to a lesser extent, by Rabbi Jacob Emden (1697-1776), some of whose decisions were remarkably liberal for the period. The philosophy and practice of the Haskalah justified secular study, the study of the language of the Jews' host country, the study of Hebrew, the philological study of the Bible, and, in the 19th century, the beginning of critical and historical study of rabbinic literature and of the synagogue liturgy.

Except in London and Amsterdam, where the Jews did not suffer from any legal restrictions on their commercial freedom, but had no political rights nor the assurance of not being expelled at some later date, European Jews suffered from a variety of civil disabilities and extraordinary taxes that limited the expansion of their communities and their participation in the cultural and social world of their non-Jewish neighbors. As neutral social spaces like the masonic movement (*see* **Freemasonry**) and the pursuit of science emerged in hitherto exclusively Christian Europe, Jews were hesitantly permitted to participate, and then towards the end of the century, with the "Toleranz-Edict" of **Joseph II** for Austria and parts of his empire in 1782, then, implicitly, in the United States with the "no establishment of religion" clause of the First Amendment to the Constitution (1791) the spheres in which they could freely participate expanded. Finally, in France complete citizens' rights were granted, first to the Sephardim of the Bordeaux and Bayonne regions (1790), then to the Ashkenazim of Eastern France (1791). At the same time that the French State extended full civic rights to Jews, it suppressed Jewish communal autonomy. This transformed both Jewish law and practice, virtually eliminating the applicability of the codes of Jewish commercial law and subordinating many aspects of matrimonial laws to the laws of the State, while reinforcing the individual Jew's right to practice as much or as little of Jewish ritual law as he or she pleased.

It need not be decided whether the Jews of France obtained the grant of political equality exclusively because they "earned" their emancipation by their services to the State since the 1550s, when a limited number of crypto-Jews and Rhenish Jews were readmitted, as David Feuerwerker and other French historians have argued, or because of certain elements of the philosophy of the Enlightenment. The first of these is the criticism of religion that is so prominent in the writings of David **Hume**, **Voltaire** and in numerous "**clandestine** tracts." The second derives from the arguments for religious **toleration** of Protestants that characterize the writings of John **Locke**, Pierre **Bayle**, John Toland, Jacques Basnage de Beauval, Laurent l'Angliviel de La Beaumelle, Jean Lévesque de Burigny and, especially, those of the iconoclast, Voltaire, who even implicitly included Jews in the category of non-Catholic sects to be tolerated. Together these trends weakened the traditional Christian prejudices against the Jews.

It may also have been that the emancipation of the Jews was furthered by "the logic of the Revolution," which could not support a disenfranchised ethnic group within the French State, and by Jacobinism, which sought to bring all residents of the State under State control. It is questionable, however, whether "the logic of the Revolution" adequately describes the advocacy of the abbé Henri **Grégoire,** the prime mover of the emancipation law in the National Assembly for political rights for Jews, black **slaves**, and actors. Several constituents of Enlightenment culture converged to recommend emancipation in France. However, certain of them were not dominant, if present at all, in the United States, where the theoretic **equality** of the Jews was incomplete while others were not dominant, if at all present, in the Jesuit-dominated circle around Joseph II where the Toleranz-Edict granted limited rights. At any event, Napoleon's troops carried the French laws emancipating the Jews into Holland, Germany and the lands to the East, which had not yet devised the emancipation of their own Jews, where they remained valid even after Napoleon effectively rescinded certain elements of that emancipation in France.

Bertram Eugene Schwarzbach

JOHNSON, Samuel (1709-1784). Probably the dominant literary figure in England from roughly the mid-18th century to his death, a period that is often referred to as the "Age of Johnson." He achieved this position of eminence despite having begun his career writing for money and living little better than other hacks on **Grub Street**, and without having produced a work comparable to the great novels of Samuel **Richardson**, Henry **Fielding** or Laurence **Sterne**. Johnson's reputation rested, rather, on his incisive intelligence, comprehensive learning, enormous energy and forceful personality, admiringly yet fairly portrayed by James Boswell in one of the great biographies in English, the *Life of Johnson*.

Johnson was born in Lichfield, the son of a bookseller. He attended the local grammar school, and then studied at Oxford from 1728 to

1729, but was forced to leave without taking a degree because of financial constraints. The death of his father in 1731 exacerbated an already bad situation. To make his living Johnson had recourse to the usual methods of educated but impecunious young men with literary ambitions.

Rather than tutoring, Johnson opened a school near Lichfield, but it did not solve his economic problems. With a former student, David Garrick, who was to become a great actor, Johnson set off for London in 1737, and there began in earnest his long career in letters. He had already written for the periodical press and done a translation for a bookseller, and in London continued in the same vein, writing anything he would be paid for (Boswell reported Johnson as saying "No man but a blockhead ever wrote, but for money." *Life of Johnson*, p.731) including articles for the *Gentleman's Magazine*, among them reports of debates in **Parliament** (which neither he nor any non-member of the House was allowed to attend), poetry, biography and essays.

Johnson is almost as noteworthy for his sociability as for his writing. We are particularly well informed about his relations with friends and other writers thanks to James Boswell, whom he met in 1763, when his reputation was established. Boswell minutely chronicled Johnson's relations with friends such as Mr. and Mrs. Thrale, and his role in the Literary Club, which was founded in 1764 and which met in the Turk's Head tavern, and over which he presided grandly (*see* **Clubs**). Its members included many of the leading personalities in the arts and letters of the time, such as Oliver Goldsmith, Sir Joshua Reynolds, Garrick, Edmund **Burke,** and later Boswell, Edward **Gibbon**, Adam **Smith** and others.

As an author, Johnson's output was considerable, but uneven. He has to his credit several minor classics, such as the whimsical short novel *Rasselas*, published the same year as *Candide*, and in many ways similar to it, the periodical essays, the *Rambler* (1750-1752) and the *Idler* (1758-1760), which bring to mind those of the *Spectator*, and a number of poems, particularly *London* (1738) and *The Vanity of Human Wishes* (1749). He also edited the *Literary Magazine* for a time, contributed to many other periodicals, produced a number of political pamphlets for the government and wrote an account of his journey in 1773 with Boswell to the Hebrides.

Apart from *Rasselas* and his essays, Johnson is today remembered for a number of projects that he undertook at the request of booksellers. These include his famous *Dictionary*, published in 1755 after years of arduous labor, and the first comprehensive dictionary in the English language; his edition of **Shakespeare**, which appeared in 1765 and contributed to the foundation of serious scholarship on the bard; and *Lives of the Poets*, which were published between 1779 and 1781. In the hands of lesser authors these works would likely have been mediocre and easily forgettable commercial enterprises. The force of Johnson's intellect and the energy of his style have made them works of lasting value.

JOSEPH II (1741-1790). Son of Maria Thesesa, empress of the Holy Roman Empire, co-regent with her from 1765 to 1780, and then Emperor. While Maria Theresa was traditional and even pious, her chancellor, Wenzel Anton von Kaunitz, who also worked with Joseph and survived him, was one of the leading enlightened politicians of the time. Joseph was the brother of **Leopold**, who ruled Tuscany as grand duke from 1765 to 1790, and who succeeded him as Emperor on his death. Leopold's intelligent and far-reaching reforms in Tuscany justify our regarding him as one of the most successful enlightened despots. Joseph's sister was Marie-Antoinette, Queen of France and wife of **Louis XVI**. Probably Joseph was the most earnest and unfortunate of the major **enlightened despots**.

In international relations Joseph was as keen to extend Austrian territory as were **Catherine II** and **Frederick II** to extend theirs. However, he was not so successful. He failed to restore Silesia to Austria through the Seven Years' War, and was prevented by Frederick and Catherine from adding Bavaria to his dominions. Austria did make territorial gains at the expense of **Poland**, but only in collaboration with Russia and Prussia, and she was not the chief beneficiary of the dismemberment of the Polish state.

Joseph's reforms included the usual compilation of law codes for the entire realm as measures of centralization and modernization, and educational reforms in the same spirit. His religious reforms were particularly far-reaching. On the one hand, he extended civil rights to non-Catholic Christians and, exceptionally, also to **Jews**. On the other, he took vigorous measures, in many ways comparable to those of the **French Revolution** on ecclesiastical matters, to subordinate the Church to the State. He sharply restricted the authority of the pope in lands under his jurisdiction, and disbanded the monasteries. His social measures also went further than those of other monarchs. Most notably, he sought to force the abolition of serfdom.

Such measures were undoubtedly enlightened. But they were not popular, and Joseph could not impose their implementation on the basis of his good intentions and authority alone. He had tried to go too far, too fast. Not long before his death he found it necessary to rescind many of the laws he had labored so hard to implement.

The reasons for Joseph's failure are many. Sovereign of territories so geographically dispersed and culturally different as Austria, Tuscany, Hungary and Belgium, he faced a far harder task than his fellow absolute monarchs of the east. His doctrinaire (the term appears in almost all accounts of his reign) approach to reform made him perhaps the most philosophical, but the least practical, of the enlightened despots. His conviction of the rightness of his ideals and objectives caused him to underestimate the strength of the attachment of local populations to their customs and liberties, or the interests of the nobilities of his realms in maintaining serfdom. Moreover, Joseph's industry and drive could not offset mediocrity of ability, lack of sympathy for views differing from his own, and a certain coolness of personality. His disappointment was commensurate with the extent and intensity of his aspirations. There is something tragic about so much good will and energy achieving so little, and about a man who tried so hard being unable to avoid consciousness of his failure.

JOURNAL ENCYCLOPÉDIQUE. A French-language journal published from 1756 to 1793, first in Liège, and then, from 1760, in Bouillon. It was part of the vibrant French-language publishing business that flourished outside France, but whose main market was within the country.

In the course of a year the *Journal Encyclopédique* published eight duodecimo volumes of between 432 and 566 pages each in installments that appeared two weeks apart. The cost was initially 24 *livres* for an annual subscription, not including postage, which could easily increase the price by half. At its peak it probably had something like 2,000 subscribers.

Each volume was divided into three parts. The first was devoted to book reviews, and the second to letters to the editor, articles, poems, announcements and occasional pieces. So far it was broadly similar in content to the *Année Littéraire*. Its third section was devoted to international news, a clear advantage of the foreign journal over its Parisian counterpart in an age in which the demand for news was great but closely controlled by the government.

The *Journal Encyclopédique* was founded by Pierre Rousseau of Toulouse. An aspiring writer himself, Rousseau turned to journalism when it became clear to him that he was unlikely to make a name for himself as a creative writer. When the Elector Palatine suggested in 1755 that he begin a journal in territory under his jurisdiction, Rousseau agreed. Though Rousseau actively wrote for and edited the *Journal Encyclopédique* himself, a project of that scope was beyond the capabilities of one man. He was fortunate in attracting a competent team of collaborators, prominent in which were Jean-Louis Castilhon, Frédérick-Emmanuel Grunwald, Jean-Baptiste René Robinet, Charpentier, Maignard, Jean Castilhon, Meusnier de Querlon, Jean Deschamps, Jean Henri Samuel Formey and the future Girondin, Brissot de Warville.

In addition to writing and editing the *Journal Encyclopédique*, Rousseau also established his own printing business, the Société Typographique de Bouillon, which printed the journal and other projects. Rousseau and his partners are thus a rare example of journalists who also had the business sense to organize a profitable printing venture.

As its name suggests, the *Journal Encyclopédique* identified with and acted as a spokesman for the mainstream Enlightenment. It discussed favorably the works of key *philosophes* such as **Voltaire**, **Montesquieu** and Jean-Louis Leclerc de **Buffon**, but distanced itself from materialism and radical views on religion, and it was consistently hostile to the work of Jean-Jacques **Rousseau**. Though it has sometimes been described as antithetical to Elie Catherine **Fréron**'s *Année Littéraire*, in its views the *Journal Encyclopédique* was remarkably similar to it. The differences between these two important periodicals had more to do with their evaluations of the abilities and characters of certain writers, such as Voltaire and Rousseau, than with their acceptance of the Enlightenment and its values.

JULIE, OU LA NOUVELLE HÉLOÏSE **(1761)**. Jean-Jacques **Rousseau**'s great epistolary novel, which proved one of the most successful best-sellers of the 18th century, but which most people today find hard going. Still, like almost everything that Rousseau produced, it is beautifully and movingly written.

The novel recounts the vicissitudes of an unusual triangle. A young commoner, Saint-Preux, who acts as the tutor in the home of a provincial noble, falls in love with his pupil, Julie d'Etange, who returns his affection. The notion of love transcending class was unusual at the time, especially if the man was of lower social standing. As Julie herself put it in referring to her father, "this proud gentleman does not even imagine that a mere commoner might fall in love with his daughter" (part I, letter xxxii). The assertion of the right and power of emotional affinity is one of the romantic features of the novel. In an age in which **marriage** was generally seen as a business transaction, and in a culture in which divorce was not permitted, this subtly presented notion of a relationship based on a great love must have been appealing, especially for women. However, in the novel, as in life, the course of true love ran neither straight nor long.

Julie's father, the baron d'Etange, was an army officer. In an encounter with the enemy, his friend, Wolmar, saved his life. Partly from gratitude the baron offered his daughter's hand to his friend, without the formality of consulting her. Rousseau has Julie accept the marriage from a sense of duty to her family, despite her still ardent love for Saint-Preux.

Far from making Wolmar a Swiss version of Squire Western, Rousseau portrays him as an intelligent, cultured, caring and beneficent, albeit manipulative, husband and master. It has been suggested that Rousseau modeled Wolmar on his acquaintance, the Baron d'**Holbach**. Wolmar manages the estate and its inhabitants efficiently and humanely, treats his wife with consideration and even undertakes to cure her former lover of his infatuation for, and excessive dependence on, his wife. The three live together at Clarens, Julie devoting herself to raising her children and her duties as lady of the estate while remaining faithful to her husband and emotionally committed to Saint-Preux.

The situation is, of course, impossible, for a person cannot live indefinitely in obedience to two conflicting value systems, and Julie does the sensible thing and dies. Romantic love, as so often happens in literature, is followed by romantic death. In *The Sorrows of Young Werther*, which treats the same theme, though without the psychological depth or social acuity of *Julie*, Johann Wolfgang von **Goethe** has the disappointed hero take his own life.

K

KANT, Immanuel (1724-1804). Probably the most important and influential philosopher of the 18th century. Whether his work properly belongs to the Enlightenment, or goes beyond it, is open to question.

Though his family is known to be of Scottish origin, Kant was born and lived his whole life in Königsberg, Prussia. His father was a modest harness maker, and the family sincerely pietist. Kant had an exceptionally warm and close relationship with his mother, and seems to have benefited from a positive home environment.

Someone of Kant's social standing would not normally have received much of an education, but a perceptive and well-intentioned pastor noticed the boy's unusual abilities, and thanks to him Kant received a solid secondary **education** at the local **college**. At the age of 16 he entered the **University** of Königsberg, initially studying theology, and graduated with a bachelor's degree in 1746. For the next nine years Kant, like many an impecunious intellectual at the time, worked as a tutor, winning the respect and affection of the students entrusted to his care and their families. In 1755 he received his master's degree from the same university, and was licensed to teach as a *privatdocent*. This position gave its holders the right to teach and to collect fees, but provided no salary, an arrangement that probably appeals to contemporary entrepreneurs of education, who may try to revive it.

As a *privatdocent* Kant taught mostly mathematics and the natural sciences, though he was also an accomplished classicist. In 1770 the University of Königsberg finally offered the gifted and popular instructor a professorship of logic and metaphysics, which he accepted and filled with distinction, teaching actively until 1796. As in Scotland, the universities of Protestant Germany contributed significantly to the articulation and dissemination of Enlightenment thought.

Kant was not only a profound and original thinker, but also an articulate and popular teacher. He lived a highly disciplined private life, devoting fixed and long hours to study, but he also valued company, and was socially accomplished. By the end of his long life he had lapsed into senility.

Kant's major works are *The Critique of Pure Reason*, published in 1781 and devoted to metaphysics, *The Critique of Practical Reason*, published in 1788 and treating ethics, and *The Critique of Judgment*, published in 1790 and concerned with esthetics. In 1775 he had published a scientific treatise, the *Universal Natural History and Theory of the Heavens*. Interestingly, his first and last significant publications both concerned theology. *The Only Possible Ground for Demonstration of the Existence of God* appeared in 1763, and *Religion Within the Bounds of Pure Reason* in 1793. Kant also published a number of seminal essays, among them "On Perpetual Peace" (1795), and

"What is Enlightenment?" (1784). This latter piece, which was written for a Berlin newspaper, has served as the basis for the development of the notion of **public opinion** in the work of Jürgen Habermas and those who follow him.

Kant's main contribution to philosophy was to restore its transcendental, or metaphysical, element. The dominant **empirical** methodology and assumptions of the Enlightenment tended to focus on facts that could be determined by observation or experience and verifiable relations among such facts. Problems or questions that fell outside of the areas of fact and law were viewed by most Enlightenment thinkers as unanswerable, with the result that it was agreed that a great many things could not be known with certainty. Kant reformulated this position by asserting that "things in themselves," or noumena, could not be known, while aspects of things perceived through the senses, or phenomena, could be known. This claim did not diverge from the basic empiricist position. His argument, put forward in the *Critique of Pure Reason,* that pure sensation or experience was never in fact available to us, did.

Broadly speaking, the Enlightenment had rejected the claims of **rationalism**, and accepted those of empiricism. This meant that the world was to be understood in terms of experience, and the mind in terms of sensation. Kant showed that if the mind was conceived as simply a mechanism for registering sensations, it would be purely passive, and so could not perform even that function. For the mind to work at all, there must be certain concepts or principles inherent in it, and knowledge must be independent of sensation. Kant thus restored metaphysics to a central place in philosophy, against the empiricist tendency to minimize, or do away with it completely. Whether this achievement puts Kant in the center of certain Enlightenment projects, or at the beginning of quite different ways of thinking, is an open question.

KIT-CAT CLUB. An important London **club** founded toward the end of the 17th century and identified with the **Whig** cause. The name of the club was taken from the patron of the Cat and Fiddle, the tavern where it first met. Christopher Cat was a pastry cook whose mutton pies were referred to as kit-cats. The club was not, however, primarily political in focus, being rather a place of meeting where writers, artists and politicians sympathetic to Whiggism could meet to talk and socialize, and to engage in a form of cultural politics.

Although the membership of the club was firmly Whig, there was nothing narrowly partisan about its attitudes and activities. One of the more prominent members of the Kit-Cats, the publisher Jacob Tonson, happily produced works by **Tory** authors if they would bring him a profit, and the club generously covered the funeral expenses for the poor but eminent poet John Dryden, who was identified with the Tories.

The social composition of the Kit-Cat Club was mixed, including many Whig magnates with artistic tastes, among them the Earl of Dorset, men of letters, such as Joseph **Addison**, Richard **Steele**, Richard Congreve and Sir John Vanbrugh, who managed a theater, artists, such as Sir Godfrey Kneller, and the occasional businessman, such as the publisher Tonson. The Kit-Cat Club was similar to **salons** in that it brought together men of different social backgrounds with similar cultural interests, but differed from them in lacking feminine guidance and having a distinctly party-political coloring.

The near-contemporaneous **Club de l'Entresol** in Paris was also exclusively male, but tended to be more serious and more interested in political theory than were the Kit-Cats, who were either in, or close to, political power and office at a time of almost unbroken Whig ascendancy. The Kit-Cat Club exemplified a particularly British form of sociability in which aristocrats would meet happily with wealthy or talented commoners with whom they shared cultural or political interests. While maintaining polite, external relations of **equality**, the wealthy and powerful were prepared to provide **patronage** for their less fortunate, but usually still useful, fellows. The tendency to find in the framework of a club a setting in which it was suitable to treat talented but impecunious commoners as equals was something which the ethos of the French nobility made more difficult.

L

LAMBERT, Anne Thérèse de Marganat de Courcelles, Marquise de (1647-1733). Best known for hosting informal meetings of writers, intellectuals and artists, which became the model for the **salons** of the high Enlightenment, Mme Lambert was also an author in her own right. She was born to a family of magistrates, and at the age of 19 was married to the Marquis de Lambert, to whom she bore two children. Untypically for a woman of her social standing, she was a devoted wife and mother. Mme de Lambert was widowed in 1686, and handsomely provided for.

Beginning in 1710 she opened her house to selected guests on a weekly basis. On Tuesdays men of letters, scholars and artists met at her home on the rue de Richelieu, just north of the old Bibliothèque Nationale. Wednesdays were intended for ladies and gentlemen of high social standing, and were the continuation of a traditional aristocratic form of sociability. There was, however, some overlap and movement between the two sets of guests, so Mme Lambert can be seen as having begun the trend toward the integration of talent and wealth that characterized the salon of the High Enlightenment.

The tone of Mme Lambert's salon was serious and restrained. It rejected the license of the **Regency**, required good manners from guests and avoided subjects that might lead to overly heated exchanges, particularly in the areas of politics and religion. While not a *dévôte*, Mme Lambert maintained a respectful attitude toward Christianity and exemplified the virtues of traditional morality. Nevertheless, she favored the moderns over the ancients, praised **Montesquieu**'s *Persian Letters* and helped assure that *philosophe*'s election to the **Académie française**. Her salon included numerous female guests, among them Mme de **Tencin**.

Mme Lambert was not merely a hostess to writers and artists, but was also an author in her own right. In addition to two works on **education**, the *Avis d'une mère à son fils* (1726) and *Avis d'une mère à sa fille* (1728), she also published *Reflexions sur les femmes* (1727) *Traité de l'amitié* (1732) and *La Viellesse* (1732). On her death in 1733 many of her guests passed to the salon of Mme de Tencin.

LA METTRIE, Julien Offray de (1709-1751). One of the most radical of the *philosophes*, who was known for his materialist and hedonist views.

La Mettrie was born in Saint Malo in Brittany to a comfortable merchant family. He received most of his secondary education at the **Jesuit** *collège* of Caen, before moving to the Collège d'Harcourt in Paris for his final two years of philosophy. Having taken his Bachelor of Arts degree in 1727, he then studied medicine at Paris for five years, though for reasons of economy he acquired his well-deserved medical degree from the University of Reims. He continued his medical studies from 1733 to 1735 at Leiden, where he followed the classes of the celebrated Dutch physician Hermann Boerhaave.

His medical training complete, La Mettrie returned to his native town, opened his own practice and married. It appeared that the young doctor had embarked on a comfortable, provincial, middle-class career. But this was not the case. By 1742 La Mettrie had begotten two children and a number of published works on medicine, and in that year he abandoned his wife and children to take up the position of doctor to the Duke of Grammont, and surgeon to the French Guards, whose officer the Duke was.

La Mettrie enjoyed the pleasures of the capital, and while there met Bernard **Fontenelle**, Mme du **Châtelet**, and Pierre Louis Moreau de **Maupertuis**. He also accompanied the troops under his care to a number of battles of the War of Austrian Succession (1741-1748), among them the Battle of Fontenoy, and continued to publish. As things turned out, his books proved more dangerous to him than his work as a military doctor.

In 1745 La Mettrie brought out a work entitled *Natural History of the Soul*, in which he argued that what had traditionally been regarded as the soul was, from the point of view of medical science, merely an epiphenomenon of the functioning of bodily organs. This was not the sort of thing to endear him to the established Church, and his book was condemned by the magistrates of the **Parlement** of Paris and burned by the public hangman. Fearing that the authorities might turn their attention from book to author, La Mettrie prudently withdrew to Leiden. There, in 1747, he published *Man a Machine*, one of the most radical materialist works of the time, and found that Dutch **toleration**, too, had its limits.

La Mettrie was fortunate to be invited by **Frederick II** to come to Prussia, which he did at the beginning of 1748. Frederick's court maintained the tradition of aristocratic libertinism, something that an outspoken bourgeois could not benefit from in France or Holland. Frederick not only offered La Mettrie asylum, he also conferred the positions of reader and physician to the king on him, and had him made a member of the **Academy** of Berlin. La Mettrie continued to write on medical subjects and ethics, and according to a tradition which seems too good to be true, died of overeating at the age of 42. His eulogy before the Academy of Berlin was delivered by the king.

LAW, FACULTY OF. One of the three senior faculties of the 18th century **university**, and the most practical from a professional and economic point of view. It was also intellectually the most attractive, for of the other two faculties, theology was in decline and medicine had not yet reached the level of a science. Still, the history of men of letters in the 18th century is full of instances, beginning with Bernard **Fontenelle** and **Voltaire**, of prudent parents sending their sons off to the university to study law, and those sons turning from the boredom of their legal studies to the pleasures and promises of literature.

In the 16th and 17th centuries practicing lawyers had contributed significantly to political theory. By the 18th century this function had been largely taken over by writers. In England, William Blackstone's commentaries on the common law commanded a far wider audience than such a work would today, while in France the **Jansenist** lawyer Louis-Adrien Le Paige produced some important oppositionist tracts. Sara Maza has shown that the briefs of members of the Paris bar circulated widely and had significant impact on **public opinion**. In Prussia and Austria whole batteries of lawyers worked hard to produce the voluminous codifications dear to **enlightened despotism**. Still, practicing lawyers played a less significant role in the elaboration of political theory in the Enlightenment than they had done previously. But a great deal of political theory was produced by men who had once been engaged in legal practice.

Montesquieu, for example, had sat as a magistrate in the *Parlement* of Bordeaux before retiring to his chateau of La Brède to meditate on the regularities behind social and historical phenomena and to produce his *Spirit of the Laws*. Similarly, Giambattista **Vico**'s legal studies and his aspiration to unity and harmony stimulated him to try to uncover a single principle or law that would explain the development of societies and cultures. The works on legal reform produced by Jacques Pierre Brissot, who abandoned the drudgery of a lawyer's office for a literary career in Paris, by Simon Nicolas Henri **Linguet**, a lawyer turned journalist, or the Italian nobleman, Cesare **Beccaria**, all far exceeded the narrow bounds of positive law (*see* **Law, Positive**) to raise larger questions of social and political organization. The legal profession thus made important contributions, both direct and indirect, to the social criticism and political theory of the Enlightenment, and it would soon provide a disproportionately large contribution to the personnel of the **French Revolution**.

LAW, NATURAL. One of the pivotal concepts of the Enlightenment, and one that serves to distinguish an older enchanted view of the world from a newer, scientific one.

Early in the development of European thought, natural phenomena were assumed to be the results of the behavior and will of divine or occult forces. The Sumerians, Greeks and other ancient peoples were aware of certain regularities of **nature**, but they did not separate these perceived regularities from their religious beliefs, philosophies and **superstitions**. This separation was not made until late in the Enlightenment. Isaac **Newton** took the order he discovered in nature as proof of the existence of a Divine Artificer, and was followed in this by **Voltaire** and other advocates of **deism**. Materialists such as Denis **Diderot**, the baron d'**Holbach** and Julien Offray **La Mettrie** explained the world in purely naturalistic terms. This attitude is well illustrated in an encounter between Napoleon and the astronomer Pierre Simon Laplace. When the scientist had finished his exposition of the workings of the solar system for the general, the latter asked, "And what of God?" The answer he received was, "Sire, I have no need of that hypothesis."

Montesquieu defined law as "the necessary relations that derive from the nature of things" (*Spirit of the Laws*, Bk. I, chap. 1). It was this element of necessity and inevitability that contributed powerfully to purging the world of spirits, goblins, the diabolical and, in some cases, the divine, all of which were believed to act by will and whim. In their place scientists and thinkers put the observed and calculable regularities that followed from "the nature of things."

That nature had its laws that were not subject to arbitrary modification came to be widely accepted after Newton (*see* **Miracles**). That there were laws of the same sort that applied to society was a proposition that was first put forward consistently by the thinkers of the Enlightenment, and it was during the Enlightenment that the groundwork for the sciences of society, particularly sociology and economics, was laid. But the concept of natural law had different implications for society than it did for the exact sciences.

The assumption that there were laws that existed necessarily and of their own right with respect to social and political arrangements provided a point of reference by which to judge the positive **laws** existing at any time in a given society, laws which were often the result of historical accident, or the expression of the interests of dominant groups. Thinkers who adhered to the natural law tradition had in that tradition a set of values and a model of social relations that could be presented as objectively based alternatives to existing conditions. Natural law thus added a dimension to social thought, and served as a useful and authoritative tool for reformers, especially reformers advocating sweeping changes.

The doctrine of natural law was not, however, universally accepted in the 18th century, even among the *philosophes*. Social conservatives, such as David **Hume** and Edmund **Burke,** insisted on the primacy and legitimacy of existing social relations and of tradition, and by denying the relevance of natural law to society, grounded their defenses of the status quo in a uni-dimensional social vision that precluded feasible alternatives. Nor did all of those committed to reform find the doctrine of natural law congenial. Jeremy **Bentham,** for example, utterly rejected it, but worked energetically to effect a wide range of reforms using utility as a criterion instead.

LAW, POSITIVE. Laws put in place (posited), or made, by man. Influenced by circumstance, tradition, the temperaments of rulers and socially determined norms and values, positive laws vary infinitely from place to place and time to time. Natural **law,** by contrast, is taken as constant and universally valid. It is usually said to be based on **reason,** whereas positive law is simply the determination of the legislator, or legislative body, of a given state, and is valid only in territories controlled by that state. Natural law is descriptive, formulating perceived regularities in the relations between things; positive law is prescriptive, requiring that people do, or refrain from doing, certain things.

Most Enlightenment thinkers recognized the need for, and legitimacy of, positive laws, both because there was no general agreement on the precise content of natural law or ways it could be applied to particular societies, and because differences in objective conditions between societies required differences in laws. During the 18th century, however, there was a tendency among progressive thinkers to judge positive laws in the light of natural law, and where the former deviated excessively from the latter, to call for their reform. Thus, for example, punishments that were out of all proportion to the crime, or were considered unreasonable or inhumane, such as capital punishment for the expression of an opinion, were criticized by reform-minded thinkers such as **Voltaire** and Cesare **Beccaria,** the formal legitimacy of such positive laws notwithstanding.

If the gap between the positive laws of a society and natural law were thought to be too great, the result might be to delegitimize the former to the point that they not only became objects of demands for reform, but also of revolution.

LEIBNIZ, Gottfried Wilhelm (1646-1716). One of the most brilliant but least focused minds of the early Enlightenment. The son of a professor of moral philosophy in the **University** of Leipzig, Leibniz took a degree in law, which he used more in an administrative than in a properly legal capacity.

Leibniz earned his living as a counselor to a number of courts of petty German princes, most consistently that of Hanover, and toward the end of his life he also held a post and a stipend from the court of St. Petersburg. He was a curious blend of courtier, administrator, political advisor and not infrequently pamphleteer, technical advisor, think-tanker and philosopher who recommended himself by his sheer intelligence and energy. He also curiously combined traditional and new motives and interests. On the one hand, he was an accomplished humanist who had translated two of Plato's dialogs from Greek to Latin; he had a lifelong interest in alchemy (as did many of his employers, and no less a figure than Isaac **Newton**); and he was perhaps the last major intellectual figure in the West seriously to aspire to heal the schism in the Church caused by the Protestant Reformation. On the other hand, he worked on such technical problems as drainage of mines, improved designs for coaches and mechanical calculating machines; and he proposed a wide variety of projects for social, economic and administrative reform. In Leibniz it was as if the interests and abilities of thinkers such as Erasmus, Pico della Mirandola and Leonardo da Vinci had been concentrated in one person, and that person had succeeded, moreover, in coming to terms with the court culture and philosophy of his time, in many ways anticipating before the event the problematics of **enlightened despotism.**

Throughout his career Leibniz exhibited a profound concern for the organization and expansion of knowledge. From 1676 his duties in Hanover included overseeing the library, and in 1690 he was named chief librarian of the Bibliotheca Augusta at Wolfenbüttel. He tried to institute new cataloging techniques to provide comprehensive subject indexes, but because of the inertia of the institutions and the costs involved was unable to do so. He also aspired to produce a universal encyclopedia, something between already existing compilations and Denis **Diderot**'s *Encyclopédie*, but this project too, like so many others, remained incomplete.

Leibniz had greater success in his attempts to organize and expand knowledge in the framework of **academies**. He was elected to the **Royal Society** in London and the Royal Academy of Sciences in Paris, was directly responsible for the founding of the Berlin Academy and put in motion the machinery for founding academies in Vienna and St. Petersburg (*see* **Academies, State-Sponsored**). He contributed numerous papers to be read before the academies, and printed in their proceedings. He also carried on a massive correspondence with other savants, and wrote frequently for the periodical press.

One of the most original philosophers of his time, Leibniz sought to harmonize the views of René **Descartes** with those of the atomists, such as Thomas Hobbes and Pierre Gassendi. Like the other great system-builders of the 17th century, he insisted on the importance of metaphysics, which caused him to be looked at askance by the empirically inclined thinkers of the High Enlightenment. Indeed, he was most widely remembered for the vicious satire of his notions of sufficient cause and optimism in *Candide*. Because he wrote as many papers and memoranda as he did, and took on projects, such as the history of the Guelphs, which he was unable to complete, he left little in the way of fully worked out treatises. His *Discourse on Metaphysics* (1687), *Essays on Theodicy* (1710) and *Monadology*, already developed in an article in the *Acta Eruditorum* of 1698, are the main works published during his lifetime.

LEOPOLD II (1747-1792). A member of the royal House of Habsburg, Leopold was Grand Duke of Tuscany from 1765 to 1790 and Holy Roman Emperor from 1790 to 1792. His brother was **Joseph II**, and his sister Marie Antoinette. Though for most of his life left to rule a minor Habsburg territory in Italy, he is remembered as one of the most successful and most humane of the enlightened monarchs.

As ruler of Tuscany Leopold provided sound and careful government, contributing to both the stability and prosperity of this historically rich region. He also carried out a series of reforms to improve the efficiency of the machinery of government and to modernize society. Among other measures he replaced the standing army with a militia, something of which the great Florentine political thinker Machiavelli would have approved enthusiastically, reformed the legal system and intended to enact a written constitution that would have limited his own powers. This he was prevented from doing by his brother, the emperor.

Leopold was perhaps the most genuinely progressive and generous of the contemporary practitioners of **enlightened despotism**, and he was certainly one of the most successful. But as the ruler of a minor Italian state he receives less attention than the rulers of the great northern monarchies. In contrast to his brother, Leopold was pragmatic and careful to make reforms that, while progressive, were acceptable to most of the population.

When Joseph died in 1790 Leopold succeeded him, and was immediately confronted with the widespread opposition, sometimes to the point of rebellion, which Joseph's far-reaching and forcefully imposed reforms called forth from the privileged. Leopold had first to restore order, which required annulling considerable parts of Joseph's program, the substance of which he agreed with. He did not, however, rescind Joseph's legislation on **toleration**, and he salvaged what he could in the way of tax reform and peasant emancipation. The crisis dealt with, Leopold loosened **censorship**, allowed public political discussion and limited police jurisdiction. He also, wisely, sought to avoid involvement with affairs in France, his sister's appeals notwithstanding.

Since he reigned as Holy Roman Emperor for only two years it is impossible to know how successful Leopold would have been in this capacity. The indications, however, are that, able to distinguish the feasible from the desirable, and having a gift for negotiation which made it possible to avoid recourse to force in imposing his policies, an extended tenure of imperial power for Leopold would have resulted in a more moderate but more lasting set of reforms than those attempted by his well-intentioned but overly forceful brother.

LESPINASSE, Julie de (1732-1776). An important and exceptional *salonnière*. She was born to the Countess d'Albon, a noblewoman from the Lyonnais who was separated from her husband. The fact that Mlle de Lespinasse was illegitimate had a number of important consequences. First, she could not inherit family property, and so, while of genteel origin, she was relatively poor. Secondly, her mother kept her with her, so Julie benefited from a close and warm maternal bond, something that was unusual at the time.

In 1748 Julie's mother died and it was decided to send her to live with her half-sister and her husband, the Count Gaspard de Vichy, who was both the brother of Mme du **Deffand** and, as it happens, Julie's father. With great discretion the count treated her as a lesser servant, and any preference he might have had for her as his natural daughter was unapparent. On the estate of Chamrond Julie acted as governess to the children of her half-sister and brother-in-law/father. This was a situation that could not be sustained indefinitely, and there was talk of putting her into a convent. She was saved from the fate of a nunnery without a vocation by a visit of Mme du Deffand to Chamrond.

By 1754 Mme du Deffand's sight was much impaired. While at Chamrond Julie frequently read to her, and her intelligence and good nature impressed the older woman, who suggested that she come to Paris as her companion and reader. Julie accepted readily. Moving from a provincial backwater to the highest circles of Parisian society could not have been easy, but with the direction of Mme du Deffand and her own tact and good sense, she made the transition successfully. Too successfully, perhaps.

Julie's charm and intelligence resulted in some of Mme du Deffand's guests giving precedence to the companion over the lady of the house. In 1764, when Mme du Deffand discovered that Jean le Ronde d'**Alembert** and some other members of her **salon** had been meeting Julie in her room before the formal reception hours, the two quarrelled and the older woman dismissed the younger one.

Julie de Lespinasse still had no fortune, but she did have friends and a perceived function in Parisian society. Mme de Geoffrin generously settled an annuity of 3,000 *livres* on her, and other friends helped in different ways. She took lodgings in the rue Bellechasse, and there held a somewhat different sort of salon. She received guests daily from 5:00 to 9:00 instead of only certain days of the week as was the custom in other salons. Lacking means, Julie was unable to keep an "open table" in the aristocratic manner, and provided only the contemporary equivalent of peanuts and pretzels. As one of her guests said with malicious charm, "One goes there to digest." But go there one did.

Julie de Lespinasse's salon became a key meeting point for those most closely identified with Enlightenment thought, among them d'Alembert, who was in love with Mlle de Lespinasse, and only left his adoptive family to take the apartment above hers, the Marquis de **Condorcet,** Jean-Baptiste Suard, the Marquis de Chastellux, Jean-François **Marmontel,** Anne-Robert-Jacques **Turgot** and Christian-Guillaume de Lamoignon de **Malesherbes.** As in most other salons, there was a significant female presence, which in this case included the Countess de Boufflers, the Maréchale de Luxembourg and Mme Geoffrin. As in other salons, too, a good deal of informal politicking took place, and many an academician had his election smoothed in the salon of Mlle de Lespinasse.

Where Julie's salon differed from others was in appealing more to men of letters and less to social elites. The hostess was also less formal than was the case in most other salons, and possibly her gifts for encouraging discussion and easing social situations was greater than that of other *salonnières*. Certainly she was remarkably bright, animated, articulate and intelligent, and she had a great capacity for both friendship and love. She was not physically robust, however, and used opium medicinally.

Her deep friendship with d'Alembert lasted as long as she lived. She was also passionately in love. In 1766 she met the Count de Mora, a Spanish noble, with whom she enjoyed a mutually affectionate relationship bedevilled by her unsuitability as a match in the eyes of his family and by his ill health. Mora died in 1774. In 1772, while Moira was absent from Paris, she met and fell in love with the Count de Guibert. Her letters to him reflect an exceptionally honest and passionate character. When Guibert married sensibly in 1775 her already precarious health was further undermined, and she died in 1776 at the age of only 44.

Where a number of the important *salonnières* of the earlier generation had participated in the sexual freedom of the **Regency**, there was nothing of the libertine about Mlle de Lespinasse. On the contrary, she seemed to embody the sensibility and the deeply moral approach to love advocated by Jean-Jacques **Rousseau,** and her death, like that of the heroine of *Julie, ou Nouvelle Héloïse*, seems to have resulted from the incompatibility of her emotional needs with the social values of the society in which she lived.

LESSING, Gotthold Ephraim (1729-1781). One of the key figures of the Enlightenment in Germany. Born in Kamenz in Saxony to the pastor of the place, Lessing received his first and very adequate education from his father at home. Like Christian **Thomasius** and Christian **Wolff**, he studied at the **University** of Leipzig, but unlike them, he did not go on to make his career as a university teacher. Rather, his search for employment was more like that of intellectuals of the Enlightenment who lacked independent incomes or unusually good luck. Lessing worked for a time as a journalist in Berlin, served as a private secretary, and finally, as of 1770, was appointed to the post of librarian of the Duke of Brunswick.

Much of Lessing's literary output was devoted to the stage and esthetic theory. He was involved in the attempt to establish a German national theater in Hamburg between 1767 and 1769. In a work on the theory of theater he criticized classical norms and the influence of French theater, praised the plays of **Shakespeare** and showed sympathy for realistic plots with middle-class characters of the sort known as the *drame*, and favored by Denis **Diderot** (*see* **Bourgeois**

Drama). He also wrote a number of plays, among them *Miss Sara Sampson* (1755), *Minna von Barnhelm* (1767), *Emilia Galotti* (1772) and *Nathan the Wise* (1779), a drama of ideas arguing for natural religion and **toleration**, and using the figure of Moses **Mendelssohn**, a Jewish thinker and writer, and a personal friend, as the model for the main character.

Perhaps Lessing's best-known work is *Laocoön*, a treatise on esthetics that takes as its starting point the interpretation of the statue group of this name. Against the great contemporary classicist Johann Joachim Winckelmann, Lessing argued that the statues reflected less the classical values of dignity and restraint than the limitations of the medium in which they were made. Painting and sculpture can only portray a situation at a given moment, while literature can extend its representations over time. The unfolding of a story with a variety of scenes and situations, and with corresponding expressions, that makes up the account of the poet or prose writer was not available to the plastic artist. According to Lessing, this limitation disposed sculptors and painters in the classical tradition against portraying the most extreme forms of emotion, since these are often too harsh or too distressing for extended viewing and consideration. Emphases appropriate in poetry were not necessarily so in other art forms. Lessing here raised an important point about the relation of different art forms to each other, and about esthetics generally.

LETTERS ON ENGLAND/PHILOSOPHICAL LETTERS (1734). One of the classic formulations of Enlightenment thought. It was written by **Voltaire** as a direct consequence of his forced residence in England from 1726 to 1729, and brings attention to the **liberalism**, openness and progressiveness of British society, especially when compared to France.

The *Philosophical Letters* treat four main subjects. The first seven letters deal with religion, particularly nonconformist varieties of Christianity, and the advantages of the co-existence of a number of faiths. Politics is the subject of letters 8 and 9 and in them Voltaire emphasizes the advantages of **constitutionalism** and limited monarchy. Letters 12 to 17 give accounts of the founders of the Enlightenment, Francis **Bacon**, John **Locke**, Isaac **Newton** and René **Descartes**, and the achievements and assumptions with which they replaced the theological and Aristotelian views of the world prevalent until their time. Letters 18 to 24 deal with literature and men of letters, and point out the respect that writers, thinkers and scientists in

England enjoyed, in contrast to their counterparts in France. The last letter treats Pascal and the particular challenge that he represented to Enlightenment thinkers.

Certain values inform and vivify Voltaire's treatments of the different subjects he takes up. He views human beings as self-interested and rational, and so more in need of freedom to exercise their initiative than direction by the authorities. Whether in religion, politics, society or intellectual endeavor, he advocates freedom and **toleration**. Underlying this broad liberalism is the assumption, forcefully presented in his treatment of the founders of the Enlightenment, that human beings have no way of knowing absolute truths, and in this condition of limited and relative knowledge it is inappropriate to coerce belief or opinion. If there is no damage, there are no grounds for state intervention.

Voltaire gives his reader to understand that the freedom that the British enjoy in their arts, religion, commerce and politics is at the heart of their prosperity and **happiness**. The implications for his own country are obvious.

LIBERALISM. Narrowly defined, a political philosophy; in its broader acceptation a worldview that asserts the rights of individuals against collectivities and assumes the desirability of a wide degree of freedom for the individual.

Classical liberalism is very much a feature of Enlightenment thought, flourishing between the time of John **Locke** and John Stuart Mill. It was based on two different sets of assumptions. The first was the belief that traditional corporate structures, the expanding authority of the **absolutist** state and the predominant Churches all exercised excessive control of those subject to their authority. In the inevitable tension between collective authority and individual autonomy, liberals favor expanding the sphere of individual choice and freedom as much as possible. This new sense of the feasibility of extending the realm of individual autonomy developed, logically enough, when Christian notions of the radical corruption of **human nature** by original sin and the Machiavellian and Hobbesian assumptions that human beings were inherently egoistic, passion-driven and violent came to be challenged by a more rational and a more gentle conceptualization of what human beings were. Given the way human nature was conceived by Jean Calvin, Thomas Hobbes or Bishop Bossuet, it made no sense to reduce the degree of control exercised by church and state over the individual; in the views of John Locke, Lord

Shaftesbury, Voltaire, Jean-Jacques **Rousseau** and many other representative thinkers of the Enlightenment, this was precisely what needed to be done.

A second, less immediate set of assumptions that furthered liberalism during the 18th century concerned the emergence of new paradigms of science. The demonstration of the basically lawful nature of the universe by Isaac **Newton** made the world seem a more intelligible and hospitable place than it had been before. It also made men and women less dependent on traditional authorities, and more able to rely on their own informed **reason** for making decisions. The demystification of the world effected by Newton empowered the rational individual, and made the attribution of greater freedom to the individual more feasible. At roughly the same time, Locke's *Essay Concerning Human Understanding* laid the basis for a demystified and rational view of human nature. According to Locke, **self-interest** was the kind of constant in human affairs that gravity was in physics. Further, for Locke, unlike Hobbes, self-interest was effectively shaped and modified by reason, so that it became possible to calculate human behavior on the basis of rational, or enlightened, self-interest.

Yet if liberals tend to see human beings as generally reasonable and responsible, they have a deep and abiding mistrust of authority and those who exercise it. No doubt the historical examples of numberless ministers of state and church who exercised power arbitrarily and with excessive vigor helped to bring liberals to this point of view. It also seems, however, that endowing the individual with power interferes with the mechanism of rational self-interest on which Enlightenment liberalism relied so heavily. Though the great Victorian historian, Lord Acton, did not make his statement that "Power corrupts and absolute power corrupts absolutely" until late in the 19th century, it was a judgment with which most Enlightenment liberals would have agreed.

Liberalism found a variety of expressions and applications during the 18th century. Voltaire's strident anticlericalism and his repeated call to "crush the infamous thing" is perhaps as much, or more, a plea for **liberty** of conscience as it is a frontal attack on the more repressive features of Catholicism. The President **Montesquieu's** desire to retain intermediary powers characteristic of the medieval model of monarchy and his advocacy of the **separation of powers** may give his liberalism an aristocratic slant, but his primary concern was with retaining institutional checks on the growing power of the absolute monarchy, which he feared would result in **despotism**.

In laying the groundwork for economic liberalism, Adam **Smith**, transposing the assumptions of Newton's physics to the field of economics, argued that the market mechanism, working in conditions of unrestricted self-interest, would achieve better results than any form of **regulation** could. Denis **Diderot** wondered whether many maladies of Western societies did not follow from ignoring or repressing our natural inclinations, and gave impressive formulation to these thoughts in works he withheld from publication during his lifetime, *D'Alembert's Dream* and *Bougainville's Voyage*. In suggesting that mankind would be better off if left to follow its natural inclinations he recalls the position most forcibly advocated by his sometime friend, Jean-Jacques Rousseau.

Rousseau's relation to liberalism has been much debated. The difficulty in determining whether or not he belongs to this tradition seems to stem from his appreciation of the formative force of state and society in the development of the individual, and his recognition that the nature and extent of the realm of personal autonomy depends on social and political conditions. It is in the work of Rousseau that the equilibrium between the public and the individual spheres is most clear, and treated most sensitively.

The 18th century was an age in which corporations, church and state still exercised great power and weighed heavily in all aspects of the life of the individual. Most progressive thinkers, therefore, demanded civil rights, freedom of conscience, freedom of expression for ordinary people and the moderation of the exercise of power by the authorities. By the end of the **Old Regime** the thinkers of the Enlightenment had succeeded in loosening somewhat the grip of church and state on the lives of most Europeans. But the balance between collective authority and individual rights still favored the former. In this context liberalism was a progressive and liberating force.

Since the 18th century, the collective structures against which the liberals of the Enlightenment struggled have lost most of their power. Not only have the "intermediary powers" so dear to Montesquieu been reduced in importance or eliminated, but the civic and political spheres have been so far eroded by the ideology of individual and private rights that it is increasingly difficult for the State to maintain its identity and to assure to its citizens services and support mechanisms that, only a generation ago, were taken for granted.

Despite a certain linguistic similarity, the present-day libertarian has little in common with the liberal of the Enlightenment. The tension between the civic and private spheres on the one hand, and the public sphere on the other, which in the 18th century still favored the latter, by the end of the 20th century had been resolved in favor of the former. Without this tension, politics as we have known it and the common good lose all validity, and economic interests replace the institutions and regulations without which an ordered and civilized polity cannot be sustained.

LIBERTY. Lack of restraint upon individuals or groups to think and behave as they see fit within accepted guidelines. Also, the rights of individuals or groups to take part in significant social and political processes. The first characterization of liberty belongs to the sphere of civil society, the second to the sphere of politics, and the two notions are distinct. It is possible to enjoy the liberty to buy and sell with only the most limited forms of restraint and yet to be totally deprived of political rights, and vice versa. It is also possible for a society to safeguard or to deny civic as well as political liberty.

The notion of political liberty is central to the tradition of **republicanism**. For classical Greeks, the right to take part in deliberation and law making was integral to **citizenship**, and citizenship was for them necessary to achieving full humanity. In the **Old Regime**, monarchy in principle denied political rights to subjects, and carried on politics through the court and in collaboration with certain recognized corporations. The notions of classical citizenship and the citizen's right to participate in government were retained in the consciousness of the educated classes in Europe during the 18th century as a result of the classically-based curriculum of secondary schools. It emerged with renewed force during the **French Revolution**.

Whether, and to what degree, liberty is suited to human beings depends on the way **human nature** is conceived. If, as in the Augustinian tradition, mankind is conceived as radically corrupt, then it is not capable of using freedom constructively. Similarly, if, as in the case of Thomas Hobbes, humans are taken as irrational creatures motivated by passion and love of dominion living in conditions of chronic scarcity, then they are again unsuited to freedom. The Enlightenment could only validate liberty if it reconceived men to be capable of curbing their passions by **reason** and **self-interest**. This shift was made pre-eminently by John **Locke**, and followed up by most of the thinkers of the Enlightenment. Jean-Jacques **Rousseau**, for example, argued that human nature was essentially good, and other *philosophes*, if they would not go so far, regarded it as neutral.

In addition to a rehabilitated human nature, the Enlightenment turn to liberty was further strengthened by the reconceptualization of **nature** as orderly and lawful. If there was an inherent order and harmony in social and political relations, it made sense to minimize the degree of state intervention in these spheres, and to rely on the rational self-interest of the individual, exercised in conditions of maximal liberty. This is the thrust of Adam **Smith's** attack on mercantilism and argument for the deregulation of the market.

It is more accurate to speak of a minimally regulated market rather than a "free" market. Markets and land are neither free nor unfree. They function or are used according to certain laws. However, human beings are properly said to be free or unfree, depending on circumstances. It is becoming increasingly apparent that the degree of deregulation of markets and the level of well-being of the population at large stand in inverse relation to each other.

It was also the view of many Enlightenment thinkers that rational self-interest renders superfluous the sort of strong police function that Hobbes regarded as essential. In the gentler view of man and the world that took root with the Enlightenment, liberty was conceived not only as possible, but also as contributing positively to social and economic well-being.

LIGNIVILLE, Anne Catherine/Mme HELVÉTIUS (1722-1800).
The daughter of a distinguished noble family from Lorraine, who married the wealthy *philosophe* and financier, Claude Adrien **Helvétius**. Mme Helvétius's aunt, Mme de **Graffigny**, took an active interest in her education, and in establishing her in the world.

Mme Helvétius first met her future husband in 1747 while staying with her aunt in Paris. She married him in 1751, and the couple enjoyed a harmonious and mutually affectionate relationship. Though she had not received a sound education, her native intelligence and acquired social graces assured that she played a central part in her husband's **salon**. The couple had two daughters, and when Helvétius died suddenly, and intestate, in 1771, she was left with a handsome annual income of about 20,000 *livres*.

In 1772 Mme Helvétius bought a comfortable property in Auteuil, just outside Paris, and there began one of the longest lasting salons of the Enlightenment, and the only one to survive into the **French Revolution**. On first being established the regular guests included such central figures of the Enlightenment as Jean le Ronde d'**Alembert**, Denis **Diderot** and the Baron d'**Holbach**. Second generation *philosophes* such as Anne Robert Jacques **Turgot** and the Marquis de **Condorcet** also made their way to Mme Helvétius's salon, and during the Revolution her Auteuil residence became a meeting place for such **ideologues** as Pierre Jean Georges Cabanis, who had already benefited from Mme Helvétius's hospitality and kindness before 1789, Antoine Louis Claude **Destutt de Tracy** and the Marquis de Volney. Mme Helvétius's salon thus provided a meeting place that, exceptionally, brought together successive generations of Enlightenment thinkers.

Other prominent figures to frequent Mme Helvétius's salon include Benjamin **Franklin** and the abbé **Morellet**. Helvétius had been involved with **freemasonry**, and his wife continued the connection with the movement. Mme Helvétius sought to honor her husband's memory in the Paris Lodge of the Seven Sisters, and many members of her salon were themselves also masons.

Not only did Mme Helvétius receive friends in her salon, she also invited some of the poorer members of the enlightened community to stay with her. For a number of years before the Revolution she housed the abbé Morellet, the abbé de La Roche, and the young Cabanis and his wife. In her circle Mme Helvétius was affectionately known as "Our Lady of Auteuil." She was buried in accordance with her wishes in her garden in Auteuil.

LINGUET, Simon Nicolas Henri (1736-1794). A forceful writer and leading political journalist of the last decades of the **Old Regime**, but also something of a maverick. He can be seen as a *philosophe* who found himself at odds both with other *philosophes* and with the establishment.

Linguet began his career as an admirer of **Voltaire** and a lawyer working in the *Parlement* of Paris. He became involved with a number of highly publicized cases, usually on the side of progressive causes. He defended the Chevalier de la Barre (1766), whom Voltaire subsequently vindicated, the Duc d'Aiguillon in the celebrated Brittany Affair (1770), the Comte de Morangies (1772) and the Comtesse de Béthune (1774), shortly after which he was disbarred.

Linguet became disenchanted with the *philosophes*, expressing this feeling publicly in a pamphlet entitled *Le Fanatisme des philosophes* (1764). However, his relation to the *philosophes* was complex. He shared many of their basic assumptions, and in 1770 published a long treatise on legal reform, the *Théorie des lois civiles*, which in many ways was a typical product of the Enlightenment. Yet a deeply felt pessimism prevented his expecting significant improvement from the kinds of measures acceptable to most *philosophes*, and he came to be a supporter of royal **absolutism**.

Having been disbarred, Linguet turned to journalism as his main activity. But unlike most journalists of the time he insisted on dealing explicitly with politics. This was something the government was not inclined to tolerate. In 1776 the official permission to publish his *Journal politique et littéraire*, which he had begun in 1774, was revoked. He founded the *Annales politiques, civiles et littéraires du dix-huitième siècle* in 1777 in London. Though often idiosyncratic, this journal was one of the most important **periodicals** of the time.

The frankness and independence of the *Annales*, in which neither the government nor its critics were spared, won Linguet many enemies. Having returned to France on business in 1781, he was arrested and imprisoned in the Bastille for two years. During this time the highly competent Swiss journalist, Jacques Mallet du Pan, took over the running of the *Annales*. **Joseph II** was impressed by Linguet's writing and invited him to Vienna where he conferred on him a title of **nobility** and a generous cash grant.

Linguet returned to France in 1789, and in 1791 argued the case of the black slaves of Santo Domingo against their masters before the National Assembly. Too outspoken and tactless to negotiate the complex byways of revolutionary politics, he was arrested and executed in 1794. *See also* **French Revolution; Slavery**.

LITERACY. The ability to read, often, but not necessarily, accompanied by the ability to write. For the 18th century, historians usually define literacy in terms of the ability to sign one's name. This is the case largely because literacy data for this and preceding periods are usually based on a person's ability to sign his or her name in the parish register at the time of marriage, or in marriage contracts. Because the ability to write had practical value, primary schools sometimes charged higher fees for writing than for reading lessons, and in any case taught reading first. The ability to sign one's name therefore probably underestimates somewhat the ability to read.

As a movement, the Enlightenment was characterized by extensive use of the written and printed word. However, it was not itself responsible for the extensive spread of literacy. In most of Protestant Europe, the Reformation with its emphasis on Bible reading and assuring the individual's access to other religious texts had achieved reasonably high levels of literacy by the end of the 17th century. In England, for example, the average rate of male literacy in the mid-17th century was roughly 30 percent, and by the end of the 18th century had doubled. In France, which as a Catholic country typically had lower rates of literacy, 29 percent of males could sign their names in 1690, and this figure rose to 47 percent by the end of the following century. The corresponding figures for French **women** were 14 percent and 27 percent.

Literacy rates varied in relation to cultural, economic and geographic factors. It has already been noted that Protestantism tended to favor literacy. However, in both Catholic and Protestant countries, literacy correlated positively to urbanism. In the great urban centers of Western Europe during the second half of the 18th century male literacy rates often reached 80 percent and 90 percent, while female rates followed not far behind. Occupational need was a major reason for acquiring the skills of literacy, so that while poorer peasants and unskilled laborers had low rates of literacy, skilled artisans often had significantly higher ones. As school attendance imposed some economic burden on families, the poorer they were, the less likely they were to send their children to school. However, during the 18th century opportunities for informally acquiring the skills of literacy, say through the good offices of a local cleric, were probably greater than they are today. It should also be noted that in Catholic countries even regular school attendance for a number of years would not guarantee acquisition of the skills of literacy, since education was conceived more in terms of religious instruction and acculturation than is the case today.

The culture of the Enlightenment was based on a reasonably wide distribution of literacy, at least among the middle and upper classes, for it was these skills that gave a larger public access to books and **periodicals** through which the ideas and values of the Enlightenment spread. There was a consensus within the enlightened community that favored making the ability to read and write general. However, it was not thought that the skills of literacy were by themselves sufficient to bring those who possessed them to share in Enlightenment culture. On the one hand, the clergy had long used the skills of literacy to propagate and defend church doctrines; on the other, there was throughout Europe a large body of popular literature made up of fairy tales, almanachs, romances and hagiographies that provided working people with fantasy and escape from the harsh and demanding world in which they lived without helping them to understand or control it any better. A high level of competence in the skills of literacy was a precondition for the spread of enlightenment, but it was not a sufficient condition for participation in Enlightenment culture.

LOCKE, John (1632-1704). One of those responsible for laying the bases of Enlightenment thought, and possibly one of the most influential European philosophers of all time. Though he began his career as an Oxford academic, Locke became actively engaged in politics, experienced extensive periods of exile in France and Holland and finally became a beneficiary of the settlement following the Glorious Revolution of 1688, for which he was also an apologist. His philosophical work treats the fields of religion, politics and **epistemology**.

Both Locke's parents came from small trading families, and both were Puritan. Locke's father fought as a cavalry officer with the Roundheads during the Civil War. Though unable to enter the gentry, he did achieve some upward mobility in his career, practicing law on a modest level, and acquiring some land. Partly with the help of **patronage** he was able to send his son to Westminster School, and then, from 1652, to Oxford. Locke was deeply interested in religious questions throughout his life, but instead of preparing himself for a career in the Church, he opted for medicine. This was a decision with far-reaching consequences.

Locke's career changed dramatically when in 1667 he accepted the offer of Lord Ashley, better known as the Earl of Shaftesbury, to become his personal physician and secretary. Shaftesbury being a **Whig** magnate, and a leading figure opposing concentration of power in the monarchy and the restoration of Catholicism as the state religion in England, Locke became actively involved in the stormy and dangerous politics of the time. To avoid some of the rigors of opposition, Locke spent most of the years 1675-1679 in France, and then 1683-1689 in Holland, returning to England only once William of Orange had established himself and James II had left the country.

During 1690 a number of works for which he is best known were published, though he had written most of them while abroad. His *Two Treatises of Government*, the second of which is a key text in the development of modern **liberalism**, justified the Glorious Revolution by arguing that political legitimacy depended on the consent of the governed and asserting a right of resistance. The *Letters on Toleration* (1689-1692) are more cautious and restricted than Pierre **Bayle**'s *Philosophical Commentary*, and in its denial of tolerance to Catholics, which reflects historical and denominational tensions in England, seem odd to modern readers.

The most influential of his 1690 publications, and the only one to appear under his name, was the *Essay Concerning Human Understanding*. In it Locke proposed models of **human nature** and of the mechanisms for the acquisition of knowledge that were firmly based on sense experience and free from traditional metaphysical considerations. Though Locke was certainly not alone in working for the renovation of European thought, the *Essay* was an exceptional text that had immense influence on the way the Enlightenment conceived mankind and problems of epistemology. By showing not only how knowledge was acquired, but also what sorts of things could not be known with certainty, Locke helped to lay the basis for an intellectual humility that was fundamental to liberalism.

Among Locke's other publications are *Some Thoughts Concerning Education* (1693), the *Reasonableness of Christianity* (1695), a typical and sincere attempt to conciliate traditional religion with science, and a late treatment of method, *Of the Conduct of the Understanding*, which did not appear during his lifetime, and which was in a way an extension of the *Essay*. As a part of the Whig ruling elite Locke also served on a number of government commissions, and wrote extensively on economic and administrative issues. His lasting legacies, however, were his contributions to liberal political theory, to the Enlightenment reconceptualizations of human nature and of epistemology, and to a lesser degree, to church-state relations.

LOUIS XV (1710-1774). Grandson of Louis XIV and King of France from 1723 to 1774. His reign marked a period of critical decline for the French state. Of the two major wars fought under Louis XV, the first, the War of Austrian Succession (1741-1748), waged against Austria, resulted in a reasonably favorable outcome for France, while the second, the Seven Years' War (1756-1763), fought in alliance with Austria against Britain and Prussia, was catastrophic, as France lost almost her entire overseas empire as a result of it. Also, once engaged in war, it is more financially burdensome to lose than to win. The outstanding diplomatic event of the reign of Louis XV was the alliance with Austria, which reversed centuries of mutual hostility.

Internally, Louis XV's reign was marked by serious dissention, which undermined the authority of the crown. Dominant elements within the Church tried to repress what remained of **Jansenism** by using coercive measures. In what is known as the "affaire des billets," the Church authorities decided to refuse the last rites to those who could not provide a note showing that they had made confession to a priest untainted by Jansenism. The *Parlement* of Paris intervened on the side of the Jansenists, and the king, whose sympathies were with the orthodox Church, ruled that both sides were to remain silent on the issue, but could not enforce his directive. In this episode the king made the mistake of invoking the authority of the state in a matter of conscience in which there was little room for compromise, and little chance of effective repression.

Louis and his ministers had been reasonable and responsible in attempting to deal with the worsening condition of state finances. In this undertaking they were consistently opposed by the magistrates of the *parlements*, who sought to keep the crown within the limits of traditional fiscal practice. By using their right of refusal to register fiscal legislation, the *parlements*, which represented the interests of the **nobility**, were able to block significant measures of fiscal reform. To overcome this opposition Louis XV backed his Chancellor, René Nicolas Charles Augustin **Maupeou,** in closing the existing *parlements*, and replacing them with new courts. This measure was effective in clearing the way for the kind of fiscal reform that was necessary if the regime was to survive, but the heavy-handed and unconstitutional way it was carried out alienated a considerable portion of **public opinion**, which regarded it as despotic. Many historians today believe that the Maupeou reforms compromised the legitimacy of the crown in the eyes of the public and contributed to its loss of popularity, and even legitimacy. Moreover, when Louis XV died in 1774, his successor restored the *parlements*, and the advantages of the reform were lost without the damage to the image of the monarchy being correspondingly improved.

Early in his reign Louis XV had been given the sobriquet "the well beloved." By the time of his death, he was generally despised. The reason for this change in attitude probably relates more to the king's private life than his policies. Neither of Louis's two most important mistresses, Madame de **Pompadour** and Madame du Barry, was popular, and it became known that he kept a virtual harem at the Parc-aux-Cerfs in Versailles. A greater degree of sexual freedom has traditionally been accorded monarchs than ordinary citizens, but in Louis XV's case his private life was widely publicized in the scandalous pamphlets, or *libelles*, which intentionally used pornography for political purposes. The authors of these pamphlets, who in effect had a good deal to work with, are now often viewed as having effectively used scandal to compromise the standing of the monarchy.

LOUIS XVI (1754-1793). Grandson of **Louis XV** and King of France from 1774 to his death by guillotine in 1793. During the Restoration his younger brothers ruled France as Louis XVIII and Charles X (1814-1830). Louis XVI was, by most standards, a decent, honorable and upright person, and well intentioned and responsible in his public functions. It was his misfortune that these qualities were inadequate to the exceptionally complex and difficult circumstances he faced.

The problems of France during the reign of Louis XVI were critical. The country was caught in an extended economic downturn. State expenditures grew faster than revenues, and the national debt became more and more unmanageable. With the cooperation of the elites, and particularly their acceptance of a greater portion of the tax burden, a feasible solution to the situation might have been found. However, the **nobility** was inclined to use the fiscal distress of the government to exact political concessions from it. An exceptionally gifted or an exceptionally lucky monarch might have managed to overcome this set of circumstances. Louis XVI was neither.

Louis XVI was quiet and somewhat introverted, and took more pleasure in hunting and his hobby of making locks than in the social round of the court. Unlike his grandfather, he was a model of domestic virtue, as was his wife, the Austrian princess Marie Antoinette. Louis was married at the age of 16, but was unable to consummate the marriage until seven years later. Whether the root of this problem was psychological or physiological, it was overcome, and the couple had four children. By the time this had happened, however, the reputations of both king and queen had been severely compromised by the gutter press that, contrary to fact, made Louis out to be impotent and a cuckold, and Marie Antoinette to be promiscuous. It is ironical that the smut that was with some basis in fact directed against Louis XV, was just as effectively, but without justification, directed at his successor. It was true in the 18th century, as it is today, that the power of the press is not necessarily connected to its veracity.

There is a case to be made for Louis XVI as an enlightened monarch. His annulment of the **Maupeou** reforms was motivated by the desire to respect constitutional norms and **public opinion**, and his collaboration with politicians such as Anne Robert Jacques **Turgot,** Christian-Guillaume Lamoignon de **Malesherbes** and Jacques **Necker** indicate a considerable openness to progressive ideas. It was also during the reign of Louis XVI that judicial torture was abolished in France, and that Protestants achieved civil status again. The regulations drawn up for the convocation of the Estates General in 1789 were exceptionally liberal and inclusive for the time. However, the events set in motion by the meeting of this body soon escaped the control of the king, and anyone else, and as the **French Revolution** became more radical, Louis came increasingly into conflict with it.

Moderate and well intentioned though he was, Louis XVI would not abandon his basic loyalty to the **Old Regime** and the Catholic Church. He attempted to flee the country in June of 1791, then formally accepted the attenuated form of monarchy prescribed by the Constitution of 1791. Increasing tensions with the Legislative Assembly and the popular movement led to his being forcibly removed from office following the uprising of 10 August 1792. He was tried by the Convention and executed on 21 January 1793. He faced death with composure and dignity.

LUXURY. Whether the enjoyment of comforts and conveniences by certain sections of the population was a good thing or not was a matter of debate during the Enlightenment. Both the Christian and the **republican** traditions were hostile to luxury, the former as a consequence of its otherworldly emphasis, the latter because it saw luxury, on the one hand, as a threat to the **equality** necessary to the republican polity, and on the other, as part of a wider process of corruption.

During the Enlightenment some thinkers and writers, usually with worldly and liberal outlooks, undertook a defense of luxury. In part this was to be expected, since the validation of this world and its pleasures would naturally include acceptance of material and cultural refinement. The Enlightenment rehabilitation of **happiness** logically extended to luxury. But other, more pragmatic arguments were also induced in its favor.

Writers such as **Voltaire** and Bernard **Mandeville** argued that far from being an indication of corruption, luxury was socially beneficial. By desiring and ordering superfluous but pleasing and refined consumer goods, the wealthy provided work for artisans and income for middlemen. Though the motives of the rich were no doubt selfish, their self-indulgence stimulated the economy, made wealth circulate and provided work for many who depended on the trade in luxury items for a living. From this point of view, however useless the goods in question, and whatever the motives of the consumers of luxury items, the result was socially beneficial. However, not all contemporaries found this line of argument convincing.

One obvious difficulty with luxury in the social conditions of the 18th century concerned context. In a society in which poverty was so deeply rooted and widespread, the presence of luxury could not but create a harsh impression. It is one thing to enjoy gourmet cooking in superfluity when others in the immediate vicinity are reasonably well fed; it is another when it is known that people are hungry, suffering malnutrition or even dying of want. This was a situation that moralists would not justify.

Other writers, such as Jean-Jacques **Rousseau**, retained a belief in the validity of that part of the republican political tradition which insisted on the importance of a significant degree of equality in any healthy society. Perceiving luxury as an expression of extreme inequality, they were hostile to it. Among traditionalists and some moralists, luxury was seen as part of a complex of values, such as **egoism**, which reflected corruption and threatened the stability as well as the moral fabric of society.

There was no clear outcome to the debate on luxury in the 18th century. The progressives and liberals had a point in arguing that some sections of the working population and the economy benefited from the demand for luxury goods. By the same token, social critics were right to call attention to the contrast of luxury and poverty, and to the problem of extreme inequality, which it highlighted.

M

MABLY, Gabriel Bonnot, abbé de (1709-1785). An example of a worldly cleric whose main commitment was to the Enlightenment while his dress remained that of the Church. Mably belonged to an affluent family. His father was a financial official who was sufficiently wealthy to achieve **nobility** by buying the very expensive office of Secretary to the King. He was also particularly well connected. His brother was the abbé **Condillac**, and for a time in the early 1740s, Jean-Jacques **Rousseau** was employed in the Mably household in Lyon as a tutor. Mably was also related to Madame de **Tencin**, whose **salon** he attended, and whose brother, the Cardinal de Tencin, a minister of state from 1742, employed him for a number of years, first as his secretary, and then in diplomacy. In 1746 this relationship ended, and with it Mably's active role in politics.

Retired to a studious leisure, Mably wrote a number of works on **history**, politics and economics. His historical works include *Observations sur l'histoire de la France* (1765), *De l'Etude de l'histoire*, which appeared as a volume of Condillac's published course of studies for the Prince of Parma (1773), *De la Manière d'écrire l'histoire* (1783) and *Droits et devoirs du citoyen*, which was written in 1758, but not published until the crisis of the pre-Revolution in 1789. Mably expressed his views on economics in a polemic against the **physiocrats**, which appeared in 1768. His last published book, reflecting the Enlightenment's deep concern for ethics, was *Principes de la morale* (1784).

MALESHERBES, Chrétien Guillaume de Lamoignon de (1721-1794). A figure of rare integrity, compassion and intelligence who not only adhered to the main values of the Enlightenment, but also held responsible positions that allowed him to attempt to implement them.

Malesherbes was born into a family of the high magistrature of the capital. He held the office of President of the Cour des Aides, one of the chambers of the ***Parlement*** of Paris, from 1750 to 1771. His father, who served as Chancellor of France, also conferred on him supervision of the book trade, or *librairie,* an office he held from 1750 to 1763, a critical time for the ***philosophes*** and their friends. Malesherbes also twice held ministerial office, once as Minister of the King's Household in 1775-1776, shortly after the accession of **Louis XVI**, who greatly admired him, and again in 1787-1788, when he served as Minister without Portfolio.

As head of the *librairie* Malesherbes strove to carry out his responsibilities fairly, and as far as possible to liberalize **censorship** procedures, and to render them more flexible. During his direction of the *librairie* the categories of tacit permission and simple tolerance were used more frequently to allow the publication of books that the authorities could not properly grant formal approval. In this way the administration modified and liberalized its censorship practices without abandoning them in principle. Malesherbes was clearly sympathetic to the *philosophes*, and used his office to assure that they received a fair hearing. He went out of his way to see to it that the ***Encyclopédie*** could continue to be published, and that Jean-Jacques **Rousseau**'s *Émile* would appear in France.

Malesherbes was also an active participant in the culture of the Enlightenment in his own right. He was elected to the Academy of

Sciences in 1750, to the Academy of Inscriptions in 1759 and to the **Académie française** in 1775 (*see* **Academies, State-Sponsored**). Most of the major *philosophes* figure in his correspondence. He wrote memoirs on the freedom of the press, on taxation and on the rights of minorities, particularly the Protestants, the regularization of whose civil standing he helped effect by 1787, and the **Jews**. Throughout his life he maintained a strong and active interest in botany.

When the Convention decided to try Louis XVI, Malesherbes offered to act as defense counsel, and did so to the best of his considerable ability. Louis XVI was executed in January of 1793. Malesherbes was arrested in December of that year and executed at the height of the Terror in April 1794, together with his daughter and granddaughter. The former Lamoignon residence in the Marais today houses the Historical Library of the City of Paris. Malesherbes is the subject of a major monograph by Pierre Grosclaude.

MANDEVILLE, Bernard (1670-1733). An important moralist and author, who argued for the critical importance of **self-interest**, the passions and even vices in the organization and functioning of advanced societies. Born to a respected family of medical practitioners in Holland, Mandeville attended the Erasmian school of Rotterdam until 1685, then studied at the **University** of Leiden, where he took his medical degree in 1691. Like his father, he specialized in nervous disorders and internal medicine.

Mandeville moved to England in 1692, settling in London. He married, and had two children that survived to adulthood. His medical practice allowed him and his family to live comfortably. In that he became a controversial figure with an international reputation, remarkably little is known of his mature years.

In addition to a number of medical works, he published several collections of fables in English between 1703 and 1705, among them *The Grumbling Hive: or Knaves Turn'd Honest*, which became the core of his famous *Fable of the Bees*. He also published a series of social commentaries and satires, which include *Free Thoughts on Religion, the Church and National Happiness* (1720), *A Modest Defence of Publick Stews* (1724), *An Enquiry into the Causes of the Frequent Executions at Tyburn* (1725) and *An Enquiry into the Origin of Honour, and the Usefulness of Christianity in War* (1732).

MARIVAUX, Pierre Carlet de Chamblain de (1688-1763). Born to a comfortable family headed by a financial official in Riom, Marivaux was sent to Paris to study law. There he began to frequent the **salons** of Mme **Lambert** and Mme de **Tencin**, and was drawn into the literary and cultural life of the capital. He married in 1717, but lost his wife's dowry in a speculation in Law's system. Marivaux wrote a great deal, much of which was appreciated, and on the basis of this output was elected to the **Académie française** in 1743.

Marivaux's writing falls into three main catgories. He wrote a number of novels, two of which, though never completed, have entered into the canon of French literature. These are *La Vie de Marianne* (1731-1741) and *Le Paysan parvenu* (1735-1736). He also worked on a number of periodicals, among them *Le Spectateur français*, an imitation of Joseph **Addison** and Richard **Steele's** *Spectator,* and the *Nouveau Mercure*. Marivaux is best known, however, as a dramatic author, particularly of comedies. In 1722 he wrote *La Surprise de l'amour*, a work which is regarded as a masterpiece, and which was followed by many others, the best known among them being *La Double Inconstance* (1723), *Le Jeu de l'amour et du hasard* (1730) and *Les fausses confidences* (1737). Marivaux's writing is distinguished by psychological insight and fine analysis of emotion. The term "marivaudage," which is derived from him, refers to elegantly formulated and subtle analysis of **sentiment**.

MARMONTEL, Jean François (1723-1799). One of the more important literary figures of the later Enlightenment. Of modest family, Marmontel owed his education to the local *curé* who recognized his ability, and after providing him with basic lessons, saw to it that he continued his studies at the secondary level. Like many aspiring but impecunious intellectuals of the time he taught in a *collège* before devoting himself to literature.

Marmontel owed his considerable success to a combination of talent and **patronage**. He won writing contests proposed by the Académie des jeux floraux (*see* **Academies, Provincial**) and by the **Académie française**. He received encouragement from **Voltaire**, whose abilities he admired and whose values he shared. Through the influence of Mme de **Pompadour** he was appointed in 1758 to the lucrative editorship of the *Mercure de France*. In 1763 Marmontel won election to the Académie française, and he eventually became its secretary when Jean le Ronde d'**Alembert** died. He was also appointed historiographer of France, a post that brought a pension as well as enhanced status. Marmontel was a regular member of a number of Parisian **salons**, and married the niece of the abbé **Morellet**.

Like many 18th-century intellectuals, Marmontel wrote in a wide variety of genres. Some of his poetry won competitions, a number of his plays were staged successfully, and he contributed many of the articles on literature to the *Encyclopédie*. Probably his greatest contemporary success was a series of moral tales which he first published one at a time in the *Mercure* beginning in 1756, and then as a collection called simply *Contes moraux* in 1761. The warm reception of this work, which had 13 editions by 1780, reflects the interest of contemporaries in moral agency as a solution to social problems. Marmontel's novel *Bélisaire* was published in 1767 and condemned by the Faculty of Theology of the Sorbonne for its defense of **toleration**. Though the author found it expedient to leave France for a time, he received the sympathy not only of liberal circles in Paris, but also of Stanislaus, **Frederick II** and **Catherine II**. In his memoirs, which provide valuable insights into Parisian culture and society, Marmontel states that *Belisaire* sold over 40,000 copies.

Having successfully established himself in the framework of the **Old Regime**, Marmontel had little sympathy for the **French Revolution**, which he regarded with suspicion and to which he was not reconciled until after the Thermidorean reaction. Like most *philosophes* whose careers extended beyond 1789, Marmontel's experience suggests that the relationship between the Enlightenment and the French Revolution is far from straightforward.

MARRIAGE. During the 18th century an arrangement by which a man and woman lived together, joined their property, and usually had children. In the Catholic and Anglican religions marriage was viewed as a sacrament, and was consequently indissoluble in all but the most exceptional cases. In the legislation of the **French Revolution** it was treated as a civil contract.

Anthropologists have described marriage in early modern Europe as primarily a mechanism for passing property from one generation to the next. Certainly the economic component of marriage was dominant at this time for all social groups. In order to marry it was almost always necessary for **women** to have a dowry. The heroine of Daniel **Defoe**'s novel *Moll Flanders* reflects on a basic social reality of the time, namely "that marriages were here the consequences of politick schemes for forming interests, carrying on business, and that love had no share, or but very little in the matter" (James Sutherland, ed., Riverside, pp. 59-60). Whether a financier or a simple laborer, potential husbands were unwilling, and toward the lower levels of the social scale unable, to do without the contribution to establishing the household that the dowry represented.

However, it was around the middle of the 18th century that the ideal of marriage based on the mutual affection of the spouses emerged. The best known spokesman of affective or romantic marriage, which also allowed a central role to children, was Jean-Jacques **Rousseau**. *See also* Mme de **Warens**; Sophie **Volland**.

MASTER FICTION(S). A term from literary criticism, sometimes used in history to designate beliefs and values that are widely accepted and used to structure and to give meaning to the narratives by which societies and cultures make sense of themselves and the world.

The term "fiction" is useful in avoiding making determinations about the truth-status of beliefs and values. While of key philosophical importance, the question of the truth of ideas and values held by societies is often impossible to determine. Leaving aside the truth-status of ideas and values has a number of effects that are relevant here.

First, ascribing the status of "fictions" to key values of a society is to opt for a form of **relativism**. It relieves the investigator of the burden of determining the validity of beliefs or ideas in question, and so facilitates less ethnocentric comparisons of cultures. It also reduces claims to priority or superiority of the values of one's own culture, making possible a more open and critical attitude to that culture.

Secondly, by reducing the **epistemological** status of social values, this approach tends to reduce the scope and intensity of conflicts between societies. There is abundant evidence of people being prepared to suffer, to kill and to commit all manner of abominations for the sake of values to which they attribute absolute validity. It makes less sense to go to such lengths for the sake of fictions.

Thirdly, once it is recognized that a set of values derives its validity from convention and consensus, and not from its truth-value, then it becomes clear that adherence to one set of values is a matter of choice, not of recognition of an objective or scientific principle. Historically, the most effective way of undermining the master fictions of any society or cultural movement has been to show that they are incompatible with principles that have a higher truth-status. Thus, for example, the **Enlightenment** value of **beneficence** was undercut by the principle of parsimony in Malthusian demography and social thought, a principle that required the systematic refusal of charity or support for those who could not fend for themselves. Arguably, however, the Malthusian principle of parsimony was simply one of the master fictions of a culture that validated unlimited individual acquisition over social solidarity.

It is questionable, then, whether the master fictions of the thinkers of the Enlightenment, the values of **equality**, **liberty**, **humanity**, **toleration**, **progress**, **utility**, **virtue** and the rest, which were used to promote a better organized state, a more productive economy, fairer distribution of material goods and a higher level of well-being, are on a different epistemological level from the values, or fictions, that displaced them. The choice between the master fictions of liberty, equality, humanity, beneficence and the rest that were used by the thinkers of the Enlightenment to structure their narratives and formulate their aspirations for the future, and master fictions, such as the efficacy of the unregulated market, social Darwinism, the superiority or inferiority of certain races, or predatory nationalisms, is not a choice between ethical propositions on the one hand, and scientific ones on the other. They are, rather, choices between sets of ethical propositions that facilitate the functioning and direct the aspirations of different societies and cultures. That the master fictions of the Enlightenment were in any way inferior to, or less firmly based than, the master fictions of the 19th and 20th centuries is far from evident.

MAUPEOU, René Nicolas Charles Augustin de (1714-1792). A member of a family of magistrates who held high office in the *Parlement* of Paris, Maupeou's name is associated less with the intellectual than the political history of the 18th century.

Himself having occupied the positions of counselor, *président à mortier* and first president in the *Parlement* of Paris, Maupeou was appointed to the key post of chancellor in the central government in 1768. With the abbé Terray, who was in charge of finances, Maupeou was obliged to deal with the serious fiscal problems that then confronted the royal exchequer.

Through their prerogative of refusing to register fiscal legislation, the *parlements*, or sovereign courts, were able to exercise a virtual veto on government financial policy. The core of the problem was that in order to move toward balancing its books the government needed to change existing laws so as to be able to tax the wealthiest elements of the population, who were protected by constitutional **privilege** from paying taxes in proportion to their wealth.

In 1771 Maupeou asked for and received the support of **Louis XV** in tackling the problem at its root. He convinced the king to eliminate the existing sovereign courts and to replace them with courts that were designed to be less independent and less obstructive, as well as less expensive and more efficient. This program, which was put into effect and seemed to be working reasonably effectively until it was annulled following the sudden death of Louis XV in 1774, had both advantages and shortcomings.

The main advantage of Maupeou's reform was to eliminate the obstructionist powers of the aristocracy, working through the sovereign courts, and to clear the way for necessary and substantial fiscal reform. In this light these reforms have been seen by certain historians as the last chance of the **Old Regime** to set its house in order and avoid the more dramatic and radical changes that began in 1789. On the other hand, the measures that Maupeou took were clearly unconstitutional, and thus raised serious questions about the legitimacy of the monarchy. **Voltaire** was one of the few *philosophes* to support Maupeou. Most others were critical of the administration's heavy-handed methods and disdain for legality. They also objected to his socially conservative outlook and willingness to use **censorship** to repress views of which he disapproved.

A vigorous pamphlet literature attacked Maupeou and his reform as despotic and harmful to the basic liberties of the French people. Together with this properly political line of criticism another, sometimes blended with it, condemned the immorality and corruption of Louis XV and his court.

Many historians are of the opinion that the propaganda directed by the magistrates of the sovereign courts and their allies against Maupeou and Louis XV significantly weakened the reputation and standing of the monarchy, thus contributing to the destabilization of the regime. This is not unlikely. Unfortunately for the old-regime state and House of Bourbon, the Maupeou reforms seem to have resulted in the crown having had the worst of both worlds. On the one hand, the government lost the practical advantages that the reform had conferred on it when **Louis XVI** annulled them on his accession to the throne; on the other hand, the damage done to the reputation and prestige of the regime and its ruling house was serious, and was not subsequently reversed, despite the good intentions of the new king.

MAUPERTUIS, Pierre Louis Moreau de (1698-1759). An important scientist and mathematician. In recognition of his work in geometry he was admitted to the Academy of Sciences in 1723. He was one of the first advocates of Newtonian science in France, publishing a *Mémoire sur les lois d'attraction* and the *Discours sur la figure des astres* in 1732. He also helped to convert **Voltaire** to Newtonianism. In 1736 Maupertuis was selected to head an expedition to Lapland to measure the length of a degree along the meridian. A parallel mission headed by Charles-Marie de La Condamine in Peru allowed scientists to confirm Isaac **Newton**'s hypothesis about the shape of the globe. Typically for a scientist of the time, Maupertuis refused to be restricted within the boundaries of a specific discipline, and wrote on a range of subjects. In addition to works such as the *Essai de cosmologie* (1750), he also produced an *Essai de philosophie morale* (1749).

Maupertuis enjoyed a high reputation throughout Europe. Mme de **Châtelet**, who was herself a serious student of physics, invited Maupertuis to her estate of Cirey while Voltaire was there. He was made a member of the **Royal Society** of London, in 1743 was elected to the **Académie française** and was invited by **Frederick II** to head the Academy of Berlin. He actively and successfully filled this position from 1746 to 1756, during which time he lived in Berlin. Though a respected scientist and academician, Maupertuis had troubled relations with many of his fellow men of letters. Koenig, a German mathematician, accused him of borrowing from Gottfried Wilhelm **Leibniz** without appropriate acknowledgment. He also fell afoul of both Denis **Diderot** and Voltaire, with the latter satirizing him mercilessly in his *Diatribe du docteur Akakia.* Apparently Maupertuis did not have a pleasing or easy personality. Still, his differences with other *philosophes* seem to be the result more of academic politics (Maupertuis did not agree to Voltaire's request to have the abbé **Raynal** admitted to the Academy of Berlin) and personal difficulties than of issues of substance.

MENDELSSOHN, Moses (1729-1786). A leading figure of the German Enlightenment in the second half of the 18th century. Son of a traditional Torah scribe, Moses son of Mendel was born in Dessau. In 1743 he followed his teacher, Rabbi David Fraenkel, to Berlin, where, by his own arduous efforts, he acquired a general education, something that was rare for a **Jew** of his time and place. It was only in 1763 that he was given legal right to live in Berlin. Throughout his lifetime he supported himself as a merchant.

Fluent in German and Hebrew, Mendelssohn was also familiar with Latin, Greek, French and Italian. He established a close friendship with the writer and playwright Gotthold Ephraim **Lessing**. In 1763 his composition *Abhandlung ueber die Evidenz in metaphysischen Wissenschaften* was awarded first prize in a competition sponsored by the Prussian Royal Academy of Sciences (a competition to which Immanuel **Kant** had also submitted an essay). An attempt to elect him a member of the Academy in 1771 was scuttled by **Frederick II**, who was not ready to have an unconverted Jew sitting in the Prussian Royal Academy.

Mendelssohn's writings on aesthetics (collected in *Philosophische Schriften* [2 vols., 1761]) influenced Friedrich Schiller, Johann Wolfgang von **Goethe** and Kant, and were crucial for Lessing's *Laokoon*. In his *Morgenstunden* (1785) and *Phaedon* (1767) Mendelssohn broke no new ground, giving expression to standard Enlightenment views of natural religion and human immortality, respectively.

Well-known in his lifetime as a philosopher and literary critic, Mendelssohn was forced by circumstances to be a representative of Judaism, especially in his controversy with John Casper Lavater (1741-1801), a Swiss clergyman who challenged the most famous Jew (at least among Gentiles) of his day to defend his loyalty to his ancestral faith and justify his failure to convert to Christianity.

Mendelssohn's final statement is in his book *Jerusalem* (1783), the work which earned him his place as one of the foremost exponents of Judaism in the modern world. In this book Mendelssohn argues that Judaism is a religion, not of revealed dogma (the beliefs in Judaism being precisely those of universal natural, which is to say, rational, religion), but of revealed law. God designed this law, Mendelssohn maintained, in order to educate the Jews toward acceptance of the rational teachings of natural religion. He implicitly criticizes Christianity for being based on dogmas contrary to reason.

Disappointed by the unwillingness of much of the Gentile world to accept him as he was, Mendelssohn devoted more and more of his energies to the intellectual and spiritual betterment of the Jews of his day, and involved himself deeply in efforts to ameliorate the legal restrictions under which Jews in the Germanic lands of his day labored.

Mendelssohn translated the Pentateuch and the Psalms into German (written in Hebrew characters); to the former he appended his famous commentary (*Bi'ur*), written in classical Hebrew. This work aroused great controversy and was roundly condemned by traditionalist Jews, who saw in it a tool through which Jews could become acquainted with German, and through German, with Western culture.

Mendelssohn's grandson was the composer Felix Mendelssohn-Bartholdy.

Menahem Kellner

MERCIER, Louis Sébastien (1740-1814). One of the most prolific and most interesting writers of the Enlightenment. Mercier was born in Paris to a comfortable but by no means affluent artisanal family. He received his secondary education at the Collège des Quatre Nations, which today houses the Institut. Following the expulsion of the **Jesuits** from France in 1762, he taught for a time in one of their former *collèges* in Bordeaux. He returned to Paris, however, and began his career as a writer.

Mercier was one of the few men of letters of the time who was able to make a living from his pen. He produced a series of reasonably successful plays, worked as a journalist and before the **French Revolution** produced the two books for which he is best remembered. One is a utopia entitled *The Year 2440*. It was first published in 1771, and according to the findings of Robert **Darnton** proved to be the most popular clandestine best seller of the last decades of the **Old Regime**. The other is the *Tableau de Paris*, a collection of vignettes on all aspects of Paris life, some of them written with remarkable force and color. This work was first published in two volumes in 1782, but by 1788 had grown to twelve volumes, over 1,000 chapters, and in its modern edition, about 3,000 pages. Despite its late appearance, it too ranks high on the list of clandestine best sellers. In addition to the *Tableau de Paris* Mercier also produced a voluminous collection of miscellaneous thoughts entitled *Mon Bonnet de nuit*, and a two-volume study of political thought, *Idées claires sur le gouvernement,* during the 1780s. To modern eyes the sheer volume of Mercier's output is mind-boggling. It explains, though, how he was able, unlike so many of his contemporaries, to make a living from writing.

Some literary critics have observed that Mercier wrote too much for it to be much good. One might argue conversely that it is remarkable how good so much of his output was: contemporaries seem to have thought so. While no democrat, Mercier showed considerable interest in and sympathy for the common people. His readiness to write about the seedier and more grotesque aspects of life drew considerable criticism from the predominantly classicist literary establishment of his day. So too did the insistent **moralism** which permeates much of his work.

With the outbreak of the Revolution Mercier engaged in journalism, then in 1792 was elected a deputy to the Convention. There he sided with the Girondins, voting against the execution of the King and protesting the arrest of his fellow Girondin deputies following the popular uprising of 2 June 1793. He was imprisoned for nearly a year, and released only after the fall of Maximilien Robespierre and the Mountain.

In the conservative regimes following the Thermidorean reaction Mercier achieved a degree of recognition that had eluded him under the Old Regime. He became a member of the Council of Five Hundred, was appointed to a professorship of history in the prestigious new Central Schools and gained a seat in the **Institut**. Nor did he cease to write. Mercier produced a sort of continuation to the *Tableau de Paris*, which he entitled *Le Nouveau Paris* and which appeared in 1800, and a book on linguistic innovations that accompanied the Revolution, *Néologie,* in 1802. Too independent, or perhaps too much of a *frondeur* and too cranky to accept the subservience imposed by Napoleon, he ended his life in relative obscurity. Both his career and his works deserve more attention than they have usually been given.

MERCURE DE FRANCE. A mainstream, widely diffused **periodical** with official status. It was founded in 1724 by Antoine de La Roque, and cost 24 *livres* for a year's subscription in Paris and 36 *livres* in the provinces for 12 volumes of roughly 200 pages each. For the most part it avoided the ideological struggles that were being carried on, and shied away from controversy. As a result it was somewhat bland, but nevertheless was widely distributed.

The greater part of the journal was devoted to book reviews, as was the case with most other important literary journals of the time, such as the *Année Littéraire* and *Journal Encyclopédique*. However, the *Mercure* gave more space to occasional pieces, such as letters to the editor, articles, poems, the theater and reports on the activities of **academies** than did the more engaged periodicals. It also carried announcements and had a section for news.

For the most part the editors of the *Mercure* were competent but relatively unknown men of letters, acceptable both to the owners of the privilege of the journal, who indeed often edited it themselves, and to the authorities. During the 1750s, however, two important writers who were also *philosophes*, the abbé **Raynal** and Jean-François **Marmontel**, edited the *Mercure* and brought it closer to the concerns of the enlightened public. This was less a matter of a main-stream periodical being radicalized than of comfortable cohabitation between some of the more moderate elements of the Enlightenment and a culturally flexible establishment. Subsequent editors and journalists did include several minor Enlightenment figures, such as Frédérick-César de La Harpe and Jean-Baptiste Antoine Suard, but these were exceptions.

In 1778 Charles-Joseph Panckoucke, one of the leading publishers and perhaps the first press baron on record, acquired the privilege for the *Mercure*. Panckoucke believed, rightly enough, that the demand for news, and especially political news, was far greater than that for literary subjects. With outstanding vision and acumen as a business-man, Panckoucke arranged for a privilege for the publication of political news. This meant that other journals either had to pay him to get his permission to publish political news, or refrain from doing so. This is a good example of old-regime business practices, which functioned in the framework of government and guild restrictions, being combined with a modern and aggressive sense of the market.

In his reorganization of the *Mercure*, Panckoucke merged it with another of his papers which was based abroad, and published it as a separate section on political news under the title *Journal politique de Bruxelles*. This stroke, together with the incorporation of other periodicals owned by Panckoucke into the *Mercure*, affected subscriptions to the paper dramatically. From less than 2,000 subscribers in 1778, it rose to 7,000 in 1779 and then to 20,000 in 1783, a pressrun larger than that for any other periodical published in France under the **Old Regime**. Though this high level of subscriptions was not sustained uniformly, it did not fall below 10,000 before the outbreak of the **French Revolution**, and when in 1792 sales of the *Mercure* fell to 8,500 copies, this was due primarily to the destruction of the system of privileges, which Panckoucke had manipulated so effectively, and to the competition now current in the newly deregulated literary marketplace.

MESLIER, Jean (1664-1729). A parish priest and militant atheist whose influence was exercised posthumously in a powerful denunciation of organized religion that he left in manuscript at his death. Meslier was the son of a comfortable merchant, and lived a life of outward conformity. He studied theology in Reims between 1684 and 1688, and from 1688 acted as *curé* of the parish of Etrepigny in the Diocese of Reims. Apart from criticizing the local seigneur for harsh treatment of his parishioners, he called little attention to himself in the exercise of his office. His *Testament* is another matter altogether.

Meslier's *Testament* is as remarkable for being produced by someone who took no public part in the intellectual debates of his time as it is for its radical materialism and atheism. The atheist *curé* would seem to have been motivated by a mixture of oppositionist theology and philosophical **Cartesianism**. Had his *Testament* been destroyed or discreetly stored away, we would never have heard of him. As it was, copies were made and it began to circulate in manuscript. In this way it reached a small but influential elite and lent support to critical **deists**, materialists, atheists and anticlericals, and helped to influence the current of radical criticism of church and society that was developing at the time. Meslier's book, which was initially too risky to publish, was only one of many radical **clandestine manuscripts** that circulated under the noses, but beyond the reach, of the authorities. **Voltaire** was among its readers and popularizers.

While the content and intent of Meslier's *Testament* is clear, one is hard-pressed to imagine how a convinced materialist, atheist and anticlerical such as Meslier could, for his entire adult life, have represented the doctrines and performed the rites of a church which in his heart he execrated.

MILLAR, John (1735-1801). A significant figure in the Scottish Enlightenment, remembered particularly for his contribution to the development of social theory.

Like so many of the key figures of the Enlightenment in Scotland, Millar was the son of a Presbyterian minister. As a boy he was sent to live with an uncle who practiced law and had a small estate not far from Glasgow. This uncle had the time and inclination to teach him to read before sending him off to a grammar school in Hamilton, where his father had a pulpit. Millar then went to the **University** of Glasgow, where he attended the classes of Adam **Smith**, and was initially supposed to prepare himself for the Church, but instead studied law.

On graduating from the university, Millar, like many an aspiring intellectual, both in Scotland and elsewhere, accepted work as a tutor, but continued to study law. He seems to have done particularly well as a tutor, as he was engaged to instruct many students from distinguished families, among them the son of Lord Kames. Later, while a professor at Glasgow, he oversaw the studies of students who boarded with him, including a cousin of Adam Smith and David

Hume's nephew. In 1760 Millar became an advocate, but the following year accepted an appointment as professor of law at the University of Glasgow, and proved as successful as a university teacher as he had been as a private tutor. Since in the 18th-century Scottish university an instructor's salary depended to a considerable degree on fees paid directly by the students to the instructor, Millar's popularity as a teacher meant that his university appointment assured him financial independence. He also inherited two modest farms, and was in a small way an agricultural improver. In addition he continued to practice a bit of law in Glasgow, sometimes serving as a mediator in commercial cases.

Millar's political views were distinctly liberal. He supported the cause of American independence, opposed the **slave** trade, favored parliamentary reform, though not universal suffrage, and supported, critically and with some reservations, the **French Revolution**. He regarded the nationalization of Church property in France as unfair, questioned the wisdom of eliminating rank altogether, condemned popular violence and preferred utility to natural rights as the criterion of legitimacy. Unlike Edmund **Burke**, however, Millar saw the French Revolution as justifiably directed against long-standing abuses, and fundamentally reasonable in its objectives. He was sympathetic towards the Gironde, and while condemning the violence and extremism of the Mountain, recognized its effectiveness and the role of the European powers in extending the revolutionary struggles. Of the thinkers of the Enlightenment who survived to see the French Revolution, Millar was among the most sympathetic, and opposed the reaction against it in Scotland.

The book for which Millar is best remembered is *The Origin of the Distinction of Ranks*, published in 1771, which builds on the work of **Montesquieu** and helped to lay the groundwork for a science of society. In 1787 he published his *Historical View of the English Government*, which took a more liberal and reformist view of English politics and society, and so stood in contrast to the **Toryism** of Hume in his famous *History of England*. Millar's book is said to have been the first constitutional history of England.

MIRACLES. A remarkable or supernatural event that deviates from, or goes against, the natural order of things. The term derives from the Latin *miraculum*, which is rendered by the *Oxford Universal Dictionary* "object of wonder." Both the Hebrew and Greek Scriptures contain numerous instances of miracles, which are taken primarily as indications of the providential interest of the Divine in human affairs, and of sheer power. Biblical miracles are usually, though not always, public.

Miracles are one of the points at which the Enlightenment came most directly into conflict with the Judeo-Christian tradition. For that tradition miracles were proofs of the power of the Divine, which, having created the world, stood above **nature** and was unconstrained by it. They were also validations of faith, and Catholicism, particularly, insisted that miracles continued to occur. For the Church a verified miracle (verification being carried out by Church authorities) was one criterion of sainthood.

The *philosophes* on the whole believed in nature as completely as traditional Christians believed in the Divine and their churches. The basic tenet of the Enlightenment faith in nature was its regularity. Events that diverged from, or ran counter to, the laws of nature were, axiomatically, either misperceptions, the result of partial information or inadequate knowledge, or outright fabrications. **Voltaire**, who was a firm believer in the Divine, asserted that the Divine always achieved its ends by acting through the laws of nature, never against them. (*Philosophical Dictionary,* art. "Catéchisme japonnais"; Besterman, p. 103). He referred to miracles as "violations of divine and eternal laws" (*Ibid*, art. "Miracles," p. 311) and David **Hume** in almost the same terms called them "violations of the laws of nature" (*Essays, "On Miracles,"* p. 536). Voltaire archly suggested that in order to properly verify miracles they be performed before the Academy of Sciences of Paris, or the **Royal Society** of London (*Philosophical Dictionary*, "Miracles," p. 316). Voltaire, and many members of the enlightened community with him, explained the miracles with which the history of the Church teems as a strategy of a cynical clergy to impose upon and exploit an ignorant people.

Thinkers and historians of the Enlightenment had little trouble showing that the original testimony and the chain of tradition by which accounts of miracles were handed down could not meet rigorous standards of proof. Thus, textual criticism and the emerging scientific view of the world combined to undermine the credibility of miracles.

MITTWOCHSGESELLSCHAFT/WEDNESDAY CLUB. A club made up of intellectuals and civil servants, which met once or twice a month on Wednesdays in Berlin between 1783 and 1798. It was a focus for the serious discussion of social and political issues, and in that many of its members occupied responsible positions or were respected thinkers, its discussions carried more weight than would the debates in coffeehouse circles (*see* **cafés**) or **clubs**. In this way it was similar to the **Club de l'Entresol** of the earlier part of the century.

Members of this club included the writer and publisher Christoph Friedrich Nicolai, the important jurist Justus Möser, the journalist Johann Erich Brechter, probably the key figure in the Jewish Enlightenment, Moses **Mendelssohn**, and Karl Wilhelm Möhsen, **Frederick II**'s doctor. It has sometimes been thought that Immanuel **Kant**, one of the greatest philosophers of the time, took part in the discussions of this club, but since Kant never left the environs of Königsberg and the club met in Berlin, this is not plausible. Kant, however, certainly knew some of the members of the club, and the fact that he published his brief but influential essay "What is Enlightenment?" in the *Berlin Monthly*, which was connected with the Mittwochsgesellschaft, suggests that he had connections with the club.

Exceptionally, this club did not admit nobles to membership. This may reflect a greater distance between nobles and the professional and cultivated levels of the middle class in Prussia than was the case in France or England.

MONTESQUIEU, Charles-Louis de Secondat, Baron de la Brède (1689-1757). One of the leading *philosophes* of the French Enlightenment. He was probably the one whose work was most widely appreciated and accepted during the 18th century, and the least controversial.

Montesquieu was born to a family of the robe **nobility** not far from Bordeaux. He received his secondary education from the Oratorians of Juilly, and then proceeded to the study of law. In 1708 he began practicing as a lawyer in the *Parlement* of Bordeaux, and in 1716 inherited from his uncle the office of judge, or president, in the same court. However, he only exercised this function until 1725 when he sold it and retired to look after his estates and devote himself to literature. Montesquieu had married in 1715 and was rather distant, though responsible, in his relations with his wife and children. As landlord and administrator of his estate he was practical, hardheaded and parsimonious, and not above personally inspecting his fields and vineyards.

Montesquieu enjoyed a rich and varied intellectual life. In 1716 he was elected to the Academy of Bordeaux, and took an active part in its proceedings (*see* **Academies, Provincial**). Between 1718 and

1721 he read a number of memoirs on physics and natural history, most of which took up the problem of causation in one way or another, before the Academy. This scientific outlook and the broader assumptions that the world was fundamentally orderly and intelligible marked his later investigations into society and politics. From 1721 to 1728 Montesquieu spent much of his time in Paris, where he frequented the **Club de l'Entresol** and the **salons** of Mme **Lambert** and Mme de **Tencin**. Late in 1727 he was elected to the **Académie française**, but then in 1728 left to travel in Germany, Austria, Italy and England, and did not return to France until the spring of 1731. Thereafter he spent more time at his estate of La Brède where he read and prepared his future works.

Montesquieu's published works reflect an age that assumed the unity of knowledge. His *Persian Letters*, published in 1721, is generally regarded as the first Enlightenment classic. It is characterized by a blend of pleasing style, social criticism, exoticism and a narrative that includes love intrigue. It succeeds in presenting the most serious subjects in a thoroughly entertaining fashion, thus breaking with the tradition of the heavy learned treatise. During the 1720s Montesquieu continued to produce both works on ethics and politics and fairly frivolous light verse, such as the *Temple de Gnide* (1725), which is mildly pornographic. In 1734 he published an important work of **history**, the *Considerations on the Causes of the Grandeur and Decadence of the Romans*. He then turned to the preparation of probably his greatest and most influential work, the *Spirit of the Laws*, which was published in Switzerland in 1748. A huge work that combines political theory, anthropology and history, and aspires to establishing sciences of society and politics, despite its size and erudition the *Spirit of the Laws* became a best seller and exercised a great influence on social and political thought not only in France and Europe, but also in the American colonies.

Montesquieu also contributed an article on taste to the *Encyclopédie*. Following his death in 1755 the editors of the *Encyclopédie* devoted the preface of their next volume to his work and memory.

MORALISM. A worldview or attitude in which ethics and ethical intent are primary, and in which social and political well-being are seen as dependent on ethical behavior.

This attitude was well developed by the 18th century, being firmly rooted in the traditions of classical **republicanism** and of Judaism and Christianity. Without a citizenry devoted to the common good of

the polity and giving precedence to **patriotism** over personal interests, the classical republic could not function. Both Judaism and
Christianity place the object of their allegiance outside the social and
political spheres, but both project back moral imperatives from it into
them.

During the Enlightenment these traditional views came to be challenged. The rise of Newtonian science (*see* Isaac **Newton**) reflected a
world inherently orderly, and encouraged a view of **nature** as beneficent. From this perspective it became possible to think in terms of
modeling one's behavior on nature, rather than on political or religious values. An extension of Newtonian physics to the realm of economics, the market mechanism, further tended to minimize the role of
ethics in human relations by assuming that an unobstructed market
would automatically dispose things for the greater good.

The appeal of the market as a self-regulating mechanism was in
large part dependent on the rehabilitation of **self-interest**, which was
occurring at about the same time. If the intelligent pursuit of self-
interest resulted in the greater good of the economy and society, there
was less need for a system of ethics to direct behavior.

Since the rehabilitation of self-interest and the emergence of the
notion of the self-regulating market are new developments in the
Enlightenment, they have been taken as characteristic of the movement, and have perhaps obscured the persistence of a powerful current of traditional ethical thought during the 18th century. The outstanding exponent of moralism in the Enlightenment is Jean-Jacques
Rousseau, whose view of politics was deeply marked by classical
thought and centered on the concept of **virtue**. Rousseau further
questioned the overall value of purely scientific and material advances. He did not deny that the sciences and the market mechanism
had logics of their own, but it did not seem to him that the workings
of these logics were socially and politically desirable. Indeed, progress in the sciences and practical arts were for him indications of
corruption (*see* **First Discourse**).

Rousseau had great influence in his own time, and was followed by
many in his denial that there were viable shortcuts to cohesive community and ethically sound politics. The emphasis on virtues such as
beneficence, **humanity** and **patriotism** in the literature of the late
Old Regime, political treatises that conceived politics in basically
ethical terms, the sub-genre known as the moral tale (*conte moral*),
and filler items in **periodicals** praising socially cohesive acts of kind-

ness and mutual support, all show that moralism remained a widely held point of view.

During the **French Revolution** a rhetoric of virtue became an important part of political discourse. This is particularly clear in the writings and speeches of the Jacobins, and finds full expression in the thought of Maximilien Robespierre, who was himself an admirer of Rousseau. Robespierre and the Jacobins, however, originated little. Rather, they worked out the basic assumptions of moralism in a political environment freed from the restraints of the Old Regime.

MORELLET, André, abbé (1727-1819). A sociable and serviceable intellectual closely associated with the *philosophes*. Though himself from a relatively humble milieu, Morellet became fully and formally integrated into the enlightened community.

Morellet's father, a paper merchant, had 14 children. His eldest son, André, was educated with the help of scholarships, first in Lyon, then in a seminary in Paris, and finally at the Sorbonne. Morellet made use of his time at the Sorbonne not only to take his bachelor's and doctor's degrees in theology (1752), but also to read widely in modern philosophy and literature. He also made lasting friendships with Anne-Robert-Jacques **Turgot** and Loménie de Brienne, both of whom achieved high political office, and both of whom employed Morellet during their tenures. Morellet's penchant for polemics, exhibited in a defense of the *philosophes* against Charles **Palissot**, and a number of pamphlets he produced upon request by the government won him the nickname "sick' em" (mords-les) from **Voltaire**.

Morellet's credentials as a representative of the Enlightenment were impressive. He contributed articles to the *Encyclopédie*, spent time in the Bastille because of one of his pamphlets, regularly attended many of the most important Parisian **salons** and translated and modified Cesare Bonesana di **Beccaria**'s *On Crimes and Punishments*. He was called upon by various administrations to put specific, usually economic, issues, before the public, and so was recognized as an effective pamphleteer. Morellet survived the **French Revolution** to achieve prominence under the Consulate and Empire as a member of both the **Institut** and the Legislative Council. His *Memoirs,* which provide a wide-ranging and colorful portrayal of the leading institutions and personalities of the High Enlightenment, are probably his most memorable work. Morellet's career provides an example of how an able young man of relatively modest origins could, by his talent and sociability, and while retaining at least a formal ecclesiastical identity, become a well integrated member of the intellectual and political elites of the Enlightenment.

MORELLY (?-?). It is not known with certainty whether Morelly was an obscure and studious recluse, or the pen name of some other writer. Morelly's name is associated with a number of books published from the early 1740s to the mid-1750s, but this association was not made until the 19th century. The best known of these works are the *Basiliade* (1753), a verse **utopia**, and the *Code de la nature*, which is generally regarded as a minor Enlightenment classic. The *Code de la nature* posits a model of man based on Lockean psychology, accepts the primacy of **self-interest**, and sketches a society in which there is a right to existence, an obligation to work, and in which private property has been eliminated. These features have given the *Code de la nature*, whoever its author may have been, a place in the history of socialist thought.

MORNET, Daniel (1878-1954). An erudite, prolific and innovative student of 18th-century literature and thought, Daniel Mornet taught in the Department of French Literature at the Sorbonne. His publications include books in French on provincial intellectual life, romanticism, the natural sciences and the literature of sentiment, all in 18th-century France. He also edited an edition of Jean-Jacques **Rousseau**'s *Julie, ou La Nouvelle Héloïse*, produced a widely used survey of 18th-century French literature and is the author of one of the most important studies ever made of the Enlightenment, namely, *Les Origines intellectuelles de la Révolution française*, which was first published in 1933.

Even slight acquaintance with Mornet's work shows that he had a remarkable mastery of the literature in his period of specialization. What distinguishes him from other scholars of 18th-century French literature, however, is the imaginative and extensive work he carried out in the sociology of literature. Mornet, of course, analyzed the content of many of the classics of the Enlightenment, but he went beyond the great texts to ask what influence they had, how they circulated, how they were popularized, what mechanisms for their diffusion existed, how they worked and what people actually read. One of his early articles, for example, is based on an analysis of the catalogues of 500 private libraries. To determine the incidence of works in them, Mornet made cards, or *fiches*, for each item, of which some libraries had thousands, and then tabulated them all. It is thanks to this piece of research that we know that Pierre **Bayle**'s *Historical and Critical Dictionary* was the most commonly found work in large libraries during the 18th century.

Mornet's masterpiece, *Les Origines intellectuelles de la Révolution française*, follows the development of key ideas and values of the Enlightenment through three periods. From 1715-1748 most of these ideas made their appearance, between 1748 and 1770 they overcame the hegemonic ideas and principles of the **Old Regime**, and between 1771 and 1787 the principles and values of the Enlightenment, together with the thinkers who advocated these views, consolidated their social and intellectual positions.

The strengths of Mornet's study, which can hardly be appreciated from a synopsis, lie in his intimate knowledge of both major and minor **authors**, and his awareness that ideas do not exist in the ether and somehow spread by virtue of their intrinsic value, but require channels of diffusion and social structures through which to move. Mornet was among the first systematically to examine **clandestine manuscripts**, pamphlets, **periodicals**, masonic lodges (*see* **Freemasonry**), **salons**, provincial and other **academies** and educational institutions as channels for the diffusion of ideas. He also moves with assurance between the *philosophes*, minor writers, mere hacks and collective bodies that, more or less integrated, formed the enlightened community. In the hands of Mornet, the Enlightenment remains a movement of ideas, but it gains a sociological specificity and awareness of the complexity of systems of communications that it had not had previously. The social history of ideas owes a great deal to him.

Given that Mornet's discipline was French literature and that his emphasis in *Les Origines intellectuelles* was the relationship between ideas and revolution in France, a relationship which he warns at the end of his study is far from simple or direct, it is not surprising that his book does not give much space to English, Scottish or German thinkers or institutions. Though it does have a chapter on the American Revolution, it does not have the European scope of, say, Ernst **Cassirer**'s *The Philosophy of the Enlightenment*, which was published only a year before, or of Paul Hazard's *La Crise de la conscience européene*, translated as *The European Mind*, published a year after. Historians may continue to debate whether the decisive phase of the Enlightenment occurred, as Mornet claimed, in the years around and after 1750, or whether, as Hazard maintained, and as Jonathan Israel has more recently argued, it took place in the later years of the reign of Louis XIV. What is clear is that the approach to the Enlightenment taken by Mornet in *Les Origines intellectuelles* inspired much of the best and most original research in the field for the rest of the 20th century.

Perhaps because of its length, perhaps because it was regarded as too narrowly specialized, perhaps because the marriage of literature, sociology and history that it effects belongs to no one discipline, *Les Origines intellectuelles* has never been translated into English. Mornet's by now classic shorter introductory text for students, *French Thought in the 18th Century*, first published in 1926, is still worth consulting. He also has an essay entitled "The Development of Literature and Culture in the 18th Century," which appears as the fifth chapter of the second volume of a collection entitled *The European Inheritance*.

MUSÉES. Unofficial cultural and educational institutions established during the 1780s. The best-known examples were in Paris. They functioned as something between centers for adult **education** and social foci for those members of the enlightened community who did not have access to **salons** or **academies**, but who sought the kind of intellectual stimulation that these more established and elitist forms of enlightened sociability provided. They reflect a broadening of the Enlightenment beyond the restricted social bases in which it originated.

The first of these organizations was established on the initiative of the Masonic Lodge of Nine Sisters, and began meeting in November 1780. It was known both by the name of Lodge and as the Apollonian Society. In 1781 Jean-François Pilâtre de Rozier, a chemist, founded the Musée de Monsieur, which specialized in giving courses in the natural sciences. After Rozier's death in 1785 in an aerostatic accident, Moreau de Saint-Mery took the lead in this institution. In 1784 it moved to the grounds of the **Palais Royal**, and survived into the **French Revolution**, changing its name to the Lycée after Rozier died, and to Lycée Républicain in 1793. It changed its name a few more times and survived through the Empire. In 1782, Court de Gébelin, a pioneer in the study of comparative religion who was also involved in the organization of the Apollonian Society, opened the Musée de Paris, which had a more literary orientation than Rozier's institute. The baronne du Plessy, who was also a novelist, founded a musée for women in 1788.

In 1781 Mammès-Claude Pahin de Lablancherie, whose high-sounding name was meant to obscure his modest social origins, established a Correspondance générale pour les sciences et les arts, and for a time published a periodical with the same title. Like other musées, this one provided lectures and classes on a variety of topics, but differed from them in also exhibiting curiosities and works of art, especially paintings, in weekly meetings. Pahin de Lablancherie has been seen as an early cultural entrepreneur who attempted to apply commercial principles to a world dominated by privileged academies and close government supervision of the arts.

Louis Sébastien **Mercier** commented on the recent appearance of musées, and speculated that they would not succeed because they represented a form of free association inimical to the spirit of **absolutism**. Mercier ironically compared the Musée de Paris, of which he was a member, to the **Académie française**, referred to the privileged status of the academicians and the payment they received, and suggested that significant cultural advances are more likely to come from free and open meetings than from the officially supervised and closed ones of the academies (*Tableau de Paris*, chaps. dxxi and cmxlvi).

N

NATIONALISM. The belief or feeling that one's belonging to a certain nation-state or national community is a primary source of identity for the individual. A key source of **particularism**, especially from the 19th century on, nationalism remained relatively weak during the Enlightenment. There are a number of reasons for this.

First, in its European context, nationalism became an ideology by which nation-states made competing claims and generated support from their citizens. During the 18th century, the nation-state was only imperfectly developed in Spain, England, France and Russia, and not at all in Italy and Austria. Prussia enlarged its territory and developed some of the institutions of a nation-state in the 18th century, but it did not become the core of a German nation until the second half of the 19th century.

Secondly, nationalism implies a degree of unity and uniformity incompatible with traditional or even absolute monarchies. France, which became a model for governmental centralization from the second half of the 17th century, remained administratively and culturally fragmented until the Revolution. The crown could not enact legislation without registration by 13 different regional sovereign courts; provincial estates moderated royal authority in a third of the country;

and two-thirds of the population spoke *patois* rather than French. Regionalism and local **privilege** colored every aspect of life.

Thirdly, kings were the symbols and foci of unity in their states, whether dynastic or relatively unified. But loyalty to kings was not so powerful a force as loyalty to a people or nation, and the nation did not replace monarchs as primary foci of loyalty until the wars of the **French Revolution**, which both destroyed many features of old-regime states and powerfully stimulated nationalist sentiment. Fourthly, cosmopolitan and international forces and interests remained strong at this time. The Catholic Church continued to exercise great influence during the 18th century, and its focus was universal rather than national. Colonialism, though certainly developed around national centers, shifted conflict between European nations at least partially away from Europe, and created new tensions between colonizers and colonized. Further, commercial rivalries involved in colonial expansion could often be more easily reconciled or compromised than conflicts over borders with neighboring states. Finally, on an ideological level, adherents of Enlightenment culture tended to give primacy to **universalism** and to a common **humanity** (*see* **cosmopolitanism**) over national differences.

NATURE. The complex of forces, things and relations of which the world is composed and which give it form. Different cultures usually have different views of what nature is and how it works.

In the medieval West nature was taken to be the handiwork of a divine Creator who might at any time intervene to reverse or change its course, so that there was no clear division between the natural and supernatural. Medieval theologians also maintained that nature existed in its pristine form only before the fall of man, and that since original sin nature, as well as man, was corrupt. In this sense the realm of nature was opposed to the realm of grace.

With the culmination of the scientific revolution of the 16th and 17th centuries in the work of Isaac **Newton**, nature came to be seen as lawful, scrutable, simple and harmonious. The supernatural was not initially purged from natural science, for Newton and the **deists** used the demonstrable orderliness of the universe as proof of the existence of an orderly and beneficent Creator (*see* **Argument from Design**). Even in the materialist and atheist philosophies of the Baron d'**Holbach** and Claude Adrien **Helvétius**, nature retained its beneficent character, serving in effect as a principle of morality immanent in the world.

Seeing nature as fundamentally good, Jean-Jacques **Rousseau** re-thought the origins of mankind without reference to the doctrine of original sin. As a purely natural creature, man, Rousseau argued in the *Second Discourse*, was endowed with an instinct to self-preservation and an equally natural, in terms of Lockean psychology, sense of compassion for other animate creatures. In Rousseau's thought nature served as the basis for an ethic of **beneficence**. Similarly, in his description of the South Seas islanders in his *Supplement to Bougainville's Voyage*, Denis **Diderot** presented the image of an uncorrupted material world and its inhabitants living sensibly and happily in Eden-like conditons.

The assumption that nature was throughout beneficent, which contrasts to the views of nature that preceded and followed the Enlightenment, is reflected in a letter to the editor of a provincial newspaper in France. The author of the letter writes that he saw a swan pick up a fish and replace it in the water. He prefaces his account of what he saw, or thought he saw, with the comment that: "I recently saw, Sir, a Bird commit an act of sensibility and of compassion which would honor humanity" (*Affiches de Picardie*, 1784, p. 148). Whatever the author of this letter in fact saw, it is clear that he viewed it as an instance of the natural goodness of at least non-carnivorous animals. For those who might wish to make the Darwinian assumption that the swan had actually intended to make a snack of the fish, it is worth pointing out that studies of the contents of stomachs of ducks and swans have found these birds to be vegetarian.

The early Enlightenment view that the Divine intervened beneficially in nature was in part made necessary by the imperfect data available to scientists such as Newton. By the end of the 18th century, when fuller and more accurate data had become available, such assumptions had become superfluous, and materialist interpretations of nature followed. Nature and the supernatural were sharply separated, with the latter dismissed as mere aberration from a properly rigorous scientific view of the world.

In the 19th century, with the new prevalence of the life sciences as reflected in the work of Thomas Malthus on population and of Charles Darwin on biology and zoology, Enlightenment views of natural beneficence were abandoned for a vision of nature as an unending struggle for existence in which strength and stealth were the only criteria: nature red in tooth and claw. This concept of nature was in turn projected onto society in the form of social Darwinism and a variety of ideologies of domination.

To a degree societies see in nature their own characteristics and preoccupations. Coming between the still sacralized and mysterious concept of nature of the Middle Ages in which man had to go in fear and trembling, and the disenchanted but brutal and pitiless world of Darwinianism, the Enlightenment view of nature, based on the Newtonian synthesis, provided a basis for an optimism about man and the world lacking in the earlier and later views of nature.

NECKER, Jacques (1732-1804). A banker and minister of finance of **Louis XVI** between 1776 and 1781 and again between 1788 and 1790. Though a Protestant who was born and raised in Geneva, Necker played an important and controversial role in the political history of France in the last decades of the **Old Regime**.

Necker was born into a respectable but not wealthy family, his father serving on the Consistory of Geneva. He was a good student, but had to abandon his studies to take up a profession. By 1756 he was a partner in a private bank, and was to become a leading figure in European finance. In 1764 he married Suzanne **Curchod**, a young Genevan woman without fortune, but with a number of excellent qualities, who had also attracted the attention of Edward **Gibbon**. Their marriage was an exceptionally happy one. Mme Necker offered consistent support to her husband, which included establishing a **salon** for the purpose of furthering his interests, and he in return was altogether devoted to her. The daughter of the Neckers, Mme Anne Louise Germaine de Staël, was an intellectual figure of considerable importance in liberal circles, and she did all she could to maintain her father's good name.

As minister of finance Necker attempted to reduce the scope of the activities of the farmers general, or private businessmen, who collected indirect taxes. He also established new provincial administrations. However, his popularity during his first ministry stemmed largely from his ability to finance France's contribution to the American War of Independence without raising taxes. Though it could not be known at the time, the increase in the national debt that his borrowing entailed would prove a heavy burden on the treasury in what turned out to be a protracted economic downturn, and was in part responsible for the decision to convene the Estates General.

During his second period in office conditions were such that Necker had little control over events. In the lead-up to the **French Revolution** he on the whole took a moderate reformist position, as in doubling the size of the deputation of the Third Estate to the Estates

General, but without mandating vote by head. His popularity was considerable, and his dismissal on 12 July 1789 was one of the causes that precipitated the uprising that ended with the taking of the Bastille. When it became clear to him that he could do little, Necker resigned his position and returned to Switzerland.

In addition to his financial and political careers, Necker also had literary aspirations. In 1769 he published a *Mémoire sur la Compagnie des Indes*, and in 1775 joined the debate on regulation of the grain trade with an *Essai sur la legislation et le commerce des grains*, subjects on which he could claim professional expertise. In 1773, however, he won the prize of the **Académie française** for that year with his essay in praise of Louis XIV's minister, Colbert. Necker also used his writings to support his political aspirations, and is sometimes regarded as one of the first politicians of the Old Regime intentionally to appeal to **public opinion**. Certainly his *Compte rendu au roi* of 1781 was so intended, though it contributed to his loss of office later that year. His *Traité de l'administration de finances*, which he wrote while out of office and published in 1784, had the same purpose. He also produced a volume entitled *De l'Importance des opinions religieuses* in 1788, which gives an insight into enlightened attitudes toward religion.

Once safely retired on his estate of Coppet near Geneva, Necker wrote a number of works with a direct bearing on the Revolution. These include *Réflexions presentées à la nation française sur le procès intenté à Louis XVI* (1792) and *De la Révolution française* (1797). In 1800 he published a *Cours de morale religieuse* in three volumes, and in 1802 *Dernières vues de politique et de finance*. He also wrote a novel that was published posthumously. Mme Necker having died in 1794, he published eight volumes of *Pensées et mélanges extraits des manuscrits de Madame Necker* (1798).

NEOCLASSICISM. A style in art that became prominent toward the end of the **Old Regime**. Its subject matter was usually taken from classical history or mythology, and its themes were generally political and ethical. The issues raised in neoclassical art include the relation of the individual to the state, and more particularly the moral obligations of the individual, or **patriotism**. The *Oath of the Horatii, Socrates, Brutus and Marat* by Jacques Louis **David** are all examples of the moral orientation of neoclassicism. In each of these canvases the limit of the individual's obligation and devotion to the state is death. The high seriousness and moral emphasis of this style reflects the currents of Enlightenment thought found in Jean-Jacques **Rousseau**'s political theory and the widely held concern about a crisis whose root causes were moral.

Scenes portrayed in neoclassical art give precedence to the public over the domestic or private spheres. While, for example, the canvases of Jean-Baptiste **Greuze** frequently portray acts of **virtue** and reconciliation, they are generally domestic. By contrast, when David paints the women in the households of the Horatii or Brutus, it is to show the cost that political virtues exact from mothers, wives and sisters. Domestic tragedy is inseparable from, but subordinated to, politics. Further, because the public sphere of the ancient world was exclusively male, the main protagonists of neoclassical art are male also, and indeed males who embody political or military virtues in a **republican** framework.

As a style, Neoclassicism relies far more on design and far less on color than did **rococo**. Apart from red, there are few if any bright colors in neoclassical canvases, which is appropriate enough in a style that appeals more to the mind than the senses. Rococo is often decorative, and has a pronounced preference for the naked human body, particularly the female nude. Neoclassicism portrays the characters in its narratives as clothed, at least for the most part. Where the rococo artist favored a sensuous portrayal of the naked female form, suggesting that the individual could find **happiness** in **nature**, the neoclassical artist focused on the artificial trappings of clothing and political forms, without which human life is not possible, but with which it is often tragic.

NEW SCIENCE, THE/SCIENZA NUOVA. One of the most innovative and challenging works produced during the period of the Enlightenment. It was written by the accomplished humanist and teacher, Giambattista **Vico**, who was born and lived almost his whole life in Naples. However, the relationship of this work to the Enlightenment was, and remains, problematic.

In *The New Science*, Vico sought to establish on objective and verifiable bases the principles of natural **law** and the laws governing **history**. This was a hugely ambitious project that concerned Vico for roughly the last 30 years of his life. He rethought the project constantly, and produced a number of versions. A "negative" version was written in 1724, but never published. The first edition, unlike most of Vico's published work, which was in Latin, appeared in Italian in 1725, a second edition in 1730, and shortly after his death, a third edition in 1744. This last edition, which has been translated and provided with scholarly apparatus by Thomas Goddard Bergin and Max Harold Fisch, is usually regarded as authoritative among English-speakers.

The New Science consists of an introduction and five "books," which are in effect chapters of varying lengths. The first is devoted to the "Establishment of Principles." The subject of the second is "Poetic Wisdom" and of the third "Discovery of the True Homer." The fourth treats "The Course the Nations Run," or the regular cycle of historical development, and the fifth, "The Recourse of Human Institutions."

In certain basic ways Vico belongs very much to the Enlightenment. His main project in *The New Science* was to establish a comprehensive science of society, which was an aspiration that he shared with thinkers as representative of the movement as **Montesquieu,** David **Hume** and the Marquis de **Condorcet.** He believed, and sought to demonstrate, that the development of mankind and society proceeded in a necessary and ordered pattern according to verifiable psychological, social, economic and political principles, and that this progression was in accordance with nature (pars. 134 and 367). Like virtually all the thinkers of the Enlightenment, Vico favored Francis **Bacon**'s method (pars. 163 and 359), and accepted sensation as the basis of knowledge (par. 816). He regarded Isaac **Newton** as well as Gottfried Wilhelm **Leibniz** as the "foremost minds of our age" (par. 347).

Like Jean-Jacques **Rousseau,** Vico attempted an analysis of human origins, but unlike Rousseau, who had recourse to physiology and logic to structure his argument, Vico depended largely on philology, especially of the classical languages, for evidence on which to reconstruct the formative stages of human development. That classical philology provided Vico with an adequate base from which to work is highly questionable. What is remarkable is the structure he was able to build on such shaky foundations. In many ways, too, Vico's view of mankind is typical of the Enlightenment. He accepts **self-interest** as the dominant motive force among men (par. 341), sees their activity directed by **utility** (par. 141) and adheres to the key value of **humanity.** These factors notwithstanding, there are aspects of Vico's thought and methodology that can hardly be made to fit with a broadly enlightened outlook.

There is, first, Vico's originality, which makes him hard to identify with any collective enterprise. Among thinkers who sought to account for the origins of mankind, he is one of the few who conceived of a basically animal primal humanoid that had to undergo a long evolutionary process in order to develop into a condition properly human. Unlike Rousseau's primal humanoid described in the *Second Discourse* as isolated but self-sufficient and naturally inclined to sympathy with its fellow creatures, Vico conceived primal humans as Hobbesian beasts whose inherent violence and nastiness precluded their joining in any form of society. What finally compelled them to enter into regular relationships was not utility, as Thomas Hobbes, John **Locke** and Rousseau had all, in varying ways, argued, but fear, or better, terror, when confronted with an unexpected natural phenomenon, namely, thunder.

This fear was providentially directed into a primitive form of religion, based on the dread of superior and unintelligible forces that alone, according to Vico, had the power to restrain the ferocious beasts that primal humans were (par. 13). Humanity socialized by the fear of unknown natural forces, Vico described as living in a "theological" stage of development, as all things were thought to be the work of divine beings. The aristocratic stage of society that developed from it and which was characterized by imaginative and poetic language, Vico called the "heroic" phase, best known through the Homeric poems. The third or "human" stage of development depended on the use of prose and the working out of ideas of fairness and equity. Thus, in contrast to Rousseau and the Scottish school, Vico conceived of society moving from one stage to the next driven by cultural, rather than biological or economic, forces.

There are also ways Vico's thought and methodology stand in contrast to basic Enlightenment positions. *The New Science* is written on the model of the systematic philosophical treatise, laying down axioms and drawing conclusions from them, all in numbered sequence. As against the Enlightenment's disdain for metaphysics, Vico repeatedly expresses his respect for this branch of philosophy and its scope (pars. 367, 374 and 400), and he even writes favorably of **scholasticism** (par. 159). Against predominant Baconian and Lockean views, Vico asserts "Man in his proper being as man, consists of mind and spirit, or, if we prefer, of intellect and will" (par. 364). And there is more. In his religious views, Vico is explicitly orthodox.

Many Enlightenment thinkers drew a distinction between the sacred and the profane and asserted that their works concerned only the profane sphere, and so could not possibly give offense to the Church and its doctrines. They then proceeded to treat the world as if it were wholly profane. Vico, who seems sincerely to have upheld Catholic orthodoxy, needed to separate the providential from the properly secular because Providence was above, or beyond, scientific analysis. He accepts the special status of the Hebrews, and then the Christians, and leaves them out of his history and science of society. His history and science apply only to the "gentiles" whose past and behavior did not benefit from direct providential intervention.

Yet, for Vico, Providence does not restrict its influence to the chosen peoples; it underlies all human justice (pars. 341-344) and is fundamental to all **law** (pars. 397-398). According to Vico, Providence allowed the brutal and mistaken forms of primitive religions as a means of raising and educating humanity.

Adhering to a far stronger form of providentialism than that advocated by the **deists**, Vico also accepted traditional views of the Bible. He asserted, for example, that sacred history was older than secular (pars. 165-169), something against which **Voltaire**, for example, protested emphatically and repeatedly. There are also elements of Renaissance syncretism in Vico's approach to the Bible, as, for example, his claim that the Mosaic Code was a form of natural law (par. 396).

It has also been argued that Vico's notions of history and culture fit poorly with basic assumptions of the Enlightenment in that they are based more on impersonal agents and unintended consequences than is usual among Enlightenment thinkers. It seems, however, that in *The New Science* Vico was engaged in a project broadly similar to that of Rousseau in the *Second Discourse* and to Montesquieu in the ***Spirit of the Laws***, though his methodology and emphasis on classical learning were different from these thinkers.

Where it has been alleged that Vico differs most from the Enlightenment is in his denial of a fixed **human nature**. Vico's portrayal of human beings with different principles of social organization, different cultures and different ways of thinking, suggests models of humanity that are mutually incompatible. This view is usually taken as indicative of a more profound view of history and historical causation than those achieved by other thinkers of the 18th century, and only came to be widely appreciated in the following century. It is not certain, however, that Vico himself regarded human beings from the three historical phases he identified as having fundamentally different natures (*see*, however, pars. 916-18). His reference to "the intelligent nature which is the proper nature of man" (par. 927) nevertheless suggests a single human nature that can adapt to very different forms of culture.

NEWTON, Isaac (1642-1727). The greatest scientist of his time, and probably the most influential culture hero of the Enlightenment. Newton's father, an obscure but well-off yeoman farmer who lived not far from Lincoln, married only a few months before his death, and died before his son was born. After attending a number of local schools, Newton was sent to Cambridge, where he took his B.A. in 1665 and his M.A. three years later. He was a fellow of Trinity College from 1667, and professor of mathematics from 1669.

Newton was indeed a thinker and mathematician of genius. Already in 1666 he had discovered the calculus, but not having troubled himself to publish his work, he became embroiled in a controversy over primacy of discovery with Gottfried Wilhelm **Leibniz,** who made the same discovery independently. Though Newton apparently had a stronger claim to first discovery, his system of notation was more cumbersome than that of the continental scholar, and it is the latter's that is in use today. In 1675 Newton became a member of the **Royal Society** in London. His greatest contribution to science, his development of the theory of gravity and demonstration of its functioning, was published in 1687, in the epoch-making *Principia Mathematica*, or *Mathematical Principles of Natural Philosophy*. This was the work that made of Newton the great culture hero of the Enlightenment, for in it he not only made the world more demonstrably intelligible than it had ever been before, but also adhered to the empirical method and subordinated his theories to fact in a way that precluded the sorts of errors common in the speculative natural philosophy of René **Descartes** and others. His other great work of science, the *Opticks*, was published in 1704.

Newton was far from being a withdrawn scholar totally committed to scientific investigation. In 1696 he left Cambridge to assume the responsible and lucrative positions of First Warden, and then Master, of the Royal Mint. In 1703 the Royal Society recognized his eminence by making him its President, and two years later he was knighted. Thus, from humble beginnings, Newton achieved the highest scientific and official recognition, something that elicited the praise of **Voltaire**, who was greatly impressed with the status granted thinkers and writers in England. Newton also received the ultimate honor of burial in Westminster Abbey.

Though today remembered as a great scientist, Newton's interests included areas that his more narrowly scientific admirers find less than congenial. As a young man he made an exhaustive study of alchemy, something that is less odd if we bear in mind that at that time the science of chemistry proper did not exist.

Newton was also a religious man. His political and religious views were generally conservative, as in his adherence to the Anglican Church, but his interests extended to the more recondite aspects of theology and biblical criticism. During his last years he devoted far more time to religious questions than to science. Of these researches, two were published posthumously, the *Observations on the Prophecies* and *Chronology of Ancient Kingdoms Amended.*

NOBILITY (FRENCH). Since the Renaissance, the French monarch decided who was a noble. True, French nobles in the 18th century often claimed descent from medieval knights or Crusaders who were their own masters, owing only limited knight-services to their overlord. This centuries-old military tradition remained the basis of one noble claim to special status in French society. But it was not the only one. Nobles also claimed privileges by their ownership of high judicial offices in the royal administration. These newer nobles became known as "nobles of the robe" distinct from the older "nobles of the sword" (*see* **Constituted Bodies**).

As the monarchy gained power and prestige from the 16th century, royal office was sought by any socially mobile family who could find the capital to buy one. Profiting from this social ambition, the Crown created offices at all levels of government and sold them. Many of these offices had titles attached, and some included hereditary nobility. Hence the robe nobility grew and eventually swamped the old sword nobility in numbers and wealth. By 1789 at least three-quarters of the French nobility owed their origins to office-holding. However, although their nobility was recent, dating from 1600 or after, robe nobles adopted a noble style of life and shared **privileges** that set them apart from other social groups. The nobles of sword and robe numbered about 40,000 families or one percent of the total population of France in 1789. This was a nobility smaller than the Spanish or Russian, but much larger than the British aristocracy.

Noble privileges were both honorific and fiscal. A noble had the privilege of a title, the right to bear arms, and claims to a preferential place in church, processions or public functions. Nobles were exempt from most taxes; they had the right to be tried in the higher courts; and they had greater testamentary freedom than other French subjects. Since land was the basis of wealth of most nobles, they were also seigneurs with the privileges pertaining to that status (*see* **Seigneurie**).

Compared to other European nobilities, French nobles were not very rich. Compared to the peasants, artisans and most of the middle class around them, however, they were wealthy. They were not innovative agriculturalists, and many of them used every privilege at their disposal to raise the rents and fees of their tenants. At the outbreak of the **French Revolution** they clung to their privileges and many joined the royalist counter-revolution. In 1789 the new French National Assembly abolished noble privileges and a year later nobility itself.

Robert Forster

NOTABLES. The notables were members of the French elite chosen by the king for purposes of consultation in matters of state. These Assemblies of Notables were summoned only for special occasions, for the French kings had no intention of convoking them on a regular basis as the kings of England had done since the 13th century. This policy had led to the development of Parliament and eventual submission of the English monarch to a representative body. In France Assemblies of Notables were therefore rare occasions when the upper clergy, nobles, high officials of state and the wealthiest burghers met in elaborate pomp, usually to give advice on public finance. They resisted taxation, defended their **privileges**, and rarely supported reforms proposed by the royal ministers. Their resistance to fiscal reforms on the eve of the **French Revolution** prepared the way for radical change in 1789.

In the 18th century, however, the term "notable" began to be applied more widely. It reflected the rapid infiltration of the old military nobility by newly ennobled members of the royal judiciary, the treasury and municipal governments. By 1789 a notable's claim to elite status in French society was not exclusively, or even primarily, based on family ancestry or illustrious military action in the distant past. It was based increasingly on a new definition of "merit" that included service in the royal administration and judiciary, and even in a few cases in banking and overseas trade.

This is not to say that a modern class system had replaced a hierarchical or corporatist one. Despite the emergence of a vigorous commercial sector in the society, agriculture remained the source of wealth of at least 80 percent of the **population** and the basis of the notables' fortunes. In fact, when Napoleon I formed his electoral colleges, which were little more than recruiting grounds for his growing administration, he had the prefects draw up "lists of notables." These were essentially lists of "leaders of **public opinion**" in each local community, and the basis of their wealth was the land, even among those who had mining or textile interests.

The term "notable" survived into the late 19th century. As France developed representative institutions, the elected members were also known as notables. Originally limited to wealthy landlords, this group gradually came to include commercial and industrial members as the economy grew in complexity. With the creation of the Third Republic in 1871 and the democratization of the countryside, the notables lost their electoral grip on the rural population and the term became increasingly ornamental.

Robert Forster

O

OLD REGIME. The set of social, economic, cultural, political and administrative institutions that characterized France, and more generally Europe, between the end of the Middle Ages and the **French Revolution**. The name was first used pejoratively by the revolutionaries to describe the regime that they set out to destroy.

The society and economy of the Old Regime were traditional, though over the 18th century significant changes began to appear unevenly, depending on region and circumstances. Old-regime demography was characterized by the natural rhythms of population growth, then massive, brutal, mortalities, usually caused by poor harvests, that kept the level of population close to what subsistence agriculture could support in bad years. However, the 18th century saw significant population growth, thanks largely to mild weather. The economic life of Europe at this time was overwhelmingly agricultural, and in France, which had a mostly free peasantry who were in their great majority smallholders, agriculture was geared to subsistence and produced only small surpluses. Nevertheless, over the 18th century large regional markets developed, and despite poor transportation, and a complicated system of tolls and excises, there are signs of the development of a national market.

Most towns were small, the majority of them functioning as markets and as centers for traditional legal and administrative activities. Usually the largest and most impressive buildings in them belonged to the Church. Some towns, however, were important for their industry, especially textile production, as in the cases of Lille, Amiens and Lyon. The mostly economically expansive towns were port cities, such as Nantes, La Rochelle and Bordeaux, engaged in the highly profitable trans-Atlantic and colonial trades. The prosperity and dynamism of the few great commercial centers contrasted with the stagnation, and sometimes regression, of the traditional market and administrative towns and of the somewhat backward agricultural sector, which supported a large population that struggled to avoid the most extreme forms of poverty.

The society of the Old Regime was hierarchical. The law recognized three different orders, each with its rights, duties and **privileges**. Membership in one of the orders, together with one's place in various corporations, defined one's standing in old-regime society. At the apex of this society was the aristocracy. Though nobles made up only one or two percent of the population, they owned roughly a quarter of national wealth. Normally noble status was attained through birth. However, it could also be acquired by service in the military, by purchase of an ennobling office, or more indirectly by purchase of a **seigneurie,** or by leading a noble lifestyle.

Social mobility was not easy in the conditions of the Old Regime, ennoblement often requiring the efforts of a number of generations, but it was possible. For a peasant family the way to noble status often began with the functions of collector of dues or rents, continued with commerce of some sort, and then entry into the liberal professions, preferably law, in which the purchase of an ennobling office was the easiest path to the public recognition of elite status that **nobility** represented. The relative openness of the nobility accounts, at least in part, for the continued wealth and political domination of this order right to the end of the Old Regime.

Politically, the Old Regime was a monarchy qualified by aristocratic interests and regional privilege. To the monarchs of medieval France, it would have seemed admirably centralized and peaceful. To any post-revolutionary regime in France, beginning with Napoleon's, it would have seemed hopelessly fragmented and diffuse. French monarchs in the 17th and 18th centuries could not impose taxes in a third of their realm without the consent of provincial **Estates**, and they could not enact laws anywhere without the formal endorsement by regional high courts, or *parlements*. At least from the time of Cardinal Richelieu and Louis XIII to the outbreak of the Revolution, the aristocracy appealed to the law of the land and its traditions to block the centralizing and innovating efforts of the monarchy. The monarchy, for its part, justified its desire to revise the late-medieval constitution in its own favor by the need to adapt to pressing changes in international relations, warfare and military technology. For the last two centuries of the Old Regime the monarchy tried to effect reforms to modernize the state, while the aristocracy adopted a conservative and **constitutionalist** stance.

The *philosophes* were divided on the long conflict between a reforming and modernizing monarchy and its opposing nobilities. The President **Montesquieu**, fearing that the loss of constitutional restraints on the monarch would result in **despotism**, argued eloquently for the retention of intermediary bodies that could secure the **separation of powers.** For him the dangers of reform and modernization entailed great risk. **Voltaire**, on the other hand, supported the reforming monarchy because he saw the weight of tradition as opposed to both the practical and necessary business of political modernization and to the furthering of Enlightenment values.

Different societies found different ways of moving beyond the principles and structures of what we term the Old Regime. The French case provides the most dramatic and the sharpest break. England was not without social and political violence, especially in the 17th century, but it managed to evolve away from the formal hierarchies, privileges and regionalism characteristic of the Old Regime gradually, with its aristocracy exhibiting greater flexibility and retaining its influence longer than in France. In Prussia, Austria and Russia an aggravated form of the Old Regime, in which serfdom played a key role, survived intact well into the 19th century.

The society, economy, politics and culture of the Old Regime in the forms that it took in different countries of Europe was the background against which enlightened thought was developed and against which it must be understood. The *philosophes* discovered the theoretical implications of **equality** in societies that were structured by formal hierarchies; their anticlericalism and demand for the separation of church and state were formulated in the face of established churches that too often preferred persecution to charity; and their economic ideas were developed in pre-industrial conditions and in the face of mercantilist policies.

The *philosophes* have sometimes been portrayed as inveterate enemies of the Old Regime who sought its overthrow. It is worth bearing in mind in this context that many of them lived comfortably, achieved satisfaction and attained lucrative and honorable positions in it. If many of the mainstream thinkers of the Enlightenment strove to modernize and improve the society in which they lived, they did so on the assumptions that in the long run the Old Regime was viable. What was needed, and what the thinkers of the Enlightenment sought to do, was to reform it. Full-scale social and political revolution was not something they desired or thought feasible.

ON CRIMES AND PUNISHMENTS/DEI DELITTI E DELLE PENE. A classic statement of Enlightenment legal and social theory written by the Italian nobleman Cesare **Beccaria** and published in 1764. The book was written at the suggestion, and with the active collaboration, of Pietro Verri and other members of the circle of socially conscious and reform-minded young gentlemen of which Beccaria was a member. The book met with an enthusiastic reception, being translated into French, English and other languages within a few years and going through many editions. Its popularity extended beyond the *philosophes* and the educated public to the courts of enlightened monarchs such as Maria Theresa of Austria, **Leopold** of Tuscany and **Catherine II**.

On Crimes and Punishments is in many ways a typical product of the Enlightenment. In it Beccaria praises Charles-Louis Secondat de **Montesquieu** for laying the groundwork for social science and Jean-Jacques **Rousseau** for his insights into the human condition and **education**. Like other enlightened thinkers he nods politely in the direction of the established authorities, and then goes on to treat religion without reference to the Church, and politics in terms that might be acceptable to enlightened rulers, but not to others. His view of man is based firmly on Lockean psychology, which accepts the primacy of **self-interest** as a fact of **nature** and sees human motivation in terms of maximization of pleasure and avoidance of pain. At many points in his discussion of law Beccaria writes in terms of the felicific calculus for which Jeremy **Bentham** later became famous.

Methodologically, Beccaria blends an **empiricist** respect for fact and observation with **rationalist** assumptions. He asserts the primacy of natural **law** and uses it as a criterion by which to evaluate positive **laws**, and adheres to a theory of natural **rights**. Similarly Beccaria uses contract theory as a means of judging existing societies by principles applicable to all of humanity. Like other Enlightenment thinkers Beccaria also believed that it was possible to construct a science of society, and the text of *On Crimes and Punishments* is full of mathematical and Newtonian images.

In giving the individual priority over the state, *On Crimes and Punishments* is typically liberal. Beccaria's reservations about capital punishment, his insistence on publicity as essential to legal procedure, and his narrow classification of crime and acceptance of all behavior that does not fall within this definition as well as his emphasis on the importance of the freedom of the individual likewise reflect his **liberalism**.

Beccaria works through the problem of justice from a **utilitarian** point of view, asserting repeatedly that the true objective of politics and jurisprudence is to assure the greatest **happiness** of the greatest number. He argues that the ability to withstand torture reflects the physical strength of the victim, and is unrelated to his innocence or guilt. The appropriate degree of punishment is that which inflicts the minimum necessary degree of pain while assuring an effective degree of deterrence. Defining crime as an action that causes harm to society, Beccaria insists that the holding or expression of unorthodox opinions should not be actionable at law. He summarizes his treatise by stating: *"In order for punishment not to be, in every instance, an act of violence of one or of many against a private citizen, it must be essentially public, prompt, necessary, the least possible in the given circumstances, proportionate to the crimes, dictated by the laws"* (Paolucci ed., p. 99; section xlii).

In light of the popularity of *On Crimes and Punishments*, it is not surprising that historians have often attributed to it a significant role in moderating the brutality and excesses of European legal systems. Certainly the work contributed to these changes. However, it does not now appear that it, or indeed the Enlightenment, was primarily responsible for such reforms. Historians of the law have pointed out that prosecutions for witchcraft and crimes such as infanticide were reduced drastically during the 17th century, and lighter penalties imposed when such cases were brought. The main reason appears to have been stricter notions of proof within the legal profession. The Enlightenment, then, may with justice be seen as having provided a more humane and general view of legal practice and having accelerated a trend toward a more moderate and humane criminal code. But it does not appear that it can claim to have originated this trend.

ON MIND/DE L'ESPRIT. A book by Claude-Adrien **Helvétius** published in 1758. It is one of the clearest, if not the most subtle, statements of Enlightenment philosophy, and on its appearance occasioned one of the great scandals associated with the movement.

In this work Helvétius offers a purely naturalistic account of man's biological and social development. He sets forth the main principles of Lockean psychology, asserting that the senses are the exclusive source of all knowledge, and that the maximization of pleasure and avoidance of pain is the overriding motive for all mankind. Further, **self-interest** is the natural and universal motive of all human beings. Like other Lockeans, Helvétius regards human beings as almost indefinitely malleable and hence readily modified by **education**.

In his methodology Helvétius is a thoroughgoing and explicit exponent of **empiricism**. He treats morality scientifically, as if it were "experimental physics" ("Preface" to *De l'Esprit*). The discussion of politics is sympathetic to **republicanism** and critical of **despotism**, and the concern for finding a way of harmonizing private and public interests, or making the public interest primary, brings to mind Jean-Jacques **Rousseau**.

Helvétius used the standard ploy of enlightened writers in formally acknowledging the authority of church and state, then saying that he was not challenging them, but writing on a detached, theoretical level. Many of the more radical works of the Enlightenment were published anonymously and abroad. Helvétius's decision to submit the work to the **censorship**, which in somewhat irregular circumstances approved it, and to have it published with official approval in France is probably what laid him open to the exceptional degree of criticism that he experienced. A less wealthy and less well connected writer would almost certainly have seen the inside of the Bastille as a result of a book of this sort.

Helvétius's assertion that it was not possible to determine with certainty whether the spiritualist or materialist position was correct notwithstanding, it was clear that his working assumption was materialist. Similarly, his references to the obscuritanism of "false" religions and of "despotic" governments were too transparent to fool anyone. Conservatives of various sorts had been troubled around this time by the appearance of the *Encyclopédie* and other more daring works of the *philosophes* and their circle, and they were in no mind to let a work so openly heterodox as *De l'Esprit* pass quietly. The royal court, the Archbishop of Paris, the Sorbonne and the *Parlement* of Paris all condemned the book. The author unheroically recanted, and thanks to his wealth and connections, and to the protection of powerful friends, among them Mme de **Pompadour** and Christian-Guillaume de Lamoignon de **Malesherbes**, he suffered neither exile nor imprisonment.

P

PAINE, Thomas (1737-1809). Probably the most important revolutionary of the 18th century, as he played significant roles in both the American and the **French Revolution**. In both cases his contributions were more ideological than practical.

Paine was born in England to a father who was a staymaker by profession and a Quaker by religion, and a mother who was an Anglican and from a family in the liberal professions, and so above the artisanate. Paine attended a primary school until the age of 13, and then began to learn his father's craft. As a young man he married and opened his own shop, but his wife died and the shop failed within the year. Thereafter he engaged in a variety of undertakings that included artisanal work, shopkeeping, teaching school and working as a minor clerk for the excise. He also remarried in 1771. In the following year he represented the excise men against the government, but without success. By 1774 his marriage had failed, he had lost his shop, and he had been dismissed from his excise position. He appealed to Ben **Franklin** for letters of recommendation, and sailed for America.

Paine's fortunes in the New World were, initially at least, as favorable as they had been disappointing in the Old. He immediately found work tutoring, and soon came to be employed as a journalist on the *Pennsylvania Magazine*. In January 1776 he published *Common Sense*, a pamphlet in favor of independence from England, which was immensely popular and has often been credited with shifting opinion in that direction. When at the end of 1776 the fortunes of the republic were at their lowest, he wrote the first of the *Crisis* papers with the intention of rallying support to the endangered cause. The famous staccato first sentence of monosyllables, "These are the times that try men's souls" opened a work that, as much as words were able, helped lift morale and give courage to those whose cause seemed in danger of collapse.

There can be no doubt but that Paine deserved well of his adoptive country. And that country responded to a reasonable degree to his merit. However, whether because of his social origins, excessive independence or some other reason, Paine was unable to fit into the elite of landed proprietors and businessmen who ruled the newly independent United States of America. Though remaining on good personal terms with figures as important as George Washington and Thomas **Jefferson**, he retired to a property given him by the State of New York to farm and work on inventions. One of these, a single span iron bridge, which he could not have built in the United States, took him back to England in 1787. There both the bridge and designer were well received.

Paine met Edmund **Burke** during the first part of his stay in England, and the two men seem to have gotten along well. When Burke published his *Reflections on the Revolution in France* in 1790 and Paine replied with the *Rights of Man*, the first part of which was published in 1791 and the second part the following year, the two men became the main spokesmen for opposing points of view in one of the great political debates in the history of the English-speaking world. When Paine was about to face prosecution and virtually certain conviction for the second part of the *Rights of Man* in the fall of 1792, he left England for France.

Paine was greeted in France as an important defender of the Revolution, and was elected to the Convention. Despite his not speaking French, he attended sessions of the Convention and served actively on its Committee for the Constitution, where his colleagues included the Marquis de (by now simple citizen) **Condorcet**. Paine openly advocated a republic, but argued against the execution of the king, as did most of the Girondins, with whom he identified. He was imprisoned in December 1793, and remained in jail for nearly a year. During that time he composed the first part of *The Age of Reason*, a **deist** tract which later caused him considerable unpopularity. He returned to the Convention and continued to write on a variety of issues until returning to the United States in 1802. His last years there were not happy, and when he died in 1809, his funeral was generally ignored. When the English radical William Cobbett tried to repatriate his remains and to erect a memorial to Paine, he mislaid his bones.

Whether Tom Paine properly belongs to the Enlightenment is a moot question. His social background and lack of formal education were unusual, and can be paralleled in the United States by Ben Franklin and in France by Jean-Jacques **Rousseau**, but by few others who played any active role in the enlightened community. Paine's main contribution to the culture of his time was political, and it was unmitigated by allegiance to any party or administration. He was an outsider who, in his political pamphlets, succeeded in reaching an audience which included many of the disenfranchised. Not only did *Common Sense* and *The Rights of Man* sell well over 100,000 copies each, but they were accessible to, and purchased by, often in cheap editions, ordinary working people.

It is difficult to associate Paine with any of the main trends in Enlightenment political thought because for the most part this thought was paternalist and elitist, even if it was responsible and well-intentioned, and Paine was fundamentally **democratic**. In this sense he begins a new radical and popular trend in politics. By the same token, his social vision, as expressed in the second part of *The Rights of Man* and in *Agrarian Justice* (1796), included a clearly articulated notion of the state's responsibility toward its citizens, concretely framed in programs of social security based on a system of progressive taxation. In this, too, he was far ahead of his time.

Although Paine was more radical and democratic than most of the thinkers of the Enlightenment, this is not to say that he should be placed outside the movement. He should be situated, rather, on its cutting edge, though his voice remains distinctive. It is uninfluenced by the classical training and learned allusions that inform so much of the writing of the Enlightenment, reflecting instead the life experience of an unquestionably intelligent man who came to his politics by way of labor disputes, a varied working life, a tavern debating society and positions as teacher and journalist that were the lot of so many at the fringes of the enlightened community. From that background, and with the resources of his own personality, Paine was able to address both the learned of his age and the artisanal levels of the population on issues from which the latter had been largely excluded. His achievement is a remarkable one, and marks the democratic and radical limits of Enlightenment thought.

PALAIS ROYAL. A monumental building in Paris situated a short distance north of the Louvre palace, and running north to south. The structure is a long rectangle, and contains in its interior a garden several hundred meters long and perhaps a hundred wide, as well as arcades lined with expensive shops. During the later **Old Regime** the Palais Royal was one of the main centers of leisure and cultural activity in the capital.

The Palais Royal was built by the Cardinal de Richelieu, but it subsequently passed into the hands of the Orléans family as an apanage. The area of the Palais Royal received more or less its present form in renovations made by the Regent, Philippe d'Orléans, at the beginning of the 18th century, and by Louis Philippe d'Orléans, the future Philippe-Egalité, in the 1780s. That the Palais Royal belonged to the princes of the blood is a point of some importance because their property was not subject to police jurisdiction, and so enjoyed virtual extraterritorial status. The area known as the Temple, toward the northeast of the city, belonged to the Artois branch of the royal family, and enjoyed the same quasi-autonomy. To modern observers the special legal status enjoyed by the highest levels of the **nobility** seems an odd and potentially dangerous anomaly, and in the event it proved to be so.

Initially the Palais Royal was a meeting place for the aristocracy and for social elites, but in the last decade or so of the Old Regime its space was increasingly commercialized, and to a degree, democratized. Though spies could not have been excluded from the grounds, normal police activities were not permitted there. The Palais Royal was famous for its restaurants and **cafés**, **clubs** of various sorts, popular entertainments, shops dealing in **luxury** goods and booksellers, who were able to sell over the counter items that could not be freely traded in most other places in the city. It was also a well-known meeting place for dissolute young (and not so young) men and prostitutes.

Following its controversial and successful renovation and commercialization in the early 1780s, the Palais Royal broadened its appeal and became in many ways the center for the unofficial cultural life of the capital. Its privileged status as property of the untiringly *frondeur* Orléans family, the absence of an overt police presence, and the free and lively atmosphere prevailing there helped to make it a focus of discussion and agitation in the years preceding the **French Revolution**.

The Palais Royal figures prominently in the literature of the time. In *Rameau's Nephew* Denis **Diderot** describes it as a place where one could choose between relative solitude and informal café sociability, while in his *Tableau de Paris* Louis Sébastien **Mercier** both describes it nostalgically as the place where, in the company of half a dozen friends, he learned to think and argue independently (chap. dcccxx), as well as the place where the corruption prevalent in the capital was at its most extreme (chap. dcccxxi).

PALISSOT, Charles (1730-1814). A writer remembered for polemics with the *philosophes*. He was the son of a court official of the Duke of Lorraine, and proved to be an outstandingly precocious student. After briefly considering a career in the Church with the Oratorian Order, he opted for secular literature.

Palissot moved to Paris in 1749 and began writing for the stage. In 1755 a comedy directed against the *philosophes* entitled *Les Originaux ou le Cercle* was performed in Nancy, and the following year he published a satire entitled *Petites lettres contre de grands philosophes* in which Denis **Diderot** in particular came in for harsh treatment. Diderot was not more gentle with Palissot, portraying him, along with Élie Catherine **Fréron**, as a sycophant and parasite in *Rameau's Nephew*. Palissot's best-known attack on the thinkers of the Enlightenment was his 1760 play *Les philosophes* in which, among other things, he portrayed Jean-Jacques **Rousseau** going on all fours and munching a lettuce. This was not profound criticism, but much of it was clever and suited to the genre in which it was expressed. This comedy caused something of a stir, and helped to make Palissot's reputation. In 1762 he produced another comedy directed against the *philosophes*, and in 1764, on the request of the pope, a poem on the same theme entitled *La Dunciade ou la Guerre des sots*. Palissot also wrote some **history** and a book on the literature of his time.

Palissot's relation to the Enlightenment was not altogether negative. He corresponded with **Voltaire**, and later helped to edit a collection of his works (1792-1798). Rousseau intervened on his behalf when his comedy *Le Cercle* brought him criticism. Palissot was a member of the Academies of Nancy and Marseilles (*see* **Academies, Provincial**), and later of the **Institut**. As a journalist he edited the *Journal français* (1777-1778) and collaborated with Fréron as well as contributing to the *Journal Encyclopédique*.

If the **French Revolution** did not appeal to most of the *philosophes* who lived long enough to experience it, those regarded as opponents of the Enlightenment can hardly be expected to have been more welcoming. Palissot, however, not only survived the Revolution, he took part in 1797 in the founding of Theophilanthropy, a quasi-religious cult of masonic inspiration that was intended as a substitute for Christianity, and under Napoleon he was accorded the post of administrator of the Bibliothèque Mazarine.

PARLEMENTS. Not to be confused with the British **Parliament**, the French *parlements* were sovereign courts of law and served as the highest instances of regular justice in the realm. The size of their jurisdictions varied considerably, with that of the *Parlement* of Paris being by far the largest, but every part of the kingdom was subject to the authority of one of these courts, of which there were 14 by the later 18th century. They were termed "sovereign" because initially they formed part of the King's Council, the medieval *curia regis,* and rendered justice in the king's name. The magistrates of these courts had, and were required to have, noble status, and their offices were venal, so they were in fact irremovable. The chief functions of these courts were to act as final instances for appeals and to register royal legislation. Without registration by a sovereign court, a law was invalid. The *parlements* also had the right of remonstrance, by which they could criticize proposed laws and exercise a temporary veto over them. The monarch, however, could override the objections of the magistrates in a special session known as a *lit de justice.*

The importance of the *parlements* for the Enlightenment is considerable. As guardians of the existing laws, they were naturally inclined to conservatism and acted as leading critics of royal reform projects. As **nobles**, the magistrates of the sovereign courts became advocates of the rule of law and respect for the status quo, and by the same token, leading critics of **absolutism.** The *parlements* served as foci of opposition to royal authority throughout the early modern period. In 1762 under the influence of a minority of determined **Jansenist** magistrates, the *Parlement* of Paris forced the expulsion from France of the **Jesuits**, a religious order closely associated with the Crown. During the last decades of the Old Regime, the *parlements* both obstructed royal programs of reform and helped organize ideological criticism of royal policies around the themes of respect for the constitution, fear of arbitrary central power and protection of the **people**. Some of the leading spokesmen of the Enlightenment, such as the President **Montesquieu** and Christian-Guillaume de Lamoignon de **Malesherbes,** served as magistrates in the sovereign courts. But then so too did some of the most devoted servants of the crown, such as René-Nicolas **Maupeou** and Anne-Robert-Jacques **Turgot.**

PARLIAMENT. The British Parliament is an example of medieval estates that were an integral part of the feudal monarchy. In France the parallel institution was the Estates General, which had fallen into disuse after 1614. Like the British Parliament, it represented not the people, but the estates of the realm, namely, the clergy (First Estate; Lords Spiritual), the **nobility** (Second Estate; Lords Temporal, and particularly the peers), and those without special status (Third Estate; Commons, mostly municipal and corporate office holders). Rooted in the medieval practice of consultation, the British Parliament and the French Estates General usually acted as advocates of **constitutionalism. Voltaire** pointed out that in its long, interrupted history the British Parliament had often been subservient to the Crown, to the point that during the Wars of the Roses and under Henry VIII it allowed itself to become the agent for judicial murders that elsewhere in Europe were carried out without any pretense of legality (*Essay on Manners*, chap. clxvii).

The British Parliament figures prominently in the famous chapter 6 of book XI of **Montesquieu**'s *Spirit of the Laws,* which analyzes the British constitution in terms of the theory of the **separation of powers**. Montesquieu portrays the Crown as exercising the executive power, and Parliament, independently, the legislative. He also posits, but does not emphasize, a separate judicial power. According to Montesquieu the **liberty** of the English people was assured by each authority maintaining its own jurisdiction and respecting the integrity of those of the other branches of government.

As an illustration of the principle of the separation of powers, Montesquieu's analysis works well. As history, however, it is wanting. Lewis Namier demonstrated that the British government of the 18th century, which effectively led England to a position of commercial, military and political hegemony in Europe and beyond, ran under the de facto control of the Crown, which used the places in its gift and the pensions at its disposal to control Parliament. It is difficult to see this manipulation and **patronage** as other than corruption. Though the application of Montesquieu's theory of the separation of powers to England was inappropriate, this does not invalidate the theory itself.

PARTICULARISM. The existence of significant differences among societies, and more especially, recognition of the legitimacy of such differences. The Enlightenment is sometimes viewed as subordinating the autonomy of individual societies to general views of **human nature** and morality, and thus of favoring **univeralism** over particularism. The balance is not easily determined, as both points of view existed among Enlightenment thinkers, and not infrequently were maintained in different contexts by the same writer.

Jean-Jacques **Rousseau**, for example, tried to show in the *Second Discourse* that there existed a universal core human nature based on physiology and psychology. At the end of this work he argued that the form of society based on private **property** ran counter to the basic needs of human nature. In the *Social Contract* he went on to suggest how a society in conformity with the basic needs of this core human nature could be established. Like **Montesquieu** and **Voltaire**, Rousseau saw in physiology and psychology grounds for a universalist approach to mankind, and in culture the source of diversity and particularism.

Enlightenment thinkers such as Montesquieu and Voltaire strove to bring the attention of their contemporaries to the significant differences between cultures, in large part because they sought in this way to negate the claims of European religious authorities to absolute legitimacy. In cultural **relativism** they found a powerful tool for discrediting tyranny and fanaticism. But their relativism was limited to the realms of taste and the indifferent. Various cultures were fully entitled to set their standards of dress, cuisine, poetry and worship as they liked. They were not entitled to infringe on basic human **rights**, which were generally conceived to be based on biology, psychology and a concept of dignity to which freedom was integral.

None of the thinkers of the Enlightenment condoned, for example, burning human beings on the grounds of differences of opinion. All of them regarded as matters of legitimate cultural difference preferences for wearing a hat or refraining from doing so, for praying in whatever position one cared to adopt, whether standing, sitting, kneeling or prostrate, or for using any language one chose for prayer.

PATRIOTISM. A sense of loyalty or devotion to one's country or fatherland. Patriotism is often used interchangeably with **nationalism**. However, in that fatherland (*patrie*) has historical and cultural connotations, "patriotism" has a broader meaning than "nationalism," which refers to devotion to a certain geographical and political structure at a given time.

The 19th century is sometimes called an "Age of Nationalism." Partly because the nation-state was not yet well developed in many parts of 18th-century Europe, partly because the main categories of Enlightenment thought were largely indifferent to national boundaries, little emphasis was placed on nationalist sentiment before the **French Revolution**. And when it was discussed it was in terms quite different from those of the 19th and 20th centuries.

One of the first important discussions of patriotism in the Enlightenment was the abbé **Coyer**'s *Dissertation sur le vieux mot patrie* (*Dissertation on the Old Term "Patrie"*) of 1755. In this brief but influential essay Coyer pointed out that the classical notion of patriotism, which implied the rule of law, a degree of **equality** among **citizens** and devotion to the common good, was no longer current in Europe. With respect to basics, Coyer's characterization of patriotism is similar to **Montesquieu**'s better-known description of political **vir-**

tue in a **republic** (*Spirit of the Laws*, Bk. II, chap. 2, Bk. III, chap. 2 and Bk. IV, chap. 5).

Unlike the situation in the 19th century, when nationalism tended to be exclusive and confrontational, during the 18th century patriotism belonged with such inclusive and cohesive values as **humanity** and **beneficence**. In the discourse of the second half of the 18th century, a person who provided relief for the poor, or objected to excessively harsh penal laws, or who criticized institutions such as serfdom or **slavery**, was likely to be described as a good patriot. The common good to which patriotism was directed in the 18th century was socially cohesive in nature, and typically crossed social boundaries.

During the 19th and 20th centuries religion was often used to reinforce a sense of national identity. During the 18th century, at least among thinkers identified with the Enlightenment, it was used differently. In the conditions of the **Old Regime** established churches had great influence in cultural matters and in administration. The classical notion of patriotism was often used to assert the claims of the State against the Church and the autonomy of things secular more generally. This was the case, for example, in the field of **education**, where it was argued that clerics should not act as teachers, because their *patrie* being heaven, they could not form the hearts of their students to the love of their fatherland.

Probably the outstanding spokesman for the classical notion of patriotism in the 18th century was Jean-Jacques **Rousseau**.

PATRONAGE. Almost every 18th-century Western society was hierarchically organized, ill policed and governed through institutions that were inefficient and limited in their effectiveness, if not in their claims. Those societies tended to be patriarchal and clannish to a degree we find hard to imagine.

Lines of authority ran from the political centers to the regions through those men who could accomplish the purposes of the rulers or the ruling class. They tended to be the greater regional **nobility** whose own followers would take their cues from the greatest among them who had at their disposal many informal means of achieving their ends. These ran from simple coercion through a range of economic and social benefits, such as good marriages and jobs in the churches or other institutions, political positions and a myriad of other inducements to act as the patron desired his clients to act. Everywhere European societies worked through the social layers on those lines.

This regime was not effectively challenged intellectually until Jean-Jacques **Rousseau** and not politically until the American and **French Revolution**s offered political models, which were in principle, if not in actuality, more egalitarian, even **democratic**. Patronage was the normal way of rewarding loyalty, getting things done and providing for social mobility. Nowhere in the 18th century had it been efficiently replaced by the coercive mechanisms of meritocratic states, and by the force of **public opinion**.

In the context of the Enlightenment, patronage also affected those who promoted the values of the enlightened and who gave places and opportunities to those who espoused them. Without the favor of rulers and great officers of state, reformers like Anne-Robert-Jacques **Turgot** or Jacques **Necker**, the Marquis de Pombal or Johan Friedrich Streunsee would have been mere idealists unable to effect changes; all had royal patrons but all started life relying on the patronage of humbler men.

What was true of politics was also true of the cultural world. Kings, aristocrats and sovereign states, including such entities as the free cities of Germany, sponsored and gave positions to all sorts of artists and skilled workers during the 18th century. Increasingly, such patronage was being matched by that given by the middling classes—the gentry, civic functionaries and professional men, minor landowners and skilled artisans. Their patronage was increasingly market-oriented and often extended to **women** who wrote and drew. It deeply affected those who produced and bought books, **periodicals** or cheap art works, such as prints or the objects mass-produced in European porcelain factories.

During the 18th century patronage also tended to be marked by an interest in cultural producers from beyond one's own frontiers. Angelica Kaufmann worked all over Europe, as did many musicians and some skilled scientist/engineers, such as Benjamin Thompson, Count Rumford. Places given by patrons in the **universities** and government offices were of great importance too. And, without the appointments of men such as Turgot in a variety of institutions, the French state would not have developed into the meritocracy that it aspired to become. Without judicious appointments made by patrons, the Dutch and Scottish universities would never have shone as they did.

Roger Emerson

PEOPLE. This term had distinct political and social meanings in the 18th century. Its political use is rooted in the republican tradition (*see*

Republicanism), and refers back to a world in which the people, or citizen body, was sovereign. By the time of the Enlightenment, however, no properly democratic or popular regimes existed in Europe, and this form of government was treated mostly as a theoretical, though impractical, alternative to monarchy and aristocracy. Divested of its sovereignty, the people was likewise deprived of its dignity. **Voltaire** reports that when a member of the British **Parliament** used the phrase "the majesty of the English people" it was greeted with derision. He adds, however, that when repeated with firmness, it was accepted (Voltaire, *Letters on England*, Letter 8).

In its social sense, the "people" were all those who lacked **privileges** or the special status conferred by membership in the clergy or **nobility**. The author who perhaps did more than any other to define the term people in the 18th century, and to rehabilitate it, the abbé **Coyer**, described the process by which the learned, talented and wealthy withdrew from the "people," leaving it a residual category for workers and peasants who had neither the wealth nor the leisure to educate themselves. As the poor, rabble or riff-raff, the "people" posed a key problem for the men and women of the Enlightenment, who debated the degrees to which they were educable and improvable.

There was no unanimity here. Coyer's essay on the people reached a broad public not in its original form, but as the substance of the Chevalier **Jaucourt**'s article "Peuple" in the *Encyclopédie*, and in other major reference works that followed it. The hesitant rehabilitation of the people begun in the Enlightenment largely on the grounds of the utility of the working population to the State was completed when the people reclaimed its sovereignty during the **French Revolution** and joined the two main meanings of the term that had for centuries been separated.

PERIODICALS. Serial and periodical publication began in Europe during the 17th century, subsequently developing into a significant and varied literary genre, and playing an important role in the Enlightenment.

Periodicals seem to have begun as an attempt to make more widely available the results of recent humanistic and theological learning. In some cases, such as the *Journal des Savants*, which was founded in France in 1665, the initiative for these projects came from governments, in others, as in the case of Pierre **Bayle**'s *Nouvelles de la République des Lettres,* which appeared between 1684 and 1687, a writer and a commercial publisher conceived and printed the journal. These publications, and others, such as the *Acta Eruditorum*, which was published in Leipzig, consisted almost exclusively of substantial reviews of serious recent works in the fields of art, science, philosophy and theology.

Literary periodicals were the logical development of the original learned journals of the 17th century. Responding to a shift among writers, and not unrelated to a widening of the reading public, more popular journals, such as the ***Mercure de France,*** the ***Année Littéraire***, the ***Journal Encyclopédique*** and the *Gentleman's Magazine* continued to provide reviews of recent publications, usually including considerably more fiction than had been the case earlier, and added to them articles, letters, poems, announcements and anecdotes in different proportions. Installments of periodicals of this sort would often appear weekly or once in two weeks.

A quite distinct form of periodical was the original literary essay, often in the form of moral or social comment. Intended primarily as a form of refined entertainment, periodicals of this sort were usually written by one main **author**, or perhaps a few associated writers, and because of the demands of daily composition and publication, usually lasted only a year or two. The founding and hugely influential model of this kind of periodical was the ***Spectator*** of Joseph Steele and Joseph **Addison**. The *Rambler* of Dr. **Johnson** is another well -known instance of the genre.

One of the more common forms of periodical publication of the 18th century that has received relatively little attention is the paper specializing in commercial announcements and local news. Historians of ideas naturally privilege journals dealing with literature, the arts and sciences. While papers giving details of local events and useful information, such as ships in port, property for sale and services available, are of little intellectual importance today, they might also include items of more general interest and tended to be economically viable and to have large readerships. In England such papers were common from the beginning of the 18th century, while in France they proliferated mostly after mid-century and were known as *Affiches*, literally notices.

Today most daily papers emphasize news in its various forms. In the 18th century there was certainly a demand for such publications, but it was met and obstructed in different ways in different countries. England was relatively free in its press laws, having done away with preliminary **censorship** early in the century, though it denied journalists access to **Parliament,** taxed periodicals and maintained vigorous laws against slander. In **absolutist** regimes, however, political news was regarded as a matter of state, and such political news as was allowed to see the light of day did so only after close government scrutiny.

The *Gazette de France*, for example, was founded on government initiative and provided an official version of the news. There was in France no free political press until the collapse of censorship in the spring of 1789. Papers dealing with current affairs and politics published abroad were, however, allowed into the country under scrutiny. The ***Journal Encyclopédique***, which was published in Belgium, contained a news section, and the *Gazette de Leyde* was devoted largely to current affairs. To be sure that their treatment of politics was acceptable to the authorities, control was exercised both through prior censorship and the post office.

Government control of the postal system made it virtually impossible for periodicals that sold their papers openly to circumvent state supervision. The only known example of a clandestine periodical to have operated successfully in France for an extended period was the *Nouvelles Ecclésiastiques*, which was an organ of the persecuted and highly motivated **Jansenist** movement, and which apparently was able to operate from the Temple, to which the police were denied entry.

The growth of the periodical press was one of the more striking aspects of cultural change over the 18th century. Great Britain had roughly 25 periodicals of all sorts in 1700, and by the 1780s more than six times that number. France not only had far more government regulation than Britain, but also an effective system of economic regulation of the printing trade imposed by guilds. Nevertheless, the growth of the periodical press there did not lag much behind that of England. While only 15 or so titles were available at the beginning of the century, there were some 80 toward the end of the **Old Regime**. It should be borne in mind, however, that this figure includes French-language publications from abroad, and, for purposes of comparison, that the population of France was roughly three times that of Britain.

How widely were periodicals read? This is a subject on which there is no shortage of contemporary estimates, but little hard information. Literary periodicals like the *Année Littéraire* or *Journal Encyclopédique* would not normally have much more than 2,000 subscribers, and could profitably survive on a quarter of that number. Highly successful journals in France might have pressruns as high as, or exceeding, 10,000 copies, while in England the *Spectator* and *Gentleman's Magazine* also reached this figure. Periodicals with pressruns approaching 20,000 copies were not unknown in the 18th century, and at its end the *Hamburg Correspondent* was publishing 30,000 copies of each number. Conditions of publication changed significantly with the **French Revolution**, however, and it is not fair to compare pressruns of the revolutionary period with those from an earlier one.

To know the size of pressruns during the Old Regime is not the same as knowing the readership of a paper. It is generally agreed that that each copy of a periodical had many readers. Estimates for the proportion of readers to copies of papers vary from 10 to one to 20 to one. Where subscriptions to periodicals were taken out by **cafés** or reading rooms, a common practice at the time, the proportion would have been much higher. It is fair to say that periodicals played a central role in popularizing Enlightenment literature and views, and that a variety of institutions of the enlightened community contributed to disseminating them.

***PERSIAN LETTERS/LETTRES PERSANES* (1721).** An epistolary novel by **Montesquieu** in which the exchange of letters between Usbek, a Persian noble traveling in France, and his friends allows discussion of a wide range of topics, and for the interweaving of a story of frustrated love into what is at once a vehicle for social criticism and a brilliant work of literature. Though this book is the first classic of the French Enlightenment, it is also remarkably radical.

Montesquieu had the book published anonymously in Holland in 1721. It was an immediate best seller, and went through many editions before the **French Revolution**. The *Persian Letters* reflect the reaction against the authoritarianism, orthodoxy and dogmatism of the reign of Louis XIV, and a new atmosphere of freedom during the **Regency**.

Using the Persian state as a foil to Europe, Montesquieu develops a criticism of **absolutism** based on the supposed **despotism** of Persia. In eastern notions of monarchy, Montesquieu maintains, there is security of neither person nor property, and the whim of the ruler rather than the law of the land is the dominant principle of politics. In this situation the subject stands in relation to the ruler as the slave does to his master. The master-slave relationship is also amplified in the series of letters dealing with Usbek's seraglio, which becomes more unruly the farther he is distant and the longer he is away. Montesquieu implies that the lot of the subject of a despotic regime is on a level with that of a woman in a seraglio, thus giving a powerful emotional twist to his denunciation of political relations of domination.

There are many places in the *Persian Letters* where the Catholic Church is satirized and criticized. But Montesquieu's criticism of religion is most powerful, though also most subtle, where he juxtaposes the traditions of different revealed religions in such a way as to show their incompatibility, and so to have one orthodoxy negate the others, as he does in the parable of the hare (Letter 46). The claim of one revelation, be it Jewish, Christian or Muslim, to absolute validity is negated by the same claim made by the other traditions. Though faith may assert the superiority of one dispensation over another, **reason** cannot. The implication, Montesquieu suggests, is that man's true religious duty consists in the observation of a simple and universal ethical code, on the one hand, and in **toleration** in matters of ritual and dogma, on the other.

As far-reaching as is the criticism of politics and religion in the *Persian Letters*, the criticism of **gender** relations is even more radical. The depiction of the seraglio as a condition of degradation and dehumanization for women and eunuchs alike is a heightened portrayal of gender relations based on domination. Montesquieu also shows his reader that there are alternatives to such relations. In invoking a world in which women have seraglios of handsome and willing men at their disposal (Letter 141), the claims of female sexual autonomy are recognized. Montesquieu even goes so far as to question the taboo on marriage between siblings (Letter 67).

In the concluding passage of the book Montesquieu shows that despite the horrendous price it exacts from those subject to it, despotism cannot satisfy those who exercise unlimited power, and that with sufficient courage and resourcefulness there are ways to freedom within the most restrictive constraints that despots can devise. There are not many heroes in works of satire and criticism such as the *Persian Letters*, but if there is one, it is Usbek's favorite wife, Roxane, who finds a way to deceive her despot-husband and fulfil herself while in the seraglio, and who having been discovered, takes her own life as a last act of independence and autonomy (Letter 161).

The criticisms of church and state with which the *Persian Letters* abounds are often adduced to present the book as an example of the debunking and reformist aspects of Enlightenment thought. This is legitimate. But it is the portrayal and analysis of the deeper and inter-related structures of oppression in politics and gender relations that gives the book its real power and lasting value. Underlying the criticisms of **prejudice, superstition** and abuse of power are Montesquieu's core values of natural **law** and the dignity of the individual.

PHILOSOPHE. Originally simply the French for philosopher. However, during the 18th century the term took on a new meaning, and came to designate a new cultural model, that of the engaged intellectual. Though a minority of *philosophes* could also be regarded as philosophers in the traditional sense, namely, as disinterested seekers for wisdom or truth, what defined the *philosophe* was a commitment to the material and moral well-being of ordinary people. A *philosophe* was expected to be independent, and so beyond the influence of patrons who might seek to further particular interests. Moreover, the *philosophe* was expected to use his independence to enlighten both the public and the authorities and to advocate reforms to further the well-being of the citizenry, to increase the degree of freedom accorded it and to render social and political arrangements more fair and more efficient. Some *philosophes* sought to cooperate directly with monarchs in achieving these goals (*see* **Enlightened Despotism**) while others appealed to the public by the printed word.

Unlike earlier philosophers, such as René **Descartes** and Benedict **Spinoza**, the *philosophes* sought to influence social and political policy according to views and doctrines that they developed independently, and unlike many members of the intelligentsia of the 19th century, the *philosophes* of the 18th century were moderate and reformist rather than revolutionary. Traditionally, philosophers were given to abstract thought, and more than that, to abstraction from society. The *philosophe* of the 18th century, by contrast, was expected to be polite and sociable. Serious pursuit of the truth was deemed to be compatible with concern for one's fellows.

According to the article "*Philosophe*" in the *Encyclopédie*, "**reason** is to the *philosophe* what grace is to the Christian." The author of this article then specifies that the reason to which the model *philosophe* of the 18th century had recourse was fact-based, inductive reason, and that induction allows one to distinguish what can be known from what cannot, and what is certain from what is merely probable. Recognizing a wide scope for the unknowable and the merely probable, induction leads the *philosophe* to accept that there are many things of which he cannot achieve certain knowledge, and this disposes him to suspend judgment and toward **toleration**. Furthermore, the reason advocated by the *philosophes* was supported and directed by the values of usefulness, **humanity** and honesty.

The *philosophes* were no doubt at the center of the Enlightenment, playing dominant roles in **salons**, **academies** and the progressive print media. They were leaders and opinion makers who set the tone for a broader enlightened community, and to appreciate their role in the Enlightenment it is necessary to consider this broader constituency to which they referred. Among the leading *philosophes* were **Montesquieu, Voltaire**, Denis **Diderot**, Jean-Jacques **Rousseau**, the Baron d'**Holbach** and Claude Adrien **Helvétius**, the abbé **Morelly** and Jean-François **Marmontel**.

PHILOSOPHICAL DICTIONARY/DICTIONNAIRE PHILOSO-PHIQUE **(1764).** One of **Voltaire**'s books that could not be sold legally, but which nevertheless was highly popular. Composed of short, incisive articles, the *Philosophical Dictionary* grew freely, with new articles and additions to older articles added at the author's discretion.

Voltaire said of the Holy Roman Empire that it was neither holy, nor Roman, nor an empire. We might say with equal justice that his *Philosophical Dictionary* is neither philosophical nor a dictionary. Rather it is a scintillating polemic against certain values and institutions of the **Old Regime** in modular form, and its alphabetical ordering is incidental. It does not attempt definitions, and its articles are far too long to be dictionary entries. More a weapon of ideological warfare than a work of reference, the *Philosophical Dictionary* is a typical work of enlightened criticism, readily accessible to intelligent and educated laymen, ironical, devastating, often hilarious.

In its first edition, the *Philosophical Dictionary* was made up of 73 articles, 31 of which treated some aspect of religion. Most other articles were devoted to ethics, politics and society. Only a few were concerned with properly philosophical subjects. In the editions appearing between 1765 and 1769 the number of articles grew to 114, of which 61, or more than half, treated religion. Sixteen of these were devoted to the Hebrew Scriptures ("Abraham," "Circumcision," "Ezechiel," "the Flood," "Jewish Kings," "Jephtah," "Joseph," "Moses," "Solomon," "Adam," "Babel," "David," "Genesis," "Job," "Judaea," "Prophets"); 20 to Christianity ("Apocalypse," "Baptism," "Christianity," "Convulsions," which treats the **Jansenists** of Saint-Médard, "Grace," "Peter," "**Abbé**," "Antitrinitarian," "Arius," "Confession," "Council," "Credo," "Divinity of Jesus," "Gospels," "Inquisition," "Julian the Philosopher," "Martyr," "Papism," "Paul —questions concerning," "Transubstantiation"). The 25 more general articles on religious issues include "Angel," "Atheism," four articles beginning "Catechism of," "God," "Hell," "**Fanaticism**," "Idolatry," "Law—Civil and Ecclesiastical," "**Miracles**," "**Prejudice**," "Religion," "Resurrection," "**Superstition**," "**Tolerance**," "Dogma," "**Enthusiasm**," "Faith," "Persecution," "Priests," "Sect," "Theist" and "Theologian."

Voltaire himself was a **deist**. He directs withering criticism against the brutality of some of the biblical narratives, the unintelligibility of much Christian theology, and the harm caused by dogmatism and persecution, but not against the Supreme Being that made the world.

The vast range of subject matter in the *Dictionary*, extending from the ancient Near East to 18th-century Paris, and the modular mode of composition, which deprives the work of any coherent structure, tend to obscure the consistency of Voltaire's basic positions. Throughout the *Philosophical Dictionary* Voltaire maintains a rigorously Lockean and Newtonian scientific point of view, which he effectively uses to discredit superstition, metaphysics and dogma. He holds it a scientific truth that the order observable in the physical universe is proof of a divine Creator, and he just as firmly maintains that this Creator "never acts by partial will, but by general laws" (art. "Catechism of the Japanese"). For a miracle to be properly attested, he archly suggests, it would have to be performed before the Academy of Sciences (art. "Miracle").

Voltaire's ethical theory is simple and comprehensive. In his view there is an objective and universally binding moral code. In his own words, "morality is the same for all men who use their reason. Therefore morality comes from God like light" (art. "Morality"). In his social theory Voltaire is moderate. On the one hand, he wants governments to correct abuses; on the other, he does not seek to undermine the existing order. While Voltaire asserts that all men are by nature equal, he does not think that this general truth should interfere with each person performing his duties in the position in which he finds himself in the society in which he lives (art. "**Equality**").

PHYSIOCRACY. Labelled a narrow philosophical sect by their critics, the Physiocrats were French economists with a precise public policy. Their writings and propaganda constituted much more than a mathematical theory of the circulation of wealth; these economists gained the attention of royal ministers after 1760, and their influence can be seen in the electoral system created by the **French Revolution** and lasting until 1848.

"Physiocracy" literally means "rule of **nature**." The Physiocrats postulated that all wealth came ultimately from the land. The produce of the land was Nature's bounty, what they called a "Net Product." Trade, manufacture and finance only transformed this net product and were essentially "sterile" economic activities. Larger landed proprietors, and eventually smaller peasant owners as well, were the focus, even the heroes, of physiocratic economics. It followed that the function of government was to encourage agriculture in every way possible.

The grain trade must be left to market forces and unhindered by price controls and distribution requirements. Consumption and sales taxes should be eliminated and all taxes be consolidated in a single land tax. Customs barriers should disappear and the **guilds** be abolished. In a phrase reminiscent of Adam **Smith**, *laissez-faire, laissez-aller* became their reform slogan.

The Physiocrats were a diverse lot. Some, like François Quesnay, wrote highly theoretical works, others like, the Marquis de Mirabeau, wrote about the moral superiority of landed society over the "bloodsuckers" of the court and cities, and still others, like Dupont de Nemours and Controller-General Jacques **Turgot**, attempted to put physiocratic ideas into practice. After 1760 there were periods when controls on grain prices and market conditions were removed in the hope of increasing grain production by market incentives. Unfortunately, the larger landlords used the open market to hoard grain and sell at the highest price. Given the rapid rise in the French **population** and only minimal increases in productivity, food prices rose catastrophically and forced the government to intervene after every period of free trade in grain.

The political influence of the Physiocrats is often overlooked. The importance they attached to landownership had much to do with a definition of **citizenship** that ascribed greater civic capacity to landowners, especially resident local landowners. The *propriétaire*, large and small, was a vital *mediator* between the individual and the nation. Indeed, this role of the individual should be contrasted with John **Locke**'s view of property as an *extension* of the individual and a barrier to state action. Before the Revolution of 1789, the royal government sponsored local assemblies of landowners (*see* **Notables**). The Constitution of 1791 distinguished property-owning "active citizens" from propertyless "passive citizens." Indeed, voting rights were defined by property qualifications in France until 1848 when universal manhood suffrage was instituted.

Robert Forster

PIDANSAT DE MAIROBERT, Mathieu-François (1727-1779). Until recently known largely for his editorship of the *Mémoires secrets* from 1771 to 1779 and as a participant in the **salon** of Mme de **Doublet,** but lately, thanks to the researches of Robert **Darnton,** recognized as one of the best-selling authors of clandestine literature in the closing decades of the **Old Regime.**

Little is known of Pidansat's family or early years. He was born in Champagne, but was raised by Mme de Doublet in Paris, and remained associated with her salon. There is speculation that he may have been the natural child of Mme de Doublet and Louis Petit de **Bachaumont,** but this can neither be proved nor disproved.

According to the *Biographie Universelle,* Pidansat lived the life of a cultivated and economically independent gentleman. He took an interest in literature and the arts, attending first nights of plays and collecting brochures. But he was not merely a passive member of the enlightened community. He was a member of the Academy of Caen (*see* **Academies, Provincial**), and in the capacity of royal censor he had a say in determining what his contemporaries were able to read in printed form. He was also familiar with Christian-Guillaume de Lamoignon de **Malesherbes,** the director of the book trade and minister of **Louis XVI,** and with a number of directors of the police, among them Antoine Raymond Jean Galbert Gabriel de Sartine, Jean Charles Pierre Lenoir and Le Camus de Neuville. That he held a secretaryship in the household of the Duc de Chartres and the expensive ennobling office of secretary of the king reinforces the impression that he belonged to the comfortable world of the Enlightenment establishment.

Pidansat was suspected of involvement in dubious proceedings associated with the Marquis de Brunoy, and was arrested by the police. On being released he is said to have been so outraged that he committed suicide.

A very different picture of Pidansat's role in the literary world of the late Old Regime emerges from the researches of Robert Darnton. Rather than merely an editor and contributor to an interesting newsletter, he figures prominently in the world of clandestine literature. Of the 15 illegal works that sold most widely, three were by Pidansat: in second place, the *Anecdotes de Mme la Comtesse du Barry* (authorship uncertain, but Pidansat is the best bet); in sixth place a highly subversive *Journal historique* of the reforms attempted by the Chancellor **Maupeou** (with Mouffle d'Angerville); and in 13th place *L'Observateur anglais*. In Darnton's list of clandestine authors whose works sold most widely, Pidansat comes third, after **Voltaire** and the Baron d'**Holbach** (Darnton, *Forbidden Best-Sellers*, Tables 2.5 and 2.6).

In addition to holding so notable a place in the production of clandestine literature, Pidansat also appears to belong to the world of **Grub Street** rather than that of the salons and academies. Using a police report from mid-century Darnton has found that Pidansat lodged with a washerwoman, had been imprisoned in the Bastille for distributing verses against Mme de **Pompadour** and was regarded as "the worst tongue in Paris" (*Great Cat Massacre*, pp. 162, 159 and 178). It is unusual, but not impossible, that the same person could live both in the worlds of Enlightenment high culture and that of the underclass of 18th-century literature. *Rameau's Nephew*, for example, contains a forceful literary portrayal of this sort of character. But there is something odd about the same man being portrayed as familiar with the official responsible for the direction of the book trade and a number of police inspectors, while at the same time producing highly subversive literature and being sent to prison for distributing verses offensive to the court.

It would seem that Pidansat, largely by underground opposition to government reforms, and by criticism of corruption in high places, contributed to the destabilization of the Old Regime. What is less clear is whether he did so as a comfortable and established member of the enlightened community, or as a Grub Street hack, or, what would be the more interesting option, as a combination of the two.

PLANTATIONS. Plantations in tropical produce–sugar, coffee, indigo, cotton–were the basis of French colonial wealth in the late 18th century (*see* **Colonies**; **Slavery**). The plantation system was the most advanced sector of the European economy in terms of technology and geographic reach, uniting four continents–Africa for labor supply, the West Indies and Brazil for production and processing, and Europe and North America for markets and provisions. Aside from the peculiarity of the labor force, the plantation resembled a modern agroindustrial factory.

How was the plantation system organized? Taking the booming French island of Saint-Domingue (today Haiti) as an example, sugar was the big money-maker. A plantation in sugar cane need not be large. Two hundred acres of cane worked by 200 slaves might produce 200 tons of sugar annually for a gross income of about 60,000 French *livres* or 3,000 English pounds, a handsome return. Expenses for new African slaves, livestock, provisions, mill materials, shipping and insurance might consume a third to half of this, still leaving a good profit.

For a newly arrived white settler, the main challenge was finding sufficient capital to equip a plantation. A third to a half of the capital value of a plantation was in black slaves. Much faster than capital equipment such as the mill and processing houses, slaves wore out quickly. Seven years was the average life span of a slave in the islands. The work was hard. During the six months' harvesting and processing season it demanded round-the-clock labor. Death rates among the slaves outdistanced birth rates by two to one. Abortions were frequent, but the main causes of death were overwork and undernourishment. Only marginal land was used for provisions, and plantation owners were very sparing with imports of food. No wonder European planters in the West Indies–French, British, Spanish, Dutch–imported four million Africans in the 18th-century alone to replace heavy losses.

The slaves fought back against this labor regime. Flight, poisonings of whites and cattle, suicides, theft, work slowdowns and petty sabotage were answered with severe physical punishments ranging from 50 lashes of the whip to the iron collar, from imprisonment in four-foot high sheds to mutilation. The plantation may have been a profitable enterprise; it was also a seething cauldron of hate and despair for blacks and of fear and anxiety for whites.

What explains the establishment of such a system? Despite high death rates, African slaves resisted malaria and yellow fever much better than white labor. Despite heavy loses on the Atlantic crossing and in the first year of acclimatizing to the island, and despite the large number of children, the aged and the sick, slave labor was still profitable. **Racism** also made such exploitation acceptable to whites. To profit and racism, one might add a sense of European hubris, a belief in technological and economic superiority of which the plantation system was an example. The Age of Reason was also an age of racial exploitation.

Robert Forster

PLUCHE, Noël Antoine, abbé (1688-1761). The author of, among other things, the *Spectacle de la nature*, one of the most widely read books on natural history during the 18th century. Pluche is interesting as a sincere cleric who made a significant contribution, though by popularization rather than original research, to the scientific culture of the Enlightenment. He was not alone in bridging the gap between traditional, ecclesiastically based learning and the newer culture of the time.

Pluche began his career as a teacher in *collèges*, first in Reims, then in Laon. However, he refused to accept the bull Unigenitus (1713), which was used as a sort of Test Act directed against **Jansenists**, and was consequently deprived of his teaching position. He readily found work as a tutor, however, and continued in that capacity until the success of the *Spectacle de la nature,* which appeared in 1732, allowed him to devote himself to writing. In 1739 he produced a similar work on astronomy entitled *Histoire du ciel.*

The *Spectacle de la nature,* which appeared in nine volumes between 1732 and 1750, was in effect a textbook on science intended for children. Like Bernard **Fontenelle**'s *Conversations on the Plurality of Worlds,* the *Spectacle* is written in dialog form so as to break up the text and help maintain the interest of the reader. Unlike Fontenelle's early work of scientific popularization, Pluche's has abandoned the principles of **Cartesian** science, and presents the world in **Newtonian** terms.

POLAND. A central European state situated between Russia, Austria and Prussia, which disappeared over the course of the 18th century.

Socially, Poland was characterized by a particularly large **nobility** that comprised some 7 or 8 percent of the population (in France the comparable figure is less than 1 percent), and a large peasantry, mostly in a condition of serfdom. The urban population was proportionately smaller than in western European states at the time, and the Jewish population much larger. Poland, which in the 18th century included Lithuania, shared in the demographic expansiveness characteristic of Europe at the time. Its population increased from roughly 12 million souls in 1700 to 14 million by the 1770s.

Politically, Poland is an example of a state in which the nobility retained its hold on power. The Polish monarchy remained elective, and hence weak. Their interests opposing centralization, the nobility effectively prevented its development. Early in the 18th century the nobility restricted the size of the army, thus depriving the monarch of an essential tool of state building. The Sejm, or Parliament, was rendered ineffective by a regulation, the *liberum veto,* which allowed any individual noble to veto any measure he opposed.

The price for this political disorganization and weakness was exacted by Poland's neighboring centralizing monarchies. Russia, Prussia and Austria, the three outstanding examples of **enlightened despotism** of the time, partitioned Poland in 1772, 1793 and 1795. With the third partition Poland disappeared as an independent state. The first two partitions were preceded by failed attempts at reform, the third by a failed rebellion. Poland is a classic example of the inability of a decentralized state dominated by its aristocracy to safeguard its national interests in the face of aggressive centralized monarchies.

Jean-Jacques **Rousseau** was requested by some Polish patriots in 1769 to evaluate the political situation of Poland. He agreed, and completed the *Considerations on the Government of Poland* in 1772. This work was not published during his lifetime. A practical application of his political theory as put forward in his *Social Contract* and elsewhere, it is a valuable indication of the way Rousseau approached concrete and specific problems in politics.

POLITICS. The making and carrying out of policy has been understood in two distinct ways by historians of the 18th century. In the first and commonsense definition, politics was a matter of decision-making, raising taxes, allocating resources and diplomacy. These activities were in the hands of the king and his ministers, whom he appointed and dismissed at will. In France and Russia the king or czar was in theory unrestrained in the making of policy and the appointment of ministers, and so far was **absolute**. In Britain the king's authority was limited by **Parliament**. In France there were constituted bodies that did not have properly political functions. These were the Church, the *parlements* and provincial **estates** that were found on the peripheries of the kingdom and that fulfilled fiscal and administrative functions. The Estates General did have a properly political role to play, but it had not met since 1614. These bodies generally represented the **nobility** in its long and losing struggle with the centralizing monarchy. They were, however, to enjoy a revenge of sorts as the *parlements* were to become centers of opposition to the crown in the last decades of the **Old Regime**, and the revived Estates General were to play a central role in the early **French Revolution**.

The second way politics has been understood in recent historiography is largely cultural, and emphasizes the notion of **public opinion.**

Historians influenced by cultural anthropology, literary criticism, the notion of discourse developed by Michel Foucault and the concept of the **public sphere** put forward by Jürgen Habermas have seen in language and communication more fundamental and formative social forces than had been the case previously. They placed far greater emphasis on metaphors such as "tribunal of public opinion" or "**republic of letters**" than earlier scholars had done. They also tended to privilege symbolic representation, language and opinion in their work to the degree that distinctions between the practical business of raising taxes, allocating resources and keeping public order, on the one hand, and discourse on rights and duties, on the other, were blurred or overlooked, and politics came to be treated as a matter of who wrote what and how it might have been received. This trend now seems to have peaked. Though perhaps unconvincing in its broad outlines, this emphasis in historiography has inspired much new and welcome research on the print and image-based cultures of especially the later decades of the Old Regime and the French Revolution.

POMPADOUR, Jeanne Antoinette Poisson, Marquise de (1721-1764). Mistress of **Louis XV**, and a key figure in the political and cultural life of the mid-century. She was from a relatively modest family engaged in finance, but received a good education thanks to the interest of her mother's wealthy and influential lover, who also saw to an advantageous marriage when she was 20.

As Madame Le Normant d'Étiolles, the future Marquise de Pompadour had considerable freedom and began to frequent the **salons** of the capital. In 1745 she was introduced to the king, and by the end of the year was recognized as his official mistress and given the title by which she is best known. Her relationship with Louis XV and her place at court were complex. Not only a lover, but also a valued companion of the king and an intelligent participant in the politics and culture of the time, she was influential both at the court and in Paris.

David Wick has argued that royal mistresses played an important role at court, in that the circle of which they became the center served to offset the influence of the queen and her circle, who usually tended toward conservatism and orthodoxy. This situation allowed the king to choose between two rival centers of influence. The failure of **Louis XVI** to take a mistress, according to Wick, deprived him of a choice of societies and outlooks that his predecessors had enjoyed, and made him more dependent on Marie Antoinette than might otherwise have been the case.

There is general agreement among historians that the Marquise de Pompadour played an active role in court politics, and was especially influential in making appointments up to and including the ministerial level. She also had a large part in setting standards of taste at court, the *style Louis XV* owing a good deal to her. Her **patronage** of the arts was extensive, and well placed. As against the traditionalist and pious circle of the Queen, Marie Leszcynska, the Marquise de Pompadour advocated the ideas and values of the Enlightenment. She acted as protector of **Voltaire** at court, and supported the project of the *Encyclopédie.* Indeed, a famous portrait of her by the painter Quentin La Tour has a volume of the *Encyclopédie* displayed in the background.

POPE, Alexander (1688-1744). The outstanding poet of the early Enlightenment in England, and as such an illustration of why poetry is not considered one of the areas in which the Enlightenment excelled.

Pope was the son of a comfortable draper who had converted to Catholicism. He learned to read at home, and was then tutored by a Catholic priest. By the age of eight he was learning Latin and Greek, and was a promising and diligent student. He attended a number of Catholic schools, and as a Catholic was not obliged to waste his time in the intellectual backwaters of Oxford or Cambridge of that time. While a youth Pope contracted an illness that interfered with his growth and seriously affected him in later life.

Pope achieved recognition for his writing at an early age. His *Pastorals* (1709), *Essay on Criticism* (1711) and mock epic, *The Rape of the Lock* (1712), were all well received. His main early success, however, was his translation of the *Iliad* (1715-1720). Pope's scholarship was not above reproach–a contemporary commented that "it was a pretty poem, but not Homer"–but his literary skill was much appreciated, and his *Iliad* sold well enough to leave him financially independent. This was highly unusual. Himself something of a businessman, Pope hired collaborators to produce a translation of the *Odyssey* (1725-1726), for which they did the bulk of the work, and for which he had the greater part of the considerable profits. However, the profits were sufficient for Pope's collaborators also to do well out of the enterprise.

At roughly the same time that he was engaged in his translations from the Greek, Pope also edited the works of **Shakespeare** (1725), but this project did poorly. Pope had a propensity to engage in literary polemics, and two of his most important works, the *Dunciad* (1728) and the *Epistle to Arbuthnot* (1734-1735), are satires of this sort. To carry on the quarrel begun by the earlier poem Pope founded and ran the *Grub Street Journal*, which appeared between 1730-1737. Two of his other main poems, the *Essay on Man* (1733) and the *Moral Essays* (1733-1735), were composed under the influence of Viscount **Bolingbroke**, and are admirable formulations of a moderate, rationalist, theistic and socially conservative outlook common in the early Enlightenment.

Though issuing from a moderately well-off commercial family, Pope, thanks to his talent, was received into the most aristocratic society. He was also active in some of the literary **clubs** of the time, among them the Scriblerus Club to which such figures as his friends Jonathan Swift, Dr. John Arbuthnot, William Congreve and John Gay belonged.

Despite his literary success, Pope in many ways remained an outsider: he was a Catholic in an overwhelmingly Anglican country; a **Tory** in an age dominated by **Whigs**; and his physical disabilities prevented him from taking part in many activities of his friends and possibly heightened his susceptibility to polemics. There is also something slightly incongruous in his insisting on treating in verse so many subjects, both satirical and philosophical, that were properly prosaic.

POPULATION. Before the Industrial Revolution, when muscle power was the basic force of production, the number of human beings in a country was not a bad indication of that country's economic strength. At that time the muscles of animals could supplement those of people, but they could not replace them. Only with the advent of effective and widespread machine-driven technologies did the importance of the size of a country's population for its economic standing decrease significantly.

Up to the 19th century the movements of population in Europe had been determined by weather patterns, disease and the ability to distribute basic foods. Old-regime demographic patterns were basically Malthusian, with steady growth in population continuing until the means of subsistence fell behind necessary minimal consumption. A population that had reached the limits of agricultural resources to sustain it would experience low wages and undernourishment, or more typically, would suffer massive and brutal mortalities, often as the consequence of unusually cold weather that caused harvest failures. Mortality was selective, disproportionately affecting the most vulnerable, that is, the aged, the very young and the malnourished.

The 18th century was a watershed in demographic history in that it was a period of protracted population growth that was not followed by a dramatic reversal. Historians are divided on the causes of this. It appears that the most general one was an improvement in the weather, and consequently of harvests. The horrendous mortalities that followed the exceptionally cold winters of the late 17th century and of 1709 did not recur after the reign of Louis XIV, nor were there widespread outbreaks of plague after the case in Marseilles in the early 1720s. From roughly 1730 to 1770 the population of France, and of Europe generally, grew significantly.

Human agency may have helped in a small way, since inoculation against smallpox, the only significant Enlightenment medical innovation to help preserve human life on a large scale, was developed and began to be used at this time. What ultimately made it possible to sustain the large and growing populations of the 18th century, however, were improved agricultural methods, the development of more extensive and more effective systems of transportation and other aspects of the Industrial Revolution.

Because the Industrial Revolution had only begun and still had little effect during the 18th century, most thinkers of the Enlightenment continued to look upon a large population as the key to economic prosperity and national strength. And because the gains in population throughout Europe were not even, and were not clear to contemporaries, they were not, at the time, seen as permanent. The thinkers of the Enlightenment were, with a few exceptions, such as David **Hume**, haunted by a fear of depopulation, even as the population of Europe grew dramatically.

From John **Locke** to the President **Montesquieu,** Jean-Jacques **Rousseau** and beyond, Enlightenment thinkers regarded the size of the population of a country as a main criterion of its well-being. According to an important reference work of the time, "the prosperity of a State derives from its population" (*Dictionnaire universel des sciences,* art. "Politique," vol. XVI, p. 510). It was also generally believed that population depended more on moral than on physical causes. According to the Baron d'**Holbach** population naturally proportioned itself to the laws and liberty a government provided as well as to geography (*Système social,* Part III, pp. 34-35). However, even the apparently exaggerated claim of Cerfvol that "Population is proportioned to morality, independent of all other causes" (*Mémoire sur la population,* p. 20) was not unusual at the time.

PREJUDICE. To pre-judge or form an opinion before considering the evidence.

Most societies function on the basis of received opinions or traditions that are passed on uncritically in the process of socialization. **Montesquieu** and **Voltaire**, for example, did not question the propriety of wearing wigs and breeches, or of bowing elaborately by way of greeting in the society in which they moved. Provided that new situations do not arise and new challenges are not made, established traditions usually continue in force. For the social and intellectual elites, at least, the 18th century was a time when accepted opinions were being challenged increasingly. The proper way to meet such challenges for the thinkers of the Enlightenment was to examine the rationality and functionality of the practices or beliefs at issue. Deciding a question before doing so was an instance of prejudice. Prejudice was unacceptable to the thinkers of the Enlightenment because it precluded the kinds of improvements and reforms that they regarded as desirable and necessary.

PRELIMINARY DISCOURSE to the *Encyclopédie/DISCOURS PRÉLIMINAIRE* à l'*Encyclopédie.* The introduction to and credo of the *Encyclopédie,* written by Jean le Ronde d'**Alembert,** and published at the beginning of the first volume of the *Encyclopédie* in 1751. More than an introduction to a reference work, the *Preliminary Discourse* is one of the great programmatic statements of the Enlightenment.

Traditionally, encyclopedias contained summaries of a wide range of subjects organized in alphabetical order. D'Alembert explains in the *Preliminary Discourse* that the work that he and Denis **Diderot** were editing was intended to be something more than that. They had in mind a "reasoned dictionary" that would not only provide information, but would also show "the order and connection of the parts of human knowledge" (*Preliminary Discourse,* R. N. Schwab trans., p. 4). However, d'Alembert begins the *Preliminary Discourse* not with a discussion of the principles of the ordering of knowledge, but with a review of the principles of **Lockean** epistemology, and moves from there to a discussion of scientific method.

The key issue that d'Alembert takes up at the beginning of the *Preliminary Discourse* is thus not what is known or how knowledge is organized, but how we are able to know things at all, and what the limits of knowledge are. Like most Enlightenment thinkers, he maintains that all knowledge is derived from sensation and experience, and so is a thoroughgoing **empiricist**. He denounces speculation and hypothesis as leading to barren and unverifiable verbal exercises. D'Alembert implies that prior to any true or fruitful knowledge, it is necessary to learn to distinguish the realms of the knowable from the unknowable. To this end the empirical method is the most reliable means. In this sense the Enlightenment is less about extending knowledge than about recognizing and refusing to enter the realms of the unverifiable.

D'Alembert praises Francis **Bacon** as the main inspiration of the *Encyclopédie*, and cites his "tree of knowledge" as the model on which the work he is introducing is based. The first branch of this tree includes sciences based on memory, or knowledge received most directly from the senses, and which is hence the most reliable. These include the sciences (natural history as it was known at the time) and history. The second branch of the tree includes sciences of reflection, such as theology, philosophy and, Alembert suggests, the sciences of man. The third branch includes the fine arts in which imagination plays a larger role than in the sciences of memory or reflection. But all, as the image of the tree suggests, are interconnected.

The *Preliminary Discourse* also includes a historical sketch of the development of Western culture. Typically for the Enlightenment it is hostile to the religious emphasis and **scholasticism** of the Middle Ages, and sympathetic to the revival of classical values that occurred during the Renaissance. As a mathematician, however, d'Alembert is particularly appreciative of the achievements of the scientific revolution of the 17th century, and sees in the empirical method of Bacon and the achievements in physics and astronomy of Galileo and Isaac **Newton** the way towards a better understanding of the world and a mastery of the world that will greatly improve the lot of mankind.

PRÉVOST, Antoine François, abbé (1697-1763). A man who moved throughout his life between the secular and religious spheres without being able to fully integrate himself into, or abandon, either. As a writer he was responsible for the production of an enormous amount of print, but is remembered primarily for a short novel, *Manon Lescaut*, which is a masterpiece.

Prévost was one of nine children. His father was a legal official of Hesdin in Artois. He studied with the **Jesuits** and at 16 became a novice in that Order. However, he could not decide between the Church and the army until in 1720 he joined the Benedictine Order and was assigned to a number of abbeys, among them Saint-Germain-des-Prés. There his scholarly abilities were recognized and he was set to work on the *Gallia Christiana*, the great 16-volume folio history of the Catholic Church in France published in Latin between 1715 and 1865. It says much about the age that the same author should have contributed to a work of ecclesiastical history and hagiography and written a novel such as *Manon Lescaut*.

By 1727 Prévost had had enough of Saint-Germain-des-Prés, and asked to be transferred to Cluny. When permission was refused, he left anyway, and so was in an irregular situation. He then went to Holland and to England. During his stays in these Protestant countries he wrote a long novel, the *Mémoires et aventures d'un homme de qualité* (1728-1731), of which *Manon Lescaut* was volume seven, familiarized himself with English literature, carried on a number of love affairs, spent time in debtor's prison and began an important periodical, *Le Pour et le Contre* (1733-1740). In 1734 he was granted permission to return to France on condition that he wear ecclesiastical dress.

Prévost's career seems sometimes to belong to the upper levels of **Grub Street**, sometimes to rise above it. He was appointed almoner to a princely house, but nevertheless continued to write, compile and translate endlessly. He thus became one of the few **authors** in the 18th century to have made a reasonable living from his work in the book trade.

His fiction includes *Le Philosophe anglais, ou histoire de M. Cleveland* (1731), *Le Doyen de Killerine* (1735), *L'Histoire d'une greque moderne* (1740), *Mémoires d'un homme de qualité* (1743) and *Le Monde morale, ou mémoires pour servir à l'histoire du coeur humain* (1760). He translated Samuel **Richardson** and David **Hume**, produced a two-volume dictionary and worked on editing and compiling a huge *Histoire générale des voyages* (1746-1789). These undertakings, as well as his work on another periodical, the *Journal étranger* (1754-1756), indicate that Prévost had to rely on publishers for a living.

Prévost retired to the country north of Paris with the intention of writing in defense of religion. This suggests that he never lost the interest in things spiritual that drew him first to the Jesuits and then to the Benedictines. His end was as strange as his life, and not happier. Having fainted and being believed dead, he was killed by a surgeon who believed he was doing an autopsy.

PRIVILEGE. Literally, a private law; in practice, a benefit or exemption which certain estates, social groups or regions enjoyed to the exclusion of others. Privileges were both practical and honorific, and the central place of privilege in the polity and society of the **Old Regime** was one of its distinguishing features.

The privileges of the clergy and **nobility** included precedence in processions, in seating in church and in other formal settings, and in the kinds of clothing and accoutrements they might wear. Both clerics and nobles had the right to be judged before particular courts and both enjoyed fiscal privileges, the chief of which was exemption from the *taille* and from most indirect taxes. Fiscal privilege was not, however, restricted to members of the first and second orders of old-regime society. A member of the Third Estate with formal bourgeois status (*droit de bourgeoisie*) was also exempt from the *taille*.

Privilege was also regional. This was a situation that followed from the retention of certain rights and prerogatives by various regions as they were incorporated into the French monarchy, usually by written treaties and agreements. The crown thus became the guarantor of local law codes, and all manner of particularistic administrative and fiscal arrangements that diverged from the practices of the central core of the French monarchy, the Ile de France. As a rule of thumb it is fair to say that the more privileged regions of the kingdom were on the peripheries.

The privileges which the elites of old-regime society enjoyed followed from the intense localization of political and administrative organization of the Middle Ages, which was retained, largely for pragmatic reasons, by the old-regime monarchy, which aspired to centralization, but had at its disposal few of the fiscal and technological means necessary to realizing it.

The existence of so much privilege complicated the task of government significantly. The privileged classes, particularly the aristocracy, remained broadly conservative, seeking to protect and maintain their special rights and exemptions. The Crown found that it could not meet its financial obligations while respecting the fiscal privileges of the elites, and it was in part the mismanaged negotiations between the Crown and the aristocracy over this issue that resulted in the convocation of the Estates General in 1789.

For most of the thinkers of the Enlightenment privilege represented the weight of the past and negation of the qualities they valued most, such as talent, industriousness, openness and **progress**.

PROGRESS. The assumption that social conditions and human life can be significantly and consistently improved. This assumption, which was not widely held before the 18th century, is itself dependent on a number of other developments and assumptions, among them **secularization** and the rise of modern science.

The notion of progress is largely foreign to the Christian worldview. This is because for the Christian the most important business of life is achieving salvation. The drama of salvation is played out in a limited number of variations an infinite number of times. It always begins from the same point, and the possible conclusions are limited. If the meaning of life is defined in these, or similarly spiritual terms, then there is no objective or certain way of measuring degrees of success or failure.

One of the preconditions for the emergence of the idea of progress was the validation of material life and of the understanding of the physical world. For Francis **Bacon** and his many disciples in the 18th century, the understanding of the workings of nature took on a new and practical importance. Science for them was not only a matter of more adequate theory and a better understanding of natural phenomena. It also entailed the application of such knowledge to assuring a greater degree of control over **nature** and a more comfortable way of life. Further, as scientific knowledge and its application were cumulative, a notion of progress was built into the model of scientific research.

Another force contributing to the idea of progress was **utilitarianism**, and more particularly, the utilitarian notion of **happiness**. Once happiness was defined in terms of the senses, such factors as life expectancy, poverty, hunger and disease became central to evaluating the well-being of individuals and societies. These and similar considerations are readily quantifiable, and the lines on graphs plotting their fluctuations can be taken as showing whether or not conditions are improving. The expectation that conditions can and should improve is itself necessary to a clearly defined idea of progress. The application of medicine and rational administrative techniques will usually have the effect of improving material conditions.

While progress inclines toward reform, it is broadly inimical to revolutionary change. The incremental and meliatory nature of change reflecting progress renders sudden and violent change super-fluous. In this sense an important current of Enlightenment thought opposed revolution. The view of **history** widely held at the time that saw intellectual advances, especially from the Renaissance on, lead-ing to improved material conditions and a more open civic order, suggested sudden and violent interventions in the running of coun-tries would result in more harm than good.

Jean-Jacques **Rousseau** did not deny that Europe had undergone considerable cultural progress, but he argued that this progress came at a prohibitively high cost in social and ethical terms. His analysis of the development of European society saw a process of moral regres-sion that would not gradually set itself right. Though he explicitly warned against the dangers of revolution in his writings, the logic of his position, which denied progress, called for some sort of basic change of direction.

Perhaps the best-known expression of the Enlightenment's faith in progress is the Marquis de **Condorcet**'s *Sketch of the Progress of the Human Mind.*

PROJECT OF ENLIGHTENMENT. A currently fashionable term for summarizing what the Enlightenment was about. From the point of view of a moral philosopher Alasdair Macintyre wrote of "the Enlightenment's project to provide a rational foundation for and justi-fication of morality" (*After Virtue*, 1981, p. 43). Other historians and thinkers have, in accordance with their points of view, presented the Enlightenment as a project in secularization, or in liberalization, or in the assertion of mastery.

There is a problem with the formulation of this notion in the singu-lar, as it is not clear that there was a single project in which all major figures in the Enlightenment, let alone others, saw themselves par-ticipating. **Montesquieu**'s main project was to uncover the laws gov-erning society and politics; **Voltaire**'s was to destroy what he be-lieved to be the life-denying aspects of Catholicism, and to have as pleasant a time as possible while doing so; and Jean-Jacques **Rous-seau**'s was to try to understand himself (which entailed a good deal of autobiographical writing), to uncover the processes by which he had become as depraved as he was and to imagine conditions in which he and others might become, or have been, better. As for Denis **Diderot**, editor of the *Encyclopédie* and author of *Rameau's Nephew*, it is not easy to point to any single project in which he was primarily engaged.

It probably makes more sense to talk about "Enlightenment projects" in the plural. There was certainly a widely shared desire among the *philosophes* to understand **nature** so as to dominate and use it, and this we might see as a scientific and technological project. There was an attempt to extend scientific methods to the study of man and of society, or a project to establish social sciences. The aspirations to understand the workings of the economy so as to increase wealth, as well as the attempts to reform society and the state so as to increase human well-being, might be termed the **utilitarian** project. The criticism of traditional theologies and of **superstitions**, both popular and learned, can be seen as part of the **deist** project. And the attempt to reconceptualize human relations in terms of affection and self-fulfillment rather than duty, obligation and property may be termed the romantic project.

The question that comes to mind at this point is, may there not be a common denominator among these various specific projects that would justify our speaking of a single "Enlightenment project"? If there is, it is probably a variation of the utilitarian project, and might be described as the intention to reduce human suffering. The two main aspects of this project would then be limiting the potential for self-inflicted cultural damage (the criticism by Voltaire and others of the suffering caused by superstition and **fanaticism**) and the maximization of the means to material well-being (reformers of the state and economy).

The formulation given here for a single project of Enlightenment is negative. So conceived, this project is a matter of taking away or moderating things that are harmful, such as conditions of scarcity, natural and artificial. The emphasis is on removing causes of suffering, and not on directing people to specific sets of beliefs or actions. So conceived, the project of Enlightenment does not include a positive ethical component. The reason for this is the assumption, which is both positive and **liberal**, that human beings in conditions of plenty and freedom would be capable of defining and effecting their own **happiness**.

Far from containing an overall logic of control and domination, the project of Enlightenment, insofar as it is possible to speak of it as a single or unified notion, calls for the elimination of social and material evils, and leaves the individual free to find his or her way in a more intelligible and more hospitable world. This is a well-intentioned and modest program. If people subsequently have found that they have been unable to find satisfaction in conditions of relative plenty and freedom, this was not an eventuality about which the thinkers of the Enlightenment were concerned. There were far more pressing issues to which they felt it imperative to address themselves. That abundance and freedom, which were at least partially achieved in the West only once the economy had been industrialized and the welfare state put in place, would not have been adequate for diffusing happiness widely throughout society would not have occurred to most thinkers struggling to remove obstacles in the way of achieving material prosperity and social openness.

PROPERTY. A key institution in the civil society of the 18th century which functioned in part as an alternate criterion of self-definition to norms dominant in old-regime society. The traditional means of defining oneself in the **Old Regime** was membership and status within overlapping corporate structures. The tendency to define oneself in terms of what one owned and the power that one's property gave one over the world and other people was of course not new in the 18th century, but it grew in importance as other criteria lost force.

As a criterion of social definition, property was dynamic in that it was relatively easily acquired and lost. In this way it was opposed to **privilege**, which was a more static principle of old-regime social organization, and which could also be gained or lost, but generally more slowly and elaborately.

Property was also more elastic and egalitarian, in that all members of society could acquire as much property as their ability and industry allowed, though it was recognized that basic inequalities of opportunity prevented some people from achieving their potential, economically and otherwise. Nevertheless, it was optimistically assumed, as it sometimes still is, that individual determination and industry would overcome adverse circumstances. It is on the basis of this assumption that progressive thinkers made of property the main criterion of civic competence and political participation.

During the Enlightenment poverty was regarded as depriving those subject to it of independence, and it precluded their receiving an extensive **education**. There is hardly surprise to find that the aristocratic President **Montesquieu** approved of the Roman constitution in which "it was the means and the wealth at one's disposal that conferred suffrage, rather than the persons" (*Spirit of the Laws*, Bk. II, chap. 2). However, thinkers as radical as Jean-Jacques **Rousseau** and Thomas **Paine** also thought that a minimal amount of property was a necessary prerequisite for full **citizenship**.

Rousseau, who admired the Romans, noted that at Rome "only the owners of hearths had the right to defend them" and that the politically, the propertyless were "regarded as absolutely nil" (*Social Contract*, Bk. IV, chap. 4). In his "Discourse on Political Economy" Rousseau asserted that property was "the true foundation of civil society, and the real guarantee of the undertakings of citizens," while later, in his "Constitutional Project for Corsica" he made full citizenship dependent on a man having "two living children, a house of his own, and land enough to live on" (Cole, p. 151; Watkins, p. 302). Similarly, Paine approved the provision of the French Constitution of 1791 that required a property qualification to qualify a citizen for the right to vote (*Rights of Man*, Penguin, p. 83).

As a principle of social organization, property was, compared to the alternatives in place during the 18th century, progressive and dynamic. But it hardly justified the claims that came to be made in its name. The 17th article of the Declaration of the Rights of Man and the Citizen of 1789 states that property was an "inviolable and sacred right." The same article then goes on to describe conditions in which the public good justified the violation of this right, but it did not qualify the strange attempt to sacralize property in an otherwise desacralized world. It would make as much sense to speak of sacred chickens (sometimes a real danger in France) or sacred cows. It would seem that the articulate and inspired men of the Constituent Assembly sought a phrase to describe the importance they ascribed to property, and in their enthusiasm, finding nothing appropriate, opted for an outdated term that in effect meant nothing more than "very important."

What the Revolution did do for property was to disencumber it of the rights of eminent domain and various ecclesiastical dues. This was no small accomplishment, and might have been described in terms that had contemporary significance.

PUBLIC OPINION. There are two main ways public opinion has been conceptualized by historians of the Enlightenment. One is to see it as majority opinion, the ideas and views held by most of the public that form a loose consensus on any range of issues. This approach is empirical, seeking only to determine what opinions are held by most people and withholding judgment on the opinions themselves. Today the most obvious tool for determining public opinion is the public opinion poll. Historians cannot of course poll populations of the early-modern period, and must therefore base their statements about public opinion on sources such as newspapers, journals and correspondences, which usually permit only rough approximations. Nevertheless, because public opinion is a significant social force, historians try to determine its content to the degree that they are able.

A second notion of public opinion has developed from the important study of Jürgen Habermas, *The Structural Transformation of the Public Sphere* (1962; English translation 1989). Habermas posited a rational, autonomous and normative notion of public opinion that emerged from a "**public sphere**" that was intermediate between the state and the purely private domestic sphere. The rationality of public opinion as defined by Habermas makes it independent of the opinions and **prejudices** of ordinary people, and enabled its spokesmen to claim normative authority for it. Public opinion was presented as a "tribunal" before which the government could be hailed, and which played a key political role. Habermas's notions of the public sphere and public opinion have been favorably received by historians of a wide variety of periods and countries.

PUBLIC SPHERE. A category between the realm of state authority and the properly private domestic sphere. This notion was developed by Jürgen Habermas in what was almost certainly the most influential doctoral dissertation of the 20th century. It was published in German in 1962, but was not translated into English until 1989 under the title *The Structural Transformation of the Public Sphere: An Inquiry into a Category of Bourgeois Society* (trans. T. Burger and F. Lawrence, MIT Press). In this study Habermas, who was, and has remained, a Marxist, sought to analyze the relations between state, society and culture in a way that allowed a more comprehensive and sophisticated appreciation of cultural phenomena than that provided by the assumption, given excessive weight in simplistic versions of Marxism, that culture, as part of the superstructure of society, was directly determined by a social and economic substructure. As a highly sophisticated and creative Marxist, Habermas maintained a firm emphasis on socio-economic forces, but accorded to culture a wider degree of autonomy.

Some of those who have developed and used the concept of the public sphere have been at pains to reify and reduce the sociological and economic aspects of it, so prominent in Habermas, to insignificance. Regardless of how it has been used, the notion of the public sphere has become one of the most important and widely used analytical concepts in cultural studies and in history in recent decades.

Located between the political authority of the state and the paternal authority of the European family, the public sphere is conceived as a realm of rational freedom. Incompatible with the authority and **patronage** predominant at the courts of absolute monarchs, the public sphere develops where economic and social conditions make possible the free and independent concourse of like-minded individuals. The institutions that shape the public sphere are typically those based on voluntary association, and regulated, to the degree that they are regulated at all, by norms of rational discourse and persuasion. These institutions, or at least enough of them to make a difference, emerged first in England and Holland in the 17th century, and then in France, the Germanic states and Italy during the 18th century, for the most part in its second half.

The cultural foci of this emerging civil society were the **cafés**, which initially also played an important role as places of commercial activity, reading rooms, *musées*, Masonic lodges (*see* **Freemasonry**), and on a rather grander scale, **salons**, in which **women** played a significant role, and **academies** that normally had government patronage. Habermas conceived the public sphere as an arena in which propertied males met in the institutions described above, or communicated with each other, whether by manuscript letter or printed **periodicals** or books. Authority, whether that of the **noblility**, the State or the Church, tended to be politely disregarded, the discourse of those participating in the public sphere being regulated by **reason**.

The public sphere could only come into being when the near monopoly of intellectual life held by the Church during the Middle Ages and the power exercised by the nobles and crown had been moderated by a new class, based in commerce and the liberal professions. The continued existence of an independent and rational public sphere is a matter of concern for Habermas, who sees the emergence of mass culture and commercialization as threats to the vital, rational and independent (and perhaps idealized) notion of the public sphere that flourished during the 18th century.

PUBLISHING. The activity of making printed works available to the public. Over the 18th century publishing underwent significant changes both in scale and organization.

At a period during which **population** grew throughout Europe, sometimes by as much as 20 percent or more, and levels of **literacy** increased, one would expect that the demand for printed materials would increase also. In effect, it did, and even more sharply than rates of population and literacy. In England the number of titles produced annually doubled from the beginning to the end of the century, and in France it more than trebled. To explain such sharp increases it is also necessary to take into account the general economic prosperity of at least the period around mid-century, which put more people in the position of being able to buy or rent printed materials, and changing cultural tastes, which included a demand for **periodicals**, novels and lighter forms of literature. This trend further broadened the reading public, bringing into it a significant female component, which had previously been lacking.

The business of publishing also changed over the 18th century. Broadly speaking, market considerations grew in importance, while corporate control of the industry weakened. In England this process went farther than elsewhere, but even in France, which retained formally corporate social and economic structures until the end of the **Old Regime**, market forces had increasing impact. This was clearly the case in the clandestine book trade, which sought profits in defiance of government regulation, but it was also true of members of the booksellers **guild**, who learned to work with, or around, the authorities in order to provide the public with works it wanted.

Although the scale of publishing was limited by the technology of the hand press, there was still a tendency over the 18th century for printing to separate from the more entrepreneurial activities of commissioning manuscripts and marketing. Publishers thus came to stand as key intermediaries between **authors** and the public. With the introduction of copyright legislation in England at the beginning of the century and in France during the 1770s, and with the denial of perpetual copyright to publishers in both countries, the condition of more popular authors improved somewhat. Hack writers on **Grub Street** who provided compilations or translations to order, however, benefited little from new notions of literary property. Publishing remained a business, and those who did best at it economically were the sharpest businessmen, who, while in search of profit, also acted as key cultural intermediaries.

R

RACISM. The "Age of Reason" did not end racism even among the *philosophes*. Although most of them opposed **slavery**, their views toward race were much less egalitarian. Indeed, the development of "scientific" racism made racism more intractable, especially regarding black Africans. Europeans in the 18th century knew little about the interior of black Africa compared to the Americas and even Asia. They classified all humankind into a hierarchy of races with the Europeans at the apex, Asians, especially the Chinese, in the second rank, followed by the Amerindians (sometimes "noble savages") and the black Africans at the bottom. The older biblical justification for black inferiority—the sin of Ham—was replaced in scholarly circles by authoritative works of biology, psychology and anthropology, which demonstrated with empirical "evidence" that different races had distinct characteristics both physiological and cultural. And given European hubris these cultures were not equal.

Georges-Louis Leclerc **Buffon** and **Montesquieu** attributed the primitiveness of black Africans to their climate, nourishment and mores, while **Voltaire** and Jean-Jacques **Rousseau** blamed the absence of monotheism and law, respectively. Claude-Adrien **Helvétius** argued that blacks lacked vivacity and mental agility, deprived of the creative edge that the Europeans possessed. Denis **Diderot**—surely the most cosmopolitan of the *philosophes*—concluded that black Africans were at an "early stage" in the long process of human evolution, although he thought African "spontaneity" and "emotion" offered Europeans something their high civilization had repressed. Thomas **Jefferson** and George Washington in North America may have agonized over slavery; they viewed the African as a child unfit for full autonomy. Blackness was not only closely associated with slavery. It was also a sign of primitive behavior, childlike and unpredictable if not immoral and violent.

These Western attitudes were formed by the juncture of two broad developments. On the one hand, biological and anthropological science, represented by Carolus Linnaeus, Buffon and Georges Léopold Cuvier, was dominated by classification–evolutionary and diffusionist. On the other hand, by the late 18th century, Europe had established a clear technological, political and economic superiority over the other continents. It seemed logical therefore to ascribe these accomplishments to a developed culture that could be classified in racial terms. By the early 19th century, light skin and specific facial features were closely associated with a creative European civilization, while "yellow," "red" and "black" skin color were signs of stagnation or barbarism. By the late 19th century racism would take another turn when invidious biological distinctions were made within Europe itself. *See also* **Equality**.

Robert Forster

RAMEAU, Jean-Philippe (1683-1764). Rameau was the leading French composer of his time, and made a significant and lasting contribution to musical theory. Born in Dijon, two years before George Frederick Handel, Johann Sebastian Bach and Domenico Scarlatti, Rameau spent the earlier part of his career principally as organist at the Cathedral of Clermont.

His father, an organist at the Dijon cathedral, intended him to study law, but he was so precocious a musician that his parents were requested to remove him from the **Jesuit** *collège* where they had placed him, as he spent all his time playing and studying music.

Rameau's parents consented to his pursuing a musical career, and sent him to Milan to study. He did not, however, remain long in Italy. Instead he joined a tour through the south of France as first violinist, and then opted for a career as a harpsichordist. In 1702 he was appointed *maître de musique* at Avignon Cathedral, but later in the same year he moved to Clermont. In 1706 he was in Paris as organist of the Jesuit *collège* of Louis-le-Grand. In 1709 Rameau returned to Dijon as organist at Notre Dame, by 1713 he was in Lyons, and in 1715 he was back in Clermont with a 29-year contract as organist.

In 1722 Rameau settled in Paris and published his famous *Traité de l'harmonie*, or *Treatise on Harmony*, which gained him the wide respect and attention of musicians. He continued his theoretical writings throughout his life, and corresponded with other theorists and writers. His theories of harmonic generation, or harmonic inversion, and of fundamental bass influenced theorists for the next 200 years. Despite the admiration of his other works, such as his harpsichord pieces, cantatas and theater music, he was not able to gain a post as organist in Paris.

Rameau's ambition was to compose an opera, and in 1733, at the age of 50, he had his first opera, *Hippolyte et Aricie*, produced at the Opéra. While it aroused great excitement and admiration among most of the audience, there were also those who had reservations about it. The opera was fairly successful, as were the other operas that followed in the ensuing years; his *opéra-ballet, Les Indes galantes* had 64 performances over two years, and the least successful, *Castor et Pollux*, had an initial run of 21 performances.

Rameau's early compositions are all for the harpsichord. A fine harpsichordist at an early age, he wrote masterful, virtuoso pieces. His 65 keyboard works are compiled into four books. Some are lute-like and filled with expressive arpeggios, some are indebted to François Couperin and some look backward to older styles. Others are filled with orchestral, sonorous textures never before heard in music for the harpsichord.

Rameau had various patrons, notably the financier Alexandre-Joseph Le Riche de La Poplinière and his wife, for whom he named one of his pieces of chamber music. He also moved in intellectual circles and counted **Voltaire** among his friends. In 1745 he was appointed a royal chamber music composer; thereafter several of his works had their premieres at court theaters. Nine new theater works followed in the mid-to-late 1740s, beginning with *La princesse de Navarre* and the comedy *Platée*, but from 1750 onwards he wrote only two major works, for Rameau was increasingly involved with theory and with a number of disputes, notably with Jean-Jacques **Rousseau**, Friedrich Melchoir Grimm and even former friends, pupils and collaborators, such as Denis **Diderot** and Jean Le Ronde d'**Alembert**. Diderot praised his ability to distinguish the tender, the voluptuous, the impassioned and the lascivious. When Rameau died in 1764 he was widely respected and admired, though he was also seen as unsociable and avaricious. Both this side of him and his musical genius figure prominently in Diderot's masterpiece, *Rameau's Nephew*.

Kalman Maler

RAMEAU'S NEPHEW. A dialog composed by Denis **Diderot** approximately in 1762 and then revised by him repeatedly over the next 20 years, but not published during his lifetime; it is perhaps the outstanding production of the Enlightenment. It is at once a masterpiece of literature and a searching examination of key Enlightenment values, and of the limits of those values.

The publishing history of this work is more than a little curious. When Diderot died it was sent, together with his library and his other papers, to Russia. A copy of it eventually found its way into the hands of Johann Wolfgang von **Goethe**, who translated it into German and published it in 1805. Thereupon it was re-translated back into French, and did not appear in a version derived directly from an original manuscript until 1823.

Rameau's Nephew is presented as an account of a chance meeting between Diderot and an acquaintance, the thoroughly historical Jean-François Rameau, ne'er-do-well nephew of the great composer, Jean-Philippe **Rameau**. Their conversation touches on art, **education**, genius, the family, the nature of social and political association, human motivation, the cultural life of Paris and other subjects. The discussion gains dramatic force from the contrast in characters, the one ("moi"), a rather restrained philosopher who combines elevated with middle-class values and an honest recollection of his economically and professionally marginal past; the other, the Nephew ("lui"), a talented musician but a thoroughly amoral and completely frank bohemian. In their discussion "moi" argues the case for social responsibility and other-regarding virtues, "lui" that for unmitigated **egoism** conceived in materialistic terms. The discussion makes apparent the utter moral debasement of the nephew, but does not show him getting the worse of the argument.

Why did Diderot not publish *Rameau's Nephew*, which he revised and copied repeatedly, and which is almost certainly the best thing he wrote? There is, first, a high probability that the daring of his speculations, especially on moral questions, would have been unacceptable to the authorities, and prudence led him to avoid the complications that publication would likely have brought. Secondly, *Rameau's Nephew* can be read as a critique of key Enlightenment values. Specifically, there is the question of the arts and sciences, their utility and the cost at which they are acquired and cultivated. And there is the even larger issue of the adequacy of **self-interest** as a motive. If the character of the Nephew reflects an artist of great ability and a radical egoist whose indifference to moral and social responsibility effectively withstands the criticism of the representative of the Enlightenment in the dialog, this may not have been an image he wished to make available to the critics of the movement of which he was a leading spokesman.

There may also be a third and more personal reason that Diderot did not want to publish this work in which he invested so much of himself. *Rameau's Nephew* can be read as a sort of accounting with his former friend, Jean-Jacques **Rousseau,** with whom he had broken at around the time of the writing of this dialog. Rousseau questioned the social value and moral costs of the arts and sciences in his *First Discourse*, and he brought attention to the corruption, oppression and degradation that he believed were inseparable from societies in which extreme inequalities of wealth and status were accepted in the *Second Discourse*. Living in Paris, Diderot was part of such a society, and while his position seemed more morally justifiable than that of the Nephew or of the financier Bertin and his household as portrayed in *Rameau's Nephew*, nor was his position above criticism, as the Nephew makes clear. Rousseau with his bright eyes, over-sensitivity and fear of dependence may well have been half mad, but he had distanced himself from the **salons** of Paris and dependence on enlightened monarchs, and so had avoided, if not solved, the problems that Diderot analyzed so acutely in *Rameau's Nephew*. Rousseau, for all his extravagance, had a point in his writings and in his life. If Diderot could not well share this accounting with his former friend with him, to which of his contemporaries would he have wanted to show it?

RATIONALISM. A methodology that gives primacy to **reason** and logic. It is usually opposed to **empiricism**. Until the Enlightenment, rationalism was the dominant methodology in philosophy and theology, though it was already being significantly qualified in the natural sciences from the 16th century on.

Rationalism depends on two main conditions. The first is a proven or indisputable truth from which a chain of reasoning can begin; the second, sound application of logic. Generally, rationalism proceeds by deduction, that is to say, by logically drawing conclusions contained within main propositions or axioms. It moves from the general to the particular. Both scholastic philosophers and the great system-builders of the 17th century, such as René **Descartes**, Benedict **Spinoza** and Gottfried Wilhelm **Leibniz**, favored rationalism as a method.

As a methodology, rationalism has a number of advantages. Since the whole philosophy is embedded in its initial axioms, it provides the comfort of allowing us to know where we are going before we get there. It is rather like playing a game of solitaire secure in the knowledge that it will work out. Another advantage of rationalism is that it is highly comprehensive. Reason being supreme, and its function being to order things, all things are put in their proper place. Whether in the thought of Saint Thomas Aquinas, Descartes or Spinoza, there are no loose ends. However, as a methodology rationalism also has drawbacks.

A minor shortcoming of rationalism is that deduction may be faulty. Since a more competent logician can identify and correct such errors, they are not serious. The great drawback of rationalism concerns the initial premises or axioms. If these are true, much is well. If, on the other hand, initial axioms are either unconvincing or demonstrably false, then the whole enterprise is compromised. From an initial nonsensical premise nonsensical or untrue consequences will be drawn.

The propositions from which scholastic philosophers proceeded were usually either scriptural truths, whose validity was assured by the authority of the Church, or principles taken from Aristotle. The system-builders of the 17th century made a major break with the rationalism of **scholasticism** by insisting that their initial axioms be rationally or naturally compelling. For the thinkers of the Enlightenment this did not really solve the main problem, which was to determine the truth-value of the initial proposition.

An axiom is by definition a proposition that cannot be proven. Most Enlightenment thinkers denied that it was possible to do valid or worthwhile work in science or philosophy on the basis of unproven assumptions. They preferred the more limited, more modest and more arduous method of collecting facts, verifying them and trying to move from more particular to more general (and empirically verifiable) statements about the subjects they were investigating. In this sense Peter **Gay** was perfectly justified in writing that "In its treatment of the passions, in its treatment of metaphysics, the Enlightenment was not an age of reason but a revolt against rationalism" (*The Enlightenment*, vol. II, p.189).

RAYNAL, Guillaume Thomas, abbé (1713-1796). The principal author of the best-selling *Histoire des deux Indes,* and a key figure in the intellectual milieus of Paris in the second half of the 18th century. Raynal was from a modest commercial family. He carried out his secondary studies in the **Jesuit** *collège* of Rodez, and apparently intended to enter the order himself. He taught for a number of years in other Jesuit *collèges* in the provinces, but never took his final vows and left the Order in 1747.

Like many aspiring intellectuals, Raynal gravitated toward Paris. His luck there was better than many. After a relatively short period fulfilling clerical functions, he frequented literary **cafés**, was received in leading **salons**, and developed friendships with other bright young men about town, among them Jean-Jacques **Rousseau**. In 1750 Raynal gained the lucrative editorship of the *Mercure de France* through **patronage**, and then that of the *Nouvelles littéraires*. His affability, tact, literary abilities and wide network of friends and associates made him a focus for aspiring writers of progressive views.

In 1770 the first edition of the *Histoire des deux Indes*, the work for which Raynal is best known, appeared. Following the condemnation of this work by the *Parlement* of Paris in 1781 a warrant was issued for his arrest, and like Rousseau before him, he fled the country. He was able to return two years later, but settled in Marseilles, well outside the jurisdiction of the *Parlement* of Paris.

Like most *philosophes* who lived to see the **French Revolution**, Raynal became critical of it before it had progressed very far. He denounced it in mid-1791 and was enthusiastically welcomed by writers associated with the Counter-Revolution. His hostility to the movement grew during the Terror, but he was reconciled to it after the Thermidorean reaction and was honored with a place in the **Institut**. Raynal is another example of a *philosophe* who began his career in the Church, and then moved substantially but incompletely into secular society. Though a freethinker and critic of his society, he retained his clerical dress and remained a bachelor, preferring good conversation and polite society to the responsibilities of a family.

REASON. A way of examining questions based on logic and evidence. The Enlightenment attitude to reason was ambivalent. On the one hand, it favored reason over most forms of unreason; on the other, it feared reason running wild, out of touch with the actual workings of **nature** and society.

There was general agreement among the *philosophes* that reason was invaluable as a means of undermining and restricting the practical damage done by various forms of opinion and behavior that could not be justified on rational grounds. **Superstitions** of the common people and the most sophisticated theological constructs of the world's major revealed and dogmatic religions were subjected to the acid criticism of reason, and where the beliefs or assertions in question were found to be incompatible with logic or the demonstrable course of nature, these beliefs were treated as invalid. **Voltaire**, for example, ingenuously asked that **miracles** be performed before the Paris Academy of Sciences so that they could be verified (***Philosophical Dictionary***, art. "Miracles," Besterman, p. 316). This is a case of reason militant being pressed into the service of the Enlightenment critique of religion. For the negative task of criticism, the category of reason was admirable.

In seeking a grounding for their own philosophy, the thinkers of the Enlightenment generally did not opt for reason. The great system-builders of the 17th century, such as René **Descartes**, Benedict **Spinoza** and Gottfried Wilhelm **Leibniz**, all produced magnificently structured and impressively coherent accounts of the world. The problem was that the most incisive and scrupulous use of logic when applied to unprovable or false premises resulted in majestic and logical structures that were unrelated to the real world. Having seen **rationalism** run amok in the work of the brilliant system-builders of the

17th century, as well as the **scholasticism** that still had a strong hold on most **universities**, the thinkers of the Enlightenment preferred to avoid reliance on reason, even if this meant, as it did, considerably restricting the scope of things that could be known.

If it is fair to call the 18th century an "Age of Reason," this is only in the sense of reason militant. Most Enlightenment thinkers from Pierre **Bayle** to David **Hume** to Immanuel **Kant,** were aware of the limitations of reason. Particularly important was the recognition that reason could determine the accuracy or logical consistency of certain propositions, but that in itself it could not relate to questions of right and wrong, or determine the ends of conduct. It was competent to pronounce only on means. Reason could measure efficiency, but not morality.

In attempting to work out their ethical positions, most Enlightenment thinkers turned to the senses or the heart as their starting point (*see* **Sentiment**). In their methodology they consistently preferred **empiricism** and reliance on fact to rationalism and reliance on logic.

RÉAUMUR, René Antoine Ferchault de (1683-1757). One the leading scientists of the 18th century. A member of a well-off family of the legal profession, Réaumur's career was marked by ease and quick and sustained success. He received his secondary education from the **Jesuits**, then proceeded to study law. However, his interest in science quickly asserted itself and he was able to devote his life to research and writing.

Réaumur came to Paris in 1703, and in the same year was accepted into the Academy of Sciences (*see* **Academies, State-Sponsored**) in a subordinate position. His first work was in geometry, but shifted to natural history, in which he distinguished himself. In 1711 Réaumur was named a full member of the Academy of Sciences, of which he repeatedly served as director. His European reputation is reflected in his membership in the **Royal Society** of London, the Berlin Academy and the Academy of Saint Petersburg. Like **Buffon**, Réaumur spent a good part of each year on his rural estates, where he had the leisure and resources to pursue his research. When in Paris he spent much of his time on the business of the Academy of Sciences, but also attended the salon of Mme de **Tencin**.

In two memoirs of 1732 Réaumur proposed a thermometer based on the freezing and boiling points of water, but using a scale of 80 degrees. His wide interests also extended to metallurgy. Réaumur's great work was a study of the *History of Insects*, set forth in a series of memoirs between 1734 and 1742, in which he investigated, largely on the basis of his own observations, the behavior of insects rather than their morphology. Réaumur was also appointed by the Academy of Sciences to oversee the publication of the multi-volume *Description des arts et métiers*, which in some ways resembled the **Encyclopédie**, which, he alleged, had pirated some of the plates of the Academy's collection.

REGENCY. The period in French history between the death of Louis XIV in 1715 and the majority of **Louis XV** in 1723. During this time Philippe, duc d'Orléans, ruled France as regent. In many ways this period was a reaction against the austerity and formality of the later part of the rule of Louis XIV.

The regent was both a freethinker and a libertine, and set the tone for the social elites with his loose personal behavior. Extreme pleasure seeking replaced the religious restraint of the last years of Louis XIV, and an attitude that validated material and physical **happiness**, often, at least within the upper levels of the aristocracy, found expression in a high degree of sexual freedom. The "orgies of the Regency" became proverbial. Both the validation of pleasure and a permissive ideal of sexuality continued to influence hedonist strains of Enlightenment thought.

Politically there was a reaction against the extreme centralization of power practiced by Louis XIV. Instead of the direct and effective rule of the king favored by **absolutism**, the great noble families, at whose expense the absolutist state had extended its powers, demanded, and for a time received, a system of government by councils, which they controlled. The regent tried this system, called the *polysydonie,* for the first three years of his rule, but then, having found that the great nobles were more interested in the status attached to high office than in doing the serious work such positions required, reverted, with modifications, to the greater efficiency of the system of Louis XIV. Though the court aristocracy was found wanting in its first opportunity to return to a position of political authority, the aspirations of the **nobility** to political power remained, and were to have important consequences for the history of France over the course of the century.

It was during the Regency, too, that France experienced a major economic trauma. The regent was persuaded by John Law, a Scottish financier of considerable ingenuity, to establish a bank that was to issue paper money, and later to found a company to develop the French areas of North America. The stocks of the *Compagnie d'Occident* rose in value by hundreds of percent in a short while, the boom became a craze, then ended in a bust. Established families who had not sold in time were ruined, while those who were clever or fortunate enough to have bought while the cost of shares was low and sold before the crash became wealthy overnight. **Montesquieu** describes the social dislocation caused by the crash of Law's company and bank and its impact on contemporary attitudes in the *Persian Letters* (Letter 138) and discusses the theoretical implications of the system in the *Spirit of the Laws* (Bk. XXII, chaps. 6 and 10, and Bk. XXIX, chap. 6).

REGULATION. A commonsense position that maintains that it is the obligation and responsibility of the authorities to regulate social, economic and political relations for the common good. It stands in opposition to **liberalism**, which assumes the overall rationality of people and a natural lawfulness in social and economic relations that makes government intervention appear superfluous or harmful.

The main assumption of the regulatory outlook is that the constituted authorities understand better than the subject or citizen what the common good consists in and how it is best achieved. The authorities are deemed to be wiser and more responsible than private persons motivated by **self-interest**.

Regulation was least contested in politics, where clearly understood sets of rules determined who could and who could not take part in the political process, and in what capacities. Mercantilism was the economic policy of **absolutism**. It assumed that economics were an aspect of necessarily conflict-driven international relations, and required regulation as close as that in politics. Internally, old-regime economic policy assumed that both the production and the distribution of goods required corporate and government supervision. This is particularly clear in the grain trade. The government agreed that it had an obligation to assure that basic necessities were provided to the working population at manageable prices. To achieve this goal the government subsidized grain prices, imported grain and limited its circulation. The assumption here, as in the regulatory mentality generally, was that unless the authorities took appropriate measures to effect the desired objectives, these objectives would not be achieved.

Economic liberals, who were usually responsible neither for public order nor for assuring subsistence, favored the deregulation of the grain trade. They did so on the grounds that a deregulated market would in the long run increase production of grains, improve provisioning and reduce prices, thus benefiting all. Whatever the virtues of this theory, in practice the poorer consumers of grains did not have a long term available to them, and so had recourse to the traditional expedient of forcible price fixing (*see* **Taxation Populaire**). An instance of this is Anne-Robert-Jacques **Turgot**'s deregulation of the grain trade and the **Flour War** that followed in response.

REID, Thomas (1710-1796). A Scottish cleric, teacher and writer who was the leading exponent of "common sense" philosophy.

Reid was born near Aberdeen. His father and grandfather were Presbyterian ministers, while his mother's side of the family included a number of mathematicians and academics. Reid received his first education at home, then was sent to Marischal College, Aberdeen. Upon graduation he studied theology, and, after a number of years as a librarian, served as minister in a rural parish near Aberdeen from 1737 to 1751, after which he took up a teaching position in King's College, Aberdeen. In 1764 he was offered and accepted the chair in moral philosophy at the University of Glasgow, previously held by Francis **Hutcheson** and Adam **Smith**. Reid taught in this post until 1780, and thereafter was the nominal professor while a conjoint appointee did his teaching.

Reid's interest in philosophy was stimulated by his reading of the works of Isaac **Newton**, Bishop George Berkeley and David **Hume**'s *Treatise of Human Nature*, which he read while minister of the parish of New Machar. Troubled by Hume's critique of causality and the skepticism central to his work, Reid set about constructing a philosophy that would allow objective validity both to the data of sense experience and to certain categories of ideas. Reid's philosophical project, which has been termed "common sense" philosophy, was directed against the skepticism, subjectivism and potential solipsism of certain trends of 18th-century thought. By asserting the objectivity of the material world and the validity of **empiricism**, Reid sought to develop a metaphysic that would justify religious belief and be suited to the practical, down to earth, improving trends that were central to the Enlightenment.

Reid did not, however, take the term "common sense" in its usual meaning. Rather, he used "sense" to designate judgment, and "common" to indicate qualities or conditions that were preconditions of communication and understanding. "Common" thus implies universality and objectivity. The regular and objective features that Reid found in **nature** also inclined him, as they did Newton and **Voltaire**, toward belief in a divinely created and orderly universe, which, for Reid, was compatible with and even required, the revelation of the Church of which he was a member.

Reid's first book, *An Inquiry into the Human Mind on the Principles of Common Sense,* appeared in 1764. Apparently his teaching duties left him little time for writing, since he retired from his professorship in 1780 in order to prepare other works for publication. In 1785 his *Essays on the Intellectual Powers of Man* appeared, and three years later, the *Essays on the Active Powers of Man.*

Reid had great influence in his time and in the generation after, not only in Britain, but also in France and America. However, as the strength of voluntarism and subjectivism grew, his philosophy, and the mainstream currents and assumptions of Enlightenment thought which they exemplified, were largely eclipsed.

RELATIVISM, CULTURAL. Cultural relativism maintains that different cultures evaluate the same things differently, and that these differences are grounded in custom and tradition. The customs of one society are not necessarily truer or more valid than those of another society, and there are no objective grounds for preferring one set of cultural values over another. This is an approach that validates difference and encourages **toleration**.

The position opposed to cultural relativism maintains that certain beliefs and forms of behavior are completely or absolutely right or true. This position, which was dominant for most of the Middle Ages and the 17th century, only came to be extensively challenged during the Enlightenment. The main sources of what we might call cultural absolutism are theologies that assert that they embody divine revelations (usually exclusive) and philosophies that assert that the essences of things can be known.

Two of the distinguishing features of Enlightenment thought are rejection of the validity of the revelations of the main monotheistic religions and denial that the essences of things can be known. Historians such as Pierre **Bayle, Voltaire** and David **Hume** denied that the historical evidence justified the claims to divine revelation made by Judaism, Christianity and Islam. **Montesquieu** and others, by comparing contradictory rituals and dogmas of religions each of which claimed to embody the truth absolutely and exclusively, showed that ritual and custom have no intrinsic validity (*see Persian Letters*).

The philosophical assumption that we can know the essences of things also inclines toward cultural absolutism. This was a position that the Enlightenment designated metaphysics, and opposed consistently. John **Locke** had argued that the human mind was incapable of achieving reliable knowledge that extended beyond empirical evidence, and so was incapable of grasping essences. Voltaire brilliantly and repeatedly mocked those who took mere assumptions or assertions of belief for certain knowledge. In more cumbersome terms, Immanuel **Kant** argued that philosophy had to restrict itself to the phenomena, or the empirical manifestations of objects, for it was incapable of knowing things-in-themselves, or "noumena."

The implication of absolute theological or philosophical knowledge was that, insofar as truth is preferable to error, it was the duty of those who had the truth to share it with others, even if this meant imposing it on them. The thinkers of the Enlightenment not only denied the legitimacy of imposing beliefs or behaviors on people, they also denied that theologians or philosophers could know what beliefs were absolutely true, and what behaviors appropriate. They used cultural relativism as a means of delegitimizing intolerance. They did not, however, deny the objective existence of ethical values.

In the 19th and 20th centuries relativism has often been taken to imply that there are no objective values whatever, and that morality is as much a matter of personal taste as the choice of a flavor of ice cream. With rare exceptions, this was not the view held in the 18th century. Most thinkers of the Enlightenment held a few basic propositions about human beings to be true in all times and all places, and they derived from these principles a simple code of ethics. They assumed that people sought to maximize pleasure and to avoid pain, and that they were with respect to fundamentals equal. From these simple propositions they derived an ethic of **beneficence**, or doing to others what we would have them do unto us, or minimally, abstaining from harming others needlessly, and they asserted a broad value of **humanity** to underpin it.

Those who criticize the Enlightenment for abandoning the absolutist theologies and systems of ethics that predominated in the West before the 18th century, and thus opening the way to the moral relativism, **egoism** and nihilism of subsequent times, should bear in mind that these positions became tenable only after the abandonment of key values of Enlightenment ethics. The notions that we are free to treat others less well than we would be treated ourselves, or that some people or nations are somehow outside of humanity, do not derive from the Enlightenment, and all the ills of modernity cannot well be traced back to it.

REPUBLIC OF LETTERS. A metaphor popular with certain intellectuals of the 17th and 18th centuries and some historians of the 20th century.

The model of republican organization in the arts and sciences was, of course, opposed to prevalent monarchical principles of political organization. While 18th-century monarchies, especially in their **absolutist** form, assumed the necessity of authority concentrated in the hands of the ruler and his or her agents, a republic posited **equality** of **rights** and obligations among **citizens**, with decisions reflecting what the majority thought to be the most reasonable course of action, or that most in conformity with the common good.

The "Republic of Letters" was not a dominant reality in the 18th century any more than it had been during the Renaissance, or would be in the 19th and 20th centuries. Writers and artists were in most cases narrowly subordinated to the needs and interests of their patrons during the 16th and 17th centuries, and they came to be just as narrowly dependent on the market thereafter. This is not to say, however, that the degree and nature of the control exercised by patrons was the same as that exercised by the public in the form of an audience that would, or would not, buy cultural products made available by publishers and other entrepreneurs.

Arguably, the 18th century was a period during which cultural life was influenced to a lesser degree by traditional **patronage**, but in which the market had not yet established its grip as firmly as it was subsequently to do with the progressive commercialization of culture. There are thus grounds for arguing that the "Republic of Letters" was not altogether illusory.

To the degree that **authorship** was meritocratic, it was at least in part compatible with the ideal of a "Republic of Letters." Nevertheless, during the 18th century appointments to state-sponsored **academies** and conferral of pensions by the State meant that patronage retained a key role in cultural production. At the other end of the cultural spectrum, hack writers of **Grub Street** labored in conditions of dependence and deprivation, though their productions often helped raise their employers to considerable affluence. There was, then, no more of a "republic" in Grub Street than there was in the major academies and great **salons** of Paris.

The organization of writers and artists in the 18th century was more oligarchical than democratic, and it retained significant elements of patronage while also incorporating principles of capitalist production. It appears that the metaphor of a "Republic of Letters" was used either to promote a more egalitarian form of cultural association or to mask the harsh and hierarchical reality of the cultural life of the time.

REPUBLICANISM. The set of ideals and values associated with the Greek city-state and Roman Republic. Among them **liberty, citizenship**, the common good and independence figure prominently. Republicanism was irrelevant to the practical politics of Europe under the Roman Empire, under feudalism and under emerging **absolute** monarchies. It did, however, gain relevance in the state system of Renaissance Italy in small, independent urban polities in some ways similar to the city-states of classical antiquity. The republic again emerged, more by force of circumstance than by design, in the 18th century, first in America from 1776, and then in France from 1792. Though the small republics that still existed in the 18th century, such as Geneva and Venice, had negligible political influence, republicanism remained a vital cultural and ideological force.

Since the Greco-Roman classics that embodied the republican tradition and its values formed the backbone of the secondary curriculum throughout Europe during the 18th century, it was familiar to all who received this much formal **education**. It was also profoundly familiar to some, such as Jean-Jacques **Rousseau** and Madame Roland, who had not. Louis Sebastien **Mercier**'s complaint that his education in a *collège* in Paris had made him a committed republican and altogether unfit for the monarchical society in which he was to live (*Tableau de Paris*, chap. lxxxi) was no doubt exceptional. But that republicanism offered a set of social and political values at variance with those of the Church and State of the **Old Regime** there can be no doubt. In the language and values of republicanism the revolutionaries of France found ready tools with which to carry out both the demolition of old-regime institutions and the construction of new ones.

RESTIF DE LA BRETONNE, Nicolas Edme (1734-1806). One of the most prolific writers of the 18th century, and one of few who found his way to literature without the benefit of a secondary **education** or the assistance of a **patron**. Restif was born to a family of comfortable peasants. He was apprenticed to a printer in Auxerre and then moved to Paris, where he exercised his profession sucessfully and worked for a number of different employers. He began writing novels in 1765 with a work entitled *The Virtuous Family*, but did not achieve success with the public until 1775 when he published *Le Paysan perverti*. Thereafter he sought to make his livelihood from literature, which no doubt explains the extent of his output. Restif began to move in the literary circles of the capital, was welcomed in **salons** and in 1782 began a friendship with Louis Sebastien **Mercier**, whom he in many ways resembles.

Restif's best-known works include *La Vie de mon père* (1779), an idealized but sharply observed portrait of his father and of the village of Sacy in which he grew up; *Les Contemporaines* (1780-1785); *La Découverte de la terre australe* (1781), an imaginative utopia; *Les Nuits de Paris* (1788-1794), a series of sketches of Paris life after dark which in some ways recall Mercier's *Tableau de Paris* and *Le Nouveau Paris*, and which are valuable for the information they provide on usually neglected aspects of life in the capital; and *Monsieur Nicolas* (1796-1797) a vast, rambling autobiography on which he worked for more than 10 years.

Restif led an adventurous and uneven life in which women appear to have played a major role. As an **author** who had to live from his writings and who often resorted to autobiography, he did not hesitate to publish accounts of his amorous doings, such as *Mon Calendrier*, which purports to be a listing of his conquests, though where to put the line between fact and fiction in that work is not easily determined. Interestingly, though Restif produced numerous works of a pornographic nature, he never abandoned the moralistic themes with which he began his literary career. It is as if the same painter had produced the works of both **Boucher** and **Greuze**. Restif's blending of the two sets of themes was not exceptional for the time.

RICCOBONI, Marie-Jeanne Laboras de Mézières (1713-1792). An important, best-selling **author** of novels during the 18th century whose works tend to be neglected today.

The child of a marriage that was annulled by the Church, the future Mme Riccoboni was deprived of any inheritance, and obliged to attend a convent school that was not at all to her liking. Though her mother withdrew her from the school at age 14, their relationship became strained and the daughter sought a means of achieving independence. She started a theatrical career in 1734, but without much success. The following year she married Antoine François Riccoboni, the son of the famous Italian comedian known as Lelio, whom she had met at the Italian **Comedy**.

In 1761 she abandoned her career as an actress, and definitively left the Italian stage. She then became involved in literature, and wrote the 12th part of *Marianne*, a novel that Pierre Carlet **Marivaux** never finished. Her imitation was successful enough to impose upon some readers. In her first original work, the *Letters of Mistress Fanny Butler*, published in 1757, she denounced the frivolous behavior of men, who were generally deficient in sensibility. This novel achieved a considerable success and led to new friendships with figures such as the Baron d'**Holbach**, David **Hume** and the famous actor, David Garrick. Her feminism culminated in the unhappy *Story of Miss Jenny Level* (1764). Like Fanny Butler, Jenny denounces the mindless and inconsistent nature of men. She also criticized social prejudices, from which only the elite could escape. Her short novel *Ernestine* (1765) illustrates the same idea.

Mme Riccoboni was strongly influenced by English writers, among them Samuel **Richardson.** She translated Henry **Fielding**'s novel *Emily* (1762) into French, as well as some plays that she published under the title of the *New English Theater*. Her other publications include *Histoire du marquis de Cressy* (1758), *Lettres de Juliette Catesby* (1759), *Milady Juliette Catesby* (1759-1760), *Lettres d'Adéleïde de Dammartin* (1766), and *The Letters of Elisabeth-Sophie de Vallière to Louise-Hortense de Cantaleu* (1772). She ended her career publishing tales set in a medieval atmosphere in the *Bibliothèque universelle des romans* (1779-1780).

Much influenced by the English novel, she borrowed the moralizing intentions, but kept her own style, which remained lively and straightforward. She sought to maintain her independence as an author and to express her views on society and on the condition of **women**. The emotion in her works remains sincere.

As a novelist Mme Riccoboni appealed to an international and a largely feminine public. Though she is largely forgotten today, during the 18th century she was a best-selling author whose works competed in circulation with the most popular writers and most influential *philosophes* of the time. She died in loneliness and poverty, and has not had the recognition which is her due.

Isabelle Martin

RICHARDSON, Samuel (1689-1761). Richardson was born in 1689 in Derbyshire. His father came from a family of "middling note" enjoying a small inheritance. He became a joiner and carpenter, gaining some knowledge of architecture. He was employed by the Duke of Monmouth and later was suspected of loyalty to the same in his rebellion. He gave up his business, and retired to the country for good. Samuel's mother was from a "not ungenteel" family, bringing with her some social connections.

Samuel himself was one of nine children. Intended for the Church, he was forced to take up a trade due to his father's financial situation. It is believed that Richardson went to Christ's Hospital for his schooling. He never acquired more than a smattering of foreign languages and was ridiculed for this later on. Never boyish, his talent for writing was recognized from the early age of 11 or 12. He easily became a favorite in the company of young women, reading to them as well as writing love letters for them.

In 1706 he was apprenticed to a stationer and worked as a compositor and corrector of the press. In 1719 he started his own business, established in Salisbury Court, Fleet Street, where he remained to the end of his life. Richardson was a "high flying" printer, married to the daughter of another printer of similar opinions. In 1723 he printed a violent opposition paper for the Duke of Wharton, yet he was prudent enough to avoid libelous publishing. Through connections he acquired the rights to publishing the *Journals* of the House of Commons.

Richardson's first wife died in 1730; all the children from this first marriage, five sons and one daughter, died in childhood. His second wife gave birth to one son and five daughters, four of whom survived Richardson himself.

Between 1736 and 1738 he published the *Daily Journal* and *Daily Gazette*, additional evidence of his unwillingness to allow "high flying" principles to interfere with business. In 1739 he was commissioned to write a volume to be entitled "Familiar Letters on Important Occasions" for semiliterate country writers. Apparently it was due to this enterprise that *Pamela* came into being, written between November 1739 and January 1740.

Pamela enjoyed a surprising and immediate success, promptly being translated into several continental languages. The novel was enthusiastically recommended from the pulpits of London, and by Parisian freethinkers such as Denis **Diderot**. Henry **Fielding**, by contrast, found the plot and characters of Richardson's novel of **sentiment** artificial and priggish, and satirized them viciously and hilariously in his own rogue novels, *Joseph Andrews* and *Shamela*. The two men henceforth became bitter rivals.

Enjoying considerable prosperity from the 1730s on, Richardson leased three country houses where he entertained a wide circle of friends including Samuel **Johnson**, William Hogarth, the actors Culiber and David Garrick, and the poet Edward Young. In 1742 he published Daniel **Defoe**'s *Tour Through Great Britain*.

Richardson began *Clarissa Harlowe* in 1744, publishing the first volumes in 1747 and the rest at the close of 1748. Richardson's European reputation was firmly established by this stage. *Sir Charles Grandison*, his bow to requests from his numerous correspondents for a hero as a good man, a counterpart to the errant hero of Fielding's *Tom Jones*, was started sometime before 1751 and published in 1753.

Richardson fully accepted the narrow moral standards of his surroundings, his novels reflecting the didacticism of the time. His work was written in extreme earnestness, espousing sentimentalism as a virtue in itself and a proper way of relating to the world. Richardson's minute realism, his almost obsessive attention to detail, conveyed the impression of truthfulness to his readers. Diderot wrote favorably of him; Jean-Jacques **Rousseau** made him a model for *Julie, ou La Nouvelle Héloïse* and Thomas Babington Macaulay was an enthusiastic reader of his, contributing to Richardson's reputation and influence in India. Richardson's great contemporary, Samuel Johnson, gave as fair an evaluation of his novels as has been made. Asked whether Richardson was not tedious, he replied, "Why, Sir, if you were to read Richardson for the story, your impatience would be so much fretted that you would hang yourself. But you must read him for the sentiment, and consider the story as only giving occasion for the sentiment" (Boswell, *Life of Johnson*, p. 480). And read him for sentiment his contemporaries did, with enthusiasm and in huge numbers.

Peter Sorek

RIGHTS. Entitlements of individuals or citizens to certain forms of activity, liberties or things. Normally rights are claimed on behalf of individuals or groups and recognized and assured by the State or community. A discourse of rights is usually subordinate in disturbed conditions, such as those in which Thomas Hobbes wrote his *Leviathan*, and in which the main problem to be faced is one of order. The rights of the individual are also a secondary consideration for thinkers, such as Edmund **Burke**, for whom a historically constituted community is the main point of reference. The discourse of rights usually flourishes in conditions of relative prosperity when individuals feel less dependent on corporate and state authority, and when they desire greater **liberty**. It is often the function of rights to assure individual liberty and independence. In Western Europe and North America, the 18th century was a period in which social and political theorists discussed rights extensively.

The source from which rights are derived significantly influences the way their extent and nature are conceived. Rights are derived either from convention or from **nature**. Where it is recognized that rights are properly conferred by the society or state to which one belongs, there is usually little tension between what rights the state is willing to confer and what individuals feel they are entitled to demand. If, however, rights recognized as traditional are denied or retracted, conventional rights can also become the basis for serious conflict between the State and those it governs. This was the case in the American colonies before the outbreak of the War of Independence, and Burke, later famous as the great spokesman of conservatism, supported the claims of the American colonists to representation and greater consideration from the government in England on the grounds that these things were the traditional rights of freeborn Englishmen.

Rights derived from nature lend themselves more readily to challenges to established governments. Indeed, the assumption that human beings are born with, and should continue to possess, certain prerogatives and entitlements that derive directly from their relation to nature, often defined by contemporary thinkers in terms of a primal state of nature, was often intended to provide a basis for challenging legal and constitutional arrangements laid down by positive **law**. In functional terms, the notion of natural rights becomes an issue, or a source of tension, when the distance between the rights the state is prepared to confer and whatever are seen as natural rights is deemed excessive.

According to thinkers such as Jean-Jacques **Rousseau** and Thomas **Paine**, history can provide an account of how states have come to be constituted, but it cannot legitimize social and political arrangements. Natural **law** served as a basis for natural rights, and these rights could be, and were, used as bases for claims against existing institutions and arrangements. In referring to the "inalienable rights" of all men conferred by their Creator, and to the "natural, inalienable and sacred rights of man," the American Declaration of Independence of 1776 and the French Declaration of the Rights of Man and the Citizen of 1789 intentionally distanced themselves from existing arrangements and appealed to abstract and universal sources of legitimacy.

Another basic distinction made during the 18th century was between civil and political rights. The **absolutist** state gave precedence to control and security over individual rights. However, it did recognize a firm legal right to **property**, and also recognized minimal civil rights, though it could, and did, infringe on these with ease. Liberal thinkers of the Enlightenment demanded comprehensive civil rights with strong guarantees in order to protect individuals from undue interference by the State in their private lives. However, they did not believe that the right to participate in political processes should automatically be granted to all. With rare exceptions, such as the Marquis de **Condorcet**, the thinkers of the Enlightenment excluded **women** from political rights. They also made participation in politics dependent on a minimal property qualification, and this was true not only of moderates, such as Anne-Robert-Jacques **Turgot** in his *Memoir on Municipalities*, but also of more radical thinkers such as Rousseau and Paine.

ROBERTSON, William (1721-1793). Presbyterian minister, professor, then Principal of the University of Edinburgh from 1762, member of the General Assembly of the Church of Scotland, and then Moderator of the Assembly from 1763, and one of the outstanding historians of the Enlightenment. Of the great historians of the time, Robertson's reputation has survived less well than those of **Voltaire**, David **Hume** or Edward **Gibbon**.

Robertson was born in Midlothian, one of six children of a Presbyterian minister. His early education took place in the local parish and grammar schools, and he entered the University of Edinburgh in 1733. In 1741 he was licensed to preach, and two years later succeeded to the living of Gladsmuir, previously held by an uncle. He was elected to the General Assembly of the Church of Scotland in 1746, and in 1756 he received a parish in Edinburgh. His career took off dramatically in 1759 with the appearance of his *History of Scotland*.

Robertson had published little to this time, and the extent of the success of his work, and the recognition that came with it, were a pleasant surprise. As was often the case in the 18th century, celebrity brought with it preferment. The author of the *History of Scotland* was soon provided with sinecures in the Church, and was moved to a more prestigious pulpit in the capital. In 1762 he was made Principal of the University of Edinburgh, and the following year Moderator of the General Assembly of the Church of Scotland and Historiographer Royal of Scotland. In Robertson's case, recognition did not exceed ability. He was an effective academic administrator and ecclesiastical politician. His leadership of the moderates in the established Church of Scotland assured that a liberal and restrained course was followed by the national church. This contributed significantly to collaboration with other important cultural institutions, such as the university, and helped to create the atmosphere in which the Scottish Enlightenment flourished.

If the *History of Scotland* made Robertson's name, it was not his only or most popular large-scale historical study. In 1769 his *History of Charles V* appeared. It is often regarded as his masterpiece, and it certainly helped to make him a rich man, as he received over 4,000 pounds for it, a princely sum for an author at the time. The introduction to this work, entitled "A View of the Progress of the Society of Europe," offers a broad synthetic overview of the development of European society from the fall of Rome to the Renaissance, and is a minor classic in its own right. Robertson's third major work, the *History of America*, was devoted largely to discovery, conditions at first contact and the Spanish conquests. It appeared in two volumes in 1777, with a third incomplete volume, meant to contrast the British and Spanish records, published posthumously. Exceptionally, the scope of Robertson's historical interests seemed to have increased with age.

Robertson had married in 1751, and was survived by his wife and five children. His professional life was divided between his administrative responsibilities at the university and in the Church, and his research and writing. He retired from his position as manager of the Moderate interest in the Church in 1780, but continued to preach and act as principal, though he spent much of his time in the peace and quiet of the countryside not far from Edinburgh.

As a relatively young man, Robertson had been among the founders of the Select Society of Edinburgh, an informal literary **club** that had among its members many of the leading figures of the Scottish Enlightenment. Between 1777 and 1783 he received the international recognition conferred by membership in Academies of Madrid, Padua and Saint Petersburg. This was a remarkable career for a man who had begun his life as the minister of a rural parish on the periphery of Europe.

ROCHE, Daniel (1935-). Formerly professor of history at the Sorbonne, and since elevated to the even more prestigious Collège de France, Roche has made a number of distinct contributions to the study of the Enlightenment. It is hard to think of another scholar in the field who has Roche's comprehensive mastery of the social history of 18th-century France. The grounding of his study of the Enlightenment in the social history of the time is one of the distinctive features of Roche's work.

While preparing his *thèse d'état* on the provincial **academies**, Roche contributed articles to important historical journals and to a collective project of research into the history of the book headed by François Furet, published in two volumes as *Livre et Société* in 1965 and 1970. When his doctorate was published in much reduced form as *Le Siècle des lumières en province: Académies et académiciens provinciaux, 1680-1789* in 1978, it was immediately apparent that new ground had been broken in Enlightenment historiography.

Roche's research brought to light a vigorous and pragmatic current of the Enlightenment devoted to the furthering and dissemination of knowledge, but also well integrated into the structures of the **Old Regime**. The members of the provincial academies, Roche demonstrated, belonged overwhelmingly to the elites, and even to the privileged orders, of society. It was, therefore, unwise to characterize the movement as a whole as an expression of middle-class culture. The academies tended to be located in towns with typical old-regime institutions, such as *parlements*, cathedral chapters and royal intendancies rather than industrial centers. Hence it did not seem appropriate to associate the Enlightenment with commerce and industry, as was often done. And since the programs advocated and supported by academies were progressive but moderate, and concerned with modifying old-regime structures without overthrowing them, the Enlightenment that Roche uncovered was far from revolutionary. Thus Roche brought to the attention of students of the 18th century a moderate and established current of the Enlightenment, much as Robert **Darnton**, with whom Roche has collaborated productively, has brought to light in his studies on **Grub Street** a radical current.

Roche's study of the provincial academies has not been translated into English, but its main findings are available in virtually all textbooks that have been published since. A number of his other important works have been translated. These include *The People of Paris: An Essay in Popular Culture in the 18th Century*, a study firmly based in archival sources of all aspects of the lives of working people, and the *Journal of My Life* by Jacques-Louis Ménétra, a rare autobiography by a Parisian worker, the manuscript of which Roche discovered in a Parisian library and edited, also supplying a richly informative accompanying essay.

In 1993 Roche published a large synthesis on 18th-century France, and five years later it appeared in English translation as *France in the Enlightenment*. It is a remarkable work, and a fitting summation of a long and productive career. More than a summary of the author's vast knowledge of the field, it presents a challenging view of what the Enlightenment was and how it originated. It is very much the book of a social historian, and it was appropriate to call it *France in the Enlightenment* rather than *The Enlightenment in France*.

Unlike historians who believe that the Enlightenment grew out of scientific or philosophical developments, or specific forms of discourse, or modified kinds of sociability, Roche presents the Enlightenment as a product of basic social and economic changes that occurred over the 18th century. Underlying the movement we know as the Enlightenment, Roche shows, are an expansive demography that justified a more optimistic attitude toward life, growing urbanization that increased impersonal, non-status-oriented interactions among individuals, a growing prosperity that allowed even the poorer levels of the **population** to enjoy more consumer goods than had been common previously, and attempts by bureaucrats to run the country in a more orderly and efficient way. Enlightenment, as Roche presents it, is rooted in changes in a number of basic, broad, impersonal forces that imply and direct modifications of attitude in the population at large. To be sure, there were *philosophes* and **salons,** and of course academies, and an expanding **periodical** press and all the other facets of enlightened thought and sociability that historians have written about. But these things by themselves do not account for the hold that the Enlightenment took in the country at large. Roche seeks to go beyond specific sets of ideas and channels of dissemination to show how broad and deeply rooted a cultural phenomenon the Enlightenment was.

ROCOCO. An artistic style developed over the first half of the 18th century, especially in France, and within France, particularly among the aristocratic circles of the capital. This style is characterized by lightness, grace, charm, and a direct appeal to, and validation of, pleasure and sensuality. To its critics rococo is merely decorative and without serious content. Whether this is a vice or a virtue depends on one's point of view.

Rococo art began to take root during the last years of the rule of Louis XIV, for the most part as a reaction against the heavy, classical and official style that that monarch favored and effectively imposed through government control of the **Royal Academy of Painting**. The art commissioned and produced for the crown, most prominently in the great palace of Versailles, was intended to enhance the glory and grandeur of the king and his regime. As such, it portrayed Louis XIV, his symbols of power and his military exploits according to the formal rules of the classical esthetic favored by the court. It is against the pompousness, formality and idealization of **absolutism** central to classical art that the freedom, spontaneity, playfulness and frivolity of the rococo should be seen.

The first and probably greatest of the rococo artists was Jean-Antoine **Watteau**. The genre of painting he established was the *fête galante*, or informal gathering of young adults for relaxation, pleasure and social interaction, often with a hint of eroticism. These scenes were usually set in a park or meadow, allowing a portrayal of **nature** at its gentlest and most lovely. The atmosphere was one of pleasurable, free and fleeting sociability and openness. No authority. No armor. No glory. Rather, sociability, playfulness and enjoyment in a natural, though still cultivated, setting.

In the canvases of François **Boucher** the predominant motif is the female nude, often presented in a mythological setting altogether extrinsic to the true purpose of the picture, which was the contemplation and enjoyment of the female form. The coloring of such paintings is delicate and sensuous, and the effect often erotic. It is common to dismiss this kind of painting as shallow and insignificant, but this is to overlook an important point. There was a time when pleasure and worldly **happiness** had not yet achieved legitimacy as themes in art. The rococo made this shift, and in so doing gave expression to a secularizing, hedonistic and life-enhancing strain of Enlightenment thought that sometimes overflowed into libertinism. It was very much in harmony with the outlook and atmosphere of the **Regency**.

As the rococo had opposed the claims of privacy, delicacy and sensibility to the political, grand and heavy style of the court art of Louis XIV, so, after a generation or so, contemporaries began to feel that the themes and methods of the rococo neglected matters of vital importance. The Enlightenment had validated the private and the personal, but it also recognized the legitimacy of the claims of the public and political. During the last decades of the **Old Regime**, **Neoclassicism** reasserted the claims of the public, though in a more egalitarian and democratic way than had the classicism of the 17th century, and in so doing largely eclipsed rococo.

ROUSSEAU, Jean-Jacques (1712-1778). Of the major *philosophes*, Rousseau's life was the most troubled and his work perhaps the most significant.

Rousseau was born in Geneva, the son of a watchmaker and a mother of somewhat higher social standing who died shortly after giving birth to him. His father, while a competent craftsman, was not stable and failed to provide Rousseau with either a home or an education. However, Rousseau had warm memories of his aunt, of his cousins and, for the most part, of the pastor Lambercier at whose home he boarded and received the only formal instruction, that of a seminary for converts to Catholicism aside, in his life. He was the only *philosophe* not to have attended at least a *collège*.

Between 1724 and 1728 Rousseau was apprenticed first to a clerk, then to an engraver. Having decided to abandon Geneva and his harsh master at age 16, Rousseau faced life as a virtually penniless vagabond. He found some resources in converting to Catholicism, and worked for a time as a lackey. The direction of his life was determined by his liaison with Mme de **Warens** with whom he lived from 1733 to 1739. While staying with her he worked as a clerk and as a music master, but for the most part he was allowed the leisure to educate himself, and he made the best of it. Mme de Warens was charming, generous and intelligent, but she was not a good manager. She died in a poorhouse. In recounting her end in his *Confessions*, Rousseau said that he should have taken whatever he had and gone to her. Given the extent of his debt to her, he probably should have.

Like Denis **Diderot** in his early years, Rousseau found it difficult to make a living. He gave music lessons, and in 1740-1741 acted as tutor in the **Mably** household in Lyon. In 1742 he went to Paris where he presented a new system of musical notation to the Academy of Sciences and published a pamphlet on music. During 1742 and 1743 he acted as secretary to the French ambassador in Venice. On his return to Paris he worked for the financier Dupin, began his lifelong association with Thérèse Levasseur, and began actively to be associated with the Enlightenment. He struck up a friendship with

Diderot, met regularly with other encyclopedists and contributed the articles on music as well as that on political economy to the *Encyclopédie*.

In October 1749 on his way to visit Diderot, who was imprisoned in the chateau of Vincennes, Rousseau experienced a revelation or "illumination." The advertisement for an essay contest asking whether the arts and sciences had benefited humanity led him to consider the moral costs at which the arts had been acquired, and turned him into perhaps the greatest critic, while at the same time remaining one of the greatest exponents, of Enlightenment values. His essay on the arts and sciences, known as the *First Discourse*, won first prize of the Academy of Dijon for 1750 and gave Rousseau a sudden prominence in French letters.

In 1752 Rousseau's light opera, *Le Divin du village*, was successfully produced before the court, and would have gained him a royal pension had he not failed to keep an appointment with the king to accept it. In 1755 his essay on the origin of inequality, or *Second Discourse*, a work of great passion and insight and far superior to the *First Discourse*, was accorded second place by the Academy of Dijon.

Unlike most philosophers, Rousseau sought to bring his way of life into line with his ideas. His critique of modern civilization led him to withdraw from Paris in 1756 and to take up residence first at the Hermitage on the estate of Mme d'**Épinay**, and then in Montmorency. Between 1756 and 1762 three of his most famous works were written, the immensely popular novel, the *Julie, ou La Nouvelle Héloïse* (published 1761), the scarcely less popular treatise on education, *Émile* (1762), and his main work on political theory, *The Social Contract* (1762).

Due to a decision of the *Parlement* of Paris to have him arrested for a section of the *Émile* that offended Catholic orthodoxy, Rousseau fled France, lived for a time in Switzerland and then in 1766 went with David **Hume** to England. There he had a famous quarrel with the Scottish philosopher, and refused the offer of a pension from the king. In 1767 he returned to France, first to the provinces, then in 1770 to Paris.

During his years of exile and wandering Rousseau developed what is generally regarded as a severe case of paranoia, believing that he was the victim of a conspiracy directed by his former friends. His psychological condition notwithstanding, he continued to produce works of admirable lucidity on politics, particularly the *Letters Writ-*

ten from the Mountain (1764), the *Constitutional Project for Corsica* (1765) and the *Considerations on the Government of Poland* (1771). Rousseau's important autobiographical writings were in part apologetic, but also represent a sincere and often profound attempt at self-understanding. His *Confessions* (completed 1770), *Rousseau Judge of Jean-Jacques* (completed 1776) and the hauntingly beautiful *Reveries of the Solitary Walker* (not in final form at his death) focus on inwardness and attempt to understand the self in ways that transcend the memoir format of the time.

ROYAL ACADEMY OF PAINTING AND SCULPTURE/ ACADÉMIE ROYALE DE PEINTURE ET DE SCULPTURE (1648-1793). The Académie Royale de Peinture et de Sculpture was the second of seven French **academies** established under Louis XIV. Formed to enhance the reputation of French art, it also served to diminish the power of the **guild** of decorative painters and sculptors. By the 1660s, academicians dominated the lucrative Paris art market and nearly every 17th-century and 18th-century French artist now considered worthy of study was once its student, a member, or both.

The new institution was one of only two royal academies (the other being Architecture) to have both instructional and intellectual missions; and the Académie is in fact better celebrated for its school than its contributions to aesthetic theory. Education was a three-stage process in which students copied drawings, drew from statuary and then drew from the model. Only the life-drawing studio (where, in 1764, 400 students competed for 120 seats) received regular faculty supervision. The high point of instruction was the annual Grand Prix for history painters and sculptors, first-prize being subsidized study in Rome.

Membership in the Académie de Peinture was a two-stage process, with full affiliation offered to any painter, sculptor or engraver judged to have satisfactorily executed a reception piece of specified type and subject matter. While academicians of every rank could exhibit at the Académie's **salons**, held intermittently until 1751 and biennially thereafter, those who were not officers had no voice in their hierarchical institution. Resentment at this circumstance surfaced with the **French Revolution**, and the last years of the Académie were marked by internecine quarrels in which dissidents demanded structural reforms that the leadership alternately rejected and pretended to develop. The educational program survived when the Convention abolished all academies in 1793, and in 1795 the Academy itself was given new life when it was folded into the newly formed **Institut** de France.

Reed Benhamou

ROYAL SOCIETY. Founded in London in 1660, the Royal Society soon became one of the leading scientific **academies** in Europe. Among its founders were Abraham Cowley and Robert Boyle. The Society was not initially intended exclusively for natural science, and over the 18th century often had as fellows more writers, philosophers and amateurs than scientists. In its mixed membership the Royal Society resembled the **Académie française.**

Though it received a charter from the crown in 1662, the Royal Society was very different from academies established and influenced by governments (*see* **Academies, State-Sponsored**) on the continent. Organized as an independent and self-administering **club**, the Royal Society enjoyed no support from the British state, and its members, elected without direct government influence by the fellows themselves, received none of the material support that academicians of Paris, Berlin or Saint Petersburg enjoyed. On the other hand, the fellows of the Royal Society enjoyed more independence than did their colleagues on the continent.

Partly because of its independence from state influence and lack of state support, the Royal Academy seems to have had a more uneven career than parallel institutions in France. After an auspicious beginning, the quality of its work and membership fell off toward the end of the 17th century, but was effectively revived and given a more properly scientific emphasis under the energetic presidency of Isaac **Newton** from 1703 to 1727. Following Newton's death, the interests and membership of the Society again broadened, so that only a minority of members were scientists. Among them, however, were leading figures in the British scientific community, such as Joseph Priestly, Henry Cavendish and James Watt.

Unlike the French Académie Royale des Sciences, which devoted most of its energies to theory, the Royal Academy showed sustained interest in the practical applications of science. Over the 18th century, for example, it became actively involved in issues such as weights and measures, calendar reform and overseas exploration. At the same time its *Philosophical Transactions* maintained high standards, and compared favorably with series of *Mémoires* published by the more formally organized continental academies.

S

SADE, Donatien Alphonse François, Marquis de (1740-1814). A third-rate writer remarkable for the tediousness of his prose and the brutality of his narratives. Sade challenged the Lockean conception of man as other-regarding and the moral sense school of ethical thought by positing a radically egoistic individual unrestrained by moral or prudential considerations. Exploring the unrestrained use of power by strong individuals against weaker ones, his work is intentionally and necessarily pornographic.

In his description of a "violent reasoner" who put the case for radical egoism in his *Encyclopédie* article "Droit naturel" ("Natural **Law**") and in his portrayal of the Nephew in *Rameau's Nephew*, Denis **Diderot** treated the basic problem that Sade raised in a more concise, searching and insightful way.

If Sade's works are without significant literary or philosophical merit, they may nevertheless still express a genuine reaction against the unrealistic and saccharine literature of selfless morality found ad nauseam in the moral tales of Jean François **Marmontel** and others, and in the accounts of deeds of **beneficence** that proliferated in the journalism and in separate collections toward the end of the **Old Regime**. This literature, which has not received much attention, reflects in a reified form the anxiety of a society in economic and moral crisis. Sade showed how inadequate was the view of human nature underlying this literature of moral concern. But his own work did nothing but deepen the crisis of moral values that marked the closing decades of the Old Regime and became part of the legacy of the Enlightenment to the 19th century.

SAINT-PIERRE, Charles Irénée Castel de, abbé (1658-1743). One of the first Enlightenment figures to think extensively in terms of social and political reform, and the originator of the term **beneficence** (*bienfaisance*).

Saint-Pierre was born to a noble family from Normandy. He was educated by the **Jesuits**, first in Rouen, then in Caen. Having been ordained a priest, he went to Paris in 1680. There he met Bernard **Fontenelle** and began to move in advanced intellectual circles. He lost his faith, at least to the point of becoming a **deist**, but this did not prevent his retaining ecclesiastical positions and the income attached to them. He was elected to the **Académie française** in 1695, apparently because he was well connected, for at this time he had not written anything of significance. In 1718 he was excluded from the Academy for his published criticism of Louis XIV. Saint-Pierre was among the moving spirits behind the forward-looking **Club de l'Entresol** that met in the house of President **Hénault** from 1724-1731, and he frequented the **salons** of Mmes **Lambert, Geoffrin** and de **Tencin.**

Saint-Pierre is best remembered for his many reform projects that reflect the rationalizing and humanitarian strains of Enlightenment thought. These projects dealt with subjects ranging from methods of political administration to public finance and taxation and poor relief. His first published reform project was a plan to assure perpetual peace in Europe (1712). Saint-Pierre had an advantage over many of those who followed his example in that he was well connected and could often get government ministers to consider his projects. His disadvantage was that despite being intelligent and well intentioned, he was a poor stylist. Jean-Jacques **Rousseau** was asked to work on the abbé's papers to try to get them into more acceptable form, and he did provide a revised summary of the project on universal peace and one or two other subjects, but he was unable to provide a complete edition of his works. In recognizing the impracticality of many of Saint-Pierre's ideas, Rousseau called them the daydreams of a good man. The abbé de Saint-Pierre is an example of a cleric who retained the outer trappings of orthodoxy once he had adopted a more worldly set of values.

SALONS. Informal meetings normally held once or twice a week, usually by a hostess who provided a meal as well as a comfortable social ambience and who carefully selected her guests. The salon was the framework for an aristocratic form of sociability that over the 18th century was opened to include talented and amusing individuals of lesser social standing. There were also some exclusively male salons, of which the Baron d'**Holbach**'s was the most famous.

Salons performed a number of important functions. One was to bridge social and cultural gaps. Though the salon of Mme **Lambert** at the beginning of the 18th century had different days to receive men of letters and the social elites and that of Mme **Necker** at the end of the century retained this separation, the distinction was not maintained rigorously, and the tendency was for the elites of wealth and social preeminence on the one hand, and of talent on the other, to come together with the salon as perhaps the most conspicuous locus for this meeting.

Salons were generally not only hosted by **women**, but also had a significant female presence. For men of letters to make themselves readily understood to the women and intellectually untrained elite males present, it was necessary for them to express themselves in terms that were readily accessible. The mixing of writers and thinkers with an unspecialized public of both genders resulted in the discourse of the Enlightenment becoming more open and appealing. The *philosophes* abandoned Latin for the languages their compatriots understood, and strove to write in a readily intelligible and pleasing manner.

It has also been argued that salons formed the framework in which certain privileged women whose educations had been neglected in their youths could effect their own educations. While this would not have been so in the cases of Mme Necker, who received an excellent education from her father, or Mlle de **Lespinasse**, whose wide reading and quick mind made her more of a facilitator than a student in her own salon, it may well have been relevant in other cases. The main functions of the salon seem, however, to lie elsewhere.

It may perhaps be obvious, but it is nevertheless worth pointing out, that one of the key functions of the salon was social. It was a framework in which men and women of a certain social standing could meet for conversation, recreation and amusement. Before radio and television people were far more dependent on their own resources for entertainment than they are today. The reading of works in progress was perhaps instructive, and responses to those readings may well have played a significant critical role, but the entertainment value of such readings was also important and should not be overlooked. Similarly, for polite society the salon was a place where members of the two sexes could meet. Claude-Adrien **Helvétius** was introduced to his wife in the salon of Mme de **Graffigny**, Mme **Necker** met her husband at the salon of Mme de Vermenoux, and the libertine salons, such as Mme de **Tencin**'s, were both intellectually stimulating and in some ways the equivalent of long cocktail parties.

No less importantly, the salons were also centers of informal cultural politics. Mme Lambert's salon has been called the "antichamber of the Academy" and the same could be said of most of the great literary salons of the time. Women such as Mme **Lambert,** Mme Tencin, Mme **Geoffrin,** Mme du **Deffand** and even Mlle de Lespinasse were well connected and wielded great influence and powers of **patronage**. The salons were thus centers of cultural politics, and the women who ran them were power brokers whom few could afford to ignore.

Salons were undoubtedly central institutions of the Enlightenment at its highest levels. They should, however, be seen as part of the larger mosaic of which they were a part. Intellectuals who lacked the credentials to be invited to join the elite company of the salons could still frequent **cafés**, reading rooms, **clubs**, the theater and other institutions, such as **musées**, and that were founded toward the end of the Old Regime.

SALONS, ART. From its inception in 1663 to its apogee in the 1780s the Enlightenment art salon was under the auspices of the **Royal Academy of Painting and Sculpture**, which had been founded in 1648. The 18th century was to augur the salons' increased freedom from government controls and a concomitant responsiveness to the taste of the public for both esthetic achievement and commercial success. The first salon, in April 1667, commemorated the 1648 founding of the Royal Academy of Painting, which had the responsibilities of overseeing the scope of the exhibits, assigning a *décorateur*, and appointing an official jury for setting the salons' standards. For the next two hundred years the jury's rigorous process of admission made the acceptance of an artist's work a privilege and an honor. Presenting a work to be exhibited at the Academy, an artist would come under the jury's scrutiny for his *réception*, followed two years or more later by his *agrégation*, or entry into the ranks of the Academy.

The salons were remarkable as both cultural and political phenomena. Held annually and then biannually and with between 224 and 432 works of art, the salons were housed in the Louvre. When no room remained in the Salon carré and Grande galérie, paintings and sculptures overflowed into the Galérie d'Apollon, the Jardin de l'Infante, the stairwells, the courtyard and the studios below the Grande galérie. Some were even exhibited on doors. As the salons gained in popularity among the capital's aristocratic and bourgeois classes, it also generated a plethora of written documents. Ranging from the esthetic reviews of La Font de Saint-Yenne, the Academy's official pamphlets, and Denis **Diderot**'s *Salons* in the international newsletter, the *Corréspondance littéraire*, to the works of literary reviewers moonlighting as art critics, this sometime cacophony, sometime concurrence of critical voices, gave birth to modern art criticism.

From the outset the works showcased by the Royal Academy of Painting and Sculpture in the salons attracted the attention of French monarchs. Louis XIV's de facto minister of culture, Jean-Baptiste Colbert, was in attendance at the 1667 salon and future generations of royal emissaries were to represent the crown's interest in these artistic exhibitions that obviously had great potential for propaganda. The king's Director of Buildings made the final decision from a list of possible dates for the salons submitted by the members of the Academy. Moreover, the regent himself subsidized a portion of the costs for each exhibit and visited the salons on opening day to inspect the *décorateur*'s arrangement of the artwork: the king's portrait always occupied the center of the Grande galérie, and religious paintings hung on only the most illuminated walls. If the government regulated all aspects of the holding of the salons, enthusiasm for art from the French citizenry imposed itself with unprecedented zeal.

Open and free to the public, the salons helped erode the traditional barriers that separated the wealthy, educated elite from an increasingly well-heeled and well-read middle class. Aristocrats rubbed elbows with lackeys, intellectuals mixed with bourgeois and artists could find themselves in the company of potential **patrons** amidst the lords in attendance. The salons of the 18th century popularized France's high art, thereby resulting in an increasingly popular form of spectatorship that left an indelible mark on the **Republic of Letters**.

Dianah Leigh Jackson

SALONNIÈRES. Hostesses of private social and cultural gatherings central to the development of enlightened sociability and thought. **Salons** were predominantly, but not always, headed by a woman. With the growth of interest in the history of **gender** and of **women**, salons have received more attention, for they provide a rare instance of women playing a dominant role in elite culture.

The legal system of the **Old Regime** completely subordinated women to their fathers and husbands. It is therefore understandable that independence for a woman often came through widowhood. If the deceased husband left his widow well provided for, then in addition to legal independence, she also had the means to live as she liked. Some of the leading *salonnières* of the 18th century, such as Mme de **Doublet**, Mme **Lambert** and Mme **Geoffrin** were widows.

Since divorce was not an option in a Catholic society such as old-regime France, among the aristocracy couples that could not get along sometimes separated and lived independently, an arrangement that could give the wife as much personal freedom as the husband. Mme du **Deffand** and Mme d'**Épinay** both belong to this category. It also happened that happily married women who shared their husbands literary or cultural interests also held salons, as in the cases of Mme **Helvétius** and Mme **Necker**. We also find that unmarried women with the means or support also functioned successfully as *salonnières*, as did the aristocratic Mme **Tencin** and the distinctly less well-off Mlle de **Lespinasse**.

The motives of women who ran salons varied considerably. For some the activity was primarily social and recreational, for others an project of self-education and for yet others a means of exercising power and patronage. That these motives were mutually exclusive or that their proportions could be readily identified in specific cases is unlikely.

SCHOLASTICISM. An integrated system of philosophy and theology that was worked out in European **universities** during the Middle Ages, and which remained dominant in higher education and was the official doctrine of the Catholic Church until the early 18th century. Basically a form of Christian Aristotelianism, this philosophy combined Aristotle's logic and physics with Christian theology. Some early Enlightenment figures, such as Pierre **Bayle** and Giambattista **Vico**, were trained in scholasticism and used it in a limited and constructive way. However, most thinkers of the Enlightenment regarded scholasticism as fundamentally misconceived and a major barrier to intellectual progress.

The hostility of the Enlightenment to scholasticism was fundamental. Scholasticism was a comprehensive, indeed all-inclusive, system that believed itself able to provide satisfactory answers for all questions, spiritual, ethical and natural. It was also committed to the principle that **reason** and religion were compatible and mutually supporting, though religion was treated as the senior partner in this relationship. Enlightenment thought, by contrast, dissociated dogma from investigations of the natural world, and was, moreover, satisfied with limited explanations of phenomena, provided they met its methodological criteria.

Methodologically, scholasticism was deductive, moving by logical steps from great *a priori* truths to their consequences, working in abstract categories and giving great weight to linguistic distinctions. The Enlightenment favored the inductive method, beginning from specific instances and building generalizations, or laws, on them, and it systematically favored "things" over "words." In both cases method suited objective: the scholastics strove to ascertain the inner essences of things, while the thinkers of the Enlightenment sought to get at the workings, or mechanics, of the phenomena they investigated.

Scholasticism worked in primarily metaphysical categories. So too did the philosophies of the great system builders of the 17th century, such as René **Descartes,** Benedict **Spinoza** and Gottfried Wilhelm **Leibniz.** For most of the thinkers of the Enlightenment, the natural and human worlds were the proper concern of philosophers, and they favored a concrete and **empirical** approach to them. The terms "metaphysics" or "metaphysical" were treated as equivalents of charlatanry and served as terms of abuse. As for the authority of the Church in scholastic philosophy and science, the Enlightenment, having asserted the autonomy of the natural sciences, rejected it utterly.

Little wonder, then, that there developed no dialog between scholastics, of whom plenty remained in the 18th century, and the thinkers of the Enlightenment. Basic assumptions about what philosophy and science were, the methods by which they should proceed and their proper objectives were so different that there was no common ground for debate. To the scholastics the *philosophes* were infidels, and to the *philosophes* the scholastics were obscurantists. Rather than treating scholasticism as a valid intellectual alternative to their own intellectual orientation, they dismissed it out of hand.

Voltaire's comment on Francis **Bacon**'s attitude to the older philosophy is typical. Bacon, Voltaire wrote, "had very early scorned what the Universities called Philosophy, and he did everything in his power to prevent these institutions, set up for the perfection of human reason, from continuing to spoil it with their *quiddities*, their *abhorrence of a vacuum*, their *substantial forms* and all the inappropriate expressions which not only ignorance made respectable, but which a ridiculous confusion with religion made almost sacred" (*Letters on England*, Letter 12; Tancock ed., pp. 58-59).

SECOND DISCOURSE, or DISCOURSE ON THE ORIGIN AND FOUNDATIONS OF INEQUALITY AMONG MEN (1755). One of the most profound and brilliant works of the Enlightenment, and one which has been called the foundation of modern social criticism. Jean-Jacques **Rousseau** wrote the *Second Discourse* in response to the essay contest set by the Academy of Dijon: "What is the origin of inequality among men, and is it authorized by natural **law**?" In the context of a society of orders based on **privilege**, such a question invited a rationale for the necessity and utility of inequality. Rousseau, however, offered a delegitimizing analysis and denunciation. This essay, which is in every way superior to the *First Discourse,* was awarded second place by the Academy (*see* **Academies, Provincial**) and published in 1755.

The first part of the *Second Discourse* attempts to explain how solitary, primal humanoid creatures, in behavior similar to the orangutan, developed into human beings with language, society, technology and culture. In this brilliant piece of speculative anthropology Rousseau incisively used contemporary zoology, posited a geological notion of time and a rough version of evolution long before Charles Lyell and Charles Darwin, and provided a far more searching concept of the state of nature than either Thomas Hobbes or John **Locke** had done. The primal, isolated humanoid that Rousseau constructs has two basic instincts, self-preservation and pity, or sympathy in the sense of the Lockean mechanism of automatically identifying with the sense experiences of others that one has oneself experienced. This physiological reflex becomes the basis of concern for others, as the physiology of need is the basis of one's **self-interest** or self-love (*amour de soi*).

Isolation requires that the primal humanoid be independent, and the fact of this independence is taken as the basis of the value of freedom. In Rousseau's creation myth man is inherently good, in that he is disposed to seek his own well-being, but not the harm of other creatures. Rousseau has thought so long and hard to reconstruct a plausible version of the primal condition of mankind because he shared the historicist assumption of his time, namely, that what a thing or creature is originally is what it is essentially. For Rousseau mankind is essentially self-regarding, compassionate and free.

Unlike most of his contemporaries, Rousseau saw that the family is a social construct and does not exist naturally. It is in the emergence of the first associations of couples and their children that Rousseau sees the emergence of creatures similar to human beings and the development of the rudiments of culture, which include language (the origin of which he is unable to determine), the simplest technologies and the most basic forms of cooperation. This stage of stable family units in loose groupings that impose little if any mutual dependence or competition (the source of self-regard in the sense of **egoism**, or *amour propre*) is for Rousseau the happiest condition for mankind. **Progress** beyond that stage, which occurs as a result of agriculture, metallurgy and the institutionalization of private **property**, increases the wealth and power of society, but in moral terms is a fall. Social and civilized mankind has, according to Rousseau, inflicted vastly more suffering and misery on itself than the primal humanoid had suffered in the state of nature.

Mankind in civilization is neither happy, nor concerned for others, nor free. The source of the misery of civilized mankind, Rousseau argues, is a fraudulent contract by which the wealthy legitimized their power, property and dominion, and laid the basis for keeping the majority in a state of dependence and deprivation. Rousseau's denunciation of this condition is among the most powerful passages in Enlightenment social theory. His way out of this situation is set forth in the *The Social Contract*. *See also* **Equality**.

SECULARIZATION. A shift in categories of conceptualization from religious and mystical to scientific and materialistic. This process is also referred to as disenchantment.

As a function of its **empiricism** and **utilitarianism,** the Enlightenment tended to emphasize and validate material things, and to question the reality of things hypothetical or spiritual. By assuming that the world was governed by laws, the Enlightenment discredited the age-old belief that occult and inscrutable forces, representing the wills of divine or diabolical agents, influenced events. Matter and motion were taken to be subject to regular and invariable principles from which deviation was not possible (*see* **Miracles**). The thinkers of the Enlightenment also assumed the existence of, and sought, comparable laws for the social and political spheres.

By ascribing great importance to the material world, and through the better understanding of this world achieved by science, the Enlightenment contributed to extending man's control of **nature**. Calling into question the existence of the supernatural, or restricting it within the narrow, rationalistic bounds of **deism**, resulted in far-reaching consequences. On the one hand, the process of secularization discredited the existence of dark or diabolical forces. The persecution of witches, already receding in the 17th century, came to an end in enlightened Europe during the 18th century. By removing the grounds for fear of witches, goblins and devils, the process of secularization demystified the world and helped men and women to feel more at home in it. On the other hand, the same process made it difficult, if not impossible, for the enlightened to hear the sounds that Caliban took such pleasure in on his enchanted island (*The Tempest*,

Act III, scene iii) or to credit the voices that Joan of Arc heard (*see* David **Hume**, *History of England*, chap. 20).

Secularization and disenchantment freed mankind from the fear of satanic forces, but, at the same time, deprived them of the comfort of personal providence in an impersonal and indifferent world. The Enlightenment represents the historical moment when the gains of disenchantment appeared immediate and valuable, and the disadvantages were hardly suspected.

SEIGNEURIE. In France the *seigneurie* was a manorial jurisdiction or lordship. It had existed since the 11th century though it had evolved into something quite different from its original structure by the 18th century. In its beginnings the *seigneurie* was an extensive block of land or domain governed by a noble lord who claimed knight-service from his vassals and rents and labor services from his serfs. Over the centuries, however, the nobility of France sold or "alienated" large sections of their domain land to meet expenses, especially for military outlays that their revenues could not cover. They alienated most of this land to freedmen, peasants or townspeople, who paid for it with a perpetual rent, something like a modern mortgage that could never be liquidated. Recall that in the Middle Ages there were no specialized banking institutions and that interest was prohibited by the Catholic Church, so that multiple small land sales replaced loans of large capital as the prime means of transferring money and property.

As a result of this centuries-long process, known to historians as the "alienation of the domain," the *seigneurie* evolved into a two-fold structure. One part consisted of land still owned directly by the lord (the *domaine proche*) and another, larger part consisted of claims to dues and monopolies on the lands previously alienated (the *mouvances*). The domain land was like modern property and was usually leased out to tenant farmers for either a money or a produce rent. The *mouvances*, however, were not fully private property even though the small holders who occupied them could will, divide, sell or exchange this land like modern property owners. They still owed a cluster of obligations and fees to the seigneur that could be burdensome. These included a portion of the harvest or a fixed charge per acre, fees paid when the land changed hands by sale or inheritance, the obligation to use only the seigneur's mill, oven or wine press, and to share use of the common meadow and wood with the seigneur. In addition, the seigneur was also judge at the lowest judicial level, which gave him considerable leverage in disputes where he was a party.

In the later half of the 18th century, this form of landowning was increasingly contested. Lawsuits instigated by townspeople and even groups of peasants focused especially on the seigneur's justice, his claims to meadow and wood, and his efforts to tighten the collection of fees. The **French Revolution** abolished the *seigneurie* in 1793, that is, it declared the end of seigneurial dues and rights. It did not touch the domain, however, which now had the status of absolute property protected by the new regime.

Robert Forster

SELF-INTEREST. The rehabilitation of self-interest was one of the most important developments in ethics during the Enlightenment, and has continuing relevance for the present. Because it is now taken for granted, the novelty of the views on self-interest adopted during the 18th century deserves comment.

The self rehabilitated by the Enlightenment was the biological and psychological individual together with his or her particular interests. This went against three important traditions of social and political thought.

First, Christianity held a spiritual and theologically-centered view of the universe in which the material being and interests of the individual were subordinated to their spiritual well-being, to love of the Divine and to the imperative of charity in relations with their fellow, fallen human beings. Materially interpreted, self-interest was not far from sin.

Secondly, classical **republicanism** defined **virtue** as preference for the common good over the interests of the individual (**Montesquieu**, *Spirit of the Laws*, Bk. IV, chap. 5 and Bk. V, chap. 2). **Patriotism**, in a **democracy**, required suppression of self-interest. This broadly secular political attitude had no more sympathy for self-interest as a value than did Christian theology.

Thirdly, one of the basic assumptions of **absolutism** was that social order necessitated the control of potentially anarchic individual impulses by the authority of the state. The main religious and political schools of thought at the end of the 17th century thus had little inclination to see self-interest as either legitimate or beneficial.

The rehabilitation of self-interest posed a basic problem to Enlightenment thought in that it undermined existing principles of social and political order and cohesion. The thinkers of the Enlightenment nevertheless maintained that self-interest could and should be legitimized. It was argued that self-interest was natural, and as such, a fact of our existence that could not well be denied. During the Enlightenment, the argument from **nature** was considered a strong one. Beyond this, self-interest, in its specifically 18th-century incarnation as *enlightened* self-interest, was said to contain within itself a principle of order. It was believed that self-interest in society played the same role that gravity did in Isaac **Newton**'s physics.

Considered inherent to **human nature**, self-interest provided the constant on which human behavior could be structured and calculated. It could thus serve as the basis of realistic sciences of society and politics. Nor would the constant pursuit of self-interest by rational and calculating people threaten the social order, since they would constructively adjust their aspirations to things they might achieve without antagonizing others excessively. Rational or enlightened self-interest was deemed to be fully compatible with the general good. In the phrase of Alexander **Pope**, self-interest and social were the same (*An Epistle on Man*, Epistle III, lines 317-18).

Making self-interest theoretically coincide with the general good was an elegant solution to the problem of assuring social order in the absence of compelling collective ideals or values, but it was not regarded as completely effective. The Enlightenment was haunted by the prospect of self-interest uninfluenced by rational reflection and social responsibility. The notion of **egoism**, understood as irresponsible self-indulgence, and as a self-centered disregard for others and for cohesive social values, became a prominent theme of the late Enlightenment. It received its most profound treatment in Denis **Diderot**'s dialog, *Rameau's Nephew*, and a pathological formulation in the works of the Marquis de **Sade**. More commonly, writers concerned about the social effects of selfishness criticized the condition of bachelorhood, whether in the obvious case of libertines, or that of monks and nuns.

Thanks to its Newtonian underpinning, the notion of self-interest during the Enlightenment was for the most part thought to be socially beneficial. In place of the equilibrium of centripetal force and gravity in Newton's physics, liberal social thinkers posited a self-regulating market mechanism, in which self-interest was the driving force, and prudence or rational calculation, the limiting factor. Ultimately, however, the system did not depend on human intelligence. The market worked according to what were thought to be objective laws that were sometimes described as the product of a **hidden hand**.

It is perhaps an anomaly that the orderliness of the Newtonian universe having been abandoned in the face of theories of evolution and the big bang, most economists in developed countries continue to maintain that the unregulated market disposes things for the best for all concerned. Common sense would lead one to believe that in conditions of competition the strongest would do best, and arrange things in their own interests, without much regard for others. Actually, this is not a bad description of the way the market in fact works. The assumption that the market automatically disposes things for the common good is a more optimistic view of the situation than experience justifies.

Voltaire maintained that "self-love is the basis of all our feelings and all our actions" and further that: "This self-love is the instrument of our conservation; it resembles the instrument that perpetuates the species: it is necessary, it is dear to us, it gives us pleasure, and it must be hidden" (*Philosophical Dictionary*, art. "Amour-propre," Besterman, p. 35). Whether the workings of self-interest are as beneficial as Voltaire optimistically suggests is questionable, but he was certainly right about the need to hide it.

SENTIMENT. A thing felt or perceived through the senses. In physiology perceptions were referred to as sensations, while in ethics they were usually termed sentiments, as in Adam **Smith**'s *Theory of Moral Sentiments* of 1759. There was also a prominent school of ethical thought in the 18th century known as the "moral sense" school (*see* Francis **Hutcheson**).

Sensation and sentiment were not always clearly distinguished from each other or from related terms, such as sensibility, in the 18th century, and indeed their common semantic root made too formal a distinction artificial. However, both in its narrow physiological use and its broader moral and literary acceptations, sentiment played a central role in the thought of the Enlightenment.

In his *Essay Concerning Human Understanding* of 1690 John **Locke** argued that human beings were born without innate ideas, and developed their ideas, no matter how complex or abstruse, from sense impressions and reflection. Over the eighteenth century thinkers such as the abbé **Condillac** and Claude Adrien **Helvétius** reduced these two faculties to one, maintaining, in effect, that reflection was a comparison of sensations, and so not properly a faculty in its own right. The implications of this position were momentous.

First, sensationist psychology, while explicitly a denial of innate ideas, is implicitly a negation of original sin. The image Locke used for a newborn infant was *tabula rasa*, or blank sheet of paper. This image was deliberately chosen to indicate pure potential, without either the benefit of preformed ideas or the burden of sin insuperable by natural means.

Secondly, Locke's psychology made experience the key to knowledge, and this in turn made **empiricism** the appropriate methodology by which to approach the study of human beings as well as **nature**.

Thirdly, in the hands of Locke and his followers sensationist psychology became the basis of a system of ethics. By defining sensations that gave pleasure as good, and those that caused discomfort as evil, Locke laid the groundwork for **utilitarianism**. If given a radically egotistical interpretation, a moral system with such a basis could easily become a thoroughly asocial form of hedonism. However, Locke and most thinkers of the Enlightenment following him saw man as a moral agent directed not by external command or rational imperatives, but by the need to avoid various forms of distress and by a desire to maximize comforts across society as a whole.

Whatever the differences among the *philosophes*, they agreed in accepting, and working within, the paradigm of Lockean sensationism. Most of them agreed, too, that ethics could better be derived from sentiment than from **reason**.

It was a widely held assumption, not just among adherents of the "moral sense" school, but also among thinkers as diverse and mutually acrimonious as **Voltaire** and Jean-Jacques **Rousseau,** that certain standards of goodness were, in a phrase popular at the time, "inscribed in the heart of man." This was not taken to mean that human beings were endowed with innate moral ideas, but rather that by the psychological mechanism of association, humans, and indeed many animals, projected their own physiologically based aversion to suffering onto other beings of the same species. Which is the equivalent of saying that we are programmed by nature to sympathize with other sentient beings (*see Second Discourse*).

The notion that our sensations incline us toward sympathy with others, and hence contained an ethical element, was a central and distinctive feature of Enlightenment thought. It was, moreover, widely disseminated beyond the works of moral philosophers in the most popular literary genres of the time, such as the novel and the **periodical** press. The *Spectator*, for example, made it one of its main goals to spread the values of politeness and decency, and in this it had many imitators. Rousseau's best-selling novel, *Julie, ou La Nouvelle Héloïse*, Samuel **Richardson**'s *Pamela* and other novels, and Denis

Diderot's plays were all built around a thoroughly moralized notion of sentiment.

The vogue of sentiment in the literature and arts of the time peaked roughly during the 1770s, and thereafter the term sentimentalism carried a negative connotation. This did not mean, however, that it had lost all importance. Romanticism was significantly influenced by notions of sentiment developed during the Enlightenment, and the set of values described elsewhere as **moralism** drew directly from it. It is also arguable that it was less the core assumptions of the philosophy and literature of sentiment that lost favor toward the end of the century than the overly didactic and melodramatic ways it was presented.

SEPARATION OF POWERS. A political doctrine that maintains that the individual is best protected from arbitrary interference by the authorities when the various branches of government retain their independence from each other. This doctrine, which was central to Enlightenment **liberalism**, is found in the *Second Treatise on Government* of John **Locke**, and was further developed in the President **Montesquieu**'s *Spirit of the Laws*. In the form given it by Montesquieu this doctrine had a direct influence on the American Constitution.

The government powers that figure in this theory are the executive, the legislative and the judiciary. According to Montesquieu, the separation of these powers, which requires the independence of the agents, such as monarchs, assemblies and courts, that perform the functions involved with them, are the necessary guarantee of individual **liberty**, while the concentration of all three powers in the same hands results in **despotism**.

The importance of the separation of powers for liberals follows from a number of assumptions. First, a mistrust of authority and the belief that left to itself authority will go beyond its proper limits to encroach on the liberties of the individual. As Montesquieu put it: "constant experience shows that every man invested with power is apt to abuse it" (*Spirit of the Laws*, Bk. XI, chap. 4). Secondly, most liberals assume that power cannot be checked by moral considerations, but only by countervailing power. As Montesquieu says in the same place, "it is necessary from the very nature of things that power should be a check to power." Thirdly, it is assumed that if maintained in independence, the executive, legislative and judicial powers will check each other and create a political equilibrium favorable to liberty.

SHAFTESBURY, THIRD EARL OF; Anthony Ashley Cooper **(1671-1713).** Member of a family of **Whig** magnates, who served in both houses of **Parliament**, and a philosopher who emphasized the benevolent and altruistic sides of human nature.

The first Earl of Shaftesbury was a key figure in English politics during the late 17th century, and employed John **Locke** as his private secretary and physician. He made Locke responsible for the education of his grandson, and Locke took the unusual step of hiring a woman, Elizabeth Birch, as young Shaftesbury's tutor. Completely fluent in Greek and Latin, Birch taught these languages to her charge while he was still a small boy. He was then sent to Winchester School, and thereafter on the grand tour for several years from 1686.

Between 1695 and 1698 Shaftesbury sat in the House of Commons, but because of poor health decided not to stand for election again. However, on inheriting the title of Earl in 1699, he attended sessions of the House of Lords. Shaftesbury married in 1709, but because of his health moved to Italy in 1711, and died there two years later.

Beginning in 1699 Shaftesbury published a series of essays on religious, moral and esthetic subjects. In 1711 he collected and published them as the *Characteristics of Men, Manners, Opinions, Times.* This work, which contains the core of Shaftesbury's thought, was much praised by contemporaries, and continued to enjoy a high reputation until roughly the 1770s. This may be because in it Shaftesbury expresses a set of views representative of aspects of Enlightenment thought that lost favor as the century progressed.

One of the main themes of the *Characteristics* was a questioning of the Hobbesian view of man as radically individualistic, driven by his interests and passions and inclined to seek domination. Shaftesbury examined the premises of Hobbes's thought and found that a creature such as Hobbes described could not form societies and would most likely end in self-destruction. In place of the passion and **egoism** that characterized humanity for Hobbes, Shaftesbury proposed a concept of man at the heart of which was a "moral sense." **Virtue,** defined as an inclination toward the common good, which Shaftesbury took to be natural and central to **human nature,** was the basis of this value. Hence, man tended naturally toward **beneficence,** and Shaftesbury has a good claim to be regarded as the first systematic theoretician of this key Enlightenment value.

It is probably fair to say that on the one hand, the notion of self-interest, as developed most brutally by Bernard **Mandeville,** and most convincingly by Adam **Smith,** came to be more widely accepted than the notion of man as fundamentally benevolent, while on the other hand, the need for widespread acts of beneficence became increasingly apparent. The "moral sense" philosophy of Shaftesbury was taken up by Francis **Hutcheson**, David **Hume** and Adam Smith among others, though it was not incompatible with other strains of Enlightenment thought.

Other areas in which Shaftesbury's relation to the Enlightenment are ambivalent include religion and **epistemology**. Like Pierre **Bayle**, whom he had met in Holland, Shaftesbury maintained that it was possible to separate religion from morality. And while himself a **deist**, he was willing openly to discuss the question of atheism. He believed in a beneficent Creator of the universe, and adhered to a Platonic kind of spirituality. Formally, he was a latitudinarian Anglican. Furthermore, he presented **enthusiasm**, seen as a form of heightened spirituality, as a positive value. These were positions that displeased the orthodox, but could not satisfy radicals.

In order to maintain a substantive and positive view of human nature, Shaftesbury asserted, against the dominant and growing influence of John Locke, a doctrine of innate ideas. The notion of mankind being inherently endowed with the ability to distinguish between ugliness and beauty, and between good and evil, and inclined toward an appreciation of harmony, certainly served to support a favorable view of human nature, but it hardly squared with the view of man as a *tabula rasa*. On the other hand, it fits well with Jean-Jacques **Rousseau**'s assumption that man is naturally good.

SHAKESPEARE, William (1564-1616). Shakespeare's reputation as England's greatest playwright was far from assured in the 18th century. Enlightenment models of dramatic form and propriety dictated a strict adherence to Aristotle's unities of plot, time and place. This orderly, artistic predisposition of Restoration England was in part due to the influence of French literary fashion, and partly a result of a desire during the Restoration to enthrone **reason** and order as the guiding lights of civil and artistic culture in the wake of the upheavals of the English Civil War.

That the tanner's son from Stratford-upon-Avon had left a body of work with unmistakable marks of genius was the unanimous opinion of even the sternest neoclassical critics of Shakespeare's plays. Nevertheless, they were unsparing in their criticism of his faults. Among the most dismissive judges of Shakespeare was **Voltaire**, who was willing to admit that the Englishman's dramatic poetry was "full of naturalness and sublimity," yet concluded that he "was without the slightest spark of good taste, or the least knowledge of the rules of drama" (Voltaire, *Letters on England*, Letter 18, Tancock, p. 92). Indeed, in Voltaire's view "the excellence of this author has ruined the English theater" (ibid.).

Two major English poet-critics, John Dryden and Alexander **Pope**, took upon themselves the task of "regularizing" Shakespeare's plots and language, and each did his part to establish Shakespeare's credentials. Dryden's revised versions of Shakespeare's plays reflect his strict adherence to the codes of **Neoclassicism**. Though he voices great admiration for Shakespeare's "natural" poetic genius, Dryden also concludes that "the fury of his fancy often transported him beyond the bounds of judgment" (Dryden, "Shakespeare's Characteristics," in his Preface to *Troilus and Cressida*).

Pope excuses Shakespeare's transgressions of Aristotelian form by pointing to the relative barbarism of the Elizabethan audiences for whom he wrote: "To judge therefore of Shakespeare by Aristotle's rules, is like trying a man by the Laws of one Country, who acted under those of another. . . He writ to the People; . . . without assistance or advice from the Learned. . . without that knowledge of the best models, the Ancients, to inspire him with an emulation of them (Pope, "Excellences and defects of Shakespeare," in the Preface to his 1725 edition of Shakespeare's works). Like Dryden, he focuses on Shakespeare's lack of classical background as the main source of his flaws.

Perhaps the best measure of Shakespeare's place in the Enlightenment literary canon is found in Samuel **Johnson**'s Preface to his 1765 edition of Shakespeare's works. Like the others, Johnson praised Shakespeare as "the poet of nature; the poet that holds up to his readers a faithful mirror of manners and of life." Shakespeare's style was sometimes uneven and flawed, particularly by his love of the quibble, "the fatal Cleopatra for which he lost the world, and was content to lose it." On the other hand, Johnson reflects a shift to a less rigid adherence to neoclassical unities: he argues that Shakespeare typically mixed comedy with tragedy and hence the unities of Aristotelian tragedy are not pertinent to the mixed genre of his plays, if he knew of them at all. In the end, Johnson concludes that only the unity of action remains essential, and the unities of time and place are rules Shakespeare often violated: "such violations of the merely positive become the comprehensive genius of Shakespeare;" after Shakespeare, violating these rules becomes the rule.

Johnson describes Shakespeare as opening "a mine which contains gold and diamonds in unexhaustible plenty, though clouded by incrustations, debased by impurities, and mingled with a mass of meaner metals." This metaphor aptly summarizes Enlightenment views of the genius of Shakespeare.

Michael Yogev

SKETCH OF THE PROGRESS OF THE HUMAN MIND*/ESQUISSE D'UN TABLEAU HISTORIQUE DES PROGRES L'ESPRIT HUMAIN (1793-1794).** Often regarded as the testament of the Enlightenment, the *Sketch* was written by the Marquis de **Condorcet** while in hiding during the Terror of the **French Revolution**. The manuscript of the work was completed by October 1793, and Condorcet was captured and committed suicide in March of the following year. Similar in many ways to **Voltaire's *Letters on England and ***Essay on Manners*** and d'**Alembert's *Preliminary Discourse***, Condorcet's *Sketch* is one of the great programmatic statements of Enlightenment ideals and values.

The *Sketch* consists of an introduction and ten chapters or periods. The first two treat prehistory and the problem of origins of society, but unlike Jean-Jacques **Rousseau** in the ***Second Discourse***, Condorcet views the arts and sciences as compatible with morality. The third period treats the first literate societies and the fourth to sixth ancient Greece to the Crusades. Condorcet here develops the theme of the conflict between true philosophers on the one hand and the coalition of despots and priests on the other. Chapters seven through nine consider the liberating influence of the Crusades and the contribution of printing, the Renaissance, the Reformation, the Scientific Revolution and the Enlightenment to the development of Western culture.

The final and most original chapter of the *Sketch* treats the future. Thanks to the broad dissemination of knowledge, advances in the natural and social sciences, greater equality and improved morality, Condorcet argued that mankind could look forward to indefinite physical, social and moral **progress**. Condorcet's last work is noteworthy not only for its optimism, but also for its generosity and humanity. In it the ***philosophe*** expressed sympathy for the oppressed and wretched of the world, from **slaves**, serfs and the poor to victims of European colonization and **women**, asserted their dignity as human beings and their rights to **liberty** and a comprehensive **education**. The humanity and generosity of these views are heightened by the tragic circumstances in which they were set down.

SLAVERY. The end of the 18th century witnessed the beginnings of a movement to abolish the slave trade and slavery itself. The Chevalier de **Jaucourt**, one of the principal collaborators of the *Encyclopédie*, stated the issue strongly: "Can it be legitimate to rob mankind of its most sacred rights solely to satisfy one's avarice . . .?" Jaucourt was seconded by the President **Montesquieu**, **Voltaire**, Jean-Jacques **Rousseau**, Denis **Diderot** and the abbé **Raynal**, who warned of a Black Spartacus.

However, outside the philosophic circles and a small group known as the "Friends of the Blacks," resistance to abolition in France was well financed by the colonial lobby, and indifference among the population at large was widespread. Unlike Britain, France was quite dependent on its sugar islands for its overseas trade surplus. The island of Saint-Domingue alone produced about 40 percent of the world's sugar and 70 percent of its coffee. It had a population of almost 500,000 slaves, and by the 1780s some 30,000 slaves were imported yearly. The colonial lobby made its case succinctly: "No slaves, no sugar. No sugar, no colonies."

The British public was more energized for abolition than the French for many reasons. The Protestant sects, especially the Quakers, Methodists and Anglican Evangelicals, lent a moral earnestness to the abolitionist movement that was lacking in France, where the Catholic Church was lukewarm to the issue. The British abolitionists were also well led by Thomas Clarkson and William Wilberforce, who knew how to organize a national campaign in the press, in pamphlets, sermons and in **Parliament**. Moreover, by the end of the century, Britain was building an empire in which the sugar islands were relatively unimportant. For all these reasons, the abolitionists came very close to success in Parliament before 1789; the war with France delayed action until 1807 to end the slave trade, and until 1833 to abolish slavery in the colonies.

At first, the French revolutionaries were too occupied with domestic issues to devote much attention to slavery. However, the campaign of the people of color for civil rights bore fruit in May 1791, despite fierce planter resistance. But the major event was the massive slave revolt in Saint-Domingue in August 1791, which became an independence movement and continued for 13 years of brutal fighting. The Jacobin government abolished slavery in February 1794, but this was essentially the acceptance of a *fait accompli* in Saint-Domingue. It was based on the hope that the freed slaves would fight against the British and Spanish invaders and keep the island French. The black leader, Toussaint Louverture, was eventually able to maneuver all three European powers out of the new Haiti.

Robert Forster

SMITH, Adam (1723-1790). One of the key figures of the Scottish Enlightenment, best known today as the founder of liberal economic theory.

Smith's family on both sides belonged to the respectable landowning and office-holding strata of the area just north of Edinburgh. His father, who both owned land and held a number of important administrative positions, died while Smith was still a small child. His education was fairly typical, as he attended the burgh school of Kirkaldy, the town of his birth, and then went on, at 14, to a secondary education in the University of Glasgow, where he had the good fortune of studying with the celebrated Francis **Hutcheson**. In 1740 he won a scholarship to Oxford, where he was left largely to his own devices for the six years of his residence.

On leaving Oxford Smith returned to Kirkaldy, and had to face the issue of career choice. Not having taken a professional degree, he welcomed the opportunity to give a series of public lectures in Edinburgh from 1748-1751. His success here led to his being offered a teaching position in the University of Glasgow in 1751, and the following year he succeeded Hutcheson in the chair of moral philosophy. Smith proved a conscientious and effective teacher, and his reputation for absentmindedness notwithstanding, a capable administrator. He might easily have continued as a university professor at Glasgow for his entire career, but in 1764 he was offered the prestigious and well-paid tutorship of the Duke of Buccleuch.

Smith accompanied his student to the continent, where they stayed in Toulouse, then Geneva, where Smith met **Voltaire**, whom he admired greatly, and finally Paris, where he frequented **salons** and met many of the leading *philosophes* and **physiocrats**. On his return to England in 1767, as had been previously agreed, Smith continued to receive as a life annuity the same sum that he had had as his salary as tutor, and so was comfortably off. Between 1767 and 1773 Smith returned to Kirkaldy, where he lived with his mother, and continued to work on the book for which he is most famous today. In 1773 he moved to London, and three years later saw his *Wealth of Nations* through the press. On receiving the lucrative post of Commissioner of Customs for Scotland in 1778, he established a comfortable household in Edinburgh, had his mother come to live with him there and conscientiously carried out his official duties. According to Alexander Carlyle, who knew him personally, Smith was both exceptionally absentminded and exceptionally beneficent.

Today Smith is best known as the author of the *Wealth of Nations*, the founding text of economic liberalism. In his own time, however, it was his *Theory of Moral Sentiments*, first published in 1759, to which he primarily owed his reputation. This work went through numerous editions, was translated into French and German and its appeal was such that it attracted students from outside the British Isles to study with its author. While recognizing the force of **self-interest**, in this work Smith emphasized the effectiveness of sympathy and **beneficence**, based on an inherent tendency to identify with the experiences of others, very much in the spirit of John **Locke**'s psychology.

SOCIAL CONTRACT. A theory designed to account for the origin and legitimacy of civil and political society. With its emphasis on consent as the basis of political association it tends toward **liberalism**, but it has also been made to serve conservative purposes.

During the 17th century it was widely assumed that complex structures such as societies needed to be explained in terms of their component parts. All contract theorists posit an initial state of nature in which lack of agreed authority led to constant conflict and violence. The point at which the uncertainty and anarchy of the state of nature become intolerable is the point at which the need for agreed rules becomes inescapably necessary. This approach both makes the individual prior to society and sees society as the result of an agreement among free individuals.

In the version of the social contract produced by Thomas Hobbes, under the intolerable conditions of the state of nature men agreed to appoint a ruler with sufficient powers to repress the aggressive and anarchic propensities of individuals. The ruler himself is not bound by this irrevocable founding contract, but stands outside and above it. Hobbes thus used contract theory to legitimize **absolutism**. John **Locke**, on the other hand, gave contract theory probably its most influential liberal formulation. Locke agreed that men could not live together without rules, but conceived of **human nature** as less aggressive and irrational than Hobbes. Accordingly, the level of **authority** required by society to function was much less than it was for Hobbes. No member of society was outside of Locke's contract, and the validity of the contract continued to depend on the consent of the parties to it, who remained free to amend or annul it. Locke's *Second*

Treatise on Government remains a classic statement of political liberalism.

During the 18th century contract theory enjoyed broad acceptance, and saw perhaps its most influential and controversial formulation in Jean-Jacques **Rousseau**'s *The Social Contract* (1762). However, it was at this time that criticisms of contract theory came to prevail. Some thinkers, such as David **Hume**, pointed out that the social contract was ahistorical, and that no known instance of the formulation of such a contract could be adduced. Others suggested that the notion was superfluous, as human beings do not, cannot, and need not exist outside of society. All are born into families, which precede civil societies and are themselves a form of society (**Montesquieu, Voltaire**, Giambattista **Vico**, Adam **Ferguson**). In his *Reflections on the Revolution in France* (1791) Edmund **Burke** argued that society was indeed based on a contract, but defined it in such restrictive and traditionalist terms as to subvert its original intent and limit the freedom of the individual to the benefit of society.

Though contract theory was in disfavor among most important thinkers after 1750, it continued to provide a way of thinking about society that gave precedence to the individual and to individual freedom, and so retained its appeal to liberals such as Thomas **Paine** and to the legislators of the **French Revolution**.

SOCIAL CONTRACT, THE (1762). During the 18th century the least popular of Jean-Jacques **Rousseau**'s major works. It can be viewed as the answer to the basic problem raised in the *Second Discourse*: How can people live together while fulfilling themselves, but without making each other miserable?

Rousseau's response consists in rejecting force and fraud as bases for political association (Bk. I, chaps. 3-4), and in adopting instead the principle of consent as embodied in the free making of an original contract. So far his position is broadly **liberal**. Unlike many liberals, however, Rousseau emphasizes the importance of community and insists on the necessity of **equality** in achieving community. Unlike most liberals, too, he is not satisfied with determining the will of the community by a simple head count. Instead he posits an objectively existing and necessarily correct general will that can be realized only if citizens take as their objective the general good. Most liberals treat **self-interest** and partial interests in politics as legitimate. Much discussion of the *Social Contract* has been concerned with the notion of the general will and with its potential for totalitarianism.

A less commented upon, but perhaps more important feature of the *Social Contract* concerns its notion of community. According to Rousseau, the social contract is not simply a matter of establishing agreed upon rules to avoid the inconveniences of the state of nature; more than this, it calls for a transformation of **human nature** (Bk. I, chap. 8 and Bk. II, chap.7).

A political treatise calling for a basic transformation of human nature would seem utopian. Yet Rousseau tells us at the outset of his book that he is taking "men as they are, and laws as they might be" (foreword to Bk. I). Further, according to the argument of the *Second Discourse*, a basic change is not just an historical possibility, it is a fact. The choice is between qualitatively different models of **humanity** and of society: there is no question of reverting to earlier or original ones. Finally, if we consult Rousseau's *Considerations on the Government of Poland*, we will see that he believed it possible to move gradually toward a polity based on principles he regarded as legitimate.

Rousseau's basic insight in the *Social Contract* is that without community there cannot be legitimate political association and that neither community nor polity exist of themselves, but must be shaped by those who make them. His analysis of the conditions necessary for achieving political legitimacy are not conducive to political theories compatible with radical **individualism**, but they are no less incisive on that account.

SOCIETY THEATER/*THÉÂTRE DE SOCIÉTÉ*. This is the title of a compilation published by Charles Collé in 1768, but the genre includes a whole set of short plays written during the century to be performed in private, and especially in the homes of aristocrats, financiers and the wealthy, as simple entertainments on festive occasions. The phenomenon is important, and develops between 1700 and 1790. There were about 50 private stages in Paris in 1732, but by 1748 Friedrich Melchior Grimm estimated there to be 160. Others, like J. Moynet, have put their number at more than 200 by the end of the century.

Often written in prose, these plays were intended for amateurs, and were usually brief. They belong to the comic genre, and since they did not have to take **censorship** or the prejudices of the actors into account, they could be a lot freer in their tone and content than plays performed by professional companies. The *théâtre de société* is divided into a number of categories: parades, small comedies, proverbs and edifying or pedagogical theater.

The parade was at its beginning a brief sketch that acrobats or artists performed in front of the theater to attract the public. Toward 1711, the word took another meaning. Thomas Simon Gueulette began to write and play some of them for young people of high social standing, and they became a specific genre. A compilation entitled *Théâtre de boulevards* attributed to the same author was published in 1756. However, since the parades used crude language in coarse, provocative and sometimes scatological scenes, especially when they used "poissard" style (an imitation of popular speech with doubtful word links), the genre predictably degenerated. In its parody of the higher genres and of the attitudes of the upper classes, the parade demonstrated a rich verbal resourcefulness, and due to its freedom, threatened the more serious and high-minded theatrical companies and genres.

Another variety of the *theater de société* is the dramatic proverb. The genre came from a society game, which required some of the participants to illustrate, by an improvised sketch, a proverb that the others had to guess. The performers never spoke or used as a title the key sentence. At the end of the 17th century Madame de Maintenon had already written some for her orphan boarders of the famous school she had established at Saint-Cyr. In 1768 Louis Carrogis, dit Carmontelle, published a compilation of the genre entitled *Dramatic Proverbs*. This kind of theatrical social entertainment met with real success. Alexandre de Moissy published a collection of them in 1770, some clearly pedagogical in intent and meant for children.

Isabelle Martin

SPECTATOR. A **periodical** founded by Richard **Steele** and to which he and Joseph **Addison** contributed roughly equally. Among the occasional contributors to the paper were Alexander **Pope** and Thomas Tickell. The *Spectator* appeared daily in 555 numbers between 1 March 1711 and 6 December 1712, and was revived by Addison for another 80 numbers in 1714. The format of the paper was normally a single essay of two or two-and-a-half pages, though it sometimes was made up of several letters, supposedly from the public, but in fact by the journalists. For a number of reasons this periodical holds an important place in the literary and intellectual history of the 18th century.

In contrast to the *Acta Eruditorum* of Leipzig, or the *Nouvelles de la République des lettres* of Pierre **Bayle**, and against the active political journalism of the time, the *Spectator* was intended primarily to amuse. Unlike the learned periodicals that specialized in book reviews of recent scholarship in theology, history and science, it was directed at a broad readership that explicitly and intentionally included **women**. From the outset, the *Spectator* was a great commercial success, and reached a wide audience. According to the authors themselves, it was soon being printed in pressruns of 3,000, and each copy was said to have 20 readers (*Spectator*, no. 10). Shortly after the project was suspended the collected papers were printed in a pressrun of 9,000 copies, and the journal continued to be reprinted and imitated for the rest of the century, both in Britain and on the continent.

The success of the *Spectator* can be accounted for in a number of ways. It was widely regarded as a model for informal English prose. Many of the papers radiate a warm, kindly sense of humor that still retains its appeal. Certain of the characters, such as Sir Roger de Coverly, combine a basic decency with personal foibles in a way that remains attractive. And much of the social criticism is done with a light touch that is amusing without being offensive, and suggests a certain sympathy with the weaknesses of humanity. But there are also more deep lying reasons for the popularity of the paper.

Numerous critics have observed that the *Spectator* is one of the earliest and most effective advocates of the value of politeness in the 18th century. This value extends far beyond formal manners. According to John Brewer, "The aim of politeness was to reach an accommodation with the complexities of modern life and to replace political zeal and religious bigotry with mutual **toleration** and understanding" (*Pleasures of the Imagination*, p. 102). It is important to appreciate the harshness of the political and religious conflicts in England during the late 17th and early 18th centuries in order to understand the appeal of the ethic of the *Spectator*, which offered an alternative to conflict by advocating mutual restraint in personal relations and harmonious forms of association, such as **clubs** of like-minded people who could meet voluntarily, without prejudice to other groups, or the public. There is, too, in the emphasis on domesticity and the validation of privacy prominent in the papers, a shift away from the main foci of political and religious confrontation.

Despite its early date, the *Spectator* can also be seen as an important agent for the diffusion of Enlightenment ideas and values. The ideas of Francis **Bacon**, Isaac **Newton** and John **Locke** are presented clearly and sympathetically, and beyond this Addison and Steele see the world in the partially disenchanted but thoroughly orderly and **beneficent** fashion that follows from the Newtonian synthesis. They already refer positively to the values such as **humanity**, explore how the traditional notion of **virtue** can be applied in modern life and offer scathing criticism of an unrestrained ethic of **self-interest**, as in the tale of Inkle and Yarico (no. 11).

Further, the notion of "Spectator," which indicates a person standing outside of specific groups and their interests, and so able to take an independent view of what is going on around him, also appealed to the Enlightenment ideal of objective and impartial observation of all phenomena, including social ones. The pose of Addison and Steele's spectator appears in recognizable form in the ethical theory of Adam **Smith** as an "impartial spectator" in the *Theory of Moral Sentiments*, and it provided the model for a large number of British and European periodicals over the 18th century.

SPINOZA, Benedict (1632-1677). With René **Descartes** and Gottfried Wilhelm **Leibniz**, Spinoza was one of the great rationalist philosophers of the 17th century.

Spinoza was born in Amsterdam to a **Jewish** family engaged in commerce. The Amsterdam Jewish community benefited from the exceptional degree of **toleration** that Holland maintained, and was itself more open than many Jewish communities elsewhere. Spinoza's education included comprehensive **literacy**, with his studies primarily directed to the Hebrew Scriptures and rabbinic literature.

Unsatisfied by this traditional curriculum, Spinoza wished to study contemporary philosophy, and to this end his father engaged a Latin tutor for him. Under the influence of Descartes, the leading European philosopher of the time, Spinoza found that his worldview was no longer compatible with that of Judaism. The Jewish community of Amsterdam was willing to accept a formal and external acquiescence in its forms of observance, but unwilling to compromise his integrity, the young Spinoza refused this not unreasonable accommodation. In 1656 he was excommunicated.

Spinoza was also, on the request of the Jewish community, required to leave Amsterdam. This can have been no great hardship for him, as he could lead his modest train of life and devote himself to his studies as easily in one place as another in the liberal atmosphere of Holland. Spinoza apparently made a modest living by grinding lenses, working only as much as necessary to meet his needs, and devoting the rest of his time to study. He never married or frequented **salons**, but was pleasant and easygoing in his relations with others, and enjoyed a favorable reputation in his personal life among his intellectual peers and neighbors alike. This is worth mentioning since the charge of atheism that came to be leveled against him implied, for contemporaries, debased morals. For Pierre **Bayle**, who found his philosophy repugnant, Spinoza was an example of a thoroughly moral unbeliever.

In 1663 Spinoza published a work in Latin (the language of all his philosophical works) entitled *Principles of the Philosophy of Descartes*, which gives an indication of his orientation. In 1670 he published the *Tractatus Theologico-Politicus*, a daring and innovative work that included one of the earliest secular and critical assessments of the Bible, that subordinated theology to philosophy, and that argued earnestly for religious freedom and toleration. The book was not to the liking of orthodox theologians of any denomination, and aroused sufficient controversy to dissuade Spinoza from publishing anything else during his lifetime. Shortly after his death in 1677 a number of his manuscripts were published. The most important of them was his *Ethics*, which today is his most highly regarded work. The others include *On the Improvement of the Intellect*, a Hebrew grammar and an unfinished treatise on politics.

Spinoza's relation to the Enlightenment is not altogether clear. Some scholars regard him as the pivotal figure, not only of the early Enlightenment, but of the movement as a whole. The *Tractatus* provides some basis for this position, but it is doubtful whether, had this work been all that Spinoza had written, his place in intellectual history would have been very different from, for example, the French Oratorian and biblical scholar, Richard Simon, or the English **deists**, John Toland or Anthony Collins. Spinoza's reputation and place in history depend basically on his *Ethics*, and the relation of this work to the Enlightenment is problematic.

The *Ethics* is written in Latin and directed to a restricted public. Methodologically it is highly systematic, proceeding by laying down axioms and drawing their consequences, very much in the Cartesian tradition. It is as far from the dominant **empiricism** of the Enlightenment as one could get. And the argument is devilishly difficult to follow. The philosophy of the *Ethics* begins and ends with the notion of the divine, and is permeated throughout by an elevated spirituality. Spinoza's religiosity is altogether unorthodox, and his pantheism, or identification of the divine with the material world, is unacceptable, if not downright offensive, to the Judeo-Christian tradition. There is no parallel to his profound spirituality in Enlightenment thinkers, who are more concerned with understanding this world and moderating the evils we suffer in it.

Though Spinoza was often denounced as an atheist, the German romantic Novalis showed more insight in referring to him as "this God-intoxicated man." There were few atheists among the thinkers of the Enlightenment, and fewer, if any, who approached Spinoza's level of spirituality. For some a secular saint, for others a particularly deep philosopher, Spinoza is not a thinker who can easily be classified, or identified with the Enlightenment in the way that, for example, his contemporary Pierre Bayle could be.

SPIRIT OF THE LAWS/DE L'ESPRIT DES LOIS (1748). Montes-quieu's classic work of political theory, which, despite its bulk and scope, quickly became and remained a best seller. Though clerics and conservatives attacked the work on its appearance, within the enlightened community it was probably the most admired and most widely praised work of its kind.

The popularity of the *Spirit of the Laws* stems in part from Montesquieu's having drawn on and successfully blended a number of currents of thought. Montesquieu was intimately familiar with the Greek and Roman classics, the common cultural heritage of the educated classes of the time, and used that literature as a modern researcher would use a database. In addition to this traditional literature, Montesquieu was also familiar with, and frequently drew on, the travel literature that showed Europeans other societies with values and principles of organization fundamentally different from their own.

But it was not so much the content of his sources as the way he used them that appealed to contemporaries. One important feature of Montesquieu's project was to establish a science of society and politics, and he used information on classical civilization and the societies of the East, Africa and the Americas as raw data from which he could discover universally applicable social and political laws. To create a science of society was a deep-lying aspiration of the thinkers of the Enlightenment, and Montesquieu's success in laying the groundwork for such sciences explains something of the wide popularity his work enjoyed. Methodologically he combined a **Cartesian** faith in the ubiquity of law with a Newtonian respect for fact.

Among the regularities that Montesquieu found in social and political spheres were correlations between climate and culture, between the size of a state and the kind of regime appropriate to it, between the nature of a crime and the punishment appropriate to it and between the degree of concentration of powers and **liberty** or its absence. His classification of governments into republican, monarchical and despotic, each with its own principle of motivation, was the first significantly new classification of governments since Aristotle, and had the virtue of being more in tune with the political realities of his time. This large and loosely structured work also devotes two long books (Bks. XXX and XXXI) to the early history of feudalism.

There are at least two other reasons the *Spirit of the Laws* enjoyed wide popularity. Not only did it expand the boundaries of knowledge, it was also written with the incisiveness, elegance and sometimes irony that the enlightened public relished. Whether in a novel or a treatise, Montesquieu was a master stylist. Beyond this, he was a moralist whose values appealed to his enlightened contemporaries. Because of concerns about objectivity, it is not usual today to intrude moral issues into academic or scientific works. This was not the case in the 18th century. The *Spirit of the Laws* is infused with a passionate concern for liberty and for the dignity of the individual. In a work that has the status of a founding text of sociology, Montesquieu did not hesitate to put a powerful imaginary condemnation of the Inquisition and of persecution into the mouth of one of its victims (Bk. XXV, chap. 13). And typically he not only warmly advocated the value of freedom, he also presented a carefully reasoned and argued analysis of the conditions in which freedom could, or could not, exist. *See also* **Despotism; Republicanism.**

STEELE, Richard (1672-1729). An important figure in the history of English literature who also played a significant role in the literary politics of the early 18th century.

Steele was born in Dublin, but received his education in England, where he attended the Charterhouse school, together with Joseph **Addison**, with whom he was later to collaborate on a number of projects. Steele began his career in the army, but soon moved to literature. He wrote for the stage without great success. The area in which he enjoyed conspicuous success was journalism. His initial work on newspapers, or gazettes, was neither original nor particularly well received, but when he offered the public amusing and instructive short essays, as he did in the *Tatler* (1709-1711), the popularity of the new journal was immediate. Addison collaborated occasionally on this paper, but more or less equally on another, even more famous **periodical** that Steele began, the *Spectator* (1711-1712). Steele also engaged in political journalism, and founded a number of other periodicals, but none met with the success of the *Spectator*.

In his politics Steele was a **Whig**. His career prospered when this party was in power, and suffered when the **Tories** held office. He was elected to **Parliament** in 1713, and was knighted in 1715. Conflicts among the Whigs resulted in his losing favor, and he fell out with his old friend and collaborator, Addison. By 1724 his financial situation had deteriorated, causing him to leave London. Little was heard of him from then until his death five years later.

STERNE, Laurence (1713-1768). Remembered primarily as an innovative novelist, Sterne was for most of his life a provincial clergyman who made a career in the Anglican Church, though without having much of a clerical vocation.

Sterne was from a prominent Yorkshire family, but was himself the son of a younger son, a circumstance that to a considerable degree shaped his life. Sterne's father made an only moderately successful career in the army, serving as ensign, and rising to the rank of lieutenant. He married a woman without fortune, and his salary was insufficient to keep his small family comfortably.

Laurence Sterne, the second of seven children, was born in Ireland, where his father was stationed. His youth included many changes of location as the family followed the father to his different postings. At age 10 he was sent to school in England, and stayed with an uncle. Thanks to the generosity of a cousin, Sterne was able to go to Cambridge in 1733. He graduated in 1737, and immediately began his career in the Church.

Sterne's career reflects the harsh social realities of his time, and particularly the importance of family connections, old-boy networks and **patronage** generally. He took holy orders on the advice of an uncle well placed in the Church in Yorkshire, not because he had any sort of religious calling, but because the uncle, who was also an active **Whig**, would be able through his influence to provide the young man with what the British so frankly called a "living." In 1738, largely through the good offices of his uncle, Sterne was named vicar of the parish of Sutton-in-the-Forest, just north of York. He soon, thanks to the same patronage network, received a number of sinecures, and then the vicarage of a parish adjoining Sutton, which he held conjointly. Sterne courted a well-off young woman whom he married in 1741, and though the marriage turned out to be far from happy, it further consolidated his economic position. His annual income soon reached the comfortable figure of 200 pounds. He also owned some land, which he farmed with little success, and was involved, as a landowner, in furthering enclosures in his neighborhood from which he benefited personally.

In 1760 a friend offered him the affluent living of Coxwold, which alone was worth 160 pounds a year. Sterne accepted the position, and was able to keep his other two vicarages, simply installing curates in them at something approaching a minimal wage. Though practices of this sort had helped bring about the Reformation more than 200 years earlier, they were still common in the Anglican Church during the 18th century.

Sterne was a highly successful ecclesiastical careerist, but he made a poor showing as a clergyman. He is said once to have set out to give a sermon, but when his dogs roused some game birds he went home for his gun and abandoned preaching for hunting. His frequent absences from his parishes and what was regarded as unseemly levity on his part did not endear him to his parishioners. Nor did the fact that he never took his clerical duties seriously. He was, moreover, an inveterate womanizer. Had he not taken to writing late in his career, Sterne would have been remembered, if at all, as a country clergyman who used the institution of the Church to sustain a standard of living that he could not have achieved outside of it, and who gave little in return. As things turned out, he is known as one of the most original and imaginative writers of the 18th century.

During 1759 Sterne wrote and published at his own expense the first two volumes of *Tristram Shandy*. These were an immediate success, and won their author a great reputation. Sterne went to London the following year to arrange for regular commercial publication and to sell a continuation of the work. Robert Dodsley, a leading London publisher who also worked with Dr. **Johnson** and Edmund **Burke**, paid him handsomely for his novel, and further agreed to publish some of his sermons. While in London Sterne's whimsical sense of humor and easy social manner won him many friends, and he thoroughly enjoyed his personal popularity and the active social round that it opened for him. He returned to Yorkshire, where he continued to enjoy his literary success, and to add to it by extending his novel. Bad health led to his making an extended trip to France from 1762 to 1764. He made another such trip to France and Italy in 1765 and

1766, and this was to provide the material for his other main published work, *A Sentimental Journey through France and Italy.* He died in 1768 at the age of 55, a short time after *A Sentimental Journey* was published.

Contemporaries were deeply divided about the merits of *Tristram Shandy.* The whimsy, some of the satire and the warm humanity of some of the characters, such as Uncle Toby, appealed to many, while the constant digressions and frequent lack of coherence, which were part of intentional innovation in literary form, and Sterne's tendency to hint at sexual or indecent subjects without explicitly describing them, offended others. Dr. Johnson thought that the book was odd, and that it would not last, and when a female acquaintance told him that she had been affected by it, responded, "that is, because, dearest, you're a dunce" (Boswell, *Life of Johnson,* pp. 696 and 1148). Sterne himself, referring to reviews of *Tristram* wrote, "The scribblers use me ill, but they have used my betters much worse" (letter to Bishop Warburton, 9 June 1760). Among Sterne's admirers was Denis **Diderot**, whose *Jacques le fataliste* shares many of the disconcerting features of Sterne's masterpiece.

SUPERSTITION. A belief held on the basis of assumptions that cannot be proven on either a rational or an empirical basis. Generally such beliefs exclude the directives or dogmas of the major revealed religions. Superstition is radically anti-scientific in that it is usually a projection of a fear or an attempt to propitiate or ward off some evil whose nature is not understood. Thus, for example, the practice common in early modern France of parish priests anathematizing insect hordes may be regarded as superstitious.

During the 18th century superstition was regarded as unsystematic, and typically the intellectual heritage of the dependent, the poor and the oppressed. It was only regarded as a positive evil if it resulted in harm. The ignorant masses could not be expected to rise to much more, and whether or not the working population as a whole could or should be educated, and if so to what degree, was debated among the men and women of the enlightened community. Superstition was related to the more active and harmful phenomenon of **fanaticism**. *See also* **Prejudice**.

SYSTEM, SPIRIT OF. The great philosophers of the 17th century, such as René **Descartes**, Thomas Hobbes and Benedict **Spinoza**, were system builders. That is to say that they based their philosophies on what they regarded as unassailable truths or principles, then proceeded on these foundations to elaborate their philosophies. The validity of any proposition was then judged on the basis of its compatibility with the system as a whole. Typically, such systems worked by deduction, or moving from a known or certain principle to specific logical consequences thereof. The most comprehensive systematic philosophy of the early modern period was **scholasticism**, which still predominated in European **universities** during the 17th century and into the 18th century.

For the *philosophes*, system building was the wrong way to do science or philosophy. The thinkers of the Enlightenment rejected this approach for two main reasons. First, they denied that basic principles or truths could either be posited or arrived at by logic alone. Secondly, the thinkers of the Enlightenment believed that the appropriate method for both science and philosophy was inductive, and that both areas of endeavor were limited in terms of what they could achieve. As **empiricists** they held that true knowledge could be arrived at only by ascertaining facts, and then proceeding as far as the facts, supplemented by calculation, would allow.

The thinkers of the Enlightenment were uniformly hostile to what they termed the "spirit of system," whether in scholasticism or **Cartesianism**. The primary reason for this was that system building and deduction were compatible with the production of castles of words that had no necessary relation to reality, and that the systems so produced could not be definitively proved or disproved in their own terms, for a nonsensical or counterfactual proposition could well be compatible with a nonsensical system. The reality check of logical compatibility favored by the system builders was rejected by the thinkers of the Enlightenment in favor of a reality check based on fact.

The universal condemnation of system building, hypothesis and deduction by Enlightenment thinkers is not simply a matter of theoretical preference. Sciences of words unrelated to things no doubt perpetuated ignorance and illusion, but beyond this they encouraged the formation of dogmas and appeals to authority and imposed positively harmful ideas and values on society.

While the thinkers of the Enlightenment condemned the "spirit of system" they themselves advocated what they termed a "systematic spirit," by which they meant working methodically and according to plan. In their case, however, the method in question was inductive.

T

TAXATION POPULAIRE. A traditional mechanism by which working people collectively responded to sharp rises in grain prices. It involved a crowd, usually including significant numbers of **women**, descending on the marketplace and forcibly setting the price of grain and bread at affordable levels. These prices were then paid by the crowd, and the merchants were forced to accept the price imposed. Pillaging rarely occurred in this process, largely because it reflected the values of settled members of the community who themselves owned some **property**, and so respected this right for others, even when they insisted that it be mitigated by the criteria of fairness and need.

The authorities often accepted the legitimacy of the notions of affordable prices and limited property rights on which popular price fixing depended, and regulated prices accordingly. *Taxation populaire* normally occurred only when the authorities failed to assure adequate supplies of grain and bread at affordable prices. This phenomenon was common throughout western Europe, and the assumptions upon which it was based have been explained in the English context by E. P. Thompson in his now classic article, "The Moral Economy of the Crowd in the Eighteenth Century."

TENCIN, Claudine Alexandrine Guerin, Marquise de (1681-1749).

An intelligent, capable and uninhibited society woman who is remembered for her **salon**, her colorful private life, her competence in informal politics and her published work.

Mme Tencin, who never married, was born to a family of the **nobility** of the robe in Grenoble. Like many aristocratic women, she was intended by her family for the Church. She took vows, but found life in a convent contrary to her inclinations, and was successful in being freed from her obligations toward the Church.

On returning to the world Mme de Tencin went to Paris where she found the new atmosphere of liberty and levity of the **Regency** to her taste. She took a long series of lovers, including the Regent, Bernard le Bovier de **Fontenelle**, and the Chevalier Destouches, by whom she conceived a child that she abandoned, and who became the celebrated mathematician and thinker, Jean Le Ronde d'**Alembert**. Highly competent in the informal politics of intrigue, Mme de Tencin made herself useful to the Court by providing **Louis XV** with mistresses, and it is alleged that she played a key role in obtaining a cardinal's hat for her brother. Though moving in the highest social circles, she was imprisoned in the Bastille for a short time on a charge of extortion levelled at her by a lover who took his own life.

Mme de Tencin began her salon in 1718. After the death of Mme **Lambert** in 1733 she continued the Tuesday meetings of her friend and turned them into what has been called the first salon with a European reputation. Among those who frequented it were Fontenelle, **Montesquieu**, the abbé **Saint Pierre**, the abbé **Prévost** and Pierre Carlet de **Marivaux**. With aristocratic haughtiness she sometimes referred to her salon as her "menagerie" and those who frequented it as "beasts." Nevertheless she took her responsibilities to her guests seriously enough to exert her considerable abilities in informal politics on their behalves when she wished to further their candidatures for the **Académie française**, which she did with marked success.

Mme de Tencin's main writings were, fittingly enough, fiction. Her novels include the Mémoires du Comte de Commiges (1735), Le Siège de Calais (1739) and Les Malheurs de l'amour (1747). The Anecedotes de la Cour et du règne d'Edouard II, roi d'Angleterre and two volumes of letters were published posthumously.

THEODICY. The problem of evil. The term is derived from the Greek words "theos" deity, and "diké," justice, and so refers to the moral and theological conundrum of the existence of evil in a world created by a **beneficent** Deity. In the Hebrew Scriptures, the book of *Job* addresses this issue. In both the Jewish and Christian traditions the contradiction of the wicked prospering and the righteous suffering in this life is resolved by projecting the ultimate accounting to an afterlife, in which each is judged, and each is rewarded or punished according to his or her actions. For the **deists** of the 18th century, who did not believe in an afterlife, this solution was not available. The problem of evil, however, continued to trouble many of the thinkers of the Enlightenment.

Voltaire, for example, accepted the existence of an irreducible amount of evil in the world that human prudence could mitigate, but never eliminate. *Candide* is in part a savage satire on those who, like Gottfried Wilhelm **Leibniz,** maintained that the overall good of the world required so many particular ills. In that work he returned to the catastrophe of the Lisbon earthquake, which killed thousands and destroyed large parts of the city. An earlier poem on this earthquake shows Voltaire questioning providence. Jean-Jacques **Rousseau** wrote Voltaire a long letter criticizing this position, and asserting his belief in providence. If men had continued to live dispersed in the countryside, Rousseau observed, they would have been less vulnerable to the damage of earthquakes, which are, after all, an act of **nature**. And, we might add, when built to appropriate specifications, cities themselves are much safer.

The problem of theodicy also occupied materialistic thinkers such as Claude Adrien **Helvétius** and the Baron d'**Holbach**. In their view nature was as all-powerful and beneficent as was the Deity in traditional theology, so for them the problem of providence remained relevant, though in a secularized form. Only when **human nature** came to be viewed as inherently aggressive and the world as the arena of an unending and inevitable struggle for existence of all living creatures, as happened following popularizations of the work of Thomas Malthus and Charles Darwin, did the notion of theodicy lose relevance, and evil, however defined, come to be seen as inevitable, and so no longer in need of explanation.

THOMAS, Antoine Léonard (1732-1785). Generally the personnel of the systems of **university** and secondary **education** in France contributed little to Enlightenment culture. Thomas is a striking exception to this rule. He began his career as a teacher in the *Collège* de Beauvais in Paris. When in 1759 the **Académie française** began a series of essay contests devoted to great men in French politics, Thomas entered and won. He also entered and won the next five contests. Such prowess in eloquence was rewarded with election to the Academy itself in 1766. From there his entry into the elite centers of Enlightenment culture was guaranteed. By attending the salon of **Mme Necker**, he came to work for her husband.

The rhetorical style of the 18th century, of which Thomas proved himself a master, is not much valued today, and his reputation has suffered accordingly. It has never been claimed that he was a great writer. However, he was among the first to suggest that the absolute monarchy might structure itself by means of a constitution, and his poem on the **people** and essay on **women** show interests in subjects that were only beginning to be treated.

THOMASIUS, Christian (1655-1728). A key figure in the early stages of the Enlightenment in Germany. Thomasius was born in Leipzig, where his father was a jurist and **university** instructor. He studied at the University of Leipzig, but took his law degree at Frankfurt an der Oder in 1679. Upon graduation Thomasius returned to

Leipzig where he taught, practiced law and founded the *Monatsgespräche*, one of the first German **periodicals** written in the vernacular. His fiery disposition and a tendency to become involved in controversy made it prudent for Thomasius to leave Leipzig.

In 1690 Thomasius moved to Halle in Brandenburg, where four years later he had a hand in the founding of the University of Halle, of which he became president in 1710. Thomasius's career, like that of Christian **Wolff**, who also taught at the same institution, was thus closely bound up with a newly founded Protestant university. This was a situation similar to that in Scotland, where the universities were centers for the working out and dissemination of Enlightenment culture, but different from that in Catholic France and Anglican England, where these institutions, completely dominated by the professional faculties, engaged in little more than professional training, or providing the social elites with a rite of passage.

Thomasius's career reflects the intellectual concerns of his time, which is to say of the early Enlightenment. His Latin treatises were directed to the late humanists and reformed theologians who still thought and wrote primarily in that language. But in his German works, including his journalism, he reached out to a broader public, much as his contemporary, Pierre **Bayle**, did in his works of popularization. Addressing this broader public on social issues and questions at the margins of contemporary religion, such as witchcraft and penal practice, certainly indicates a direction that would be taken up by the thinkers and publicists of the High Enlightenment. It should be noted, however, that many of his Latin works were translated into German, an indication that the broader public for which he wrote was serious and well educated.

In his philosophy Thomasius continued the project, begun by Samuel Pufendorf, of separating natural **law** from theology. However, this was not simply an aspect of a program of **secularization** in which he was engaged. Thomasius regarded natural law as dependent on the divine will, but he thought the realm of knowledge to which this law gave access could be reached by **reason** without need of revelation. This was not to deny the need for revelation in other areas of life. Thomasius remained a Lutheran, and if he diverged from strict orthodoxy, it was in the direction of spiritualism and mysticism, a tendency that he shared with his near contemporary, Lord **Shaftesbury**. Like Shaftesbury, too, he based his ethics on love rather than duty, and made of **humanity** a key value.

Thomasius's main works include *Institutions of Divine Jurisprudence* (1688; Latin), *Introduction to the Theory of Reason* (1691; German), *Introduction to Moral Philosophy* (1692; German), and *Foundations of the Law of Nature and of Nations, deduced from Common Sense* (1705; Latin).

TOLERATION. One of the key values of the Enlightenment that calls for the acceptance of ideas, beliefs, and customs different from one's own. The implications of toleration are pluralism within a society and peace among societies. In practice, toleration has always been a part of social relations, for there have always been actions and ideas that fell between things defined as crimes and things defined as virtues, and such things were generally tolerated with different degrees of approbation or disapproval. Before the Enlightenment toleration was generally held as a least harmful, or only practical alternative, and seldom, if ever, as a positive value in its own right. There are a number of reasons for the validation of toleration in the 18th century.

First, the **epistemology** based on sense psychology as worked out by John **Locke** disposed Enlightenment thinkers to accept a far greater degree of uncertainty in considering what things could be known and what could not than was the case with either theologians or systematic philosophers. This tendency was reinforced by the **empiricism** of the movement that not only limited the sphere of the knowable, but also validated the material world above abstraction.

Secondly, by the 18th century more people were tired of theological conflict and saw less justification for engaging in war and violence for the sake of dogma. Revulsion against religiously-motivated violence, whether a massive outbreak such as the Saint Bartholomew's Day massacre, or the quasi-legalistic, individualized, ritualized brutality of the Inquisition, was typical of the thinkers of the Enlightenment. There was a tendency to see theological issues as matters of opinion rather than as questions of absolute truth on which the destinies of peoples depended for all eternity. Convinced of the wrongness and futility of coercing opinion, heartily sick of the human consequences of religious conflicts, and aspiring primarily to a more secure and comfortable worldly existence, the *philosophes* and their followers counseled allowing those who held views that differed from their own to live quietly, and claimed the same right for themselves.

A third important aspect of the rise of the value of toleration in the 18th century concerns a shift in the formal status of religion within society. Through the 17th century, religion was considered a matter of public policy, and deviation from the dogma of the dominant religion was treated as a crime subject to a whole range of punishments, including death. One of the issues on which virtually all thinkers of the Enlightenment agreed was the need to decriminalize religion by shifting it from the public to the private sphere and by taking religious convictions as matters of opinion rather than verifiable, absolute truths. **Montesquieu** explicitly argued against the appropriateness of subjecting matters of religious belief to criminal procedures (*Spirit of the Laws*, Bk. XII, chaps. 4-10 and Bk. XXVI, chaps. 2 and 8-11), and he was followed in this by Cesare **Beccaria** in his classic *On Crimes and Punishments* (chap. 11; Paolucci, p. 29). Nor is it a coincidence that **Voltaire's** *Treatise on Toleration* (1764) was begun as a polemic against an instance of religious persecution. Against the positions of virtually all established Churches, the thinkers of the Enlightenment argued that questions of religion belonged to the private rather than the public sphere, and so were a matter of individual conscience properly beyond the reach of the civil magistrate.

TORY. One of the two main parliamentary parties of 18th-century Britain. According to the *Oxford English Dictionary* the term was first used to designate Irish bandits, and during the exclusion crisis was applied by the opponents of James II to the supporters of the House of Stuart. The Tories were generally identified with support of the Court and Church against the aristocratic **constitutionalism** of the **Whigs**. During the 19th century the term "conservative" came to replace "Tory," though down to the present the Conservative Party in Britain is sometimes referred to as "Tory."

Apart from a brief period between 1710 and 1714, the Tories found themselves in opposition during the earlier part of the 18th century. In British politics of the time the great majority of the population was without representation of any sort, so while the Whigs represented the interests of the great landed magnates together with the commercial interests of the capital, the Tories were seen as spokesmen of the smaller rural gentry, or the "country." Until the Hanoverian dynasty came to be accepted beyond question, roughly at the time of the accession of George III in 1760, the Tories remained sympathetic to the Stuarts. Throughout the century they adhered strictly to the Church of England. After 1760 the distinction between Whigs and Tories became blurred. The ministries of William Pitt the Younger from 1783 to the early 19th century are considered broadly Tory. Tory policy remained consistent in opposing liberalization of religious policy and reform of **Parliament**.

Many of the outstanding figures of British literature in the 18th century are identified with the Tories. These include John Dryden, Jonathan Swift, Alexander **Pope**, Viscount **Bolingbroke** and Dr. **Johnson**. Something of the fluidity in the distinction between Tories and Whigs by the late 18th century is reflected in the fact that the founder of modern conservatism, Edmund **Burke**, was throughout his life an active and convinced Whig politician and theoretician.

TRAGEDY. In its development from the 17th to the 18th century, French tragedy was influenced by popular theories of sensibility. It is generally qualified as "neoclassical." In fact, the real neoclassical tragedy (i.e. a direct imitation of the classical, which is to say of the antique) appeared only in the last 20 years of the century. It cannot be better illustrated than by the neo-Greek style of André Chénier in literature and of Jacques-Louis **David** in painting. The best example of its kind was achieved by Louis-Jean "Népomucène" Lemercier in his *Agamemnon*.

In treating neoclassical tragedy, it is important to realize that it was impossible for contemporaries to distance themselves from certain of the archetypes inherited from Corneille and Racine. Two authors of the 18th century epitomize this genre and its evolution: the elder Crébillon and **Voltaire**. Crébillon tried to move the hearts of the spectators while confronting them with agonizing situations and horrible crimes. Voltaire, for his part, wrote 28 tragedies, not counting librettos of tragedies for the opera. He saw himself as the successor of Corneille and Racine, but tried to renew tragic emotion while giving an epic dimension to his characters. Influenced by the English, and in some respects following **Shakespeare**, for whom he had mixed admiration and disdain, he made impressive use of local color, a new element in French dramaturgy, and showed an insistent preoccupation with realism. For example, he dared, despite the rule concerning decorum, to have the body of Caesar, covered with a bloody sheet, brought on stage.

The tragedy of the 18th century further innovated by treating philosophical themes and topics and put on stage characters belonging to French history or from exotic locations, thus refusing to limit inspiration to mythology or ancient history. Some characters, who take pleasure in moral or political professions of faith, express the opinions of Voltaire, such as the heroes of *Brutus* (1730) and *Du Guesclin* (1734).

Also remarkable in the period are the numerous theoretical writings about tragedy like those of Jean-François **Marmontel,** Louis Sébastien **Mercier,** Antoine Houdar de la Motte and others. The latter, advocate of tragedy in prose, even recommended the rejection of the classical unities. One can also note in this context the works of the authors meditating on their art in treatises and prefaces.

Isabelle Martin

TREATISE OF THE THREE IMPOSTORS/TRAITÉ DES TROIS IMPOSTEURS. This is one of the earliest and most corrosive of the **clandestine** tracts, written very close to 1709. There have been several guesses regarding its author, the best being Silvia Berti's that he was a Dutch diplomat, Jan Vroese (1672-1725). Other candidates are Jean Maximilien Lucas (died in 1697), because it is a traditional attribution and because several of its stylistic traits are shared with *La Vie de Spinosa* (between 1678 and 1688), which is also traditionally attributed to him, and Peter Friedrich Arpe (1652-1740). It was first published in 1719, together with a biography of **Spinoza,** under the title, *La vie et l'esprit de Mr Benoît de Spinosa,* with six intercalated chapters drawn from Pierre Charron's *Les livres de la Sagesse* (1601), and reissued several times later in the century without those intercalations. In 1768, when he apparently first encountered it, **Voltaire** considered it to be a scandalous and vulgar tract! A critical edition by Françoise Charles-Daubert has appeared in the series "Libre pensée literature clandestine" directed by Antony McKenna.

Any traditional religion, traditional in the literal sense of having been handed down from generation to generation, is hostage to the good faith of its founders, who are supposed to have received a revelation of God's will (religious law) or information about his nature (theology). Since very early times (Deut. xiii.2-6; I Cor. xii.1-3; Koran xxi.3-10), the danger of imposture was recognized, and, since the Renaissance, the possibility that the three monotheistic religions were the results of impostures by Moses, by Jesus and finally by Mohammed was, in Ernest Renan's phrase, the "nightmare" of the religious philosophers. Christian polemics had long treated Islam as an imposture; the recent "imposture" of Shabbetai Zvi (1666) was still all too evident and scandalous to **Jew** and Christian alike, though for different reasons, so it took much daring but little imagination to actually write a three-impostor treatise. In fact at least two have survived, a

Latin treatise dated 1598 on the title page but actually composed around 1680 and published in 1753, and the French treatise under discussion here.

Recent scholarship has shown that the *Trois imposteurs* borrowed freely from Spinoza's *Ethics*—the author was remarkably receptive to its pantheism—from his *Tractatus theologico-politicus*, from Hobbes, and more fragmentary borrowing from Pierre **Bayle**'s *Dictionnaire historique et critique* (1698) and Bernard Le Bouvier de **Fontenelle**'s *Histoire des oracles* (1687). The sixth and last chapter, on the soul, is taken from Guillaume Lamy's *Discours anatomiques* (1675), and there are extensive borrowings from Giulio-Cesare Vanini's *De admirandis* (1616) and from François La Mothe Le Vayer's *La vertu des payens* (1642). La Mothe Le Vayer was one of the "libertins érudits", as was Charron, whose work provided the late but well-adapted intercalations added in the 1719 edition, so the tract can be seen as a product of Padovan "naturalism" as it was received in 17th-century France. It can be claimed that the thesis that Moses was an impostor, a position sometimes identified with Vanini, is necessarily a part of any three-impostor argument, and that the resemblances with Vanini's *De admirandis* are coincidental and possibly even drawn from a very late refutation by Johann Moritz Schramm, *De vita et scriptis famosi athei Julii Cæsaris Vanini* (Custrine, 1709). This is not absolutely inconsistent with the earliest dated manuscript (1709).

There are several interesting aspects of the treatise, aside from the light it casts on the sources of early 18th-century iconoclasm. One is its thesis that the Pentateuch was written by several authors, each defending his own interest or that of his caste, which was a new and useful slant on the documentary analysis of the Bible which had already been launched by Richard Simon (1678) and Jean Leclerc (1685), and that the documents that were the least inconsistent with rabbinic theology were edited together and then canonized. Another is that demonology is still alive for this author, who copies passages about demons from Hobbes. He is indeed a vigorous, vehement and daring iconoclast, even a nihilist, denying the traditional moral hierarchies, but the world of natural science lies outside his philosophical and literary culture, which still contains many archaisms.

Actually, though in a strange way, this is a very religious tract, one that expresses a nature-mysticism that transcends the laws, norms and values of Christian Europe, rather than being the vulgar application of reductive atheism that Voltaire and most subsequent critics have taken it to be. Many manuscript copies of this tract, possibly as many as 200, have been preserved, so it clearly had wide diffusion.

Bertram Eugene Schwarzbach

TURGOT, Anne-Robert-Jacques, baron de l'Aune (1727-1781). An important Enlightenment thinker who held a number of high posts in the royal administration. Turgot came from an established family of the robe **nobility**. Initially intended for the Church, he studied theology extensively, but then abandoned this subject in his mid-twenties. He then began his career according to family tradition as a counsellor in the *Parlement* of Paris. After acquiring the office of Master of Requests, which was a prerequisite for more responsible positions in the royal administration, he was appointed Intendant of Limousin in 1761. From August of 1774 to May 1776 he held the post of minister of finance. During his tenure of these positions he strove to give practical expression to his enlightened and physiocratic ideas (*see* **Physiocracy**).

As Intendant of Limousin Turgot sought to advance agriculture by serving as president of the local agricultural society, by founding a veterinary school and by significantly modifying the *corvée*, an obligation on peasants to maintain royal roads passing through their parishes without pay. His solution to this last problem was to levy a tax for road maintenance on all members of the community, and from the funds so raised to pay for materials and for the labor of those who did the work. In his brief but active tenure as finance minister, Turgot generalized his reform of the *corvée* throughout France and deregulated important areas of the economy, among them **guild** organization and the grain trade (*see* **Flour War**).

Turgot contributed a number of articles to the *Encyclopédie*, wrote an early defense of **toleration** (1753-1754), and in his *Réflexions sur la formation et distribution des richesses* (1758) argued for increased economic freedom. The *Mémoire sur les municipalités*, which was written for Turgot by Dupont de Nemours and presented to **Louis XVI**, advocated replacing status with wealth as the basis for local government. Though Turgot's collected works make up five large volumes, much of it went unpublished during his lifetime. He was, however, closely connected to most leading *philosophes*. The significance of his career is to be found in part in his reformist and progressive ideas, but more particularly in his having achieved high office and having attempted to implement these ideas.

U

UNIVERSALISM. The view that basic tendencies, phenomena and processes remain constant wherever they are found, and interact with other forces in a regular and predictable way.

With respect to natural phenomena, verified regularities are termed **laws**. During the 18th century the laws of Newtonian physics were believed to be valid throughout time and space. With the emergence of quantum physics and relativity theory, the overall validity of Newtonian physics was seen to be inadequate. However, the assumption of the uniform and regular behavior of different forms of matter and energy in given conditions was retained.

Thinkers of the Enlightenment, seeking to develop sciences of man and of society, for the most part on the model of physics, tended to assume fundamental similarities in the make-up of human beings, and basic regularities in their motivation and behavior. Most enlightened thinkers posited a uniform **human nature** based in biology and recognized the primacy of **self-interest**. John **Locke**, for example, argued that all human beings are born in the same basic state, and develop in accordance with the sense impressions they receive and the associations that accompany them. For Locke, pain and pleasure were physiological givens to which humans reacted in predictable ways, avoiding the former, maximizing the latter and calculating courses of action accordingly.

Voltaire accepted these assumptions and argued from them that human nature was everywhere the same. In his *Second Discourse*, Jean-Jacques **Rousseau** imagined a primal humanoid in whom self-preservation and pity (understood in Lockean terms as an involuntary physiological reflex to a discomfort perceived in another that the viewer had experienced) were the only instincts natural to human beings. However these inclinations were articulated in the course of the development of societies, and however submerged they might become, they nonetheless remained the constants of human nature in all times and in all places.

For **deists**, such as Voltaire and Rousseau, the existence of a Creator or Supreme Being was also a given, or a fact subtending **nature**. Arguing sometimes from first principles, and sometimes from the ethnography available to them that showed that there were no known societies without some concept of the divine, deists maintained that religion was also universal.

The universalism of the Enlightenment has sometimes been seen as an abstraction that was used to undermine the legitimacy of certain particular societies. There is some validity to this claim. Certainly Rousseau and others viewed societies that subjected the great majority of their members to unnecessary or extreme discomforts, deadened their moral sense or deprived them of attainable levels of freedom as less legitimate than those that met core human needs more adequately.

By basing their views of universal human nature in the first instance on biology and physiology, the thinkers of the Enlightenment grounded it in physical reality. This is a modest, if practical way, of asserting the common humanity of the whole species. Moreover, this universalism, which was grounded in nature, and to a lesser degree in deist theology, did not exclude recognition of the uniqueness and **particularism** of different social and political constructs that were the consequences of culture.

UNIVERSITIES. In the 18th century universities were institutions for professional training, and apart from the preparatory Faculty of Arts, which in effect consisted in the colleges attached to the University, they had only three faculties. These were the Faculties of Theology, **Law** and Medicine. The great medieval universities of England, France and Italy that led the intellectual life of their time were by the 18th century stagnating in tradition, dogma and the requirements of professional training. Accounts by contemporaries such as Edward **Gibbon** or Adam **Smith** of their experiences at the colleges of Oxford are uniformly and justifiably harsh. The universities of France and England contributed little or nothing to the Enlightenment, and it is largely to their intellectual nullity that the **clubs** and **academies** in these countries owe their prominence.

In Scotland, Holland and Germany, however, universities, especially the more recently founded ones, did play a significant role in intellectual life. In Germany university professors such as Christian **Thomasius** at Leipzig and Halle, Christian **Wolff** at Halle and Marburg and Immanuel **Kant** at Königsberg played, together with princely courts, a central role in the Enlightenment. Scotland, however, is where personnel of the universities made the greatest contribution to Enlightenment thought and culture. Francis **Hutcheson**, Adam **Smith** and John **Millar** at Glasgow, William **Robertson**, Adam **Ferguson** and Hugh Blair at Edinburgh and Thomas **Reid** at Aberdeen and then Glasgow, combined university teaching and original research in a way that has rarely if ever been equaled. David **Hume** applied for a teaching position in the University of Edinburgh, but was not deemed worthy of it, and contented himself for a time with the position of librarian to the advocates of the city. Like Giambattista **Vico** at the University of Naples, most of these men taught in the preparatory Faculty of Arts and not the professional faculties.

UTILITARIANISM. An ethical doctrine that makes **happiness**, understood as the maximization of pleasure and minimization of pain, the criterion of good. The calculation of net pleasure or pain in this system is known as "felicific calculus." The doctrine of utilitarianism is commonly summarized as "the greatest good of the greatest number." This phrase is often associated with the Englishman, Jeremy **Bentham**, the most constant exponent of utilitarianism, but it is also found in Claude Adrien **Helvétius**, and was first used by Francis **Hutcheson**. It accurately reflects the main ethical current of the Enlightenment. Indeed, the groundwork for the doctrine was laid by John **Locke** when, in his *Essay Concerning Human Understanding* (Bk. II, chaps. 20 and 27), he defined pleasure as good and pain as bad, thus pointing toward a physiologically based ethic.

Utilitarianism has been subjected to a range of criticisms. There is the basic problem of definition, and the fact that undergoing the same experience may result in pleasure for some but pain for others, as would be sufficiently clear if the audiences of classical and acid rock concerts were to be transposed. There is also the argument, made by John Rawls and others, that certain things that are beneficial to society as a whole may be unjust to individuals. And there is, too, a sense that life is too complicated and too elevated an affair adequately to be accounted for in terms of mere pleasure and pain. Perhaps the most elegant refutation of utilitarianism is John Stuart Mill's *Autobiography*, which demonstrates, at least in his case, the inadequacy of utilitarianism for the imaginative and emotive aspects of life. And yet, certainly in the historical moment of the Enlightenment, utilitarianism has a good deal to be said for it.

One of the great advantages of utilitarianism is the modesty of its objectives. To reduce the quantum of pain (disease, hunger, abuse, persecution and the like) in a society, and to increase the level of material well-being is a limited and down-to-earth objective. Yet until such goals are articulated, the project cannot begin to be implemented. Moreover, the significance of this project can only be grasped in its historical context. The transcendental ethical systems that preceded and followed the Enlightenment allowed for torture and capital punishment on theological and metaphysical grounds. Utilitarianism is the dialectical negation of such systems and the assertion of the primacy of the well-being of the individual over values such as theology and **nationalism**.

There is, further, a consistent balance between the individual and the collective in utilitarianism that is lacking in some other ethical systems. Defining human beings in basically material and physiological terms, utilitarianism is egalitarian. Until special conditions, such as illness or incapacity, are introduced, it is presumed that none have a right to special treatment. Utilitarianism supports a strong form of **individualism**, which allows a person to define pleasures and pains for himself or herself. Thus, in a system based on utilitarian ethics, no one would be obliged to listen to music that the authorities favored, but that they themselves did not appreciate.

The limit of the individual's rights, however, stop, in typically liberal fashion, at the point at which significant discomfort to others begins. Utilitarianism thus provides the basis for a limited individualism and a restricted notion of the state. What it does not provide is a set of positive values by which the individual is expected to live. Coming between theologically justified persecution characteristic of the period preceding the Enlightenment, and often equally fanatical nationalism that began with the Napoleonic wars, utilitarianism marks a moment when men and women were thought to be broadly rational, concerned (at least to some degree) with the rights and needs of others and self-sufficient.

UTOPIA. A genre of social criticism that compares, implicitly or explicitly, an imaginary set of social and political relations with existing ones, usually to the detriment of, and with the intent of modifying, the latter. The term is derived from the Greek "ou," meaning not, and "topos," meaning place, as in Thomas More's *Utopia* of 1516, a place without geographical specificity or reality, and so designates an ideal or alternate polity.

If the basic function of **absolutist** and conservative political ideology is to demonstrate the validity of existing arrangements and accepted principles, thus precluding an appeal to other criteria of social or political organization and seeking to maintain a uni-dimensional ideological space, then the basic function of utopian literature is to open the minds of its readers to alternate social and political values and arrangements. As the utopia is, by definition, a fantasy without objective existence, its purpose is to appeal to that which does not exist as a means for changing things that do. The act of imagining sets of social and political values and institutions that avoid the worst forms of injustice and exploitation current in a given society is a way of creating conceptual space for change. To the degree that the utopian model appeals to contemporaries, a tension is created between the imaginary and the real, and a demand for change is generated. Utopian literature is inherently critical and reformist.

Unlike the Renaissance, the Enlightenment cannot be said to have produced any great utopias. Yet the utopian impulse was central to a movement oriented toward practical and progressive change, and the taste for kinds of literature that explored alternate forms of social and political organization was strong. It was this proclivity that provided a ready readership for travel literature and practical reform projects as well as for properly utopian works. That the government did not look kindly upon this genre is evident from the fact that Louis Sebastien **Mercier**'s *L'An 2440*, a utopia removed in time rather than geographical distance from the contemporary world, could not be published and distributed legally in France. That the book had great appeal to the public is clear from the fact that it was, according to the findings of Robert **Darnton**, the number one clandestine best seller of the **Old Regime**.

Perhaps utopias played a smaller role in the Enlightenment than one might have expected because by the 18th century authors who chose to address social and political issues, or to advocate specific reforms, could do so more openly than they had formerly. In any case, there is no shortage of examples of this literature in this period. Fénelon's *Telemachus* (1699) continued to be read during the Enlightenment, while Daniel **Defoe**'s *Robinson Crusoe* (1719), Jonathan Swift's *Gulliver's Travels* (1726), the *Basiliade* (1553) of the abbé **Morelly,** the portrayal of Eldorado in **Voltaire**'s **Candide** (1758), **Restif de la Bretonne**'s *La Découverte australe* (1777) and Denis **Diderot**'s posthumous *Supplément au voyage de Bougainville* are only a few of the works that show that the genre developed, diversified and retained its appeal during the Enlightenment.

V

VAUDEVILLE. The term "vaudeville" is ancient but its meaning evolved appreciably between the time when it described a genre marked by music. Today it is more related to light comedy, and associated with street theater.

A "vaudeville" is a song on which original tunes, known to all, provide the melody for new words. The name of the original song, or the first verse of the chorus written above the new song, designated the air, and is called the tone (*timbre*). The air itself is the hum (*fredon*). In the 18th century the word had a more precise meaning and designated a popular song, particularly Parisian. The vaudeville was used indifferently by tightrope walkers, puppet manipulators or sellers of ointments, and generally accompanied their sketches. The successful ones were sold on printed sheets, illustrated with engravings.

From the end of the 18th century, through the **fairground theaters**, the vaudeville was introduced into plays and so contracted with the new genre of this theater a promising union. Tunes known to all, of which only the words were modified, were inserted in theatrical plots. To be precise, at this time, the dramatic vaudeville was indifferently called vaudeville comedy or later, opéra-comique. With Alain-René Lesage, Louis Fuselier and Dorneval at the beginning of the 18th century appears this first "manner" of the opéra-comique. Later, under the influence of Charles Simon Favart, the genre of the opéra-comique took another form around 1750. It became more delicate, more sensitive and more precious, a worthy ancestor of the operetta. In 1753, for the first time, the composer and the librettist were brought together to take care of the theatrical and purely musical effect of the airs. The plays then included exclusively ariettas, musical scores specially written for the stage, often borrowed from existing opéras-comiques, and not from popular tunes. It was the beginning of the comedy "à ariettes." The arietta (new air) later superseded the vaudeville.

The opéra-comique was thus distinctly differentiated from the "comédie à vaudevilles", that would, nevertheless, make a comeback after a brief eclipse, during the **French Revolution**, with the creation of the Vaudeville Theater (1792). The term then designated a new theatrical comic genre that, thanks to inventive authors, created original types and met with an extraordinary success that continued on into the Empire and Restoration.

Isabelle Martin

VICO, Giambattista (1668-1744). The son of a bookseller of Naples, Vico became a professor in the faculty of arts of the **university** of his native city, a position more like that of a high school teacher than that of a modern university professor, and considerably less well paid. Though he lived in quiet respectability, he also produced some of the most original writing on society and history of the 18th century.

During the late 17th and early 18th centuries Italy was more influenced by the Catholic Church than many other parts of Europe. In his studies Vico was trained in **scholasticism** and the classics, and with his father's encouragement studied **law**. Despite his striking originality, however, his language and mentality remained in many ways those of Renaissance humanism. Probably the greatest disappointment of his professional life was his failure in 1723 to win a lucrative chair in law at the university in which he taught rhetoric.

Vico worked for a time as a tutor in a noble household, and then, in 1699, was appointed professor of rhetoric in the University of Naples. He led an interesting if arduous professional life teaching at the university, writing occasional poetry on request for the local **nobility** and belonging to a number of **clubs** and learned societies that no doubt offered more stimulation than he received from his regular teaching duties.

Vico published a youthful poem in 1693, a philological and historical treatise in Latin entitled *On the Ancient Wisdom of the Italians* in 1710, a biography in Latin of a 17th-century Neapolitan noble and politician in 1716, and another Latin treatise, *Universal Law,* stimulated in part by his reading of Grotius, between 1720 and 1722. In 1725 he published the first edition of *The New Science*, the work for which he is remembered. It was his only major work to be written in Italian.

In *The New Science* Vico sought to show how natural law applied to social phenomena. The result is a work that, far from asserting a simple notion of historical uniformity, seeks to demonstrate the existence of fundamentally different forms of culture and of mentalities that are nevertheless logically and progressively connected to each other. Vico saw mankind moving from a quasi-animal stage of being, in many ways similar to that described by Jean-Jacques **Rousseau** in the *Second Discourse*, to mentalities that he characterizes as theological, heroic and human. Each phase had its linguistic and imaginative specificity that made it seem strange to other phases of development, but which was nevertheless intelligible. Vico produced expanded editions of *The New Science* in 1730 and 1744, but the work, its originality and profundity notwithstanding, and despite certain similarities to the *Spirit of the Laws* of Charles-Louis Secondat de

Montesquieu, remained largely unappreciated in the 18th century, and did not gain wide recognition until the 19th century.

VIRTUE. In its original Latin formulation, virtue denoted manliness, from the Latin *vir,* which means man. The term derived immediately from the political context of the classical city-state, in which the virtue of the citizen was paramount, consisting in his ability and willingness to serve the state on the field of battle and to participate actively in the making and administration of policy. The virtue of the citizen in the **republican** tradition was bound up with both the freedom of the state from domination by outside forces, and with the freedom of the citizen within the framework of the state. Civic freedom was usually deemed to be assured by **constitutionalism** and the rule of **law**.

By shifting the focus of human activity from living responsibly and well within a demanding political framework to achieving personal salvation, Christianity deprived the idea of virtue of its classical significance. Further, for theologians such as Augustine, who emphasized the radical corruption of **human nature**, it did not make sense for creatures as flawed as human beings to think in terms of virtues to which they could not properly aspire. At the same time, once dogma and ritual had begun to be formulated, adherence to the currently accepted versions of these things came loosely to be referred to as virtues.

One of the ways the Enlightenment worked to effect the **secularization** of society was to restore to virtue its political and social significance, and to adapt the notion to contemporary circumstances. The original republican notion of virtue retained its ideological appeal, but it was seen as largely irrelevant to contemporary European political practice. **Montesquieu**, for example, made virtue the principle of what he defined as republican government, but relegated it to the distant and irretrievable classical past (*Spirit of the Laws*, Bk. II, chap. 2, Bk. III, chap. 3 and Bk. V, chaps. 2-3). By the 18th century the real business of politics was carried out by monarchs and their agents, and in that context the values and workings of the traditional city-state did not have much to contribute.

In some cases, enlightened thinkers sought to apply the notion of virtue to the civil society of their time. This required applying the ideals of personal integrity and **liberty** of the classical tradition to conditions of the 18th century, a development that opened the way for the feminization of virtue. It is not easy to identify a hero in Montesquieu's *Persian Letters*, but if there is one it is likely Roxane, Usbek's favorite wife, who has the integrity to deny her status as an object of the will of another, the resourcefulness to circumvent the restrictions on her liberty by the regime of the seraglio and the courage to take her own life (as ancient Romans did) once her position had become untenable. The behavior of the heroine of *Julie, ou La Nouvelle Héloïse* is less defiant, but hardly less dramatic or less heroic.

To a degree, then, the Enlightenment mused nostalgically about republican virtue, but it also sought to modify and update it. However, there was also an important, and possibly dominant, trend of Enlightenment thought that sought to do without the notion altogether and to replace it with an alternate motive force.

The key feature of republican virtue is the devotion of the citizen to the common good embodied in the city-state. Having rehabilitated the notions of self and **self-interest**, the thinkers of the Enlightenment found subordinating one's own interests to the common good unnatural and problematic. Thinkers such as Bernard **Mandeville**, David **Hume**, Adam **Smith**, **Voltaire** and the **physiocrats** argued that the pursuit of enlightened self-interest in a context of minimal restraints was the best way of maximizing social well-being. This myth, which depends in large part on the transposition of a natural order and harmony from Isaac **Newton**'s concept of **nature** to the spheres of politics, society and economics, is one of the most lasting influences of the Enlightenment.

Among Enlightenment thinkers it was Jean-Jacques **Rousseau** who insisted most forcefully and eloquently that the common good could only be achieved by direct and intentional efforts of the citizens. In modern liberal democracies the very notion of a common good has been eroded, and advocates of the magical transformation of self-interest into the public good have almost complete control of public discourse.

VOLLAND, Louise-Henriette (1716-1784). Born to a well-off family engaged in tax collection and finance with a town house in Paris as well as a country residence, Louise-Henriette Volland, better known as Sophie, played an indirect, but still significant, role in the Enlightenment. She was the love of Denis **Diderot**'s life, and it is thanks to her (and her mother, who sought to keep her away from the married and disreputable philosopher) that we have one of the most intimate portraits of Diderot and his friends in long series of letters he wrote her.

Diderot and Sophie met in 1755 or 1756. Sophie (the name apparently was bestowed by Diderot) was a bright, intelligent, spirited woman to whom Diderot was drawn intellectually as well as emotionally. It is highly probable, but not certain, that they were lovers. Be that as it may, their friendship outlived any other passion, as Diderot was known to have taken another mistress in 1768, while still close to Sophie. Certainly they were unquestionably drawn to each other intellectually and emotionally. Diderot wrote her over 550 letters, of which 187 are extant. The first of these dates from the summer of 1759. Sophie apparently destroyed the letters of the first years of their friendship, as well as many others, likely because they contained passages more personal than she would have wanted to come into the public domain. None of her letters to Diderot exist. Nor is there a portrait of her. Diderot refers to her wearing glasses, but does not say much more about her appearance in the extant letters.

There is always an interest in great love stories. The story of Sophie and Denis, however, needs to be understood in terms of its social background. The Catholic religion did not, and with remarkable consistency still does not, permit divorce. In the 18th century **marriage** was, with few exceptions, and even among the working population, regarded primarily as a business transaction. Where considerable **property** was involved, the personal preferences of the principals was seldom consulted. So the odds for feeling a strong emotional bond with one's spouse were not much better than having such feelings for one's grocer, real estate agent or bank manager. With the exception of men who were both independently wealthy and free from family pressures, unconstrained choice of a spouse was rare. For most, marriage was an emotional desert. Of the few happy long-term marriages among the enlightened are those of M and Mme **Helvétius** and M and Mme **Necker**, examples that give the impression that in the 18th century marital bliss favored tax collectors and bankers.

Diderot's marriage was indeed a love match, but as is well known, it was not happy. The outgoing and persuasive young philosopher was able to convince the lovely Mlle Champion of his love for her (no doubt sincere), and her family to accept the match. The philosopher, however, then went out into the wide world, where he mixed with the brightest and many of the better off in Parisian society. As he developed new interests and acquired new friends and the occasional mistress, M and Mme Diderot drifted apart. Mme has often been described as a shrew, and M complained of her harshness and refusals even to speak to him. Not a pleasant situation. But hardly one for which Mme must bear the main responsibility.

Separations of spouses were known in the 18th century, but Diderot would have found this solution difficult for two reasons. First, his means were not up to supporting two households. Secondly, he had one surviving daughter, Angélique, whom he loved dearly. So, divorce, which was impossible, aside, there was no satisfactory solution to Diderot's domestic problem. Like many before and since, he sought emotional and erotic satisfaction outside the home. Hence the relationship with Sophie Volland, which appears to have been deeply satisfying for both.

VOLTAIRE/AROUET, François Marie (1694-1778). While not the most original or profound of the thinkers of the Enlightenment, Voltaire was perhaps the most indefatigable, and the best example of the engaged intellectual. By the end of his career he represented the Enlightenment triumphant as well as the Enlightenment militant.

Voltaire's father was a Parisian notary who was able to give his son the best education available. Between 1704 and 1711 Voltaire attended the elite *collège* of Louis-le-Grand, where he learned from his **Jesuit** teachers the literary skills that he was subsequently to use so effectively against them. As expected by his family he studied law, but was drawn to literature and never practiced.

Voltaire's literary output is as remarkable for its variety as for its volume. He began his career writing plays and poetry in the classical tradition. His first play, *Oedipus,* was performed successfully in 1718, and his epic poem, *La Henriade,* was first published in 1723 and won its author what is today regarded as a greatly exaggerated reputation as a poet. Following a quarrel with the Chevalier de Rohan in 1726 Voltaire spent a short time in the Bastille (not his first visit), and then was allowed to go abroad to England. It was thanks in large part to his English experience that Voltaire developed from a fashionable poet and dramatist into an engaged intellectual, or *philosophe*.

His *Letters on England*, also known as *Philosophical Letters,* published in 1734, are one of the great programmatic statements of the Enlightenment. In England Voltaire discovered the virtues of Baconian and Newtonian science, of John **Locke**'s psychology, the **utility** and dignity of commerce, the respect accorded to ability, and the advantages of **toleration** and **liberty**. On his return to France he began his long association with Mme du **Châtelet**, with whom he lived and studied science and the Bible. In 1745 he was named royal historiographer, and the following year was elected to the **Académie française**. But he was too independent and pugnacious to remain within the boundaries of established authority.

Voltaire never stopped writing plays, but he did feel the need to find a new vehicle for what he had to say. He was among the inventors, and perhaps the most accomplished practitioner, of a new literary genre, the *conte*, or philosophical tale in which ideas count for more than character, plot or verisimilitude. His best-known work, *Candide* (1759) is of this genre. In 1764 he published his *Philosophical Dictionary*, which while not particularly philosophical and only incidentally alphabetical, provided an admirable framework from which to carry on his polemics against religious dogma and excessive secular authority. Some of his historical work, especially the *Essay on Manners* (1756), had the same purpose. Here Voltaire continued his polemic against **superstition** and violence, but also laid the foundations for cultural history. This work is probably the first in the Western tradition to try seriously to incorporate the great cultures of India and China into a wider historical narrative.

Voltaire's literary output reflects only part of his activities. During the 1740s he performed some diplomatic missions for the French government. He was also invited to the court of Stanislas at Lunéville and in the early 1750s to that of **Frederick II**. His experience there was not a happy one and does not support the view that **enlightened despotism** was a great success.

Voltaire found a new and characteristic outlet for his energies in his efforts to rehabilitate three victims of miscarriages of French justice, Jean Calas (1762-1763), the Chevalier de la Barre (1766) and the Sirven family (1760-1771). All these cases involved religious intolerance and abuse of judicial procedure. Here Voltaire was able to give practical application to values he had so often advocated in theory. No other major *philosophe* was either able or willing to become so directly engaged in defending the values in which they believed.

For most of his adult life Voltaire had lived in the provinces, or beyond the borders of France. Not long before dying he returned to Paris and was received with the enthusiasm appropriate to the man who more than any other represented the Enlightenment to his contemporaries.

W

WARENS, Louise Eléonore de (1699-1762). The first great love of Jean-Jacques **Rousseau**, and the person without whom Rousseau would most probably have been yet another young man whose potential could not be realized for lack of opportunity. There are those who would say that she has a good deal to answer for.

Mme de Warens did not lead a happy life, and in conventional terms it was not a successful one. Born into the noble Protestant family of La Tour de Pil in eastern France, she was married in her early teens to an army officer considerably her senior. Like most arranged matches of the time it provided little emotional satisfaction for the spouses, and as was usual at the time and in those circumstances, husband and wife were free, provided they observed certain social niceties, to seek companionship where they chose. Mme de Warens was exceptional in being more independent in spirit and aspirations than were most women of her position. Partly for personal and partly for practical reasons she sought a way out her **marriage**, and found it in a short trip to neighboring Savoy and conversion to Catholicism. She was given a pension from the King and Church of Savoy on the understanding that she help in the good work of encouraging Protestants to accept Catholicism. It was in this capacity that she met Rousseau.

Rousseau met Mme de Warens shortly after running away from Geneva, and in the course of his project of converting to Catholicism. He describes her at their first meeting, which occurred on Palm Sunday 1728, as follows: "a face full of charm, large and blue eyes beaming with such kindness, a dazzling complexion and the outline of an enchanting neck. . . . in a moment I was hers, and certain that a faith preached by such missionaries would not fail to lead to paradise" (*Confessions,* Bk. II; Cohen, p. 55). Mme de Warens was, indeed, very attractive, and in addition kind, generous, sociable and loving. Unfortunately, she was under constant economic pressure, and while energetic and imaginative in seeking to assure her economic independence (in her case, a chateau of one's own), she was impractical and an unsuccessful business-woman. Eventually she was reduced to poverty.

Rousseau's debt to Mme de Warens was twofold. First, she offered this sensitive and emotionally starved adolescent affection and eventually, love. Rousseau was unusual in finding that the object of his youthful admiration, a beautiful woman more than 10 years his senior, was also prepared to become his lover and companion. This, perhaps, could only have happened in the context of the strange, resourceful, marginal household of which Mme de Warens was the center, and in the case of a woman whose divorce not being recognized in the country where she lived, could not hope for social advancement by the usual means of an advantageous marriage. This is not to suggest that Rousseau was mistaken about the nature of the emotional bond he shared with Mme de Warens and its importance to him.

Secondly, it was during his long stay with Mme de Warens, between 1730 and 1737, first at Annecy, then at Chambéry and Les Délices, that Rousseau was given the opportunity to change from a starry-eyed and ignorant youth into an informed, self-educated young man. Having attended no institution of secondary or higher education, Rousseau, thanks to an exceptional woman, had the leisure and, be it said, the self-discipline to educate himself to a very high level. No doubt Mme de Warens hoped that Rousseau would make something serviceable of himself, but this should not diminish our appreciation of her generosity and kindness. Certainly Rousseau's comments about her when he learned of her death reflect respect and admiration, as well as love (*Confessions*, Bk. 12; Cohen, p. 572).

WATTEAU, Antoine (1684-1721). Antoine Watteau, renowned for *fêtes galantes* or celebrations of fantasy and leisure, came to Paris from Valenciennes around 1702. After brief stints with a scene-painter at the Opera and a wholesale producer of devotional subjects, he studied with the decorative painter Claude Gillot, innovator of *fêtes champêtres* (depictions of festive occasions in a rustic setting), absorbing genre, subject matter and love for *commedia dell'arte*. At Gillot's urging, Watteau then moved to the atelier of Claude Audran, another decorative painter, where he expanded his repertoire by copying from the Luxembourg collection curated by his new mentor.

Although not a student of the **Royal Academy of Painting**, he received second prize in its 1709 Grand Prix; returned to Valenciennes when this achievement failed to garner patrons; then came back to Paris with new paintings in his portfolio. In 1712 he brought two works to the royal institution, hoping to qualify for subsidized study in Rome. Impressed by his approach, the Academy instead extended him associate membership. In 1717, he became a full member of the royal institution, accepted as a painter of *fêtes galantes*, a category it invented for Watteau, and then retired in 1728 with the induction of Watteau's only student, Jean-Baptiste Pater.

Prolific but rarely satisfied, Watteau destroyed many paintings and drawings prior to his premature death from tuberculosis. Among the best known of his surviving oils are *Pilgrimage to the Island of Cythera* (1717), *The Embarkation to Cythera* (c. 1718) and *Gersaint's Shopsign* (1721). His evocative drawings in red chalk, such as *Sheet of Eight Heads* (c. 1716) are famous in their own right. His fascination with the unconventional world of street theater is revealed in such well-regarded works as *Pierrot* (c. 1719) and *The Italian Comedians* (c. 1720), which feature subjects dressed in theatrical costumes from his private collection.

Reed Benhamou

WEALTH OF NATIONS, THE. See INQUIRY INTO THE NATURE AND CAUSES OF THE WEALTH OF NATIONS, AN.

WHIGS. According to the *Oxford English Dictionary*, the term "Whig" was first applied to Presbyterian Scots who in the mid-17th century rebelled against the crown. In English politics it designated those interests that opposed the return of a Catholic monarch to the throne of England, and therefore wished to exclude James, Duke of York, who ruled as James II from 1685 to 1688, from the kingship. When it became known that he was to have an heir, and thus threatened a return to a Catholic ruling house, he was removed. The Whigs were the architects and main beneficiaries of the Glorious Revolution of 1688, and upholders of the revolutionary settlement. As such they advocated a constitutionally limited monarchy, the supremacy of **Parliament** and a degree of religious freedom. The outstanding ideologist of Whig political theory was John **Locke**. During the 18th century the parliamentary party opposing the Whigs was the **Tory**. In the course of the 19th century the term "Whig" was replaced by "Liberal."

The social bases of the Whigs consisted in most of the great landed families of the realm, together with commercial and moneyed interests in London, and more latitudinarian elements of the established church. Though more liberal in politics and general outlook than the Tories, the Whigs were far from representing the interests of the population at large, as the right to be represented in Parliament was the prerogative of a small minority.

After getting the better of the great constitutional conflict around the Glorious Revolution, the Whigs controlled British politics for most of the 18th century. Their domination was unbroken from 1714 to 1760. It was during the ascendancy of Sir Robert Walpole from

1720 to 1742 that, despite the predominant cronyism and corruption, a notion of cabinet government essential to effective parliamentary rule was developed. The outstanding spokesman for at least one branch of Whigs in the later part of the century was Edmund **Burke**. Prominent among the Whig writers and thinkers of the time were Daniel **Defoe**, William Congreve, Joseph **Addison** and Richard **Steele**.

WOLFF, Christian (1679-1754). An academic, and one of the main figures of the Enlightenment in Germany. Wolff was born at Breslau, and studied at the Universities of Jena and Leipzig, where he received his master's degree in 1706. The intellectual milieu of northern Germany exposed students there to a variety of faiths and philosophies, but the main influence on Wolff was Gottfried Wilhelm **Leibniz**, as whose disciple and popularizer he is often seen.

It was in part thanks to a recommendation from Leibniz that Wolff was offered a position teaching mathematics and the natural sciences at the recently founded University of Halle in 1706. Wolff had the misfortune of making enemies among theologians and orthodox philosophers who objected to the implications of some of his teachings, which included the assumption, already publicized by Pierre **Bayle**, that an adequate system of ethics could be worked out on the basis of **reason** alone. When a complaint was made about Wolff to Frederick William I of Prussia, the king, in a striking demonstration of the efficiency of **absolutism**, ordered Wolff to leave the kingdom within two days on pain of death. He did not bother with the formality of an investigation.

An experience of this sort cannot but be traumatic. The immediate consequence of Wolff's exile was mitigated by his being offered a post at the University of Marburg. However, as a result of this experience he abandoned the vernacular for Latin in his published work. When **Frederick II** acceded to the throne in 1740 he invited the distinguished philosopher to return to Halle. Wolff did so, and was made chancellor of the University three years later.

As a philosopher Wolff was more systematic than original. While his interests were encyclopedic in scope, his method was broadly rationalistic. He also retained a faith in purely logical tools, such as the syllogism, longer than more advanced thinkers in England and France. There can be little doubt that Wolff's model of deductive encyclopedism differed from the more empirical French model that was just being developed during his last years. Whether the French model of encyclopedism is somehow more typical of the Enlightenment, or whether Wolff's model is a variant of equal validity, is open to question.

Wolff's complete works include 29 volumes in German and 41 in Latin.

WOLLSTONECRAFT, Mary (1759-1797). The founder of modern feminism. She was born to a downwardly mobile family whose condition was aggravated by the incompetence and brutality of the father. Wollstonecraft's career is a striking instance of a woman without means struggling to make a living, to keep a troubled family together and to educate herself.

To make a living Wollstonecraft had recourse to the standard options of a woman of her time. She acted as companion to a wealthy woman at Bath, she established and ran, with her sisters, a school in Newington Green and she worked as governess for the Kingsboroughs, a family of Irish landlords. The condition of upper servant grated on this young woman with a sense of self worth and social injustice, and the economic rewards were hardly adequate to the needs of Wollstonecraft and her family, for whom she continued to take responsibility.

In 1787 Wollstonecraft came to London with the intention of earning her living by writing. The previous year she had published *Thoughts on the Education of Daughters*, and was fortunate to fall in with the circle of Joseph Johnson, a principled and kindly publisher who helped make Wollstonecraft's early literary career both intellectually challenging and economically rewarding. It is probably not too much to say that he saved her from the perils and exploitation typical of **Grub Street**. Johnson provided her regular work as a reviewer for his journal, the *Analytical Review*, and published her novel *Mary, or the Wrongs of Woman* (1788) and another educational text, *Original Stories from Real Life*, for the second edition of which he got another member of his circle, William Blake, to do the engravings.

Johnson's shop was a meeting place for a remarkable group of liberals and radicals, among them the Swiss artist and polymath Henry Fuseli, the poet William Blake, the author and Wollstonecraft's future husband, William Godwin, the biblical scholar Alexander **Geddes**, Johnson's co-founder of the *Analytical Review*, Thomas Christie, and on occasion Thomas **Paine**. Meeting and talking with so varied and informed a group as she read and wrote to produce reviews and other writing for Johnson greatly contributed to Wollstonecraft's intellectual development.

Wollstonecraft's first contribution to the political debates of the time was her response to Edmund **Burke**'s *Reflections on the Revolution in France*, a brief pamphlet entitled *A Vindication of the Rights of Men*, which appeared early in 1791. The work for which she is most famous, *A Vindication of the Rights of Woman*, appeared in early 1792. In it she criticized the formal and informal limitations imposed on women in contemporary society, and demanded that the rights being newly acquired by men be extended to women also.

Attracted by events in France, Wollstonecraft moved there at the end of 1792. The results of her stay in revolutionary Paris were an affair with an American businessman, Gilbert Imlay, by whom she had a child, and another book, *An Historical and Moral View of Origins and Progress of the French Revolution* (1794). In 1796 she travelled in Scandinavia, apparently in connection with one of Imlay's business ventures. On returning to London she attempted suicide, but was saved. She then entered into a warm relationship with William Godwin, who had published one of the most important radical works of the period in Britain, the *Enquiry Concerning Political Justice*. When Mary became pregnant they married. Mary died shortly after giving birth to a daughter, the future Mary Shelley.

WOMEN. In the high culture of Western Europe women have seldom played key roles, though the princely courts of the early-modern period do provide some exceptions. During the Enlightenment, however, women expanded their cultural activities in a numbers of ways.

So long as they were excluded from institutions of higher education and provided with a limited curriculum in convent schools at the secondary level, women had little opportunity to make their mark in formal erudition. Nevertheless, the 18th century did see significant exceptions to this trend, such as Mme du **Châtelet,** who excelled in the natural sciences and undertook serious biblical studies, and Catherine Macaulay, who wrote a substantial history of England. Mary **Wollstonecraft**, who began her literary career as a novelist and who also wrote on **education** (as did Mme d'**Épinay** and Mme de **Genlis**), is primarily remembered for her polemics against Edmund **Burke** and Jean-Jacques **Rousseau,** and her feminist social criticism.

With the broadening of the literary marketplace to include realistic works of fiction, women were no longer so seriously disadvantaged, and began to appear as **authors** in growing numbers. Though now little remembered, Mme **Riccoboni** was one of the best-selling novelists of her time. Other important female novelists of 18th-century France were Mme de **Graffigny**, Mme de Charrière, Marie Le Prince de Beaumont, Françoise Albine Benoît and Mme de **Tencin**. In England women novelists and professional writers included the remarkable Aphra Behn and Mary Delariviere Manley from the turn of the century, and Jane Baker, Mary Davys, Penelope Aubin, Eliza Haywood, Sarah Fielding (sister of Henry **Fielding**), Frances Sheridan (mother of the playwright Richard Brinsley Sheridan), Charlotte Lennox, Elizabeth Inchbald, Charlotte Smith, Mary Wollstonecraft and Frances Burney. It has been argued that roughly half the novels produced in Britain in the 18th century were written by women. Before this time certainly no other area of print culture could claim female participation anywhere near this level.

Another way women made an impact on the literary world of the Enlightenment was as an audience. As levels of **literacy** rose, and in most of Europe they rose proportionately faster for women than for men, women made up a growing part of the reading public. Not only did women take an active role in producing literature, but they were also significant consumers of the printed page, and their interest may in part explain the striking popularity and success of the novel. Certainly the participation of women in the reading public is an integral part of a process of literary democratization occurring at the time.

Perhaps the most distinct cultural role played by women in the Enlightenment was as **salonnières**. It was not unprecedented for women to write, or even to achieve significant levels of erudition before the 18th century, but there are few if any examples of women in key positions of cultural leadership, which was the case for Mmes **Lambert**, du **Deffand**, **Geoffrin**, de Tencin, de **Doublet, Necker,** Mme Helvétius (*see* **Ligniville**, Anne Catherine) and Mlle **Lespinasse**. While these were all highly competent and able women, it was not just their personal qualities, but also the fact that **salons** were a recognized and important part of the culture of the Enlightenment that accounted for their wide influence.

While it is not correct to maintain that the 18th century was the time that women achieved equality to men in the cultural domain, and while it is necessary to recognize the views of thinkers such as Jean-Jacques **Rousseau** that women properly belonged in the private sphere, it is probably fair to say that it was during the Enlightenment that women began to be recognized as having an important place, as producers, consumers and intermediaries, in the world of high culture. *See also* **Gender.**

Bibliography

Introduction

This bibliography is divided into broad headings to facilitate investigations of main areas of Enlightenment thought. Since many works deal with more than one aspect or subject of concern to the thinkers of the Enlightenment, some overlap has been inevitable. In general, a work is placed in the broadest category that can accommodate it. With one exception, works are listed only once. The exception concerns collections of essays, the more general of which are listed in the section "Some Useful Collections of Essays." When an article appearing in one of these collections is cited later in the bibliography, an abbreviated reference is given to the collection.

For more important works the original date of publication is given after the date of publication of the edition cited or consulted. In these cases the two dates are separated by a semicolon. One of the most important publications devoted to the Enlightenment, *Studies on Voltaire and the Eighteenth Century*, puts out both monographs and collections of articles. Articles appear in quotation marks with page numbers following the volume number and date of appearance, while the titles of monographs are in italics and do not include page numbers. From its inception to volume number 381 *Studies on Voltaire and the Eighteenth Century* volumes were numbered consecutively. Since 2000 they appear with the year of publication and number of the volume of that year. References to this periodical necessarily follow this change.

Orientation, Reference, Basics

Reference Works

Black, Jeremy, and Porter, Roy, eds., *A Dictionary of Eighteenth-Century World History* (Oxford, Blackwell, 1994)

Craig, Edward, ed., *Routledge Encyclopedia of Philosophy* (London, Routledge, 10 vols., 1998)

Delon, Michel, ed., *Encyclopedia of the Enlightenment*, trans. Gwen Wells (Chicago, Fitzroy Dearborn, 2 vols., 2001)

Didier, Beatrice, *Le Siècle des lumières* (Paris, MA Editions, 1987)

Edwards, Paul, ed., *The Encyclopedia of Philosophy* (London and New York, Macmillan and The Free Press, 8 vols., 1967)

Grente, Georges, Cardinal, and Moreau, François, *Dictionnaire des lettres françaises: Le XVIIIe siècle* (Paris, Fayard, 1995)

Hardin, James, ed., *German Baroque Writers, 1661-1730: Dictionary of Literary Biography*, vol. 168 (Detroit, Gale Research, 1996)

———, and Schweitzer, Christopher E., eds., *German Writers of the Age of Goethe, Sturm und Drang to Classicism: Dictionary of Literary Biography*, vol. 94 (Detroit, Gale Research, 1990)

Harvey, Sir Paul, and Hesteltine, Janet E., eds., *The Oxford Companion to French Literature* (Oxford, Clarendon Press, 1969; 1959)

———, *The Oxford Companion to English Literature* (Oxford, Clarendon Press, 1958; 1932)

Kors, Alan Charles, ed., *Encyclopedia of the Enlightenment* (Oxford, Oxford University Press, 4 vols., 2003)

Michaud, Louis Gabriel, ed., *Biographie Universelle* (Paris, Michaud frères, 45 vols., 1854)

Newman, Gerald, ed., *Britain in the Hanoverian Age, 1714-1837* (New York, Garland, 1997)

Reill, Peter Hanns and Wilson, Ellen Judy, eds., *Encyclopedia of the Enlightenment* (New York, Facts on File, 1996)

Roth, John K., ed., *World Philosophers and Their Works* (Pasadena, Calif., Salem Press, 3 vols., 2000)

Stephen, Leslie, and Lee, Sidney, eds., *The Dictionary of National Biography* (Oxford, Oxford University Press, 22 vols., 1921-1922)

Viguerie, Jean de, *Histoire et Dictionnaire du temps des lumières* (Paris, Robert Laffont, 1995)

Weiner, Philip P., ed., *Dictionary of the History of Ideas* (New York, Scribner, 5 vols., 1968)

Yolton, John W., Porter, Roy, Rogers, Pat, and Stafford, Barbara Maria, eds., *The Blackwell Companion to the Enlightenment* (Oxford, Blackwell, 1992)

———, Price, John Vladimir and Stephens, John, eds., *The Dictionary of Eighteenth-Century Philosophers* (Bristol, Thoemmes Press, 2 vols., 1999)

Important and Representative Primary Sources

Alembert, Jean le Rond d', *Preliminary Discourse to the Encyclopedia of Diderot,* trans. Richard N. Schwab and Walter E. Rex (New York, Bobbs-Merrill, 1963; 1751)

Andrews, John, *Comparative View of the French and English Nations, in their Manners, Politics and Literature* (London, Longman and Robinson, 1785)

Bayle, Pierre, *Historical and Critical Dictionary: Selections,* trans. Richard H. Popkin (New York, Bobbs-Merrill, 1965; 1697)

Beccaria, Cesare, *On Crimes and Punishments,* trans. David Young (Indianapolis, Hackett, 1986; 1764)

Bentham, Jeremy, *The Principles of Morality and Legislation,* ed. Laurence J. Lafleur (New York, Hafner, 1948; 1789)

Boswell, James, *Life of Johnson* (London, Oxford University Press, 1957; 1791)

Carlyle, Alexander, *The Autobiogrpahy of Dr. Alexander Carlyle of Inveresk,* ed. John Hill Burton (Bristol, Thoemmes, 1990; 1860)

Condorcet, Jean Antoine Nicolas Caritat de, *Sketch of the Progress of the Human Mind* (London, Weidenfield and Nicolson, 1955; 1793)

Diderot, Denis, *Rameau's Nephew and D'Alembert's Dream,* trans. Leonard Tancock (Harmondsworth, Penguin, 1966)

Gibbon, Edward, *Autobiography*, ed., Dero A. Saunders (New York, Meridian, 1961; 1796)

———, *The Decline and Fall of the Roman Empire* (New York, Modern Library, 3 vols., n. d. ; 1776-1788)

Goethe, Johann Wolfgang von, *The Sufferings of Young Werther*, trans. Bayard Quincy Morgan (New York, Ungar, 1980; 1774)

Helvétius, Claude Adrien, *Essays on the Mind* (New York, Ben Franklin, 1970; 1758)

———, *A Treatise on Man, His Intellectual Faculties and His Education*, trans. W. Hooper (New York, Ben Franklin, 1970; 1772)

Holbach, Paul-Henri Thiry d', *The System of Nature; Or Laws of the Moral and Physical World*, trans. H. D. Robinson (New York, Ben Franklin, 1970; 1770)

Hume, David, *A Treatise of Human Nature: Being An Attempt to Introduce the Experimental Method of Reasoning into Moral Subjects* (Oxford, Clarendon Press, 1967; 1739)

———, *Essays Moral, Political and Literary*, ed. Eugene F. Miller (Indianapolis, Liberty Press, 1985; 1741-1758)

Kant, Immanuel, *Critique of Pure Reason*, trans. Norman Kemp-Smith (London, Macmillan, 1964; 1781)

———, *On History*, trans. Lewis White Beck, Robert E. Anchor and Emil L. Fackenheim (New York, Bobbs-Merrill, 1963)

La Mettrie, Julien Offray, *Man a Machine*, ed. Gertrude Carman Bussey (La Salle, Illinois, Open Court, 1912; 1748)

Leibniz, Gottfried Wilhelm von, *Monadology and Other Philosophical Essays*, trans. Paul and Anne Martin Schrecker (New York, Bobbs-Merrill, 1965; 1714)

Montesquieu, Charles-Louis Secondat de, *Persian Letters*, trans. C. J. Betts (Harmondsworth, Penguin, 1987; 1721)

———, *The Spirit of the Laws*, trans. Thomas Nugent (New York, Hafner; 1748)

Rousseau, Jean-Jacques, *The First and Second Discourses*, trans. Roger D. and Judith R. Masters (New York, St. Martin's Press, 1964; 1750 and 1755)

———, *On the Social Contract*, trans. Judith R. Masters, ed. Roger D. Masters (New York, St. Martin's Press, 1978; 1762)

———, *Emile, or On Education*, trans. Allan Bloom (New York, Basic, 1979; 1762)

———, *Confessions*, trans. J. M. Cohen (Harmondsworth, Penguin, 1954; 1781)

Schmidt, James, ed., *What Is Enlightenment? Eighteenth-Century Answers and Twentieth-Century Questions* (Berkeley, University of California Press, 1996)

Smith, Adam, *The Theory of Moral Sentiments*, eds. A. L. Macfie and D. D. Raphael (Indianapolis, Liberty Press, 1981; 1759)

————, *An Inquiry into the Nature and Causes of the Wealth of Nations*, eds. R. H. Campbell and A. S. Skinner (Indianapolis, Liberty Press, 2 vols., 1981; 1776)

Vico, Giambattista, *The New Science*, trans., Thomas Goddard Bergin and Max Harold Fisch (Ithaca, N.Y., Cornell University Press, 1968; 1744)

Voltaire, *Letters on England* [*Philosophical Letters*], trans. Leonard Tanckock (Harmondsworth, Penguin, 1986; 1734)

————, *Candide, or Optimism*, trans. John Butt (Harmondsworth, Penguin, 1987; 1759)

————, *Philosophical Dictionary*, trans. Theodore Besterman (Harmondsworth, Penguin, 1972; 1764)

Relevant Periodicals

British Journal for Eighteenth-Century Studies
Consortium on Revolutionary Europe
Dix-huitième siècle
Eighteenth-Century Life
Eighteenth-Century Studies
European Legacy
French Historical Studies
French History
History of European Ideas
History of Political Thought
Journal of the History of Ideas
Studies in Eighteenth-Century Culture
Studies in the Eighteenth Century
Studies on Voltaire and the Eighteenth Century
The Eighteenth-Century: Theory and Interpretation

Some Useful Collections of Essays

Baker, Keith Michael, ed., *The French Revolution and the Creation of Modern Political Culture*, vol. I: *The Political Culture of the Old Regime* (Oxford, Pergamon, 1987)

Barber, Giles and Courtney, C. P., eds., *Enlightenment Essays in Memory of Robert Shackleton* (Oxford, Voltaire Foundation, 1988)

Barber, W. H., Brumfitt, J. H. *et al., The Age of Enlightenment: Studies Presented to Theodore Besterman* (Edinburgh, Oliver and Boyd, 1967)

Barnes, Barry and Shapin, Steven, eds., *Natural Order* (London, Sage, 1979)

Bingham, Alfred J. and Topazio, Virgil W., eds., *Enlightenment Studies in Honour of Lester G. Crocker* (Oxford, Voltaire Foundation, 1979)

Brewer, John and Porter, Roy, eds., *Consumption and the World of Goods* (London, Routledge, 1993)

Bronson, Bertrand Harris, *Facets of the Enlightenment: Studies in English Literature and Its Contexts* (Berkeley, University of California Press, 1968)

Brown, S. C., ed., *Philosophers of the Enlightenment* (Brighton, Harvester Press, 1979)

Campbell, Roy Harold and Skinner, Andrew, eds., *The Origins and Nature of the Scottish Enlightenment* (Edinburgh, John Donald, 1982)

Crimmins, James E., ed., *Religion, Secularization and Political Thought: Thomas Hobbes to John Stuart Mill* (London, Routledge, 1989)

Dooley, Brendan and Baron, Sabrina Alcorn, eds., *The Politics of Information in Early Modern Europe* (London, Routledge, 2001)

Gay, Peter, *The Party of Humanity* (New York, Knopf, 1964)

Gilmour, Peter, ed., *Philosophers of the Enlightenment* (Edinburgh, Edinburgh University Press, 1989)

Gordon, Daniel, ed., *Postmodernism and the Enlightenment: New Perspectives in Eighteenth-Century French Intellectual History* (New York, Routledge, 2001)

Hont, Istvan and Ignatieff, Michael, eds., *Wealth and Virtue: The Shaping of Political Economy in the Scottish Enlightenment* (Cambridge, Cambridge University Press, 1983)

Hulme, Peter and Jordanova, Ludmilla, eds., *The Enlightenment and Its Shadows* (London, Routledge, 1990)

Jones, Peter, ed., *Philosophy and Science in the Scottish Enlightenment* (Edinburgh, John Donald, 1988)

Kolving, Ulla and Mervaud, Christiane, eds., *Voltaire et ses combats: Actes du Congrès International Oxford-Paris* (Oxford, Voltaire Foundation, 2 vols., 1997)

Kors, Alan Charles and Korshin, Paul, J., eds., *Anticipations of the Enlightenment in England, France and Germany* (Philadelphia, University of Pennsylvania Press, 1987)

Lough, John, *The Encyclopédie in Eighteenth-Century England and Other Studies* (Newcastle upon Tyne, Oriel, 1970)

Maccubbin, Robert Purks, ed., *'Tis Nature's Fault: Unauthorized Sexuality during the Enlightenment* (Cambridge, Cambridge University Press, 1987)

Micale, Mark S. and Dietle, Robert L., eds., *Enlightenment, Passion, Modernity: Historical Essays in European Thought and Culture* (Stanford, Calif., Stanford University Press, 2000)

Pagden, Anthony, ed., *Languages of Political Theory in Early Modern Europe* (Cambridge, Cambridge University Press, 1987)

Pappas, John, ed., *Essays on Diderot and the Enlightenment in Honor of Otis Fellows* (Geneva, Droz, 1974)

Phillipson, Nicolas T. and Mitchison, Rosalind, eds., *Scotland in the Age of Improvement* (Edinburgh, Edinburgh University Press, 1970)

———, and Skinner, Quentin, *Political Discourse in Early Modern Britain* (Cambridge, Cambridge University Press, 1993)

Porter, Roy and Rousseau, G. S., eds., *The Ferment of Knowledge: Studies in the Historiography of Eighteenth-Century Science* (Cambridge, Cambridge University Press, 1980)

———, and Teich, Mikulas, eds., *The Enlightenment in National Context* (Cambridge, Cambridge University Press, 1981)

———, and Roberts, Marie Mulvey, eds., *Pleasure in the Eighteenth Century* (London, Macmillan, 1996)

———, and Ole, Peter Grell, eds., *Toleration in Enlightenment Europe* (Cambridge, Cambridge University Press, 2000)

Shackleton, Robert, *Essays on Montesquieu and on the Enlightenment*, ed. David Gilson (Oxford, Voltaire Foundation, 1988)

Stewart, Michael Alexander, ed., *Studies in the Philosophy of the Scottish Enlightenment* (Oxford, Clarendon Press, 1990)

Van Kley, Dale, ed., *The French Idea of Freedom: The Old Regime and the Declaration of Rights of 1789* (Stanford, Calif., Stanford University Press, 1994)

Venturi, Franco, *Italy and the Enlightenment: Studies in a Cosmopolitan Century*, trans. Susan Corsi (London, Longman, 1972)

Vovelle, Michel, ed., *Enlightenment Portaits*, trans. Lydia G. Cochrane (Chicago, University of Chicago Press, 1997; 1992)

Wasserman, Earl, ed., *Aspects of the Eighteenth Century* (Baltimore, Johns Hopkins University Press, 1971)

Wooton, David, ed., *Republicanism, Liberty and Commercial Society, 1649-1776* (Stanford, Calif., Stanford University Press, 1994)

Syntheses

Allan, David, *Virtue, Learning and the Scottish Enlightenment* (Edinburgh, Edinburgh University Press, 1993)

Anchor, Robert, *The Enlightenment Tradition* (New York, Harper & Row, 1967)

Becker, Carl, *The Heavenly City of the Eighteenth-Century Philosophers* (New Haven, Conn., Yale University Press, 1932)

Besterman, Theodore, *Voltaire* (London, Longman, 1969)

Bredvold, Louis I., *The Brave New World of the Enlightenment* (Binghamton, N.Y., University of Michigan Press, 1961)

Brewer, John, *The Pleasures of the Imagination: English Culture in the Eighteenth Century* (New York, Farrar, Straus and Giroux, 1997)

Brumfitt, John Henry, *The French Enlightenment* (Cambridge, Mass., Schenkman, 1973)

Cassirer, Ernst, *The Philosophy of the Enlightenment*, trans. Fritz C. A. Koelln and James P. Pettegrove (Boston, Beacon Press, 1960; 1932)

Chaunu, Pierre, *La Civilisation de l'Europe des lumières* (Paris, Arthaud, 1971)

Cobban, Alfred, *In Search of Humanity: The Role of the Enlightenment in Modern History* (New York, George Braziller, 1960)

Crocker, Lester G., *An Age of Crisis: Man and the World in Eighteenth-Century French Thought* (Baltimore, Johns Hopkins University Press, 1959)

———, *Nature and Culture: Ethical Thought in the French Enlightenment* (Baltimore, Johns Hopkins University Press, 1963)

Darnton, Robert, "In Search of Enlightenment: Recent Attempts to Create a Social History of Ideas," *Journal of Modern History* 43 (March 1971): 113-32

Ford, Franklin, "The Enlightenment: Towards a Useful Definition," in R. Brissenden, ed., *Studies in the Eighteenth Century* (Canberra, Australian National University Press, 1968)

Gascoigne, John, *Joseph Banks and the English Enlightenment: Useful Knowledge and Polite Culture* (Cambridge, Cambridge University Press, 1994)

Gay, Peter, *The Enlightenment: An Interpretation* (New York, Knopf, 2 vols., 1967-1969)

———, *The Bridge of Criticism: Dialogues among Lucian, Erasmus and Voltaire on the Enlightenment* (New York, Harper & Row, 1970)

Giarrizzo, Guisepe, "Enlightenment: The Parabola of an Idea," *Proceedings of the American Philosophical Society* 141 (1997): 436-53

Goldman, Lucien, *The Philosophy of the Enlightenment: The Christian Burgess and the Enlightenment*, trans. Henry Maas (Cambridge, Mass., MIT Press, 1973; 1968)

Goodman, Dena, *The Republic of Letters: A Cultural History of the French Enlightenment* (Ithaca, N.Y., Cornell University Press, 1994)

Guéhenno, Jean, *Jean-Jacques Rousseau*, trans. John and Doreen Weightman (London, Routledge and Kegan Paul, 2 vols., 1966)

Gusdorf, Georges, *Les Principes de la pensée au siècle des lumières* (Paris, Payot, 1971)

———, *L'Avènement des sciences humaines au siècle des lumières* (Paris, Payot, 1973)

Hampson, Norman, *A Cultural History of the Enlightenment* (New York, Pantheon, 1968)

Harari, Josué V., *Scenarios of the Imaginary: Theorizing the French Enlightenment* (Ithaca, N.Y., Cornell University Press, 1987)

Havens, George R., *The Age of Ideas: From Reaction to Revolution in Eighteenth-Century France* (New York, Henry Holt, 1955)

Hayes, Julie Chandler, *Reading the French Enlightenment: System and Subversion* (Cambridge, Cambridge University Press, 1999)

Hazard, Paul, *The European Mind: 1680-1715,* trans. J. Lewis May (New York, Meridian, 1967; 1935)

———, *European Thought in the Eighteenth Century: From Montesquieu to Lessing*, trans. J. Lewis May (New York, Meridian, 1967; 1946)

Im Hof, Ulrich, *The Enlightenment*, trans. William E. Yuill (Oxford, Blackwell, 1994)

Israel, Jonathan I., *Radical Enlightenment: Philosophy and the Making of Modernity, 1650-1750* (Oxford, Oxford University Press, 2001)

Jacob, Margaret C., *The Radical Enlightenment: Pantheists, Freemasons and Republicans* (London, Allen & Unwin, 1981)

———, *Living the Enlightenment: Freemasonry and Politics in Eighteenth-Century Europe* (New York, Oxford University Press, 1991)

———, "The Enlightenment Redefined: The Formation of Modern Civil Society," *Social Research* 58 (Summer 1991): 475-95

Kors, Alan Charles, *D'Holbach's Coterie: An Enlightenment in Paris* (Princeton, N.J., Princeton University Press, 1976)

Krieger, Leonard, *Kings and Philosophers: 1689-1789* (New York, Norton, 1970)

Martin, Kingsley, *French Liberal Thought in the Eighteenth Century: A Study of Political Ideas from Bayle to Condorcet* (New York, Harper & Row, 1963; 1929)

Meysonnier, Simone, *La Balance et l'horloge: La Genèse de la pensée libérale en France au XVIIIe siècle* (Paris, Editions de la Passion, 1989)

Mornet, Daniel, *French Thought in the Eighteenth Century,* trans. Lawrence M. Levine (New York, Prentice Hall, 1929)

———, *Les Origines intellectuelles de la Révolution française* (Paris, Colin, 1954; 1933)

Munck, Thomas, *The Enlightenment: A Comparative Social History, 1721-1794* (New York, Arnold and Oxford University Press, 2000)

Outram, Dorinda, *The Enlightenment* (Cambridge, Cambridge University Press, 1995)

Porter, Roy, *The Creation of the Modern World: The Untold Story of the British Enlightenment* (New York, Norton, 2000)

———, *The Enlightenment* (Hong Kong, Macmillan, 1990)

Roche, Daniel, *France in the Enlightenment*, trans. Arthur Goldhammer (Cambridge, Mass., Harvard University Press, 1998; 1993)

Rothkrug, Lionel, *Opposition to Louis XIV: The Political and Social Origins of the French Enlightenment* (Princeton, N.J., Princeton University Press, 1965)

Shackleton, Robert, *Montesquieu: A Critical Biography* (Oxford, Oxford University Press, 1961)

Stephen, Leslie, *The History of English Thought in the Eighteenth Century* (New York, Harcourt, Brace & World, 2 vols., 1962; 1876)

Vyverberg, Henry, *Human Nature, Cultural Diversity and the French Enlightenment* (New York, Oxford University Press, 1989)

Wade, Ira O., *Structure and Form in the French Enlightenment* (Princeton, N.J., Princeton University Press, 2 vols., 1977)

———, *The Intellectual Origins of the French Enlightenment* (Princeton, N.J., Princeton University Press, 1971)

Wilson, Arthur M., *Diderot* (Oxford, Oxford University Press, 1972)

Thematic Studies

Acomb, Frances, *Anglophobia in France, 1763-1789: An Essay in the History of Constitutionalism and Nationalism* (New York, Octagon, 1980; 1950)

Baczko, Bronislaw, *Utopian Lights: The Evolution of the Idea of Progress*, trans., Judith L. Greenberg (New York, Paragon House, 1989; 1978)

Baker, Keith Michael, *Condorcet: From Natural Philosophy to Social Mathematics* (Chicago, University of Chicago Press, 1975)

Berlin, Isaiah, *Three Critics of the Enlightenment: Vico, Hamann, Herder*, ed. Henry Hardy (Princeton, N.J., Princeton University Press, 2000)

Berman, Marshall, *The Politics of Authenticity: Radical Individualism and the Emergence of Modern Society* (New York, Simon and Schuster, 1970)

Butterfield, Herbert, "Toleration in Early Modern Times," *Journal of the History of Ideas* 38 (1977): 573-84

Charlton, D. G., *New Images of the Natural in France: A Study in European Cultural History* (Cambridge, Cambridge University Press, 1984)

Chartier, Roger, *The Cultural Origins of the French Revolution*, trans. Lydia G. Cochrane (Durham, N.C., Duke University Press, 1991)

Chisick, Harvey, *The Limits of Reform in the Enlightenment: Attitudes toward the Education of the Lower Classes in Eighteenth-Century France* (Princeton, N.J., Princeton University Press, 1981)

———, "The Ambivalence of the Idea of Equality in the French Enlightenment," *History of European Ideas* 13 (1991): 215-23

Coward, David, *The Philosophy of Restif de La Bretonne, Studies on Voltaire and the Eighteenth Century* 283 (1991)

Darnton, Robert, *Mesmerism and the End of the Enlightenment in France* (Cambridge, Mass., Harvard University Press, 1968)

———, *The Great Cat Massacre and Other Episodes in French Cultural History* (New York, Basic, 1984)

Dwyer, John, *Virtuous Discourse: Sensibility and Community in Late Eighteenth Century Scotland* (Edinburgh, John Donald, 1987)

Ehrard, Jean, *L'Idée de nature en France dans la première moitié du XVIIIe siècle* (Paris, S. E. V. P. E. N., 1963)

Gordon, Daniel, "On the Supposed Obsolescence of the French Enlightenment," in Daniel Gordon, ed., *Postmodernism and the Enlightenment*, 27-43

Grafton, Anthony, *Defenders of the Text: The Traditions of Scholarship in an Age of Science, 1450-1800* (Cambridge, Mass., Harvard University Press, 1991)

Grosclaude, Pierre, *Malesherbes Témoin et Interprète de son temps* (Paris, Fischbacher, 1961)

Head, Brian William, *Ideology and Social Science: Destutt de Tracy and French Liberalism* (Dordrecht, Martinus Nijhoff, 1985)

Hope, Vincent, *Virtue by Consensus* (Oxford, Clarendon Press, 1989)

Horkheimer, Max and Adorno, Theodore W., *Dialectic of Enlightenment*, trans. John Cumming (New York, Continuum, 1998; 1944)

Jack, Malcolm, *Corruption and Progress: The Eighteenth Century Debate* (New York, AMS Press, 1989)

Jenkinson, Sally, "Two Concepts of Tolerance: Or Why Bayle Is Not Locke," *Journal of Political Philosophy* 4 (1996): 302-22

Kamen, Henry, *The Rise of Toleration* (London, Weidenfeld and Nicolson, 1967)

Kennedy, Emmet, *A Philosophe in the Age of Revolution: Destutt de Tracy and the Origins of "Ideology"* (Philadelphia, American Philosophical Society, 1978)

Laski, Harold, *The Rise of European Liberalism* (London, Allen & Unwin, 1958)

Lough, John, *Essays on the Encyclopédie of Diderot and D'Alembert* (Oxford, Oxford University Press, 1968)

Mansbridge, Jane, *Beyond Self-Interest* (Chicago, University of Chicago Press, 1990)

Manuel, Frank E., *The Prophets of Paris* (New York, Harper & Row, 1965)

Mauzi, Robert, *L'Idée du bonheur dans la littérature et la pensée française au XVIIIe siècle* (Geneva, Slatkine, 1979; 1960)

McMahon, Darrin M., *Enemies of the Enlightenment: The Counter-Enlightenment and the Making of Modernity* (New York, Oxford University Press, 2001)

Meek, Ronald L., *Social Science and the Ignoble Savage* (Cambridge, Cambridge University Press, 1976)

Mercier, Roger, *La Rehabilitation de la nature humaine, 1700-1750* (Villemomble, La Balance, 1960)

O'Brian, Karen, *Narratives of Enlightenment: Cosmopolitan History from Voltaire to Gibbon* (Cambridge, Cambridge University Press, 1997)

O'Neal, John C., *The Authority of Experience: Sensationist Theory in the French Enlightenment* (University Park, Pennsylvania State University Press, 1996)

Oz-Salzburger, Fania, *Translating the Enlightenment: Scottish Civil Discourse in Eighteenth-Century Germany* (Oxford, Clarendon Press, 1995)

Perkins, Jean A., *The Concept of the Self in the French Enlightenment* (Geneva, Droz, 1969)

Roberts, Warren, *Morality and Social Class in Eighteenth-Century French Literature and Painting* (Toronto, University of Toronto Press, 1974)

Schlereth, Thomas J., *The Cosmopolitan Ideal in Enlightenment Thought: Its Form and Function in the Ideas of Franklin, Hume and Voltaire* (Notre Dame, Indiana, University of Indiana Press, 1977)

Sekora, John, *Luxury: The Concept in Western Thought, Eden to Smollet* (Baltimore, Johns Hopkins University Press, 1977)

Spadafora, David, *The Idea of Progress in Eighteenth-Century Britain* (New Haven, Conn., Yale University Press, 1990)

Staum, Martin S., *Cabanis: Enlightenment and Medical Philosophy in the French Revolution* (Princeton, N.J., Princeton University Press, 1980)

————, *Minerva's Message: Stabilizing the French Revolution* (Montreal, McGill-Queen's University Press, 1996)

Trenard, Louis, *Lyon: De l'Encyclopédie au Préromantisme* (Paris, Presses Universitaires de France, 2 vols., 1958)

Vereker, Charles, *Eighteenth-Century Optimism: A Study of the Interrelations of Moral and Social Theory in English and French Thought between 1689 and 1789* (Liverpool, Liverpool University Press, 1967)

Viner, Jacob, *The Role of Providence in the Social Order: An Essay in Intellectual History* (Princeton, N.J., Princeton University Press, 1976)

Volkov, Shulamit, "Exploring the Other: The Enlightenment's Search for the Boundaries of Humanity," in Robert Wistrich, ed., *Demonizing the Other: Antisemitism, Racism and Xenophobia* (Amsterdam, Harwood, 1999)

Vyverberg, Henry, *Historical Pessimism in the French Enlightenment* (Cambridge, Mass., Harvard University Press, 1958)

Wade, Ira O., *The Clandestine Organization and Diffusion of Philosophic Ideas in France from 1700 to 1750* (Princeton, N.J., Princeton University Press, 1938)

Willey, Basil, *The Eighteenth-Century Background: Studies on the Idea of Nature in the Thought of the Period* (Boston, Beacon Press, 1961; 1940)

Religion

Religious Life and Thought

Acosta, Ana M., "Conjectures and Speculations: Jean Astruc and Biblical Criticism in Eighteenth-Century France," *Eighteenth-Century Studies* 35 (2002): 256-66

Adams, Geoffrey, *The Huguenots and French Opinion 1685-1787: The Enlightenment Debate on Toleration* (Waterloo, Ont., Canadian Corporation for Studies in Religion, 1991)

Aston, Nigel, *Religion and Revolution in France, 1780-1804* (China, Macmillan, 2000)

Bien, David, *The Calas Affair: Persecution, Toleration and Heresy in Eighteenth-Century Toulouse* (Princeton, N.J., Princeton University Press, 1960)

Boss, Ronald I., "The Development of Social Religion: A Contradiction of French Free Thought," *Journal of the History of Ideas* 34 (1973): 577-89

Bradley, James E. and Van Kley, Dale, eds., *Religion and Politics in Enlightenment Europe* (Notre Dame, Indiana, University of Notre Dame Press, 2001)

Byrne, James M., *Religion and the Enlightenment: From Descartes to Kant* (Louisville, Kentucky, Westminster John Knox Press, 1997)

Callahan, W. J. and Higgs, D., eds., *Church and Society in Catholic Europe of the Eighteenth Century* (Cambridge, Cambridge University Press, 1979)

Corrigan, John, *The Prism of Piety: Catholick Congregational Clergy at the Beginning of the Enlightenment* (New York, Oxford University Press, 1991)

Cragg, Gerald R., *The Church and the Age of Reason* (Harmondsworth, Pelican, 1972)

Delumeau, Jean, *Catholicism between Luther and Voltaire*, trans. Jeremy Moiser (London, Burnes and Oates, 1977)

Ditchfield, G. M., "Religion, 'Enlightenment,' and Progress in Eighteenth-Century England," *Historical Journal* 35 (1992): 681-87

Donakowski, Conrad L., "God in Man's Image: Religious Ritual as Mass Media during the Aufklärung," *Consortium on Revolutionary Europe* 15 (1985): 441-52

Frei, Hans, *The Eclipse of the Biblical Narrative: A Study in Eighteenth and Nineteenth Century Hermeneutics* (New Haven, Conn., Yale Uni- versity Press, 1974)

Fuller, Reginald C., *Alexander Geddes, 1737-1802: Pioneer of Biblical Criticism* (Sheffield, The Almond Press, 1984)

Garrett, Clarke, *Spirit Possession and Popular Religion: From the Camissards to the Shakers* (Baltimore, Johns Hopkins University Press, 1987)

Gilkey, Langdon, "The New Watershed in Theology," *Soundings* 64 (1981): 118-31

Gilley, Sheridan. "Christianity and Enlightenment: An Historical Survey," *History of European Ideas* 1 (1981): 103-21

Golden, Richard, ed., *Church, State and Society under the Bourbon Kings* (Lawrence, Kansas, Coronado Press, 1982)

Graham, Ruth, "The Revolutionary Bishops and the *Philosophes*," *Eighteenth-Century Studies* 16 (1982-1983): 117-40

Grimsley, Ronald, *Rousseau and the Religious Quest* (Oxford, Clarendon Press, 1968)

Haakonssen, Knud, ed., *Enlightenment and Religion: Rational Dissent in Eighteenth-Century Britain* (New York, Cambridge University Press, 1996).

Herrick, James A., *The Radical Rhetoric of the English Deists* (Columbia, University of South Carolina Press, 1997)

Heyd, Michael, "A Disguised Atheist or a Sincere Christian? The Enigma of Pierre Bayle," *Bibliothèque d'humanisme et renaissance* 39 (1997): 157-65

Kors, Alan Charles, *Atheism in France, 1650-1729: The Orthodox Sources of Disbelief* (Princeton, N.J., Princeton University Press, 1990)

Krieger, Leonard, "The Heavenly City of the Eighteenth-Century Historians," *Church History* 47 (1978): 279-97

Lebrun, François, *Histoire des Catholiques en France du XVe siècle à nos jours* (Toulouse, Privat, 1980)

Leung, Cécile, *Etienne Fourmont (1683-1745): Oriental and Chinese Languages in Eighteenth-Century France* (Louvain, Leuven University Press, 2002)

MacMillan, Ken, "John Wesley and the Enlightened Historians," *Methodist History* 38 (2000): 121-32

Manuel, Frank E., *The Eighteenth Century Confronts the Gods* (Cambridge, Mass., Harvard University Press, 1959)

———, *The Changing of the Gods* (Hanover, New Hampshire, University Press of New England, 1983)

McManners, John, *French Ecclesiastical Society under the Old Regime* (Manchester, Manchester University Press, 1960)

———, *Death in the Enlightenment: Changing Attitudes to Death in Eighteenth-Century France* (Oxford, Clarendon Press, 1981)

———, *Church and Society in Eighteenth-Century France* (Oxford, Oxford University Press, 2 vols., 1998)

Merrick, Jeffrey W., *The Desacralization of the French Monarchy in the Eighteenth Century* (Baton Rouge, Louisiana State University Press, 1990)

Miller, Samuel J., *Portugal and Rome, c. 1748-1830: An Aspect of the Catholic Enlightenment* (Rome, Universita Gregoriana, 1978)

Nourry, Emile, "La Bible et la critique catholique au XVIIIe siècle: Les idées de Dom Calmet," *Annales de philosophie chrétienne*, n. s., 37 (1897): 184-97

Palmer, R. R., *Catholics and Unbelievers in Eighteenth-Century France* (Princeton, N.J., Princeton University Press, 1970; 1939)

Payne, Harry, "Review Essay: Remaking One's Maker—The Career of Religion in the Eighteenth Century," *Eighteenth-Century Life* 9 (1984): 107-15

Po-Chia Hsia, R., *The World of Catholic Renewal 1540-1770* (Cambridge, Cambridge University Press, 1990)

Poland, B. C., *French Protestantism and the French Revolution: A Study in Church and State, Thought and Religion* (Princeton, N.J., Princeton University Press, 1957)

Pomeau, René, *La Religion de Voltaire* (Paris, Nizet, 1969)

Popkin, Richard H., ed., *Millenarianism and Messianism in English Literature and Thought, 1650-1800* (Leiden, Brill, 1988)

Ravitch, Norman, *Sword and Mitre: Government and Episcopate in France and England in the Age of Aristocracy* (The Hague, Mouton, 1966)

Redwood, John, *Reason, Ridicule and Religion: The Age of Enlightenment in England 1660-1750* (Cambridge, Mass., Harvard University Press, 1976)

Schmidt, James, "Kant and the Politics of Enlightenment: Reason, Faith, and Revolution," *Studies in Eighteenth-Century Culture* 25 (1996): 225-44

Schmidt, Leigh Eric, "From Demon Possession to Magic Show: Ventriloquism, Religion, and the Enlightenment," *Church History* 67 (1998): 274-304

Schwarzbach, Bertram Eugene, *Voltaire's Old Testament Criticism* (Geneva, Droz, 1971)

———, "Dom Augustin Calmet: Homme des Lumières malgré lui?" *Dix-huitième siècle* 34 (2002): 451-64

———, "Etienne Fourmont, *Philosophe* in Disguise?" *Studies on Voltaire and the Eighteenth Century* 102 (1973): 65-119

———, "L'Étude de l'hébreu en France au XVIIIe siècle: La grammaire d'Étienne Fourmont," *Revue des Études juives* 151 (1992): 43-75

Sullivan, Robert, "Rethinking Christianity in Enlightened Europe," *Eighteenth-Century Studies* 34 (2001): 298-309

Tackett, Timothy, *Priest & Parish in Eighteenth-century France: A Social and Political Study of the Curés in a Diocese of Dauphiné, 1750-1789* (Princeton, N.J., Princeton University Press, 1977)

Trevor-Roper, Hugh "The Religious Origins of the Enlightenment," in H. Trevor-Roper, *Religion and Social Change* (London, Macmillan, 1967)

Van Kley, Dale, *The Religious Origins of the French Revolution: From Calvin to the Civil Constitution* (New Haven, Conn., Yale University Press, 1996)

———, "Church, State and the Ideological Origins of the French Revolution: The Debate over the General Assembly of the Gallican Clergy in 1765," *Journal of Modern History* 51 (1979): 629-66

———, "The Religious Origins of the Patriot and Ministerial Parties in Pre-Revolutionary France," in Thomas Kselman, ed., *Belief in History: Innovative Approaches to European and American Religion* (Notre Dame, Indiana, University of Notre Dame Press, 1991)

Vovelle, Michel, *Piété baroque et déchristianisation en Provence au XVIIIe siècle* (Paris, Plon, 1973)

Young, B. W., *Religion and Enlightenment in Eighteenth-Century England: Theological Debate from Locke to Burke* (Oxford, Clarendon Press, 1998)

Jansenism

Adam, Antoine, *Du Mysticisme à la révolte: les jansénistes au XVIIe siècle* (Paris, Fayard, 1968)

Cognet, Louis, *Le Jansénisme* (Paris, Que Sais-je, 1968)

Cottret, Monique, *Jansénismes et Lumières: Pour un autre XVIIIe siècle* (Paris, Albin Michel, 1998)

Doyle, William, *Jansenism: Catholic Resistance to Authority from the Reformation to the French Revolution* (Hong Kong, Macmillan, 2000)

Gazier, Augustin, *Histoire générale du mouvement janséniste* (Paris, Champion, 2 vols., 1922-1924)

Kreiser, B. R., *Miracles, Convulsions, and Ecclesiastical Politics in Early Eighteenth-Century Paris* (Princeton, N.J., Princeton University Press, 1978)

Maire, Catherine, *De la Cause de Dieu à la cause de la nation: Le Jansénisme au XVIIIe siècle* (Paris, Gallimard, 1998)

McManners, John, "Jansenism and Politics in the Eighteenth Century," *Church, Society and Politics: 13th and 14th Meetings of the Ecclesiastical History Society*, Oxford, 1975: 253-73

O'Brien, Charles H., "The Jansenist Campaign for the Toleration of Protestants in the Late Eighteenth Century: Sacred or Secular?" *Journal of the History of Ideas* 46 (1985): 523-38

O'Keefe, Cyril B., "The Jansenists and The Enlightenment in France," *Religion in the Eighteenth Century* (New York: Garland, 1979): 25-39

Orcibal, Jean, and Barnes, A., *Les Origines du jansénisme* (Louvain, Vrin, 5 vols., 1947-1962)

Préclin, Edmond, *Les Jansénistes au XVIIIe siècle et la Constitution Civile du Clergé: Le développement du richerisme, sa propagation dans le bas clergé, 1713-1791* (Paris, Gamber, 1929)

Tavenaux, René, *Jansénisme et Politique* (Paris, Colin, 1965)

Van Kley, Dale, *The Jansenists and the Expulsion of the Jesuits from France* (New Haven, Conn., Yale University Press, 1975)

———, *The Damiens Affair and the Unravelling of the Old Regime, 1750-1770* (Princeton, N.J., Princeton University Press, 1984)

———, "The Jansenist Constitutional Legacy in the French Pre-revolution, 1750-1789," *Historical Reflections/Réflexions Historiques* 13 (1986): 393-453

Williams, William H., "Jansenism Revisited," *Catholic Historical Review* 63 (1977): 573-82

———, "The Significance of Jansenism in the History of the French Catholic Clergy in the Pre-Revolutionary Era," *Studies in Eighteenth Century Culture* 7 (1978): 289-306

Judaism

Abramsky, Chimen, "The Crisis of Authority within European Jewry in the Eighteenth-Century," in Siegfried Stein and Raphael Loewe, eds., *Studies in Jewish Religious and Intellectual History* (London, Institute of Jewish Studies and University of Alabama Press, 1979)

Altmann, Alexander, "The Philosophical Roots of Moses Mendelssohn's Plea for Emancipation," *Jewish Social Studies* 36 (1974): 191-202

Arkush, Allan, *Moses Mendelssohn and the Enlightenment* (Albany: State University of New York Press, 1994)

———, "Voltaire on Judaism and Christianity," *AJS Review* 18 (1993): 223-43

Badinter, Robert, *Libres et Égaux: L'Emancipation des juifs, 1789-1791* (Paris, Fayard, 1989)

Birnbaum, Pierre and Katznelson, Ira, eds., *Paths of Emancipation: Jews, States and Citizenship* (Princeton, N.J., Princeton, University Press, 1995)

Breuer, Edward, *The Limits of Enlightenment: Jews, Germans and the Eighteenth-Century Study of Scripture* (Cambridge Mass., Harvard University Press, 1995)

Chisick, Harvey, "Ethics and History in Voltaire's Attitudes toward the Jews," *Eighteenth-Century Studies* 35 (2002): 577-600

———, "Community and Exclusion in Rousseau and Voltaire: The Case of the Jews," in *Inclusion and Exclusion: Perspectives of Jews from the Enlightenment to the Dreyfus Affaire*, ed. Ilana Zinguer and Sam Bloom (Leiden, Brill, 2003): 77-103

Dubin, Lois C., *The Port Jews of Habsburg Trieste: Absolutist Politics and Enlightenment Culture* (Stanford, Calif., Stanford University Press, 1999)

Endelman, Todd, *The Jews of Georgian England 1714-1830: Tradition and Change in a Liberal Society* (Bloomington, Indiana University Press, 1990)

Erspamer, Peter R., *The Elusiveness of Tolerance: The "Jewish Question" from Lessing to the Napoleonic Wars* (Chapel Hill, University of North Carolina Press, 1997)

Felsenstein, Frank, *Anti-Semitic Stereotypes: A Paradigm of Otherness in English Popular Culture, 1660-1830* (Baltimore, Johns Hopkins University Press, 1995)

Feuerwerker, David, *L'Emancipation des Juifs de France de l'Ancien Régime à la fin du Second Empire* (Paris, Albin Michel, 1976)

Hertzberg, Arthur, *The French Enlightenment and the Jews* (New York and Philadelphia, Columbia University Press and Jewish Publication Society, 1968)

Israel, Jonathan I., *European Jewry in the Age of Mercantilism, 1550-1750* (Oxford, Clarendon Press, 1989)

Katz, Jacob, *Out of the Ghetto: The Social Background of Jewish Emancipation* (Cambridge, Mass., Harvard University Press, 1973)

Liberles, Robert, "From Toleration to *Verbesserung*: German and English Debates on the Jews in the Eighteenth Century," *Central European History* 21 (1989): 1-31

Librett, Jeffrey S., *The Rhetoric of Cultural Dialogue: Jews and Germans from Moses Mendelssohn to Richard Wagner and Beyond* (Stanford, Calif., Stanford University Press, 2000)

Malino, Frances, *The Sephardic Jews of Bordeaux* (University of Alabama, University Press, 1978)

———, "Attitudes toward Jewish Communal Autonomy in Pre-Revolutionary France," in Frances Malino and Phyllis Cohen Albert, eds., *Essays in Modern Jewish History* (Rutherford, N.J., Farleigh Dickinson University Press, 1982)

———, "Competition and Confrontation: The Jews and the Parlement of Metz," in Bernard Blumenkranz and Gilbert Dahan, eds., *Les Juifs au regard de l'histoire* (Paris, Picard, 1985)

———, "Resistance and Rebellion: The Jews in Eighteenth-Century France," *Jewish Historical Studies* 30 (1987-1988): 55-70

Manuel, Frank E., *The Broken Staff: Judaism through Christian Eyes* (Cambridge, Mass., Harvard University Press, 1992)

Meyer, Paul H., "The Attitude of the Enlightenment toward the Jew," *Studies on Voltaire and the Eighteenth Century* 26 (1963): 161-205

Perry, Thomas W., *Public Opinion, Propaganda and Politics in Eighteenth-Century England: A Study of the Jew Bill of 1753* (Cambridge, Mass., Harvard University Press, 1962)

Poliakov, Léon, *The History of Anti-Semitism*, trans. R. Howard (London, Routledge & Kegan Paul, 4 vols., 1965-1985)

Ruderman, David B., *Jewish Enlightenment in an English Key: Anglo-Jewry's Construction of Modern Jewish Thought* (Princeton, N.J., Princeton University Press, 2000)

Schechter, Ronald, *Obstinate Hebrews: Representations of Jews in France, 1715-1815* (Berkeley, University of California Press, 2003)

Schwarzbach, Bertram Eugène, "Voltaire et les juifs: bilan et plaidoyer," *Studies on Voltaire and the Eighteenth Century* 358 (1998): 27-91

Sorkin, David, *Moses Mendelssohn and the Religious Enlightenment* (Berkeley, University of California Press, 1996)
————, "Jews, the Enlightenment and Religious Toleration: Some Reflections," *Leo Baeck Institute Yearbook* 37 (1992): 3-16
Sutcliffe, Adam, *Judaism and Enlightenment* (Cambridge, Cambridge University Press, 2003)

Society

Social Background and Social Thought

Barnard, F. M., "Metaphors, Laments, and the Organic Community," *Canadian Journal of Economics and Political Science* 32 (1966): 281-301
Becker, Marvin B., *The Emergence of Civil Society in the Eighteenth Century: A Privileged Moment in the History of England, Scotland and France* (Bloomington, Indiana University Press, 1994)
Berry, Christopher J., *The Social Theory of the Scottish Enlightenment* (Edinburgh, Edinburgh University Press, 1997)
Bryson, Galdys, *Man and Society: The Scottish Inquiry of the Eighteenth-Century* (New York, Kelley, 1968; 1945)
Cameron, David, *The Social Thought of Rousseau and Burke: A Comparative Study* (London, Weidenfeld and Nicolson, 1973)
Chartier, Roger, ed., *A History of Private Life*, vol. III, *Passions of the Renaissance*, trans. Arthur Goldhammer (Cambridge, Mass., Harvard University Press, 1989)
Davis, David Brion, *The Problem of Slavery in the Age of Revolution, 1770-1823* (Ithaca, N.Y., Cornell University Press, 1975)
Davis, Natalie Zemon and Farge, Arlette, eds., *A History of Women in the West*, vol. III, *Renaissance and Enlightenment Paradoxes* (Cambridge, Mass., Harvard University Press, 1993)
Duchet, Michèle, *Anthropologie et histoire au siècle des lumières* (Paris, Maspero, 1971)
Goubert, Pierre, *L'Ancien Régime: French Society, 1600-1750*, trans. Steve Cox (New York, Harper & Row, 1974)
Kelley, Donald R., *The Human Measure: Social Thought in the Western Legal Tradition* (Cambridge, Mass., Harvard University Press, 1990)
Kettler, D., *Social and Political Thought of Adam Ferguson* (Columbus, Ohio State University Press, 1965)

Lehmann, W., *Adam Ferguson and the Beginnings of Modern Sociology* (New York, Columbia University Press, 1930)

Leroy, Maxime, *Histoire des idées socials en France de Montesquieu à Robespierre* (Paris, Gallimard, 1947)

Lindgren, J. R., *The Social Philosophy of Adam Smith* (The Hague, Martinus Nijhoff, 1973)

Lough, John, *An Introduction to Eighteenth-Century France* (London, Longman, 1960)

Mandrou, Robert, *Introduction to Modern France, 1500-1750: An Essay in Historical Psychology*, trans. R. E. Hallmark (London, E. Arnold, 1975)

Melzer, Arthur M., *The Natural Goodness of Man: On the System of Rousseau's Thought* (Chicago, University of Chicago Press, 1990)

Payne, Harry, *The Philosophes and the People* (New Haven, Conn., Yale University Press, 1976)

Pocock, J. G. A., *Barbarism and Religion*, vol. II, *Narratives of Civil Government* (Cambridge, Cambridge University Press, 1999)

Riley, Patrick, *The General Will before Rousseau: The Transformation of the Divine into the Civic* (Princeton, N.J., Princeton University Press, 1986)

Spierenburg, Pieter, *The Broken Spell: A Cultural and Anthropological History of Preindustrial Europe* (London, Macmillan, 1991)

Waszek, Norbert, *The Scottish Enlightenment and Hegel's Account of "Civil Society"* (Boston: Kluwer Academic, 1988)

The Nobility

Chaussinand-Nogaret, Guy, *The French Nobility in the Eighteenth Century*, trans. W. Doyle (Oxford, Oxford University Press, 1985)

Dewald, Jonathan, *The Formation of a Provincial Nobility: The Magistrates of the Parlement of Rouen* (Princeton, N.J., Princeton University Press, 1980)

———, *The European Nobility, 1400-1800* (Cambridge, Cambridge University Press, 1996)

Ford, Franklin L., *Robe and Sword: The Regrouping of the French Nobility after Louis XIV* (New York, Harper & Row, 1962)

Forster, Robert, *The Nobility of Toulouse in the Eighteenth Century* (Baltimore, Johns Hopkins University Press, 1960)

———, *The House of Saulx-Tavannes* (Baltimore, Johns Hopkins University Press, 1971)

————, "The Provincial Noble: A Reappraisal," *American Historical Review* 68 (1963): 681-91

Goodwin, Albert, *The European Nobility in the Eighteenth Century* (New York, Harper & Row, 1967; 1953)

————, "The Social Origins and Privileged Status of the French Eighteenth-Century Nobility," *Bulletin of the John Rylands Library* 47 (1965): 382-403

Howarth, David, *Lord Arundel and His Circle* (New Haven, Conn., Yale University Press, 1985)

Meyer, Jean, *La Noblesse bretonne au XVIIIe siècle* (Paris, S. E. V. P. E. N., 1966)

Mingay, G. E., *The Gentry: The Rise and Fall of a Ruling Class* (London, Longman, 1976)

Shovlin, John, "Towards a Reinterpretation of Revolutionary Antinobilism: The Political Economy of Honor in the Old Regime," *Journal of Modern History* 72 (2000): 35-66

Smith, Jay, *The Culture of Merit: Nobility, Royal Service and the Making of Absolute Monarchy in France, 1600-1789* (Ann Arbor, University of Michigan Press, 1996)

————, "Social Categories, the Language of Patriotism, and the Origins of the French Revolution: The Debate over *Noblesse commerçante*," *Journal of Modern History* 72 (2000): 339-74

The Middle Classes

Adams, Christine, *A Taste for Comfort and Status: A Bourgeois Family in Eighteenth-Century France* (University Park, Pennsylvania State University Press, 2000)

Barber, Elinor, *The Bourgeoisie in Eighteenth-Century France* (Princeton, N.J., Princeton University Press, 1973)

Bell, David, *Lawyers and Citizens: The Making of a Political Elite in Old-Regime France* (New York, Oxford University Press, 1994)

Berlanstein, Lenard R., *The Barristers of Toulouse in the Eighteenth Century: 1740-1793* (Baltimore, Johns Hopkins University Press, 1975)

Cobban, Alfred, "The 'Middle-Class' in France, 1815-1848," *French Historical Studies* 5 (1967): 41-52

Corcia, Joseph, "*Bourg, Bourgeois, Bourgeois de Paris* from the Eleventh to the Eighteenth Century," *Journal of Modern History* 50 (1978): 207-33

Forster, Robert, *Merchants, Landlords and Magistrates: The Depont Family in Eighteenth-Century France* (Baltimore, Johns Hopkins University Press, 1980)

Garrioch, David, *The Formation of the Parisian Bourgeoisie, 1690-1830* (Cambridge, Mass., Harvard University Press, 1996)

Groethuysen, Bernard, *The Bourgeois: Catholicism versus Capitalism in Eighteenth-Century France*, trans. Mary Ilford (London, Cresset Press, 1968; 1927)

Hufton, Olwen, *Bayeux in the Late Eighteenth Century: A Social Study* (Oxford, Oxford University Press, 1967)

Kaplow, Jeffry, ed., *New Perspectives on the French Revolution: Readings in Historical Sociology* (New York, Wiley, 1967)

Maza, Sarah, *The Myth of the French Bourgeoisie: An Essay on the Social Imaginary, 1750-1850* (Cambridge, Mass., Harvard University Press, 2003)

Pernoud, R., *Histoire de la bourgeoisie en France*, vol. II (Paris, Seuil, 1981)

The Poor and Laboring Population

Adams, Thomas McStay, *Bureaucrats and Beggars: French Social Policy in the Age of the Enlightenment* (Oxford, Oxford University Press, 1990)

Appleby, Andrew, "Grain Prices and Subsistence Crises in England and France, 1590-1740," *Journal of Economic History* 39 (1979): 865-87

Fairchilds, Cissie, *Poverty and Charity in Aix-en-Provence* (Baltimore, Johns Hopkins University Press, 1978)

Farge, Arlette, *Fragile Lives: Violence, Power and Solidarity in Eighteenth-Century Paris*, trans. Carol Shelton (Cambridge, Mass., Harvard University Press, 1993; 1986)

———, and Revel, Jacques, *The Vanishing Children of Paris: Rumor and Politics before the French Revolution*, trans. Claudia Miéville (Cambridge, Mass., Harvard University Press, 1991; 1988)

Gagliardo, John G., *From Pariah to Patriot: The Changing Image of the German Peasant, 1770-1840* (Lexington, University Press of Kentucky, 1969)

Gutton, Pierre, *La Société et les pauvres en Europe: XVIe-XVIIIe siècles* (Paris, Presses Universitaires de France, 1974)

———, *La Société et les pauvres: L'exemple de la généralité de Lyon, 1534-1789* (Paris, Les Belles Lettres, 1971)

Himmelfarb, Gertrude, *The Idea of Poverty: England in the Early Industrial Age* (New York, Vintage, 1985)

Hufton, Olwen, *The Poor of Eighteenth-Century France* (Oxford, Clarendon Press, 1974)

Jones, Colin, *Charity and Bienfaisance: The Treatment of the Poor in the Montpellier Region, 1740-1815* (Cambridge, Cambridge University Press, 1982)

————, *The Charitable Imperative: Hospitals and Nursing in Ancien Régime and Revolutionary France* (London, Routledge, 1989)

Jutte, Robert, *Poverty and Deviance in Early Modern Europe* (Cambridge, Cambridge University Press, 1994)

Kaplan, Steven L., and Koepp, Cynthia J., eds., *Work in France: Representations, Meaning, Organization and Practice* (Ithaca, N.Y., Cornell University Press, 1986)

Kaplow, Jeffry, *The Names of Kings: The Parisian Laboring Poor in the Eighteenth Century* (New York, Basic, 1972)

Lindeman, Mary, *Patriots and Paupers: Hamburg, 1712-1830* (New York, Oxford University Press, 1990)

Lis, Catharina and Soly, Hugo, *Poverty and Capitalism in Pre-Industrial Europe* (Hassocks, Sussex, Harvester Press, 1979)

McCloy, Shelby T., *Government Assistance in Eighteenth-Century France* (Philadephia, Porcupine Press, 1977; 1946)

Norberg, Kathryn, *Rich and Poor in Grenoble, 1600-1804* (Berkeley, University of California Press, 1985)

Oxley, Geoffrey W., *Poor Relief in England and Wales, 1601-1834* (Newton Abbot, David and Charles, 1974)

Roche, Daniel, *The People of Paris: An Essay in Popular Culture in the 18th Century,* trans. Marie Evans and Gwynne Lewis (Leamington Spa, Berg, 1987; 1981)

Root, Hilton L., *Peasants and King in Burgundy* (Berkeley, University of California Press, 1987)

Rozbicki, Michael J., "To Save them from Themselves: Proposals to Enslave the British Poor, 1698-1755," *Slavery & Abolition* 22 (2001): 29-50

Rudé, George, *Ideology and Popular Protest* (New York, Pantheon, 1980)

————, *Paris and London in the Eighteenth Century: Studies in Popular Protest* (New York, Viking, 1971)

Rule, John, *The Experience of Labour in Eighteenth-Century Industry* (London, Croom Helm, 1981)

Schwartz, Robert N., *Policing the Poor in Eighteenth-Century France* (Chapel Hill, University of North Carolina Press, 1988)

Sewell, William, *Work and Revolution in France: The Language of Labor from the Old Regime to 1848* (Cambridge, Cambridge University Press, 1980)

Sonenscher, Michael, *The Hatters of Eighteenth-Century France* (Berkeley, University of California Press, 1987)

Thompson, E. P., "The Moral Economy of the English Crowd in the Eighteenth Century," *Past & Present* 50 (1971): 71-136

Truant, Cynthia M., *The Rites of Labor: Brotherhoods of Compagnonnage in Old and New Regime France* (Ithaca, N.Y., Cornell University Press, 1994)

Woolf, Stuart, *The Poor in Western Europe in the Eighteenth and Nineteenth Century* (London, Methuen, 1986)

Popular Culture

Brennan, Thomas, *Public Drinking and Popular Culture in Eighteenth-Century Paris* (Princeton, N.J., Princeton University Press, 1988)

———, "Beyond the Barriers: Popular Culture and Parisian Ginguettes," *Eighteenth-Century Studies* 18 (1984): 153-69

Burke, Peter, *Popular Culture in Early Modern Europe* (New York, Harper & Row, 1978)

Harris, Tim, ed., *Popular Culture in England, c. 1500-1850* (Cambridge, Cambridge University Press, 1995)

Isherwood, Robert M., *Farce and Fantasy: Popular Entertainment in Eighteenth-Century Paris* (New York, Oxford University Press, 1986)

Malcolmson, R. W., *Popular Recreations in English Society, 1700-1850* (Cambridge, Cambridge University Press, 1973)

Mandrou, Robert, *De La Culture populaire aux 17e et 18e siècles: La Bibliothèque bleue de Troyes* (Paris, Stock, 1975)

Martin, Isabelle, *Le Théâtre de la foire: Des tréteaux aux boulevards, Studies on Voltaire and the Eighteenth Century* (2002) : 10

Mitchell, Harvey, "The World between the Literate and Oral Traditions in Eighteenth-Century France: Ecclesiastical Instructions and Popular Mentalities," *Studies in Eighteenth-Century Culture* 8 (1979): 33-67

———, "Rationality and Control in French Eighteenth-Century Medical Views of the Peasantry," *Comparative Studies in Society and History* 21 (1979): 82-113

Muchembled, Robert, *Popular Culture and Elite Culture in France, 1400-1750*, trans. Lydia Cochrane (Baton Rouge, Louisiana State University Press, 1985; 1978)

Payne, Harry, "Elite versus Popular Mentality in the Eighteenth Century," *Historical Reflexions* 2 (1975): 183-208

Rogers, Pat, *Literature and Popular Culture in Eighteenth-Century England* (Totowa, N.J., Barnes & Noble, 1985)

Thompson, E. P., "Patrician Society, Plebeian Culture," *Journal of Social History* 7 (1974): 382-405

———, "Eighteenth-Century English Society: Class Struggle without Class," *Social History* 3 (1978): 133-65

The Family

Ariès, Philippe, *Centuries of Childhood: A Social History of Family Life*, trans. Robert Baldick (New York, Vintage, 1962)

Fairchilds, Cissie, *Domestic Enemies: Servants and Their Masters in Eighteenth-Century France* (Baltimore, Johns Hopkins University Press, 1984)

Flandrin, Jean-Louis, *Families in Former Times: Kinship, Household and Sexuality*, trans. R. Southern (Cambridge, Cambridge University Press, 1979; 1976)

Maza, Sarah, *Servants and Masters in Eighteenth-Century France: The Uses of Loyalty* (Princeton, N.J., Princeton University Press, 1983)

Mitterauer, Michael and Sieder, Reinhard, *The European Family: Patriarchy to Partnership from the Middle Ages to the Present*, trans. K. Oosterveen and M. Horzinger (Chicago, University of Chicago Press, 1983; 1977)

O'Day, Rosemary, *The Family and Family Relationships, 1500-1900: England, France and the United States of America* (London, Macmillan, 1994)

Okin, Susan Moller, "Women and the Making of the Sentimental Family," *Philosophy and Public Affairs* 11 (1982): 65-88

Shorter, Edward, *The Making of the Modern Family* (New York, Basic, 1977)

Sussman, George D., *Selling Mother's Milk: The Wet-Nursing Business in France 1715-1914* (Urbana, University of Illinois Press, 1982)

Traer, James F., *Marriage and the Family in Eighteenth-Century France* (Ithaca, N.Y., Cornell University Press, 1980)

Troyansky, David G., *Old Age in the Old Regime: Image and Experience in Eighteenth-Century France* (Ithaca, N.Y., Cornell University Press, 1989)

Women

Backer, Dorothy Anne Liot, *Precious Women: A Feminist Phenomenon in the Age of Louis XIV* (New York, Basic, 1974)

Barber, W. H. *et al., Woman and Society in Eighteenth-Century France: Essays in Honour of John Stephenson Spink* (London, Athlone, 1979)

Darrow, Margaret, "French Noblewomen and the New Domesticity, 1750-1850," *Feminist Studies* 5 (1979): 41-65

DeJean, Joan, *Tender Geographies: The Politics of Female Authorship under the Late Ancien Régime* (New York, Columbia University Press, 1991)

Ehrman, Esther, *Mme du Châtelet: Scientist, Philosopher, and Feminist of the Enlightenment* (Leamington Spa, Berg, 1986)

Fauré, Christine, *Democracy without Women: Feminism and the Rise of Liberal Individualism in France*, trans. Claudia Gorbman and John Barks (Bloomington, Indiana University Press, 1991; 1985)

Fermon, Nicole, *Domesticating Passions: Rousseau, Woman and Nation* (Hanover, N.H., Wesleyan University Press, 1997)

Fox-Genovese, Elizabeth, "Women and the Enlightenment," in *Becoming Visible: Women in European History,* Renate Bridenthal, Claudia Koontz and Susan Stuard, eds. (Boston, Houghton Mifflin, 1987)

Gelbart, Nina Rattner, *Feminine and Opposition Journalism in Old Regime France:* Le Journal des Dames (Berkeley, University of California Press, 1987)

Goodman, Dena, "Enlightenment Salons: The Convergence of Female and Philosophic Ambitions," *Eighteenth-Century Studies* 22 (1989): 329-50

Gutwirth, Madelyn, *The Twilight of the Goddesses: Women and Representation in the French Revolutionary Era* (New Brunswick, N.J., Rutgers University Press, 1992)

Harth, Erica, *Cartesian Women: Versions and Subversions of Rational Discourse in the Old Regime* (Ithaca, N.Y., Cornell University Press, 1992)

Hesse, Carla, "Reading Signatures: Female Authorship and Revolutionary Law in France, 1750-1850," *Eighteenth-Century Studies* 22 (1989): 469-87

Kelly, Joan, "Early Feminist Theory and the *Querelle des Femmes, 1400-1789," Signs* 8 (1982): 2-28

Landes, Joan, *Women and the Public Sphere in the Age of the French Revolution* (Ithaca, N.Y., Cornell University Press, 1988)

Laqueur, Thomas, *Making Sex: Body and Gender from the Greeks to Freud* (Cambridge, Mass., Harvard University Press, 1990)

Lee, Vera, *The Reign of Women in Eighteenth-Century France* (Cambridge, Mass., Schenkman, 1975)

Merrick, Jeffrey, "Royal Bees: The Gender Politics of the Beehive in Early Modern Europe," *Studies in Eighteenth-Century Culture* 18 (1988): 7-37

Miller, Nancy K., "Men's Reading, Women's Writing: Gender and the Rise of the Novel," *Yale French Studies* 75 (1988): 40-55

Offen, Karen, "Defining Feminism: A Comparative Historical Approach," *Signs* 14 (1988): 119-57

Schwarz, Joel, *The Sexual Politics of Jean-Jacques Rousseau* (Chicago, University of Chicago Press, 1984)

Spencer, Samia I., ed., *French Women and the Age of Enlightenment* (Bloomington, Indiana University Press, 1984)

Tomaselli, Sylvana, "The Enlightenment Debate on Women," *History Workshop Journal* 20 (1985): 101-24

Weiss, Penny A., *Gendered Community: Rousseau, Sex and Politics* (New York, New York University Press, 1993)

Wexler, Victor, "'Made for Man's Delight:' Rousseau as Antifeminist," *American Historical Review* 81 (1976): 266-91

Wiesner, M. E., *Women and Gender in Early Modern Europe* (Cambridge, Cambridge University Press, 1995)

Zerilli, Linda M. G., *Signifying Woman: Culture and Chaos in Rousseau, Burke and Mill* (Ithaca, N.Y., Cornell University Press, 1994)

The Economy and Economic Thought

Background and Context

Bowles, P., "The Origin of Property and the Development of Scottish Historical Science," *Journal of the History of Ideas* 46 (1985): 197-209

Braudel, Fernand, *Civilization and Capitalism: 15th-18th Century,* vol. I, *The Structures of Everyday Life: The Limits of the Possible,* trans. Siân Reynolds (New York, Harper & Row, 1981)

————, et al., *Histoire économique et sociale de la France*, vol. II (Paris, Presses Universitaires de France, 1970)

Brewer, J. D., "Adam Ferguson and the Theme of Exploitation," *British Journal of Sociology* 37 (1986): 461-78

Deane, Phyllis, *The Evolution of Economic Ideas* (Cambridge, Cambridge University Press, 1978)

Dobb, Maurice Herbert, *Theories of Value and Distribution since Adam Smith* (Cambridge, Cambridge University Press, 1973)

Hall, John A., *Liberalism, Politics, Ideology and the Market* (London, Paladin, 1988)

Hirschsman, A., *The Passions and the Interests: Political Arguments for Capitalism before Its Triumph* (Princeton, N.J., Princeton University Press, 1977)

Hutchison, Terence W., *Before Adam Smith: The Emergence of Political Economy, 1622-1776* (Oxford, Oxford University Press, 1988)

Letwin, William, *The Origins of Scientific Economics: English Economic Thought, 1660-1776* (London, Methuen, 1963)

Mackrell, J. Q. C., *The Attack on "Feudalism" in Eighteenth-Century France* (London, Routledge & Kegan Paul, 1973)

McNally, David, *Political Economy and the Rise of Capitalism* (Berkeley, University of California Press, 1988)

Meek, Ronald L., *Economics and Ideology and Other Essays* (London, Chapman and Hall, 1967)

Rotwein, Eugene, *David Hume: Writings on Economics* (Edinburgh, Thomas Nelson and Sons, 1955)

Routh, Guy, *The Origin of Economic Ideas* (London, Macmillan, 1975)

Schumpeter, Joseph A., *History of Economic Analysis* (London, Allen & Unwin, 1954)

Skinner, Andrew S., "The Shaping of Political Economy in the Enlightenment," *Scottish Journal of Political Economy* 37 (1990): 145-65

Spengler, J. J., *French Predecessors of Malthus* (Durham, N.C., Duke University Press, 1942)

Stein, Robert Louis, *The French Slave Trade in the Eighteenth Century: An Old Regime Business* (Madison, University of Wisconsin Press, 1979)

Steiner, Philippe, *La "Science nouvelle" de l'économie politique* (Paris, Presses Universitaires de France, 1998)

Tribe, Keith, *Governing Economy: The Reformation of German Economic Discourse, 1750-1840* (Cambridge, Cambridge University Press, 1988)

Tully, James, *A Discourse on Property: John Locke and His Adversaries* (Cambridge, Cambridge University Press, 1980)

Winch, Donald, *Riches and Poverty: An Intellectual History of Political Economy in Britain, 1750-1834* (Cambridge, Cambridge University Press, 1996)

Work, Trade and Provisioning

Bouton, Cynthia, *The Flour War: Gender, Class and Community in Late Ancien Régime Society* (University Park, Pennsylvania University Press, 1993)

Hufton, Olwen, "Social Conflict and Grain Supply in Eighteenth-Century France," *Journal of Interdisciplinary History* 14 (1983): 303-32

Kaplan, Steven Laurence, *Bread Politics, and Political Economy in the Reign of Louis XV* (The Hague, Martinus Nijhoff, 2 vols., 1976)

———, *The Famine Plot Persuasion in Eighteenth-Century France* (Philadelphia, American Philosophical Society, 1982)

———, *Provisioning Paris: Merchants and Millers in the Grain and Flour Trade during the Eighteenth Century* (Ithaca, N.Y., Cornell University Press, 1984)

———, and Koepp, Cynthia J., eds., *Work in France: Representations, Meaning, Organization and Practice* (Ithaca, N.Y., Cornell University Press, 1986)

Miller, Judith A., *Mastering the Market: The State and the Grain Trade in Northern France, 1700-1860* (Cambridge, Cambridge University Press, 1999)

Root, Hilton, *The Fountain of Privilege: Political Foundations of Markets in Old Regime France and England* (Berkeley, University of California Press, 1994)

———, "The 'Moral Economy' of the Pre-Revolutionary French Peasant," *Science and Society* 54 (1990): 351-61

Rosenthal, Jean-Laurent, "Credit Markets and Economic Change in South-eastern France, 1630-1788," *Explorations in Economic History* 30 (1993): 129-57

Rotberg, Robert I. and Rabb, Theodore K., eds., *Hunger and History: The Impact of Changing Food Production and Consumption Patterns on Society* (Cambridge, Cambridge University Press, 1985)

Sewell, William H., *Work and Revolution in France: The Language of Labor from the Old Regime to 1848* (Cambridge, Cambridge University Press, 1980)

Sonenscher, Michael, *Work and Wages: Natural Law, Politics and the Eighteenth-Century French Trades* (Cambridge, Cambridge University Press, 1989)

Stevenson, John, "The Moral Economy of the English Crowd," in *Order and Disorder in Early Modern England*, ed. A. Fletcher and John Stevenson (Cambridge, Cambridge University Press, 1985)

Tilly, Charles, *The Contentious French* (Cambridge, Mass., Harvard University Press, 1985)

————, "Food Supply and Public Order in Modern Europe," in *The Formation of National States in Western Europe*, ed. Charles Tilly (Princeton, N.J., Princeton University Press, 1975)

Tilly, Louise A., "The Food Riot as a Form of Political Conflict in France," *Journal of Interdisciplinary History* 2 (1971): 23-58

Physiocracy

Beer, Max, *An Enquiry into Physiocracy* (London, Allen & Unwin, 1939)

Bloomfield, Arthur J., "The Foreign Trade Doctrine of the Physiocrats," *American Economic Review* 28 (1938): 716-35

Delamas, Bernard, Demals, Thierry and Steiner, Philippe, eds., *La Diffusion internationale de la Physiocratie: XVIIIe-XIXe* (Grenoble, Presses Universitaires de Grenoble, 1995)

Einaudi, Mario, *The Physiocratic Doctrine of Judicial Control* (Cambridge, Mass., Harvard University Press, 1938)

Foley, V., "An Origin of the *Tableau Economique*," *History of Political Economy* 5 (1973): 121-50

Fox-Genovese, Elizabeth, *The Origins of Physiocracy: Economic Revolution and Social Order in Eighteenth-Century France* (Ithaca, N.Y., Cornell University Press, 1976)

Groenewegen, Peter D., *The Economics of A. R. J. Turgot* (The Hague, Martinus Nijhoff, 1977)

Higgs, Henry, *The Physiocrats: Six Lectures on the French Economists of the Eighteenth Century* (London, Macmillan, 1897)

Kuczynski, Marguerite, and Meek, Ronald L., *Quesnay's Tableau économique* (London, Royal Economics Society, 1972)

Laugier, Lucien, *Turgot, ou le mythe des réformes* (Paris, Albatross, 1979)

Meek, Ronald L., *The Economics of Physiocracy: Essays and Translations* (London, Allen & Unwin, 1962)

Miller, J., *The Pragmatic Economy: Liberal Reform in the Grain Trade in Upper Normandy, 1750-1789* (Durham, N.C., Duke University Press, 1987)

Samuels, Warren J., "The Physiocratic Theory of Property and State," *Quarterly Journal of Economics* 76 (1962): 145-62

Saricks, Ambrose, *Pierre Samuel Du Pont de Nemours* (Lawrence, University of Kansas Press, 1965)

Steiner, Philippe, "Wealth Power: Quesnay's Political Economy of the Agricultural Kingdom," *Journal of the History of Economic Thought* 24 (2002): 91-110

Vaggi, Giuanni, *The Economics of François Quesnay* (Hong Kong, Duke University Press, 1987)

Weulersse, Georges, *Le Mouvement Physiocratique en France, 1756-1770* (Paris, Mouton, 2 vols., 1968; 1910)

Adam Smith and Liberal Economics

Brown, Vivienne, *Adam Smith's Discourse: Canonicity, Commerce and Conscience* (London, Routledge, 1994)

Campbell, T. D., *Adam Smith's Science of Morality* (London, Allen & Unwin, 1971)

Chisick, Harvey, "The Wealth of Nations and the Poverty of the People in the Thought of Adam Smith," *Canadian Journal of History* 25 (1990): 325-44

Cropsey, J., *Polity and Economy: An Interpretation of Adam Smith* (The Hague, Martinus Nijhoff, 1957)

Dickey, Laurence, "Historicizing the 'Adam Smith Problem:' Conceptual, Historiographical and Textual Issues," *Journal of Modern History* 58 (1986): 579-609

Fitzgibbons, Athol, *Adam Smith's System of Liberty, Wealth and Virtue: The Moral and Political Foundations of the* Wealth of Nations (Oxford, Clarendon Press, 1995)

Grisworld, Charles L., *Adam Smith and the Virtues of Enlightenment* (Cambridge, Cambridge University Press, 1999)

Hollander, Samuel, *The Economics of Adam Smith* (Toronto, Toronto University Press, 1973)

Jones, Peter, and Skinner, Andrew, eds., *Adam Smith Reviewed* (Edinburgh, Edinburgh University Press, 1992)

Lindgren, J. Ralph, *The Social Philosophy of Adam Smith* (The Hague, Martinus Nijhoff, 1973)

Macfie, Alec Lawrence, *The Individual in Society: Papers on Adam Smith* (London, Allen & Unwin, 1967)

———, "The Invisible Hand of Jupiter," *Journal of the History of Ideas* 32 (1971): 595-99

Malloy, Robin Paul, and Evensky, Jerry, eds., *Adam Smith and the Philosophy of Law and Economics* (Dordrecht, Kluwer, 1994)

Meek, Ronald L., "Adam Smith and the Classical Concept of Profit," *Scottish Journal of Political Economy* 1 (1954)

———, *Smith, Marx and After* (London, Chapman & Hall, 1977)

Peil, John, *Adam Smith and Economic Science: A Methodological Reinterpretation* (Cheltenham, E. Elgar, 1999)

Redman, Deborah A., "Adam Smith and Isaac Newton," *Scottish Journal of Political Economy* 40 (1993): 210-30

Reisman, David A., *Adam Smith's Sociological Economics* (London, Croom Helm, 1976)

Robertson, John, "Scottish Political Economy beyond the Civic Tradition: Government and Economic Development in the *Wealth of Nations*," *History of Political Thought* 4 (1983): 137-78

Ross, Ian Simpson, *The Life of Adam Smith* (Oxford, Clarendon Press, 1995)

Salter, J., "Adam Smith on Feudalism, Commerce and Slavery," *History of Political Thought* 13 (1992): 219-41

Skinner, Andrew, and Wilson, T., eds., *Essays on Adam Smith* (Oxford, Clarendon Press, 1975)

Taylor, W. L., *Francis Hutcheson and David Hume as Predecessors of Adam Smith* (Durham, N.C., Duke University Press, 1965)

Teichgrabber, Richard F. III, *"Free Trade" and Moral Philosophy: Rethinking the Sources of Adam Smith's* Wealth of Nations (Durham, N.C., Duke University Press, 1986)

Walther, Rudolf, "Economic Liberalism," *Economy and Society* 13 (1984): 178-207

Werhane, Patricia Hogue, *Adam Smith and His Legacy for Modern Capitalism* (Oxford, Oxford University Press, 1991)

Politics

States and Government

Behrens, C. B. A., *Society, Government and the Enlightenment: The Experiences of Eighteenth-Century France and Prussia* (New York, Harper & Row, 1985)

Bernard, Paul, *The Limits of Enlightenment: Joseph II and the Law* (Urbana, University of Illinois Press, 1979)

Blanning, T. C. W., *The Culture of Power and the Power of Culture: Old-Regime Europe, 1660-1789* (Cambridge, Cambridge University Press, 2002)

Brewer, John, *The Sinews of Power: War, Money and the English State, 1688-1783* (Oxford, Oxford University Press, 1989)

Campbell, Peter Robert, *Power and Politics in Old-Regime France, 1720-45* (London, Routledge, 1996)

Clark, J. C. D., *English Society, 1688-1832* (Cambridge, Cambridge University Press, 1985)

Collins, James B., *The State in Early Modern France* (Cambridge, Cambridge University Press, 1995)

Dickinson, H. T., *The Politics of the People in Eighteenth-Century Britain* (New York, St. Martin's Press, 1995)

Dickson, Peter George Muir, *Finance and Government under Maria Theresa, 1740-1780* (Oxford, Clarendon Press, 2 vols., 1987)

Doyle, William, *The Old European Order, 1660-1800* (Oxford, Oxford University Press, 1978)

———, "The Parlements of France and the Breakdown of the Old Regime, 1771-1788," *French Historical Studies* 6 (1970): 415-58

Dukes, Paul, *The Making of Russian Absolutism, 1613-1801* (London, Longman, 1990)

Echeverria, Durand, *The Maupeou Revolution: A Study in the History of Libertarianism; France, 1770-1774* (Baton Rouge, Louisiana State University Press, 1985)

Ellis, Harold A., *Boulainvilliers and the French Monarchy: Aristocratic Politics in Eighteenth-Century France* (Ithaca, N.Y., Cornell University Press, 1988)

Ford, Franklin, *Robe and Sword: The Regrouping of the French Aristocracy after Louis XIV* (Cambridge, Mass., Harvard University Press, 1953)

Gagliardo, John, *Germany under the Old Regime, 1600-1790* (London, Longman, 1991)

Gascoigne, John, "Politics, Patronage and Newtonianism: The Cambridge Example," *Historical Journal* 27 (1984): 1-24

Hardman, John, *French Politics, 1774-1789: From the Accession of Louis XVI to the Fall of the Bastille* (London, Longman, 1995)

Ingrao, Charles, *The Habsburg Monarchy, 1618-1815* (Cambridge, Cambridge University Press, 1994)

Johnson, Hubert C., *Frederick the Great and His Officials* (New Haven, Conn., Yale University Press, 1975)

Kann, Robert A., *A History of the Habsburg Empire, 1526-1918* (Berkeley, University of California Press, 1974)

Le Roy Ladurie, Emmanuel, *The Ancien Régime: A History of France, 1610-1774*, trans. Mark Greengrass (Oxford, Blackwell, 1996; 1991)

Lukowski, J. T., *Liberty's Folly: The Polish-Lithuanian Commonwealth in the Eighteenth Century* (London, Routledge, 1991)

Méthivier, Hubert, *L'Ancien Régime en France: XVIe-XVIIe-XVIIIe siècles* (Paris, Presses Universitaires de France, 1981)

Mousnier, Roland E., *The Institutions of France under the Absolute Monarchy, 1589-1789*, trans. Brian Pearce and Arthur Goldhammer (Chicago, University of Chicago Press, 2 vols., 1979-1984; 1974-1980)

Namier, Lewis, *The Structure of Politics at the Accession of George III* (New York, St. Martin's Press, 1963; 1929)

O'Gorman, Frank, *Voters, Patrons and Parties: The Unreformed Electorate of Hanoverian England, 1734-1832* (Oxford, Oxford University Press, 1989)

Parker, David, *Class and State in Ancien Régime France: The Road to Modernity* (London, Routledge, 1996)

Rosenberg, Hans, *Bureaucracy, Aristocracy and Autocracy: The Prussian Experience, 1660-1815* (Cambridge, Mass., Harvard University Press, 1958)

Shennan, J. H., *Liberty and Order in Early Modern Europe: The Subject and the State, 1650-1800* (London, Longman, 1986)

———, *The Parlement of Paris* (Stroud, Sutton, 1998; 1968)

Smith, Jay M., *The Culture of Merit: Nobility, Royal Service and the Making of Absolute Monarchy in France, 1600-1789* (Ann Arbor, University of Michigan Press, 1996)

Stone, Bailey, *The French Parlements and the Crisis of the Old Order* (Chapel Hill, University of North Carolina Press, 1986)

Strakosch, Henry E., *State Absolutism and the Rule of Law: The Struggle for the Codification of Civil Law in Austria, 1753-1811* (Sydney, Sydney University Press, 1967)

Swann, Julian, *Politics and the Parlement of Paris under Louis XV, 1754-1774* (London, Routledge, 1996)

Wangermann, Ernst, *The Austrian Achievement: 1700-1800* (London, Thames and Hudson, 1973)

Political Theory

Althusser, Louis, *Montesquieu, Rousseau, Marx: Politics and History*, trans. Ben Brewster (London, Verso, 1982)

Appleby, Joyce, "Republicanism in Old and New Contexts," *William and Mary Quarterly* 43 (1986): 20-34

Baker, Keith Michael, *Inventing the French Revolution: Essays on French Political Culture in the Eighteenth Century* (Cambridge, Cambridge University Press, 1990)

Bates, David, "Between Error and Enlightenment: Condorcet and the Theory of Political Decision," *The Eighteenth Century: Theory and Interpretation* 36 (1995): 55-74

Bell, David A., *The Cult of the Nation in France: Inventing Nationalism, 1680-1800* (Cambridge, Mass., Harvard University Press, 2003)

Bourke, Richard, "Edmund Burke and Enlightenment Sociability: Justice, Honour and the Principles of Government," *History of Political Thought* 21 (2000): 632-56

Caplow, Theodore, "St. Pierre and the Project of Perpetual Peace," *Tocqueville Review* 8 (1986-1987): 111-123

Carcassonne, E., *Montesquieu et le problème de la Constitution française au XVIIIe siècle* (Paris, Presses Universitaires de France, 1927)

Carrithers, David A., Mosher, Michael A., and Rahe, Paul A., eds., *Montesquieu's Science of Politics: Essays on* The Spirit of the Laws (Lanham, Md., Rowman & Littlefield, 2001)

Chisick, Harvey, "Utopia, Reform and Revolution: The Political Assumptions of L. S. Mercier's *L'An 2440*," *History of Political Thought* 22 (2001): 648-68

Colley, Linda, *Britons: Forging the Nation, 1707-1837* (New Haven, Conn., Yale University Press, 1992)

Confer, Vincent, "French Colonial Ideas before 1789," *French Historical Studies* 3 (1964): 338-59

Cranston, Maurice, *Philosophers and Pamphleteers: Political Theorists of the Enlightenment* (New York, Oxford University Press, 1986)

Crocker, Lester G., "Interpreting the Enlightenment: A Political Approach," *Journal of the History of Ideas* 46 (1985): 211-31

Cumming, Robert D., *Human Nature and History: A Study of the Development of Liberal Political Thought* (Chicago, University of Chicago Press, 1969)

Danford, John W., "'The Surest Foundation of Morality': The Political Teaching of Hume's *Dialogues Concerning Natural Religion*," *Western Political Quarterly* 35 (1982): 137-60

Derathé, Robert, *Jean-Jacques Rousseau et la science politique de son temps* (Paris, Vrin, 1970)

Diaz, Furio, "La Représentation dans la formation du système démocratique: une esquisse historique," *Parliaments, Estates & Representation* 8 (1988): 115-24

Dickinson, H. T., *Liberty and Property: Political Ideology in Eighteenth-Century Britain* (London, Weidenfield and Nicolson, 1977)

Durkheim, Emile, *Montesquieu and Rousseau: Forerunners of Sociology*, trans. Ralph Manheim (Ann Arbor, University of Michigan Press, 1965)

Ellis, Harold A., "Montesquieu's Modern Politics: *The Spirit of the Laws* and the Problem of Modern Monarchy in Old-Regime France," *History of Political Thought* 10 (1989): 665-700

Farr, James, "Political Science and the Enlightenment of Enthusiasm," *American Political Science Review* 82 (1988): 51-69

Fontana, Biancamaria, ed., *The Invention of the Modern Republic* (Cambridge, Cambridge University Press, 1994)

Garrard, Graeme, "Rousseau, Maistre, and the Counter-Enlightenment," *History of Political Thought* 15 (1994): 97-120

Gay, Peter, *Voltaire's Politics: The Poet as Realist* (New Haven, Conn., Yale University Press, 1988; 1959)

Ghachem, Malick W., "Montesquieu in the Caribbean: The Colonial Enlightenment between Code Noir and Code Civil," *Historical Reflections* 25 (1999): 183-210

Goodman, Dena, *Criticism in Action: Enlightenment Experiments in Political Writing* (Ithaca, N.Y., Cornell University Press, 1989)

Gordon, Daniel, *Citizens without Sovereignty: Equality and Sociability in French Thought, 1670-1789* (Princeton, N.J., Princeton University Press, 1994)

Gough, J. W., *The Social Contract: A Critical Study of Its Development* (Oxford, Oxford University Press, 1957; 1936)

Gunn, J. A. W., *Beyond Liberty and Property: The Process of Self-Recognition in Eighteenth-Century Political Thought* (Kingston and Montreal, McGill-Queen's University Press, 1983)

Haakonssen, Knud, *The Science of a Legislator: The Natural Jurisprudence of David Hume and Adam Smith* (Cambridge, Cambridge University Press, 1981)

———, "Moral Philosophy and Natural Law: From the Cambridge Platonists to the Scottish Enlightenment," *Political Science* 40 (1988): 97-110

———, "The Science of a Legislator in James Mackintosh's Moral Philosophy," *History of Political Thought* 5 (1984): 245-80

Higonnet, Patrice, *Sister Republics: The Origins of French and American Republicanism* (Cambridge, Mass., Harvard University Press, 1988)

Horne, Thomas A., *Property Rights and Society: Political Argument in Britain, 1605-1834* (Chapel Hill, University of North Carolina Press, 1990)

Houston, Alan Craig, *Algernon Sidney and the Republican Heritage in England and America* (Princeton, N.J., Princeton University Press, 1981)

Hulliung, Mark, *Montesquieu and the Old Regime* (Berkeley, University of California Press, 1976)

Hundert, Edward J., *The Enlightenment's Fable: Bernard Mandeville and the Discovery of Society* (New York: Cambridge University Press, 1994)

———, "Market Society and Meaning in Locke's Political Philosophy," *Journal of the History of Philosophy* 15 (1977): 33-44

Kaiser, Thomas E., "The Evil Empire: The Debate on Turkish Despotism in Eighteenth-Century French Political Culture," *Journal of Modern History* 72 (2000): 6-34

Keohane, Nannerl O., *Philosophy and the State in France: The Renaissance to the Enlightenment* (Princeton, N.J., Princeton University Press, 1980)

Kramnick, Isaac, *Bolingbroke and His Circle: The Politics of Nostalgia in the Age of Walpole* (Cambridge, Mass., Harvard University Press, 1968)

———, *Republicanism and Bourgeois Radicalism: Political Ideology in Late Eighteenth-Century England and America* (Ithaca, N.Y., Cornell University Press, 1990)

Landes, Joan B., *Visualizing the Nation: Gender, Representation and Revolution in Eighteenth-Century France* (Ithaca, N.Y., Cornell University Press, 2001)

La Vopa, Anthony J., "The Politics of Enlightenment: Friedrich Gedikeand and German Professional Ideology," *Journal of Modern History* 62 (1990): 34-56

Levinger, Matthew, "Kant and the Origins of Prussian Constitutionalism," *History of Political Thought* 19 (1998): 241-63

Levy, Darline Gay, *The Ideas and Careers of Simon-Nicolas-Henri Linguet: A Study in Eighteenth-Century French Politics* (Urbana: University of Illinois Press, 1980)

Loft, Leonore, "The Repudiation of Tradition and the Status Quo in Brissot's Pre-Revolutionary Pamphlets," *Consortium on Revolutionary Europe* 23 (1994): 324-31

Luke, Timothy W., "On Nature and Society: Rousseau versus the Enlightenment," *History of Political Thought* 5 (1984): 211-43

Lukowski, J. T., "Towards the Ideal Constitution: Rousseau, Montesquieu and 3 May 1791," *Parliaments, Estates & Representation* 15 (1995): 59-66

Lüthy, Herbert, *Calvin to Rousseau: Tradition and Modernity in Socio-Political Thought from the Reformation to the French Revolution*, trans. Salvator Attanasio (New York, Basic, 1970)

Mali, Joseph, "The Poetics of Politics: Vico's Philosophy of Authority" *History of Political Thought* 10 (1989): 41-69

Mason, Sheila Mary, *Montesquieu's Idea of Justice* (The Hague, Martinus Nijhoff, 1975)

Masters, Roger D., *The Political Philosophy of Rousseau* (Princeton, N.J., Princeton University Press, 1968)

McDowall, Gary L., "Commerce, Virtue and Politics: Adam Ferguson's Constitutionalism," *Review of Politics* 45 (1983): 536-52

Melton, James Van Horn, "From Enlightenment to Revolution: Hertzberg, Schlozer, and the Problem of Despotism in the Late Aufklärung," *Central European History* 12 (1979): 103-23

Merrick, Jeffrey, *The Desacralization of the French Monarchy in the Eighteenth Century* (Baton Rouge, Louisiana State University Press, 1990)

———, "Conscience and Citizenship in Eighteenth-Century France," *Eighteenth-Century Studies* 21 (1987): 48-70

———, "Patriarchalism and Constitutionalism in Eighteenth-Century Parlementary Discourse," *Studies in Eighteenth-Century Culture* 20 (1990): 317-30

———, "Subjects and Citizens in the Remonstrances of the Parlement of Paris in the Eighteenth Century," *Journal of the History of Ideas* 51 (1990): 453-60

Miller, David, *Philosophy and Ideology in Hume's Political Thought* (Oxford, Clarendon Press, 1981)

Moore, James, "Hume's Political Science and the Classical Republican Tradition," *Canadian Journal of Political Science* 10 (1977): 809-39

Morgenstern, Mira, *Rousseau and the Politics of Ambiguity: Self, Culture and Society* (College Park, Pennsylvania State University Press, 1996)

Mori, Jennifer, "The Political Theory of William Pitt the Younger," *History* 83 (1998): 234-48

Newman, Gerald, *The Rise of English Nationalism: A Cultural History, 1740-1830* (New York, St. Martin's Press, 1987)

Pagden, Anthony, "The Genesis of 'Governance' and Enlightenment Conceptions of the Cosmopolitan World Order," *International Social Science Journal* 50 (1998): 7-15

Pangle, T. L., *Montesquieu's Philosophy of Liberalism: A Commentary on "The Spirit of the Laws"* (Chicago, University of Chicago Press, 1973)

Plamenatz, John, *Man and Society: Political and Social Theory, Machiavelli through Rousseau* (New York, McGraw-Hill, 2 vols., 1963)

Pocock, J. G. A., *Politics, Language and Time: Essays on Political Thought and History* (New York, Atheneum, 1971)

———, *The Machiavellian Moment: Florentine Political Thought and the Atlantic Republican Tradition* (Princeton, N.J., Princeton University Press, 1975)

———, *Virtue, Commerce and History: Essays on Political Thought and History, Mostly in the Eighteenth Century* (Cambridge, Cambridge University Press, 1985)

———, "Gibbon's *Decline and Fall* and the World View of the Late Enlightenment," *Eighteenth-Century Studies* 10 (1977): 287-303

Popkin, Jeremy, "The Business of Political Enlightenment in France, 1770-1800," in John Brewer and Roy Porter, eds., *Consumption and the World of Goods* (London, Routledge, 1993)

Rahe, Paul A., *Republics: Ancient and Modern* (Chapel Hill, University of North Carolina Press, 3 vols., 1992-1994)

Resnick, David, "Locke and the Rejection of the Ancient Constitution," *Political Theory* 12 (1984): 97-114

Ripley, Randall B., "Adams, Burke and Eighteenth-Century Conservatism," *Political Science Quarterly* 80 (1965): 216-35

Robbins, Caroline, *The Eighteenth-Century Commonwealthman: Studies on the Transmission, Development and Circumstances of English Liberal Thought from the Restoration of Charles II until the War with the Thirteen Colonies* (Cambridge, Mass., Harvard University Press, 1959)

Rosen, F., "Crime, Punishment and Liberty," *History of Political Thought* 20 (1999): 173-85

Saint-Amand, Pierre, *The Laws of Hostility: Politics, Violence, and the Enlightenment*, trans. Jennifer Curtiss Gage (Minneapolis, University of Minnesota Press, 1996; 1992)

———, "Original Vengeance: Politics, Anthropology, and the French Enlightenment," *Eighteenth-Century Studies* 26 (1993): 399-417

Salmon, J. H. M., "Renaissance Jurists and 'Enlightened' Magistrates: Perspectives on Feudalism in Eighteenth-Century France," *French History* 8 (1994): 387-402

Sarubbi, Antonio, "Representation in the Late Reformist Period and in Southern Italian Jacobinism," *Parliaments, Estates & Representation* 19 (1999): 151-62

Shklar, Judith N., *Men and Citizens: A Study of Rousseau's Social Theory* (Cambridge, Cambridge University Press, 1985; 1969)

———, *Montesquieu* (Oxford, Oxford University Press, 1987)

Simonutti, Luisa, "Between Political Loyalty and Religious Liberty: Political Theory and Toleration in Huguenot Thought in the Epoch of Bayle," *History of Political Thought* 17 (1996): 523-54

Sorenson, L. R., "Rousseau's Liberalism," *History of Political Thought* 11 (1990): 443-66

Spragens, Thomas A., Jr., "The Politics of Inertia and Gravitation: The Functions of Exemplar Paradigms in Social Thought," *Polity* 5 (1973): 288-310

Striner, Richard, "Political Newtonianism: The Cosmic Model Of Politics in Europe and America," *William and Mary Quarterly* 52 (1995): 583-608

Strugnell, Anthony, *Diderot's Politics: A Study in the Evolution of Diderot's Political Thought after the Encyclopédie* (The Hague, Martinus Nijhoff, 1973)

Swenson, James, *On Jean-Jacques Rousseau Considered as One of the First Authors of the Revolution* (Stanford, Calif., Stanford University Press, 2000)

Velema, Wyger R. E., *Enlightenment and Conservatism in the Dutch Republic: The Political Thought of Elie Luzac, 1721-1796* (Assen, Netherlands, Van Gorcum, 1993)

Vile, M. C. J., *Constitutionalism and the Separation of Powers* (Oxford, Oxford Univeristy Press, 1967)

Vernon, Richard, *Citizenship and Order: Studies in French Political Thought* (Toronto, Toronto University Press, 1986)

Waddicor, Mark H., *Montesquieu and the Philosophy of Natural Law* (The Hague, Martinus Nijhoff, 1970)

Walicki, Andrzej, *The Enlightenment and the Birth of Modern Nationhood: Polish Political Thought from Noble Republicanism to Tadeusz Kosciuszko* (Notre Dame, Indiana, University of Notre Dame Press, 1989)

Whelan, Frederick G., "Oriental Despotism: Anquetil-Duperron's Response to Montesquieu," *History of Political Thought* 22 (2001): 619-47

Wilson, Arthur M., "Why Did the Political Theory of the Encyclopedists not Prevail? A Suggestion," *French Historical Studies* 1 (1960): 283-94

Wilson, David A., *Paine and Cobbett: The Transatlantic Connection* (Kingston and Montreal, McGill-Queen's University Press, 1988)

Winch, Donald, *Adam Smith's Politics: An Essay in Historiographic Revision* (Cambridge, Cambridge University Press, 1978)

Wright, Johnson Kent, *A Classical Republican in Eighteenth-Century France: The Political Thought of Mably* (Cambridge, Cambridge University Press, 1995)

———, "Conversations with Phocion: The Political Thought of Mably," *History of Political Thought* 13 (1992): 391-415

Zuckert, Michael, *Natural Rights and the New Republicanism* (Princeton, N.J., Princeton University Press, 1994)

Public Opinion

Baker, Keith Michael, "Politics and Public Opinion under the Old Regime: Some Reflections," in *Press and Politics in Pre-Revolutionary France*, ed. Jack Censer and Jeremy Popkin (Berkeley, University of California Press, 1987), 204-46

———, "Defining the Public Sphere in Eighteenth-Century France: Variations on a Theme by Habermas," in *Habermas and the Public Sphere*, ed. Craig Calhoun (Cambridge, Mass., MIT Press, 1993), 181-211

Bell, David A., "'Public Sphere,' the State and the World of Law in Eighteenth-Century France," *French Historical Studies* 17 (1992): 912-34

Brewer, John, "The Misfortunes of Lord Bute: A Case Study in Eighteenth-Century Political Argument and Public Opinion," *Historical Journal* 16 (1973): 7-43

Chisick, Harvey, "Public Opinion and Political Culture in France during the Second Half of the Eighteenth Century," *English Historical Review* 117 (2002): 48-77

Cowans, Jon, *To Speak for the People: Public Opinion and the Problem of Legitimacy in the French Revolution* (New York, Routledge, 2001)

———, "Habermas and French History: The Public Sphere and the Problem of Political Legitimacy," *French History* 13 (1999): 134-60

Desan, Susan, "What's after Political Culture?" *French Historical Studies* 23 (2000): 163-96

Downie, James Alan, *Robert Harley and the Press: Propaganda and Public Opinion in the Age of Swift and Defoe* (Cambridge, Cambridge University Press, 1979)

Farge, Arlette, *Subversive Words: Public Opinion in Eighteenth-Century France*, trans. Rosemary Morris (Cambridge, Polity Press, 1994; 1992)

Graham, Lisa Jane, *If Only the King Knew: Seditious Speech in the Reign of Louis XV* (Charlottesville, University Press of Virginia, 2000)

———, "Crimes of Opinion: Policing the Public in Eighteenth-Century Paris," in Christine Adams, Jack R. Censer and Lisa Jane Graham, eds., *Visions and Revisions of Eighteenth-Century France* (University Park, Pennsylvania State University Press, 1997), 79-103

Gunn, J. A. W., *Queen of the World: Opinion in the Public Life of France from the Renaissance to the Revolution, Studies on Voltaire and the Eighteenth Century* 328 (1995)

Habermas, Jürgen, *The Structural Transformation of the Public Sphere: An Inquiry into a Category of Bourgeois Society,* trans. Thomas Burger with Frederick Lawrence (Cambridge, Mass., MIT Press, 1991; 1962)

Kaiser, Thomas E., "The *Abbé* de Saint Pierre, Public Opinion, and the Reconstruction of the French Monarchy," *Journal of Modern History* 55 (1983): 618-43

———, "The Abbé Dubos and the Concept of Public Judgement," *Eighteenth-Century Studies* 23 (1989-1990): 182-99

———, "Money, Despotism, and Public Opinion in Early Eighteenth-Century France: John Law and the Debate on Royal Credit," *Journal of Modern History* 63 (1991): 1-28

La Vopa, Anthony J., "Conceiving a Public: Ideas and Society in Eighteenth-Century Europe," *Journal of Modern History* 44 (1992): 79-116

Melton, James Van Horne, *The Rise of the Public in Enlightenment Europe* (Cambridge, Cambridge University Press, 2001)

Merrick, Jeffrey, "'Disputes over Words' and Constitutional Conflict in France, 1730-1732," *French Historical Studies* 14 (1986): 497-520

Nathans, Benjamin, "Habermas's 'Public Sphere' in the Era of the French Revolution," *French Historical Studies* 16 (1990): 620-44

Ozouf, Mona, "Public Opinion at the End of the Old Regime," *Journal of Modern History* 40 (1988), supplement, S1-S21

Porter, Roy, "Science, Provincial Culture and Public Opinion in Enlightenment England," in Peter Borsay, ed., *The Eighteenth-Century Town: A Reader in English Urban History, 1688-1820* (London, Longman, 1990), 243-67

Van Kley, Dale, "In Search of Eighteenth-Century Parisian Public Opinion," *French Historical Studies* 19 (1995): 215-26

Reform

Bailyn, Bernard, "Political Experience and Enlightenment Ideas in Eighteenth-Century America," *American Historical Review* 67 (1962): 339-51

Blanning, T. C. W., *Reform and Revolution in Mainz, 1743-1830* (Cambridge, Cambridge University Press, 1974)

———, *Reform in Great Britain and Germany, 1750-1850* (Oxford, Oxford University Press, 1999)

Bosher, John F., *The Single Duty Project: A Study of the Movement for a French Customs Union in the Eighteenth Century* (London, Athlone, 1964)

———, *French Finances, 1770-1795: From Business to Bureaucracy* (Cambridge, Cambridge University Press, 1970)

Carey, John A., *Judicial Reform in France before the Revolution of 1789* (Cambridge, Mass., Harvard University Press, 1981)

Dakin, Douglas, *Turgot and the Old Regime in France* (New York, Octagon, 1980; 1939)

Engstrand, Iris H. W., "The Enlightenment in Spain: Influences upon New World Policy," *Americas* 41 (1985): 436-44

Harris, Robert D., *Necker: Reform Statesman of the Ancien Régime* (Berkeley, University of California Press, 1979)

Henderson, Nicholas, "Joseph II," *History Today* 41 (1991): 21-27

Ingrao, Charles, *The Hessian Mercenary State: Ideas, Institutions and Reform under Frederick II, 1760-1785* (Cambridge, Cambridge University Press, 1987)

Jacobson, David Y., "The Trois Roues Case and the Debate over Criminal Law Reform in Late Eighteenth-Century France," *Proceedings of the Annual Meeting of the Western Society for French History* 4 (1976): 168-73

Keller, Katrin, "Retablissement and Enlightened Absolutism," *German History* 20 (2002): 309-31

Kern, Edmund M., "An End to Witch Trials in Austria: Reconsidering the Enlightened State," *Austrian History Yearbook* 30 (1999): 159-85

Klaits, Joseph, "Men of Letters and Political Reform in France at the End of the Reign of Louis XIV: The Founding of the *Académie politique*," *Journal of Modern History* 43 (1971): 577-99

Klang, Daniel M., *Tax Reform in Eighteenth-Century Lombardy* (Boulder, Colorado, East European Quarterly, 1977)

———, "Reform and Enlightenment in Eighteenth-Century Lombardy," *Canadian Journal of History* 19 (1984): 39-70.

Letzring, Monica, "Teresa Margarida da Silva e Orta and the Portuguese Enlightenment," *Studies in Eighteenth-Century Culture* 15 (1986): 111-26

Nicassio, Susan Vandiver, "Reform in Modena," *Consortium on Revolutionary Europe* 21 (1992): 320-27

Shepherd, Robert Perry, *Turgot and the Six Edicts* (New York, AMS, 1970; 1903)

Stoddard, Eve W., "A Serious Proposal for Slavery Reform: Sarah Scott's Sir George Ellison," *Eighteenth-Century Studies* 28 (1995): 379-96

Szabo, Franz A., "Haugwitz, Kaunitz, and the Structure of Government in Austria under Maria Theresia, 1745 to 1761," *Historical Papers* (1979): 111-30

Venturi, Franco, *Utopia and Reform in the Enlightenment* (Cambridge, Cambridge University Press, 1971)

———, "Church and Reform in Enlightenment Italy: The Sixties of the Eighteenth Century," *Journal of Modern History* 48 (1976): 215-32

Enlightened Despotism

Alexander, John T., *Catherine the Great: Life and Legend* (New York, Oxford University Press, 1989)

Balazs, Eva H., *Hungary and the Habsburgs, 1765-1800: An Experiment in Enlightened Absolutism*, trans. Tim Wilkinson (London, Central European University Press, 1997)

Beales, Derek, *Joseph II* (Cambridge, Cambridge University Press, 1987)

Behrens, Betty, "Enlightened Despotism," *Historical Journal* 18 (1975): 401-8

Bernard, Paul P., *From the Enlightenment to the Police State: The Public Life of Johann Anton Pergen* (Urbana, University of Illinois Press, 1991)

Blanning, T. C. W., *Joseph II and Enlightened Absolutism* (London, Longman, 1970)

Brennan, James F., *Enlightened Despotism in Russia: The Reign of Elisabeth, 1741-1762* (New York, Peter Lang, 1987)

Bruun, Geoffrey, *The Enlightened Despots* (New York, Holt, Rinehart and Winston, 1967; 1929)

Campbell, Leon G., "Recent Research on Bourbon Enlightened Despotism, 1750-1824," *New Scholar* 7 (1978): 29-50

Cavallar, Georg, "Kant's Judgment on Frederick's Enlightened Absolutism," *History of Political Thought* 14 (1993): 103-32

Cavanaugh, Gerald J., "Turgot: The Rejection of Enlightened Despotism," *French Historical Studies* 6 (1969): 31-58

Dixon, Peter, "Joseph II's Reshaping of the Austrian Church," *Historical Journal* 36 (1993): 89-114

Duffy, C., *Frederick the Great: A Military Life* (London, Routledge, 1988)

Gagliardo, John G., *Enlightened Despotism* (New York, Crowell, 1967)

Grab, Alexander J., "The Politics of Subsistence: The Liberalization of Grain Commerce in Austrian Lombardy under Enlightened Despotism," *Journal of Modern History* 57 (1985): 185-210

Griffin, Frederick C., "Catherine The Great and Voltaire," *Studies in History and Society* 4 (1972): 12-18

Herr, Richard, *The Eighteenth-Century Revolution in Spain* (Princeton, N.J., Princeton University Press, 1958)

Ingrao, Charles, "The Problem of 'Enlightened Absolutism' and the German States," *Journal of Modern History* 58 (1986): S161-S180

Kiraly, Bela K., "The Political and Social Legacy of the Enlightenment to the Hungarian National Revival," *Canadian Review of Studies in Nationalism* 10 (1983): 5-15

Klingenstein, Grete, "Revisions of Enlightened Absolutism: 'The Austrian Monarchy is like No Other'," *Historical Journal* 33 (1990): 155-67

Krieger, Leonard, *An Essay on the Theory of Enlightened Despotism* (Chicago, University of Chicago Press, 1975)

Lentin, A., *Enlightened Absolutism (1760-1790): A Documentary Sourcebook* (Newcastle-upon-Tyne, Avero, 1985)

Maxwell, Kenneth, *Pombal, Paradox of the Enlightenment* (New York, Cambridge University Press, 1995)

Mueller, Christine L., "Enlightened Absolutism," *Austrian History Yearbook* 25 (1994): 159-83.

Omel'chenko, O. A., "The 'Legitimate Monarchy' of Catherine the Second: Enlightened Absolutism in Russia," *Russian Studies in History* 33 (1995): 66-94

Paret, Peter, *Frederick the Great: A Profile* (London, Macmillan, 1968)

Parry, G., "Enlightened Government and Its Critics in Eighteenth-Century Germany," *Historical Journal* 6 (1963): 89-114

Petrie, Charles, *King Charles III of Spain: An Enlightened Despot* (London, Constable, 1971)

Raeff, Marc, *The Well-Ordered Police State: Social and Institutional Change through Law in the Germanies and Russia, 1600-1800* (New Haven, Conn., Yale University Press, 1983)

Reddaway, William Fidian, ed., *Documents of Catherine II: The Correspondence with Voltaire and the Instruction of 1767 in the English Text of 1768* (Cambridge, Cambridge University Press, 1971; 1931)

Ritter, Gerhard, *Frederick the Great*, trans. Peter Paret (Berkeley, University of California Press, 1978; 1954)

Salmonowicz, Stanislaw, "Was Frederick the Great an Enlightened Absolute Ruler?" *Polish Western Affairs* 22 (1981): 56-69

Scott, H. M., ed., *Enlightened Absolutism: Reform and Reformers in Later Eighteenth-Century Europe* (Ann Arbor: University of Michigan Press, 1990)

———, "Whatever Happened to the Enlightened Despots?" *History* 68 (1983): 245-57

Szabo, Franz A., *Kaunitz and Enlightened Absolutism, 1753-1780* (Cambridge, Cambridge University Press, 1994)

———, "Reevaluating the Habsburg Monarchy from Counter-Reformation to Enlightened Absolutism," *Dalhousie Review* 68 (1988): 336-56

Wangermann, Ernst, *Government Policy and Public Opinion in the Habsburg Dominions in the Period of the French Revolution* (Oxford, Oxford University Press, 1959)

———, *From Joseph II to the Jacobin Trials* (Oxford, Oxford University Press, 1969)

Weis, Eberhard, "Enlightenment and Absolutism in the Holy Roman Empire: Thoughts on Enlightened Absolutism," *Journal of Modern History* 58 (1986): S181-S197

Institutions, Sociability, Literacy and Education

Academies and Broader Structures

Cochrane, Eric W., *Tradition and Enlightenment in the Tuscan Academies, 1690-1800* (Chicago, University of Chicago Press, 1961)

Daston, Lorraine, "The Ideal and Reality of the Republic of Letters in the Enlightenment," *Science in Context* 4 (1991): 367-86

Evans, Joan, *A History of the Society of the Antiquaries of London* (Oxford, Oxford University Press, 1956)

Goldgar, Anne, *Impolite Learning: Conduct and Community in the Republic of Letters* (New Haven, Conn., Yale University Press, 1995)

Gossman, Lionel, *Medievalism and the Ideologies of the Enlightenment* (Baltimore, Johns Hopkins University Press, 1968)

Hahn, Roger, *The Anatomy of a Scientific Institution: The Paris Academy of Sciences, 1666-1803* (Berkeley, University of California Press, 1971)

Lough, John, "Did the *Philosophes* Take over the Académie française?" *Studies on Voltaire and the Eighteenth Century* 336 (1996): 153-94

Lowood, Henry E., *Patriotism, Profit and the Promotion of Science in the German Enlightenment: The Economic and Scientific Societies, 1760-1815* (New York, Garland, 1991)

Lux, David, *Patronage and Royal Science in Seventeenth Century France: The Académie de physique at Caen* (Ithaca, N.Y., Cornell University Press, 1989)

Lyons, Henry, *The Royal Society* (Cambridge, Cambridge University Press, 1944)

McClellan, James E., *Science Reorganized: Scientific Societies in the Eighteenth Century* (New York, Columbia University Press, 1985)

Roche, Daniel, *Le Siècle des lumières en province: Académies et académiciens provinciaux, 1680-1789* (Paris, Mouton, 2 vols., 1970)

Schofield, Robert E., *The Lunar Society of Birmingham: A Social History of Provincial Science in Eighteenth-Century England* (Oxford, Clarendon Press, 1963)

Sturdy, David J., *Science and Social Status: The Members of the Académie des Sciences, 1666-1750* (Woodbridge, Boydell Press, 1995)

Terrall, Mary, "The Culture of Science in Frederick the Great's Berlin," *History of Science* 28 (1990): 333-64

Salons

Arendt, Hannah, *Rahel Varnhagen: The Life of a Jewish Woman* (New York, Harcourt Brace Jovanovich, 1974; 1957)

Craveri, Benedetta, *Madame du Deffand and Her World*, trans. Teresa Waugh (Boston, Godine, 1994; 1982)

Glotz, Marguerite and Maire, Madeleine, *Salons du XVIIIe siècle* (Paris, Hachette, 1945)

Goldsmith, Elizabeth, *Exclusive Conversations: The Art of Interaction in Seventeenth-Century France* (Philadelphia, University of Pennsylvania Press, 1988)

Goodman, Dena, "Enlightenment Salons: The Convergence of Female and Philosophic Ambitions," *Eighteenth-Century Studies* 22 (1989): 329-50

———, "Filial Rebellion in the Salon: Madame Geoffrin and Her Daughter," *French Historical Studies* 16 (1989): 27-47

Hammel, Frank, *Famous French Salons* (London, Methuen, 1908)

Heller, Deborah, "Bluestocking Salons and the Public Sphere," *Eighteenth-Century Life* 22 (1998): 59-82

Hertz, Deborah, *Jewish High Society in Old-Regime Berlin* (New Haven, Conn., Yale University Press, 1988)

Marchal, Roger, *Madame de Lambert et son milieu, Studies on Voltaire and the Eighteenth Century* 289 (1991)

McNiven, Ellen, "Madame de Lambert, Her Sources and Her Circle: On the Threshold of a New Age," *Studies on Voltaire and the Eighteenth Century* 102 (1973): 173-91

Myers, Sylvia Harcstark, *The Bluestocking Circle: Women, Friendship and the Life of the Mind in Eighteenth-Century England* (Oxford, Oxford University Press, 1990)

Pekacz, Jolanta T., *Conservative Tradition in Pre-revolutionary France: Parisian Salon Women* (New York, Peter Lang, 1999)

———, "The Salonnières and Philosophes in Old-Regime France: The Authority of Aesthetic Judgment," *Journal of the History of Ideas* 60 (1999): 277-97

Spiel, Hilde, *Fanny von Arnstein: Daughter of the Enlightenment, 1758-1818* (Oxford, Oxford University Press, 1991)

Clubs and Associations

Agulhon, Maurice, *Pénitents et Francs-Maçons de l'ancienne Provence: Essai sur la sociabilité méridionale* (Paris, Fayard, 1968)

Allen, Robert J., *The Clubs of Augustan London* (Cambridge, Mass., Harvard University Press, 1933)

Auricchio, Laura, "Palin de la Blancherie's Commercial Cabinet of Curiosity, 1779-1787," *Eighteenth-Century Studies* 36 (2002): 47-61

Benhamou, Paul, "The Reading Trade in Lyons: Cellier's *cabinet de lecture,*" *Studies on Voltaire and the Eighteenth Century* 308 (1993): 305-21

Burke, Janet M., "Freemasonry, Friendship and Noblewomen: The Role of the Secret Society in Bringing Enlightenment Thought to Pre-revolutionary Women Elites," *History of European Ideas* 10 (1989): 283-94

Childs, Nick, *A Political Academy in Paris, 1724-1731: The Entresol and Its Members, Studies on Voltaire and the Eighteenth Century* 2000: 10

Clark, Peter, *Sociability and Urbanity: Clubs and Societies in the Eighteenth Century* (Leicester, Leicester University Press, 2000)

———, *British Clubs and Societies, 1580-1800: The Origins of an Associational World* (Oxford, Oxford University Press, 2000)

Clive, John, "The Social Background of the Scottish Renaissance," in *Scotland in the Age of Improvement*, ed. Nicolas T. Phillipson and Rosalind Mitchison, 225-44

Coser, Lewis A., *Men of Ideas: A Sociologist's View* (New York, Free Press, 1967)

Coutura, Johel, "Le Musée de Bordeaux," *Dix-Huitième Siècle* 19 (1987): 149-64

Emerson, Roger L., "The Social Composition of Enlightened Scotland: The Select Society of Edinburgh, 1754-1764," *Studies on Voltaire and the Eighteenth Century* 94 (1973): 291-329

Guénot, Hervé, "Musées et lycées parisiens (1780-1830)," *Dix-huitième siècle* 18 (1986): 249-67

————, "Une nouvelle sociabilité savante: Le Lycée des Arts," in Jean-Claude Bonnet, ed., *La Carmagnole des muses: L'homme de lettres et l'artiste dans la Révolution* (Paris, Colin, 1988)

Halevi, Ran, *Les Loges maçonniques dans la France d'Ancien Régime* (Paris, Colin, 1984)

Jacob, Margaret C., *Living the Enlightenment: Freemasonry and Politics in Eighteenth-Century Europe* (New York, Oxford University Press, 1991)

Lynn, Michael R., "Enlightenment in the Public Sphere: The Musée de Monsieur and Scientific Culture in Late-Eighteenth-Century Paris," *Eighteenth-Century Studies* 32 (1999): 463-76

McElroy, Davis D., *Scotland's Age of Improvement: A Survey of Eighteenth-Century Literary Clubs and Societies* (Pullman, Washington State University Press, 1969)

Pailhès, Jean-Louis, "En marge des bibliothèques: l'apparition des cabinets de lecture," in *Histoire des bibliothèques françaises* ed. Claude Jolly, (Paris, Promodis, 1998): 415-21

Smeaton, William A., "The Early Years of the Lycée and the Lycée des Arts: A Chapter in the Lives of A. L. Lavoisier and A. F. Fourcroy," *Annals of Science* 11 (1955): 257-67 and 309-19

Coffeehouses

Ellis, Aytoun, *The Penny Universities* (London, Secker & Warburg, 1956)

Haine, Scott W., *The World of the Paris Café: Sociability among the French Working Class, 1789-1914* (Baltimore, Johns Hopkins University Press, 1996)

Lillywhite, Bryant, *London Coffeehouses* (London, Allen & Unwin, 1963)

Money, John, "Taverns, Coffeehouses and Clubs: Local Politics and Popular Articulacy in the Birmingham Area in the Age of the American Revolution," *Historical Journal* 14 (1971): 15-47

Pincus, Steve, "Coffee Politicians Does Create: Coffeehouses and Restoration Political Culture," *Journal of Modern History* 67 (1995): 807-34

Literacy, Education and Reading

Baumann, Gerd, ed., *The Written Word: Literacy in Transition* (Oxford, Clarendon Press, 1986)

Brockliss, L. W. B., *French Higher Education in the Seventeenth and Eighteenth Centuries: A Cultural History* (Oxford, Clarendon Press, 1987)

Chartier, Roger, Compère, Marie Madeleine and Julia, Dominique, *L'Éducation en France du XVIe au XVIIIe siècle* (Paris, SEDES, 1976)

Chisick, Harvey, "Institutional Innovation in Popular Education in Eighteenth-Century France: Two Examples," *French Historical Studies* 10 (1977): 41-73

———, "Literacy, School Attendance and Acculturation: *Petites écoles* and Popular Education in Eighteenth-Century France," *Europa* 3 (1980): 185-220

———, "French Charity Schools in the Seventeenth and Eighteenth Centuries: With Special Reference to the Case of Amiens," *Histoire Sociale / Social History* 16 (1983): 241-77

Coward, D. A., "Restif as a Reader of Books," *Studies on Voltaire and the Eighteenth Century* 205 (1982): 89-132

Darnton, Robert, "First Steps toward a History of Reading," *Australian Journal of French Studies* 23 (1986): 5-30

Durkheim, Emile, *The Evolution of Educational Thought: Lectures on the Formation and Development of Secondary Education in France*, trans. Peter Collins (London, Routledge & Kegan Paul, 1977)

Emerson, Roger, *Professors, Patronage and Politics: The Aberdeen Universities in the Eighteenth Century* (Aberdeen, Aberdeen University Press, 1992)

Furet, François, and Ozouf, Jacques, eds., *Reading and Writing: Literacy in France from Calvin to Jules Ferry* (Cambridge, Cambridge University Press, 2 vols., 1982; 1977)

Gawthrop, R., and Strauss, G., "Protestantism and Literacy in Early Modern Germany," *Past & Present* 104 (1984): 31-55

Goody, Jack, ed., *Literacy in Traditional Societies* (Cambridge, Cambridge University Press, 1975)

Graff, Harvey J., *The Legacies of Literacy: Continuities and Contradictions in Western Culture and Society* (Bloomington, Indiana University Press, 1987)

Houston, Robert Allan, *Literacy in Early Modern Europe: Culture and Education, 1500-1800* (London, Longman, 1988)

———, "Literacy, Education and the Culture of Print in Enlightenment Edinburgh," *History* 78 (1993): 373-92

Melton, James Van Horne, *Absolutism and the Eighteenth-Century Origins of Compulsory Schooling in Prussia and Austria* (Cambridge, Cambridge University Press, 1988)

Raven, James, Small, Helen, and Tadmor, Naomi, eds., *The Practice and Representation of Reading in England* (Cambridge, Cambridge University Press, 1996)

Ridder-Symoens, Hilda de, ed., *A History of the University in Europe,* vol. 2, *Universities in Early Modern Europe, 1500-1800* (Cambridge, Cambridge University Press, 1996)

Roche, Daniel, "Urban Reading Habits during the French Enlightenment," *British Journal for Eighteenth-Century Studies* 2 (1979): 221-31

Rosbottom, Ronald C., "A Matter of Competence: The Relationship between Reading and Novel-Making in Eighteenth-Century France," *Studies in Eighteenth-Century Culture* 6 (1977): 245-63

Sher, Richard, *Church and University in the Scottish Enlightenment: The Moderate Literati of Edinburgh* (Princeton, N.J., Princeton University Press, 1985)

Vincent, David, *Literacy and Popular Culture: England 1750-1914* (Cambridge, Cambridge University Press, 1989)

Wittman, Reinhard, "Was There a Reading Revolution at the End of the Eighteenth Century?" in *A History of Reading in the West*, ed. Guglielmo Cavallo and Roger Chartier, trans. Lydia Cochrane (Amherst, University of Massachusetts Press, 1999)

Print Culture and the Book Trade

Production and Control of Print

Bachman, Albert, *Censorship in France from 1715 to 1750: Voltaire's Opposition* (New York, Burt Franklin, 1974; 1934)

Barber, Giles, *Studies in the Booktrade of the European Enlightenment* (London, 1993)

Birn, Raymond, "The Profits of Ideas: *Privilèges en librairie* in Eighteenth-Century France," *Eighteenth-Century Studies* 4 (1971): 131-68

Censer, Jack R., "The History of the Book in Early Modern France: Directions and Challenges," *Eighteenth-Century Life* 19 (1995): 84-95

Chartier, Roger, *The Cultural Uses of Print in Early Modern France*, trans. Lydia G. Cochrane (Princeton, N.J., Princeton University Press, 1987)

————, *The Order of Books: Readers, Authors and Libraries in Europe between the Fourteenth and Eighteenth Centuries*, trans. Lydia G. Cochrane (Cambridge, Polity, 1994)

————, Martin, Henri-Jean, and Vivet, Jean-Pierre, eds., *Histoire de l'édition française* (Paris, Promodis, 4 vols., 1983-1985)

Darnton, Robert, *The Business of Enlightenment: A Publishing History of the Encyclopédie* (Cambridge, Mass., Harvard University Press, 1979)

————, *The Forbidden Best-Sellers of Pre-revolutionary France* (New York, Norton, 1996)

————, *The Corpus of Clandestine Literature in France, 1769-1789* (New York, Norton, 1995)

————, and Roche, Daniel, eds., *Revolution in Print: The Press in France, 1775-1800* (Berkeley, University of California Press, 1989)

Duke, A. C., and Tamse, C. A., *Too Mighty to Be Free: Censorship and the Press in Britain and the Netherlands* (Zutphen, De Walburg, 1987)

Eisenstein, Elizabeth, *The Printing Press as an Agent of Change* (Cambridge, Cambridge University Press, 2 vols., 1974)

————, *Grub Street Abroad: Aspects of the French Cosmopolitan Press from the Age of Louis XIV to the French Revolution* (Oxford, Clarendon Press, 1992)

Feather, John, *The Provincial Book Trade in Eighteenth-Century England* (Cambridge, Cambridge University Press, 1985)

————, *A History of British Publishing* (London, Croom Helm, 1988)

————, *Publishing, Piracy and Politics: An Historical Study of Copyright in Britain* (London, Mansell, 1994)

Febvre, Lucien, and Martin, Henri-Jean, *The Coming of the Book: The Impact of Printing, 1450-1800*, trans. David Gerard (London, Verso, 1984; 1958)

Furet, François, ed., *Livre et société dans la France du XVIII siècle* (Paris, Mouton, 2 vols., 1965-1970)

Hermann-Mascard, Nicole, *La Censure des livres à Paris à la fin de l'ancien régime, 1750-1789* (Paris, Presses Universitaires de France, 1968)

Korshin, Paul J., ed., *The Widening Circle: The Diffusion of Literature in the Eighteenth Century* (Philadelphia, University of Pennsylvania Press, 1976)

McLeod, J., "Provincial Book Trade Inspectors in Eighteenth-Century France," *French History* 12 (1998): 77-112

Martin, Henri-Jean, *Livre, Pouvoirs et Société à Paris au XVIIe siècle, 1598-1701* (Geneva, Droz, 1969)

————, *The History and Power of Writing*, trans. Lydia G. Cochrane (Chicago, University of Chicago Press, 1994; 1988)

————, *The French Book: Religion, Absolutism and Readership, 1585-1715*, trans. Paul Saenger and Nadine Saenger (Baltimore, Johns Hopkins University Press, 1996)

Mason, Haydn, *French Writers and Their Society: 1715-1800* (London, Macmillan, 1982)

————, *The Darnton Debate: Books and Revolution in the Eighteenth Century, Studies on Voltaire and the Eighteenth Century* 359 (1998)

Mitchell, C. J., "Provincial Printing in Eighteenth-Century Britain," *Publishing History* 21 (1987): 5-24

Myers, Robin, and Harris, Michael, eds., *Censorship and Control of Print in England and France* (Winchester, St. Paul's Bibliographies, 1992)

————, and Harris, Michael, eds., *The Development of the English Book Trade, 1700-1793* (Oxford, Oxford Press, 1981)

————, eds., *Spreading the Word: The Distribution Networks of Print, 1550-1850* (Winchester, St. Paul's Bibliographies, 1990)

Goldsmith, Elizabeth C., and Goodman, Dena, *Going Public: Women and Publishing in Early Modern France* (Ithaca, N.Y., Cornell University Press, 1995)

Pottinger, David Thomas, *The French Book Trade in the Ancien Regime, 1500-1791* (Cambridge, Mass., Harvard University Press, 1958)

Rivers, Isabelle, ed., *Books and Their Readers in Eighteenth-Century England* (Leicester, Leicester University Press, 1982)

Rose, Mark, "The Author as Proprietor: Donaldson v. Beckett and the Genealogy of Modern Authorship," *Representations* 23 (1988): 51-85

Saunders, David, *Authorship and Coypright* (London, Routledge, 1992)

Tucoo-Chala, Suzanne, *Charles-Joseph Panckoucke et la librairie française, 1736-98* (Pau, Marrimpouey, 1977)

Tyson, Gerald P., *Joseph Johnson: A Liberal Publisher* (Iowa City, University of Iowa Press, 1979)

Ward, Albert, *Book Production, Fiction and the German Reading Public, 1740-1800* (Oxford, Oxford University Press, 1974)

Williams, Raymond, *The Long Revolution* (New York, Harper & Row, 1966; 1961).

Thinking, Writing and the Profession of Letters

Beljame, Alexander, *Men of Letters and the English Public in the Eighteenth Century* (London, Kegan, Paul, Trench, Trubner, 1948)

Brockliss, L. W. B., *Calvet's Web: Enlightenment and the Republic of Letters in Eighteenth-Century France* (Oxford, Oxford University Press, 2002)

Collins, Arthur Simon, *Authorship in the Days of Johnson* (London, Routledge, 1927)

Commanger, Henry Steele, "America and the Eighteenth-Century Community of Learning," *Studies in Eighteenth-Century Culture* 2 (1972): 13-31

Darnton, Robert, "The High Enlightenment and the Low-Life of Literature in Pre-Revolutionary France," *Past & Present* 51 (1971): 81-115

———, "The Facts of Literary Life in Eighteenth-Century France," in *The French Revolution and the Creation of Modern Political Culture,* vol. 1, *The Political Culture of the Old Regime,* ed. Keith Baker, 261-91

———, *The Literary Underground of the Old Regime* (Cambridge, Mass., Harvard University Press, 1982)

Gallagher, Catherine, *Nobody's Story: The Vanishing Act of Women Writers in the Marketplace, 1670-1820* (Berkeley, University of California Press, 1994)

Korshin, Paul, "Types of Eighteenth-Century Literary Patronage," *Eighteenth-Century Studies* 7 (1974): 453-73

La Vopa, Anthony J., *Grace, Talent and Merit: Poor Students, Clerical Careers and Professional Ideology in Eighteenth-Century Germany* (Cambridge, Cambridge University Press, 1998)

———, "Herder's *Publikum*: Language, Print and Sociability in Eighteenth-Century Germany," *Eighteenth-Century Studies* 29 (1995): 5-24

Lough, John, *Writer and Public in France: Middle Ages to the Present Day* (Oxford, Clarendon Press, 1978)

————, "Who Were the *Philosophes*?" in *Studies in Eighteenth-Century French Literature Presented to Robert Nicklaus*, ed. J. H. Fox, M. H. Waddicor and D. A. Watts, 139-50

Masseau, Didier, *L'Invention de l'intellectuel dans l'Europe du XVIIIe siècle* (Paris, Presses Universitaires de France, 1994)

Rogers, Pat, *Grub Street: Studies in a Subculture* (New York, Wiley, 1964)

Roustan, M., *The Pioneers of the French Revolution*, trans. Frederick Whyte (London, Ernest Benn, 1926)

Saunders, John Whiteside, *The Profession of English Letters* (London, Routledge and Kegan Paul, 1964)

Shackleton, Robert, "When Did the French *Philosophes* become a Party?" *Bulletin of the John Rylands Library* 60 (1977): 181-99

Spencer, Jane, *The Rise of the Woman Novelist: From Aphra Behn to Jane Austen* (Oxford, Blackwell, 1986)

Turner, Cheryl, *Living by the Pen: Women Writers in the Eighteenth Century* (London, Routledge, 1992)

Walter, Eric, "Sur l'intelligensia des lumières," *Dix-huitième siècle,* 5 (1973): 1-24

The Periodical Press

Bellanger, Claude, *et al., Histoire générale de la presse française* (Paris, Presses universitaires de France, 5 vols., 1969-1974)

Birn, Raymond, *Pierre Rousseau and the Philosophes of Bouillon, Studies on Voltaire and the Eighteenth Century* 29 (1964)

Black, Jeremy, *The English Press in the Eighteenth Century* (Philadelphia, University of Pennsylvania Press, 1987)

————, "Journalism and Its Problems in Late Eighteenth-Century England," *Journal of Newspaper and Periodical History* 7 (1991): 31-38

Botein, Stephen, Censer, Jack R., and Ritvo, Harriet, "The Periodical Press in Eighteenth-Century English and French Society," *Comparative Studies in Society and History* 23 (1981): 464-90

Bots, Hans, ed., *La Diffusion et la lecture des journaux de langue française sous l'Ancien Régime* (Amsterdam, APA-Holland University Press, 1988)

Censer, Jack R., *The French Press in the Age of Enlightenment* (London, Routledge, 1994)

————, and Popkin, Jeremy, eds., *Press and Politics in Prerevolutionary France* (Berkeley, University of California Press, 1987)

Clark, Charles E., *The Public Prints: The Newspaper in Anglo-American Culture, 1665-1740* (New York, Oxford University Press, 1994)

Craig, M. E., *The Scottish Periodical Press, 1750-1789* (Edinburgh, 1931)

Harris, Bob, *A Patriot Press: National Politics and the London Press in the 1740s* (Oxford, Clarendon Press, 1993)

————, *Politics and the Rise of the Press: England and France, 1620-1800* (London, Routledge, 1996)

Harris, Michael, *London Newspapers in the Age of Walpole: A Study in the Origins of the Modern English Press* (Rutherford, N.J., Farleigh Dickinson University Press, 1987)

————, "The Management of the London Newspaper Press during the Eighteenth Century," *Publishing History* 4 (1978): 95-112

————, "The Structure, Ownership and Control of the Press, 1620-1780," in James Curran, George Boyce and Pauline Wingate, eds., *Newspaper History from the Seventeenth Century to the Present Day* (London, Constable, 1978)

Helmuth, Eckhart, "Enlightenment and Freedom of the Press: The Debate in the Berlin Mittwochsgesellschaft, 1783-1784," *History* 83 (1988): 420-44

Labrosse, Claude, and Rétat, Pierre, *L'Instrument périodique: La fonction de la presse au XVIIIe siècle* (Lyon, Presses Universitaires de Lyon, 1985)

O'Keefe, Cyril B., *Contemporary Reactions to the Enlightenment (1728-1762): A Study of Three Critical Journals: The Jesuit Journal de Trévoux, the Jansenist Nouvelles Ecclésiastiques, and the Secular Journal des Savants* (Geneva, Slatkine, 1974)

Olivier, Louis, "Bachaumont the Chronicler: A Doubtful Renown," *Studies on Voltaire and the Eighteenth Century* 143 (1975): 161-79

Pappas, John N., *"Berthier, The Journal de Trévoux and the Philosophes,"* *Studies on Voltaire and the Eighteenth Century* 3 (1957)

Popkin, Jeremy D., *News and Politics in the Age of Revolution: Jean Luzac's Gazette de Leyde* (Ithaca, N.Y., Cornell University Press, 1989)

————, "The Pre-Revolutionary Origins of Political Journalism," in *The Political Culture of the Old Regime*, ed. Keith Baker, 203-23

Rétat, Pierre, ed., *Le Journalisme d'Ancien régime* (Lyon, Presses Universitaires de Lyon, 1982)

Sgard, Jean, ed., *Dictionnaire de journalistes* (Grenoble, Presses Universitaires de Grenoble, 1976)

————, ed., *Dictionnaire des journaux, 1600-1789* (Paris, Universitas, 1991)

————, *La Presse provinciale au XVIIIe siècle* (Grenoble, Centre de Recherches sur les Sensibilités, 1983)

————, *Bibliographie de la presse classique, 1600-1789* (Geneva, Slatkine, 1984)

Tate, Robert S. Jr., *Petit de Bachaumont: His Circle and the Mémoires secrets*, Studies on Voltaire and the Eighteenth Century 65 (1968)

Werkmeister, Lucyle Thomas, *The London Daily Press, 1772-1792* (Lincoln, University of Nebraska Press, 1963)

Wiles, Roy, *Freshest Advices: Early Provincial Newspapers in England* (Columbus, Ohio State University Press, 1965)

Fiction

Armstrong, Nancy, *Desire and Domestic Fiction: A Political History of the Novel* (Oxford, Oxford University Press, 1987)

Astbury, Katherine, *The Moral Tale in France and Germany, 1750-1789*, Studies on Voltaire and the Eighteenth Century 2002: 7

Brissenden, R. F., *Virtue in Distress: Studies in the Novel of Sentiment from Richardson to Sade* (London, Macmillan, 1974)

Davis, Lenard J., *Factual Fictions: The Origins of the English Novel* (New York, Columbia University Press, 1983)

Denby, David, *Sentimental Narrative and the Social Order in France, 1760-1820* (Cambridge, Cambridge University Press, 1994)

Hunter, Paul J., *Before Novels: The Cultural Context of Eighteenth-Century English Fiction* (New York, Norton, 1990)

McGhee, Dorothy Madeleine, *The Cult of the "Conte Moral": The Moral Tale in France—Its Emergence and Progress* (Menasha, Wisconsin, George Banta, 1960)

McKeon, Michael, *The Origins of the English Novel, 1600-1740* (Baltimore, Johns Hopkins University Press, 1987)

Mullan, John, *Sentiment and Sociability: The Language of Feeling in the Eighteenth Century* (Oxford, Clarendon Press, 1988)

Richetti, John, *The Cambridge Companion to the Eighteenth-Century Novel* (Cambridge, Cambridge University Press, 1996)

Ross, Deborah, *The Excellence of Falsehood: Romance, Realism and Women's Contribution to the Novel* (Lexington, University Press of Kentucky, 1991)

Showalter, English, *The Evolution of the French Novel, 1641-1782* (Princeton, N.J., Princeton University Press, 1972)

Van Sant, Ann Jessie, *Eighteenth-Century Sensibility and the Novel* (Cambridge, Cambridge University Press, 1993)

Warner, William, *The Elevation of Novel Reading in Britain, 1684-1750* (Berkeley, University of California Press, 1998)

Watt, Ian, *The Rise of the Novel: Studies in Defoe, Richardson and Fielding* (Berkeley, University of California Press, 1957)

Science

Background and Context

Ashworth, William J., "England and the Machinery of Reason: 1780 to 1830," *Canadian Journal of History* 35 (2000): 1-36

Broman, Thomas, "The Habermasian Public Sphere and Science in the Enlightenment," *History of Science* 36 (1998): 123-49

Brooke, John Hedley, "Science and the Secularization of Knowledge: Perspectives on Some Eighteenth-Century Transformations," *Nuncius* 4 (1989): 43-65

Burtt, Edwin Arthur, *The Metaphysical Foundations of Modern Science* (London, Kegan Paul, Trench & Co., 1932; 1924)

Butterfield, Herbert, *The Origins of Modern Science, 1300-1800* (London, Bell and Sons, 1949)

Clark, William, Golinski, Jan, and Schaffer, Simon, eds., *The Sciences in Enlightened Europe* (Chicago, University of Chicago Press, 1999)

Daumas, Maurice, *Scientific Instruments of the Seventeenth and Eighteenth Centuries*, trans. Mary Holbrook (London, Batsford, 1972)

Emerson, Roger L., "Science and the Origins and Concerns of the Scottish Enlightenment," *History of Science* 26 1988: 333-66

Freudenthal Gideon, *Atom and Individual in the Age of Newton: The Genesis of Mechanistic Natural and Social Philosophy* (Dordrecht, Reidel, 1986)

Gavroglu, Kostas, ed., *The Sciences in the European Periphery during the Enlightenment* (Dordrecht, Kluwer, 1999)

Gelbart, Nina R., "Science in the Utopias of the French Enlightenment," *Proceedings of the Annual Meeting of the Western Society for French History* 6 (1978): 120-28

Gillispie, Charles Coulston, *The Edge of Objectivity* (Princeton, N.J., Princeton University Press, 1960)

Hall, A. Rupert, *The Scientific Revolution, 1500-1800: The Formation of the Modern Scientific Attitude* (Boston, Beacon, 1966; 1954)

Hankins, Thomas L., *Jean d'Alembert: Science and the Enlightenment* (Oxford, Clarendon Press, 1970)

———, *Science and the Enlightenment* (New York: Cambridge University Press, 1985)

Jacob, Margaret C., *The Cultural Meaning of the Scientific Revolution* (New York, Knopf, 1988)

———, *Scientific Culture and the Making of the Industrial West* (New York, Oxford University Press, 1997)

Jardine, Nicolas, Secord, James, and Wokler, Robert, eds., *Cultures of Natural History* (Cambridge, Cambridge University Press, 1996)

Jordanova, Ludmilla, ed., *Languages of Nature: Critical Essays on Science and Literature* (London, Free Association Books, 1986)

Koyré, Alexandre, *From the Closed World to the Infinite Universe* (Baltimore, Johns Hopkins University Press, 1957)

Kronick, David A., *A History of Scientific and Technical Periodicals: The Origins and Development of the Scientific and Technical Press, 1665-1790* (New York, Scarecrow, 1962)

Kuhn, Thomas, *The Structure of Scientific Revolutions* (Chicago, University of Chicago Press, 1962)

Liedman, Sven-Eric, "Condorcet and the Postmodernists: Science, Ethics, the Arts and Progress," *History of European Ideas* 19 (1994): 691-97

Paul, Charles B., *The Eloges of the Paris Academy of Science, 1699-1791* (Berkeley, University of California Press, 1980)

Reill, Peter Hanns, "Vitalizing Nature and Naturalizing the Humanities in the Late Eighteenth Century," *Studies in Eighteenth-Century Culture* 28 (1999): 361-81

———, "Science and the Construction of the Cultural Sciences in Late Enlightenment Germany: The Case of Wilhelm von Humboldt," *History and Theory* 33 (1994): 345-66

Ruler, Han van, "Minds, Forms, and Spirits: The Nature of Cartesian Disenchantment," *Journal of the History of Ideas* 61 (2000): 381-95

Sparry, E. C., *Utopia's Garden: French Natural History from Old Regime to Revolution* (Chicago, University of Chicago Press, 2000)

Taton, René, ed., *The Beginnings of Modern Science: From 1450 to 1800* (London, Thames and Hudson, 1964)

Terrall, Mary, *The Man Who Flattened the Earth: Maupertuis and the Sciences in the Enlightenment* (Chicago, University of Chicago Press, 2002)

Thomas, Keith, *Man and the Natural World: Changing Attitudes in England, 1500-1800* (London, Allen Lane, 1983)

Vartanian, Aram, *Diderot and Descartes: A Study of Scientific Naturalism in the Enlightenment* (Princeton, N.J., Princeton University Press, 1953)

——, *Science and Humanism in the French Enlightenment* (Charlottesville, Rockwood Press, 1999)

Wolf, Abraham, *A History of Science, Technology and Philosophy in the Eighteenth Century* (New York, Harper, 2 vols., 1961)

Science and Society

Carneiro, Ana, Simoes, Ana, and Diogo, Maria Paula, "Enlightenment Science in Portugal: The Estrangeirados and Their Communication Networks," *Social Studies of Science* 30 (2000): 591-619

Dooley, Brendan, *Science, Politics and Society in Eighteenth-Century Italy: The Giornale de letterati d'Italia and Its World* (New York, Garland, 1991)

Findlen, Paula, "Science as a Career in Enlightenment Italy: The Strategies of Laura Bassi," *Isis* 84 (1993): 440-69

Fox, Christopher, Porter, Roy and Wokler, Robert, eds., *Inventing Human Science: Eighteenth-Century Domains* (Berkeley, University of California Press, 1995)

Gascoigne, John, *Cambridge in the Age of the Enlightenment: Science, Religion, and Politics from the Restoration to the French Revolution* (New York: Cambridge University Press, 1989)

Gillispie, Charles Coulston, *Science and Polity in France at the End of the Old Regime* (Princeton, N.J., Princeton University Press, 1980)

Goodman, David, "Science and the Clergy in the Spanish Enlightenment," *History of Science* 21 (1983): 111-40

Heyd, Michael, *Between Orthodoxy and the Enlightenment: Jean-Robert Chouet and the Introduction of Cartesian Science in the Academy of Geneva* (Boston: Martinus Nijhoff, 1982)

Jackson, Myles W., "Labor, Skills, and Practices in the Scientific Enterprise: Recent Works in the Cultural History of Science," *Journal of Modern History* 71 (1999): 902-13

Kramnick, Isaac, "Eighteenth-Century Science and Radical Social Theory: The Case of Joseph Priestley's Scientific Liberalism," *Journal of British Studies* 25 (1986): 1-30

Lafuente, Antonio, "Enlightenment in an Imperial Context: Local Science in the Late-Eighteenth-Century Hispanic World," *Osiris* 15 (2000): 155-73

Logan, Gabriella Berti, "The Desire to Contribute: An Eighteenth-Century Italian Woman of Science," *American Historical Review* 99 (1994): 785-812

Lynn, Michael R., "The Consumption of Natural Philosophy in Enlightenment France," *Proceedings of the Annual Meeting of the Western Society for French History* 23 (1996): 105-13

Money, John, "From Leviathan's Air Pump to Britannia's Voltaic Pile: Science, Public Life and the Forging of Britain, 1660-1820," *Canadian Journal of History* 28 (1993): 521-44

Sokolow, Jayme A., "Count Rumford and Late Enlightenment Science, Technology, and Reform," *The Eighteenth Century: Theory and Interpretation* 21 (1980): 67-86

Stewart, Larry, *The Rise of Public Science: Rhetoric, Technology and Natural Philosophy in Newtonian Britain, 1660-1750* (New York, Cambridge University Press, 1992)

Sutton, Geoffrey V., *Science for a Polite Society: Gender, Culture, and the Demonstration of Enlightenment* (Boulder, Colorado, Westview, 1995)

Umbach, Maiken, "Visual Culture, Scientific Images and German Small-State Politics in the Late Enlightenment," *Past & Present* 158 (1998): 110-45

Vidal, Mary, "David among the Moderns: Art, Science, and the Lavoisiers," *Journal of the History of Ideas* 56 (1995): 595-623

Biology

Blunt, W., *The Complete Naturalist: The Life of Linnaeus* (London, Collins, 1971)

Burckhardt, R. J., *The Spirit of System: Lamark and Evolutionary Biology* (Cambridge, Mass., Harvard University Press, 1977)

Dawson, Virginia P., *Nature's Enigma: The Problem of the Polyp in the Letters of Bonnet, Tremblay and Réaumur* (Philadelphia, American Philosophical Society, 1987)

Frängsmyr, Tore, ed., *Linnaeus: The Man and His Work* (Berkeley, University of California Press, 1983)

Glass, Bentley, Temkin, Oswei and Straves, William L., Jr., eds., *Forerunners of Darwin* (Baltimore, Johns Hopkins University Press, 1968; 1959)

Jacob, François, *The Logic of Living Systems* (London, Allen Lane, 1974)

Larson, James L., *Interpreting Nature: The Science of Living Form from Linnaeus to Kant* (Baltimore, Johns Hopkins University Press, 1994)

Moravia, Sergio, "From *Homme Machine* to *Homme Sensible*: Changing Eighteenth-Century Models of Man's Image," *Journal of the History of Ideas* 39 (1978): 45-60

Rigotti, Francesca, "Biology and Society in the Age of Enlightenment," *Journal of the History of Ideas* 47 (1986): 215-34

Roe, Shirley A., *Matter, Life and Generation: Eighteenth-Century Embryology and the Haller-Wolff Debate* (Cambridge, Cambridge University Press, 1981)

Roger, Jacques, *The Life Sciences in Eighteenth-Century France*, trans. Robert Ellrich (Stanford, Calif., Stanford University Press, 1997; 1963)

———, *Buffon: A Life in Natural History*, trans. Sara Lucille Bonnefoi (Ithaca, N.Y., Cornell University Press, 1997; 1989)

Rosenfield, L. C., *From the Beast-machine to Man-machine* (London, Oxford University Press, 1940)

Vila, Anne C., *Enlightenment and Pathology: Sensibility in the Literature and Medicine of Eighteenth-Century France* (Baltimore, Johns Hopkins University Press, 1998)

Williams, Elizabeth A., *The Physical and the Moral: Anthropology, Physiology and Philosophical Medicine in France, 1750-1850* (Cambridge, Cambridge University Press, 1994)

Chemistry

Anderson, Wilda C., *Between the Library and the Laboratory: The Language of Chemistry in Eighteenth-Century France* (Baltimore, Johns Hopkins University Press, 1985)

Clericuzio, Antonio, "From Van Helmont to Boyle: A Study of the Transmission of Helmontian Chemical and Medical Theories in Seventeenth-Century England," *British Journal for the History of Science* 26 (1993): 303-34

Donovan, Arthur, *Antoine Lavoisier: Science, Administration and Revolution* (Cambridge, Cambridge University Press, 1993)

———, "Pneumatic Chemistry and Newtonian Natural Philosophy in the Eighteenth Century: William Cullen and Joseph Black," *Isis* 67 (1976): 217-28

Duncan, Alistair, *Laws and Order in Eighteenth-Century Chemistry* (Oxford, Clarendon Press, 1996)

Golinski, Jan, *Science as Public Culture: Chemistry and Enlightenment in Britain, 1760-1820* (Cambridge, Cambridge University Press, 1992)

Holmes, Frederick L., *Eighteenth-Century Chemistry as an Investigative Enterprise* (Berkeley, University of California Press, 1989)

————, *Antoine Lavoisier: The Next Crucial Year* (Princeton, N.J., Princeton University Press, 1998)

————, and Levere, Trevor H., *Instruments and Experimentation in the History of Chemistry* (Baltimore, Johns Hopkins University Press, 1999)

Simpson, A. D. C., ed., *Joseph Black 1728-1799: A Commemorative Symposium* (Edinburgh, Royal Scottish Museum, 1982)

Physics

Heilbron, J. L., *Elements of Early Modern Physics* (Berkeley, University of California Press, 1982)

————, *Weighing Imponderables and Other Quantitative Sciences around 1800* (Berkeley, University of California Press, 1993)

Jungnickel, Christa and McCormmach, Russell, *Cavendish: The Experimental Life* (Lewisburg, Pa., Bucknell University Press, 1999)

Lynn, Michael R., "The Fashion for Physics: Public Lecture Courses in Enlightenment France," *Historian* 64 (2002): 335-50

Schofield, Robert, *Mechanism and Materialism: British Natural Philosophy in an Age of Reason* (Princeton, N.J., Princeton University Press, 1970)

Snelders, H. A. M., "Physics and Chemistry in the Netherlands in the Period 1750-1850," *Janus* 65 (1978): 1-20

Newton and Newtonianism

Calinger, Ronald, "Kant and Newtonian Science: The Pre-Critical Period," *Isis* 70 (1979): 349-62

Casini, P., "Newton's *Principia* and the Philosophers of the Enlightenment," *Notes and Records of the Royal Society of London* 42 (1988): 35-52

Chandler, Philip, "Clairaut's Critique of Newtonian Attraction: Some Insights into His Philosophy of Science," *Annals of Science* 32 (1975): 369-78

Christianson, Gale E., *In the Presence of the Creator: Isaac Newton and His Times* (New York, Free Press, 1984)

Dobbs, Betty Jo Teeter and Jacob, Margaret C., *Newton and the Culture of Newtonianism* (Atlantic Highlands, N.J., Humanities, 1995)

Downing, Lisa J., "Locke's Newtonianism and Lockean Newtonianism," *Perspectives on Science* 5 (1997): 285-310.

Epstein, Julia L. and Greenberg, Mark L., "Decomposing Newton's Rainbow," *Journal of the History of Ideas* 45 (1984): 115-40

Evans, James, "Fraud and Illusion in the Anti-Newtonian Rear Guard: The Coultaud-Mercier Affair and Bertier's Experiments, 1767-1777," *Isis* 87 (1996): 74-107

Ferrone, Vincenzo, *The Intellectual Roots of the Italian Enlightenment: Newtonian Science, Religion, and Politics in the Early Eighteenth Century* (Atlantic Highlands, N.J., Humanities, 1995)

Force, James E., *William Whiston, Honest Newtonian* (New York, Cambridge University Press, 1985)

Gascoigne, John, "From Bentley to the Victorians: The Rise and Fall of British Newtonian Natural Theology," *Science in Context* 2 (1988): 219-56

Gillespie, Neal C., "Natural History, Natural Theology, and Social Order: John Ray and the 'Newtonian Ideology'," *Journal of the History of Biology* 20 (1987): 1-49

Goldish, Matt, "Newtonian, Converso, and Deist: The Lives of Jacob (Henrique) De Castro Sarmento," *Science in Context* 10 (1997): 651-75

Guerrini, Anita, "James Keill, George Cheyne, and Newtonian Physiology, 1690-1740," *Journal of the History of Biology* 18 (1985): 247-66

Guicciardini, Niccolo, *The Development of Newtonian Calculus in Britain, 1700-1800* (New York, Cambridge University Press, 1989)

Hall, A. Rupert, *Philosophers at War: The Quarrel between Newton and Leibniz* (Cambridge, Cambridge University Press, 1980)

———, "Newton in France: A New View," *History of Science* 13 (1975): 233-50

Hanley, William, "Voltaire, Newton, and the Law," *Library* 13 (1991): 48-65

Home, Roderick W., "Leonhard Euler's 'Anti-Newtonian' Theory Of Light," *Annals of Science* 45 (1988): 521-33

———, "'Newtonianism' and the Theory of the Magnet," *History of Science* 15 (1977): 252-66

Jackson, Myles W., "A Spectrum of Belief: Goethe's 'Republic' versus Newtonian 'Despotism'," *Social Studies of Science* 24 (1994): 673-701

Jacob, Margaret C. *The Newtonians and the English Revolution, 1679-1720* (Hassocks, Sussex, Harvester, 1976)

———, "Early Newtonianism," *History of Science* 12 (1974): 142-46

———, "Newtonianism and the Origin of the Enlightenment: A Reassessment," *Eighteenth-Century Studies* 11 (1977): 1-25

Koyré, Alexandre, *Newtonian Studies* (Chicago, University of Chicago Press, 1965)

Nakata, Ryoichi, "Joseph Privat de Molieres: Reconciler between Cartesianism and Newtonianism in Collision Theory," *Historia Scientiarum* 3 (1994): 201-13

———, "Non-Newtonian Elements in French Newtonian Physics: A Perspective on a History of Science of Eighteenth-Century France," *Historia Scientiarum* 7 (1998): 205-11

Pierson, Stuart, "Two Mathematics, Two Gods: Newton and the Second Law," *Perspectives on Science* 2 (1994): 231-53

Redman, Deborah A., "Adam Smith and Isaac Newton," *Scottish Journal of Political Economy* 40 (1993): 210-30

Ruderman, David, "On Defining a Jewish Stance toward Newtonianism: Eliakim Ben Abraham Hart's *Wars of The Lord*," *Science in Context* 10 (1997): 677-91

Stewart, Larry, "Samuel Clarke, Newtonianism, and the Factions of Post-Revolutionary England," *Journal of the History of Ideas* 42 (1981): 53-72

Sysak, Janusz, "Coleridge's Construction of Newton," *Annals of Science* 50 (1993): 59-81

Verlet, Loup, "'F=Ma' and the Newtonian Revolution: An Exit from Religion through Religion," *History of Science* 34 (1996): 303-46

Art

Aesthetics, Society and the Arts

Barker, Emma, "Painting and Reform in Eighteenth-Century France: Greuze's *L'Accordée de Village*," *Oxford Art Journal* 20 (1997): 42-52

Barrel, John, *The Dark Side of the Landscape: The Rural Poor in English Painting, 1730-1840* (Cambridge, Cambridge University Press, 1980)

———, *The Political Theory of Painting from Reynolds to Hazlitt* (New Haven, Conn., Yale University Press, 1986)

Baxandall, Michael, *Shadows and Enlightenment* (New Haven, Conn., Yale University Press, 1995)

Bazin, Germain, *Baroque and Rococo* (London, Thames and Hudson, 1964)

Brookner, Anita, *Greuze: The Rise and Fall of an Eighteenth-Century Phenomenon* (London, Elek, 1972)

———, *Jacques-Louis David* (London, Thames and Hudson, 1980)

Bryson, Norman, *Word and Image: French Painting of the Ancien Régime* (Cambridge, Cambridge University Press, 1981)

Coleman, Francis X. J., *The Aesthetic Thought of the French Enlightenment* (Pittsburgh, Pa., University of Pittsburg Press, 1971)

Consibee, Philip, *Painting in Eighteenth-Century France* (Ithaca, N.Y., Cornell University Press, 1981)

Crow, Thomas E., *Painters and Public Life in Eighteenth-Century Paris* (New Haven, Conn., Yale University Press, 1985)

———, *Emulation: Making Artists for Revolutionary France* (New Haven, Conn., Yale University Press, 1995)

Fried, Michael, *Absorption and Theatricality: Painting and Beholder in the Age of Diderot* (Berkeley, University of California Press, 1980)

Friedlander, Walter, *David to Delacroix* (Cambridge, Mass., Harvard University Press, 1952)

Hauser, Arnold, *The Social History of Art*, vol. 3, *Rococo, Classicism, Romanticism*, trans. Stanley Godman (New York, Vintage, 1958)

Hunt, J. D., *The Figure in the Landscape: Poetry, Painting and Gardening during the Eighteenth Century* (Baltimore, Johns Hopkins University Press, 1976)

Kavanagh, Thomas, *Esthetics of the Moment: Literature and Art in the French Enlightenment* (Philadelphia, University of Pennsylvania Press, 1996)

Leith, James A., *The Idea of Art as Propaganda in France, 1750-1799: A Study in the History of Ideas* (Toronto, University of Toronto Press, 1965)

Levey, Michael, *Painting and Sculpture in France, 1700-1789* (New Haven, Conn., Yale University Press, 1994)

Lipking, Lawrence, *The Ordering of the Arts in Eighteenth-Century England* (Princeton, N.J., Princeton University Press, 1970)

Paulson, Ronald, *Breaking and Remaking: Aesthetic Practice in England, 1700-1820* (New Brunswick, N.J., Rutgers University Press, 1989)

Pears, Iain, *The Discovery of Painting: The Growth in the Interest in the Arts in England, 1680-1768* (New Haven, Conn., Yale University Press, 1988)

Pugh, Simon, ed., *Reading Landscape: Country, City, Capital* (Manchester, Manchester University Press, 1990)

Rosenblum, Robert, *Transformations in Late Eighteenth Century Art* (Princeton, N.J., Princeton University Press, 1967)

Saisselin, Rémy, G., *Taste in Eighteenth-Century France: Critical Reflections on the Origins of Aesthetics, or An Apology for Amateurs* (Syracuse, N.Y., Syracuse University Press, 1965)

Solkin, David, *Painting for Money: The Visual Arts and the Public Sphere in Eighteenth-Century England* (New Haven, Conn., Yale University Press, 1993)

Wakefield, David F., *French Eighteenth-Century Painting* (London, Gordon Fraser, 1984)

Wendorf, Richard, *The Elements of Life: Biography and Portrait Painting in Stuart and Georgian England* (Oxford, Clarendon Press, 1990)

Whinney, Margaret, *English Sculpture, 1720-1830* (London, Her Majesty's Stationery Office, 1971)

Rococo

Allen, Brian, *Rococo: Art and Design in Hogarth's England* (London, Victoria and Albert Museum, 1984)

Ashton, Dore, *Fragonard in the Universe of Painting* (Washington, D.C., Smithsonian, 1988)

Clements, Candace, "The Academy and the Other: *Les Graces and le Genre Gallant*," *Eighteenth-Century Studies* 25 (1992): 469-94

Crown, Patricia, "British Rococo as Social and Political Style," *Eighteenth-Century Studies* 23 (1990): 269-82

Fried, Michael, "Absorption: A Master Theme in Eighteenth-Century French Painting and Criticism," *Eighteenth-Century Studies* 9 (1975): 139-77

Harries, Karstein, *The Bavarian Rococo Church: Between Faith and Aestheticism* (New Haven, Conn., Yale University Press, 1983)

Hart, Clive and Stevenson, Kay Gilliland, *Heaven and the Flesh: Imagery of Desire from the Renaissance to the Rococo* (New York: Cambridge University Press, 1995)

Levey, Michael, *Rococo and Revolution* (London, Thames and Hudson, 1966)

McEwen, John, "Fragonard: Rococo or Romantic?" *Art in America* 76 (1988): 84-95

McKay, Sherry, "The 'Salon de La Princesse': 'Rococo' Design, Ornamented Bodies and the Public Sphere," *RACAR* 21 (1994): 71-84

Milam, Jennifer, "Playful Constructions and Fragonard's Swinging Scenes," *Eighteenth-Century Studies* 33 (2000): 543-59

Minor, Vernon Hyde, *Baroque and Rococo: Art and Culture* (New York, Abrams, 1999)

Newlin, Thomas, "Rural Ruses: Illusion and Anxiety on the Russian Estate, 1775-1815," *Slavic Review* 57 (1998): 295-319

Park, William, *The Idea of Rococo* (Cranbury, N.J., University of Delaware Press, 1993)

Pitou, Spire, *The Paris Opera: An Encyclopedia of Operas, Ballets, Composers, and Performers.* Vol. II, *Rococo and Romantic, 1715-1815* (New York, Greenwood, 1990)

Rauser, Amelia, "Empiricism and Rococo Aesthetics: Reclaiming the Enlightenment as a Moment of Liberation," *The Eighteenth Century: Theory and Interpretation* 40 (1999): 80-86

Scott, Katie, *The Rococo Interior: Decoration and Social Spaces in Early Eighteenth-Century Paris* (New Haven, Conn., Yale University Press, 1995)

Snodin, Michael, ed., *Rococo: Art and Design in Hogarth's England* (Totowa, N.J., Allanheld & Schram, 1985)

Timpe, Eugene, "Metastasio and the Beginning of Rococo Literature in Austria," *Italian Quarterly* 30 (1989): 17-27

Varriano, John L., *Italian Baroque and Rococo Architecture* (New York, Oxford University Press, 1986)

Vidal, Mary, *Watteau's Painted Conversations* (New Haven, Conn., Yale University Press, 1992)

Wittkower, Rudolf, *Art and Architecture in Italy, 1600-1750.* Vol. III, *Late Baroque and Rococo, 1675-1750* (New Haven, Conn., Yale University Press, 1999)

Neoclassicism

Boime, Albert, *Art in an Age of Revolution, 1750-1800* (Chicago, University of Chicago Press, 1987)

Buxton, John, *The Grecian Taste: Literature in the Age of Neo-Classicism, 1740-1820* (New York, Barnes & Noble, 1979)

Fischer, Michael, "The Collapse of English Neoclassicism," *Centennial Review* 24 (1980): 338-59

Greene, Donald, "What Indeed Was Neo-classicism? A Reply to James William Johnson's 'What Was Neo-classicism'," *Journal of British Studies* 10 (1970): 69-79

Hicks, Philip, *Neoclassical History and English Culture: From Clarendon to Hume* (London, Macmillan, 1996)

Honour, Hugh, *Neo-classicism* (Harmondsworth, Penguin, 1968)

Johnson, James William, "What Was Neo-Classicism?" *Journal of British Studies* 9 (1969): 49-70

Levin, Miriam R., "'Ideology' and Neoclassicism: The Problem of Creating a Natural Society through Artificial Means," *Consortium on Revolutionary Europe* 11 (1981): 177-87

Potts, Alex, *Flesh and the Ideal: Winckelmann and the Origins of Art History* (New Haven, Conn., Yale University Press, 1994)

———, "Beautiful Bodies and Dying Heroes: Images of Ideal Manhood in the French Revolution," *History Workshop Journal* 30 (1990): 1-21

Rykwert, Anne and Rykwert, Joseph, *Robert and James Adam: The Men and the Style* (New York, Rizzoli, 1985)

Saisselin, Rémy G., "Neo-Classicism: Images of Public Virtue and Realities of Private Luxury," *Art History* 4 (1981): 14-36

Schumann, Robert A., "Virility and Grace: Neoclassicism, Jacques-Louis David, and the Culture of Pre-revolutionary France," *Consortium on Revolutionary Europe* 16 (1986): 519-28

Sleigh, Sylvia, "Angelica Kauffmann," *Women's Studies* 6 (1978): 35-41

Sonderen, Peter C., "Beauty and Desire: Frans Hemsterhuis' Aesthetic Experiments," *British Journal for the History of Philosophy* 4 (1996): 317-45

Stillman, Damie, *English Neoclassical Architecture* (London, A. Zwemmer, 2 vols., 1988)

Van Meter, Lorna, "The Czartoryski Family and Stanislas August Poniatowski: Promoters of Neoclassical Architecture in Poland," *East European Quarterly* 20 (1986): 257-72

Voss, Hermann, *Baroque Painting in Rome*, vol. II, *The High and Late Baroque, Rococo and Early Neoclassicism, 1620-1790* (San Francisco: Alan Wofsy Fine Arts, 1997)

West, Alison, *From Pigalle to Préault: Neoclassicism and the Sublime in French Sculpture, 1760-1840* (New York, Cambridge University Press, 1998)

About the Author

Harvey Chisick was born in London, England, in 1946. With his family he moved to Vancouver, British Columbia, where he attended elementary and secondary schools, and did his B. A. He received his doctorate from The Johns Hopkins University, and is the author of a number of books and articles on the social and intellectual history of the eighteenth century.